Principles of
Transaction Processing

The Morgan Kaufmann Series in Data Management Systems (Selected Titles)

Principles of
Transaction Processing
Second Edition

Philip A. Bernstein

Eric Newcomer

ELSEVIER

AMSTERDAM · BOSTON · HEIDELBERG · LONDON
NEW YORK · OXFORD · PARIS · SAN DIEGO
SAN FRANCISCO · SINGAPORE · SYDNEY · TOKYO
Morgan Kaufmann Publishers is an imprint of Elsevier

MORGAN
KAUFMANN

Morgan Kaufmann Publishers is an imprint of Elsevier

30 Corporate Drive, Suite 400, Burlington, MA 01803, USA

Library of Congress Cataloging-in-Publication Data
Bernstein, Philip A.
Principles of transaction processing/Philip A. Bernstein, Eric Newcomer.—2nd ed.
 p. cm.—(The Morgan Kaufmann series in data management systems)
Includes bibliographical references and index.
ISBN 978-1-55860-623-4 (pbk.)
1. Transaction systems (Computer systems) I. Newcomer, Eric. II. Title.
QA76.545.B47 2009
005.74′5–dc22

2009003605

For information on all Morgan Kaufmann publications,
visit our Web site at www.mkp.com or www.elsevierdirect.com

Printed in the United States of America
09 10 11 12 13   5 4 3 2 1

Working together to grow
libraries in developing countries

www.elsevier.com | www.bookaid.org | www.sabre.org

ELSEVIER   BOOK AID International   Sabre Foundation

For Jim Gray, wherever he may be

Contents

Preface

WHY READ THIS BOOK?

Transaction processing has been an important software technology for 40 years. Large enterprises in transportation, finance, retail, telecommunications, manufacturing, government, and the military are utterly dependent on transaction processing applications for electronic reservations, banking, stock exchanges, order processing, music and video services, shipment tracking, government services, telephone switching, inventory control, and command and control. Many large hardware and software vendors receive much of their revenue from components of transaction processing systems, such as IBM, HP, Oracle, Microsoft, Dell, Red Hat, and EMC. The market for transaction processing products and services is many tens of billions of dollars per year. As consumers, we all use this technology every day to withdraw cash, buy gas, rent movies, and make purchases on the Internet.

How exactly do these transaction processing systems work? This question was once of interest only to computer professionals in the commercial data processing field. Now, given the widespread use of transaction processing in today's economy, it is of interest to a much broader engineering audience. Despite this interest, there is little written for a system professional to get a readable, technically solid introduction to this complex technology. This book fills the gap.

The software environment of most large-scale transaction processing systems is based on transactional middleware, which helps knit together many software components. These components include front-end applications to drive web browsers and other devices, middle-tier applications to route requests to the server that can run them, and server applications that execute business logic. Examples of transactional middleware include IBM's CICS; Microsoft's .NET Enterprise Services; and Java Enterprise Edition products, such as IBM WebSphere Application Server, Oracle's WebLogic Server, and Red Hat's JBoss Application Server. The first half of this book focuses on transactional middleware technology.

For many software engineers, transactional middleware is obscure technology—strange software glue that seems to be needed beyond operating systems, database systems, communication systems, and application programming languages. This book demystifies transactional middleware by explaining how it contributes to the performance, security, scalability, availability, manageability, and ease-of-use of transaction processing systems. The first half of the book explains transactional middleware outside and in—the features it offers to application programmers and how it is constructed to offer these features.

The transaction abstraction itself is largely implemented by database systems. They ensure that each transaction executes in its entirety, is isolated from interference by other transactions, and generates results that will survive hardware and software failures. This behavior is implemented by locking, logging, communication protocols, and replication. These technologies are the subject of the second half of this book.

This book is an introduction to transaction processing, intended to meet the needs of a broad audience, including:

- Application programmers with an interest in building transaction processing applications
- Database administrators who manage database systems used for transaction processing
- Application analysts who design applications for deployment on transaction processing systems
- Product developers in related areas, such as database systems, operating systems, and communications

- Marketing and technical support engineers for both systems and application products
- Computer science undergraduates and graduate students looking for an introduction to this topic

Our focus is on the principles of transaction processing, not on a prescription for how to build a transaction processing application—"how come?" not "how to." We include examples from many products, to illustrate how the principles have been applied and where ideas originated. But we do not dwell heavily on any one product. We present technology that is practical and used in products and pay only modest attention to good ideas that are not commonly used in practice.

We do not assume any special prerequisites, other than "system sophistication." We expect most readers will have some familiarity with SQL and database systems, but this background isn't necessary.

After finishing the book, you will understand how transactional middleware works and when to use it, and how transactional middleware and database systems work together to support reliable distributed transaction processing applications. You will be able to learn quickly how to use any transactional middleware product or database system to support the development and management of transaction processing applications.

WHAT'S NEW IN THIS SECOND EDITION?

The short answer is "a lot." There are several new chapters and rewritten chapters, and many new and revised sections of the rest.

Two main goals drove these changes. Our first goal was to present the new and revised transaction architectures and technologies that have appeared since we published the first edition twelve years ago. Back then, Internet-based electronic commerce was just beginning. Now, it is established as a major segment of many business-to-consumer and business-to-business markets. The growth of this segment, along with the commoditization of server hardware and operating systems, has led to major changes in transaction processing products. Web browsers are now a dominant technology for interacting with transaction processing systems. Transactional middleware has evolved from on-line transaction processing monitors to many new product categories that are designed to work well over the Internet, such as application servers, object request brokers, message-oriented middleware, and workflow systems. Object-oriented programming and service-oriented architecture have become mainstream. And database systems have become more complete transaction processing environments. These changes are all reflected in this second edition.

Our second main goal was to add coverage and depth of classical transaction processing topics, to make the book more complete. In part, this is based on the first author's experience in using the book as a textbook for a graduate computer science course for professional masters' students at the University of Washington. It is also in response to technological improvements, where formerly exotic technologies are now widely used.

Concretely, the major changes are as follows: The three chapters on transactional middleware have been entirely rewritten—two on principles and a long one on example products and standards, including details of Java Enterprise Edition and Microsoft .NET. There is a new chapter on business process management. The chapter on locking has new sections on optimistic concurrency control, B-tree locking, multigranularity locking, and nested transactions. There are new sections on the TPC-E benchmark, state management, scalability, shadow-paging, data sharing systems, consensus algorithms, log-based replication, and multimaster replication. Concepts of service-oriented architecture (SOA), REST, and Web Services are sprinkled throughout the book. There are numerous smaller additions of technical detail in many sections. Significant changes can be found in every chapter.

Supplementary material will be available on the publisher's web page for this book. Initially, it will include a selection of problems, grouped by chapter. We will add other technical material over time.

SUMMARY OF TOPICS

The enterprise that pays for a transaction processing system wants it to give fast service, be inexpensive to buy and operate, and be scalable as usage grows and new applications are added. Application programmers want to be insulated from the complexity of the many different kinds of technologies required to run a transaction processing system, such as transaction protocols, message protocols, transactional remote procedure calls, persistent queues, multithreaded processes, resource pooling, session management, and replication protocols. An application programmer's job is to understand what the business wants the transaction to do and to write a program that does it. The system software should make it possible to run that program on a system that is fast, efficient, scalable, and reliable. This is what transactional middleware does, which is the main subject of the first half of this book, Chapters 1 through 5. Today's products and standards for transactional middleware are described in Chapter 10.

Users of a transaction processing system want to think of it as a sequential processor of transactions, one that's infinitely reliable, gives them its full and undivided attention while it executes their transaction, executes the whole transaction (not just part of it), and saves the result of their transaction forever. This is a tall order and doesn't at all describe what's really going on inside the system: The system executes many transactions concurrently; it fails from time to time due to software and hardware errors, often at the worst possible moment (when it's running *your* transaction); and it has limited storage capacity. Yet, through a combination of software techniques, the system approximates the behavior that users want. Those techniques are the main subject of Chapters 6 through 9.

As computing technology evolves, transaction processing technology will evolve to support it. We discuss some major trends in Chapter 11: cloud computing, scalable distributed computing, flash storage, and streams and event processing.

Here is a summary of what you'll find in each chapter:

Chapter 1, Introduction: Gives a broad-brush overview of transaction processing application and system structure. It describes service-oriented computing, the ACID properties of transactions, the two-phase commit protocol, the industry-standard TPC performance benchmarks, high availability requirements, and the relationship of transaction processing to batch processing, real-time, and data warehousing systems.

Chapter 2, Transaction Processing Abstractions: Describes the main software abstractions found in transaction processing systems: transactions; processes and threads; remote procedure call; techniques for managing shared state, such as transaction context, sessions, and cookies; and scalability techniques, such as caching, resource pooling, partitioning, and replication.

Chapter 3, Transaction Processing Application Architecture: Explains the value of multitier application architecture and then delves into each tier in detail: front ends that use forms and web servers to communicate with end-user devices; request controllers that bracket transactions; and transaction servers that execute transactions. It also explains how transactional middleware and database servers structure these activities.

Chapter 4, Queued Transaction Processing: Shows how a persistent message queue adds reliability. It gives detailed walk-throughs of recovery scenarios and shows how queues drive publish-subscribe, broker-based and bus-based message-oriented middleware. It also explains the internals of queue managers, with IBM's Websphere MQ and Oracle's Stream AQ as examples.

Chapter 5, Business Process Management: Describes mechanisms to support the creation, management, and monitoring of business processes that execute as multiple related transactions. It explains how to obtain suitable atomicity, isolation, and durability of multitransaction requests. It summarizes the business process execution language (BPEL) standard and, as an example, business process mechanisms in Microsoft SQL Service Broker.

Chapter 6, Locking: Shows how and why two-phase locking works and how application programmers affect its correctness and performance. It describes lock manager implementation and deadlock handling. It then explains in detail how performance can be controlled by lock granularity, optimistic methods, batching, avoiding hot spots, avoiding phantoms, and supporting query-update workloads using lower degrees of isolation and multiversion methods. Finally, it covers B-tree locking and multigranularity locking used in SQL database systems, and nested transaction locking.

Chapter 7, System Recovery: Identifies what causes failures, and how transactions help mask their effects. It discusses checkpoint-based application recovery, using stateless servers to simplify recovery, and warm and hot standby systems that use process pairs to reduce recovery time. It then explains how database systems use logging to recover from transaction failures, system failures, and media failures. It explains the undo and redo paradigm, how and why logging algorithms work, log checkpointing, recovery algorithms, shadow paging, some fancy popular logging optimizations (including the ARIES algorithm), and archive recovery.

Chapter 8, Two-Phase Commit: Explains the two-phase commit protocol in detail. It carefully walks through recovery situations and shows where and why the user must get involved. It presents popular optimizations such as presumed abort, phase zero, and transfer of coordination. And it explains how database systems and transaction managers interoperate using the XA interface of the X/Open transaction management architecture.

Chapter 9, Replication: Describes the tradeoffs of replicating servers versus replicating resources and shows how the correctness criterion, one-copy serializability, applies to each of them. It presents the two most popular approaches to replication: primary-copy replication, where updates to a primary are propagated to secondaries; and multimaster replication, where updates are applied to any copy and then propagate to other copies. It also explains synchronization of replicated caches that connect to a shared database. It covers algorithms for electing a primary, quorum consensus, establishing the latest state, and replica recovery.

Chapter 10, Transactional Middleware Products and Standards: Describes popular products and standards for transactional middleware, such as Java Enterprise Edition, Microsoft's .NET Enterprise Services, legacy transaction processing monitors (CICS, IMS, Tuxedo, ACMS, and Pathway), and other service-oriented middleware. Component technologies include Windows Communications Foundation, Enterprise Java Beans, Java Database Connectors, Java Transaction API, and the Spring Framework, which appear in products from IBM, Oracle, Progress, and in open source software. It also describes transaction standards from OMG and X/Open, and Web Services standards from OASIS.

Chapter 11, Future Trends: Discusses major directions where transaction processing technology is headed: cloud computing platforms, composing scalable systems using distributed computing components, the use of flash storage to replace disks, and data and event streams from sensor devices as a source of transaction requests.

GUIDANCE FOR INSTRUCTORS

The first author has taught transaction processing courses several dozen times over the past 25 years. Details of his most recent offerings are on the web site of the Department of Computer Science and Engineering at the University of Washington, http://www.cs.washington.edu/education/courses/csep545/, where you'll find assignments, projects, and video-recorded lectures.

The syllabus that has worked best for a formal university course is to use the first half of the course to cover Chapter 1 of this book followed by principles of concurrency control (Sections 6.1–6.4 of Chapter 6) and recovery (Chapter 7). These topics immerse students in challenging technical details that are best learned through structured homework assignments and are amenable to a conventional exam. This gets students to the point where they can work on a course project.

Transaction processing is a systems engineering problem, with many interacting parts. We have tried three different kinds of course projects to help students deepen their understanding of how the parts fit together: case studies of applications; building an application using commercial products (such as Microsoft .NET or Java Enterprise Edition); and building a transactional middleware system for running distributed transactions. The last of these projects has been the most effective by far, from both the students' and instructor's viewpoint. So in recent offerings, we require that all students do this project.

The project involves building a skeleton of a travel reservation system for flights, hotel rooms, and rental cars. This requires them to build a resource manager with locking and recovery, a two-phase commit protocol, and transactional middleware to move requests around. We found this was too much work for a 10-week quarter, even for graduate students who are full-time professional programmers. So we give them some of the components to start with. The software is downloadable from the course web site.

ACKNOWLEDGMENTS

This book began over 20 years ago as course notes developed by the first author. Over the years, the course has been presented to over a thousand people at Digital Equipment Corp., the Wang Institute of Graduate Studies (gone, but not forgotten), Microsoft Corp., and University of Washington. The "students," most of them practicing engineers, suggested countless ideas that have become part of this book. We thank them all for the rich detail they provided.

Many people gave generously of their time to review selected chapters. They corrected our blunders, pointed out holes, and often filled them in. We are very grateful to Brian Milnes, who reviewed the entire book in detail and added much from his experience in running large Internet TP systems. We greatly appreciate the help we received on various chapters from John Apps, Darach Ennis, Mike Keith, David Kubelka, Mark Little, Peter Niblett, Betty O'Neil, Pat O'Neil, Gera Shegalov, Tony Storey, Satish Thatte, Roger Wolter, and especially Lev Novik, who was a partner in developing the new section on multimaster replication.

It was a major challenge to include many examples of products, applications, and benchmarks, and to get them right. We could never have done it without the substantial assistance of the engineers who work on those artifacts. They reviewed several iterations, to help us think through every detail. While we take full responsibility for any errors that slipped through, we are pleased to share the credit with Keith Evans, Max Feingold, Tom Freund, Jonathan Halliday, Jeurgen Hoeller, Rajkumar Irudayaraj, Jim Johnson, Ed Lassettre, Charles Levine, Anne Thomas Manes, Miko Matsumura, Laurence Melloul, Dean Meltz, Geoff Nichols, Greg Pavlik, Mike Pizzo, Ian Robinson, Adrian Trenaman, Steve Vinoski, John Wells, and Jesse Yurkovich.

Although much of this edition is new, much is not. In writing the first edition, we benefited enormously from the help of Jim Gray and Joe Twomey. We also appreciate the help we received from Mario Bocca, Dexter Bradshaw, Ian Carrie, Ed Cobb, Gagan Chopra, Dick Dievendorff, Keith Evans, Wayne Duquaine, Terry Dwyer, Ko Fujimura, Per Gyllstrom, Vassos Hadzilacos, Brad Hammond, Pat Helland, Greg Hope, Larry Jacobs, Roger King, Walt Kohler, Barbara Klein, Dave Lomet, Susan Malaika, Michael C. Morrison, M. Tamer Ozsu, Wes Saeger, David Schorow, Randy Smerik, Alex Thomasian, Karen Watterson, and Tom Wimberg.

We thank Vassos Hadzilacos, Nat Goodman, and the Addison-Wesley Publishing Company for permission to republish excerpts from *Concurrency Control and Recovery in Database Systems*, by P. Bernstein, V. Hadzilacos, and N. Goodman, primarily in Chapter 8.

We thank our editors, Rick Adams, Diane Cerra, and Denise Penrose for their encouragement, flexibility, and good advice, as well as the production staff at Elsevier, and especially Jeff Freeland, for their efficiency and careful attention in the production of the book.

Finally, we thank our families and friends for indulging our moaning, keeping us happy, and accepting our limited companionship without complaint, while all our discretionary time was consumed by this writing. It's over … for awhile ☺.

Trademarks

The following trademarks or registered trademarks are the property of the following organizations:

Dreamweaver is a trademark or registered trademark of Adobe Systems Incorporated.

AMD is a trademark or registered trademark of Advanced Micro Devices, Inc.

Amazon.com is a trademark or registered trademark of Amazon.com, Inc.

Netscape is a trademark or registered trademark of AOL, LLC.

Apache, Apache API, Apache ActiveMQ, Apache CXF, Apache HTTP Server, Apache Kandula2, Apache Tomcat, Apache OpenJPA, Apache Qpid, and Apache ServiceMix are trademarks or registered trademarks of The Apache Software Foundation.

ARM is a trademark or registered trademark of ARM Limited.

Atomikos is a trademark or registered trademark of Atomikos BVBA.

Raima RDM is a trademark or registered trademark of Birdstep Technology ASA.

VisiBroker is a trademark or registered trademark of Borland Software Corporation.

SiteMinder and Unicenter are trademarks or registered trademarks of CA.

RabbitMQ is a trademark or registered trademark of Cohesive Flexible Technologies Corporation and Lshift Ltd.

Eclipse, SOA Tools Platform Project, Rich Client Platform, and Higgins are trademarks or registered trademarks of The Eclipse Foundation.

Delphi is a trademark or registered trademark of Embarcadero Technologies, Inc.

Google is a trademark or registered trademark of Google, Inc.

ACMS, DATATRIEVE, DECforms, DECdtm, Guardian, HP, Non-Stop, OpenView, OpenVMS, Pathway, Reliable Transaction Router, TDMS, TP Ware, TP Web Connector, VAX, VMSCluster, and Web Services Integration Toolkit are trademarks or registered trademarks of Hewlett-Packard Development Company.

TPBroker is a trademark or registered trademark of Hitachi Computer Products, Inc.

OpenAMQ is a trademark or registered trademark of iMatix Corporation.

Intel is a trademark or registered trademark of Intel Corporation.

i5/OS, AIX, CICS, DB2, IBM, IMS, Informix, OS/400, Power PC, Tivoli, Tx Series VSE, UDB, WebSphere, and zOS are trademarks or registered trademarks of International Business Machines Corporation.

Linux is a trademark or registered trademark of the Linux Mark Institute.

eXtremeDB and McObject are trademarks or registered trademarks of McObject LLC.

Active Directory, BizTalk, Expression, Microsoft, SQL Server, Visual Basic, Visual C#, Visual J#, Visual Studio, Windows, Windows Cardspace, Windows Server, Windows Vista, and Xbox are trademarks or registered trademarks of Microsoft Corporation.

Introduction

1.1 THE BASICS

The Problem

A **business transaction** is an interaction in the real world, usually between an enterprise and a person or another enterprise, where something is exchanged. For example, it could involve exchanging money, products, information, or service requests. Usually some bookkeeping is required to record what happened. Often this bookkeeping is done by a computer, for better scalability, reliability, and cost. Communications between the parties involved in the business transaction is often done over a computer network, such as the Internet. This is **transaction processing (TP)**—the processing of business transactions by computers connected by computer networks. There are many requirements on computer-based transaction processing, such as the following:

- A business transaction requires the execution of multiple operations. For example, consider the purchase of an item from an on-line catalog. One operation records the payment and another operation records the commitment to ship the item to the customer. It is easy to imagine a simple program that would do this work. However, when scalability, reliability, and cost enter the picture, things can quickly get very complicated.

- Transaction volume and database size adds complexity and undermines efficiency. We've all had the experience of being delayed because a sales person is waiting for a cash register terminal to respond or because it takes too long to download a web page. Yet companies want to serve their customers quickly and with the least cost.

- To scale up a system for high performance, transactions must execute concurrently. Uncontrolled concurrent transactions can generate wrong answers. At a rock concert, when dozens of operations are competing to reserve the same remaining seats, it's important that only one customer is assigned to each seat. Fairness is also an issue. For example, Amazon.com spent considerable effort to ensure that when its first thousand Xboxes went on sale, each of the 50,000 customers who were vying for an Xbox had a fair chance to get one.

- If a transaction runs, it must run in its entirety. In a retail sale, the item should either be exchanged for money or not sold at all. When failures occur, as they inevitably do, it's important to avoid partially completed work, such as accepting payment and not shipping the item, or vice versa. This would make the customer or the business very unhappy.

- Each transaction should either return an acknowledgment that it executed or return a negative acknowledgment that it did not execute. Those acknowledgments are important. If no acknowledgment arrives, the user doesn't know whether to resubmit a request to run the transaction again.

- The system should be incrementally scalable. When a business grows, it must increase its capacity for running transactions, preferably by making an incremental purchase—not by replacing its current machine by a bigger one or, worse yet, by rebuilding the application to handle the increased workload.

- When an electronic commerce (e-commerce) web site stops working, the retail enterprise is closed for business. Systems that run transactions are often "mission critical" to the business activity they support. They should hardly ever be down.

- Records of transactions, once completed, must be permanent and authoritative. This is often a legal requirement, as in financial transactions. Transactions must never be lost.

- The system must be able to operate well in a geographically distributed environment. Often, this implies that the system itself is distributed, with machines at multiple locations. Sometimes, this is due to a legal requirement that the system must operate in the country where the business is performed. Other times, distributed processing is used to meet technical requirements, such as efficiency, incremental scalability, and resistance to failures (using backup systems).

- The system should be able to personalize each user's on-line experience based on past usage patterns. For a retail customer, it should identify relevant discounts and advertisements and offer products customized to that user.

- The system must be able to scale up predictably and inexpensively to handle Internet loads of millions of potential users. There is no way to control how many users log in at the same time or which transactions they may choose to access.

- The system should be easy to manage. Otherwise, the system management staff required to operate a large-scale system can become too large and hence too costly. Complex system management also increases the chance of errors and hence downtime, which in turn causes human costs such as increased stress and unscheduled nighttime work.

In summary, transaction processing systems have to handle high volumes efficiently, avoid errors due to concurrent operation, avoid producing partial results, grow incrementally, avoid downtime, never lose results, offer geographical distribution, be customizable, scale up gracefully, and be easy to manage. It's a tall order. This book describes how it's done. It explains the underlying principles of automating business transactions, both for traditional businesses and over the Internet; explores the complexities of fundamental technologies, such as logging and locking; and surveys today's commercial transactional middleware products that provide features necessary for building TP applications.

What Is a Transaction?

An **on-line transaction** is the execution of a program that performs an administrative function by accessing a shared database, usually on behalf of an on-line user. Like many system definitions, this one is impressionistic and not meant to be exact in all its details. One detail is important: A transaction is always the *execution* of a program. The program contains the steps involved in the business transaction—for example, recording the sale of a book and reserving the item from inventory.

We'll use the words **transaction program** to mean the program whose execution is the transaction. Sometimes the word "transaction" is used to describe the message sent to a computer system to request the execution of a transaction, but we'll use different words for that: a **request message**. So a transaction always means the execution of a program.

We say that a transaction performs an administrative function, although that isn't always the case. For example, it could be a real-time function, such as making a call in a telephone switching system or controlling a machine tool in a factory process-control system. But usually there's money involved, such as selling a ticket or transferring money from one account to another.

Most transaction programs access shared data, but not all of them do. Some perform a pure communications function, such as forwarding a message from one system to another. Some perform a system administration function, such as resetting a device. An application in which no programs access shared data is not considered true transaction processing, because such an application does not require many of the special mechanisms that a TP system offers.

There is usually an on-line user, such as a home user at a web browser or a ticket agent at a ticketing device. But some systems have no user involved, such as a system recording messages from a satellite. Some transaction programs operate **off-line**, or in batch mode, which means that the multiple steps involved may take longer than a user is able to wait for the program's results to be returned—more than, say, ten seconds. For example, most of the work to sell you a product on-line happens after you've entered your order: a person or robot gets your order, picks it from a shelf, deletes it from inventory, prints a shipping label, packs it, and hands it off to the shipping company.

Transaction Processing Applications

A **transaction processing application** is a collection of transaction programs designed to do the functions necessary to automate a given business activity. The first on-line transaction processing application to receive widespread use was an airline reservation system: the SABRE system developed in the early 1960s as a joint venture between IBM and American Airlines. SABRE was one of the biggest computer system efforts undertaken by anyone at that time, and still is a very large TP system. SABRE was spun off from American Airlines and is now managed by a separate company, Sabre Holdings Corporation, which provides services to more than 200 airlines and thousands of travel agencies, and which runs the Travelocity web site. It can handle a large number of flights, allow passengers to reserve seats and order special meals months in advance, offer bonuses for frequent flyers, and schedule aircraft maintenance and other operational activities for airlines. Its peak performance has surpassed 20,000 messages per second.

Today, there are many other types of TP applications and new ones are emerging all the time. We summarize some of them in Figure 1.1. As the cost of running transactions and of managing large databases decreases, more types of administrative functions will be worth automating as TP applications, both to reduce the cost of administration and to generate revenue as a service to customers.

In its early years, the TP application market was driven primarily by large companies needing to support administrative functions for large numbers of customers. Such systems often involve thousands of terminals, dozens of disk drives, and many large processors, and can run hundreds of thousands of transactions per day. Large TP systems are becoming even more important due to the popularity of on-line services on the Internet. However, with the downsizing of systems has come the need for small TP applications too, ones with just a few browsers connected to a small server machine, to handle orders for a small catalog business, course registrations for a school, or patient visits to a dental office. All these applications—large and small—rely on the same underlying system structure and software abstractions.

Application	Example Transaction
Banking	Withdraw money from an account
Securities trading	Purchase 100 shares of stock
Insurance	Pay an insurance premium
Inventory control	Record the fulfillment of an order
Manufacturing	Log a step of an assembly process
Retail point-of-sale	Record a sale
Government	Register an automobile
Online shopping	Place an order using an on-line catalog
Transportation	Track a shipment
Telecommunications	Connect a telephone call
Military Command and Control	Fire a missile
Media	Grant permission to download a video

FIGURE 1.1

Transaction Processing Applications. Transaction processing covers most sectors of the economy.

TP systems also are being offered as services to other companies. For example, Amazon.com hosts other companies' web storefronts. Some airlines develop and operate reservation services for other airlines. Some vendors of packaged applications are now offering their application as a service that can be invoked by a third party's application over the Internet, which in turn helps the third party offer other TP services to their customers. Given the expense, expertise, and management attention required to build and run a high-quality TP system, this trend toward out-sourcing TP applications is likely to grow.

A Transaction Program's Main Functions

A transaction program generally does three things:

1. Gets input from a web browser or other kind of device, such as a bar-code reader or robot sensor.
2. Does the real work being requested.
3. Produces a response and, possibly, sends it back to the browser or device that provided the input.

Each invocation of the transaction program results in an independent unit of work that executes exactly once and produces permanent results. We'll have more to say about these properties of a transaction program shortly.

Most TP applications include some code that does not execute as a transaction. This other code executes as an ordinary program, not necessarily as an independent unit of work that executes exactly once and produces permanent results. We use the term TP application in this larger sense. It includes transaction programs, programs that gather input for transactions, and maintenance functions, such as deleting obsolete inventory records, reconfiguring the runtime system, and updating validation tables used for error-checking.

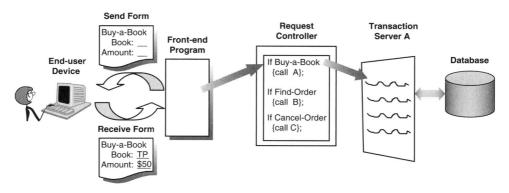

FIGURE 1.2

Transaction Application Parts. A transaction application gathers input, routes the input to a program that can execute the request, and then executes the appropriate transaction program.

1.2 TP SYSTEM ARCHITECTURE

A **TP system** is the computer system—both hardware and software—that hosts the transaction programs. The software parts of a TP system usually are structured in a special way. As you can see from Figure 1.2, the TP system has several main components. Different parts of the application execute in each of these components.

1. End-user device: An **end user** is someone who requests the execution of transactions, such as a customer of a bank or of an Internet retailer. An end-user device could be a physical device, such as a cash register or gasoline pump. Or it could be a web browser running on a desktop device, such as a personal computer (PC). If it is a dumb device, it simply displays data that is sent to it and sends data that the user types in. If it is a smart device, then it executes application code that is the front-end program.

2. Front-end program: A **front-end program** is an application code that interacts with the end-user device. Usually it sends and receives menus and forms, to offer the user a selection of transactions to run and to collect the user's input. Often, the device is a web browser and the front-end program is an application managed by a web server that communicates with the browser via HTTP. The front-end program validates the user's input and then sends a request message to another part of the system whose job is to actually execute the transaction.

3. Request controller: A **request controller** is responsible for receiving messages from front-end programs and turning each message into one or more calls to the proper transaction programs. In a centralized system, this is simply a matter of calling a local program. In a distributed TP system, it requires sending the message to a system where the program exists and can execute. If more than one program is needed, it tracks the state of the request as it moves between programs.

4. Transaction server: A **transaction server** is a process that runs the parts of the transaction program that perform the work the user requested, typically by reading and writing a shared database, possibly calling other programs, and possibly returning a reply that is routed back to the device that provided the input for the request.

5. Database system: A **database system** manages shared data that is needed by the application to do its job.

For example, in an Internet-based order processing application, a user submits orders via a web browser. The front-end program is managed by a web server, which reads and writes forms and menus and perhaps maintains a shopping cart. A request controller routes requests from the web server to the transaction server that can process the order the user requested. The transaction server processes the order, which requires accessing the database that keeps track of orders, catalog information, and warehouse inventory, and perhaps contacts another transaction server to bill a credit card for the order.

The transaction programs that run in the server are of a limited number of types that match operational business procedures, such as shipping an order or transferring funds. Typically there are a few dozen and usually no more than a few hundred. When applications become larger than this, usually they are partitioned into independent applications of smaller size. Each one of these programs generally does a small amount of work. There's no standard concept of an average size of a transaction program, because they all differ based on the application. But a typical transaction might have between zero and 30 disk accesses, a few thousand up to a few million instructions, and at least two messages, but often many more depending on how distributed it is. It may be distributed because different application services are needed to process it or because multiple machines are needed to handle the application load. The program generally is expected to execute within a second or two, so that the user can get a quick response. Later on we'll see another, more technical reason for keeping transactions short, having to do with locking conflicts.

Database systems play a big role in supporting transaction programs, often a bigger role than the application programs themselves. Although the database can be small enough to fit in main memory, it is often much larger than that. Some databases for TP require a large number of nonvolatile storage devices, such as magnetic or solid state disks, pushing both storage and database system software technology to the limit. To scale even larger, the database may be replicated or partitioned onto multiple machines.

Another major category of TP software products is **transactional middleware**, which is a layer of software components between TP applications and lower level components such as the operating system, database system, and system management tools. These components perform a variety of functions. They can help the application make the most efficient use of operating system processes, database connections, and communications sessions, to enable an application to scale up. For example, they may provide functions that client applications can use to route requests to the right server applications. They can integrate the transaction abstraction with the application, operating system, and database system, for example, to enable the execution of distributed transactions, sometimes across heterogeneous environments. They can integrate system management tools to simplify application management, for example, so that system managers can balance the load across multiple servers in a distributed system. And they may offer a programming interface and/or configurable properties that simplify the use of related services that originate in the operating system and database system.

Transactional middleware product categories have evolved rapidly over the past fifteen years. Before the advent of the World Wide Web (WWW), transactional middleware products were called TP monitors or on-line TP (OLTP) monitors. During the mid 1990s, application server products were introduced to help application developers cope with new problems introduced by the Web, such as integrating with web servers and web browsers. Initially, application servers formed a bridge between existing commercial systems managed by TP monitors and the Internet. In a relatively short time, the functionality of application servers and TP monitors converged. During the same period, message-oriented transactional middleware and object request brokers became popular. Message-oriented middleware became the foundation of a product category called enterprise application integration systems. The adoption of standard Internet-based protocols for application communication, called Web Services, has led to the enterprise service bus, another transactional middleware product. And finally, workflow products have become popular to help users define and manage long-running business processes. Although transactional middleware products usually are marketed as a complete environment for developing and executing TP applications, customers sometimes use components from multiple transactional middleware products to assemble their TP environments.

Service Oriented Computing

Service Oriented Architecture (SOA) is a style of design in which applications are composed in whole or in part of reusable services. SOA aligns information systems technology well with business objectives by modeling an application as a composition of reusable services. In contrast to the object-oriented (OO) paradigm, services are designed to model functions rather than things. They are a natural abstraction of the concept of business services; that is, services that a business provides to its customers and partners. A service can be implemented using an object, but it need not be. For example, it may be implemented using a procedure, stored procedure, asynchronous message queue, or script. Services are characterized by the messages they exchange and by the interface contracts defined between the service requester and provider, rather than by the programs that are used to implement them.

Service orientation has been around for a long time as a concept. However, only recently has it become mainstream, with many large-scale web sites for web search, social networking, and e-commerce now offering service-oriented access to their functions. In part, this wide availability is due to the advent of standard Web Services protocols. Web Services is an implementation technology that enables independent programs to invoke one another reliably and securely over a network, especially the Internet. Many vendors now support Web Services protocols. This enables one to implement SOA in a multivendor environment, which is a requirement for most enterprises.

A TP system that is created in whole or in part using the SOA approach may include multiple reusable services offered by a single transaction program or by multiple distributed services. An SOA-based TP system may include both synchronous and asynchronous communications mechanisms, depending on the message exchange patterns that a given service supports and the execution environment in which it runs. SOA-based TP systems may be assembled using a combination of services from a variety of applications and using a variety of operating systems, middleware platforms, and programming languages.

Figure 1.3 illustrates the components of a service-oriented architecture. They include a service provider that offers a service, a requester that invokes a service, and a registry (sometimes called a repository) that publishes service descriptions. The service descriptions typically include the service interface, the name and format of data to be exchanged, the communications protocol to be used, and the quality of service that the interaction is required to support (such as its security and reliability characteristics and its transaction behavior).

A caller communicates with a service by sending messages, guided by a message exchange pattern. The basic pattern is a one-way asynchronous request message, where a caller sends a request message to the service provider and the service provider receives the message and executes the requested service. Other common patterns are request-response and publish-subscribe.

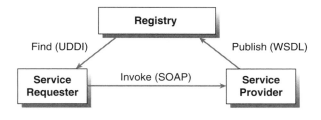

FIGURE 1.3

Basic Architecture of Service Orientation. A service provider publishes its interface in the registry. A service requester uses the registry to find a service provider and invokes it. The corresponding Web Service technologies are WSDL, UDDI, and SOAP.

The registry is an optional component because the requester can obtain service description information in other ways. For example, a developer who writes the requester can find the service description on a web site or be given the service description by the service's owner.

One mechanism to implement SOA is Web Services, where a service requester invokes a service provider using the protocol SOAP.[1] The service interface offered by the service provider is defined in the Web Services Description Language (WSDL). The service provider makes this interface known by publishing it in a registry. The registry offers access to service descriptions via the Universal Description, Discovery, and Integration (UDDI) protocol. A service requester and provider can be running in different execution environments, such as Java Enterprise Edition or Microsoft. NET.

Web Service interfaces are available for virtually all information technology product categories: application servers, object request brokers, message oriented middleware systems, database management systems, and packaged applications. Thus, they provide **interoperability**, meaning that applications running on disparate software systems can communicate with each other. Web Services support transaction interoperability too, as defined in the Web Services Transactions specifications (discussed in Section 10.8).

Services simplify the assembly of new applications from existing ones by combining services. Tools and techniques are emerging to simplify the assembly of services, such as the Service Component Architecture for Java and the Windows Communication Foundation for Windows.

A TP application may exist as a combination of reusable services. The use of reusable services doesn't change the functions of the front-end program, request controller, or transaction server. However, it may affect the way the functions are designed, modeled, and implemented. For example, in Figure 1.2, the decision to build the request controller as a reusable Web Service may affect the choice of implementation technologies, such as defining the interface to the request controller using WSDL and invoking it using SOAP. That decision may also affect the design by enabling an end-user device such as a web browser to call the request controller service(s) directly, bypassing the front-end program. We'll talk a lot more about TP software architecture in Chapter 3.

Representational State Transfer (REST) is another approach to SOA, rather different than that of Web Services. The term REST is used in two distinct but related ways: to denote the protocol infrastructure used for the World Wide Web, namely the Hypertext Transfer Protocol (HTTP); and to denote a software architectural pattern that can be implemented by web protocols. We use it here in the former sense, which we call REST/HTTP. We will discuss the REST architectural pattern in Section 3.3.

REST/HTTP focuses on the reuse of resources using a small set of generic HTTP operations, notably GET (i.e., read), PUT (i.e., update), POST (i.e., insert), and DELETE. This is in contrast to Web Services, which uses services that are customized for a particular application. Each HTTP operation is applied to a resource identified by a Uniform Resource Identifier (URI). A registry function, as shown in Figure 1.3, is needed to translate each URI into a network address where the resource can be found. On the Internet, this is implemented by the Domain Name System, which translates domain names such as www.mydomain.com into IP addresses.

In REST, generic HTTP operations are used to perform application-specific functions. For example, instead of invoking a Web Service AddCustomer, you could use REST to invoke the POST operation with a URI that makes it clear that a customer is being inserted, such as www.company-xyz.com/customers. In general, the application-specific information that identifies the function and its parameters must be embodied in the representation of the resource. This is why this style of communication is called representational state transfer. In practice, the representation that is transferred is often in a standard, stylized form, such as JavaScript Object Notation (JSON).

The format of the representation is specified in the HTTP header; the `content-type` and `accept` fields specify the format of the input and output, respectively. Thus, instead of specifying data types in a service's

---

[1]Originally, SOAP was an acronym for Simple Object Access Protocol. However, the SOAP 1.2 specification explicitly says it should no longer be treated as an acronym.

interface definition, the caller specifies the data types it would like to receive. This flexibility makes it easier for diverse kinds of callers to invoke the service.

REST/HTTP is popular for its speed and simplicity. Web Services require parameters in SOAP messages to be represented in XML, which is expensive to parse. XML is self-describing and highly interoperable, but these benefits are not always important, for example, for simple services. A very simple interface makes it easier and faster to manipulate in limited languages such as JavaScript.

Hardware Architecture

The computers that run these programs have a range of processing power. A display device could be a character-at-a-time terminal, a handheld device, a low-end PC, or a powerful workstation. Front-end programs, request controllers, transaction servers, and database systems could run on any kind of server machine, ranging from a low-end server machine, to a high-end multiprocessor mainframe, to a distributed system. A distributed system could consist of many computers, localized within a machine room or campus or geographically dispersed in a region or worldwide.

Some of these systems are quite small, such as a few display devices connected to a small machine on a PC Local Area Network (LAN). Big TP systems tend to be enterprise-wide or Internet-wide, such as airline and financial systems, Internet retailers, and auction sites. The big airline systems have on the order of 100,000 display devices (terminals, ticket printers, and boarding-pass printers) and thousands of disk drives, and execute thousands of transactions per second at their peak load. The biggest Internet systems have hundreds of millions of users, with tens of millions of them actively using the system at any one time.

Given this range of capabilities of computers that are used for TP, we need some terminology to distinguish among them. We use standard words for them, but in some cases with narrower meanings than is common in other contexts.

We define a **machine** to be a computer that is running a single operating system image. It could use a single-core or multicore processor, or it could be a shared-memory multiprocessor. Or it might be a virtual machine that is sharing the underlying hardware with other virtual machines. A **server machine** is a machine that executes programs on behalf of client programs that typically execute on other computers. A **system** is a set of one or more machines that work together to perform some function. For example, a **TP system** is a system that supports one or more TP applications. A **node** (of a network) is a system that is accessed by other machines as if it were one machine. It may consist of several machines, each with its own network address. However, the system as a whole also has a network address, which is usually how other machines access it.

A **server process** is an operating system process, P, that executes programs on behalf of client programs executing in other processes on the same or different machines as the one where P is running. We often use the word "server" instead of "server machine" or "server process" when the meaning is obvious from context.

1.3 ATOMICITY, CONSISTENCY, ISOLATION, AND DURABILITY

There are four critical properties of transactions that we need to understand at the outset:

- Atomicity: The transaction executes completely or not at all.
- Consistency: The transaction preserves the internal consistency of the database.
- Isolation: The transaction executes as if it were running alone, with no other transactions.
- Durability: The transaction's results will not be lost in a failure.

This leads to an entertaining acronym, ACID. People often say that a TP system executes ACID transactions, in which case the TP system has "passed the ACID test." Let's look at each of these properties in turn and examine how they relate to each other.

Atomicity

First, a transaction needs to be **atomic** (or **all-or-nothing**), meaning that it executes completely or not at all. There must not be any possibility that only part of a transaction program is executed.

For example, suppose we have a transaction program that moves $100 from account A to account B. It takes $100 out of account A and adds it to account B. When this runs as a transaction, it has to be atomic—either both or neither of the updates execute. It must not be possible for it to execute one of the updates and not the other.

The TP system guarantees atomicity through database mechanisms that track the execution of the transaction. If the transaction program should fail for some reason before it completes its work, the TP system will undo the effects of any updates that the transaction program has already done. Only if it gets to the very end and performs all of its updates will the TP system allow the updates to become a permanent part of the database.

If the TP system fails, then as part of its recovery actions it undoes the effects of all updates by all transactions that were executing at the time of the failure. This ensures the database is returned to a known state following a failure, reducing the requirement for manual intervention during restart.

By using the atomicity property, we can write a transaction program that emulates an atomic business transaction, such as a bank account withdrawal, a flight reservation, or a sale of stock shares. Each of these business actions requires updating multiple data items. By implementing the business action by a transaction, we ensure that either all the updates are performed or none are.

The successful completion of a transaction is called **commit**. The failure of a transaction is called **abort**.

Handling Real-World Operations

During its execution, a transaction may produce output that is displayed back to the user. However, since the transaction program is all-or-nothing, until the transaction actually commits, any results that the transaction might display to the user should not be taken seriously, because it's still possible that the transaction will abort. Anything displayed on the display device could be wiped out in the database on abort.

Thus, any value that the transaction displays may be used by the end-user only if the transaction commits and not if the transaction aborts. This requires some care on the part of users (see Figure 1.4). If the system actually displays some of the results of a transaction before the transaction commits, and if the user utilizes any of these results as input to another transaction, then we have a problem. If the first transaction aborts and the second transaction commits, then the all-or-nothing property has been broken. That is, some of the results of the first transaction will be reflected in the results of the second transaction. But other results of the first transaction, such as its database updates, were not performed because the transaction aborted.

Some systems solve this problem simply by not displaying the result of a transaction until after the transaction commits, so the user can't inadvertently make use of the transaction's output and then have it subsequently abort. But this too has its problems (see Figure 1.5): If the transaction commits before displaying any of its results, and the system crashes before the transaction actually displays any of the results, then the user won't get a chance to see the output. Again, the transaction is not all-or-nothing; it executed all its database updates before it committed, but did not display its output.

We can make the problem more concrete by looking at it in the context of an automated teller machine (ATM) (see Figure 1.6). The output, for example, may be an operation that dispenses $100 from the ATM. If the system dispenses the $100 before the transaction commits, and the transaction ends up aborting, then the

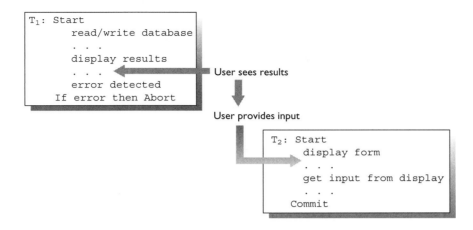

FIGURE 1.4

Reading Uncommitted Results. The user read the uncommitted results of transaction T_1 and fed them as input to transaction T_2. Since T_1 aborts, the input to T_2 is incorrect.

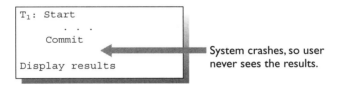

FIGURE 1.5

Displaying Results after Commits. This solves the problem of Figure 1.4, but if the transaction crashes before displaying the results, the results are lost forever.

bank gives up the money but does not record that fact in the database. If the transaction commits and the system fails before it dispenses the $100, then the database says the $100 was given to the customer, but in fact the customer never got the money. In both cases, the transaction's behavior is not all-or-nothing.

A closely-related problem is that of ensuring that each transaction executes exactly once. To do this, the transaction needs to send an acknowledgment to its caller, such as sending a message to the ATM to dispense money, if and only if it commits. However, sending this acknowledgment is not enough to guarantee exactly-once behavior because the caller cannot be sure how to interpret the absence of an acknowledgment. If the caller fails to receive an acknowledgment, it might be because the transaction aborted, in which case the caller needs to resubmit a request to run a transaction (to ensure the transaction executes once). Or it might be that the transaction committed but the acknowledgment got lost, in which case the caller must not resubmit a request to run the transaction because that would cause the transaction to execute twice. So if the caller wants exactly-once behavior, it needs to be sure that a transaction did not and will not commit before it's safe to resubmit the request to run the transaction.

Although these seem like unsolvable problems, they can actually be solved using persistent queues, which we'll describe in some detail in Chapter 4.

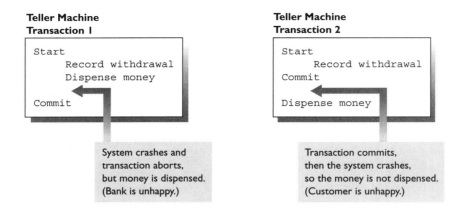

FIGURE 1.6

The Problem of Getting All-or-Nothing Behavior with Real-World Operations. Whether the program dispenses money before or after it commits, it's possible that only one of the operations executes: dispense the money or record the withdrawal.

Compensating Transactions

Commitment is an irrevocable action. Once a transaction is committed, it can no longer be aborted. People do make mistakes, of course. So it may turn out later that it was a mistake to have executed a transaction that committed. At this point, the only course of action is to run another transaction that reverses the effect of the one that committed. This is called a **compensating transaction**. For example, if a deposit transaction was in error, then one can later run a withdrawal transaction that reverses its effect.

Sometimes, a perfect compensation is impossible, because the transaction performed some irreversible act. For example, it may have caused a paint gun to spray-paint a part the wrong color, and the part is long gone from the paint gun's work area when the error is detected. In this case, the compensating transaction may be to record the error in a database and send an e-mail message to someone who can take appropriate action.

Virtually any transaction can be executed incorrectly. So a well-designed TP application should include a compensating transaction type for every type of transaction.

Multistep Business Processes

Some business activities do not execute as a single transaction. For example, the activity of recording an order typically executes in a separate transaction from the one that processes the order. Since recording an order is relatively simple, the system can give excellent response time to the person who entered the order. The processing of the order usually requires several time-consuming activities that may require multiple transactions, such as checking the customer's credit, forwarding the order to a warehouse that has the requested goods in stock, and fulfilling the order by picking, packing, and shipping it.

Even though the business process executes as multiple transactions, the user may still want atomicity. Since multiple transactions are involved, this often requires compensating transactions. For example, if an order is accepted by the system in one transaction, but later on another transaction determines that the order can't be fulfilled, then a compensating transaction is needed to reverse the effect of the transaction that accepted the order. To avoid an unhappy customer, this often involves the universal compensating transaction, namely, an apology and a free gift certificate. It might also involve offering the customer a choice of either cancelling or telling the retailer to hold the order until the requested items have been restocked.

Transactional middleware can help manage the execution of multistep business processes. For example, it can keep track of the state of a multistep process, so if the process is unable to complete then the middleware can invoke compensating transactions for the steps that have already executed. These functions and others are discussed in Chapter 5, *Business Process Management*.

Consistency

A second property of transactions is consistency—a transaction program should maintain the consistency of the database. That is, if you execute the transaction all by itself on a database that's initially consistent, then when the transaction finishes executing the database is again consistent.

By consistent, we mean "internally consistent." In database terms, this means that the database at least satisfies all its integrity constraints. There are several kinds of integrity constraints that database systems can typically maintain:

- All primary key values are unique (e.g., no two employee records have the same employee number).
- The database has referential integrity, meaning that records reference only objects that exist (e.g., the Part record and Customer record that are referenced by an Order record really exist).
- Certain data values are in a particular range (e.g., age is less than 120 and social security number is not null).

There are other kinds of integrity constraints that database systems typically cannot maintain but may nevertheless be important, such as the following:

- The sum of expenses in each department is less than or equal to the department's budget.
- The salary of an employee is bounded by the salary range of the employee's job level.
- The salary of an employee cannot decrease unless the employee is demoted to a lower job level.

Ensuring that transactions maintain the consistency of the database is good programming practice. However, unlike atomicity, isolation, and durability, consistency is a responsibility shared between transaction programs and the TP system that executes those programs. That is, a TP system ensures that transactions are atomic, isolated, and durable, whether or not they are programmed to preserve consistency. Thus, strictly speaking, the ACID test for transaction systems is a bit too strong, because the TP system does its part for the C in ACID only by guaranteeing AID. It's the application programmer's responsibility to ensure the transaction program preserves consistency.

There are consistency issues that reach out past the TP system and into the physical world that the TP application describes. An example is the constraint that the number of physical items in inventory equals the number of items on the warehouse shelf. This constraint depends on actions in the physical world, such as correctly reporting the restocking and shipment of items in the warehouse. Ultimately, this is what the enterprise regards as consistency.

Isolation

The third property of a transaction is called **isolation**. We say that a set of transactions is isolated if the effect of the system running them is the same as if the system ran them one at a time. The technical definition of isolation is serializability. An execution is **serializable** (meaning isolated) if its effect is the same as running the transactions serially, one after the next, in sequence, with no overlap in executing any two of them. This has the same effect as running the transactions one at a time.

A classic example of a non-isolated execution is a banking system, where two transactions each try to withdraw the last $100 in an account. If both transactions read the account balance before either of them updates it, then both transactions will determine there's enough money to satisfy their requests, and both will withdraw the last $100. Clearly, this is the wrong result. Moreover, it isn't a serializable result. In a serial execution, only the first transaction to execute would be able to withdraw the last $100. The second one would find an empty account.

Notice that isolation is different from atomicity. In the example, both transactions executed completely, so they were atomic. However, they were not isolated and therefore produced undesirable behavior.

If the execution is serializable, then from the point of view of an end-user who submits a request to run a transaction, the system looks like a standalone system that's running that transaction all by itself. Between the time he or she runs two transactions, other transactions from other users may run. But during the period that the system is processing that one user's transaction, the user has the illusion that the system is doing no other work. This is only an illusion. It's too inefficient for the system to actually run transactions serially, because there is a lot of internal parallelism in the system that must be exploited by running transactions concurrently.

If each transaction preserves consistency, then any serial execution (i.e., sequence) of such transactions preserves consistency. Since each serializable execution is equivalent to a serial execution, a serializable execution of the transactions will preserve database consistency too. It is the combination of transaction consistency and isolation that ensures that the execution of a set of transactions preserves database consistency.

The database typically sets locks on data accessed by each transaction. The effect of setting the locks is to make the execution appear to be serial. In fact, internally, the system is running transactions in parallel, but through this locking mechanism the system gives the illusion that the transactions are running serially, one after the next. In Chapter 6, we will describe those mechanisms in more detail and present the rather subtle argument why locking actually produces serializable executions.

A common misconception is that serializability isn't important because the database system will maintain consistency by enforcing integrity constraints. However, as we saw in the previous section on consistency, there are many consistency constraints that database systems can't enforce. Moreover, sometimes users don't tell the database system to enforce certain constraints because they degrade performance. The last line of defense is that the transaction program itself maintains consistency and that the system guarantees serializability.

Durability

The fourth property of a transaction is durability. **Durability** means that when a transaction completes executing, all its updates are stored in **stable storage**; that is, storage that will survive the failure of power or the operating system. Today, stable storage (also called **nonvolatile** or **persistent storage**) typically consists of magnetic disk drives, though solid-state disks that use flash memory are making inroads as a viable alternative. Even if the transaction program fails, or the operating system fails, once the transaction has committed, its results are durably stored on stable storage and can be found there after the system recovers from the failure.

Durability is important because each transaction usually is providing a service to the user that amounts to a contract between the user and the enterprise that is providing the service. For example, if you're moving money from one account to another, once you get a reply from the transaction saying that it executed, you expect that the result is permanent. It's a legal agreement between the user and the system that the money has been moved between these two accounts. So it's essential that the transaction actually makes sure that the updates are stored on some stable storage device, to ensure that the updates cannot possibly be lost after the transaction finishes executing. Moreover, the durability of the result must be maintained for a long period, until it is explicitly overwritten or deleted by a later transaction. For example, even if a checking account is unused for several years, the owner expects to find her money there the next time she accesses it.

The durability property usually is obtained by having the TP system append a copy of all the transaction's updates to a log file while the transaction program is running. When the transaction program issues the commit operation, the system first ensures that all the records written to the log file are out on stable storage, and then returns to the transaction program, indicating that the transaction has indeed committed and that the results are durable. The updates may be written to the database right away, or they may be written a little later. However, if the system fails after the transaction commits and before the updates go to the database, then after the system recovers from the failure it must repair the database. To do this, it reads the log and checks that each update by a committed transaction actually made it to the database. If not, it reapplies the update to the database. When this recovery activity is complete, the system resumes normal operation. Thus, after the system recovers, any new transaction will read a database state that includes all the updates of transactions that committed before the failure (as well as those that committed after the recovery). We describe log-based recovery algorithms in Chapter 7.

1.4 TWO-PHASE COMMIT

When a transaction updates data on two or more database systems, we still have to ensure the atomicity property, namely, that either both database systems durably install the updates or neither does. This is challenging, because the database systems can independently fail and recover. This is certainly a problem when the database systems reside on different nodes of a distributed system. But it can even be a problem on a single machine if the database systems run as server processes with private storage since the processes can fail independently. The solution is a protocol called **two-phase commit** (**2PC**), which is executed by a module called the **transaction manager**.

The crux of the problem is that a transaction can commit its updates on one database system, but a second database system can fail before the transaction commits there too. In this case, when the failed system recovers, it must be able to commit the transaction. To commit the transaction, the recovering system must have a copy of the transaction's updates that executed there. Since a system can lose the contents of main memory when it fails, it must store a durable copy of the transaction's updates before it fails, so it will have them after it recovers. This line of reasoning leads to the essence of two-phase commit: Each database system accessed by a transaction must durably store its portion of the transaction's updates before the transaction commits anywhere. That way, if a system S fails after the transaction commits at another system S' but before the transaction commits at S, then the transaction can commit at S after S recovers (see Figure 1.7).

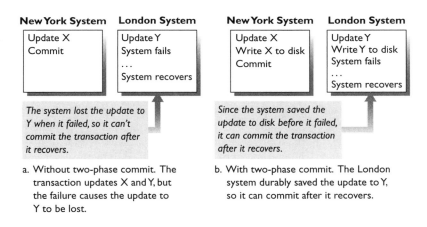

a. Without two-phase commit. The transaction updates X and Y, but the failure causes the update to Y to be lost.

b. With two-phase commit. The London system durably saved the update to Y, so it can commit after it recovers.

FIGURE 1.7

How Two-Phase Commit Ensures Atomicity. With two-phase commit, each system durably stores its updates before the transaction commits, so it can commit the transaction when it recovers.

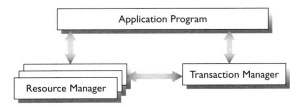

FIGURE 1.8

X/Open Transaction Model (XA). The transaction manager processes Start, Commit, and Abort. It talks to resource managers to run two-phase commit.

To understand two-phase commit, it helps to visualize the overall architecture in which the transaction manager operates. The standard model, shown in Figure 1.8, was introduced by IBM's CICS and popularized by Oracle's Tuxedo and X/Open (now part of The Open Group, see Chapter 10). In this model, the transaction manager talks to applications, resource managers, and other transaction managers. The concept of "resource" includes databases, queues, files, messages, and other shared objects that can be accessed within a transaction. Each resource manager offers operations that must execute only if the transaction that called the operations commits.

The transaction manager processes the basic transaction operations for applications: Start, Commit, and Abort. An application calls Start to begin executing a new transaction. It calls Commit to ask the transaction manager to commit the transaction. It calls Abort to tell the transaction manager to abort the transaction.

The transaction manager is primarily a bookkeeper that keeps track of transactions in order to ensure atomicity when more than one resource is involved. Typically, there's one transaction manager on each node of a distributed computer system. When an application issues a Start operation, the transaction manager dispenses a unique ID for the transaction called a **transaction identifier**. During the execution of the transaction, it keeps track of all the resource managers that the transaction accesses. This requires some cooperation with the application, resource managers, and communication system. Whenever the transaction accesses a new resource manager, somebody has to tell the transaction manager. This is important because when it comes time to commit the transaction, the transaction manager has to know all the resource managers to talk to in order to execute the two-phase commit protocol.

When a transaction program finishes execution and issues the commit operation, that commit operation goes to the transaction manager, which processes the operation by executing the two-phase commit protocol. Similarly, if the transaction manager receives an abort operation, it tells the resource managers to undo all the transaction's updates; that is, to abort the transaction at each resource manager. Thus, each resource manager must understand the concept of transaction, in the sense that it undoes or permanently installs the transaction's updates depending on whether the transaction aborts or commits.

When running two-phase commit, the transaction manager sends out two rounds of messages—one for each phase of the commitment activity. In the first round of messages it tells all the resource managers to prepare to commit by writing a copy of the results of the transaction to stable storage, but not actually to commit the transaction. At this point, the resource managers are said to be **prepared to commit**. When the transaction manager gets acknowledgments back from all the resource managers, it knows that the whole transaction has been prepared. That is, it knows that all resource managers stored a durable copy of the transaction's updates but none of them have committed the transaction. So it sends a second round of messages to tell the resource managers to actually commit. Figure 1.9 gives an example execution of two-phase commit with two resource managers involved.

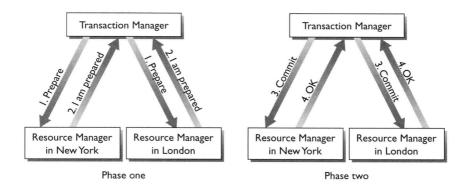

Phase one   Phase two

FIGURE 1.9

The Two-Phase Commit Protocol. In Phase One, every resource manager durably saves the transaction's updates before replying "I am Prepared." Thus, all resource managers have durably stored the transaction's updates before any of them commits in phase two.

Two-phase commit avoids the problem in Figure 1.7(a) because all resource managers have a durable copy of the transaction's updates before any of them commit. Therefore, even if a system fails during the commitment activity, as the London system did in the figure, it can commit the transaction after it recovers. However, to make this all work, the protocol must handle every possible failure and recovery scenario. For example, in Figure 1.7(b), it must tell the London system to commit the transaction. The details of how two-phase commit handles all these scenarios is described in Chapter 8.

Two-phase commit is required whenever a transaction accesses two or more resource managers. Thus, one key question that designers of TP applications must answer is whether or not to distribute their transaction programs among multiple resources. Using two-phase commit adds overhead (due to two-phase commit messages), but the option to distribute can provide better scalability (adding more systems to increase capacity) and availability (since one system can fail while others remain operational).

1.5 TRANSACTION PROCESSING PERFORMANCE

Performance is a critical aspect of TP systems. No one likes waiting more than a few seconds for an automated teller machine to dispense cash or for a hotel web site to accept a reservation request. So response time to end-users is one important measure of TP system performance. Companies that rely on TP systems, such as banks, airlines, and commercial web sites, also want to get the most transaction throughput for the money they invest in a TP system. They also care about system scalability; that is, how much they can grow their system as their business grows.

It's very challenging to configure a TP system to meet response time and throughput requirements at minimum cost. It requires choosing the number of systems, how much storage capacity they'll have, which processing and database functions are assigned to each system, and how the systems are connected to displays and to each other. Even if you know the performance of the component products being assembled, it's hard to predict how the overall system will perform. Therefore, users and vendors implement benchmarks to obtain guidance on how to configure systems and to compare competing products.

Vendor benchmarks are defined by an independent consortium called the Transaction Processing Performance Council (TPC; www.tpc.org). The benchmarks enable apples-to-apples comparisons of different vendors' hardware and software products. Each TPC benchmark defines standard transaction programs and characterizes a system's performance by the throughput that the system can process under certain workload conditions, database size, response time guarantees, and so on. Published results must be accompanied by a **full disclosure report**, which allows other vendors to review benchmark compliance and gives users more detailed performance information beyond the summary performance measures.

The benchmarks use two main measures of a system's performance, throughput, and cost-per-throughput-unit. Throughput is the maximum throughput it can attain, measured in **transactions per second (tps)** or **transactions per minute (tpm)**. Each benchmark defines a response time requirement for each transaction type (typically 1–5 seconds). The throughput can be measured only when 90% of the transactions meet their response time requirements and when the average of all transaction response times is less than their response time requirement. The latter ensures that all transactions execute within an acceptable period of time.

As an aside, Internet web sites usually measure 90% and 99% response times. Even if the average performance is fast, it's bad if one in a hundred transactions is too slow. Since customers often run multiple transactions, that translates into several percent of customers receiving poor service. Many such customers don't return.

The benchmarks' cost-per-throughput-unit is measured in dollars per tps or tpm. The cost is calculated as the list purchase price of the hardware and software, plus three years' vendor-supplied maintenance on that hardware and software (called the **cost of ownership**).

The definitions of TPC benchmarks are worth understanding to enable one to interpret TPC performance reports. Each of these reports, published on the TPC web site, is the result of a system benchmark evaluation performed by a system vendor and subsequently validated by an independent auditor. Although their main purpose is to allow customers to compare TP system products, these reports are also worth browsing for educational reasons, to give one a feel for the performance range of state-of-the-art systems. They are also useful as guidance for the design and presentation of a custom benchmark study for a particular user application.

The TPC-A and TPC-B Benchmarks

The first two benchmarks promoted by TPC, called TPC-A and TPC-B, model an ATM application that debits or credits a checking account. When TPC-A/B were introduced, around 1989, they were carefully crafted to exercise the main bottlenecks customers were experiencing in TP systems. The benchmark was so successful in encouraging vendors to eliminate these bottlenecks that within a few years nearly all database systems performed very well on TPC-A/B. Therefore, the benchmarks were retired and replaced by TPC-C in 1995. Still, it's instructive to look at the bottlenecks the benchmarks were designed to exercise, since these bottlenecks can still arise today on a poorly designed system or application.

Both benchmarks run the same transaction program. The only difference is that TPC-A includes terminals and a network in the overall system, while TPC-B does not. In both cases, the transaction program performs the sequence of operations shown in Figure 1.10 (except that TPC-B does not perform the read/write terminal operations).

In TPC-A/B, the database consists of:

- Account records, one record for each customer's account (total of 100,000 accounts)
- A teller record for each teller, which stores the amount of money in the teller's cash drawer (total of 10 tellers)
- One record for each bank branch (one branch minimum), which contains the sum of all the accounts at that branch
- A history file, which records a description of each transaction that actually executes

```
Start
  Read message from terminal (100 bytes)
  Read and write account record (random access)
  Write history record (sequential access)
  Read and write teller record (random access)
  Read and write branch record (random access)
  Write message to terminal (200 bytes)
Commit
```

FIGURE 1.10

TPC-A/B Transaction Program. The program models a debit/credit transaction for a bank.

The transaction reads a 100-byte input message, including the account number and amount of money to withdraw or deposit. The transaction uses that input to find the account record and update it appropriately. It updates the history file to indicate that this transaction has executed. It updates the teller and bank branch records to indicate the amount of money deposited or withdrawn at that teller and bank branch, respectively. Finally, for TPC-A, it sends a message back to the display device to confirm the completion of the transaction.

The benchmark exercises several potential bottlenecks on a TP system:

- There's a large number of account records. The system must have 100,000 account records for each transaction per second it can perform. To randomly access so many records, the database must be indexed.
- The end of the history file can be a bottleneck, because every transaction has to write to it and therefore to lock and synchronize against it. This synchronization can delay transactions.
- Similarly, the branch record can be a bottleneck, because all of the tellers at each branch are reading and writing it. However, TPC-A/B minimizes this effect by requiring a teller to execute a transaction only every 10 seconds.

Given a fixed configuration, the performance and price/performance of any TP application depends on the amount of computer resources needed to execute it: the number of processor instructions, I/Os to stable storage, and communications messages. Thus, an important step in understanding the performance of any TP application is to count the resources required for each transaction. In TPC-A/B, for each transaction a high performance implementation uses a few hundred thousand instructions, two or three I/Os to stable storage, and two interactions with the display. When running these benchmarks, a typical system spends more than half of the processor instructions inside the database system and maybe another third of the instructions in message communications between the parts of the application. Only a small fraction of the processor directly executes the transaction program. This isn't very surprising, because the transaction program mostly just sends messages and initiates database operations. The transaction program itself does very little, which is typical of many TP applications.

The TPC-C Benchmark

The TPC-C benchmark was introduced in 1992. It is based on an order-entry application for a wholesale supplier. Compared to TPC-A/B, it includes a wider variety of transactions, some "heavy weight" transactions (which do a lot of work), and a more complex database.

The database centers around a *warehouse*, which tracks the *stock* of *items* that it *supplies* to *customers* within a sales *district*, and tracks those customers' *orders*, which consist of *order-lines*. The database size is proportional to the number of warehouses (see Table 1.1).

Table 1.1 Database for the TPC-C Benchmark. The database consists of the tables in the left column, which support an order-entry application

Table Name	Number of Rows per Warehouse	Bytes-per-Row	Size of Table (in bytes) per Warehouse
Warehouse	1	89	.089 K
District	10	95	.95 K
Customer	30 K	655	19.65 K
History	30 K	46	1.38 K
Order	30 K	24	720 K
New-Order	9 K	8	72 K
Order-Line	300 K	54	16.2 M
Stock	100 K	306	306 M
Item	100 K	82	8.2 M

There are five types of transactions:

- **New-Order:** To enter a new order, first retrieve the records describing the given warehouse, customer, and district, and then update the district (increment the next available order number). Insert a record in the Order and New-Order tables. For each of the 5 to 15 (average 10) items ordered, retrieve the item record (abort if it doesn't exist), retrieve and update the stock record, and insert an order-line record.

- **Payment:** To enter a payment, first retrieve and update the records describing the given warehouse, district, and customer, and then insert a history record. If the customer is identified by name, rather than id number, then additional customer records (average of two) must be retrieved to find the right customer.

- **Order-Status:** To determine the status of a given customer's latest order, retrieve the given customer record (or records, if identified by name, as in Payment), and retrieve the customer's latest order and corresponding order-lines.

- **Delivery:** To process a new order for each of a warehouse's 10 districts, get the oldest new-order record in each district, delete it, retrieve and update the corresponding customer record, order record, and the order's corresponding order-line records. This can be done as one transaction or 10 transactions.

- **Stock-Level:** To determine, in a warehouse's district, the number of recently sold items whose stock level is below a given threshold, retrieve the record describing the given district (which has the next order number). Retrieve order lines for the previous 20 orders in that district, and for each item ordered, determine if the given threshold exceeds the amount in stock.

The transaction rate metric is the number of New-Order transactions per minute, denoted **tpmC**, given that all the other constraints are met. The New-Order, Payment, and Order-Status transactions have a response time requirement of five seconds. The Stock-Level transaction has a response time of 20 seconds and has relaxed consistency requirements. The Delivery transaction runs as a periodic batch. The workload requires executing an equal number of New-Order and Payment transactions, and one Order-Status, Delivery, and Stock-Level transaction for every 10 New-Orders.

Table 1.2 TPC-E Transaction Types

Transaction Type	Percent of Transactions	Database Tables Accessed	Description
Trade Order	10.1%	17	Buy or sell a security
Trade Result	10%	15	Complete the execution of a buy or sell order
Trade Status	19%	6	Get the status of an order
Trade Update	2%	6	Make corrections to a set of trades
Customer Position	13%	7	Get the value of a customer's assets
Market Feed	1%	2	Process an update of current market activity (e.g., ticker tape)
Market Watch	18%	4	Track market trends (e.g., for a customer's "watch list")
Security Detail	14%	12	Get a detailed data about a security
Trade Lookup	8%	6	Get information about a set of trades
Broker Volume	4.9%	6	Get a summary of the volume and value of pending orders of a set of brokers

The TPC-C workload is many times heavier per transaction than TPC-A/B and exhibits higher contention for shared data. Moreover, it exercises a wider variety of performance-sensitive functions, such as deferred transaction execution, access via secondary keys, and transaction aborts. It is regarded as a more realistic workload than TPC-A/B, which is why it replaced TPC-A/B as the standard TP systems benchmark.

The TPC-E Benchmark

The TPC-E benchmark was introduced in 2007. Compared to TPC-C, it represents larger and more complex databases and transaction workloads that are more representative of current TP applications. And it uses a storage configuration that is less expensive to test and run. It is based on a stock trading application for a brokerage firm where transactions are related to stock trades, customer inquiries, activity feeds from markets, and market analysis by brokers. Unlike previous benchmarks, TPC-E does not include transactional middleware components and solely measures database performance.

TPC-E includes 10 transaction types, summarized in Table 1.2, which are a mix of read-only and read-write transactions. For each type, the table shows the percentage of transactions of that type and the number of database tables it accesses, which give a feeling for the execution cost of the type.

There are various parameters that introduce variation into the workload. For example, trade requests are split 50-50 between buy and sell and 60-40 between market order and limit order. In addition, customers are assigned to one of three tiers, depending on how often they trade securities—the higher the tier, the more accounts per customer and trades per customer.

The database schema has 33 tables divided into four sets: market data (11 tables), customer data (9 tables), broker data (9 tables), and static reference data (4 tables). Most tables have fewer than six columns and less than 100 bytes per row. At the extremes, the Customer table has 23 columns, and several tables store text information with hundreds of bytes per row (or even more for the News Item table).

A driver program generates the transactions and their inputs, submits them to a test system, and measures the rate of completed transactions. The result is the **measured** transactions per second (tpsE), which is the number of Trade Result transactions executed per second, given the mix of the other transaction types. Each transaction type has a response time limit of one to three seconds, depending on transaction type. In contrast to TPC-C, application functions related to front-end programs are excluded. Thus, the results measure the server-side database management system. Like previous TPC benchmarks, TPC-E includes a measure for the cost per transaction per second ($/tpsE).

TPC-E provides data generation code to initialize the database with the result of 300 days of initial trading, daily market closing price information for five years, and quarterly company report data for five years. Beyond that, the database size scales up as a function of the **nominal** tpsE, which is the transaction rate the benchmark sponsor is aiming for. The measured tpsE must be within 80 to 102% of the nominal tpsE. The database must have 500 customers for each nominal tpsE. Other database tables scale relative to the number of customer rows. For example, for each 1000 Customers, there must be 685 Securities and 500 Companies. Some tables include a row describing each trade and therefore grow quite large for a given run.

Compared to TPC-C, TPC-E is a more complex workload. It makes heavier use of SQL database features, such as referential integrity and transaction isolation levels (to be discussed in Chapter 6). It uses a more complex SQL schema. Transactions execute more complex SQL statements and several of them have to make multiple calls to the database, which cannot be batched in one round-trip. And there is no trivial partitioning of the database that will enable scalability (to be discussed in Section 2.6). Despite all this newly introduced complexity, the benchmark generates a much lower I/O load than TPC-C for a comparable transaction rate. This makes the benchmark cheaper to run, which is important to vendors when they run high-end scalability tests where large machine configurations are needed.

In addition to its TP benchmarks, the TPC publishes a widely used benchmark for decision support systems, TPC-H. It also periodically considers new TP benchmark proposals. Consult the TPC web site, www.tpc.org, for current details.

1.6 AVAILABILITY

Availability is the fraction of time a TP system is up and running and able to do useful work—that is, it isn't down due to hardware or software failures, operator errors, preventative maintenance, power failures, or the like. Availability is an important measure of the capability of a TP system because the TP application usually is offering a service that's "mission critical," one that's essential to the operation of the enterprise, such as airline reservations, managing checking accounts in a bank, processing stock transactions in a stock exchange, or offering a retail storefront on the Internet. Obviously, if this type of system is unavailable, the business stops operating. Therefore, the system *must* operate nearly all the time.

Just how highly available does a system have to be? We see from the table in Figure 1.11 that if the system is available 96% of the time, that means it's down nearly an hour a day. That's too much time for many types of businesses, which would consider 96% availability to be unacceptable.

An availability of 99% means that the system is down about 100 minutes per week (i.e., 7 days/week × 24 hours/day × 60 minutes/hour × 1/100). Many TP applications would find this unacceptable if it came in one 100-minute period of unavailability. It might be tolerable, provided that it comes in short outages of just a few minutes at a time. But in many cases, even this may not be tolerable, for example in the operation of a stock exchange where short periods of downtime can produce big financial losses.

An availability of 99.9% means that the system is down for about an hour per month, or under two minutes per day. Further, 99.999% availability means that the system is down five minutes a year. That number

Downtime	Availability (%)
I hour/day	95.8
I hour/week	99.41
I hour/month	99.86
I hour/year	99.9886
I hour/20 years	99.99942

FIGURE 1.11

Downtime at Different Availability Level. The number of nines after the decimal point is of practical significance.

may seem incredibly ambitious, but it *is* attainable; telephone systems typically have that level of availability. People sometimes talk about availability in terms of the number of 9s that are attained; for example, "five 9s" means 99.999% available.

Some systems need to operate for only part of the day, such as 9 AM to 5 PM on weekdays. In that case, availability usually is measured relative to the hours when the system is expected to be operational. Thus, 99.9% availability means that it is down at most 2.4 minutes per week (i.e., 40 hours/week × 60 minutes/hour × 1/1000).

Today's TP system customers typically expect availability levels of at least 99%, although it certainly depends on how much money they're willing to spend. Generally, attaining high availability requires attention to four factors:

- The environment—making the physical environment more robust to avoid failures of power, communications, air conditioning, and the like
- System management—avoiding failures due to operational errors by system managers and vendors' field service
- Hardware—having redundant hardware, so that if some component fails, the system can immediately and automatically replace it with another component that's ready to take over
- Software—improving the reliability of software and ensuring it can automatically and quickly recover after a failure

This book is about software, and regrettably, of the four factors, software is the major contributor to availability problems. Software failures can be divided into three categories: application failures, database system failures, and operating system failures.

Because we're using transactions, when an application fails, any uncommitted transaction it was executing aborts automatically. Its updates are backed out, because of the atomicity property. There's really nothing that the system has to do other than re-execute the transaction after the application is running again.

When the database system fails, all the uncommitted transactions that were accessing the database system at that time have to abort, because their updates may be lost during the database system failure. A system management component of the operating system, database system, or transactional middleware has to detect the failure of the database system and tell the database system to reinitialize itself. During the reinitialization process, the database system backs out the updates of all the transactions that were active at the time of the failure, thereby getting the database into a clean state, where it contains the results only of committed transactions.

A failure of the operating system requires it to reboot. All programs, applications, and database systems executing at the time of failure are now dead. Everything has to be reinitialized after the operating system reboots. On an ordinary computer system all this normally takes between several minutes and an hour, depending on how big the system is, how many transactions were active at the time of failure, how long it takes to back out the uncommitted transactions, how efficient the initialization program is, and so on. Very high availability systems, such as those intended to be available in excess of 99%, typically are designed for very fast recovery. Even when they fail, they are down only for a very short time. They usually use some form of replicated processing to get this fast recovery. When one component fails, they quickly delegate processing work to a copy of the component that is ready and waiting to pick up the load.

The transaction abstraction helps the programmer quite a bit in attaining high availability, because the system is able to recover into a clean state by aborting transactions. And it can continue from where it left off by rerunning transactions that aborted as a result of the failure. Without the transaction abstraction, the recovery program would have to be application-specific. It would have to analyze the state of the database at the time of the failure to figure out what work to undo and what to rerun. We discuss high availability issues and techniques in more detail in Chapter 7, and replication technology in Chapter 9.

In addition to application, database system, and operating system failures, operator errors are a major contributor to unplanned downtime. Many of these errors can be attributed to system management software that is hard to understand and use. If the software is difficult to tune, upgrade, or operate, then operators make mistakes. The ideal system management software is fully automated and requires no human intervention for such routine activities.

1.7 STYLES OF SYSTEMS

We've been talking about TP as a style of *application*, one that runs short transaction programs that access a shared database. TP is also a style of *system*, a way of configuring software components to do the type of work required by a TP application. It's useful to compare this style of system with other styles that you may be familiar with, to see where the differences are and why TP systems are constructed differently from the others. There are several other kinds of systems that we can look at here:

- Batch processing systems, where you submit a job and later receive output in the form of a file
- Real-time systems, where you submit requests to do a small amount of work that has to be done before some very early deadline
- Data warehouse systems, where reporting programs and *ad hoc* queries access data that is integrated from multiple data sources

Designing a system to perform one of these types of processing is called *system engineering*. Rather than engineering a specific component, such as an operating system or a database system, you engineer an integrated system by combining different kinds of components to perform a certain type of work. Often, systems are engineered to handle multiple styles, but for the purposes of comparing and contrasting the different styles, we'll discuss them as if each type of system were running in a separately engineered environment. Let's look at requirements for each of these styles of computing and see how they compare to a TP system.

Batch Processing Systems

A batch is a set of requests that are processed together, often long after the requests were submitted. Data processing systems of the 1960s and early 1970s were primarily batch processing systems. Today, batch workloads are still with us. But instead of running them on systems dedicated for batch processing, they often execute on systems that also run a TP workload. TP systems can execute the batches during nonpeak periods, since the batch workload has flexible response-time requirements. To make the comparison between TP and batch clear, we will compare a TP system running a pure TP workload against a classical batch system running a pure batch workload, even though mixtures of the two are now commonplace.

A batch processing system executes each batch as a sequence of transactions, one transaction at a time. Since transactions execute serially there's no problem with serializability. By contrast, in a TP system many transactions can execute at the same time, and so the system has extra work to ensure serializability.

For example, computing the value of a stock market portfolio could be done as a batch application, running once a day after the close of financial markets. Computing a monthly bill for telephone customers could be a batch application, running daily for a different subset of the customer base each day. Generating tax reporting documents could be a batch application executed once per quarter or once per year.

The main performance measure of batch processing is throughput, that is, the amount of work done per unit of time. Response time is less important. A batch could take minutes, hours, or even days to execute. By contrast, TP systems have important response time requirements, because generally there's a user waiting at a display for the transaction's output.

A classical batch processing application takes its input as a record-oriented file whose records represent a sequence of request messages. Its output is also normally stored in a file. By contrast, TP systems typically have large networks of display devices for capturing requests and displaying results.

Batch processing can be optimized by ordering the input requests consistently with the order of the data in the database. For example, if the requests correspond to giving airline mileage credit for recent flights to mileage award customers, the records of customer flights can be ordered by mileage award account number. That way, it's easy and efficient to process the records by a merge procedure that reads the mileage award account database in account number order. By contrast, TP requests come in a random order. Because of the fast response time requirement, the system can't spend time sorting the input in an order consistent with the database. It has to be able to access the data randomly, in the order in which the data is requested.

Classical batch processing takes the request message file and existing database file(s) as input and produces a new master output database as a result of running transactions for the requests. If the batch processing program should fail, there's no harm done because the input file and input database are unmodified—simply throw out the output file and run the batch program again. By contrast, a TP system updates its database on-line as requests arrive. So a failure may leave the database in an inconsistent state, because it contains the results of uncompleted transactions. This atomicity problem for transactions in a TP environment doesn't exist in a batch environment.

Finally, in batch the load on the system is fixed and predictable, so the system can be engineered for that load. For example, you can schedule the system to run the batch at a given time and set aside sufficient capacity to do it, because you know exactly what the load is going to be. By contrast, a TP load generally varies during the day. There are peak periods when there's a lot of activity and slow periods when there's very little. The system has to be sized to handle the peak load and also designed to make use of extra capacity during slack periods.

Real-Time Systems

TP systems are similar to real-time systems, such as a system collecting input from a satellite or controlling a factory's shop floor equipment. TP essentially is a kind of real-time system, with a real-time response time demand of 1 to 2 seconds. It responds to a real-world process consisting of end-users interacting with display devices, which communicate with application programs accessing a shared database. So not surprisingly, there are many similarities between the two kinds of systems.

Real-time systems and TP systems both have predictable loads with periodic peaks. Real-time systems usually emphasize gathering input rather than processing it, whereas TP systems generally do both.

Due to the variety of real-world processes they control, real-time systems generally have to deal with more specialized devices than TP, such as laboratory equipment, factory shop floor equipment, or sensors and control systems in an automobile or airplane.

Real-time systems generally don't need or use special mechanisms for atomicity and durability. They simply process the input as quickly as they can. If they lose some of that input, they ignore the loss and keep on running. To see why, consider the example of a system that collects input from a monitoring satellite. It's not good if the system misses some of the data coming in. But the system certainly can't stop operating to go back to fix things up like a TP system would do—the data keeps coming in and the system must do its best to continue processing it. By contrast, a TP environment can generally stop accepting input for a short time or can buffer the input for awhile. If there is a failure, it can stop collecting input, run a recovery procedure, and then resume processing input. Thus, the fault-tolerance requirements between the two types of systems are rather different.

Real-time systems are generally not concerned with serializability. In most real-time applications, processing of input messages involves no access to shared data. Since the processing of two different inputs does not affect each other, even if they're processed concurrently, they'll behave like a serial execution. No special mechanisms, such as locking, are needed. When processing real-time inputs to shared data, the notion of serializability is as relevant as it is to TP. However, in this case, real-time applications generally make direct use of low-level synchronization primitives for mutual exclusion, rather than relying on a general-purpose synchronization mechanism that is hidden behind the transaction abstraction.

Data Warehouse Systems

TP systems process the data in its raw state as it arrives. **Data warehouse systems** integrate data from multiple sources into a database suitable for querying.

For example, a distribution company decides each year how to allocate its marketing and advertising budget. It uses a TP system to process sales orders that includes the type and value of each order. The customer database tells each customer's location, annual revenue, and growth rate. The finance database includes cost and income information, and tells which product lines are most profitable. The company pulls data from these three data sources into a data warehouse. Business analysts can query the data warehouse to determine how best to allocate promotional resources.

Data warehouse systems execute two kinds of workloads: a batch workload to extract data from the sources, cleaning the data to reconcile discrepancies between them, transforming the data into a common shape that's convenient for querying, and loading it into the warehouse; and queries against the warehouse, which can range from short interactive requests to complex analyses that generate large reports. Both of these workloads are quite different than TP, which consists of short updates and queries. Also unlike TP, a data warehouse's content can be somewhat out-of-date, since users are looking for trends that are not much affected by the very latest updates. In fact, sometimes it's important to run on a static database copy, so that the results of successive queries are comparable. Running queries on a data warehouse rather than a TP database is also helpful for performance reasons, since data warehouse queries would slow down update transactions, a topic we'll discuss in some detail in Chapter 6. Our comparison of system styles so far is summarized in Figure 1.12.

Other System Types

Two other system types that are related to TP are timesharing and client-server.

Timesharing

In a timesharing system, a display device is connected to an operating system process, and within that process the user can invoke programs that interact frequently with the display. Before the widespread use of PCs, when timesharing systems were popular, TP systems often were confused with timesharing, because they both

	Transaction Processing	Batch	Real-time	Data Warehouse
Isolation	serializable, multi-programmed execution	serial, uni-programmed execution	no transaction concept	no transaction concept
Workload	high variance	predictable	predictability depends on the application	predictable loading, high variance queries
Performance metric	response time and throughput	throughput	response time, throughput, missed deadlines	throughput for loading, response time for queries
Input	network of display devices submitting requests	record-oriented file	network of devices submitting data and operations	network of display devices submitting queries
Data Access	random access	accesses sorted to be consistent with database order	unconstrained	possibly sorted for loading, unconstrained for queries
Recovery	after failure, ensure database has committed updates and no others	after failure, rerun the batch to produce a new master file	application's responsibility	application's responsibility

FIGURE 1.12

Comparison of System Types. Transaction processing has different characteristics than the other styles, and therefore requires systems that are specially engineered to the purpose.

involve managing lots of display devices connected to a common server. But they're really quite different in terms of load, performance requirements, and availability requirements:

- A timesharing system has a highly unpredictable load, since users continually make different demands on the system. By comparison, a TP load is very regular, running similar load patterns every day.

- Timesharing systems have less stringent availability and atomicity requirements than TP systems. The TP concept of ACID execution doesn't apply.

- Timesharing applications are not mission-critical to the same degree as TP applications and therefore have weaker availability requirements.

- Timesharing system performance is measured in terms of system capacity, such as instructions per second and number of on-line users. Unlike TP, there are no generally accepted benchmarks that accurately represent the behavior of a wide range of timesharing applications.

Client-Server

In a client-server system, a large number of personal computers communicate with shared servers on a local area network. This kind of system is very similar to a TP environment, where a large number of display devices connect to shared servers that run transactions. In some sense, TP systems were the original client-server systems with very simple desktop devices, namely, dumb terminals. As desktop devices have become more powerful, TP systems and personal computer systems have been converging into a single type of computing environment with different kinds of servers, such as file servers, communication servers, and TP servers.

There are many more system types than we have space to include here. Some examples are embedded systems, computer-aided design systems, data streaming systems, electronic switching systems, and traffic control systems.

Why Engineer a TP System?

Each system type that we looked at is designed for certain usage patterns. Although it is engineered for that usage pattern, it actually can be used in other ways. For example, people have used timesharing systems to run TP applications. These applications typically do not scale very well or use operating system resources very efficiently, but it can be done. For example, people have built special-purpose TP systems using real-time systems, and batch systems to run on a timesharing system.

TP has enough special requirements that it's worth engineering the system for that purpose. The amount of money businesses spend on TP systems justifies the additional engineering work vendors do to tailor their system products for TP—for better performance, reliability, and ease-of-use.

1.8 TP SYSTEM CONFIGURATIONS

When learning the principles of transaction processing, it is helpful to have a feel for the range of systems where these principles are applied. We already saw some examples in Section 1.5 on TP benchmarks. Although those benchmark applications have limited functionality, they nevertheless are meant to be representative of the kind of functionality that is implemented for complete practical applications.

In any given price range, including the very high end, the capabilities of TP applications and systems continually grow, in large part due to the steadily declining cost of computing and communication. These growing capabilities enable businesses to increase the functionality of classical TP applications, such as travel reservations and banking. In addition, every few years, these capabilities enable entirely new categories of businesses. In the past decade, examples include large-scale Internet retailers and social networking web sites.

There is no such thing as an average TP application or system. Rather, systems that implement TP applications come in a wide range of sizes, from single servers to data centers with thousands of machines. And the applications themselves exhibit a wide range of complexity, from a single database with few dozen transaction types to thousands of databases running hundreds of millions of lines of code. Therefore, whatever one might say about typical TP installations will apply only to a small fraction of them and will likely be outdated within a few years.

A low-end system could be a departmental application supporting a small number of users who perform a common function. Such an application might run comfortably on a single server machine. For example, the sales and marketing team of a small company might use a TP application to capture sales orders, record customer responses to sales campaigns, alert sales people when product support agreements need to be renewed, and track the steps in resolving customer complaints. Even though the load on the system is rather light, the application might require hundreds of transaction types to support many different business functions.

By contrast, the workload of a large Internet service might require thousands of server machines. This is typical for large-scale on-line shopping, financial services, travel services, multimedia services (e.g., sharing of music, photos, and videos), and social networking. To ensure the service is available 24 hours a day, 7 days a week (a.k.a. 24 × 7), it often is supported by multiple geographically distributed data centers. Thus if one data center fails, others can pick up its load.

Like hardware configuration, software configurations cover a wide range. The system software used to operate a TP system may be proprietary or open source. It may use the latest system software products or ones that were introduced decades ago. It may only include a SQL database system and web server, or it may include several layers of transactional middleware and specialized database software.

The range of technical issues that need to be addressed is largely independent of the hardware or software configuration that is chosen. These issues include selecting a programming model; ensuring the ACID properties; and maximizing availability, scalability, manageability, and performance. These issues are the main subject of this book.

1.9 SUMMARY

A **transaction** is the execution of a program that performs an administrative function by accessing a shared database. Transactions can execute on-line, while a user is waiting, or off-line (in batch mode) if the execution takes longer than a user can wait for results. The end-user requests the execution of a transaction program by sending a request message.

A transaction processing application is a collection of transaction programs designed to automate a given business activity. A TP application consists of a relatively small number of predefined types of transaction programs. TP applications can run on a wide range of computer sizes and may be centralized or distributed, running on local area or wide area networks. TP applications are mapped to a specially engineered hardware and software environment called a TP system.

The three parts of a TP application correspond to the three major functions of a TP system:

1. Obtain input from a display or special device and construct a request.
2. Accept a request message and call the correct transaction program.
3. Execute the transaction program to complete the work required by the request.

Database management plays a significant role in a TP system. Transactional middleware components supply functions to help get the best price/performance out of a TP system and provide a structure in which TP applications execute.

There are four critical properties of a transaction: atomicity, consistency, isolation, and durability. Consistency is the responsibility of the program. The remaining three properties are the responsibility of the TP system.

- Atomicity: Each transaction performs all its operations or none of them. Successful transactions commit; failed transactions abort. Commit makes database changes permanent; abort undoes or erases database changes.
- Consistency: Each transaction is programmed to preserve database consistency.
- Isolation: Each transaction executes as if it were running alone. That is, the effect of running a set of transactions is the same as running them one at a time. This behavior is called serializability and usually is implemented by locking.
- Durability: The result of a committed transaction is guaranteed to be on stable storage, that is, one that survives power failures and operating system failures, such as a magnetic or solid-state disk.

If a transaction updates multiple databases or resource managers, then the two-phase commit protocol is required. In phase one, it ensures all resource managers have saved the transaction's updates to stable storage. If phase one succeeds, then phase two tells all resource managers to commit. This ensures atomicity, that is, that the transaction commits at all resource managers or aborts at all of them. Two-phase commit usually is implemented by a transaction manager, which tracks which resource managers are accessed by each transaction and runs the two-phase commit protocol.

Performance is a critical aspect of TP. A TP system must scale up to run many transactions per time unit, while giving one- or two-second response time. The standard measures of performance are the TPC benchmarks, which compare TP systems based on their maximum transaction rate and price per transaction for a standardized application workload.

A TP system is often critical to proper functioning of the enterprise that uses it. Therefore, another important property of TP systems is availability; that is, the fraction of time the system is running and able to do work. Availability is determined by how frequently a TP system fails and how quickly it can recover from failures.

TP systems have rather different characteristics than batch, real-time, and data warehouse systems. They therefore require specialized implementations that are tuned to the purpose. These techniques are the main subject of this book.

Transaction Processing Abstractions

2.1 INTRODUCTION

This chapter discusses five software abstractions that are used heavily in TP systems:

- Transactions
- Processes and threads
- Remote procedure calls
- Transaction context, sessions, and other techniques for managing shared state
- Caching, resource pooling, partitioning, and replication

These abstractions involve both the application programming interface and mechanisms to support it. Understanding them is fundamental to developing and engineering a TP system.

We start with the transaction abstraction, where we focus on the semantics of the programming model. We present pseudocode that illustrates how a transaction is delimited and thus establishes the relationship between a program and the TP infrastructure. This sets the stage to discuss the significant abstractions relevant to that infrastructure—processes, threads, and remote procedure call—where the focus shifts from the programming model to how the mechanisms work. Then we present the main abstractions involved in state management, which are at the core of the leading programming and deployment models used in transactional middleware. Finally, we talk about abstractions that are used to enhance the performance and scalability of TP applications: caching of state; pooling of sessions, threads, and other resources; and partitioning and replication of databases and server processes.

2.2 TRANSACTIONS

The transaction abstraction affects three aspects of a TP system:

- The programming model; that is, the style in which application programs are written
- The application programming interface (API); that is, the commands available to the application programmer
- Components of the system software that support TP applications

It is up to the application programmer to bracket the set of operations that should be executed as part of the same transaction. This section focuses on the semantics that is implied by the transaction brackets. For the most part, we use pseudocode to express this bracketing explicitly, because it is easy to understand and exposes the semantic issues that are at stake. Other styles of programming are described later in this section. Product-specific programming models and APIs for transaction bracketing are presented in Chapter 10. System software components that support TP applications are discussed in Chapter 3.

Transaction Bracketing

Transaction bracketing offers the application programmer commands to Start, Commit, and Abort a transaction. These are expressed explicitly in some programming models and implicitly in others, but in either case these are the commands whose execution begins and terminates a transaction.

The commands to bracket a transaction are used to identify which operations execute in the scope of a transaction. The Start command creates a new transaction. After an application invokes a Start command, all of its operations execute within that transaction until the application invokes Commit or Abort. In particular, if the application calls a procedure, that procedure ordinarily executes within the same transaction as its caller. After invoking Commit or Abort, the application is no longer executing a transaction until it invokes Start again.

Sometimes, a procedure is designed to be executed either as an independent transaction or as a step within a larger transaction. For example, consider the following two procedures:

- `DebitChecking(acct, amt)`. Withdraw a given amount of money (`amt`) from a given checking account (`acct`).
- `PayLoan(loan, amt)`. Pay back a given amount of money (`amt`) on a given loan (`loan`).

Each of these procedures could execute as an independent ACID transaction. In that case, you would expect to see Start at the beginning of the body of each of the procedures and Commit at the end. Example procedures for `DebitChecking` and `PayLoan` are shown in Figure 2.1.

```
Boolean DebitChecking(acct, amt) {
        int acct, amt;
        Start;
        Boolean success = true;
        // Code to perform the withdrawal goes here.
        // Set "success = false" if the withdrawal fails,
        // e.g., due to insufficient funds
        if success Commit else Abort;
        return success;
}


Boolean PayLoan(loan, amt) {
        int loan, amt;
        Start;
        Boolean success = true;
        // Code to perform the payment goes here.
        // Set "success = false" if the payment fails,
        // e.g., because the loan has already been paid
        if success Commit else Abort;
        return success;
}
```

FIGURE 2.1

Explicit Transaction Brackets. The `DebitChecking` and `PayLoan` procedures explicitly bracket their transactions with a Start command and a Commit or Abort command.

As long as a transaction executes a single procedure, it is quite straightforward to bracket the transaction using Start, Commit, and Abort. Things get more complicated if a procedure that is running a transaction calls another procedure to do part of the work of the transaction. For example, suppose there is a procedure PayLoan FromChecking(acct, loan, amt) that calls the DebitChecking and PayLoan procedures to withdraw money from a checking account to pay back part of a loan, as shown in Figure 2.2.

We would like the PayLoanFromChecking procedure to execute as an ACID transaction. We therefore bracket the body of the procedure with calls to Start and Commit. This PayLoanFromChecking transaction includes its calls to the DebitChecking and PayLoan procedures. However, there is a potential problem with this, namely, that DebitChecking and PayLoan also invoke the Start and Commit commands. Thus, as they're currently written, DebitChecking and PayLoan would execute separate transactions that commit independently of PayLoanFromChecking, which is not what we want. That is, we cannot compose DebitChecking and PayLoan into a larger transaction. We call this the **transaction composability problem**.

One solution is to have the system ignore invocations of the Start command when it is executed by a program that is already running within a transaction. In this approach, when the PayLoanFromChecking procedure calls the DebitChecking procedure, the Start command in the DebitChecking procedure in Figure 2.1 would not cause a new transaction to be created. However, the system cannot completely ignore this second Start command. It must remember that this second Start command was invoked, so it will know that it should ignore the execution of the corresponding Commit command in DebitChecking. That is, the Commit command in Figure 2.1 should not commit the "outer" transaction created by PayLoanFromChecking. More generally, the system maintains a start-count for each executing application, which is initialized to zero. Each execution of the Start command increments the start-count and each Commit decrements it. Only the last Commit, which decrements the count back to zero, causes the transaction to commit.

What if the DebitChecking procedure issues the Abort command? One possible interpretation is that if an inner procedure calls Abort, then the transaction that the procedure is executing really does need to abort. Thus, unlike the Commit command, the Abort command in the DebitChecking procedure causes an abort of the outer transaction created by PayLoanFromChecking. In some systems, it is simply an error for a procedure that has executed a second Start command to subsequently invoke an Abort command. In others, the invocation of Abort is ignored. Another possible interpretation is that it is an attempt to abort only the work that was performed since the last Start command executed. This semantics is discussed in the later subsection, *Nested Transactions*.

Another solution to the transaction composability problem is to remove the Start and Commit commands from DebitChecking and PayLoan, so they can be invoked within the transaction bracketed by the PayLoanFromChecking procedure. Using this approach, the DebitChecking procedure would be replaced by the one in Figure 2.3. To enable DebitChecking to execute as an independent transaction, one can write

```
Boolean PayLoanFromChecking(acct, loan, amt) {
        int  acct, loan, amt;
        Start;
        if ¬DebitChecking(acct, amt) {Abort; return false;};
        if ¬PayLoan(loan, amt) {Abort; return false;};
        Commit;
        return true;
    }
```

FIGURE 2.2

A Composite Transaction. The transaction PayLoanFromChecking is written by composing the DebitChecking and PayLoan procedures.

```
Boolean DebitChecking(acct, amt) {
        int acct, amt;
        Boolean success = true;
        // Code to perform the withdrawal goes here.
        // Set "success = false" if the withdrawal fails,
        // e.g., due to insufficient funds
        return success;
}

Boolean CallDebitChecking(acct, amt) {
        int acct, amt;
        Start;
        Boolean success = DebitChecking(acct, amt);
        if success Commit else Abort;
        return success;
}
```

FIGURE 2.3

Enabling Composability. The Start, Commit, and Abort commands are removed in this revised version of the
DebitChecking procedure (Figure 2.1), so it can be invoked in a larger transaction, such as PayLoanFromChecking
(Figure 2.2). A wrapper procedure CallDebitChecking is added, which includes the transaction brackets needed to
execute DebitChecking as an independent transaction.

a "wrapper" procedure CallDebitChecking that includes the transaction brackets, also shown in Figure 2.3.
This approach avoids the need to rewrite application code when existing procedures are composed in new ways.
Another programming model that realizes this benefit is described in a later subsection entitled, *Transaction
Bracketing in Object-Oriented Programming*.

The impact of the transaction composability problem is something that needs to be evaluated and under-
stood in the context of whichever programming model or models you are using.

Transaction Identifiers

As we explained in Chapter 1, each transaction has a unique transaction identifier (transaction ID), which is
assigned when the transaction is started. The transaction ID is assigned by whichever component is responsible
for creating the transaction in response to the Start command. That component could be a transaction manager
(see Section 1.4) or a transactional resource manager such as a database system, file system, or queue manager.

There are two major types of transaction IDs: global and local. The transaction manager assigns a global
ID, which is needed when more than one transactional resource participates in a transaction. If the transactional resource managers also assign transaction IDs, then these are local IDs that are correlated with the
global transaction ID since they all refer to the same transaction.

Whenever a transaction accesses a transactional resource, it needs to supply its transaction ID, to tell the
resource's manager on which transaction's behalf the access is being made. The resource manager needs this
information to enforce the ACID properties. In particular, it needs it for write accesses, so that it knows which
write operations to permanently install or undo when the transaction commits or aborts.

When an application program invokes Commit or Abort, it needs to pass the transaction ID as a parameter.
This tells the transaction manager which transaction it is supposed to commit or abort.

Since the application needs to supply its transaction ID to resource managers and the transaction manager,
it needs to manage its transaction ID. It could do this explicitly. That is, the Start operation could return a

transaction ID explicitly to the application, and the application could pass that transaction ID to every resource it accesses.

Most systems hide this complexity from the application programmer. Instead of returning the transaction ID to the program P that invokes Start, the system typically makes the transaction ID part of a hidden **context**, which is data that is associated with P but is manipulated only by the system, not by P. In particular, using the context the system transparently attaches the transaction ID to all database operations and Commit and Abort operations. This is more convenient for application programmers—it's one less piece of bookkeeping for them to deal with. It also avoids errors, because if the application passes the wrong transaction identifier, the system could malfunction.

Typically, the hidden context is associated with a thread, which is a sequential flow of control through a program. A thread can have only one transaction ID in its context, so there is no ambiguity about which transaction should be associated with each database operation and Commit or Abort. Threads are discussed in detail in the next section.

Notice that there are no transaction IDs in Figure 2.1 through Figure 2.3. The transaction ID is simply part of the hidden program context. Throughout this chapter, we will assume that transaction IDs are hidden in this way, although as we will see some programming models allow access to this transaction context.

Chained Transactions

In some programming models, an application is assumed to be always executing within a transaction, so there is no need for the developer to start a transaction explicitly. Instead, an application simply specifies the boundary between each pair of transactions. This "boundary operation" commits one transaction and immediately starts another transaction, thereby ensuring that the program is always executing a transaction. In IBM's CICS product, the verb called **syncpoint** works in this way. Microsoft SQL Server offers an implicit transaction mode that works this way too.

This programming style is called **chained transactions**, because the sequence of transactions executed by a program forms a chain, one transaction after the next, with no gaps in between. The alternative is an **unchained** model, where after a program finishes one transaction, it need not start the execution of another transaction right away. For example, this can be done using the Start and Commit commands for explicit transaction bracketing. Most of today's programming models use the unchained model, requiring that the developer explicitly defines the start of each new transaction.

On the face of it, the unchained model sounds more flexible, since there may be times when you would want an application to do work outside of a transaction. However, in fact there is really very little purpose in it. The only benefit is in systems where a transaction has significant overhead even if it doesn't access recoverable data. In that case, the unchained model avoids this overhead.

On the other hand, the unchained model has two significant disadvantages. First, if the code that executes outside a transaction updates any transactional resources, then each of those updates in effect executes as a separate transaction. This is usually more expensive than grouping sets of updates into a single transaction. That is, it is sometimes important to group together updates into a single transaction for performance reasons. Second, the unchained model gives the programmer an opportunity to break the consistency property of transactions by accidentally executing a set of updates outside of a transaction. For these reasons, the chained model usually is considered preferable to the unchained model.

Transaction Bracketing in Object-Oriented Programming

With the advent of object-oriented programming for TP applications, a richer style of chained transaction model has become popular. In this approach each method is tagged with a **transaction attribute** that indicates its transactional behavior, thereby avoiding explicit transaction bracketing in the application code itself. The transaction attribute can have one of the following values:

- Requires New: Every invocation of the method starts executing in a new transaction, whether or not the caller is already executing in a transaction.
- Required: If the caller is already running within a transaction, then the called method executes within that transaction. If not, then the called method starts executing in a new transaction.
- Supported: If the caller is already running within a transaction, then the called method executes within that transaction. If not, then the called method does not execute within a transaction.
- Not Supported: The called method does not execute within a transaction, even if the program that created the object is running within a transaction.[1]

This style of programming was introduced in the mid-1990s in Microsoft Transaction Server, which evolved later into COM+ in Microsoft's .NET Enterprise Services. In that system, a transaction attribute is attached to a component, which is a set of classes, and applies to all classes in the component. In its intended usage, the caller creates an object of the class (rather than calling a method of an existing object), at which time the transaction attribute is interpreted to decide whether it is part of the caller's transaction, is part of a new transaction, is not part of any transaction, or throws an exception. The called object is destroyed when the transaction ends.

The concept of transaction attribute was adopted and extended by OMG's CORBA standard and Enterprise Java Beans (EJB, now part of Java Enterprise Edition (Java EE)). It is now widely used in transactional middleware products, as well as in Web Services. In EJB, the attributes tag each method and apply per method call, not just when the called object is created. A class can be tagged with a transaction attribute, in which case it applies to all untagged methods. EJB also adds attributes to cover some other transaction options, in particular, Mandatory, where the called method runs in the caller's transaction if it exists and otherwise throws an exception.

Microsoft introduced per-method transaction attributes in Windows Communication Foundation in .NET 3.0. It uses separate attributes to specify whether the method executes as a transaction and whether the caller's transaction context propagates to the called method (i.e., the difference between Required and Requires New).

Let us call a method invocation **top-level** if it caused a new transaction to be started. That is, it is top-level if it is tagged with Requires New or is tagged with Required and its caller was not executing in a transaction. Generally speaking, a transaction commits when its top-level method terminates without an error. If it throws an exception during its execution, then its transaction aborts.

A top-level method can call other methods whose transaction attribute is Required, Mandatory, or Supported. This submethod executes in the same transaction as the top-level method. If the submethod terminates without error, the top-level method can assume that it is fine to commit the transaction. However, the top-level method is not obligated to commit, for example, if it encounters an error later in the execution of another submethod. In some execution models, a submethod can continue to execute after announcing that the transaction can be committed as far as it is concerned.

If the submethod throws an exception, then the top-level method must abort the transaction. In some execution models, the exception immediately causes the transaction to abort, as if the submethod had issued the Abort command. In other models, it is left to the top-level method to cause the abort to happen.

Instead of having a method automatically vote to commit or abort depending on whether it terminates normally or throws an exception, an option is available to give the developer more explicit control. For example,

---

[1]Microsoft supports an additional value, Disabled, which has the same transaction behavior as Not Supported. A newly created object uses the "context" of its caller, whereas for Not Supported the newly created object is given a fresh context of its own. Contexts are explained in Section 2.5.

in the .NET Framework, a program can do this by calling SetComplete and SetAbort. Java EE is similar, offering the setRollbackOnly command for a subobject to tell the top-level object to abort.

The approach of using transaction attributes is declarative in that the attributes are attached to interface definitions or method implementations. Microsoft's .NET framework also offers a runtime layer, exposed through the class TransactionScope, that allows a program to invoke the functionality of the transaction bracketing attributes shown previously. A program defines a transaction bracket by creating a TransactionScope object with one of the following options:

- Requires New: The program starts executing within a new transaction, whether or not it was previously executing in the context of a transaction.
- Required: If the program was executing in the context of a transaction, then it continues doing so. Otherwise, it starts a new transaction.
- Suppress: The program is now executing outside of a transaction.

In the case of Requires New and Suppress, if the program was running within a transaction T when it created the new transaction scope S, then T remains alive but has no activity until S exits.

Additional details of these approaches to transaction bracketing appear in Section 10.3 for .NET and Section 10.4 for Java EE.

Nested Transactions

The **nested transaction** programming model addresses the transaction composability problem by capturing the program-subprogram structure of an application within the transaction structure itself. In nested transactions, each transaction can have subtransactions. For example, the PayLoanFromChecking transaction can have two subtransactions DebitChecking and PayLoan.

Like ordinary "flat" (i.e., non-nested) transactions, subtransactions are bracketed by the Start, Commit, and Abort operations. In fact, the programs of Figure 2.1 and Figure 2.2 could be a nested transaction. What is different about nested transactions is not the bracketing operations—it's their semantics. They behave as follows:

1. If a program is already executing inside a transaction and issues a Start command, then Start creates a **subtransaction** of its parent transaction, rather than creating a new, independent transaction. For example, if DebitChecking is called from PayLoanFromChecking, the Start in DebitChecking starts a subtransaction.

2. If a program is *not* already executing inside a transaction and issues a Start command, then Start creates a new, independent transaction, called a **top-level** transaction, which is not a subtransaction of another transaction. For example, Start in PayLoanFromChecking creates a top-level transaction.

3. The Commit and Abort operations executed by a top-level transaction have their usual semantics. That is, Commit permanently installs the transaction's updates and allows them to be read by other transactions. Abort undoes all the transaction's updates. For example, Commit and Abort in PayLoanFromChecking have these effects.

4. If a subtransaction S aborts, then all the operations of S are undone. This includes all the subtransactions of S. However, the abort does not cause the abort of S's parent. The parent is simply notified that its child subtransaction aborted. For example, Abort in DebitChecking aborts the subtransaction, but not its parent transaction that was started by PayLoanFromChecking.

5. While a subtransaction is executing, data items that it has updated are isolated and hence not visible to other transactions and subtransactions (just like the flat transaction model). For example, if

PayLoanFromChecking executed its subtransactions DebitChecking and PayLoan concurrently and those subtransactions read and wrote some shared data (which they don't in this example), then DebitChecking would not see PayLoan's updates until after PayLoan commits, and PayLoan would not see DebitChecking's updates until after DebitChecking commits.

6. When a subtransaction commits, the data items it has updated are made visible to other subtransactions. For example, after PayLoan commits, any data it has updated would be visible to DebitChecking (if they shared data).

Consider the properties of subtransactions relative to the ACID properties. Rule (4) means that a subtransaction is atomic (i.e., all-or-nothing) relative to other subtransactions of the same parent. Rule (5) means that a subtransaction is isolated relative to other transactions and subtransactions. However, a subtransaction is not durable. Rule (6) implies that its results become visible once it commits, but by rule (3) the results become permanent only when the top-level transaction that contains it commits.

The nested transaction model provides a nice solution to the transaction composability problem. In our example, DebitChecking and PayLoan in Figure 2.1 can execute as subtransactions within a top-level transaction executed by PayLoanFromChecking or as independent top-level transactions, without writing an artificial wrapper transaction like CallDebitChecking in Figure 2.3.

Although nested transactions are appealing from an application programming perspective, they are not supported in many commercial products.

Exception Handling

An application program that brackets a transaction must say what to do if the transaction fails and therefore aborts. For example, suppose the program divides by zero, or one of the underlying database systems deadlocks and aborts the transaction. The result would be an **unsolicited abort**—one that the application did not cause directly by calling the Abort command. Alternatively, the whole computer system could go down. For example, the operating system might crash, in which case all the transactions that were running at the time of the crash are affected. Thus, an application program that brackets a transaction must provide error handling for two types of exceptions—transaction failures and system failures.

For each type of exception, the application should specify an **exception handler**, which is a program that executes after the system recovers from the error. To write an exception handler, a programmer needs to know exactly what state information is available to the exception handler; that is, the reason for the error and what state was lost due to the error. Two other issues are how the exception handler is called and whether it is running in a transaction.

Information about the cause of the abort should be available to the exception handler, usually as a status variable that the exception handler can read. If the abort was caused by the execution of a program statement, then the program needs to know both the exception that caused the statement to malfunction and the reason for the abort—they might not be the same. For example, it's possible that there was some error in the assignment statement due to an overflow in some variable, but the real reason for the abort was an unavailable database system. The exception handler must be able to tell the difference between these two kinds of exceptions.

When a transaction aborts, all the transactional resources it accessed are restored to the state they had before the transaction started. This is what an abort means, undo all the transaction's effects. Nontransactional resources—such as a local variable in the application program, or a communications message sent to another program—are completely unaffected by the abort. In other words, actions on nontransactional resources are not undone as a result of the abort.

It's generally best if a transaction failure automatically causes the program to branch to an exception handler. Otherwise the application program needs an explicit test, such as an IF-statement, after each and every statement, which checks the status returned by the previous statement and calls the appropriate exception handler in the event of a transaction abort.

In the chained model, the exception handler is automatically part of a new transaction, because the previous transaction aborted and, by definition, the chained model is always executing inside of some transaction. In the unchained model, the exception handler is responsible for demarcating a transaction in which the exception handling logic executes. It *could* execute the handler code outside of a transaction, although as we said earlier this is usually undesirable.

If the whole system goes down, all the transactions that were active at the time of the failure abort. Since a system failure causes the contents of main memory to be lost, transactions cannot resume execution when the system recovers. So the recovery procedure for transaction programs needs to apply to the application as a whole, not to individual transactions. The only state that the recovery procedure can rely on is information that was saved in a database or some other stable storage area before the system failed. A popular way to do this is to save request messages on persistent queues. The technology to do this is described in Chapter 4.

Some applications execute several transactions in response to a user request. This is called a **business process** or **workflow**. If the system fails while a business process is executing, then it may be that some but not all of the transactions involved in the business process committed. In this case, the application's exception handler may execute compensating transactions for the business process' transactions that already committed. Business process engines typically include this type of functionality. More details appear in Chapter 5.

Savepoints

If a transaction periodically saves its state, then at recovery time the exception handler can restore that state instead of undoing all the transaction's effects. This idea leads to an abstraction called savepoints.

A **savepoint** is a point in a program where the application saves all its state, generally by issuing a **savepoint command**. The savepoint command tells the database system and other resource managers to mark this point in their execution, so they can return their resources to this state later, if asked to do so. This is useful for handling exceptions that only require undoing part of the work of the transaction, as in Figure 2.4.

```
void Application
    {  Start;
       do some work;
       . . .
       Savepoint ("A");
       do some more work;
       . . .
       if (error)
          { Restore ("A");
            take corrective action;
            Commit;
          }
       else Commit;
    }
```

FIGURE 2.4

Using Savepoints. The program saves its state at savepoint "A." It can restore the state later if there's an error.

```
Void Application                        Void ExceptionHandlerForApplication
    {  Start;                               {  Restore ("B");
       get-input-request;                      generate diagnostic;
       Savepoint ("B");                        Commit;
       do some more work;                   }
       Commit;
    }
```

FIGURE 2.5

Using Savepoints for Broken Requests. The application's savepoint after getting the request enables its exception handler to generate a diagnostic and then commit. If the transaction were to abort, the get-input-request would be undone, so the broken request would be re-executed.

A savepoint can be used to handle broken input requests. Suppose a transaction issues a savepoint immediately after receiving an input request, as in the program `Application` in Figure 2.5. If the system needs to spontaneously abort the transaction, it need not actually abort, but instead can roll back the transaction to its first savepoint, as in `ExceptionHandlerForApplication` in Figure 2.5. This undoes all the transaction's updates to transactional resources, but it leaves the exception handler with the opportunity to generate a diagnostic and then commit the transaction. This is useful if the transaction needs to abort because there was incorrect data in the request. If the whole transaction had aborted, then the get-input-request operation would be undone, which implies that the request will be re-executed. Since the request was incorrect, it is better to generate the diagnostic and commit. Among other things, this avoids having the request re-execute incorrectly over and over, forever.

Unfortunately, in some execution models the exception handler of a transactional application must abort the transaction. In this case, a mechanism outside the transaction needs to recognize that the broken request should not be re-executed time after time. Queuing systems usually offer this function, which is described in Chapter 4.

Some database systems support the savepoint feature. Since the SQL standard requires that each SQL operation be atomic, the database system does its own internal savepoint before executing each SQL update operation. That way, if the SQL operation fails, it can return to its state before executing that operation. Since the database system supports savepoints anyway, only modest additional work is needed to have it make savepoints available to applications.

In general, savepoints seem like a good idea, especially for transactions that execute for a long time, so that not all their work is lost in the event of a failure. Although it's available in some systems, it's a feature that reportedly is not widely used by application programmers.

Using Savepoints to Support Nested Transactions

Since a savepoint can be used to undo part of a transaction but not all of it, it has some of the characteristics of nested transactions. In fact, if a transaction executes a sequential program, then it can use savepoints to obtain the behavior of nested transactions if the system adheres to the following rules:

1. When a subtransaction first accesses a resource manager, it issues a savepoint operation.
2. When a subtransaction aborts, the system restores the savepoint that the subtransaction previously established at each resource manager that the subtransaction accessed.
3. To commit a subtransaction, no special action is required by the resource managers. However, future accesses to resource managers are now done on behalf of the subtransaction's parent.

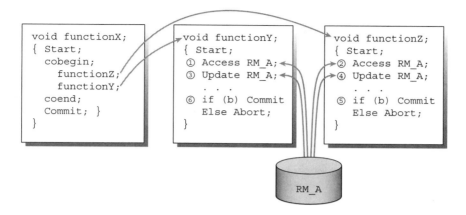

FIGURE 2.6

Savepoints Aren't Enough for Concurrent Subtransactions. If `functionZ` commits and `functionY` aborts, there is no savepoint in RM_A that produces the right state.

This implementation works only if the transaction program is sequential. If it has internal concurrency, then it can have concurrently executing subtransactions, each of which can independently commit or abort. Since a savepoint applies to the state of the top-level transaction, there will not always be a savepoint state that can selectively undo only those updates of one of the concurrently executing subtransactions.

Consider the example in Figure 2.6, where `functionX` starts a transaction and then calls `functionY` and `functionZ` concurrently, indicated by the "concurrent block" bracketed by `cobegin` and `coend`. Both `functionY` and `functionZ` access a resource manager RM_A that supports savepoints. Each of them has transaction brackets and therefore should run as a subtransaction. Since `functionY` and `functionZ` are executing concurrently, their operations can be interleaved in any order. Consider the following steps:

1. `functionY` accesses RM_A, and since this is its first access it issues a savepoint at RM_A (rule 1, in the previous list).
2. `functionZ` accesses RM_A, and therefore also issues a savepoint at RM_A (rule 1 in the previous list).
3. `functionY` performs an update at RM_A.
4. `functionZ` performs an update at RM_A.
5. `functionZ` commits its subtransaction.
6. `functionY` aborts its subtransaction.

According to rule 2 (in the previous list), in step 6 the system should restore the savepoint created on behalf of `functionY`. However, this will undo the update performed by `functionZ`, which is incorrect, since `functionZ` commits in step 5.

2.3 PROCESSES AND THREADS

Why We Need Threads

A processor has a state, called the **processor context**, that consists of a control thread and an address space. The **control thread** consists of the values stored in the processor's registers, such as the instruction counter, the stack pointer, and data registers. It also includes certain memory areas that are assigned to the processor but are not directly addressable by the program running on the processor, such as a processor stack. An **address space** is a mapping of the processor's view of memory to the physical memory, typically represented in registers that point to page tables.

In a multiprogrammed system, every active program has an associated processor state. For a program that's currently executing, it is the state of the physical processor on which it's running. For programs that were executing and are temporarily idle, the state is saved in main memory and will be reloaded into a processor when the program resumes execution.

The architecture of a TP system is affected by whether components share an address space, whether that address space has one thread or multiple threads executing, and whether there are hardware, operating system, or language mechanisms to protect programs that share an address space from inappropriately modifying each other's memory. For example, traditional timesharing systems, such as early UNIX operating systems, were structured so that each display device had its own process, each process had exactly one thread executing, and all programs that ran on behalf of that display device executed in that one process. As we'll see, TP systems don't work this way.

In the timesharing model one could implement a TP system by combining all three TP application functions into one big sequential program, rather than splitting them across front-end, middle-tier, and back-end servers. The TP application would simply be a sequential program that consists of an infinite loop that gets an input message from a display device, starts a transaction, calls the appropriate transaction server program to run the request, commits or aborts that transaction, and returns to the top of the loop to do it again. Each display device would be connected to a process that runs this program, thereby executing transactions on behalf of that display.

There are many disadvantages, however, of using this execution model. The most important is that there are just too many processes. A system with tens or hundreds of thousands of display devices would have tens or hundreds of thousands of processes, because it needs one process for every display device. Most operating systems do not work well with such a large number of processes, for many reasons:

- Some operating system functions sequentially scan lists of processes. If the list is too long, it takes too long to perform these operating system functions.

- There is a lot of context switching between these processes, which involves swapping out register values of one process and loading those of another process, including invalidating and reloading the processor's cache memory.

- There's usually a certain amount of memory for each process that has to remain in physical main memory and can't be paged at all. Given this high memory consumption, many processes may have some of their virtual memory out on disk, which has to be paged in when the transaction is invoked, adding extra delay.

- Distributing transactions on multiple nodes require even more processes, because each display device needs a process running on every system doing work on behalf of that display.

- It is difficult to control the load on such a system. The only knob you can turn is to reduce the number of active processes. Since each process is associated with a display device, shutting down a process effectively turns off a display—bad news for the person using that display. It would be better to shut down only certain low-priority types of transactions, but this is hard to control because those transaction types are buried in the application. It would require some application programming to control the load in this way.

- With a large number of processes, the complexity of sharing data structures between processes is significantly higher and requires more costly synchronization. Additionally, resources shared between processes can become orphaned under certain failure scenarios.

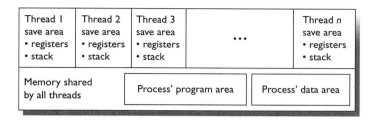

FIGURE 2.7

Memory Structure of a Multithreaded Process. In addition to the usual program and data areas, there is a save area for each thread, instead of one save area for the whole process as in a single-threaded process.

Due to all these disadvantages, from a very early stage in the history of TP systems, transactional middleware started supporting multithreaded processes. Like all abstractions supported by transactional middleware, this threading abstraction is made available in a uniform way across all the operating systems that the transaction middleware supports.

A multithreaded process supports many control threads in a single address space. Each thread is an independent path of execution through the process. All the threads in the process execute the same program and use the same process memory. But each of them has a save area for register values and private variables (e.g., the process stack). See Figure 2.7. Thus, a multithreaded process has many executions of its program running concurrently, one for each of its threads.

Threads save memory, since the process' memory is shared by many threads. It avoids some of the expense of context switching, since a processor can switch between threads without switching address spaces. And it reduces the number of processes, since threads can be used instead of processes and there can be many threads per process.

In a system with dedicated display devices, a single multithreaded process can manage multiple displays. In this case, a thread can be used to execute a program on behalf of a display. When the process switches attention between display devices, it switches to a different thread. Compared to a process-per-display, this reduces the number of processes and the number of context switches.

Initially, threads were dynamically allocated to display devices when the display was actively executing a request. Later, as the cost of processors and memory declined, a thread was statically allocated to each display device.

Implementing Threads

Threads can be implemented by middleware or by the operating system. There are benefits to each approach.

Middleware Threads

If threads are implemented by transactional middleware, then the operating system doesn't know about the threads. It's just running an ordinary process. Basically the transactional middleware is fooling the operating system by turning the process's attention to different display devices by itself. However, this may produce interference between these two levels of scheduling. Since the operating system is scheduling processes and the transactional middleware is scheduling threads within the process, they may end up working at cross-purposes.

There is one technical difficulty with having the transactional middleware implement threads. If a transaction server, executing in a multithreaded process, tries to read data from disk or tries to read a communications message, and the data that it needs is not yet available, then the operating system ordinarily will put the process to sleep. If there's only one thread running, this is the right thing to do—put the process to sleep until it has some work to do. But if there are multiple threads running inside the process, then all the threads, and therefore all the displays, end up getting delayed. This is bad, because some of those other displays could do useful work while the first display's I/O operation is in progress.

For this reason, the transactional middleware has to trap any of those synchronous I/O operations (generally reads) to avoid putting the process to sleep. Instead, it sends an asynchronous message to the disk, database system, or communications system, and asks to get a software interrupt back when the operation is complete. After the message is sent, the transactional middleware can continue operating by calling another thread that has useful work to do. When the I/O operation that corresponds to the message has finished, it will send a software interrupt to the transactional middleware, which then wakes up the thread that was waiting for that result. The cost of this approach to multithreading is that all the calls to I/O operations have to be intercepted by the transactional middleware.

For example, the mainframe version of IBM's CICS transactional middleware product has worked this way starting from its earliest implementations. It offers I/O operations that can be invoked from ordinary application programs, such as COBOL and C. Some transactional middleware products trap all synchronous I/O operations.

Operating System Threads

If the operating system supports multithreading, it keeps track of all the threads on its own. For example, since the mid-1990s, Windows and UNIX operating systems support this. When a thread issues a synchronous I/O operation, the operating system puts that thread to sleep. But it recognizes when there are other active threads that it can call and calls another thread that's ready to execute (in that process), rather than putting the whole process to sleep. This avoids unnecessary context switching. Another benefit of operating system multithreading is that if the process is running on a shared memory (i.e., symmetric) multiprocessor (SMP) or a multicore processor, it can assign the threads of the same process to different processors in the machine and thereby get parallelism among the threads of the process.

A difficulty of operating system multithreading, however, is performance overhead. Since it is the operating system that is involved in switching threads, this involves system calls. These are generally more expensive than thread operations executed at the user level, which is where the transactional middleware is operating.

There is a second disadvantage of multithreading, which is a problem whether it is implemented by the middleware or the operating system. Since there are multiple threads running inside the same process, there's little or no memory protection between them. An error in the execution of one thread could potentially damage memory for the entire process, thereby causing all the threads to malfunction. This could also lead to a security leak, if one thread reads memory that is private to another thread. With operating system threads, this problem can be somewhat mitigated by providing a protected memory area for special subsystems, such as transactional middleware functions, which can be protected from user level code. It can also be mitigated by the use of strongly-typed programming languages, such as Java and C#, which can make fairly strong guarantees that an executing program will access only memory dedicated to its use.

A third disadvantage of multithreading is that a multithreaded process cannot use a single-threaded process that retains context information for only one thread. The canonical example of this is early database system products. Until the mid-1980s, most database systems were single-threaded and could execute only one transaction at a time. The database system executed as a runtime library in each single-threaded application process. Thus, if a multithreaded process invoked a database system, all threads in the process would have to be running the same transaction, which is obviously not what is intended when using multithreaded applications for

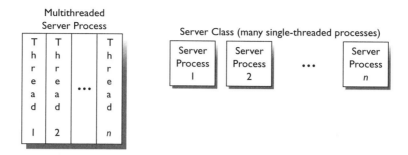

FIGURE 2.8

Multithreaded Process vs. Server Class. In both cases, there is one server program and many threads executing it. The difference is whether the threads execute in one process (multithreaded server) or many processes (server class).

TP. This problem was solved by the database system vendors who re-engineered their products to run as independent multithreaded processes, where each thread could run a different transaction. This enables each thread of a multithreaded application process to have an independent connection to a database system and have the database system execute that connection in a thread (and hence in a transaction) that's private to the connection. Most database systems today work this way, though there is still a market for database systems that run in the application process (e.g., for embedded systems). We will have more to say about multithreaded database servers in Section 3.7.

In summary, multithreading offers significant efficiency improvements, but must be used carefully to avoid blocking during I/O operations, interference between transactional middleware and operating system scheduling, performance overhead in thread context switching, and corruption of unprotected memory. Overall, for most applications, operating system multithreading is superior to transactional middleware multithreading, since it avoids the first two of these problems and can benefit from multicore and SMP configurations. For this reason, operating system multithreading has become ubiquitous in current TP products. The use of transactional middleware multithreading is now mostly limited to older products.

Server Classes

When multithreaded operating system processes are not available, a good alternative is to use a set of processes to emulate a pool of threads. That is, instead of having one multithreaded process, the system uses a set of single-threaded processes, all of which are running the same program (see Figure 2.8). This often is called a **server class**. In this case, for each server program, there is a set of server processes that runs it.

Server classes have a number of nice features. Most of them stem from the fact that each process in the server class is an ordinary single-threaded process and therefore avoids the disadvantages of multithreading, such as the following:

- Since the process is single-threaded, there's no harm in putting it to sleep if it is blocked during a synchronous I/O operation. Therefore, there is no need for the transactional middleware to trap synchronous I/O; the normal blocking behavior of the operating system is just fine.

- There's no possible conflict between process and thread scheduling and no possible memory corruption problems from threads in the same process.

- Processes in a server class fail independently. That is, a server class is largely unaffected by the failure of any individual process in the server class, since other processes continue to run. This is in contrast to a multithreaded process, where the failure of one thread can bring down the whole process, especially if it corrupts the memory of other threads.

■ Each process in a server class can use single-threaded services, such as a single-threaded database system that executes as a runtime library. This was an important benefit before the advent of multithreaded database systems.

For these reasons, and to avoid the expense of implementing multithreading, server classes were quite popular in transactional middleware products before the advent of multithreaded operating systems, as in the case of HP's ACMS and Pathway legacy TP monitors.

However, server classes do have disadvantages. One is that there is a process per thread. As we explained earlier, operating systems don't work well with too many processes. So server classes can be used only when the number of required server threads is relatively small.

Another disadvantage of server classes is that they require an additional mechanism to dispatch calls to the server class to a particular server process. The problem is how to balance the load across the servers in the server class. The caller could randomize its selection of server, thereby balancing the load across multiple servers, on the average. Or, the processes in the server class could share a queue of unprocessed requests. If a busy process receives a call, it simply adds it to the queue, where another process can pick it up. Or, the server class could have a single process that receives all requests and routes each one to an idle process. The latter is easy to implement, but costs an extra context switch, since each call has to invoke the server class's router process before going to a server. We will have more to say about load balancing in Section 2.6.

2.4 REMOTE PROCEDURE CALL

Remote procedure call (RPC) is a programming mechanism that enables a program in one process to invoke a program in another process using an ordinary procedure call, as if the two programs were executing in the same process (or more precisely, in the same address space).

There are several benefits to programming in the RPC style. First, the programmer can still write and reason about a program as if all the program's procedures were linked together in a single process. Therefore, the programmer can focus on correctly modularizing the program and ignore the underlying communications mechanism. In particular, the programmer can ignore that the program is really distributed, which would add significant complexity to the programming task if it were made visible.

Second, the RPC style avoids certain programming errors because of the simple request-response message protocol that it implies. Using RPC, a program receives a return for every call. Either the caller receives a return message from the called procedure, or the system returns a suitable exception to the caller so it can take appropriate action. By contrast, using asynchronous message passing, a program has explicit statements to send and receive messages. These send and receive operations issued by communicating programs define a communication protocol. This requires the programmer to handle the message sequences and errors directly. For example, each program must be ready to receive a message after the message is sent to it. Programs have to cope with certain error conditions, such as waiting for a message that never arrives, or giving up waiting for a message and coping with that message if it does eventually arrive later. In RPC, these problems are dealt with by the RPC implementation rather than by the application program.

Third, RPC implementations can hide the differences in parameter format between the programming languages in which the client's and server's program are written. RPC implementations also can hide differences among processors such as Intel x86, AMD, PowerPC, and SPARC and the differences among operating systems such as Windows and Linux.

To understand how RPC works, consider the example in Figure 2.9. This program consists of three procedures:

- PayCreditCard, which pays a credit card bill
- DebitChecking, which subtracts money from a checking account
- PayBill, which calls PayCreditCard and DebitChecking to pay a credit card bill from a checking account

Let us assume that these three procedures execute in separate processes, possibly on different nodes of a network. Therefore, the invocations of PayCreditCard and DebitChecking by PayBill are remote procedure calls.

```
Boolean Procedure PayBill (acct#, card#)
{ int     acct#, card#;

  long     amount;
  Boolean ok;

  Start;  /* start a transaction */
  amount = PayCreditCard(card#);
  ok = DebitChecking(acct#, amount);
  if (!ok) Abort else Commit;
  return (ok);
}

long Procedure PayCreditCard (card#);
{ int   card#;
  long amount;

  /* get the credit card balance owed */
  Exec SQL Select AMOUNT
          Into :amount
          From CREDIT_CARD
          Where (ACCT_NO = :card#);
  /* set the balance owed to zero */
  Exec SQL Update CREDIT_CARD
          Set AMOUNT = 0
          Where (ACCT_NO = :card#);
  return (amount);
}

Boolean Procedure DebitChecking (acct#, amount);
{ int   acct#;
  long amount;
  /* debit amount from checking balance if balance is sufficient */
  Exec SQL Update ACCOUNTS
          Set BALANCE = BALANCE - :amount
          Where (ACCT_NO = :acct# and BALANCE ≥ amount);
  /* SQL Code = 0 if previous statement succeeds */
  return (SQLCODE == 0);
}
```

FIGURE 2.9

Credit Card Payment Example. PayBill brackets the transaction and calls two subprograms, PayCreditCard and DebitChecking, which it calls by RPC.

PayCreditCard takes a credit card account number as input, returns the amount of money owed on that account, and zeroes out the amount owed. The first SQL statement selects the amount of money from the credit card table, which contains the amount of money owed on each account number. The second statement zeroes out that amount (i.e., the entire balance is paid off) and returns the amount actually owed for the account.

DebitChecking subtracts a given amount of money from a given account. In the SQL statement, if the balance in that account is greater than or equal to the amount of money to be debited, then it subtracts the amount of money to be debited from the account balance. In this case, the SQL statement succeeds and therefore sets SQLCODE to zero, so DebitChecking returns true. On the other hand, if the balance in that account is less than the amount of money to be debited, then the SQL statement does not update the account balance. Since the SQL statement failed, SQLCODE is not set to zero and DebitChecking returns false.

Each of these programs is useful by itself. The PayCreditCard program can be used to process credit card bills. The DebitChecking program can be used to process debits and credits against a checking account from an ATM. Using these two programs, we can easily write a PayBill program that implements a bill-paying service by paying a customer's credit card bill out of his or her checking account.

The PayBill program takes a checking account number and credit card number and tries to pay the credit card bill out of the checking account. The program starts a transaction, pays the credit card bill (which returns the amount of money owed), and tries to debit that money from the checking account. If the DebitChecking program returns true—meaning that there was enough money to pay the bill—the program commits. If it returns false, then there wasn't enough money to pay the bill and the transaction aborts. In both cases the PayCreditCard program updates the credit card table. But if the PayBill program aborts the transaction, the abort automatically undoes that update, thereby leaving the bill for that credit card account unpaid. (If DebitChecking returns false, its SQL update failed and has no effect on the ACCOUNTS table.)

Transactional RPC

The RPC runtime system has some extra work to do to allow a transaction to invoke an RPC. It has to pass the transaction context from the caller to the callee (which may be hidden, as in Figure 2.9 and earlier examples) and must throw transaction-related exceptions back to the caller. In addition to the transaction ID, the context may include security credentials, the identity of the system that started the transaction, and other system information that is required by the callee to continue operating within the same transaction. An RPC mechanism that does this additional work is called a **transactional RPC**.

A transactional RPC system may also need to do some work to support two-phase commit. For example, as part of making an RPC call, it may need to call the transaction manager on the caller's and callee's systems to notify them that the transaction has now moved to a new system. This information is needed later when the two-phase commit protocol is initiated, so the transaction managers know which systems are participants in the transaction. We'll discuss these issues at length in Chapter 8.

Sometimes, the RPC mechanism itself is used to transmit the two-phase commit messages. This is an implementation strategy for the vendor of the two-phase commit implementation. It is a sensible one, but has no effect on the functionality available to application developers. This is *not* what is meant by the term "transactional RPC."

Binding Clients and Servers

The programs shown in Figure 2.9 are incomplete in that they don't show how the caller and callee procedures discover each other's interfaces and establish connections that enable them to communicate. First of all, to make remote procedure call worthwhile in this situation, the PayBill program would probably be running in a different process, possibly on a different system, than the PayCreditCard or DebitChecking programs.

To compile and run the programs on these different systems, `PayBill` needs to reference the external procedures `PayCreditCard` and `DebitChecking`. This is done by writing an **interface definition** for each program to be called—in this case `PayCreditCard` and `DebitChecking`.

Interface Definitions

An interface definition specifies the name and type of the program and its parameters. It is processed by the **interface compiler** or **stub compiler**, which may be part of the programming language compiler if the latter has built-in RPC functionality. The interface compiler produces several outputs, one of which is a header file (consisting of data structures) for the caller to use. In this case the interface compiler would produce header files for `PayCreditCard` and `DebitChecking` that could be included with the `PayBill` program so that it can be compiled. The interface compiler also produces **proxy** and **stub** procedures, which are the programs that interface the `PayBill` caller to the `PayCreditCard` and `DebitChecking` servers via the network. The caller's program is linked with a proxy and the server's program is linked with a stub. The interface compiler produces both the header files and the proxy and stub procedures. Figure 2.10 illustrates the interface compiler operation.

Marshaling

Another function of the proxy and stub procedures is to lay out the procedure name and parameters into a stream, which can be sent in a message. This is called **marshaling**.

Some care is needed to avoid marshaling too much information, such as repeatedly copying and sending the same object class information. In addition, it is sometimes hard to maintain identity when sending items of a type. For example, Java enumerations don't maintain identity over RPC.

As part of marshaling parameters, the proxy can translate them between the format of the caller and the callee. In the previous examples, all the programs were written using the same language, but that needn't be the case. The `PayCreditCard` and `DebitChecking` programs might have been written some time ago in one language, whereas the `PayBill` program was added later to introduce the new service and was written in a different language. In this case the client proxy translates the parameters into a standard format that the callee can understand, and the server stub translates that into the appropriate format for the procedures called `PayCreditCard` and `DebitChecking`.

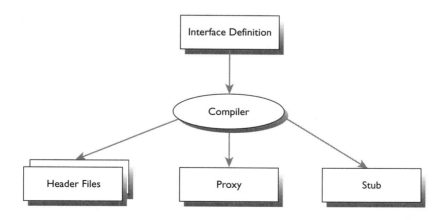

FIGURE 2.10

Interface Compiler Operation. The interface compiler produces header files for the caller and callee to use, and proxy and stub procedures that provide an interface between the caller and callee and the underlying network.

Communication Binding

Besides linking in the proxy and stub, there is the issue of creating a communication binding between these programs so they can communicate over the network. The runtime system has to know where each server process exists (e.g., PayCreditCard and DebitChecking), so it can create bindings to each server process when asked (e.g., by PayBill). Two activities are involved:

- Each server program must **export** or publish its interface, to tell all the systems on the network that it supports this interface. It must also tell where on the network it can be found.
- When the PayBill program wants to connect to the server, it must create a communications connection using that information exported by the server.

These activities are ordinarily supported by a **registry service**. For a Web Service, its interface is typically contained within a Web Services Description Language (WSDL) file that can be retrieved from a registry. A registry is used to store and retrieve the interface information and is accessible from any computer in the distributed system. For example, when the PayCreditCard program is initialized in a process, its location can be written to the registry service (step 1 in Figure 2.11). This location could be "process 17315" of network node 32.143, URL www.xyz.net (which is defined in the WSDL file). When the PayBill program asks to connect to the PayCreditCard program, it calls the registry service (one of the RPC runtime calls mentioned earlier) to find out where PayCreditCard is located (step 2). The registry service returns the instances of PayCreditCard it knows about (in this case, there is one). If there are any running, PayBill may connect to any one of them (step 3). Some implementations of communication bindings automate server selection to balance the load across multiple identical servers. Having received the network address of the server process number (in this case 32.143.17315), the PayBill process can now communicate with the server, so it can issue RPCs to PayCreditCard.

Mapping interface or server names into network addresses has to be a dynamic function, to support periodic reconfiguration. For example, if a server on one system fails, and the system manager recreates that server on another system, the mapping needs to be updated to reflect the new location of the server. The system manager may also want to move servers around to rebalance the load across servers, for example due to changing input patterns.

The registry that supports the binding activity needs to be accessible from all machines in the distributed system. This functionality ordinarily is supported by a network directory service, usually by replicating its contents

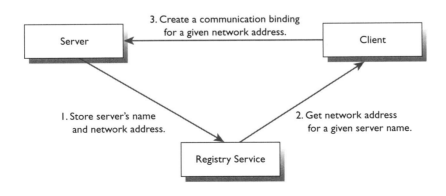

FIGURE 2.11

Using a Registry Service. When it's initialized, the server stores its name and address in the registry service. Later, the client gets the server's address and uses it to create a communication binding.

on many servers. For this reason, registries are often implemented on top of a network directory. For good performance, the network directory provides a client layer that caches recently accessed information. The client usually has connections to multiple directory services, so it can quickly switch between them if one fails.

Instead of using a replicated repository, a simpler primary-copy approach may be supported. In this approach, a central copy of the repository is maintained, and each system keeps a cached copy that is periodically refreshed. This arrangement gives fast access to the cached mapping during normal operation. When a reconfiguration requires that the central copy be updated, the central copy must notify the other systems to refresh their caches.

Much of this work is done by the RPC runtime system, but some may be exposed to the application. For example, the application may have to issue calls to get the network address and create a communications binding. Most systems hide this. A distinguishing feature among different implementations of RPC is how much of this complexity the application programmer has to cope with.

Dispatching

When an RPC call arrives at the target system, the RPC runtime library needs to invoke the designated server process. If the multithreaded process or server pool doesn't exist, then the runtime creates it. If the server is a multithreaded process, then the runtime needs to assign the call to a thread. It can create a new thread to process the call, assign the call to an existing thread, or put the call packet on a queue (e.g., if the process is already executing its maximum allowable number of active threads). If a server pool is used, then it assigns the call to a server process, or if all server processes are busy it enqueues the request.

Application Programmer's View

Although the RPC style does simplify some aspects of application programming, it may also introduce some new complexities. First, to write these programs, one may have to write interface definitions for the servers. This is a new programming task that isn't needed in the single-process case.

Second, to support synchronous waiting by the caller, one needs a multithreaded client so that blocking a caller doesn't stall the client process. Programmers find it challenging to write **thread-safe** applications for multithreaded servers. Program-level locking problems slow throughput, consume processor cycles, or worse—a single memory corruption can stop many threads. As the number of available processor cores is projected to increase dramatically in the coming years, finding ways to simplify thread-safe programming is a hot research topic in computer science.

Third, the client and server programs need startup code to connect up or **bind** the programs together before they first communicate. This includes importing and exporting interfaces, defining security characteristics, setting up communication sessions, and so on. Although much of this can be hidden, sometimes a lot of it isn't. Finally, communication failures generate some new kinds of exceptions, such as a return message that never shows up because of a communications or server failure. Such exceptions don't arise in the sequential case when the programs are running inside of the same process.

Object-Oriented RPC

In an object-oriented programming model, procedures are defined as methods of classes. There are two types of methods, **class methods** and **object methods**. A class method is invoked on the class itself, such as the method `new`, which creates an object (i.e., instance) of the class. Most methods are object methods, which are invoked on an object of the class, not the class itself. For example, the procedures in Figure 2.9 could be defined as object methods of three classes: `PayBill` as a method of the Billing class, `PayCreditCard` as a method of the CreditCard class, and `DebitChecking` as a method of the CheckingAccount class. (Class definitions are not shown in Figure 2.9.)

To invoke an object method, the caller uses a reference (i.e., a binding) to the object. This could be created by the caller when it invokes the method new. If the class is remote, then this invocation of new is itself an RPC, which returns a reference to a new object of the remote class. The object lives in the remote class, while the reference is local to the caller. The reference is thus a local **surrogate** for the remote object. The caller can now invoke an object method on the surrogate, which the caller's runtime system recognizes as an RPC to the real object that resides in the remote class.

As an optimization, the invocation of the method new usually is executed locally in the caller's process by creating the surrogate and not yet calling the method new on the remote class. When the caller invokes an object method on the newly created object for the first time, the caller's runtime system sends both the invocation of the method new and the object method in a single message to the remote class. This saves a message round-trip between the caller and the remote class. Since the only thing that the caller can do with the newly created object is to invoke methods on the object, there's no loss of functionality in grouping the remote invocation of the method new with the first invocation of a method on it.

A remote object may need to live across multiple object method calls, so that the object can retain state information that is accessible to later invocations of the object's methods. For example, the first invocation of an object could invoke an ExecuteQuery method, which executes an SQL query. Later invocations of the object could invoke a GetNext method, each of which returns the next few rows that are in the result of that query. Other examples of retained state are discussed in Section 2.5.

Callbacks

A callback enables the callee of an RPC to invoke the caller. The caller of the RPC includes a so-called **context handle** as a parameter to the RPC. The callee can use the context handle to call back to the caller. One use of callbacks is to pass along a large parameter from caller to callee a-chunk-at-a-time. That is, instead of sending the large parameter in the original RPC to the callee, the caller sends a context handle. The callee can use this context handle to call back to the caller to get a chunk of the parameter. It executes multiple callbacks until it has received the entire large parameter.

The context handle passed in a callback could be an object. In a sense, a callback is an object-oriented RPC in reverse; it is the RPC callee that holds a reference to the caller, rather than having the caller hold a reference to the callee.

An RPC Walkthrough

Now that we have explained the main components of an RPC system, let's walk through an example to see what happens, beginning-to-end. In Figure 2.12, the client application calls the server application. The client application could be the PayBill program, for example, and the server application could be PayCreditCard. As we discussed, there are proxy and stub programs and a runtime system along the path.

The client application issues a call to the server, say PayCreditCard. This "Call PayCreditCard" statement actually calls the client's PayCreditCard proxy (1). The proxy is a procedure with the same interface as the server application; it looks exactly like PayCreditCard to the client. Of course the PayCreditCard proxy doesn't actually do the work. All it does is send a message to the server.

The PayCreditCard proxy marshals the parameters of PayCreditCard into a packet (2). It then calls the communications runtime for the RPC, which sends the packet as a message to the server process (3).

The RPC runtime creates a communications binding between the processes and adds it as a parameter to subsequent send and receive operations. The client's RPC runtime sends each message to the server's RPC runtime. The server's RPC runtime contains a binding of message types to processes and procedures within them and uses it to direct each message to the right procedure.

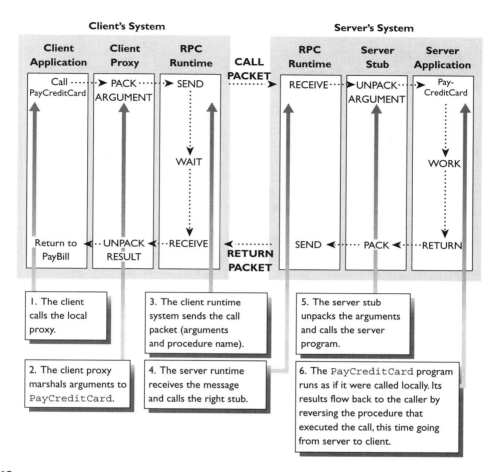

FIGURE 2.12

RPC Implementation. The numbers indicate the sequence of actions to process a call from the client to the PayCreditCard server program.

The server process's RPC runtime system receives the message (4). It looks at the packet's header and sees that this is a call to the PayCreditCard program, so it calls the PayCreditCard server stub. The server stub unmarshals the arguments and performs an ordinary local procedure call to the PayCreditCard program (5). The PayCreditCard program takes the call and runs just as if it had been called by a local caller instead of a remote caller (6).

When PayCreditCard completes, the whole mechanism runs in reverse: PayCreditCard does a return operation to the program that called it. From PayCreditCard's viewpoint, that's the server stub. When it returns to the server stub, it passes a return value and perhaps some output parameters. The server stub marshals those values into a packet and passes them back to the RPC runtime system, which sends a message back to the caller.

The caller's system receives the packet and hands it to the correct process. The process's RPC runtime returns to the correct proxy for this call, which unmarshals the results and passes them back as part of its return statement to the original PayCreditCard call, the client's call.

System Characteristics of RPC

An RPC system needs to be engineered for security, fault tolerance, performance, and manageability. Some RPC systems are engineered specifically for interoperability across multiple programming languages, data formats, and operating systems. We discuss these system issues in the following subsections.

Security of RPC

When a client binds to a server, the client first calls the runtime system to find the server's address and to create a communications binding to the server. A secure gatekeeper is needed to control the creation of these bindings, since not all clients should be able to connect to any server for any purpose. As an extreme example, it shouldn't be possible for any workstation to declare itself the network-wide electronic mail server, since it would allow the workstation to eavesdrop on everyone's mail.

In general, when a client connects to a server, it wants to know who it is actually talking to—that the server is who it says it is. Moreover, the server wants to authenticate the client, to be sure the client is who it claims to be. This requires **authentication**; that is, a secure way to establish the identity of a system, a user, a machine, and so forth. Thus, when binding takes place, the runtime system should authenticate the names of the client and the server (see Figure 2.13). This ensures, for example, that the server can prove that it really is the mail server, and the client can prove that it's really a client that's allowed to connect to this server.

Having authenticated the client, the server still needs to exercise **access control**; that is, to check whether a client is authorized to use the procedure. Access control is entirely up to the server. The server's transactional middleware or operating system may help by offering operations to maintain a list of authorized clients, called an **access control list**. But it's up to the server to check the access control list before doing work on behalf of a client.

Fault Tolerance in RPC

A common fault tolerance problem is determining what a program should do if it issues an operation but doesn't get a reply that tells whether the operation executed correctly. We saw an example of this in Section 1.3, *Handling Real-World Operations*, in dealing with a missing reply to a request to dispense $100 from an ATM. This problem also arises in RPC when a client issues a call and does not receive a reply. The key question is whether it is safe to retry the operation.

Suppose a client calls a server that processes the call by updating a database, such as the DebitChecking program in Figure 2.9. If the client does not receive a return message, it's not safe to try the call again, since it's possible that the original call executed, but the return message got lost. Calling DebitChecking again would debit the account a second time, which is not the desired outcome.

The property that says it is safe to retry is called idempotence. An operation is **idempotent** if any number of executions of the operation has the same effect as one execution. In general, queries are idempotent—it doesn't

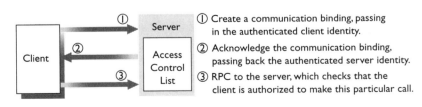

FIGURE 2.13

RPC Security. The communication system authenticates the client and server when it creates a communication binding between them (in 1 and 2). The server checks the client's authorization on subsequent calls for service (in 3).

matter how many times you call, you always get back the same answer (if there are no intervening updates) and there are no side effects. Most update operations are not idempotent. For example, `DebitChecking` is not idempotent because executing it twice has a different effect than executing it just once.

A server is idempotent if all the operations it supports are idempotent. It is useful if a server declares that it is idempotent (e.g., its operations are all queries). The RPC runtime system learns that fact when it creates a binding to the server. In this case, if the client RPC runtime sends a call but does not receive a reply, it can try to call again and hope that the second call gets through. If the server is not idempotent, however, it's not safe to retry the call. In this case, the client could send a control message that says "Are you there?" or "Have you processed my previous message?" but it can't actually send the call a second time, since it might end up executing the call twice.

Even if it resends calls (to an idempotent server) or it sends many "Are you there?" messages (to a non-idempotent server), the caller might never receive a reply. Eventually, the RPC runtime will give up waiting and return an exception to the caller. The caller cannot tell whether the call executed or not. It just knows that it didn't receive a reply from the server. It's possible that a server will reply later, after the RPC runtime returns an exception. At this point, it's too late to do anything useful with the reply message, so the RPC runtime simply discards it.

Looking at the issue a bit more abstractly, the goal is to execute an idempotent operation *at least once* and to execute a non-idempotent operation *at most once*. Often, the goal is to execute the operation *exactly once*. Transactions can help. A call executes exactly once if the server is declared non-idempotent and the RPC executes within a transaction that ultimately commits. We will explore exactly-once behavior further in Chapter 4.

System Management

We've discussed RPC assuming that both the client and server process are already up and running, but of course somebody has to make all this happen to begin with. These are system management activities: to create client and server processes and communications sessions to support RPC bindings. Sometimes these are dynamic functions that are part of the RPC system. In TP systems, they are usually static functions that are part of initializing the application, done in the transactional middleware.

The system manager also has to track the behavior of the system. This requires software to monitor all the low-level system components and make them visible with abstractions that are intelligible to the system manager. For example, if someone calls the Help Desk saying, "I can't run transactions from my PC," the system manager has to check, among other things, whether the PC is communicating with the server, whether the server processes are running, whether the client and server are running compatible versions of the proxy and stub, and so on. Similarly, if there are performance problems, the system manager has to track the message load for each of the systems, determine whether the server has enough threads to run all the incoming calls, and so on.

Interoperability of RPC

In the example, suppose that the client and server applications use different programming languages with different data formats. In that case, the client proxy and the server stub need to translate the parameters between the client's and server's format. There are two ways to do this:

- Put the parameters into a standard, canonical format that every server knows how to interpret.
- Ensure that the server's stub can interpret the client's format, known as **receiver-makes-it-right**.

Canonical forms include XML Schema, CDR (used in RMI/IIOP), and XDR (used in the Sun RPC). When using a canonical format, the client proxy translates the parameters into the standard format, the server translates them out of standard format, and likewise for the return parameters—the server stub puts them into standard format and the client proxy puts them back into client format.

This is fine if the client and server are running different languages, but what if they're running the same language? For example, suppose they're both using Java or C#. The client proxy is going through all the extra work of taking the data out of Java format and putting it into standard format, and then the server is taking it out of standard format and putting it back into Java format. For this reason, the receiver-makes-it-right technique often is used. The client proxy marshals the parameters in the client's format, not in a standard format, and tags them with the name of the format it's using. When the receiver gets the parameters, if it sees that they're in the same format that the server is using, it just passes them unmodified to the server. However, if they're not in the right format, it does the translation, either via a standard format or directly into the target format. This saves the translation expense in many calls, but requires the server to support format translations for every format it might see as input.

Even when the client and server are running the same language in the same execution environment, some machine-dependent translation may be required. This arises because there are two different ways of laying out bytes in words in computer memory, sometimes called little-endian and big-endian. The difference is whether the bytes are laid out in increasing addresses starting with the least-significant byte (little-endian) or most-significant byte (big-endian) within the word. In other words, is the low-order bit in the first or last position of the word. (Intel and compatible processors use little-endian. Motorola, PowerPC, SPARC, and Java wire format use big-endian. ARM and some PowerPC and SPARC processors are switchable.) When moving packets between systems, it may be necessary to translate between little-endian and big-endian format, even if both systems are running the same implementation of the same language. Again this can be hidden by the proxies and stubs using one of the parameter translation mechanisms.

Performance of RPC

RPC is a heavily used mechanism when a TP system is distributed. Each transaction that's split between two TP systems, such as between a client PC and a server back-end, needs at least one RPC to send the request and return the reply. It's very important that this executes quickly. If it isn't very fast, people will avoid using it, which completely defeats its purpose.

There are basically three parts to the execution, which were illustrated in Figure 2.12. One is the proxy and stub programs that marshal and unmarshal parameters. The second is the RPC runtime and communications software, which passes packets between the stub and the network hardware. And then there's the network transfer itself, which physically passes the messages through the communications hardware and over the wire to the other system.

In most RPC systems, the time spent performing a call is evenly split among these three activities, all of which are somewhat slow. In a local area network, the overall performance is typically in the range of about 10,000 to 15,000 machine-language instructions per remote procedure call, which is several hundred times slower than a local procedure call. So it's very important to optimize this. There are lower-functionality research implementations in the 1500 to 2000 instruction range. For web services that rely on text-based data formats, such as XML, performance is typically even slower. Techniques to make the system run faster include avoiding extra acknowledgment messages, using the receiver-makes-it-right technique to make the proxies and stubs faster, optimizing for the case where all the parameters fit in one packet to avoid extra control information and extra packets, optimizing the case where client and server processes are on the same machine to avoid the full cost of a context switch, and speeding up the network protocol.

How to Compare RPC Systems

RPC has become a standard feature of distributed computing systems, whether or not those systems run transactions. For example, Microsoft's Windows operating systems and Linux support RPC as a built-in function.

To get RPC integrated with transactions often requires using some transactional middleware. Many operating systems have some of this integration built in. This appeared first in Tandem's Guardian operating system and then in Digital's OpenVMS (both now part of HP).

When shopping for a transactional middleware product, simply knowing that it supports RPC, or even RPC with transactions, is not enough. You really have to go to the next layer of detail to understand the exact programming model and how difficult it is to write programs. Some of these interfaces are low-level and hard to program, whereas others are high-level and relatively easy to program.

One thing to look for when evaluating RPC systems is which languages and data types are supported. For example, some systems support only a generic proxy and stub procedure, which require application programming to marshal parameters. Most proxies and stubs are unable to translate complex data structures such as an array. Or they may handle it as a parameter, but only for a certain language. Bulk data transfer is difficult using some RPC systems, for example scrolling through a long table a portion at a time.

Another issue is whether transactional RPC is supported. If so, what types of context are transparently propagated and what types are the application programmer's responsibility? The types of context might include user context, device context, security context, file or database context, and of course transaction context.

Popular RPC implementations include the Remote Method Invocation (RMI) in Java, the Internet Inter-ORB Protocol (IIOP) from CORBA, and the Microsoft RPC on Windows. RMI, IIOP, and Microsoft RPC closely follow the concepts and implement the mechanisms described in the previous sections.

2.5 SHARED STATE

There are many situations in which components of a TP system need to share state information about users, activities, and the components themselves. Some examples of state information are the following:

- Transaction—the transaction ID of the programs executing a transaction
- Users—a user's authenticated identity or the address of the user's device
- Activities—the identity or contents of the last message that one component sent to another, or temporary information shared between a client and the system, such as the contents of a shopping cart
- Components—the identity of transaction managers that need to participate in committing a transaction, or the identity of processes that can handle a certain kind of request

The rest of this section explores these kinds of state and mechanisms to share it.

The kind of shared state we are interested in here is usually short-lived. That is, it is a state that can be discarded after a few seconds, minutes, or hours, though in some cases it may be much longer than that. Often it is information that describes a current activity of limited duration, such as a transaction or a shopping session. It is usually shared mostly for convenience or performance, to avoid having to send it repeatedly when components communicate. If this shared state is lost due to a failure, it can be reconstructed in the same way it was created in the first place—a nuisance and an expense, but not a catastrophe.

Of course, a TP system also needs to manage long-lived, permanent state. Examples of such state are databases that contain information about accounts, loans, and customers in a bank; or information about products, warehouses, and shipments in a retail business. In a sense, this information describes the state of the enterprise. This is the information that transactions are keeping track of. Unlike the short-lived state, it must not be lost in the event of a failure. This kind of long-lived state information is a very important part of TP systems, but it is *not* the kind of state that is the subject of this section.

Transaction Context

Earlier in this chapter, we saw that each transaction has a transaction ID, and that each program that executes a transaction has context information that includes its transaction ID. Thus, the transaction ID is state shared by the programs executing a transaction.

There are two design issues for any kind of shared state: how to establish the shared state and how to stop sharing and release the state. For transaction IDs, the first issue is addressed by native transactional RPC and WS-Transactions for SOAP. They propagate transaction context from caller to callee, to ensure that all programs executing the transaction have the same transaction context.

The second issue is addressed in different ways, depending on whether the program is a resource manager that needs to participate in two-phase commit. If so, then it retains the transaction context until after it processes the Commit operation in the second phase of two-phase commit. If not, and if it does not need to retain transaction state across calls, then it can release its transaction state when it returns from the transactional RPC that called it. If it does need to retain transaction state across calls, then it retains the transaction state until some later time, determined either by two-phase commit or by the program itself.

For example, in .NET, a program can release its transaction context by calling `SetComplete` or `SetAbort` before returning from a call. As we explained earlier, these operations tell the system that the transaction may or may not be committed (respectively) insofar as the caller is concerned. To retain the transaction context, the program calls `EnableCommit` or `DisableCommit`. These operations tell the system that the transaction may or may not be committed (respectively) insofar as the caller is concerned, but unlike `SetComplete` and `SetAbort`, they do not release the transaction context. These two situations—releasing or retaining transaction context—are special cases of stateless and stateful servers, which are discussed in more detail later in this section.

In Java EE, context is managed using a context object that is created when the transaction is started. The Java APIs to release context are `javax.transaction.UserTransaction.commit` and `rollback`—there's no equivalent for `SetComplete` but for `SetAbort` the Java extensions (Javax) API provides `setRollbackOnly`.

Sessions

A **communication session** is a lasting connection between two system components, typically two processes, that want to share state. The main reason to establish a session is to avoid having the components send the shared state information in each message. This saves not only the transmission cost, but also the sender's cost of obtaining the state information when composing the message and the receiver's cost of validating and saving the state information when receiving the message. The following are some examples of state information that might be shared by a session:

- The network address of both components, so they do not need to incur costly address lookups every time they send a message to each other
- Access control information, so each party knows that the other one is authorized to be sending it messages, thereby avoiding some security checks on each message
- A cryptographic key, so the components can encrypt information that they exchange in later messages
- The identity of the last message each component sent and received, so they can resynchronize in case a message is not delivered correctly
- The transaction ID of the transaction that both components are currently executing

A session is created between two components by exchanging messages that contain the state to be shared. For example, a component C_1 can send a message Request-Session(id, x) to component C_2, which asks it to

FIGURE 2.14

Three-Way Handshake to Create a Session. Component C_1 initiates the protocol by requesting to establish a session. C_2 agrees to be a party to the session. Finally, C_1 acknowledges receipt of that agreement.

become a party to a new session that is identified by id and whose initial state is x. C_2 replies with a message ACCEPT-SESSION(id), which tells C_1 that C_2 received the REQUEST-SESSION message, agrees to be a party to the session, and has retained the initial session state x. Usually, this is enough to establish the session. However, sometimes C_2 needs to be sure that C_1 received its ACCEPT-SESSION message before it sends C_1 another message. In that case it should require that C_1 acknowledge C_2's ACCEPT-SESSION message by sending a message CONFIRM-SESSION(id). In the latter case, the protocol to establish the session is called a **three-way handshake** (see Figure 2.14).

Sometimes a session is established as a side-effect of another message. For example, it might be a side-effect of the first RPC call from a client to a server, and it stays around until it times out.

Each component that is involved in a session needs to allocate some memory that holds the shared state associated with the session. This is usually a modest cost per session. However, the memory cost can be significant if a component is communicating with a large number of other components, such as server with sessions to a million clients over the Internet. This is one good reason why HTTP is not a session-oriented protocol.

Most sessions are transient. This means that if one of the components that is involved in a session fails, then the session disappears. Continuing with our example, suppose component C_2 fails and loses the contents of its main memory. Then it loses the state information that comprises the session. The other component C_1 involved in the session may still be operating normally, but it will eventually time out waiting for a message from C_2, at which point it discards the session. If C_2 recovers quickly, before C_1 times out, then C_2 might reply to C_1's attempt to re-establish contact. However, since C_2 lost the session due to its failure, it no longer has the shared state of the session when it recovers. Therefore, it should reply to C_1's message with a negative acknowledgment, thereby telling C_1 to discard the session. If C_1 and C_2 want to re-establish their session after C_2 has recovered, then they have to recreate the session from scratch.

If C_2 had sessions with only a few other components at the time it failed, then re-establishing the sessions does not cost very much. However, if it had a large number of sessions at the time it failed, then re-establishing them all at recovery time can be very time-consuming. During that time, C_2 is still unavailable. If one of the components with which C_2 is re-establishing a session is slow to respond to the REQUEST-SESSION or, even worse, is unavailable, then C_2's availability may be seriously degraded waiting for that session to be established.

A given pair of components may have more than one session between them. For example, they may have a transport session for the network connection, a session for the application state, and a session for end user information. Although in principle these sessions could be bundled into a single session between the components, in practice they are usually maintained independently, because they have different characteristics. For example, they may be established in different ways, use different recovery strategies, and have different lifetimes.

To summarize, the benefit of using sessions is to avoid resending and reprocessing the same information over and over again in every message exchange between a pair of components. The costs are the time to establish the session and to recover it after a failure, which in turn negatively affects availability.

One common use of sessions in TP is to connect an application component to a database system. The session state typically includes a database name, an authenticated user ID, and the transaction ID of the current transaction being executed by the application component. When the application component creates the session via REQUEST-SESSION, it includes the user ID and password as parameters. They are validated by the database system before it replies with ACCEPT-SESSION. The database system executes all the operations it receives from the application component on behalf of the session's user. Thus, operations only succeed if the session's user has privileges for them. All the operations execute within the session's transaction. After the application commits the transaction, the session either automatically starts a new transaction (i.e., if it uses the chained transaction model) or it no longer is operating in the context of a transaction (i.e., if it uses the unchained transaction model).

Another common use of sessions in TP is to connect transaction managers that participate in the two-phase commit protocol for a given transaction. The protocol for establishing sessions between these participants is a major part of a two-phase commit implementation and is discussed in Chapter 8.

Stateless Servers

Consider a session between a client process and a server process, where the client calls the server using RPC in the context of the session, so both the client and server can use the session's shared state. There are three problems that arise in this arrangement:

1. The session ties the client to a particular server process. In a distributed system with multiple server processes that are running the same application, it is desirable for a given client to be able to send different requests to different server processes; for example, to use the most lightly loaded one. However, if the client is relying on the server to retain state information about their past interactions, then it does not have the freedom to send different requests to different servers. All its requests have to go to the same server, namely, the one that is keeping track of their shared state.

2. If the server fails, then the session is lost. Since the client was depending on the server to remember the state of the session, the server needs to rebuild that state after it recovers. The server can do this either by having the client resend that state or by recovering the state from persistent storage, which in turn requires that the server saved the state in persistent storage before it failed.

3. If the server is servicing requests from a large number of clients, then it costs a lot of memory for it to retain a shared state. Moreover, the problem of rebuilding sessions after a failure becomes more acute.

For these three reasons, it is sometimes recommended that server processes be **stateless**. That is, there is no session between the client and server processes, and the server retains no application state after it services and replies to a client's request. Thus, it processes each request message from a clean state. Let us reconsider the preceding three problems for stateless server processes. First, if there are multiple server processes running the same application, then successive calls from a client can go to any of the server processes since none of them retain any state from the client's previous calls. Second, if a stateless server process fails, then it has no application state that it needs to recover. And third, a stateless server process does not incur the memory cost of retaining shared state.

The recommendation that servers be stateless applies mainly to communication between middle-tier servers and front-end processes associated with an end-user (i.e., clients), such as a browser or other presentation manager on a desktop device. This is a case where these three problems are likely to appear: (1) a client may want to send different requests to different servers, depending on server load; (2) re-establishing client-server sessions may be problematic, because clients can shut down unexpectedly for long periods and because a server would need a large number of these sessions since there is typically a large number of clients; and (3) the server would need to dedicate a lot of memory to retain shared state.

By contrast, this recommendation usually does not apply to communication between a middle-tier server and a back-end server, which are often database systems. As mentioned earlier, there usually *are* sessions between a middle-tier server and each back-end database system it invokes. Therefore, the back-end server is stateful with respect to the middle-tier servers that call it. Thus, the preceding three problems need to be addressed. We will discuss solutions in the next section.

It may sound a little strange to hear about stateless middle-tier server processes, because of course a TP application needs to store a lot of application state in databases. The point is that this database state is the only state that the stateless server process depends on. The server process itself does not retain state. Thus, if the server fails and subsequently recovers, it doesn't need to rebuild its internal state, because all the state that it needs is ready and waiting in the databases it can access.

A well-known example of a stateless middle-tier process is the use of a web server for HTTP requests for static web pages. All the state needed by the web server is stored in files. After servicing a request, a web server does not need to retain any state about the request or response. Since such web servers are stateless, if there are multiple web server processes, then each request can be serviced by a different web server. And if a web server fails and is then restarted, it has no state that needs to be recovered.

Stateful Applications

Having just explored reasons why stateless applications are beneficial, let us now examine cases where a middle-tier application needs to retain state information across multiple front-end requests. Here are four examples:

1. A user request requires the execution of several transactions, and the output of one transaction may need to be retained as input to the next.
2. A middle-tier server wants to retain information about a user's past interactions, which it will use for customizing the information it displays on later interactions.
3. A front end establishes a secure connection with a server using authentication information, which requires it to cache a token.
4. A user wants to accumulate a shopping cart full of merchandise before actually making the purchase.

In each of these scenarios, the state that is retained across client requests has to be stored somewhere. There are several places to put it, such as the following:

- Save it in persistent storage, such as a database system. The operation that stores the state should be part of the transaction that produces the state, so that the state is retained if and only if the transaction that produces it commits.

- Save it in shared persistent storage, but not within a transaction.

- Store it in volatile memory or in a database that is local to one server process. This makes the server stateful. Whether or not there is a communication session, future requests from the same client need to be processed by the server that has the shared state.

- Return it to the caller that requested the transaction execution. It is then the caller's responsibility to save the state and pass it back to the server on its next invocation of that server.

Wherever the state is stored, it must be labeled with the identity of the client and/or server, so that both client and server can find the state when they need it.

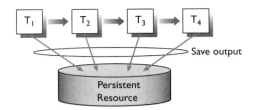

FIGURE 2.15

Retaining State in a Business Process. Each transaction in a business process saves the process state for use by the next transaction in the sequence.

Let us explore these ways of managing state and client-server identities in examples (1) to (4) in the previous list. The first scenario is a business process, that is, a user request that requires the execution of multiple transactions. A variety of state information is accumulated during a business process execution. This state includes a list of the business process steps whose transactions have committed and those that have yet to be executed. It may also include results that were returned by the transactions that committed, since these results may be needed to construct input to other transactions in the business process (see Figure 2.15). For example, if a travel reservation executes as a business process, then the arrival time of the flight that is returned by the flight reservation transaction may be needed to construct the input to a car rental reservation transaction, since that input requires a pick-up time. This information also needs to be saved so it can be returned to the client when the business process has finished executing.

Like any transaction, each transaction that executes as part of a business process should execute at most once. Therefore, the business process state must be maintained in persistent storage. If it were stored in volatile memory instead of persistent storage, and the contents of that memory were lost due to a failure, then it could not be reconstructed by executing the business process' transactions again (because transactions should execute at most once). For the same reason, the state must be updated by each transaction that executes as part of the business process. Suppose the application is written so that the result of the transaction is stored in the business process state after the transaction committed. If a failure occurs between the time the transaction commits and the time its results are supposed to be written to the business process state, then those results would be lost.

In scenario (2) the server keeps track of a user's interactions over a long period of time. For example, it may remember all the user's past orders and past window-shopping. It may use this information to suggest new products that are likely to be of interest based on that past behavior. In this case, the shared state needs to be identified by a long-lived name. The user's e-mail address commonly is used for this purpose. But in some cases it might not be good enough, since the user may access the server both from home and the office, and may switch e-mail providers from time to time. The user's full name and address might be better, although this too has problems due to variations in spelling and typos. Thus, depending on the requirements, selecting and using long-lived names can be a nontrivial design problem.

In scenario (3) a client browser establishes a secure connection with a server by exchanging authentication information. The connection establishes trust between the client and server so that the authentication information does not have to be passed on each subsequent call. The server caches the authentication token and identifies it with the connection to the browser. This is handy because then the user does not have to log in again and can submit multiple requests during the same session to the same resource. Since the connection is established as secure, the user's credentials do not have to be presented on each request.

Scenario (4) concerns creating and maintaining a shopping cart. Each item that a user selects to buy is put into the user's shopping cart. Since a user may be shopping for awhile, the shopping cart may be stored in a database or other persistent storage, to avoid the expense of using main memory for information that is infrequently accessed. This need not be written in the context of a transaction. However, the shopping cart is not the permanent state. The server system retains the shopping cart until either the user checks out and purchases the items in the cart, or until a time-out has occurred after which the server disposes of the shopping cart. The shopping cart is the shared state between the user and the system. So is the user ID that the system needs to know in order to find the user's shopping cart while processing each of the user's operations.

What user ID should be associated with the shopping cart? If the server is stateful, the session ID can be used to identify the user and hence the shopping cart. If the session goes away before the customer purchases the contents of the shopping cart, then the shopping cart can be deleted. If the server is stateless, and the user has not identified herself to the server, then the system must generate a user ID. Since the server is stateless, that user ID must accompany every call by that user to the server. One way to do this is to ensure that all calls from the client to the server, and all return messages, include the server-generated user ID. Since this is rather inconvenient, a different mechanism has been adopted for web browsers, called cookies.

A **cookie** is a small amount of information sent by a server to a web browser that the web browser then stores persistently and returns to the same server on subsequent calls. For example, when an anonymous user places his or her first item in a shopping cart, the server that performs the action could generate a user ID for that user and return it in a cookie. The user's subsequent requests to that server would contain the cookie and therefore would tell the server which shopping cart is relevant to those subsequent requests. Thus, the cookie is the shared state between the web browser and the server.

A cookie has a name, domain, and path, which together identify the cookie. It also has a value, which is the content of the cookie, such as a server-generated user ID for the shopping cart. For privacy reasons, the browser should send the cookie with HTTP requests only to the cookie's domain (e.g., books.elsevier.com). Since cookies are easily sniffed, they are also usually encrypted. Each cookie also has an expiration date, after which the browser should dispose of the cookie.

Cookies are sometimes not available, for example, because a user disabled them in the browser. In this case, the server can use a different technique, called **URL rewriting**. Before the server sends an HTML page back to the browser, it rewrites all the URLs on the page to include the user's session ID. For example, it could append ";jsessionid=1234" to every URL on the page. That way, any action that the user takes on that page causes the session ID to be sent back to the server.

URL rewriting is less secure than an encrypted cookie, since it can be seen by others. Moreover, an unsuspecting user might copy the rewritten URL into an e-mail to send to a friend, who might thereby have access to the sender's private session information.

In summary, maintaining the state across multiple requests requires a fair bit of design effort to choose where and how the state is identified and maintained. For this reason, it is worthwhile to design an application to limit the use of shared state whenever possible.

2.6 SCALABILITY

Scaling up a TP system to handle high load involves two activities. First, one can tune and grow each individual server system to handle the maximum possible load. And second, one can distribute the load across multiple interconnected server systems. The decision of which approach to take depends on cost-performance as well as other goals, such as availability, security, and manageability. In this section we focus on the mechanisms that enable scaling up system performance.

Scaling up a Server

The throughput of a server system is ultimately dependent on its hardware configuration; that is, on the speed of its processors, on the size and speed of main memory and secondary storage, and on the bandwidth and latency of its interconnects. Software too plays a major role. For a given hardware configuration, there are two techniques that are commonly used to get the most benefit from that configuration: caching and resource pooling.

Caching

A cache is an area of memory containing data whose permanent home is elsewhere, such as in secondary storage or on a remote server system. Ideally, the cache contains data that frequently is accessed by programs running on the system containing the cache and that is much cheaper to access than its permanent home. Thus, the expense of retrieving the data from its permanent home is amortized across a large number of accesses. This greatly improves performance over a system in which every access to the data requires accessing the data's permanent home.

Since many components of a TP system need to access data that is not local to the component, caches are heavily used in TP. A web browser may cache pages of frequently accessed web sites, to avoid having to go to the web site every time those pages are requested. A web server may cache information that is needed to service popular requests, such as the information displayed in response to a client's initial request to access the web site. A proxy server, which sits between the network and the web server, also offers this caching functionality. Some large data items, such as images, may be cached at a third-party's web site that is closer to the end user and can therefore offer higher speed access to the information. A server running a TP application may cache popular data whose permanent home is a remote database system. And the database system itself may cache data whose permanent home is secondary storage.

The official copy of a data item in its permanent home may be updated shortly after that copy was read and put into a cache. Therefore, once data has been put into a cache (somewhere other than its permanent home), it potentially is no longer up to date. Thus, a cache is most appropriate for data that is infrequently updated. For example, in a TP system, it is probably useful to cache catalog information, since its content changes slowly. But it may not be useful to cache the latest bid in an auction that will close shortly, since it may be updated very frequently.

The implementation of a cache requires a fast way to look up entries. This usually is done using a hash algorithm that maps the identifier of a data item to its memory location in the cache. It also requires a **replacement algorithm**, which selects an item to remove from the cache to make room for a new item that has to be inserted. A commonly used replacement algorithm is **least-recently-used**, which replaces the item whose last access was longest in the past among all items in the cache. There is a large repertoire of cache replacement algorithms used in practice. However, coverage of these algorithms is beyond the scope of this book.

Sometimes, items in the cache are **invalidated** before they need to be replaced. Invalidation is done if it is known that the item is unlikely to be fresh enough to be used. When a server stores an item in its cache, it may include an invalidation time that the cache manager enforces. For example, a web server may add an invalidation time 10 minutes in the future when it caches a copy of a headline news banner, thereby ensuring it refreshes the headline from the news server at least that often.

Alternatively, the server that is the data's permanent home may keep track of which caches have a copy of that data. After the server processes an update for that data, it can issue an **invalidation message** to every cache that has a copy, which tells the cache to invalidate its copy of that data. This helps to ensure that the caches are **coherent**; that is, that a data item has the same value in all caches that currently hold the data item. Clearly, there are limits to cache coherence due to variance in the time it takes for each cache to receive an invalidation message and process it.

A cache may be updatable. Each update to a data item in the cache must be propagated back to the data item's permanent home. Sometimes, this must be done explicitly by the client of the cache. That is, it stores the updated data item in both the cache and the data item's permanent home. If the cache manager knows how to map each cached data item to its permanent home, then the client may only need to update the cache and the cache manager propagates the update to the data item's permanent home. If the cache manager propagates the update immediately as part of the operation to update the cache, then the cache is called **write-through**. If it propagates the update lazily, potentially long after the cache was updated, then the cache is called **write-back**.

Clearly, cache coherence is affected by the way that updates to the cache are propagated. For example, if the data item's server uses invalidation messages to notify caches when the item has changed, then a write-through cache will yield better cache coherence than a write-back cache. But this better coherence has a cost. Usually, the cost of the write-back cache is lower, since multiple updates to the same cached data item within a short time period incur only one write-back, and a write-back can batch multiple updates in a single message to the data's permanent home.

Since caching mechanisms are complex and important, they are built into many types of products, notably transactional middleware and database systems. There are main memory database systems that are intended to be used for cached data. Some operate as a conventional transactional resource manager, such as Oracle's TimesTen, McObject's eXtremeDB, and Raima's RDM. Others are designed specifically for caching, for example, by offering the application explicit control of when to invalidate cached data or write-back updated cached data to its home location. Examples include Danga Interative's memcached, Oracle's Coherence and Microsoft's project codenamed "Velocity."

Resource Pooling

Another case where caching can improve performance is when a resource is costly to create and relatively inexpensive to access. Sessions are one such resource. Consider an application that requires the use of a database system. The server process that runs this application needs a session with a database system for each transaction currently running. However, each transaction typically needs the session only for a fraction of a second. Therefore, the server process can maintain a pool (i.e., cache) of sessions. Each transaction is given exclusive use of one of the sessions while it is running. After it commits or aborts, the session is returned to the pool. Thus, sessions are **serially reused** by different transactions.

Process threads are another example of resources that can be pooled and serially reused. The process has a fixed number of threads. When it receives an RPC, the RPC is assigned to a thread in which to execute. After the RPC finishes executing and returns to its caller, the thread is returned to the thread pool.

A third example is server classes, which avoid the overhead of frequent process creation. Like threads, each process receives a call. After the call completes, the process is available for reuse by another call.

Scaling Out a System

One way to scale up a system is to add more machines. This is called **scale-out**. There are two approaches to scale-out, partitioning and replication, which offer different ways of distributing the workload across the machines.

Partitioning

One way to distribute the workload is to **partition** the application and its data into different types of work and assign each type to a different machine. For example, in a bank, one might assign the credit card application to one system, the loan application to a second system, and the checking account application to a third system.

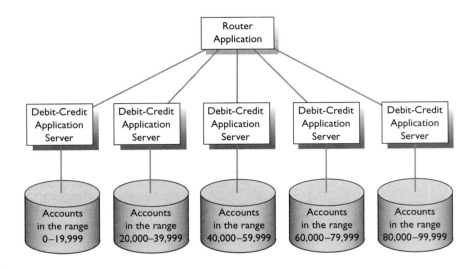

FIGURE 2.16

Parameter-based Routing. The router application forwards each request to the appropriate server based on the account number parameter in the request.

When a request arrives, it is directed to the system that supports the relevant application. This can be done by storing the mapping between applications and servers in a registry service and looking up the mapping for each request, as was described in Section 2.4.

Partitioning by application type is an effective technique. However, it is an incomplete solution if an application needs to scale up beyond the capabilities of a single machine. Then the application itself needs to be partitioned. A common way to do this is **range partitioning**, where different copies of the server handle different ranges of an input parameter. For example, a debit-credit application dealing with retail banking might be split into five servers, each of which handles a range of account numbers (see Figure 2.16). The database that supports each of these servers can be local to the system that supports those account numbers. So the first group of account numbers is stored on the same computer as the application program that supports those account numbers, and so on.

When the system is organized in this way, a routing function needs to forward each request to the correct server based not only on the identifier of the request type, but also on one or more of the input parameters. In the example, it would be the account number. This is called **parameter-based routing**.

Range partitioning can be implemented directly by the application, by having the application support the routing function. Many systems provide built-in support. For example, range partitioning and parameter-based routing are supported by many high-function database systems and some transaction middleware products.

Partitioning schemes all suffer from the problem of load balancing, especially when servers are partitioned statically. Usually, the workload varies over time. For example, in the system shown in Figure 2.16 there may be a burst of activity for accounts in the 20,000 to 39,999 range, thereby overloading the second server. This problem may arise frequently if the load is correlated with value ranges. For example, if account numbers are correlated with geographical regions, then a peak period in one time zone will cause its partition's servers to be more heavily loaded than those of other partitions. An overloaded partition will perform poorly. It doesn't help that other servers may be less heavily loaded, because they don't have the data required to service requests in the 20,000 to 39,999 range.

One way to reduce the frequency of such overload situations is to use **hash partitioning**, where a hash function is used to map each parameter value to a server partition. A well-designed hash function will, with very high probability, spread the load evenly across servers. It therefore is less likely to exhibit load-balancing problems than range partitioning. Hash partitioning commonly is used not only for partitioning a database but also for partitioning a large-scale cache that is spread across many servers.

One solution to load balancing is **automatic reconfiguration**. That is, when a partition becomes overloaded, it automatically is split into two partitions and the routing function is updated accordingly. The decision to split a partition should be based on workload trends, not a short-term spike in load. If a partition is split based on a temporary load spike, the split partitions will be underutilized after the spike dissipates.

Another solution to load balancing is to use **table-lookup partitioning**, where a mapping table explicitly maps each input parameter value to a particular server. There is a significant cost to maintaining all this mapping information when a lot of parameter values are present, though this can be mitigated with the use of some network switches, such as Layer 7 switches. This partitioning approach offers some significant benefits over range and hash partitioning. One benefit is fine-grained control over reconfiguration. When a server overflows, a new server can be allocated and newly added parameter values can be assigned to the new server. Another benefit is that different parameter values can be explicitly assigned levels of service. For example, a bank may offer two levels of service to checking accounts, depending on their minimum monthly balance. This account-type information can be stored in the mapping table and the account stored at a server that supports the appropriate level of service. A third benefit is that users can be upgraded to a new release of an application one by one. By contrast, with range or hash partitioning, the application would not know whether to access a user's data in the partition using the old or new format. Thus, all the parameter values (e.g., accounts) in a partition would be inaccessible while the upgrade was in progress.

Whatever partitioning scheme is used, configuring a system with the right amount of server capacity is important. Servers need to be configured for peak load, not average load, to ensure that they can offer good response time even in periods of high load. The more extra capacity (or **headroom**) that each system offers relative to its expected peak load, the less likely it will become overloaded.

Partitioning Sessions

Partitioning also helps scale-out when communication sessions are required. In a two-tier architecture, if there are many clients and each client requires a session with every server, the result is a polynomial explosion in the number of sessions. For example, if there are 100,000 clients and each one has to connect to all 500 servers, then each server would have 100,000 sessions, resulting in 50,000,000 sessions overall (see Figure 2.17). Each session consumes some main memory and requires some setup time. When there are too many sessions, this session overhead can be troublesome. It can limit the ability of the server system to scale out by adding more servers.

The total number of sessions can be greatly reduced by inserting a routing layer between the clients and servers that partitions the set of clients. Each router process connects to a subset of the clients and to all the servers. Thus, each client can still send messages to all servers, at the cost of an extra message hop through a router. See Figure 2.18.

Now say you have 10 routers between the clients and servers, and each client is connected to one router. Each of the 10 routers would have 10,000 sessions to their clients and 500 sessions to all the servers, resulting in 10,500 sessions per router, or 105,000 sessions overall—a huge reduction from the 50,000,000 sessions required without the routing layer.

Grouping clients by routers can be based on geographical considerations. For example, all the clients on a given local area network might be serviced by the same router. More complex groupings may be needed

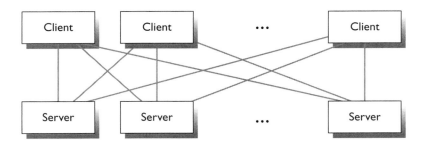

FIGURE 2.17

Polynomial Explosion in Two-Tier Model. If there are f front-end programs and t transaction servers, then there are f × t sessions.

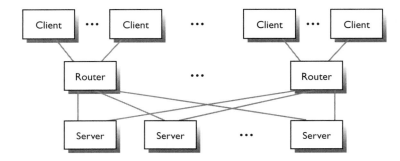

FIGURE 2.18

Multilevel Routing. By introducing routers in between clients and servers, the overall number of sessions is greatly reduced, compared to the two-tier model of Figure 2.17.

for fault tolerance reasons. For example, the ATMs at a bank branch may be split across two routers over two separate communication lines, so the failure of one router still leaves half of the ATMs operating.

Replication

Another way to distribute workload is to replicate server processes and assign the replicas to different systems. The replicas are identical, in the sense that they can all process the same kinds of requests. This works especially well if the processes are stateless. In that case, each request can be assigned to any of the replicas, even if a previous request from the same client was processed by a different replica.

As in the partitioning approach, it is desirable to balance the load across the replicated servers. This can be done by having each request randomly choose a server to process the request, sometimes called **spraying** the requests across the servers. It can be done by the client that issues the request, or it can be done in a server system. For example, a network router that connects a server system to the Internet might have built-in load balancing functionality to forward messages based on round robin, least number of active connections, or fastest response time.

Even if each client sends the same number of requests to each server, the load may not be distributed evenly, because one server may receive requests that require more time to service than those received by another server. To avoid this unbalanced load, each client can put requests into a queue that is shared by all servers, and each server dequeues a request whenever it is idle. Thus, each server obtains new work if and only if it has additional capacity to process it. The main disadvantage of this approach is the overhead of managing the queue. It needs to be accessible to all the servers, and clients and servers need to synchronize their accesses to the shared queue. We will have a lot more to say about queuing mechanisms in Chapter 4.

Replication interacts with caching. Suppose a server is replicated and a client process C issues a request r that accesses one of those server replicas, S. To process r, S may access remote data, which S saves in a cache. For example, C may be a web browser running on a desktop machine and S may be a web server at a site that has a large number of web servers running. The request may access a web page, which is cached by S. A given client often issues many similar requests. If C issues a request r' that is similar to r and hence accesses the same data as r, then it would be cheaper to process r' at S rather than at a different server replica that has not cached the data required by r'. In this case, we say that C has **cache affinity** for S. Although C can still access any of the server replicas, it performs better when accessing S than any of the other server replicas.

A more extreme example of affinity occurs when a server replica S is maintaining shared state with respect to a client C. In this case, it is essential that all requests from C be serviced by S, so the request has access to the shared state. Notice that this problem does not arise if C maintains the shared state. That is, if C includes the shared state with every request, then any server replica can process a request, because the server replicas are stateless with respect to C.

When replicas contain updatable data, updates must be propagated to all replicas to keep them identical. A common configuration is to require that all updates be applied to a primary replica, which forwards those updates to the other read-only replicas. This offers simpler synchronization than immediately broadcasting updates to all replicas, but introduces delay by passing all updates through the primary replica. Synchronization algorithms for replicated data are covered in Chapter 9.

Replication is a common feature of database systems. It can also be used to implement cache coherence. If a replicated cache is updatable, then a replication mechanism can be used to propagate updates from one cache to all the others.

Replication also is used to improve availability. If one replica is unavailable, then its workload can be handled by other replicas. Techniques for using replicas in this way are also covered in Chapter 9.

2.7 SUMMARY

This chapter covered major software abstractions needed to make it easy to build reliable TP applications with good performance: transaction bracketing, threads, remote procedure calls, state management, and scalability techniques.

Transaction Bracketing

Transaction bracketing offers the programmer commands to start, commit, and abort a transaction. The operations on data that execute after the Start command and before the Commit or Abort are part of the transaction. In the chained model, a new transaction begins immediately after a Commit or Abort, so all operations are part of some transaction.

The transaction composability problem arises when a program running a transaction calls another program. There is a choice of bracketing semantics, depending on whether the callee should or should not execute within the caller's transaction. If so, the caller's transaction ID must be passed to the callee.

In the nested transaction model, the callee executes in a subtransaction. A subtransaction abort undoes its actions, but leaves its parent transaction intact. It is up to the top-level transaction to decide whether to commit all its committed subtransactions' work, thereby making its results durable. Savepoints are a related technology that enable single-threaded transactions to back up to a previous state, much like subtransaction abort.

Another approach to transaction bracketing is to tag each component with an attribute that indicates whether an invocation of the component should run in a new transaction, in the caller's transaction, or in no transaction. This approach commonly is used in object-oriented transactional middleware products, instead of explicit commands to start, commit, and abort.

A transaction program needs to provide compensation steps and exception handling code for transaction failures and system failures. The programming model needs a way to expose the reason for the exception, the state that is available if the exception handler executes after an abort or recovery from a system failure, and whether the handler itself executes within a transaction.

Processes and Threads

Each program executing in a processor has an address space and control thread, called its processor state. In a multiprogrammed computer system, each program's processor state can be temporarily stored in main memory or on disk and reloaded when the program resumes execution. A TP system architecture must take into account whether its related programs are running in the same or different address spaces, since this can affect performance and management.

The behavior of a TP system is affected by whether the components of the system share an address space and control thread. Although it is possible to deploy all components of the TP system in a single-threaded process, it leads to a system with a large number of processes, typically at least one per executing transaction. Better performance and scalability usually is obtained with multithreaded processes, due to reduced main memory requirements, fewer context switching operations, and finer grained tuning opportunities. If middleware implements the multithreading, then it must intercept synchronous I/O to avoid blocking the entire process during such operations. The more popular approach is to use threads supported by the operating system.

When multithreading is unavailable, an alternative is server classes, where multiple copies of a TP component are replicated in multiple single-threaded servers. Executing the same code in a pool of single threaded processes can produce similar benefits to executing the same code in multiple threads of the same process.

Remote Procedure Calls

A remote procedure call (RPC) mechanism provides a programming model and runtime environment that allows a program to invoke a program in another address space as if it were a local call within the same address space. With an RPC, the programmer either receives a return from the call or an error indicating that the program didn't run, just as if the call were performed locally.

An RPC mechanism uses an interface definition language to produce a proxy linked to the local program and a stub linked to the program in the remote address space. Proxies and stubs abstract distributed computing details such as data marshaling and the communications protocol from the programs involved in the call. In an object-oriented RPC, the proxy may use a local object as a surrogate for the remote object being called. A transactional RPC uses the proxies and stubs to propagate the transaction context, including the transaction ID, from the caller to the callee.

Before performing an RPC, a client needs to create a binding to the server, for example, by looking up the server's network address in a registry service. To perform an RPC securely, the client and server need to be authenticated and the server needs to check that the client is authorized to do the call. The runtime needs to monitor each call to ensure it succeeds. If the client runtime does not receive an acknowledgment, then it can either repeat the call or ping the server, depending on whether the server is idempotent. The runtime might also translate parameters between different machine formats to enable interoperability.

All this functionality has a price. RPCs are much slower than local procedure calls and simple message passing. But since RPC functionality usually is needed, the only alternative is to move the burden to the application programmer, which makes application programming more time-consuming. Hence, transactional RPC is a popular feature of transactional middleware and underlying platforms.

Shared State

To process transaction requests correctly, components of a TP system need to share state information about users, security tokens, transaction IDs, and the locations and characteristics of other system components. When all the components are deployed within a single address space, they can easily share this state. When the components are distributed across multiple address spaces, this sharing becomes more challenging.

This problem can be circumvented by using stateless servers, which do not share state with the client that calls them. Instead of sharing state, each client request includes all state information that the server needs for processing the request. For example, a browser can retain a cookie, which is the server state that is stored at the client and passed by the client to the server in each request.

One important type of shared state is a transaction ID, which identifies a transaction context and is shared across programs that participate in the same transactional unit of work. A transaction context typically is associated with a thread of execution and can be propagated from one program to another, for example when using an RPC.

A communication session is a way of sharing state between processes on different machines. Typical session state includes transaction context and security information. By creating a shared session, two processes avoid having to pass state information on every interaction. However, sessions require messages to set up and memory to store their state. Thus, they are primarily useful when information is shared for a relatively long period.

Scalability Techniques

Several abstractions are needed to help a TP system scale up and scale out to handle large loads efficiently, including caching, resource pooling, and data partitioning and replication. Using these abstractions improves the ability of a TP system to share access to data.

Caching is a technique that stores a copy of persistent data in shared memory for faster access. The major benefit of caching is faster access to data. If the true value of the data in its permanent home needs to be updated, then synchronization is required to keep the cache values acceptably up to date.

Resource pooling is a mechanism that reuses a resource for many client programs, rather than creating a new resource for each program that needs the resource. For example database connections can be pooled. A database connection is allocated to a program when it needs to use the database and returned to the pool when a program's task is completed.

Partitioning is a technique for improving scalability by segmenting resources into related groups that can be assigned to different processors. When a resource type is partitioned, the TP system routes requests for the resource to the partition that contains it. For example, if a database is partitioned, an access to a data item is routed to the database partition that contains the data item.

Replication is a technique for improving scalability by spreading the workload across multiple identical servers. Clients can either push their work onto particular servers or enqueue the work and have the servers pull from the queues. A client may have affinity for a server that has cached data that it frequently accesses, in which case it prefers sending its workload to that server. Replication can also be used to improve availability by using backup replicas to handle the load of a failed replica. One major challenge of replication is to keep updatable replicas mutually consistent at an affordable cost.

Transaction Processing Application Architecture

3.1 INTRODUCTION

From the end user's point of view, a transaction processing (TP) application is a serial processor of requests. It is a server that appears to execute an infinite loop whose body is an ACID transaction, such as the following pseudo-program:

```
Do Forever
        /* the body of this loop is a transaction */
        receive a request
        do the requested work
        send a reply (optional)
End
```

However, as we saw in Chapter 1, the behind-the-scenes reality is more complex. Usually, the user is executing on a front-end machine that is remote from the server machine that executes the transactions. Often the server is itself a distributed system, primarily so that it can scale up to handle a large number of requests.

To process a request, the actual control flow within a TP application is more like this:

- The front-end program captures the user's request using a combination of forms and menu selections, typically executing in a web browser or more specialized input device, such as an ATM or gas pump.
- The front-end program translates the input into a request message and sends it to a server.
- A middle-tier or back-end server examines the request message to determine what type of transaction is being requested and which application program P should process the request.
- The server starts a transaction and invokes P. Typically P invokes a database system to do some of its work.
- If the transaction terminates successfully, the server commits the transaction. Otherwise, it aborts the transaction.
- The server sends some output back to the source of the request, such as a web browser or other input device, to finish processing the user's request.

TP applications that have the preceding structure require a diverse set of runtime functions. They include the functions described in Chapter 2, plus many others such as presentation services, message routing, security, and system management. These functions are typically not all packaged together in one product. Some are in the operating system. Others are in the database system. Some are in independent middleware components.

This is a fairly complicated picture: many different services, supported by a variety of products, distributed across different systems in a network. It can be a challenging environment in which to develop an application and to manage it while it is running. This chapter will try to simplify the challenge by explaining how the pieces of the environment are meant to be used together to build and operate a TP application.

3.2 APPLICATION ARCHITECTURE

There are three interrelated ways to decompose a TP system: by functional components, by hardware subsystems, and by operating system processes. The decomposition by functional components is shown in Figure 3.1. It consists of front-end programs, request controllers, transaction servers, and database systems. In the past, this was called a **three-tier architecture**, consisting of the front-end program as the first tier, the database system as the third tier, and everything in between as the middle tier. As systems have become more layered, it is no longer clear how many tiers are present. We therefore call it a **multitier architecture**.

The display device, shown in the upper left, interacts with a component that we call the **front-end program**, which is responsible for gathering input and displaying output. It captures input from forms, menu selections, and the like; validates the input; and translates it into a request message.

The front-end program communicates with the device in a device-specific format. The types of display devices change frequently based in large part on the cost of hardware to implement them. Today, a web browser running on a PC is a common device. In this case, the front-end program is a web browser connected to a web server that uses the HTTP protocol and some variant of hypertext markup language (HTML) plus some scripting.

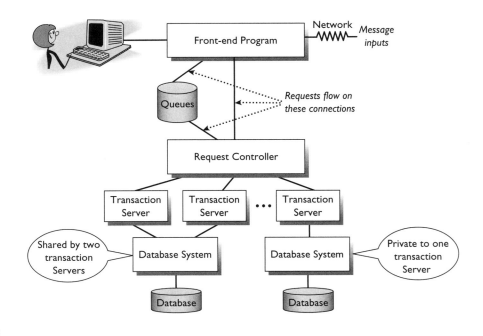

FIGURE 3.1

Multitier TP Application Architecture. The front-end program manages the user's display and outputs requests. The request controller processes a request by calling transaction servers, which access databases and other transactional resources.

The front-end program may respond to some requests itself. It sends other requests to the next stage of the system, either by storing them on a disk in a queue or forwarding them directly for processing by the application, in a component that we call the **request controller**.

The request controller component guides the execution of requests. It determines the steps required to execute the request. It then executes those steps by invoking transaction servers. The application executing in this component usually runs as part of an ACID transaction.

Transaction servers are processes that run application programs that do the actual work of the request. They almost always execute within a transaction. The transaction server usually communicates with one or more database systems, which may be private to a particular transaction server or may be shared by several of them.

Like any program, a TP application usually is constructed by composing simple components into more complex ones. Simple transaction server applications can be composed into a compound application using local procedure calls, such as composing `DebitChecking` and `PayLoan` into `PayLoanFromChecking` as we saw in Section 2.2. To compose distributed components, a distributed communications mechanism is needed, such as a remote procedure call or asynchronous message queue. Service-oriented components and workflow mechanisms can also play a part in this composition. Compound applications can then be composed into even higher level functions. This composition of components can have several levels, which sometimes makes the distinction between request controller and transaction server programs rather fuzzy. In such situations, a program may perform both request controller and transaction server functions.

This multitier TP application architecture means that the TP application itself must be split into different parts that perform these different functions: front end, request controller, and transaction server. Most of this chapter is devoted to the details of what each of the components needs to do.

Multitier Architectures

TP systems usually have two kinds of hardware subsystems, front-end systems that sit close to the display devices, and back-end systems that sit close to the databases. In a simple configuration, each front-end system may be a PC running a web browser connected to the Internet, and the back-end system may be a single machine such as a shared memory multiprocessor running a web server and a database management system. In complex configurations, both the front-end and back-end systems may contain many machines. For example, a front-end system may have multiple machines that support a large number of devices in a retail store. A back-end system may be a large server farm that supports hundreds of stores, with different machines running different applications, such as finance, order processing, shipping, and human resources.

A major architectural issue in TP systems is how to map the functional components of Figure 3.1 into processes on front-end and back-end systems. One natural way is to have each function run in a separate kind of process:

- The front-end program runs in a separate process, typically either a web browser or custom software to control relatively low-function end-user devices. On large systems, separate front-end machines are dedicated to front-end programs. On small systems, they run on the same back-end machine as other components.

- Each request controller runs in a separate process and communicates with the front-end programs via messages. It usually runs on a back-end system.

- Each transaction server runs as a process on a back-end system, preferably colocated on the same machine or local area network as the database system that it most frequently accesses. It communicates with request controllers and other transaction servers via messages.

- Each database system runs as a process on a back-end system.

Most modern TP applications are structured in this multitier architecture to get the following benefits in a distributed computing environment:

- Flexible distribution: Functions can be moved around in the distributed system without modifying application programs, because the different functions already are separated into independent processes that communicate by exchanging messages.

- Flexible configuration: Processes can be located to optimize performance, availability, manageability, and so on.

- Easier scale-out: The distribution and configuration flexibility makes it easier to scale out a system by adding more server boxes and moving processes to them.

- Flexible control: Each functional component can be independently controlled. For example, one can control the relative speeds of transaction servers by varying the number of threads in those servers without affecting the front-end program or request controller functions, which are running in separate processes.

- Easier operations: In a large system, only a few people are expert at each tier's applications. Having them isolated makes them easier to debug and independently upgradable.

- Fault isolation: Since the different functions are running in different processes, errors in one function cannot corrupt the memory of other functions, which are running in separate processes.

The main disadvantage of this multitier architecture is its impact on performance. The functional components are communicating via messages between processes, instead of local procedure calls within a single process. The former are at least two orders-of-magnitude slower than the latter. Since even the simplest transaction requires a round-trip between a front-end program and request controller and between a request controller and transaction server, there is quite a lot of message overhead in this approach.

There are other disadvantages of the multitier architecture due to its large number of moving parts. This leads to complexity of the design, deployment, configuration, and management of the multitier system. To mitigate these problems, vendors have been steadily improving their tools for development and system management. But there is still much room for improvement.

Due to communications overhead, it is common to combine functions in a single process. For example, most database systems support **stored procedures**, which are application programs that execute within the database server process. One can use this mechanism to run transaction server programs as stored procedures, thereby eliminating a layer of processes between request controllers and the database system and hence eliminating communication overhead. Of course, this reduces the degrees of flexibility of the multitier architecture, since it prevents transaction server programs from being distributed independently of the database server processes in which they run.

Taking this approach to the extreme, one can run all the functional components of the multitier architecture in a database server process. This reduces the multitier architecture to a two-tier architecture. This was a popular approach in the early days of client–server computing in the 1980s, but fell out of favor for large-scale systems due to its limited ability to scale out. However, as database servers are becoming more functional, it is looking more appealing. We will discuss this trend later, in Section 3.7.

Service-Oriented Architecture

In addition to the multitier application architecture, application design methodologies play a role in the structure of TP applications. Service-oriented architecture (SOA) is one such design methodology, which was discussed

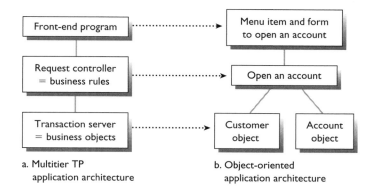

FIGURE 3.2

Mapping Object-Oriented Application Architecture to a Multitier Model. Business objects, such as "Customer," "Credit History," and "Account" run in transaction servers, and business rules such as "Open an Account" run in request controllers.

in Chapter 1. In SOA, the designer identifies a service that a business provides for its customers and partners. The designer maps this business service to a software service, which is an operation. Typically, a set of related operations are grouped together in a service interface. Each operation in a service interface is implemented as a software component that can be invoked over a network by sending it a message. In SOA, operations are intended to be relatively independent of each other, so they can be assembled into applications in different combinations, connected by different message patterns.

In a TP system, a service can implement a transaction or a step within a transaction. That is, it can play the role of a request controller or transaction server. In either case, it is invoked by sending a message to the service. In this sense, the notion of a service is nicely aligned with multitier TP system architecture.

This alignment between SOA and TP depends only on the fact that SOA decomposes applications into independent services. It does not depend on the particular technology that is used to define service interfaces or to communicate between services, such as RPC or Web Service standards.

Object-Oriented Design

Another popular application design methodology that plays a role in the structure of TP applications is object-oriented design. Object-oriented design offers a different perspective than SOA, focusing on modeling things rather than functions.

Object-oriented design maps nicely onto the TP application architecture of Figure 3.1 as shown in Figure 3.2. In this style of design, one starts by defining **business objects**, which are the elementary types of entities used by the business. In programming terms, each business object corresponds to a class in an object-oriented programming language, such as C++, Java, C#, or Visual Basic. It encapsulates the elementary operations on that type of entity, called **methods**. Typically, these methods change slowly, because they correspond to types of real-world objects whose behavior has been well-established for a long time. For example, the following could be defined as business objects:

- Customer: It supports methods to create a new customer, change address, change phone number, and return customer information in several different formats.

- Loan Account: It supports methods to create a new loan account, increase the amount owed, credit the amount paid, and associate the loan account with a different customer.

- Credit History: It supports methods to create a credit history for a given customer, add a credit event (such as a loan or loan payment), and return all its credit events for a given time period.

After defining the business objects in an application, one defines **business rules**, which are actions that the business performs in response to things that happen in the real world. For example, the business rule for opening a new loan might involve creating a new customer object (if this is a new customer), checking the customer's credit history, and if the credit history is satisfactory, then creating an account. Business rules change more frequently than business objects, because they reflect changes in the way the business operates in the real world. It is therefore useful to program business rules in modules that are separate from business objects.

One can map this object-oriented application design onto TP application architecture by running business objects as transaction servers and business rules as request controller programs. This is an efficient architecture, since business objects make frequent access to the database that stores the object's state and can be colocated with the database. It is also a flexible structure, since business rules can be changed within request controllers without affecting the business objects (i.e., transaction servers) that they call.

Applications created using objects can be service-enabled to participate in an SOA. Externally callable methods of an object-oriented application are good candidates for services. Services might expose only portions of the functionality of the objects through the service interface.

Simple Requests

In this chapter, we'll focus on simple requests. A **simple request** accepts one input message from its input device (a display device or specialized device such as an ATM), executes the transaction, and sends one message back to the input device. Examples are making a bank account deposit, placing an order, or logging a shipment. Each simple request is independent of every other simple request.

A given user interaction may actually require a sequence of related requests. For example, a user might want to arrange a trip, which requires reserving airline seats, reserving a car, and reserving a hotel room. A travel web site may offer this as one request, even though it may actually run as three separate requests. We'll look at multi-request interactions in Chapter 5. In this chapter, we'll assume that all requests are simple—one message in and one message out.

The next three sections, Sections 3.3 through 3.5, cover the main components of TP application architecture: front-end programs, request controllers, and transaction servers. They look at both the application's functions and issues related to building the underlying component. Section 3.6 looks at transactional middleware that provides support for these components. Section 3.7 revisits the two-tier versus three-tier system models, exploring in more detail the decision to group front-end programs, request controllers, and transaction servers into the database server process.

3.3 FRONT-END PROGRAM

Front-End Program Layers

A front-end program gathers input from a user and sends it as a request message to the request controller. From that point on, the TP application deals with only request messages. It doesn't need to know any details of the various devices, forms managers, or web services that capture input for the request or that interpret the output

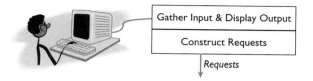

FIGURE 3.3

Layers of a Front-End Program. The front-end program gathers input by communicating with the display, then translates that input into a request message.

of the transaction that runs the request. Only the front-end program deals with that. We call this **presentation independence**, because the front-end program makes the rest of the application independent of the other software and hardware that's interacting with the user.

Typically the request controller offers a fixed application programming interface (API) for use by the front-end program. That is, the API doesn't depend on the type of front-end device or program. This enables a single TP application to interact concurrently with diverse front-end devices and programs. It also makes it easy to add new front-end devices and programs without modifying the rest of the TP application.

The front-end program has two main functions (see Figure 3.3): one that interacts with the user to gather input and display output; and one that deals with constructing request messages and interpreting replies. We'll describe each function in turn.

Gathering Input Using Forms and Menus

Form and Menu Concepts

The front-end program gathers from a display device the input required to generate a request message. If the display device is a terminal, PC, or workstation, the front-end program generally interacts with the user via menus and forms, often executing inside a web browser. The user selects a menu item—perhaps by clicking on an icon or a command button, or by highlighting an entry on a pull-down menu—to identify the type of transaction he or she wants to run. Then the front-end program displays a form or series of forms in which the user enters the input data needed for the type of request. Anyone who has made a retail purchase over the Internet using a web browser recognizes this style of interaction.

Application programmers write the programs that direct the front end's menu management, forms management, and data validation functions. One or more presentation technologies offers application programmers the ability to do the following:

- Define menus and how to navigate between them.
- Define the fields of each form and how they are laid out on the screen.
- Identify the data validation routine to be called for each field on the form to ensure that the input makes sense.

The system functions available to interact with forms and menus have changed a lot over the years, due to the evolution of desktop devices and graphical user interfaces. However, the required capabilities of forms and menus have not changed very much. We first explain the principles and then discuss how they have been embodied in various kinds of technology.

The front-end program usually performs some data validation of the input form, to ensure that the input values make sense. This validation is done for each field, either one-by-one as each field is entered, or altogether after the entire form has been filled in. The goal of the validation is to minimize the chance of attempting to execute the request with incorrect input. This would result in having the error detected downstream by a request controller, transaction server, or database system, thereby wasting system resources and increasing the delay in notifying the user of the error.

Data validation can sometimes be circumvented by offering a pick-list, such as a drop-down menu, that contains only the valid values for that field (e.g., a state or province in an address). Other checks require a cached copy of valid data values that are compared to values that the user enters in the form. For example, when requesting a flight reservation, the user needs to enter a valid city name or airport code.

When validating fields, it is usually a bad idea to compare the values entered by the end-user directly with data in the back-end database. If this were done as each input field is entered, it would generate a high load on the communication path between the user display and the database and on the database itself. This would degrade the response time to the user and the throughput of the back end. However, using a cached copy also has disadvantages. The cached copy is refreshed from the live database only periodically, so it usually isn't completely accurate. This is satisfactory for fields that don't change frequently, such as department names and product codes, but not for frequently changing fields, such as the number of items left in inventory for a popular product. Those fields can be validated only by executing the transaction itself in the transaction server, which has direct access to the database.

One problem with validation logic is that it resides on the front end but is closely associated with the back end, where the validated input is interpreted. Thus, changes in transaction server behavior can affect the data validation behavior that's required. This affects the process for developing, deploying, and managing applications.

The use of cached and potentially out-of-date data for data validation is an example of the general design principle presented in Section 2.6 for scaling up. By limiting the application's need for accurate and consistent data, the application can be replicated to scale up to a large number of web servers and browsers. If accurate data were required, then it would be more costly to keep the replicas up to date.

Form and Menu Technology

Before the advent of the PC, terminals were the dominant device for an end-user to communicate with a TP system. Terminal devices evolved from teletype terminals, to character-at-a-time cathode-ray tube terminals, to block-mode screen-at-a-time terminals. In all the cases, forms management software was used to write front-end programs to communicate with such devices. In the 1970s, this functionality was built into early TP monitor products. In the 1980s, independent forms manager products became popular. They offered a What-You-See-Is-What-You-Get (WYSIWYG) forms designer and callout functions to a standard programming language.

In the early 1990s, PCs became popular as display devices for communicating with TP applications. Early forms products were replaced by fourth generation languages (4GLs) and visual programming products, such as Microsoft's Visual Basic, Powersoft's (now Sybase's) PowerBuilder, and Borland's Delphi. The forms and menus compile into programs that run on a PC, rather than on a server as had been the case for low-function display devices. They typically use an RPC to communicate with the back-end server. This style of front-end program often is called a **thick client**, because it runs in a general-purpose operating system environment.

As web browsers became popular in the late 1990s, the **thin client** architecture emerged, where the menus and forms are hosted in a browser. Figure 3.4 illustrates the thick and thin client alternatives.

The thin client architecture gets its name from the more limited functionality of the browser environment compared to a general-purpose programming language and operating system. The basic interaction pattern is that the browser receives and displays HTML files and their embedded links, the user enters data (usually via HTML forms), and the browser returns the user's data to the web server as a query-string in an HTTP GET or as the content of an HTTP POST, which the web server then processes. The same pattern is used for XHTML, which uses XML syntax to express HTML. The web server is then responsible for invoking the back-end server.

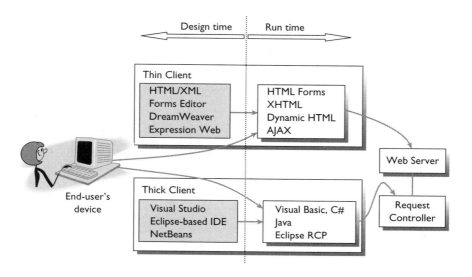

FIGURE 3.4

Sample Forms Tools. In a thick client, a general-purpose program on the user's PC communicates with the back-end server. A thin client uses a browser to display forms and gather input.

In the thin client architecture, some of the browser controls may be used instead of or in addition to the forms logic, such as the browser navigation buttons. Browser-based front-end programs also may have to compensate for browser-based navigations; for example, compensating for the case when the browser's "back" button is pushed before the form is completed.

From a TP system designer's perspective, one benefit of browsers is that there are a relatively small number of popular ones and hence a relatively small number of interfaces to support. However, early browsers did not support a very expressive programming environment. The browser has become less of a thin client over time with the development of more powerful programming constructs that can run in the browser, such as interactive plug-ins and scripting languages. Other programming models for active content include Dynamic HTML, which adds client-side scripting, cascading style sheets, and the document object model to HTML; AJAX (Asynchronous JavaScript And XML), which enables updating of small portions of a web page instead of reloading the entire page; and multimedia environments such as Adobe Flash and Microsoft Silverlight. New, more powerful browser-based technologies appear every year.

Desktop systems are much less expensive than back-end TP systems and are usually paid for by users, not by the enterprise owning the TP system. Therefore, TP system designers want to offload as much processing as possible to the front end. However, given the power of a web browser to display complex multipart pages and to execute code, some care is needed to avoid overloading a page with too much functionality and thereby negatively affecting performance. For example, displaying too many objects, with images assembled from several sources, can be a source of delay. Objects embedded in the browser also have the capability to directly invoke a transaction server, but this can introduce scalability problems such as those discussed in Chapter 2.

Forms Development

Forms and menus usually are designed graphically, by creating the form on the screen. Actions may be associated with each field and menu item to validate as the form is filled in, or there may be a single action to accept all the user input and package it in a request message.

User ID	Device ID	Request Type	Request-Specific Parameters

FIGURE 3.5

Typical Request Contents. It contains the ID of the user entering the request, the user's device, the type of transaction being requested, and parameters to the request.

Some development environments provide extensive function libraries to help build the form and process the input to it, including validation. If using HTML or a variation of it, the development environment may have fewer built-in functions, so more processing may be needed at the request controller to compensate for the lack of functionality in the front-end program environment.

Constructing Requests

A request message from a front-end program can take the form of a remote procedure call or asynchronous message. Its format usually includes the following (see Figure 3.5):

- The identifier of the user; that is, the name of the user who is operating the device and is entering the request (if a human is doing this work) or of the software component that is authorized to issue the request. For HTTP, this often is captured in a cookie and is omitted for some types of requests.

- A device identifier of the device that's producing the input. For example, this could be the network address of the device or an operating system socket that is bound to a TCP session with the device. The device's type might be available through the message protocol (e.g., in HTTP) or it may be supplied by the communications system. For example, the device type could be a particular version of a web browser or a particular asynchronous terminal device.

- A request type, which is the identifier of the type of transaction that the request is asking to execute.

- Input parameters; each request type generally requires a certain number of parameters as input. The rest of the message contains those parameters, which are different for each type of request.

There are many message format standards that define fields for some of the above information. For example, HTTP provides a default mechanism for constructing a request using a URL. Other standard formats include SOAP headers and some Web Services standards, such as WS-Addressing and WS-Security. Application-specific formats also are used. For example, some fields could be expressed in the data type part of the Web Service Description Language. They may simply be part of an XML payload that is passed in an asynchronous message, defined using XML Schema. Or they may be defined by a transactional middleware product that offers request management functions.

Ideally, a TP application uses one format for all its transaction types. However, an enterprise system often has heterogeneous components that use different request formats. In this case, a request controller may need to transform or reformat some requests into and out of different formats. This is a common function of message-oriented middleware, which is described in Chapter 4.

A request should also include a **request identifier**, which is unique relative to other request identifiers from the same client and is made visible to the user or application program that issued the request. There are two operations that should be offered to users and that need this identifier, Status and Cancel. The Status operation is issued by a user who has timed out waiting for a reply to the request. It returns the state of the request, such as whether the request has been received, has been processed and committed, or has been processed and aborted. The Cancel operation attempts to kill the request before it executes. This operation cannot be guaranteed to succeed. If the request has already executed and committed at the time the cancel operation is received by the system, it's too late, because once a transaction is committed, its results are permanent (except by running a compensating transaction). If the front-end program is allowed to have many requests outstanding, then the request identifier has a third use: to match each reply to the corresponding request, either by the front-end program or request controller.

After the front-end program has gathered the user's input, it sends a request message to the request controller. This is typically an RPC or HTTP operation. Before RPC was widely available, transactional middleware products often implemented a custom protocol to send a request message and receive a reply. These protocols are still available in many of the older products, primarily for backward compatibility. Modern SOA or web-based systems may also offer an asynchronous messaging capability.

When a front-end program is tightly integrated with a transactional middleware product, the request may be constructed by the middleware product with little application programming. By setting certain properties of the menu item and by tagging forms fields with the names of parameters required by the transaction program, the application programmer can give the front-end program what it needs to translate that menu item and form data into a request message.

Logging

Some front-end programs are able to keep a record of all the work going on at the front-end by logging messages. Sometimes the display devices themselves do this. For example, some ATMs print a record of each transaction on a paper log inside the machine, to settle later disputes. For less functional devices, the front-end program may do the message logging itself and provide an interface where system managers can go back and look at that log to reconcile any errors that might appear later. Transactional middleware often has built-in message logging functionality to help, such as that in the Java Enterprise Edition (Java EE) and the .NET Framework. We discuss such reconciliation problems further in Sections 4.4 and 5.5.

Web Servers

Although web servers reside on back-end systems, their primary purpose is to capture input from web browsers and display output in the form of static or dynamically-generated content. Since they are so closely linked to the behavior of web browsers, we usually regard them as part of the front-end layer of the multitier architecture.

Web servers are designed not only to interact with a display by sending pages to web browsers, but also to process simple requests. For example, a web server can process a request for relatively static information, such as the root page of a web site or the table of contents of a catalog. Answering this kind of request in the web server offers faster response time than forwarding the request to other middle-tier or back-end components for processing. Moreover, since the requested information is static, it can be cached in the web server, further improving efficiency. Over time, we expect web servers to continually grow in their capacity to handle not only simple requests efficiently, but also more and more complex requests.

Some simple requests require the invocation of an application program. One of the first mechanisms introduced for a web server to invoke application code was the Common Gateway Interface (CGI). A CGI program can be written in any language supported by the system on which the web server is running. A specific location is defined for the CGI programs (e.g., http://www.example.com/wiki.cgi). Whenever a request to a matching URL is received (e.g., http://en.wikipedia.org/wiki/URL), the corresponding program is called, together with any data that the client sent as input. Output from the program is collected by the web server, augmented with appropriate headers, and sent back to the client.

Each call from the web server to execute a request through CGI causes a new process to be created. The new process executes the application program required to process the request. In particular, that application program could be a request controller. This is the 1970s' time-sharing model of executing commands, namely, for every call create a process and run the called program in that process. The approach is simple, but expensive, and therefore has limited scalability. Techniques have been developed to improve the performance of CGI scripts, including the ability to execute compiled programs and an optimized version of the CGI protocol called FastCGI. FastCGI creates a limited pool of processes (i.e., a server class) that runs CGI programs with communications connections to the web server. These processes can be reused by multiple CGI calls, instead of creating a process per call.

To avoid the overhead of process creation altogether, web servers have interfaces to execute application code within the web server that invokes the application, such as Microsoft's Internet Server Application Programming Interface (ISAPI) and the Apache API. This is more efficient. But the APIs are relatively low-level, which makes applications that use these APIs somewhat complex. Moreover, applications running in a web server process are not as well protected from each other as they would be running in separate processes, as in CGI. A higher level and more portable alternative is the Java Servlet API. HTTP requests and responses are mapped to Servlet threads, which invoke Java objects to dynamically generate content and access resources external to the web server.

Higher level programming environments also have been developed that simplify application programming. Initially, a scripting language was allowed to be embedded in web pages, such as Active Server Pages (ASP) and Java Server Pages (JSP). When the web server receives a URL for such a page, it loads the page and then interprets the embedded script, which results in a page containing only HTML (for example), which is returned to the browser that requested the page. This programming model has been quite popular and therefore has been steadily improved to allow more powerful language features, more prepackaged controls, compilation of pages, and invocation of code outside pages using an RPC.

Another trend is offering more modern programming languages, such as Java and C#, which have garbage collection and type safety for higher programmer productivity and increased reliability. However, garbage collection hides from the user the amount of memory being used, so the equivalent of a memory leak may go undetected while the memory footprint increases forever. Although garbage collection often reduces application execution time, even with concurrent multithreaded garbage collectors the system must sometimes stop and collect garbage, thereby introducing latency. To avoid unacceptable response time, TP system implementers need to watch out for these issues and minimize their effects.

The functionality of web servers, and of front-end programs in general, changes relatively rapidly. These changes are driven by several factors: the continual increase in the power of end-user devices and speed of networks that connect the front-end program to that device; the desire to offer more appealing interfaces for human–computer interaction; and the demand to improve programmer productivity when developing applications for presentation services. We expect all these trends to continue indefinitely.

State Management for Web Servers

Applications running in a web server usually are designed to be stateless with respect to a browser instance. This is partly because browsers communicate with web servers using the HTTP protocol, which is stateless. Thus, different requests sent by a browser to a given back-end system may be processed by different web servers in that system. Clearly, this creates a problem if there is a state that needs to be maintained across multiple interactions between the browser and web servers. One approach is to carry along the state as application-managed parameters or cookies in each call. A second approach is to store that state on the back end by replicating it across multiple web servers. A third approach is to store it on the back end in a location that is accessible to all the web servers that can receive requests that may need that state. In the latter two approaches, the URL or a cookie needs to identify that state so the web server knows how to find it.

One reason that stateless web servers are popular is that they simplify scalability. Since web servers do not retain state, the dispatcher of HTTP requests can spray those requests randomly across all the web servers, thereby balancing the load. Moreover, there is no state management needed to scale up a back-end system comprised of web servers. One can simply add server machines, create web servers to run on the machines, and make the existence of the web servers known to the HTTP dispatcher.

Stateless web servers also simplify recovery. A web server may fail unexpectedly or be deliberately brought down for maintenance or an upgrade. Since a web server does not retain state from one request to the next, the failure of a web server affects only the specific requests it was processing at the time it failed. If a user times out waiting for a reply from a failed web server, he or she can simply reissue the request. The back-end system will dispatch the retry to an available web server, which is equally well prepared to process the request. Moreover, when the failed web server recovers, it can immediately start processing new requests, since it has no state that needs to be recovered first.

The use of stateless web servers is part of the software architectural pattern called REST (representational state transfer). An example of the architectural pattern is the REST/HTTP protocol infrastructure, which we discussed in Section 1.2. The REST architectural pattern is characterized by the following set of constraints on service-oriented systems:

- Servers are stateless.
- Operations are generic (e.g., GET and POST), so the application-specific nature of an operation must be captured in the name and content of the resource being accessed (e.g., the URL).
- The resource's (e.g., web page's) representation captures the name and parameters of operations being invoked.
- Caching is transparent, so the invocation of an operation can be answered from a cached result if it is available, such as a cached copy of a static web page being requested by a GET operation.

Together, these constraints enable scalability of clients and servers. To invoke a service, a client needs to know only the name of the resource being invoked. It does not need to know the names of operations because they are generic. Thus, a client can invoke a server as long as it has access to a service that can translate resource names into network addresses (e.g., the Internet Domain Name System (DNS)). Since servers are stateless, they scale out easily and more cheaply. And the use of caching helps avoid expensive communication and accesses to databases or files, further improving scalability.

The downside is that the REST architectural pattern, and stateless servers in general, can cause worse performance when interacting with shared data, because sometimes it leads to transferring more state than would be needed with stateful servers. For example, since a stateless server cannot cache database records, it may send a large set of records to a client, even though often only the first few are used. A stateful server S can solve this problem by maintaining a record cache. Or S can use a database session with a database server-side cursor, which caches a large query result and returns a small set of records on each fetch operation by S.

In practice many web sites do not follow all the constraints of REST, making it more like an ideal architecture against which to measure implementations of web technologies than a concrete programming model. The widespread use of cookies is a good example, since they create resources that don't have a URL, introduce state management into a stateless protocol, and can become inconsistent when a web browser's BACK button is pressed. Other common violations of REST are including parameters and methods in URLs, using POST

FIGURE 3.6

Authentication and Security. Web servers and back-end servers authenticate the identity of users that communicate with them. Additional security is provided by encrypting messages.

for every operation instead of using GET, and misapplications of caching such that a system cannot determine which representation of a resource is authoritative or expired.

Authentication and Encryption

Another function performed by the front-end program is authentication, which is the activity of determining the identity of the user (see Figure 3.6). For example, this is required when a user accesses a bank or brokerage account. Not all applications require authentication. For example, retail businesses often allow users to make purchases simply by providing billing and shipping information, without logging in. For applications that require it, authentication usually is done by having the user enter a username and password, the results of which are visible to the application as an authentication token.

Whenever the front-end program sends a request message to the request controller, the results of the user authentication process are included. This proves to the rest of the application that the message came from a certain person and allows authorization to be performed by the server.

The user also wants to be sure that she is communicating with the correct server, not a rogue server that is spoofing—that is, masquerading as the server the user really wants. This requires that the server authenticate itself to the user.

An additional level of security can be provided if the wire that connects the device to the system is encrypted, which reduces the threat of wiretapping. A good encryption algorithm makes it unlikely that a wiretapper would be able either to decrypt messages or to spoof the system by trying to convince the system that it's actually a qualified user.

When the client system is communicating with the server over the Internet, server authentication and encryption usually is obtained using Transport Layer Security (TLS) (the successor to Secure Socket Layer (SSL)) on TCP/IP. This is a protocol by which the client and server exchange enough information to establish a secure information channel, over which they exchange encrypted information that only each other can decipher.

In TLS, the client obtains from the server a certificate, which includes the server's public key. The server certificate is issued by a trusted certificate authority and signed using the authority's private key. A client can validate the certificate using the authority's public key. Thus, the certificate can be used to authenticate the server to the client web browser, so the latter is sure that it is talking to the intended server. The client and server then exchange encryption keys and message authentication codes, which enable the client and server to exchange encrypted information. Often TLS is implemented by a site's network switch, and lighter weight encryption is used within the site.

There are many ways to arrange secure communications between the front-end program and web server, depending on the desired level of security and the amount of effort devoted to performance optimization. The following is a typical scenario:

- Suppose that Alice is browsing a retail web site. She gets an encrypted cookie that identifies her as a user, whether or not she's logged in. Her browser sends the cookie back and forth over HTTP. The web server of the web site can quickly decrypt basic information about Alice and her session.

- After some browsing, Alice decides to buy what's in her shopping basket. She goes to the checkout page, which uses HTTPS (i.e., TLS). All pages in the checkout process use HTTPS and hence communication is encrypted to protect Alice's password, credit card number, and other personal information such as her address. The HTTPS connection setup is expensive as it uses public key encryption of certificates to give Alice some assurance that she's talking to the right web site. After the certificate is checked the HTTPS connection may switch to a symmetric and cheaper connection.

- The web site asks her to log in. It authenticates Alice's login information and creates an encrypted cookie, which holds a key for the session information that's stored on the back end. The web site also looks up any relevant personal information it has on file for her, such as billing and shipping address, preferred type of shipping, and credit card number. The web server caches the information in a local nondurable in-memory database and stores it as session state in a separate database that's available to all web servers.

- The web site then asks Alice to fill in or validate that personal information. It takes multiple interactions for Alice to enter all this information. Since the web site uses a layer 7 network switch, which can route messages by content, the switch will continue to direct her to the same server unless the server slows down or crashes. If one of her interactions moves to another web server, the web server uses her cookie to find her session state in the session state database.

- On the final web page, if Alice agrees to the purchase, the web site validates her credit card with a bank over another TLS connection, runs the transaction, and replies to Alice with a receipt. After that, she's back to normal HTTP for more shopping. As HTTPS is more costly than HTTP, when Alice returns to web pages that anyone can see, the web site will switch back to unencrypted HTTP connections to save cost.

Some TP applications manage their own authentication and authorization information, whereas others use an external security service, such as the operating system's security service, or an independent security service such as those provided by CA's SiteMinder, Microsoft's Windows Active Directory, or IBM's Tivoli. If the security service is made available to all back-end components, then the system can offer users a single set of credentials across all applications. It might also offer a single sign-on for users, where they receive a ticket-granting ticket that can be used by multiple applications to authenticate the user. When an external security service is used, the application has to be able to understand the external format, access the external service, and potentially federate security tokens (when more than one is used).

In some TP applications, it's quite important to know that a message arrived from a particular device, not just from any device at which a particular user logged in. This is called **geographical entitlement**, because one is entitled to provide input based on one's geographic location. An example would be in the securities trading room of a brokerage house. When the traders show up for work, they have to display their photo identification cards to a guard before entering the trading room. They then sit down at their display devices and provide pass-words to prove to the TP application that they are who they say they are. For this extra level of security to work, the system must know that the request actually came from a device in the secured trading room. If someone connects from another location, device authentication will tell the system which device entered the request, so the system can determine that the device is not entitled to enter requests, even if that someone knows the password of an authorized user.

Specifying the security of the TP system and monitoring the front-end program's behavior creates requirements for a variety of system management functions within the front end. The front end has to allow a system manager to define information needed to authenticate devices and users, such as passwords and valid network addresses. For example, the front-end program might allow the system manager to set up a default password that the device owner or the user can change after logging in. The system manager may also specify that a user is allowed to enter only certain types of requests at certain times of day. Since there may be many users of the system, the complexity of this specification can be reduced by introducing the abstraction of a **role**. Each role has a set of privileges, such as allowable requests and usage times, and a set of users that have those privileges. Instead of specifying privileges for each user, the system manager simply assigns and removes individual users from roles. The system manager needs to specify privileges for each role, but there are many fewer roles than users and the privileges for roles change less frequently than for users. Identity-based security is starting to emerge as a way to achieve more fine-grained authorization, such as Microsoft's CardSpace and Eclipse's Higgins.

Security is a major consideration when developing and deploying TP applications and is a subject for a book in itself. In-depth discussions about security mechanisms are beyond the scope of this book.

3.4 REQUEST CONTROLLER

The purpose of a request controller is to execute requests by calling the transaction server programs that can perform the request. If the execution of the request produces output, the request controller routes the response back to the front-end program that sent the request. Usually the request controller brackets transactions; that is, it issues the Start, Commit, and Abort operations. Within a transaction, there may be calls to one or more transaction servers.

Specifying Request Controller Functions

A request may require the execution of many transaction server programs and possibly of many transactions. An application-specific program in the request controller decides which transaction servers to call and in which order. On the face of it, there's nothing special about it. It simply accepts a call that contains a request and calls subroutines (transaction servers) to do most of its work. For requests that execute as a single transaction, the application really is quite simple. When multiple transactions are required to process the request, there are complications, but we'll defer those until Chapter 5.

Most transactional middleware products allow the same language to be used both for request controller and transaction server functions. So it's the application designer's job to split the request-processing function between the request controller and the transaction server, but it is not something that is forced on the developer. Nevertheless, this split is desirable for the reasons discussed in the subsection *Multitier Architectures* in Section 3.2.

Some transactional middleware products support a special programming language in which to express the request controller logic. Some of these languages were introduced in the 1980s to ensure request controller applications cannot do synchronous I/O, thereby enabling the implementation of multithreading in middleware (see Section 2.3). Examples are Task Definition Language used in HP's ACMS (originally from Digital Equipment Corporation) and Screen COBOL used in HP's Pathway TP monitor (originally from Tandem Computers).

Other languages are designed to simplify programming multi-transaction requests, such as the Web Services Business Process Execution Language. This is discussed further in Chapter 5.

Modern transactional middleware systems handle these functions using a combination of container abstractions, APIs, attributes, and configuration properties.

Transaction Bracketing

No matter what language is used to express it, the request controller generally brackets the transaction before it actually calls the program to do the work for the request—that is, it issues a Start operation to begin a transaction before it calls any transaction server programs. After all the transaction servers that execute on behalf of the request have returned, it issues a Commit operation to indicate that the transaction is done and should be committed. The Start and Commit operations are issued by the system when using an implicit programming model.

Some discipline may be required in choosing which programs issue the transaction bracketing operations Start, Commit, and Abort. For example, suppose the transactional middleware or underlying platform does not offer a solution to the transaction composability problem, e.g., by properly handling calls to Start issued within a transaction or by using transaction attributes attached to object-oriented components (as in .NET and Java EE). Then the transaction server programs should not contain the Start, Commit, and Abort operations, but rather should be pure objects. The request controller that calls the transaction server program should be the one that actually starts the transaction and commits or aborts it. That way the callee can be called from several different applications that use the same procedure in different ways, as described in the subsection *Transaction Bracketing* in Section 2.2. All the other issues related to the transaction abstraction in Section 2.2 apply here too, such as exception handing, savepoints, and chained versus unchained transaction models.

Request Integrity

One major complication related to transaction bracketing is ensuring the integrity of each transaction's request message. If a transaction aborts, its request may be lost, making it impossible to re-execute the transaction, which is very undesirable. The application should catch the abort exception and return a comprehensible message to the user. If it doesn't, the user might get back an inscrutable error message (e.g., "transaction aborted" or "HTTP 500: Internal Server Error"), or in some bad cases no response at all.

To avoid lost requests, the transaction that performs the request should include the operation that gets a request as input, say *Get-input-request* as shown in Figure 3.7. Usually, it's the first operation executed by the transaction. The system should make the Get-input-request operation recoverable. That is, if the transaction aborts, then the Get-input-request operation is undone, just like any other recoverable transaction operation. Thus, the request message is again available as input and will cause another transaction to execute later, as desired.

```
// Example A
Get-input-request;
Start;
   . . .
Commit;
```

```
// Example B
Start;
   Get-input-request;
   . . .
Commit;
```

FIGURE 3.7

Ensuring the Integrity of Requests. In (A), the Get-input-request operation executes before the transaction, so if the transaction aborts, the request is lost. In (B), Get-input-request executes within the transaction, so if the transaction aborts, the Get-input-request operation is undone and the request is restored.

A limit on the number of retries is needed to avoid looping forever on badly formed requests. If a request is determined to be badly formed, then a transaction should execute Get-input-request, report the error, and commit, thereby ensuring the request doesn't execute anymore. As discussed in Section 2.2, savepoints can be helpful in structuring this activity.

Using the explicit Get-input-request operation, the program waits until a front-end program has an input request to offer. This is common practice with dumb display devices, which was the usual situation before the advent of PCs.

The advent of client-server computing and widespread availability of RPC has made it popular for the client to invoke the server. That is, the front-end program calls the request controller program, rather than having the request controller call a Get-input-request operation. In this case, the operation that receives the client's call is the invocation of the called procedure. To avoid the request integrity problem, this "receive-the-client's-call" operation must be made explicit, so it can be invoked within the context of a transaction and undone if the transaction aborts. The details of how to recover a request if the transaction aborts are sufficiently complex so that we devote an entire chapter to them, Chapter 4, and therefore do not discuss them further here.

Process Structure

The request controller typically runs in a multithreaded process. The process may be dedicated to request controller functions. Or it may be combined with front-end program functions or transaction server functions, to save context switching overhead. For example, we saw how to combine web server functions with a request controller in Section 3.3, *Web Servers*. Combining request controller functions in the same process as transaction server functions is usually straightforward. Since a request controller usually invokes transaction servers using RPC, it is simply a matter of replacing remote procedure calls by local procedure calls.

Since the request controller application executes within a transaction, it needs to have a transaction context and to pass that context to transaction servers that it invokes. If the request controller and transaction server run in separate processes, then this is usually done with a transactional RPC. If they run in the same process, then they automatically share thread context and hence transaction context.

Usually, only a modest amount of processing time is required in the request controller to handle each request. Nevertheless, this processing time is not zero, so even a multithreaded request controller has limited capacity. If the system is required to handle a maximum request controller workload that exceeds the processing capacity of a single machine, then it may be necessary to partition or replicate the request controller. For example, a request controller could be partitioned by request type, and each partition assigned to run on a different machine. As with any scale-out scheme, if request controllers are replicated or partitioned, then it is desirable to have them be stateless with respect to their request sources, to avoid the complexity of having to route requests to the particular copy of a request controller that has the request source's state.

Session Structure

One traditional function of request controllers is to reduce the number of communication sessions by partitioning the sessions that would otherwise be required to connect front ends to transaction servers. This helps the session scale-out problem that is described in Section 2.6, *Partitioning Sessions*. For example, front ends executing in the same geographical location could be serviced by the same request controller.

More complex groupings of connections between front ends and request controllers may be needed for fault tolerance reasons. For example, the ATMs at a bank branch may be split across two request controllers over two independent communication lines, so the failure of one controller or communication line still leaves half of the ATMs operating.

Security

If the request controller is receiving requests from untrusted front ends, then requests are a potential source of security threats. The request controller therefore should not trust that the data it receives is well formed. For example, it should not assume that a buffer it receives is null terminated or that field *A* of a message really is the size for field *B*. The bottom line is that secure coding practices are essential when developing TP applications.

We assume that the request controller is part of the trusted computing base. In particular, it is safe to have it be responsible for checking user authorization. To do this, it needs to know about the authenticated user that issued the request. For example, it may need to check that the user is authorized to execute the request's request type. It also needs to pass the authenticated user ID to transaction servers, since some access control can be performed only when accessing the database. For example, permission to withdraw from a bank account should be given only to users who own that account.

In addition to user authorization, process authorization may be required. For example, a transaction server may be accessible only from request controller processes that are known to have done preliminary user authorization checks and therefore are trusted. This avoids the need for the transaction server to duplicate the request controller's check that the user is authorized to execute the request. Process authorization can be done by associating the request controller process with an authenticated application administrator, who creates the request controller process to execute on his or her behalf. Transaction servers are then configured to accept calls only from request controller processes executing on behalf of this application administrator.

A session may be established between the request controller and transaction server whose session state includes the authenticated application administrator information. This avoids requiring the transaction server to perform this security check on every access. Since the authorization state is the same for all requests, these sessions can be pooled, to avoid creating a new one for every request.

It can be time consuming for a system manager to maintain all this security information. It can also be time consuming for the transactional middleware to check all this security information at runtime. Simplicity of security management and efficiency of runtime security checking are features of transactional middleware products.

3.5 TRANSACTION SERVERS

A **transaction server** is the application program that does the real work of running the request. Part of that work usually involves reading and writing shared databases. It always executes in the context of a transaction, often created by the request controller that called it.

It can be a self-contained program or it might call other programs to do its work. Those other programs might execute on the same system as the transaction server that calls it or on a remote system that requires a communications message to go from the caller to the callee. The communications must be transactional, so that the transaction context flows along with the messages. This typically is done using transactional RPC, as discussed in Section 2.4.

For application portability, it's desirable that the transaction servers be written using a popular programming language such as COBOL, C++, C#, FORTRAN, or Java. It is also desirable that they express database accesses in a widely used data manipulation language, such as SQL. This ensures that the transaction server part of the application can be ported to different transactional middleware environments.

From the viewpoint of the application programmer, transaction servers are ordinary data access programs. The application programmer needs to ensure the program preserves database integrity, doesn't take too long to execute and thereby create a resource bottleneck, uses timeouts to detect database server failures, returns comprehensible error messages, copes with distributed databases, and so on. These are complex issues that arise for any data access program. There is little that the programmer needs to do differently to run the program in a transaction server process.

Process and Session Structure

From the viewpoint of process structure, transaction servers have several special considerations, which are related to their need to scale to high request rates and to support transaction-based communications.

For scale-out, a transaction server S needs to have enough threads to handle the system's maximum required load. Although figuring out the right number of threads is really an experimental science, the following back-of-the-envelope calculation shows which factors are at stake. Suppose each transaction requires t seconds of elapsed time to be processed by the transaction server. If the transaction server has one thread, then it can process $1/t$ transactions per second. Thus, if the system needs to handle a peak load of n transactions per second of the transaction types implemented by S, then $t \times n$ threads are required. Actually, somewhat more are required, due to variance in elapsed processing time. The latter is dependent in large part on the time it takes to process its database operations, which is usually where most of the time is spent. This varies based on database server load, which may include database operations from other transaction servers.

To access a database system, every active transaction in a transaction server process needs a database session with the database system. Thus, the number of database sessions required is comparable to the number of threads in the transaction server. Since it is relatively expensive to create a database session, it is desirable that they be pooled and reused.

The use of database sessions has security implications, because part of the database session is the ID of a database user, which usually cannot be changed after the session is created. The database system uses that ID to do an authorization check of each operation executed on that session. Usually, the user ID of the database session is that of a dedicated account with sufficient privileges to access the data needed by the transaction server. This allows sessions to be reused for different requests and hence pooled. By contrast, if the user ID were that of the end user who is issuing the request, then a new session would have to be created on that user's behalf, unless the user happens to have executed another request in the very recent past and therefore already has a database session set up. Also, if the user ID were that of an end user, then a database administrator would have to create a database user account for every end user who can access the database. This is not feasible for TP applications that are accessed by a large number of end users only occasionally, a few times a year, such as a retail e-commerce site.

The dedicated account usually is given read-write authorization on all parts of the database that may be accessed by the given transaction server. That is, the database system treats the transaction server as a trusted user. Thus, it is up to the transaction server to check that a given end-user request is authorized to perform the database operations required.

3.6 TRANSACTIONAL MIDDLEWARE

Software vendors have developed transactional middleware products that make it easier to create, execute, and manage TP applications by integrating diverse runtime functions. The main product category for this market today is the application server. Before the advent of the World Wide Web, the main product category was the TP monitor or On-Line TP (OLTP) monitor. Descriptions of transactional middleware products are presented in Chapter 10.

The main job of transactional middleware is to provide an environment that takes applications that are written to process a single request and scale them up to run efficiently on large, often distributed systems with many active users submitting requests and many servers processing requests. By enabling this scale-up, transactional middleware increases the capacity and lowers the per-transaction cost of the application. From a business perspective, it lowers the cost of retail sales, ticket reservations, funds transfers, and such.

Transactional middleware typically includes software in four major functional areas:

- An application programming interface that offers the type of runtime functions described in earlier sections of this chapter. It integrates these functions, thereby simplifying the environment in which applications are programmed. Some of these functions may be directly implemented by the transactional middleware. Others may be offered by lower-level products, which the application server passes through either as functions in its integrated API or directly through system-level APIs. Some functions may be defined using attributes embedded in class definitions, or as policies and configuration attributes of the application execution environment.

- Program development tools for building transaction programs, such as program templates for the main application components, and smooth integration of its API into a particular programming language and development environment.

- A system management interface and accompanying runtime functions to configure a TP application for a distributed system, deploy it, and then monitor and control its execution.

- Integration with popular database management systems and front-end programs.

Transactional middleware is a software framework or application execution environment in which application programs run and in which users interact with the computer system. The execution environment often is called a **container**. The container ties together the underlying system components that are needed by all TP applications—multithreading, user interface services, communications system, operating system, and the database system. It also may offer components of its own. For example, it may add transactional capability to the built-in RPC mechanism or it may add two-phase commit, if these are absent from the operating system and/or database system.

The container provides a single, smooth interface, so that developers and end users don't need to deal with each of these components independently or learn multiple low-level APIs (see Figure 3.8). Instead of writing application programs that talk independently to the forms system, web server, operating system, communication

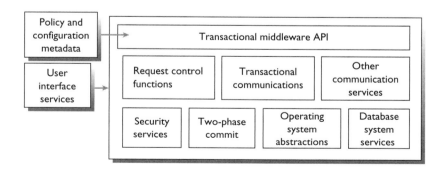

FIGURE 3.8

Transactional Middleware Container. The transactional middleware container provides services, such as request management, transactional communications, and two-phase commit. Its container provides a single abstraction to application programmers and system managers.

system, and so on, the programmer writes an application using a single interface that talks to the transactional middleware.

Some transactional middleware systems integrate their runtime functions with a particular programming language. A notable example of this is Java EE, which consists of Java classes that encapsulate the application server's functionality. Older examples of the language-specific approach developed in the 1980s are HP's Screen COBOL and Task Definition Language (see also Section 3.4).

Other transactional middleware products offer language-independent runtime functions. IBM's CICS is one example of this approach, introduced in the late 1960s and still widely used. A more recent example is Microsoft's .NET Framework, where runtime functions are available in all .NET languages. There is a trend toward exposing transactional middleware features as extensions to the normal development experience, rather than making them available only in a closed development environment.

Java EE-based application servers are **portable** in the sense that they run on a variety of **platforms**, or operating systems (e.g., Windows, IBM mainframes, and many flavors of UNIX); they support the same APIs on these platforms; and they integrate with multiple database systems and front-end programs. Thus, TP applications can usually be ported from one Java EE application server to another with moderate effort.

Interoperability is the ability of programs to participate as part of the same application. Programs may find it hard to interoperate because they were independently developed in different languages, with incompatible interfaces, and using incompatible data types. Or interoperations may be difficult because they run on different machines with different underlying platforms. This latter issue requires that there are implementations of the same protocols on the machines for communication, two-phase commit, and other shared functions.

Interoperability can be achieved by running instances of the same application server on different machines that run different platforms or by using application servers that support the same protocol. For example, two RPC protocols that are in common use by different application servers are RMI/IIOP and SOAP/HTTP. Sometimes, interoperability is sacrificed by offering custom features, by disabling features of an interoperability standard, or by using nonstandard protocols for better performance. For example, some platforms implement a custom two-phase commit protocol that has special features and better performance than standard protocols.

System management functions include load balancing, fault monitoring and repair, performance monitoring and tuning, and the ability to change the configuration by creating and destroying processes, creating and destroying communication sessions, and so on. For example, the transactional middleware may store a description of which server processes are running on which machines. Instead of just telling the system manager that an operating system process has failed, the transactional middleware might say that the bank's loan server process has failed, thereby giving the system manager a better idea of where the problem is and what to do about it. It may also automate recovery by creating a new copy of the failed process on another machine that has spare capacity. System management functions also are required to set up and maintain security information to protect access to displays and to ensure that only authorized users can access sensitive transaction control programs. These kinds of system management functions often are provided for TP applications by generic system management tools, such as CA's Unicenter, IBM's Tivoli, and HP's OpenView.

The transactional middleware also provides some application development tools to make it easier to write the code for each of the components of a multitier architecture. We'll describe examples of program development in Chapter 10.

3.7 DATABASE SERVERS VERSUS TRANSACTIONAL MIDDLEWARE

A database server is a relational database system that runs as a multithreaded server. It supports stored procedures that can be invoked by an RPC-like protocol. And, of course, it supports transactions. It therefore offers

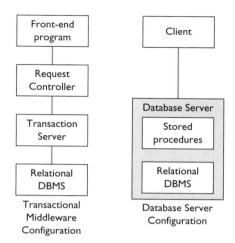

FIGURE 3.9

Transactional Middleware and Database Server Configurations. The database server architecture eliminates the request controller layer of the transactional middleware.

many of the main features of transactional middleware. It's interesting to compare database servers to transactional middleware, to see where these two technologies are similar and different.

Stored procedures are written in either a proprietary version of SQL or a general-purpose programming language, and can issue SQL requests to the database system, just like a transaction server running in an application server. Thus, a request controller can directly call stored procedures, instead of first calling a transaction server, which in turn calls a database server. Said differently, the transaction server application can be written as a stored procedure. In fact, the request controller application can be written as a stored procedure too.

Figure 3.9 shows the process structure of transactional middleware and database servers. Most relational database systems today offer this database server structure, including those from IBM, Oracle, Sybase, and Microsoft. So why might one buy a transactional middleware product if the database server supports most of the facilities that we've been discussing in this chapter?

One reason is scalability. In a multitier system running under transactional middleware, if a machine becomes overloaded, one can simply reassign request controller and transaction server processes to another machine. Today, this isn't very easy with most database servers, because the application runs in the same process and therefore on the same machine as the database server. Spreading the workload across multiple database servers requires a request controller outside the database servers to distribute the load and to multiplex sessions across a large number of users (see Section 2.6, *Scaling Out a System*). We expect this scalability advantage of transactional middleware will decrease over time as database servers add more functionality to support partitioning and scalable data sharing. The capabilities of web servers also are growing, however, and are increasingly being used to route requests directly to a database on behalf of a web browser client.

Like scalability, the issues that distinguish transactional middleware from database servers are changing with each new product release, so any list of feature distinctions we give here would be quickly outdated. However, we can identify general areas where functionality differences often are found. The main ones are as follows:

- Choice of programming language: Some database servers offer a more limited set of programming languages for stored procedures than application servers offer for transaction servers. And even when database servers support standard languages, they impose restrictions to ensure compatibility with the database software.

- Implicit transaction bracketing: Many database servers require explicit bracketing of transactions using Start, Commit, and Abort, rather than allowing components to be tagged with transaction attributes, such as Requires New, Required, and Supported. The explicit bracketing of transactions makes it more difficult to compose them.

- Transports: A TP system can offer both secure and reliable transport (written to a journal) between client and server. Most database systems don't offer this.

- Debugging: Some database servers offer weaker debugging and development tools than are available in a general-purpose program development environment. The latter are usually fully available when using a transaction server.

- Interoperable distributed transactions: Most database servers offer distributed transactions with two-phase commit. However, they often do not offer distributed transactions across database servers from different vendors and other transactional resource managers, such as record-oriented file systems and queue managers. This usually requires a two-phase commit protocol implemented by transactional middleware or the underlying platform.

- Communications efficiency: Some database server protocols are more efficient for pipelined transfer of large data sets than transactional middleware protocols.

- Protocol support: Application processes running with transactional middleware can use all platform-supported protocols. By contrast, some database servers have limited protocol support. For example, they may not support HTTP, so remote requests to a database server need to pass through an application process, such as a web server.

- Multitransaction workflow: Some transactional middleware products have more functionality than database servers in support of multitransaction workflows, such as the ability to configure resource dependencies and transactional compositions.

- System management: Some transactional middleware products offer a richer system management environment than a database server offers. For example, it may allow prioritization of applications, application-based load control, remote name resolution, geographical entitlement, or application-based security.

Over the past decade, the functionality gap between database servers and transactional middleware has been getting smaller. Only time will tell whether this trend will continue or transactional middleware will add functionality fast enough to stay ahead of database servers for decades to come.

3.8 SUMMARY

The processing of simple requests involves receiving a request, routing it to the appropriate application program, and then executing it. This activity usually is distributed across components of a multitier architecture, consisting of the following:

- Front-end programs, for interaction with an end user or special device
- Request controllers, for routing a request to the correct transaction program
- Transaction servers, to do the work necessary to fulfill the request, usually involving accesses to transactional resources, such as databases, and typically returning results to the caller

This architecture is aligned with service-oriented architecture, by mapping services to transaction servers, and with object-oriented design, by mapping business objects to transaction servers.

The front-end program is responsible for interacting with the end user via menus and forms, gathering input for the transaction request and the name of the transaction to be executed. After gathering input, the front-end program constructs the request message and sends it to the request controller. The front-end program needs a suitably secure connection to the request controller, optionally using geographical entitlement to check that the user is authorized for the specific device. Currently, the most popular technology for these functions is the web browser running on the end user's device, communicating with a web server that executes many of the front-end program's functions. When money or personally identifiable information is involved, the connection between web browser and web server often is enabled by use of Transport Layer Security.

The main goal of the request controller is routing. It decodes the request message, determines the location of the transaction program to be called, and makes the call. The request controller brackets the transaction that executes the request. Its application code is structured to solve the transaction composability problem using whatever mechanisms are available from the underlying middleware or platform. It ensures that each request is not lost if its corresponding transaction aborts. It typically runs in a multithreaded process, often partitioning front-end sessions by request controller for scalability. It also bridges the per-user security model of the front ends with the process-oriented authorization model that usually is needed for communication with back ends.

The transaction server executes program logic to fulfill the request, such as retrieve data from a database or update data with new values provided by the request. It usually is implemented as a multithreaded process, which in turn communicates with multithreaded database servers using pooled database sessions.

Transactional middleware products provide APIs, development tools, system management tools, and integration with popular database systems and front-end programs. Transactional middleware products typically provide an abstraction called a container that helps TP application developers handle the complexities of transaction management and low-level operating system functions such as multithreading, communications, and security.

Many functions previously performed only by transactional middleware products are now features of database servers. Transactional middleware products still provide features that database servers don't yet have, such as request routing, server classes, transactions distributed across multiple types of resource managers, composable transactions by setting transaction attributes, and certain system management and administrative functions for TP applications programs and systems. However, database servers are suitable for many applications and their range of applicability is growing.

Queued Transaction Processing

4.1 WHY USE QUEUES?

In direct transaction processing, a client sends a request to a server and synchronously waits for the server to run the transaction and reply. For example, using RPC, the client sends a request to the system as an RPC, which returns with a reply indicating whether or not the transaction ran.

Even though this direct TP model is widely used in practice, it has some limitations (see Figure 4.1). The first problem is dealing with the failure of a server or of client-server communications, which prevents a client from communicating with the server. If a client sends a request to this server, it immediately receives an error telling it that the server is down or disconnected and therefore is unable to receive the request message. At this point, either the client is blocked, waiting for a server to become available, or the user has to return later and resubmit the request to the client. A desirable alternative, which is not possible in direct TP, is simply to ask that the request be sent as soon as the server is available, without the user or client being required to wait on-line for the server to do so. For example, the user might want to log off and come back later to get the reply.

The second problem is the inverse of the first. The client may successfully send the request to the server. But the server, after executing the transaction, may be unable to send a reply to the client, because the client failed, client-server communications failed, or the server failed after completing the transaction and before sending the reply. In each of these failure cases, the server's reply may be lost. So even after the failed component has recovered, the client still may not receive a reply. It therefore doesn't know whether its last request actually ran, and hence whether it should resubmit the request.

The first or second problem could occur due to failed communications between the client and server. Suppose the client sends the request to the server and does not receive an immediate error. What does it do if it does not receive a reply in a timely manner? It cannot tell whether the original request failed to be delivered to the server due to a communication failure or server failure, or the request was delivered to the server but the reply failed to be delivered back to the client. Under the circumstances, it is hard to imagine how the system could be programmed to execute each request exactly once, which is usually the behavior that's desired.

A third issue is load balancing. In direct TP, if there is a pool of servers that can handle a client's request, then the mechanism for binding a client to a server must select one of the servers from the pool. As discussed in Section 2.3, *Server Classes*, one approach is to randomize the selection of a server, so on average, the same number of clients are connected to each server. However, this randomization is just a guess. At any given moment, the actual load may not be equally balanced among the servers. That is, one server could receive many requests requiring a lot of work and thereby become overloaded. At the same time, other servers may not

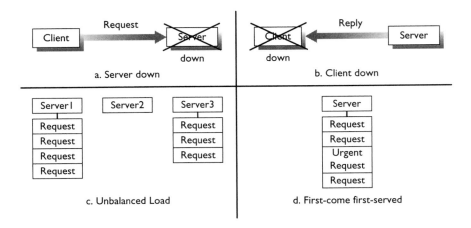

a. Server down

b. Client down

c. Unbalanced Load

d. First-come first-served

FIGURE 4.1

Problems with Direct TP. (a) Sending a request to a down server. (b) Sending a reply to a down client. (c) Balancing the request load across many servers. (d) Scheduling requests.

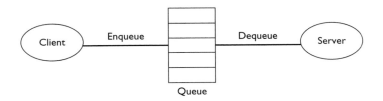

FIGURE 4.2

Queued Transaction Model. In queued TP, clients send requests to queues, and servers receive requests from queues. This is in contrast to direct TP, where clients send requests to servers.

be receiving any requests at all. When the variance in workload is high, this type of situation is rather likely, leading to poor response time for some clients some of the time.

Finally, this whole model is based on first-come, first-served scheduling of requests. There's no sense of priority in the system in which high priority requests are processed early and low priority requests are delayed until later.

We are using the term "client" here because it's more architecturally neutral than front-end program or web server. The issues of interest apply to any program that is outside the TP system and submitting requests to run transactions, rather than being a participant in the transaction itself.

Queues as the Solution

These problems are solved by using a queue as a buffer for requests and replies between the client and the server (see Figure 4.2). Instead of sending a request directly to the server, a client sends it to a queue. And the server receives those requests from the queue, instead of receiving them directly from the client. Similarly, the server sends replies to a queue, and the client receives replies from the queue.

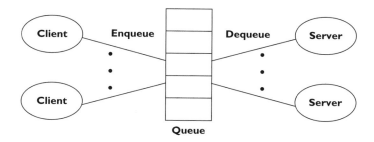

FIGURE 4.3

Load Balancing Using Multiple Servers. When a server finishes processing one request, it takes another request from the queue. This dynamically balances the load across all servers.

The queue is a transactional resource. So operations on the queue are made permanent or undone, depending on whether the transaction that issued the operations commits or aborts. Usually, the queue is persistent and is stored on disk or some other nonvolatile storage device.

This queued TP model solves the problems that we just listed. First, a client can send a request even if it is targeted for a server that is busy, down, or disconnected, as long as the queue is available. The client simply stores the request in the queue. If the server is available, it can execute the request right away. Otherwise, when the server becomes available, it can check the queue and run requests that were submitted while it was down.

Second, a server can send a reply to a client even if the client is down or disconnected, as long as the client's reply queue is available. The server simply sends the reply to the queue. When the client recovers or is reconnected to the system, it checks the queue to find any reply messages that are waiting.

By using queues to capture requests and replies, we can implement exactly-once execution of requests. For each request that a client submits, the client can tell whether the request is waiting to be processed (in the request queue), executing (absent from both queues), or processed (in the reply queue). There are some corner cases that need attention, but with queues an implementation of exactly-once execution seems within reach. We will work out the details in Sections 4.2 and 4.3.

Third, as shown in Figure 4.3, many servers can be receiving requests from the same queue, thereby balancing the load across many servers. This load balancing is fully dynamic. As soon as a server finishes processing one request, it can take another request from the queue. There is never a time when one server is overloaded while another is idle.

Fourth, queues can be used for priority-based scheduling. Each request can be tagged with a priority, which is used to guide the scheduling strategy. For example, each server can dequeue requests highest-priority-first. Alternatively, to ensure low priority requests are given some service, one server can be given the job of servicing low-priority requests while all other servers use highest-priority-first. Or each request's priority could be set to be its deadline, and requests are processed in deadline order. Requests can also be scheduled manually, by collecting them in a queue and running them under operator control. Once there is a queue in the picture, there is great flexibility in controlling the order in which requests are processed.

A queue is also useful as an intermediary between a back-end system and a remote service, for many reasons. It can buffer the effect of network delays. It can be used to localize credentials for accessing the remote service. It can be a protocol bridge by supporting different protocols for remote and local access. And it is a convenient place for auditing and performance measurement of the remote service.

This is a long list of benefits for such a relatively simple mechanism. For this reason most transactional middleware products and even some database systems support queues as one way of moving requests and replies between clients and servers. Usually, queues sit between the front-end program and the request controller, as shown in Figure 3.1. Since queues can be used in other parts of a system, in the rest of this chapter we will use the more general client-server terminology, instead of front-end program and request controller terminology. However, to be concrete, you can think about it in the latter setting without being misled.

4.2 THE QUEUED TRANSACTION PROCESSING MODEL

Server's View of Queuing

Let's look at how the queued TP model works in the context of a transaction from a server's perspective. As in our description of direct TP in previous chapters, we will assume that each request is asking for just one transaction to be executed. In the queued TP model, the server program starts a transaction and dequeues the next request from the request queue (see Figure 4.4). The server then does the work that the request is asking for, enqueues the reply to the reply queue, and commits.

  Since these queues are transactional resources, if the transaction aborts, the dequeue operation that receives the request is undone, thereby returning the input request to the request queue. If the abort happens at the very end, then the enqueue operation to the reply queue also is undone, thereby wiping out the reply from the reply queue. Therefore, whenever the client checks the queues, either the request is in the request queue, the reply is in the reply queue, or the request can't be checked because it is currently being processed. In any case, there's never any ambiguity as to the request's state. It either has not yet been processed, is in the midst of being processed, or has been completed.

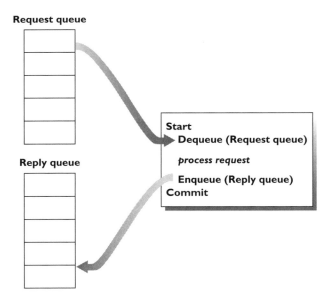

FIGURE 4.4

Managing a Queued Request within a Transaction. The request is dequeued and the reply enqueued within a transaction. If the transaction aborts, the request isn't lost.

Client's View of Queuing

In Figure 4.4 we looked at the queues from the server's viewpoint. Now let's look at the entire path from the client to the server in the queued TP model. In this model, each request executes three transaction programs (see Figure 4.5). Transaction 1 (Submit Request) receives input from the user, constructs a request, enqueues that request onto the request queue, and then commits. Then Transaction 2 (Execute Request) runs, just as described in Figure 4.4: It starts a transaction, dequeues the request, processes the request, enqueues the reply, and commits. At this point, the request is gone from the request queue, and the reply is sitting in the reply queue. Now, Transaction 3 (Process Reply) runs: It starts a transaction, dequeues the reply from the reply queue, translates the reply into the proper output format, delivers that output, and commits, thereby wiping out the reply from the reply queue.

For example, to run a debit transaction, the client runs a transaction that enqueues a request on the request queue. The debit server runs a transaction that dequeues the request, debits the account, and enqueues a reply that confirms the debit. Later, the client runs a transaction to dequeue the reply and print a receipt. By contrast, if direct TP were used, the client would send the request directly to the server, and the server would send the reply directly to the client, all within one transaction and without any queues in between.

In Figure 4.5 the client pushes a request to the queue while the server pulls it from the queue. If desired, the server (Transaction 2) can be turned into a push model by adding a dispatcher component that starts a transaction, dequeues the request, calls the rest of the Transaction 2 code (i.e., starting with "process request" in Figure 4.5), and, after the latter finishes, commits.

Because the queues are now under transaction control, they have to be managed by a database system or some other resource manager that supports transaction semantics. To optimize performance, TP systems often

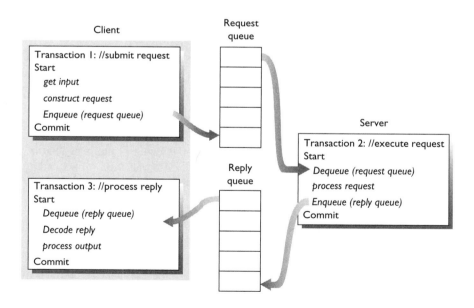

FIGURE 4.5

Running a Request as Three Transactions. The client submits a request (Transaction 1), the server processes the request and returns a reply (Transaction 2), and the client processes the reply (Transaction 3).

use a specialized queue manager that is tuned for the purpose. Today's transactional middleware products typically provide an API to an external queued messaging system that supports transaction semantics.

Notice that to run even a single request, the system executes three transactions. The client transactions may be rather lightweight, as transactions go. For example, in the simple case of Figure 4.5, they each do one access to a transactional resource, that is, a queue. But even so, queued TP uses more system resources than an ordinary direct TP system in which each request runs as a single transaction. Not only are there two client transactions, but the server transaction has two additional accesses to transactional resources—the request and reply queues. In return for this extra overhead, the system offers the benefits that we talked about previously; that is, communication with unavailable servers and clients, load balancing across servers, and priority-based scheduling.

4.3 CLIENT RECOVERY

An important reason to use queuing instead of direct TP is to address certain client and server failure situations. In this section, we systematically explore the various failure situations that can arise. We do this from a client's perspective, to determine what a client should do in each case.

We will assume the request-reply model of Figure 4.5. That is, a client runs Transaction 1 to construct and submit a request, and later runs Transaction 3 to receive and process the reply. Its goal is to get exactly-once behavior; that is, that Transaction 2 executes exactly once and its reply is processed in Transaction 3 exactly once.

Let us assume that there is no failure of the client, the communications between the client and the queues, or the queues themselves. In this case, the client's behavior is pretty straightforward. It submits a request. Since there are no failures between the client and the request queue, the client receives an acknowledgment that the request is successfully enqueued. The client then waits for a reply. If it is waiting too long, then there is presumably a problem with the server—it is down, disconnected, or busy—and the client can take appropriate action, such as sending a message to a system administrator. The important point is that there is no ambiguity about the state of the request. It's either in the request queue, in the reply queue, or being processed.

Suppose the client fails or loses connectivity to the queues, or the queues fail. This could happen for a variety of reasons, such as the failure of the client application or machine, the failure of the machine that stores the queues, a network failure, or a burst of traffic that causes one of these components to be overloaded and therefore unresponsive due to processing delays. At some point, the failed or unresponsive components recover and are running normally again, so the client can communicate with the queues. At this point the client needs to run recovery actions to resynchronize with the queues. What exactly should it do?

To keep things simple, let's assume that the client processes one request at a time. That is, it processes the reply to each request before it submits another request, so it has at most one request outstanding. In that case, at the time the client recovers, there are four possible states of the last request it submitted:

A. Transaction 1 did not run and commit. Either it didn't run at all, or it aborted. Either way, the request was not submitted. The client should resubmit the request (if possible) or else continue with a new request.

B. Transaction 1 committed but Transaction 2 did not. So the request was submitted, but it hasn't executed yet. The client must wait until the reply is produced and then process it.

C. Transaction 2 committed but Transaction 3 did not. The request was submitted and executed, but the client hasn't processed the reply yet. The client can process the reply right away.

D. Transaction 3 committed. The request was submitted and executed, and the client already processed the reply. So the client's last request is done, and the client can continue with a new request.

To determine what recovery action to take, the client needs to figure out which of the four states it is in.

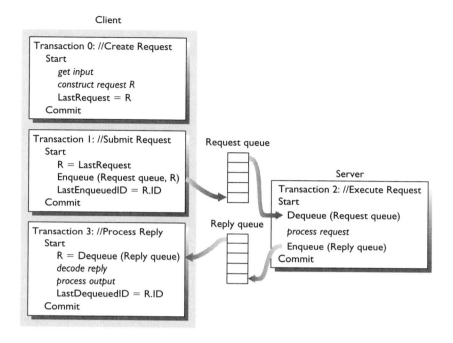

Client

Transaction 0: //Create Request
    Start
        get input
        construct request R
        LastRequest = R
    Commit

Transaction 1: //Submit Request
    Start
        R = LastRequest
        Enqueue (Request queue, R)
        LastEnqueuedID = R.ID
    Commit

Request queue

Server
Transaction 2: //Execute Request
    Start
        Dequeue (Request queue)
        process request
        Enqueue (Reply queue)
    Commit

Reply queue

Transaction 3: //Process Reply
    Start
        R = Dequeue (Reply queue)
        decode reply
        process output
        LastDequeuedID = R.ID
    Commit

FIGURE 4.6

Client Maintains Request State. The client stores the ID of the last request it enqueued and the last reply it dequeued, in Transactions 1 and 3, respectively.

If each client has a private reply queue, it can make some headway in this analysis. Since the client processes one request at a time, the reply queue either is empty or has one reply in it. So, if the reply queue is nonempty, then the system must be in state C, and the client should go ahead and process the reply. If not, it could be in states A, B, or D.

To disambiguate these states, some additional state information needs to be stored somewhere. If the client has access to persistent storage that supports transaction semantics, it can use that storage for state information. The client marks each request with a globally-unique identifier (ID) and stores the request in persistent storage before enqueuing it in the request queue (see LastRequest in Transaction 0 in Figure 4.6). In persistent storage the client also keeps the IDs of the last request it enqueued and the last reply it dequeued, denoted LastEnqueuedID and LastDequeuedID, respectively. It updates these IDs as part of transactions 1 and 3 that enqueue a request and dequeue a reply, as shown in Figure 4.6. In that figure, the expression R.ID denotes the ID of request R.

At recovery time, the client reads LastRequest, LastEnqueuedID, and LastDequeuedID from persistent storage. It uses them to analyze the state of LastRequest as follows:

- If LastRequest.ID ≠ LastEnqueuedID, then the system must be in state A. That is, the last request that the client constructed was not successfully submitted to the request queue. Either the client failed before running Transaction 1, or Transaction 1 aborted because of the client failure or some other error. The client can either resubmit the request or delete it, depending on the behavior expected by the end user.

- If LastRequest.ID = LastDequeuedID, then the client dequeued (and presumably processed) the reply to the last request the client submitted, so the system is in state D. In this case, the request ID has helped the client match up the last request with its reply, in addition to helping it figure out which state it is in.

- If the reply queue is nonempty, the client should dequeue the reply and process it (i.e., state C). Notice that in this case, LastRequest.ID = LastEnqueuedID and LastRequest.ID ≠ LastDequeuedID, so the previous two cases do not apply.

- Otherwise, the client should wait until the reply appears before dequeuing it (i.e., state B).

This recovery procedure assumes that the client uses a persistent storage system that supports transaction semantics. This is a fairly strong assumption. The client may not have such storage available. Even if the client does have it, the application developer may want to avoid using it for performance reasons. That is, since the queue manager and persistent storage are independent resource managers, the two-phase commit protocol is needed for Transactions 1 and 3, which incurs some cost.

This cost can be avoided by storing the state information in the queue manager itself. For example, the client could store LastEnqueuedID and LastDequeuedID in a separate queue dedicated for this purpose. Alternatively, the queue manager could maintain LastEnqueuedID and LastDequeuedID as the state of a persistent session between the client and the queue manager. The client signs up with the queue manager by opening a session. The session information is recorded in the queue manager's persistent storage, so the queue manager can remember that the client is connected. If the client loses connectivity with the server and later reconnects, the queue manager remembers that it already has a session with the client, because it is maintaining that information in persistent storage. So when the client attempts to reconnect, the system re-establishes the existing session. Since the session state includes the request and reply IDs, the client can ask for them as input to its recovery activity.

The recovery scenario that we just described is based on the assumption that the client waits for a reply to each request before submitting another one. That is, the client never has more than one request outstanding. What if this assumption doesn't hold? In that case, it is not enough for the system to maintain the ID of the last request enqueued and the last reply dequeued. Rather, it needs to remember enough information to help the client resolve the state of all outstanding requests. For example, it could retain the ID of every request that has not been processed and the ID of the last n replies the client has dequeued. Periodically, the client can tell the queue manager the IDs of recently dequeued replies for which it has a persistent record, thereby freeing the queue manager from maintaining that information. Many variations of this type of scheme are possible.

This scenario assumes that after a client processes a reply, it no longer needs to know anything about that request's state. For example, suppose a client runs two requests. It submits $Request_1$, the server processes $Request_1$ and sends $Reply_1$, and the client processes $Reply_1$. Then the client submits $Request_2$, the server processes $Request_2$ and sends $Reply_2$, and the client processes $Reply_2$. At this point, the client can find out about the state of $Request_2$, but not about $Request_1$, at least not using the recovery procedure just described.

Finding out the state of old requests is clearly desirable functionality. Indeed, it's functionality that we often depend on in our everyday lives, such as finding out whether we paid for a shipment that hasn't arrived or whether we were credited for mileage on an old flight. However, this functionality usually is not offered by a queuing system or queued transaction protocols like the ones we have been discussing. Rather, if it is offered, it needs to be supported by the application as another transaction type—a lookup function for old requests. To support this type of lookup function, the application needs to maintain a record of requests that it already processed. In financial systems, these records are needed in any case, to support the auditability required by accounting rules. However, even when they're not required, they're often maintained as a convenience to customers.

4.4 HANDLING NON-UNDOABLE OPERATIONS

Although the analysis of the previous section appears to cover all the cases, it still leaves one problem open if the system is in state C, namely how to handle the statement "process output" in Transaction 3 if Transaction 3 aborts. There are three cases to consider, depending on whether the process-output statement is undoable, is idempotent, or has neither of these properties.

If the process-output statement is an undoable operation, then there is no problem. If Transaction 3 aborts, then process-output is undone, just like any database operation. For example, this would be the behavior if process-output involves only recording the execution of the request in transactional persistent storage.

If the process-output statement is idempotent, then again there is no problem. The operation does not need to be undone by an abort of Transaction 3. When Transaction 3 re-executes, it re-executes the process-output statement, which is safe to do if the statement is idempotent. For example, this would be the case if process-output involves printing a receipt that has a unique identification number that is linked to the request. There is no harm in executing it twice, since it would generate two identical receipts. It would be a bit confusing to the recipient, but it might be acceptable since there is enough information to recognize the two receipts as duplicates of each other.

Often, the process-output statement is neither undoable nor idempotent. For example, this typically arises when processing the output involves asking a physical device to perform some action in the real world, such as dispensing money. As we observed in Chapter 1, it isn't clear whether this operation should be done before or after the transaction commits. If the operation is done before the transaction commits, but the transaction actually aborts, then the operation can't be undone, as it should be. And it is unsafe to run the operation again when Transaction 3 re-executes, because the operation is not idempotent. On the other hand, if the operation is done after the transaction commits, but a failure happens after the transaction commits and before the operation executes, then the operation is lost.

To solve this problem, the process-output statement must be operating on a device that has **testable state**. This means that it must be possible for Transaction 3 to read the state of the physical device, and the physical device must change its state as a result of performing the operation required by the process-output statement. That way, the transaction can record the device's state before it performs the operation and can determine if the operation ran by comparing the device's current state to the value it recorded. For example, the transaction might read the check number that is to be printed next. After printing the check, the transaction would read a different number for the new check sitting under the print head. If it reads the same number for the check, then it knows the printing operation did not execute.

Given that this device state is available, the transaction that processes replies should follow the process-a-reply transaction shown in Figure 4.7. To see why this works, suppose the client is recovering from a failure and through the previous analysis determines that it is in state C. It should therefore process the reply by running the process-a-reply transaction. If this is its first attempt at processing the reply, then there is no earlier logged device state for this reply, so the transaction performs the device operation and commits. Otherwise, in step (3) it determines whether it's safe to rerun the device operation associated with this reply. If the state of the device has changed since the previous attempt to run the transaction, then the device operation for this reply appears to have executed, so it is *not* safe. At this point, the operator must get involved to determine what really happened. For example, did the check really get printed, or was it destroyed by the device, which caused the previous execution of the reply-processing transaction to abort after logging the device's state in step (4)? In the latter case, the operator has to tell the current execution of the process-a-reply transaction whether it's safe to reprint the check.

A clever technique for logging the device's state is to read the device state *before* dequeuing the reply (i.e., before step (2) in Figure 4.7) and to attach the device state to the log record for the dequeue operation. Since

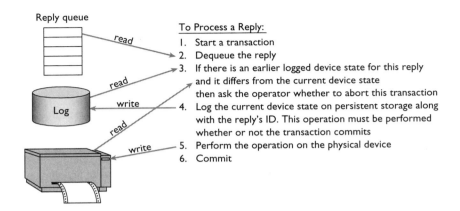

Reply queue

read

read

write

Log

read

write

To Process a Reply:

1. Start a transaction
2. Dequeue the reply
3. If there is an earlier logged device state for this reply
    and it differs from the current device state
    then ask the operator whether to abort this transaction
4. Log the current device state on persistent storage along
    with the reply's ID. This operation must be performed
    whether or not the transaction commits
5. Perform the operation on the physical device
6. Commit

FIGURE 4.7

Client Procedure for Reply Processing. Step (3) determines if the reply has already been processed. Step (4) logs the device state, in case this transaction aborts and restarts, so it can run step (3) the next time around.

the queue manager has to log the dequeue operation anyway (since it might have to undo it), it can log the device state at the same time and thereby do one write to the log, instead of two.

There is one case where step (3) is not needed—if the device's operation is idempotent. For example, suppose the operation causes a robot arm to move to a certain position, or suppose it sends a mail message describing the transaction. In these cases, there may be no harm in executing the operation a second time. That is, the operation is idempotent. So there is no reason to log the state of the device and recheck it in steps (3) and (4).

Sometime, an operation that is not normally idempotent can be made idempotent. This is important when it isn't possible to read the current state of the device. For example, sending a mail message that says "you just bought 100 shares of IBM" is not idempotent. If you issued one request to buy 100 shares and got back two acknowledgment messages like this, you would be worried whether your request executed once or twice. Moreover, at recovery time, there is no device state that the client can read to tell if the message was sent. However, if the mail message says, "your request, with confirmation number 12345, to buy 100 shares of IBM, has executed," there's no harm in sending it twice. You would recognize the second message as a duplicate and ignore it.

4.5 THE QUEUE MANAGER

To support a queuing model, the system needs a **queue manager** that stores and manages queues. A queue manager is a lot like a database system. It supports the storage abstraction of a queue store. The queue store can be a conventional relational database system or a custom storage system designed specifically for queue management. Within a queue store, the queue manager supports operations to create and destroy queues and modify a queue's attributes (e.g., owner, maximum size, queue name, user privileges). Most importantly, it supports operations on messages in queues.

Operations on Queued Messages

The main operations on messages are enqueue and dequeue. The queue manager should also support operations to examine a queue, such as to determine if it's empty, and to scan a queue's messages one by one without dequeuing them. It might also support random access to messages in a queue; for example, to read or dequeue the third message in the queue or a message with a specific ID.

Usually, the dequeue operation offers two options in dealing with an empty queue. If called with the non-blocking option, it returns with an exception that says the queue is empty. For example, this is useful if a server is polling several queues and does not want to be blocked on an empty queue since another one may be nonempty. If called with the blocking option, the dequeue operation remains blocked until a message can be returned. The latter is useful, for example, to dequeue a reply when it arrives.

Generalized Messaging

We have focused on using queued messages for the reliable processing of requests and replies. However, queuing can be used for other kinds of messages too. That is, the enqueue and dequeue operations can be used to send and receive arbitrary messages. This is a peer-to-peer messaging scenario, where the communicating parties can exchange messages in a general application-defined pattern, not just matched request-reply pairs.

In this scenario, it is sometimes useful to use volatile queues. That is, the content of the queues do not survive system failures. Volatile queues still offer many of the benefits discussed in Section 4.1, such as load balancing, priority scheduling, and the ability to communicate with an unavailable server.

Timeouts

If a message remains in a queue for too long without being processed, it may need special attention. It is therefore useful to be able to attach a timeout to a message. If the timeout expires before the message has been dequeued, then a timeout action is invoked, such as discarding the message or enqueuing the message on another queue (e.g., an error queue) with a tag that explains the timeout.

Handling Poisoned Messages

Suppose a message has faulty content that causes an abort of the transaction that dequeues it. The abort will cause the dequeued message to be returned to the queue. To avoid repeating this problem forever, a queue may have a user-configurable threshold of the maximum number of times a message can be dequeued. To avoid rejecting a message due to a transient system problem, the queue may offer control over the minimum time between the retries. If the retry threshold is exceeded, the message is moved to an error queue for manual reconciliation. This may be done by the application, queue manager, or dispatcher, depending on the implementation.

Message Ordering

The message in a queue may be ordered in a variety of ways, such as first-come, first-served, in which case an enqueue operation places the new message at the end of the queue, or highest-priority-first, in which case an enqueue operation places the new message before the first message in the queue of lower priority.

Whatever the priority mechanism, the ordering is normally made fuzzy by the possible abort of a transaction that does a dequeue. For example, suppose transaction T_1 dequeues the first message M_1 from the queue and then T_2 dequeues the next message M_2 (see Figure 4.8). If T_1 aborts, then its dequeue operation is undone, so M_1 is returned to the queue. However, T_2 might commit, in which case M_2 ends up being processed before M_1, even though it should have been processed *after* M_1.

To avoid this anomaly, T_2 should not be allowed to dequeue M_2 until after T_1 commits. For example, the queue may be set to disallow concurrent dequeues. Unfortunately, this eliminates concurrency among transactions that dequeue from the same queue, in this case T_1 and T_2, and therefore degrades performance. Since this reduction in concurrency is only to prevent the relatively infrequent out-of-order dequeuing that results from an abort, most systems allow concurrent dequeue operations and ignore the occasional out-of-order

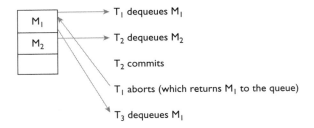

FIGURE 4.8

An Abort Destroys Priority Ordering. Although M_1 is dequeued before M_2, since T_1 aborts, M_2 is processed before M_1.

dequeuing. However, in some applications, out-of-order processing is unacceptable, for example, for legal reasons. For example, in a stock trading system, orders submitted at the same price (to buy or sell) may be legally required to be processed in strict arrival order. To obey this rule and get satisfactory concurrency, trading systems exploit the specific semantics of the trading transactions themselves, for example, by batching up a set of trades and committing them as a group (even though they were submitted separately).

Filter Criteria

Some queue managers offer clients the ability to dequeue messages based on their content. That is, rather than simply dequeuing the oldest message, the client can dequeue the oldest message that has a particular value in one of its content fields. For example, the client might first dequeue a message with a field "importance" equal to the value "high." If there are no such messages, then it could revert to dequeuing the oldest one.

Nontransactional Queuing

Most clients of the queue manager execute queue operations within a transaction. However, it is sometimes desirable to execute operations as independent transactions, so the result is recorded whether or not the surrounding transaction aborts. A classic example is a security violation. Suppose a running transaction discovers that the request it is executing is illegal—for example, it includes an illegal password. It is often important to record such violations, so they can be analyzed later to find patterns of security break-in attempts. The transaction can do this by enqueuing a security violation message on a special queue. Even if the transaction aborts, the security violation should still be persistently recorded. Therefore, the operation to enqueue the security violation message should run as a separate transaction, which commits even if the transaction that called it aborts.

Journaling

Queued messages can provide a history of all the transactions that were executed by a TP system. Therefore, some queue managers offer an option to save a description of all operations on messages in a journal. The journal may be useful for finding lost messages or for auditing purposes; for example, to prove that certain messages were submitted and/or processed, or to comply with government regulations, such as the Sarbanes-Oxley Act.

Queue Management

A queue manager usually supports operations to start and stop a queue. Stopping a queue disables enqueue and dequeue operations. While the queue is stopped, these operations return an exception. This is a way of taking a queue off-line, for example, if the server that processes its messages is down. It is also useful to enable and

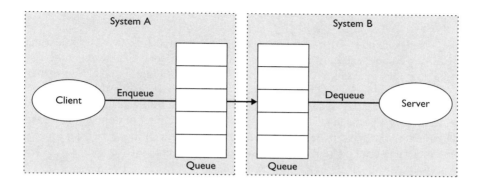

FIGURE 4.9

Forwarding with Local Enqueuing. The client enqueues requests to its local queue. Those requests are transparently forwarded to the server's queue, where the server dequeues them locally.

disable enqueue and dequeue operations independently. For example, if a queue is full, enqueue operations can be disabled so the queue will not accept any new work.

Routing

A queue manager usually supports flexible routing. For example, it may support queue forwarding, to move messages from one queue to another. This is useful to reroute a client system's input queue to another server system when the server is overloaded or down. It can also be used to save communications by batching up requests on one system and sending them later in bulk to another system, rather than sending them one by one. Queue forwarding involves reading one or more messages from one queue, moving them to the other queue, storing them on disk, and then committing, thereby removing the messages from one queue and installing them on the other queue as one transaction.

A typical configuration that exploits queue forwarding is shown in Figure 4.9. The client can reliably enqueue requests locally, whether or not the server system is available. Requests on the local queue can subsequently be forwarded to the server's queue. The queue manager might offer an option to send an acknowledgment to the client when the message reaches its final destination, in this case on System B, or when the transaction that dequeues the message has committed.

The transaction to forward a request adds a fourth transaction to the three-transaction model and a fifth if a reply is needed. Alternatively, a client could enqueue its requests directly to a server queue, without using a local queue as an intermediary. This saves the fourth transaction to forward the request and a fifth to return a reply. However, the client is unable to submit transactions when the remote queue is unavailable. Some products offer both queue forwarding and remote queuing. This allows a hybrid scheme, where the client enqueues to the remote server queue when it's available, otherwise it uses a local queue.

Of course, for a client to support a local queue, it needs a queue store. This requires additional hardware resources and system administration—the price to be paid for the additional availability.

A queue manager may also support parameter-based routing, as was described in Section 2.6. This allows a queue to be partitioned onto multiple systems for scale-out. It may also enable more flexible reconfiguration options. For example, if a queue is overloaded, messages with certain parameter values can be directed to a more lightly loaded queue simply by changing the mapping of parameter values to queue names.

Dispatcher

A queue manager usually includes a dispatcher, to support a push model as mentioned near the end of Section 4.2. Instead of requiring an application to call the queue manager to dequeue a message, the dispatcher calls the application when a new message appears on the queue. Many scheduling options are possible: It may do this (1) every time a new message arrives, (2) only if a new message arrives when the application is not currently running, (3) when the queue reaches a certain length, or (4) at fixed time intervals provided the queue is non-empty. The dispatcher may also include load control, to limit the number of application threads it can invoke. That is, if the maximum number of application threads are already executing, then a new message that appears on the queue must wait there until a thread finishes executing its current request.

4.6 PUBLISH-SUBSCRIBE

Using queued communication, each message has a single recipient—the process that dequeued the message. By contrast, some applications need to send a message to multiple recipients. For example, this arises with a notification service that broadcasts an alert when an important event occurs, such as a major change of a stock price. If the sender knows the identities of all the recipients, it can broadcast the message by sending the message to each of them. However, this is inconvenient if there is a large number of recipients. And it may not even be feasible if the sender doesn't know the identities of all the recipients.

To handle the latter case, a different communication paradigm can be used instead, called publish-subscribe. In the **publish-subscribe** paradigm, a publisher sends a message to a broker that is responsible for forwarding the message to many subscribers. Typically, the publisher tags each message by its type. Each subscriber registers interest in certain message types. After receiving a message from a publisher, the publish-subscribe broker sends the message to all subscribers that have registered an interest in that message's type.

The publish-subscribe paradigm is like queuing in three ways. First, the sender and receiver are decoupled, in the sense that they don't communicate directly with each other. Instead, they each communicate with the message broker. In fact, if one equates the notion of message type with that of queue, then the similarity is even more pronounced; in effect, senders enqueue messages to a queue for the message type and receivers dequeue them.

Second, messages can be sent or received in the context of a transaction. In that case, the operations to send or receive a message are undone in the event of an abort.

Third, subscribers can use either a pull or push model. In the pull model the subscriber can explicitly poll for new messages that satisfy its subscription. In the push model when a message arrives a dispatcher forwards the message to all subscribers whose subscriptions include that message.

Given these similarities between queuing and publish-subscribe systems, the two communications paradigms often are supported by a common queue management implementation. This has become especially common since the development of the Java Message Service (JMS) standard, which includes a programming interface for both point-to-point messaging and publish-subscribe. Other standard interfaces that offer publish-subscribe capability are the CORBA-Notification service and WS-Eventing or WS-Notification for Web Services.

In the simplest version, the message type is simply a name, sometimes called a topic. In more advanced versions, types can be grouped into a hierarchical namespace. So a type could be a path in the namespace, such as "Equity-exchange/NY-stock-exchange/IBM" rather than simply "IBM."

Some publish-subscribe systems allow subscribers to identify messages using predicates that refer to the messages' content. For example, one could subscribe to (type = "IBM") and (price > 100) where price is a field in the message content.

Publish-subscribe systems usually offer the option of having a subscription be persistent or volatile. If it is persistent, then each message is delivered to all registered recipients. If a recipient is unavailable when the message arrives, then the message broker retains the message and resends it when the recipient becomes available. If the subscription is volatile, then when each message arrives, the message broker forwards it to all registered recipients. If a recipient isn't available, then it simply doesn't receive the message; the message broker does not attempt redelivery when the recipient becomes available.

4.7 OTHER MESSAGE-ORIENTED MIDDLEWARE

Many TP systems are used in conjunction with other TP systems that offer related application functionality. We saw a simple example of this in Section 2.4, which described the integration of TP applications that support checking accounts and credit card accounts. To be used together, the systems need to be integrated.

Integration is hard because independent TP applications are usually heterogeneous in three ways. They support different communications protocols, different application functions, and different message formats. To integrate the applications, all three of these differences must be reconciled.

There are two main architectures for performing this reconciliation: **broker-based** and **bus-based**. Broker-based products, sometimes called **enterprise application integration (EAI)** systems, use a broker as intermediary between client and server to perform the integration. Bus-based products, sometimes called enterprise service buses (ESBs), enable clients to communicate directly with servers. However, the technical distinction between EAI and ESB products is not always this sharp. For example, both product categories are moving toward incorporating business process management capabilities, which will be discussed in the next chapter. As we noted in Chapter 1, the terminology for transactional middleware product categories has been evolving over the past 15 years, an evolution that seems likely to continue.

Broker-Based Architecture

In a broker-based architecture a message server provides a bridge between the heterogeneous applications (see Figure 4.10). Instead of communicating directly with the applications, a client communicates with the broker, which forwards the message to the desired application. The client can be one of the applications being integrated or an external program such as an end-user device.

The broker provides three functions, which correspond to the three differences to be reconciled. First, it supports all the communication protocols required to communicate with the applications. A client sends a message

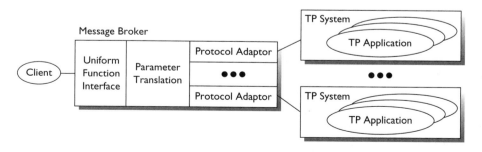

FIGURE 4.10

Broker-Based Application Integration. The Message Broker mediates message transfer from clients to TP applications.

to the broker using any of the supported protocols. The broker can forward that message to the desired application using the protocol supported by that application.

Second, the broker supports the union of all the functions offered by the applications being integrated. Usually, the broker offers a uniform interface to these functions, such as a canonical message format defined by the broker. Thus, a client can call these functions using that uniform interface, independent of the message protocol, programming language, or other technologies used by the application that implements the function. Internally the broker stores a mapping that tells it how to translate each function into the form required by the application that implements the function. This mapping often is implemented as a set of protocol adaptors, one for each of the application environments being integrated. Some brokers can also support clients that use their own protocols and formats and don't enforce the use of a single uniform interface

Third, it offers tools for translating between different parameter and message formats. The translation may be based on a calculation (such as translating between date formats), a table (such as translating between country codes), or a lookup from an external source (such as an exchange rate server to translate a money field between currencies). Some applications import or export structured documents (e.g., in XML), rather than individual parameters. In this case document translation is used, such as an XSLT program that translates one XML document into another XML document having a different format.

Some brokers also offer routing functions. A message may be routed based on the contents of a request or by requirements that are set by the client or the server. Other broker functions include logging, auditing, performance monitors, and other system management functions.

Bus-Based Architecture

In a bus-based architecture all TP applications are invoked using the same communications protocol, which is configurable for some products (such as Microsoft's WCF and Progress Software's Artix). For example, they may all support the Web Service protocols. If a TP system does not support the common protocol, then it needs to have a protocol translator that translates from the bus's common protocol to the system-specific technology for calling the TP system's applications (see Figure 4.11).

Since all TP systems can be invoked using the same protocol, the TP application interfaces are naturally exposed using the same interface definition technology, namely, the one supported by the protocol. For example, if Web Services are used, then interfaces are defined using WSDL and are made available to callers using UDDI.

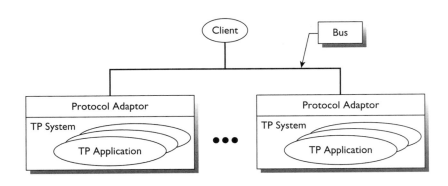

FIGURE 4.11

Bus-Based Application Integration. The client talks directly to TP applications using a standard wire protocol.

Since there is no broker between the client and the TP system it calls, the client is usually responsible for translating between formats for parameters and messages. This can be done using a shared library of translation functions that can be bound into the client's applications. Or it can be implemented as a service that the client invokes to translate parameters before invoking the target application.

Comparing Brokers and Buses

The main difference between broker-based and bus-based architectures is whether messages from client to TP system pass through an intermediate message server. If so, then it's a broker-based architecture, in which case the protocol translation usually takes place in the message server. If not, then it's a bus-based architecture, in which case the protocol translation usually takes place in the TP systems running the applications to be integrated. However, this distinction gets muddy when a bus-based architecture offers a queuing subsystem. It's in the eye of the beholder to regard the queue subsystem as another server on the bus or as a broker that mediates accesses between the client and the TP system.

The broker-based and bus-based approaches are even more similar in their approaches to the uniform definition of application functions and parameter format translation. Both architectures require a directory service to expose the interface definitions of the TP applications being integrated. For parameter translation, the main difference seems to be in choosing where the functionality is implemented: in the client, in a broker or translation service, or in the TP system.

4.8 QUEUING PRODUCTS AND STANDARDS

A variety of queue manager products are available. One of the original implementations was in IBM's IMS TP monitor, where queued TP was the default behavior. Queuing is integrated with many other transactional middleware products, such as Oracle's WebLogic and JBoss Messaging. It is also integrated in Oracle Database, called Oracle Streams AQ, and in Windows, called Microsoft Message Queue (MSMQ). Some vendors offer queuing in independent products, such as TIBCO's Enterprise Message Service, Progress' SonicMQ, Apache ActiveMQ, and IBM's Websphere MQ (MQ = Message Queuing). A consortium sponsored by JP Morgan Chase has proposed a messaging standard, called Advanced Message Queuing Protocol. We briefly describe WebSphere MQ and Oracle Streams AQ here as two examples of such products.

IBM's WebSphere MQ

IBM promotes WebSphere MQ[1] as an integration solution among its various operating system and TP environments and those of other vendors. It has a proprietary API, called Message Queuing Interface (MQI), a Java Messaging Service (JMS) API, and a non-Java equivalent of JMS. It can be used by applications running under IBM's transactional middleware such as WebSphere Application Server and CICS Transaction Server, and on any operating system supported by WebSphere MQ, including IBM AIX, i5/OS, OS/400, and z/OS, as well as HP-UX, Linux, Sun Solaris, and Microsoft Windows.

The WebSphere MQ **queue manager** accepts input from an application via the JMS API or MQI verbs. The main verbs are MQPUT to enqueue a message and MQGET to dequeue a message. A named queue can support multiple concurrent enqueuers and dequeuers.

---

[1]The information in this section is based on WebSphere MQ V6.0.

To process an MQPUT, the queue manager starts a transaction if the application is not already executing one and places the message in the queue. The operation is committed along with the rest of the transaction (which can be the normal exit from the application) or can optionally run in its own transaction as described in the subsection on nontransactional queuing in this section. The enqueued message consists of application data and the **message context**, including a variety of parameters, such as a system-generated message ID, a flag indicating whether the message is persistent, a message priority, the name of the destination queue when forwarding, the name of the reply queue (if any), message type (datagram, request, reply, report), correlation id (to link a reply to a request), priority, expiry time, application-defined format type, code page identifiers (for language localization), context information (to identify the user and application that generated the message), and report options—whether the recipient should confirm on arrival (when it's enqueued), on delivery (when it's dequeued), on expiration (if the expiry time is exceeded), on positive action (the application successfully serviced it), on negative action (the application was unable to service it), or on exception.

A message that is oversized for the queue manager or application can be decomposed into smaller segments. Moreover, several messages can be assigned to a group, which allows the application to correlate independent messages, such as those that arrive from different sources but must be processed by the same application.

An application can request that MQI operations participate in a transaction. Otherwise, by default, each individual MQPUT or MQGET executes outside a transaction, meaning that the operation completes immediately whether or not the application is executing a transaction.

WebSphere MQ offers several transaction management options for applications that are running within a transaction. If the only transactional operations are MQI operations, then the transaction can be managed as a local transaction by MQ. If the transaction needs to access other transactional resources, then MQ can play the role of a resource manager under an external transaction manager, such as the Java Transaction API in Java EE. If no external transaction manager is present, then on non-mainframe platforms MQ's XA-capable transaction manager can coordinate the transactions across MQ and databases.

Like many queuing products, WebSphere MQ offers the ability to enqueue persistent and nonpersistent messages in the same queue. Nonpersistent messages are more efficient but less reliable. They do not incur logging overhead and normally are handled in main memory, without being written to disk. Both types of messages obey transaction semantics. However, a persistent message is delivered exactly once, whereas a nonpersistent message is delivered at most once; that is, once (in the absence of failures) or not at all (if there is a failure).

Queue forwarding is handled by another component, which is much like an ordinary client that does MQGET from one queue manager and MQPUT to another, though it does have special access to the log for its sequence number management. So if MQPUT has a destination queue name that maps to a remote queue, this component forwards the message asynchronously and transactionally, using an intermediate node if necessary, to the system on which the remote queue exists (see Figure 4.12). The queue forwarding component uses a transaction that's internal to MQ to coordinate updates to the source and target queues.

An application issues an MQGET to dequeue a message. The queue manager starts a transaction upon receipt of an MQGET verb, dequeues the message from the message queue, and upon the commit from the application, physically removes the message from the queue. If the transaction aborts, the queue manager returns the message to the queue. MQGET supports a blocking option, which blocks the caller if the queue is empty and awakens it when a message is available or a timeout expires. It also supports a signaling option, where the caller can continue executing and is notified when the desired message arrives. Messages can be retrieved in order or by searching for a given ID or key. The queue can also be browsed, to examine the messages of the queue without deleting them. WebSphere MQ also includes a dispatcher that triggers the execution of an application when the first message arrives on a queue, whenever a new message arrives, or when the queue length reaches a predefined threshold.

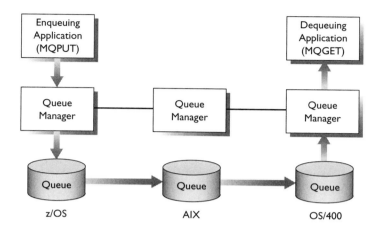

FIGURE 4.12

WebSphere MQ Architecture. Messages can be forwarded transparently between queue managers running on different platforms.

WebSphere MQ supports multiple named queues per queue manager. Each queue manager has the following components: a connection manager for managing the connections between the application and the queues; a message manager for remote communications; a data manager to manage the physical storage of the linked lists comprising the queue; a lock manager for locking queues and messages; a buffer manager for caching data, ordering writes, and flushing data to disk; a recovery manager for keeping track of active transactions in the event of a failure/restart; and a log manager for handling the recovery log. The component names differ slightly in different products.

Features of most message queuing systems that support JMS are similar to WebSphereMQ.

Oracle Streams AQ

Unlike most queue management products, which are independent middleware components, Oracle Streams AQ is a queuing facility that is built into Oracle Database.[2] It is built on top of Oracle Streams, which enables the propagation and management of information in data streams, either within a database or from one database to another. AQ can be accessed from most popular programming languages via APIs for PL/SQL, Oracle Call Interface, Oracle Objects for OLE, and extended versions of JDBC and JMS that provide access to Oracle-specific features such as those in AQ. It also offers web-based access via SOAP through the AQ XML Servlet.

In Oracle Streams AQ queues are mapped to a table that can be accessed using the standard types of queuing operations, such as enqueue and dequeue. Since queued messages are stored in a table, they can also be accessed by SQL queries.

Oracle Streams AQ is a complete queuing system offering most of the capabilities described in Section 4.5. The enqueue operation takes a queue name, payload, message properties, and enqueue options as input and returns a message ID. Message properties and enqueue options control the behavior of the enqueue operation. For example, using message properties, the sender can control the earliest time when a message is consumed,

---

[2]The information in this section is based on Oracle 11 g.

whether a message is volatile or persistent, the retry threshold after which a poison message is added to an exception queue, whether the operation is transactional, and priority ordering.

The entire history of information about a message is maintained along with the message itself. This serves as proof of the sending and receipt of messages and can be used for nonrepudiation of the sender and receiver. The history includes the name of the agent and database that performed the enqueue or dequeue operation and the time and transaction ID of the operation. After the message is propagated to the destination queue, it still includes the message ID of the source message so that the source and destination messages and their histories can be correlated. Stronger nonrepudiation can be achieved by storing the digital signature of the sender and receiver.

The following are some additional features worth highlighting:

- A message can be enqueued with an explicit set of recipients, which overrides the list of subscribers to the queue.
- A caller can batch multiple items in an enqueue or dequeue operation, which is less expensive than enqueuing or dequeuing the items one by one.
- A consumer can dequeue a message without deleting it from the queue based on the queue's retention policy. The first dequeue runs as a select query, which returns a snapshot of the messages to be dequeued. Subsequent dequeues within the same transaction are performed on the same snapshot without issuing a new select.
- A sender can split a complex message into a message group, which the consumer can process atomically.
- A caller can listen to multiple queues, waiting for a message to arrive. If the listen operation returns successfully, then the caller must issue a dequeue to retrieve the message.
- A caller can dequeue a message without retrieving the message's content. This is useful for deleting a large message whose content is irrelevant.

4.9 SUMMARY

Queued TP is an alternative to direct TP that uses a persistent queue between client and server programs. The client enqueues requests and dequeues replies. The server dequeues a request, processes the request, enqueues a reply, and commits; if the transaction aborts, the request is replaced in the queue and can be retried.

The main benefits of queued TP are:

- A client can submit a request even when the server is down (by enqueuing the request).
- A server can reply to the client even when the client is down (by enqueuing the reply).
- Communication failures do not result in lost replies or uncertain results.
- Balancing the load among multiple servers is easier.
- Priority can be given to some requests relative to others.

The cost of these benefits is the additional transactions to enqueue requests and dequeue replies.

Clients can determine whether or not a request executed by examining its queues. An unexecuted request is still in the client's request queue. An executed request has a reply in the client's reply queue. If the queue manager remembers the unique ID of the last request enqueued and reply dequeued by a client, then the client can recover from a failure by synchronizing its state with the state known to the queue manager. To cope with failures that make the result of nonredoable operations (such as printing a check) ambiguous, the client should read the state of the device and compare it to the state it logged before operating on the device.

A queue manager is needed to support the queued communication model. It may be an independent product or an integral component of a transactional middleware product. It provides operations for the storage abstraction of queues, including:

- Operations on queued messages, such as enqueue, dequeue, scan a queue, and keyed access
- Creating and destroying queues
- Modifying a queue's attributes (e.g., queue owner, size, queue name, privileges)
- Starting and stopping a queue.

A queue manager may support routing, either by enqueuing to a remote server, or by enqueuing locally and forwarding messages to a remote server. This is useful to reroute requests to another server when a primary server is overloaded or down, or to batch requests that are processed only periodically. When forwarding is done transactionally, it adds a fourth transaction to the model.

Publish-subscribe is a messaging style where a publisher sends a message to a broker that is responsible for forwarding the message to many subscribers. Subscribers register interest in certain message types and receive all published messages of that type. Publish-subscribe systems usually are based on queued messaging, where published messages are distributed to subscribers via queues.

Other types of message-oriented middleware are available to integrate independent TP applications that support different communications protocols, different application functions, and different message formats. The two main architectures for performing this reconciliation are broker-based products, often called enterprise application integration (EAI) systems, and bus-based products, often called enterprise service buses (ESBs). They include functions for bridging different protocols, routing messages to the desired application, and translating between different message formats.

Business Process Management

5.1 INTRODUCTION

A **business process** is a set of related tasks that lead to a particular goal. Some business processes automate the execution or tracking of tasks using software. Such processes can be modeled as a partially ordered set of steps. Each step may be a transaction, an execution of a program that is not a transaction, an activity performed by a person or machine, or another multistep business process. Business processes are not limited to businesses. They arise in government, academia, science, and many other complex organizations.

The term **workflow** is a commonly used synonym for the concept of a business process. The term **business transaction** is sometimes used as a synonym for a business process or a step within a business process. **Business process management** is the activity of creating, managing, adapting, and monitoring business processes. Sometimes a distinction is made between **orchestration** and **choreography**, which are essentially business process management within an enterprise and between enterprises, respectively.

Much of the work of business process management is comprised of traditional operational activities performed by business managers. This includes defining and organizing the activities of an enterprise, hiring and training people to do the work, developing accounting procedures to measure cost and productivity, and identifying ways of simplifying or automating the work to reduce cost, improve quality, improve customer satisfaction, and so on. These activities are essential ingredients for successful business process management, but they are not our main interest here. Rather, this chapter focuses on aspects of business process management that relate to the choice and use of software.

The operation of a large enterprise usually involves hundreds or thousands of business processes. Many of them offer a product or service to a customer of the enterprise, often interoperating with multiple businesses. The following are a few examples:

- Process an order for retail goods: Check the customer's credit, reserve the required material from stock, schedule the shipment, give commission credit to the salesperson, submit a request for payment from a credit card company, perform the shipment, and then validate that the order was delivered.

- Transfer money: The source bank approves the transfer and sends a message to the target bank. The target bank records the transfer, bills the account for the transfer fee, and sends an acknowledgment to the source bank. The source bank bills the account for the transfer fee and sends a written acknowledgment to the customer.

- Reserve a trip: Arrange a trip at a travel web site by reserving flights, car rentals, and hotel rooms.

- Process an order for a new computer: Analyze the configuration for feasibility. Manufacture the computer. Ship the computer. Debit the credit card. E-mail an acknowledgment to the customer. The manufacturing step is, in turn, a nested business process: identify the required components; group the components by supplier; send an order to each supplier; when all the components have arrived, issue a build order; when the computer is completed, send a notification to the parent process.

Many business processes are internal to an organization and only indirectly in support of a product or service, such as the following:

- Report a bug: A tester reports a bug in a software product. A test engineer diagnoses the problem and assigns it to the relevant design engineer. The design engineer fixes the problem. The test engineer checks that the repaired program indeed solves the problem. The test engineer adds a test to the product's regression test suite, to detect if the product exhibits the bug in a later version.

- Process a shipping request: Print the shipping order. Get the products to be shipped. Package the products. Print a shipping label and affix it to the package. Add the postage label. Record the shipment in the database. Place the package in the outbox.

This chapter focuses on business processes that are at least partially automated using software, especially using TP technology, such as those just listed. Partially automated business processes have steps that include human interaction, such as the following:

- Adjust an insurance claim: When someone submits a claim, preliminary data must be captured. Later there is an inspection of the damage, which is recorded. Then the claim is approved (or not). After the damage is repaired, receipts are submitted for reimbursement. Then a reimbursement check is issued.

- Plan a new product version: A product manager collects ideas for new product features from customers, engineers, and sales people. The engineering group estimates the feasibility, design time, and manufacturing cost of each new feature. The product manager ranks the features based on cost and incremental sales expected due to each feature. A business manager decides which features to include based on available engineering resources and on the expected increase of profit and customer satisfaction compared to other product investments being considered. The engineering manager develops a schedule to design the approved features.

- Buy a piece of real estate: Find the right property. Make an offer. If the offer is accepted, have it inspected. If the inspection reveals problems, renegotiate the offer. Arrange financing. Arrange insurance. Do the closing.

- Evaluate a book proposal: The editor receives a book proposal from an author. The editor negotiates changes to the proposal with the author. The editor sends the proposal to reviewers. The editor sends reviews to the author. The author revises the proposal. The editor either rejects the revised proposal or offers a publishing contract. The author reviews and revises the contract. The editor and author sign the contract.

Even when all steps of a business process involve human interaction, the process can benefit from software assistance from TP applications; for example, to track progress in a system for document management or case management. Many business processes are a hybrid of human and automated steps where the latter execute as transactions, such as customer relationship management. There are packaged software products for each of these applications.

Following the traditional waterfall model of software development, business process management involves the usual application development activities: specifying the business process, implementing it, deploying it, and monitoring and managing its execution. A lot of attention has focused on the specification of business processes, especially on software tools to visually display a process specification and to simulate it, thereby enabling business users to evaluate the appropriateness of the specification. Although this is an important aspect of business process management, it is more closely related to software design methodology and tools than to TP, so we will not be delving into it here.

5.2 BUSINESS PROCESS DEFINITION

A business process definition specifies the steps of the business process, the work performed by each step, the order in which the steps execute, and how steps communicate with each other. That is, it defines the control flow and data flow between steps. It also specifies the components of the state of the business process and how they relate to each other.

A business process definition can be distributed among the steps of the process. For example, consider a travel reimbursement request. The step that captures the request from the user can include logic to send a message to the appropriate manager for approval. The step that captures the manager's approval can either forward a request-for-payment to the accounting department (if approved) or return the original request to the employee (if rejected).

Alternatively, the business process definition can be expressed as a single program. In this case it is usually a relatively simple script-like program, not a complex algorithm with complex data structures. For the travel reimbursement example, this program would first receive the request input from the user and then send a message to the manager for approval. Based on the manager's reply, it would either send a request-for-payment message to the accounting department or send the rejected request to the employee.

Independent of how the business process is defined, it is best to encapsulate each step of the business process separately. This allows the business process definition to focus on the flow of control and data between steps without being cluttered by the application logic of each step. It also is consistent with the goal of reusing services in a service-oriented architecture. Each encapsulated step can be defined as a service that can be invoked in multiple business processes.

Systems that support the execution of business processes usually offer a special-purpose programming language for specifying business processes. For the most part, these are ordinary languages with local variables and the usual control flow constructs, such as if-then-else, do-while, RPCs, one-way messages, parallel execution of a set of statements, and exception handlers. In addition, there are a few constructs that are somewhat specialized for business processes. One construct is to wait for the arrival of one or all of a set of messages and events (such as timeouts). Another is to send a message to a particular instance of another business process, thereby enabling business processes on two systems to coordinate their activities by passing messages back and forth.

Business processes typically are driven by events that reflect actions in the outside world: a house purchaser receives a mortgage approval, an investor receives a trade confirmation, a programmer receives a bug report, or an author receives a draft publishing contract. It is therefore natural to specify a business process as a finite state machine. Such a machine has a finite set of states. For each state, it specifies the set of events that can occur. Each event causes the machine to perform an action and move into a different state. An example state machine appears in Figure 5.1. A finite state machine is a convenient way to specify a business process when at each point in time there are several possible events that cause the process to act, and those events can arrive in any order. This typically arises when events correspond to actions performed by people, which can happen in arbitrary orders.

One limitation of the finite state machine model is the difficulty of specifying transaction boundaries and compensating transactions. A procedural specification is often more natural for capturing these aspects of a business process definition.

A step of a business process may need to interact with a person. For example, a person may be needed to review a special order or approve a travel request. In a large organization, it is important that the business

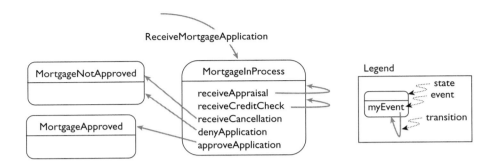

FIGURE 5.1

Finite State Machine. A mortgage approval process specified as a finite state machine.

process identify these people by their roles and not by their names. This allows multiple people to serve the same role, such as using multiple expediters to handle nonstandard orders. It also allows people to change roles dynamically, such as enabling a manager to approve travel requests for one of her subordinates when the subordinate is on vacation. The mapping of roles to people is explicitly stored and used by the runtime environment to assign a step of a given business process to the right person.

5.3 BUSINESS PROCESS EXECUTION

Many systems that support the execution of business processes offer a special-purpose runtime system. This section summarizes the main capabilities one would expect from such a runtime system.

First, the system needs to offer a way of installing business process definitions so they can subsequently be invoked. For the most part, this is no different than installing any service. One needs to store the executable, make its interface definition known to programs that will call it, and add its name to a registry so that a caller can find the service to invoke it.

Routing a request to create a business process is easy enough, since it can be guided by a registry entry. Messages that arrive for running business processes are more challenging. Each message, which corresponds to an event, needs to be routed to the proper instance of the business process. For example, when a message arrives that says a particular computer has left manufacturing, the message needs to be routed to the business process instance that is responsible for that order. This involves matching parameters in the message with process state. This matching needs to be fast, even when there is a large number of active business processes.

Many business processes that include steps performed by people need to allow people to modify the process dynamically. That is, a person performing a step might want to add a new step, skip a certain step, or reorder some steps. For example, in a mortgage application process, if an underwriter finds the customer has an unusual credit history, she may add another step for a second opinion by a more experienced loan officer. Like other process behavior, these modifications of the process should be logged so they are made available to later queries.

State Management

The runtime system needs to manage the state of a running process. For each process, it needs to know which steps have executed, the step(s) that should execute next, the business process's local variables, and other context information needed for it to run. Much of the work in managing business process execution involves managing the business process state.

The runtime system should make process state available to applications. Applications need this capability so they can tell the user about the state of his or her partially executed business process, which is important because business processes may take a long time to execute. For example, if a user places an order and doesn't receive an acknowledgment within a few days, then the user wants to be able to investigate the state of the order. A general-purpose mechanism to save the state of a business process and to query that state makes it easier for applications to offer this kind of functionality.

To maintain the state of a running process, the runtime needs to log all the interesting events that occur in a process, since the fact that those events occurred is part of the process's state. For example, for each active process, it should log when the process starts, who invoked it, and when it ends. Also, the runtime should log when each step starts and ends, perhaps including its input parameters and other information about the context in which it runs. This information should be stored in a form that makes it easy to process queries about an individual process or a large number of processes. The former is needed for answering customer questions, such as the question earlier, to investigate the state of an order. The latter is needed by system managers to monitor performance and identify slow or otherwise unhealthy processes that need attention. Aggregate information may also be useful to business process analysts, to determine the average performance of business processes (e.g., response time for certain kinds of orders), to optimize processes (e.g., certain kinds of processes that are taking too long), and to identify poorly automated processes (e.g., ones that require too many manual steps for exception handling).

A business process may execute over a long period, such as days or even months. Although a business process is long-running, it spends most of its time in an inactive state, waiting for an event to arrive to wake it up. It would be inefficient and unreliable for the process to reside in main memory throughout its execution. It would be inefficient because the process has long periods of inactivity during which its state might as well reside on less expensive persistent storage. It would be unreliable because main memory is volatile, so the business process's state would be lost in a system failure. This is a much more serious problem than the loss of a short transaction, which can simply abort and re-execute. Therefore, for safety's sake, the business process should save its state at the end of each step, as we saw in Figure 2.15.

There are two styles of process execution that relate to process state management, **document-oriented** and **message-oriented**. A document-oriented application takes a document as input, associates it with a business process, and passes the document along from one step of the business process to the next. Each step knows where to look in the document for the information that it needs for that step. Each step updates the state of the process in the document itself and saves it persistently before passing it on to the next step. Applications that evolved from the Electronic Data Interchange (EDI) standard typically work this way, as are many newer ones that use XML documents for business-to-business e-commerce.

By contrast, a message-oriented application looks more like a sequence of events, where each event arrives as a message with explicit parameters that tell the next step what to do, rather than relying on the step to find its input in a document. The state of the business process is stored in one or more databases, not in the message like in a document-oriented application.

Although most applications follow one of these two styles, there are hybrid cases that don't fall neatly into one style or the other. That is, some process state information may be retained in messages that are passed between steps, while other state information resides in databases. And document-oriented processing often invokes RPCs to execute one or more of the steps.

The system needs to offer functions for saving and restoring the state of a business process. The functions for saving a business process's state might be invoked by the business process itself or by an agent that looks for business processes that have been idle for a long time and should be moved out of main memory. The function for restoring the state of a business process could be invoked by the runtime environment when a step of the process is ready to execute. We will see other uses for state management in the next section for handling system failure and recovery.

Business process state can be used to help understand the relationships between different types of enterprise information. It is often the only place where related data entities are correlated and managed. For instance, the relationship between a sales opportunity, a sales quote, a sales order, and a contract for sales is hard to maintain. If these activities were reflected as entities and were coordinated by a single opportunity-to-contract process, then each instance of the process would have an ID that would correlate the IDs of these related activity entities as part of the business process state. In this sense business process state is central to creating integrated views of business data.

Given the importance of business process state, tools to analyze this state have become a recognized business process management capability, called **business activity monitoring**. This involves emitting business process state, such as event streams that populate a database. The database can be used by data mining and other business intelligence tools to provide visibility into every aspect of the workings of real business processes, including human-driven ones.

5.4 TRANSACTIONAL PROPERTIES

Although it is tempting to execute all the steps of a business process within one transaction, the vast majority of business processes require the execution of more than one transaction. There are many reasons for this, such as the following:

- Resource availability: At the time the request to execute the business process is taken as input, only some of the people or systems that are necessary to execute the request may be available. For example, when a customer submits an order, it is immediately stored in the order processing database. But if the request arrives after normal business hours, there may be no one to process it until the next business day. As another example, one step in processing an expense claim may be getting a manager's approval, but the manager only sets aside time to approve claims twice a week.

- Real-world constraints: Processing an automobile insurance claim may require the customer to bring in the car for damage inspection and get two estimates for the cost of the repair. This could take weeks.

- System constraints: When executing a money transfer between two banking systems (e.g., to automatically pay a credit card bill from a checking account), the two systems might not run compatible transaction protocols, such as two-phase commit, or be available at the same time. The transfer therefore has to run as multiple independent transactions on each system.

- Function encapsulation: Different business functions are managed independently by different departments. For example, in order processing, inventory management is done in manufacturing, scheduling a shipment is done by the field service group, commission reporting is done in the sales system, and credit approval is done by the finance department. Decomposing a workflow request into steps that are processed by these separate systems or by separate reusable services in an SOA is more intellectually and organizationally manageable than designing it to run as one big transaction.

- Resource contention: A long-running transaction usually holds resources, such as a lock on data or a communications device. Contention for the resource thereby slows down other transactions trying to use the resource. What starts as a performance problem, due to resource contention, may turn into an availability problem, since whole groups of transactions may be unable to run until the long-running transaction gives up its resources. For example, a money transfer between two banks could take a long time to run, because the banks are connected by slow or intermittent communication. For this reason, the operation normally runs as (at least) two transactions: one on the source system, to debit the money from the source account; and then some time later, a second one on the target system to credit the money to the target account.

So far in this book, we have assumed that each user request can be satisfied by the execution of a single transaction. When queuing is used for better availability and load balancing, we added transactions that read from and write to queues to move the request around. However, even in this case, only one transaction did the application-oriented work that was requested.

This assumption breaks down for multistep business processes. One of the most important runtime requirements of business processes is that they do not have to execute as a single transaction. Once you split the execution of a request into multiple transactions, you no longer necessarily get the benefits of a single transaction: atomicity, isolation, and durability. Let's look at how these properties might break and what can be done about it.

Isolation

Consider a money transfer operation as an example, debiting $100 from account A and then crediting that $100 to account B at another bank. If these run as separate transactions, then the money transfer request is not isolated from other transactions. For example, somebody could perform an audit of the two banks while the money is in flight, that is, after it is debited from account A and before it is credited to account B. If an auditor reads those accounts, it would look like $100 had disappeared. Thus, if the audit and money transfer are considered to be "transactions," they are not serializable; no serial execution of the audit and money transfer could result in the audit seeing the partial result of a transfer.

Of course, running the money transfer as one transaction would eliminate the problem. But as explained earlier, there are many reasons why this may not be possible or desirable. Therefore, in contrast to single-transaction requests, multitransaction business processes require special attention to the isolation problem.

The isolation problem of a multitransaction business process usually requires application-specific solutions. For example, the bank audit program must have logic that can deal with in-flight money transfers. An alternative general-purpose solution is to lock data for the duration of the business process. However, for long-running business processes, this creates major resource contention, which is usually unacceptable.

Atomicity

In the money transfer example earlier, suppose there is a failure after committing the first transaction that debits account A. This could be a failure of the business process's application code or of the system that is running that code. In either case, as a result of this failure, the first bank's message to tell the second bank to credit account B may have been lost. If this occurs, then the second transaction to credit account B will never execute. Thus, the money transfer is not all-or-nothing.

Any automated solution to this problem must include maintaining the state of the business process, that is, which steps of the business process did and did not execute. The mechanism will need this state after the recovery from the failure that caused the business process to stop prematurely. Therefore, as we noted earlier, this state should be kept in persistent storage, such as a disk. If the state is maintained in persistent storage, then it will be available after recovery from the failure even if the failure was caused by a system failure in which the content of main memory was lost.

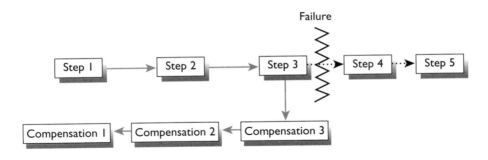

FIGURE 5.2

A Saga. This saga has five steps, each of which is a transaction. Each step's program includes a compensating transaction. Since this execution of the saga cannot proceed past step 3, it runs compensations for the three steps that did execute.

Given that the state of each business process is maintained persistently, a recovery mechanism can address the atomicity problem by periodically polling that state to determine whether to initiate recovery. If the recovery mechanism finds a business process that has remained in the same state for longer than the process's predefined timeout period, then it can initiate recovery.

One way that a recovery mechanism can repair a stalled business process is to run a compensating transaction for each of the steps of the business process that have already executed. This approach requires that for every step of a business process, the application programmer writes code for a compensating transaction that reverses the effect of the forward execution of the step. So in the money transfer example, the first transaction, which debits $100 from account A, has an associated compensating transaction that puts the money back into account A. If the system is unable to run the second transaction, which credits account B, it can run a compensation for the first transaction that debited account A. A compensating transaction may not be needed for the last step if the successful completion of that step ensures that the entire business process has completed successfully.

Some systems include a general-purpose recovery mechanism to implement this approach, for example as part of the transactional middleware. For each active business process, the transactional middleware keeps track of the sequence of transactions that have run. During its forward execution, each transaction saves all the information that is needed to allow its compensating transaction to be invoked at recovery time. For example, it might save the name of the program that implements the compensating transaction and the parameter values that should be used to invoke that program. If the recovery mechanism detects that the business process is unable to finish, then it runs compensations for all the transactions that committed and thereby brings the system back to its initial state (see Figure 5.2). Thus, it automates the execution of those compensations. This is called a **saga**: a sequence of transactions that either runs to completion or that runs a compensating transaction for every committed transaction in the sequence.

In a saga, how does the system keep track of these multiple transaction steps to ensure that at any given time it can run the compensations if the saga terminates prematurely? One possibility is to store the saga's state in queue elements. Each transaction in the saga creates a queue element, which is a request that incorporates or references the history of the steps that have run so far. If at any point the saga can't run the next step in the request, the system can look at that history and invoke the compensating transaction for each of the steps in the history. Because the queue elements are persistent, they can't get lost. Even if one of the steps is aborted many times, eventually the system will recognize the fact that the saga has not completed and will run the compensating transactions for the steps in the saga that executed.

Durability

The use of a multistep business process to implement a request does not affect the durability guarantee. The durability of a business process's updates is ensured by the durability property of the transactions that execute those updates. If all of a business process's updates to durable transactional resources execute in the context of transactions, then the result of those updates is durable.

As we saw in this section and the last, it is also important to maintain a durable copy of the intermediate state of a business process. This is not a requirement for transactions. The reason is that a transaction is atomic; that is, all-or-nothing. However, a multistep business process may not be atomic. To make it atomic, we need a durable copy of its intermediate states.

5.5 MAKING PROCESS STATE DURABLE

We have seen several reasons why business process state needs to be maintained durably. This section discusses several techniques for doing so:

- A special-purpose runtime system for business processes
- Persistent queues
- Pseudo-conversations
- Message logging

Using a Special-Purpose Runtime System

Consider a system that uses a special-purpose runtime system to support business process management. Suppose the runtime supports a function SaveState that stores the current state of a business process in persistent storage. Suppose the business process calls SaveState and then executes another step as a transaction, T. In general, executing a transaction is not an idempotent operation. So if the system fails and, after recovering, resumes executing the business process, it is important that the business process doesn't execute T a second time. This problem is reminiscent of the problem of handling non-undoable and non-idempotent operations in Section 4.4, where we wanted to process the output of a transaction (e.g., print a check) exactly once. In this case, we want to run T in the business process exactly once. It is essentially the same problem, except in this case the non-undoable operation is a transaction.

The way we solved this problem in Section 4.4 was the equivalent of invoking SaveState immediately before running T, as illustrated in Figure 5.3. Then, before invoking T, check that it didn't run once before. This assumes that T produces some testable state; that is, some persistent state that proves whether it did or did not run. This can be arranged if the invocation of the step that corresponds to T is done via a special function in the business process's runtime. That function can perform the required update of persistent storage that, if needed, can be checked later to determine if T ran.

Since T is a transaction, another possible solution is to have the business process's state be a transactional resource and make SaveState the last operation of the transaction. That way, the business process's state is saved in persistent storage if and only if T commits. If the system fails before T commits, then at recovery time the business process will continue executing with the last state that was saved before the execution of T. So T will execute again, which is what we want since T's first execution aborted as a result of the failure. If the system fails after T commits, then at recovery time the business process will continue executing with the statement that follows the SaveState operation. We would like this to be the statement that follows the execution of the commit operation for T. So we would like the SaveState operation to save the state that the transaction committed.

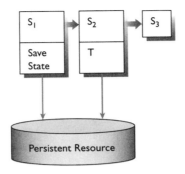

FIGURE 5.3

The SaveState Operation Runs Before Transaction T. Saving the state of the business process in step S_1 allows the state to be tested before running step S_2 to prevent re-execution of T in the event of a recovery from failure.

Notice that it is not satisfactory to invoke the SaveState operation immediately after T commits, instead of invoking it as part of T. The reason is that the system might fail after T commits and before executing the SaveState operation that follows the commit. That would result in having T execute again at recovery time, which is one of the outcomes we want to avoid.

Using Queued Requests

Another way to manage the state of a business process is to use persistent queues. The business process can be initiated by a request that is stored in a queue. Each step of the business process executes as a transaction and produces requests for the succeeding steps of the business process if and only if the step commits. Thus, the state of the process is stored in the queue elements holding the active requests of the business process.

Since the steps are separated in time, some requests in a business process may stay in a queue for a long time. However, since the queue is persistent, the request cannot be lost. Moreover, no special recovery procedure is required. If the system fails and then recovers, the recovery procedure will restart the configuration of the server processes, which includes the dispatchers associated with its queues. These dispatchers will then start dequeuing requests and invoking the appropriate programs to run them.

In this approach, there may be no one program that encapsulates the control flow of the business process. Instead, that logic could be distributed among the steps of the process. Each step of the process has an associated program that performs the work of that step, which includes defining what happens next by virtue of the requests that it produces. Since no one program defines the business process, the process has no local variables that need to be stored persistently. If step S produces any information that is needed by subsequent steps, then S needs either to pass that information along in the requests it produces or to store it in a shared database that is accessible to subsequent steps.

Instead of distributing the logic of business process steps, the business process could be encapsulated in a single program. The program executes each step as a transaction that dequeues the expected request, executes it, and enqueues output requests for the next steps. Since queue elements are persistent, the process can save its state there instead of saving it periodically in a separate transactional resource. However, it still needs to save its control state periodically in a well-known location, as we described in the previous subsection, so that at recovery time the business process can be resurrected and resume execution at the point where it left off.

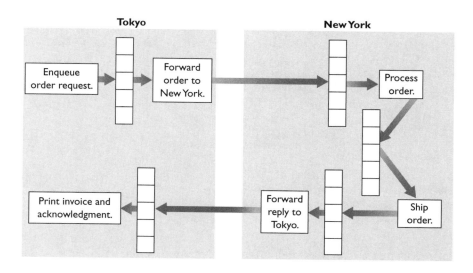

FIGURE 5.4

A Multitransaction Business Process. Each boxed action runs as a transaction. An order is entered in Tokyo, forwarded to New York for processing, processed, and shipped, and a reply is forwarded to Tokyo, which prints an invoice for the order.

The top-level request that initiates a business process often requires a reply that tells the user when the business process is completed. For example, the reply might include the itinerary for a trip, the reimbursement of an insurance claim, or the acknowledgment of a money transfer. However, intermediate steps of the workflow often do not need to reply to the originator of the step's request. Rather than sending a reply to the previous step of the business process, each intermediate step feeds a request to perform the next step of the business process. Each intermediate step might also send an e-mail or other form of notification to the end-user of the latest step that was performed (e.g., the order was received or the order was shipped), but it does not expect a reply to such notifications.

For example, consider the problem of moving orders from one office to another in a global enterprise. The Tokyo office runs a transaction to enqueue an order request (see Figure 5.4). The server recognizes the request as one that requires remote processing, so it runs a transaction that dequeues the order from the queue in Tokyo and enqueues it to another queue in New York. Now a server in New York dequeues the order, processes the order, and enqueues a shipping request. When the order ships, a transaction records that fact, enqueues a message containing an invoice and an acknowledgment that the order was filled, and perhaps sends a shipping notification to the end user. A transaction forwards the reply from the queue in New York back to the queue in Tokyo. The Tokyo server prints the invoice and acknowledgment and mails it to the customer. That final step in Tokyo is effectively a reply to the original order request. The intermediate steps are a chain of steps where each step sends a request to perform the next step.

Pseudo-Conversations

Another type of business process arises from an interactive request; that is, one that interacts with a display device. As before, due to resource contention and availability, it is wise to break up the execution into several transactions, one for each point of interaction.

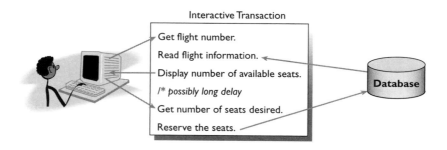

FIGURE 5.5

An Interactive Transaction. During the delay while the user is deciding how many seats to reserve, the flight information is locked, preventing other users from accessing it.

For example, consider an airline reservation transaction that gets a flight number as input from a display, reads the number of seats available on that flight from the database, and then displays that number and asks the ticket agent how many seats the customer wants to reserve (see Figure 5.5). After the customer says how many seats to reserve, this number is entered as input, the number of available seats is decremented, and the transaction commits. To make such transactions serializable, the system ordinarily holds a lock on that flight record for the duration of the transaction. This blocks other customers from making reservations on that flight. The blocking delay could be significant, while the customer is deciding how many seats to reserve. For this reason, determining the number of available seats usually runs as a separate transaction from reserving the seats. That way, the flight record isn't locked while the customer is deciding how many seats to reserve. Of course, this means that the number of available seats can change while the customer is deciding. That's why the ticket agent often reserves seats on the flight you inquire about, to make sure the seats don't go away while you're deciding; if you decide not to reserve them, the agent cancels the reservation.

In most ways, making this airline reservation is an ordinary multistep request, consisting of two transactions. The first displays the number of available seats and the second makes a reservation. Like other multistep requests, one could implement it as a business process; for example, by moving requests between client and server queues. However, these sorts of interactive situations arise often enough that some systems have a special mechanism, called **pseudo-conversations**, where the request is shuttled back and forth between client and server.

With pseudo-conversations, each time the server processes a request message, it saves some information that was gathered from that transaction step in the message that it returns to the client device (essentially a queued reply). Some of this information may be displayed to the user (e.g., number of available seats). Other information may be there just as context that can be sent back from the client to the next transaction step (e.g., an identifier for a partially-completed reservation record). The message is saved in persistent storage on the client and the server. But since there's only one message ever in transit between them, the system doesn't need a mechanism as elaborate as queues. It just needs a block of persistent storage reserved for each client. In a sense, the pseudo-conversation is a session with the message containing the state being shared by the client and server. Thus, any technique for managing persistent session state could be used. For example, the client state could be stored in a cookie in the web browser.

This way of exchanging messages is called a pseudo-conversation because it looks as if it's a conversational transaction; that is, it looks interactive. In fact, it's just a sequence of noninteractive requests, each of which has one input and one output.

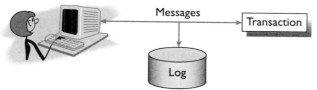

a. During normal operation, log all messages

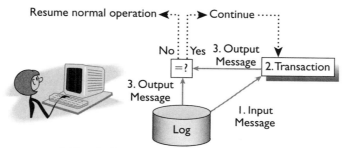

b. Use the log to recover from a transaction failure

FIGURE 5.6

Message Log for Transaction Recovery. During recovery, the transaction replays by (1) getting its input messages from the log, (2) executing until it produces output, and (3) comparing its output messages to the result of the previous execution. If the output is the same as its previous execution it continues the replay.

Using Logging

Logging is another way to make interactive requests reliable, without a pseudo-conversation or queuing. In this approach, the system runs the interactive request as one transaction (not a sequence of transactions) and logs all the transaction's input/output operations to the display or the communications system.

If the transaction aborts and restarts, then the system executes the restarted transaction in "restart mode." In this mode the system uses the log to service the transaction's input requests. That is, instead of reading from the display, the restarted transaction reads the values produced during the previous execution, which are in the log (see Figure 5.6). If there are no more logged input values to read, then the system resumes processing the restarted transaction's input operations in "normal mode," by reading from the display or communication system.

While in restart mode the system processes each of the restarted transaction's output operations by comparing it to the output that was recorded in the log during the original execution. These two outputs might differ because the restarted transaction read a different value from the database than the original transaction read. If so, then the system aborts the transaction and restarts it, but this time executing it in normal mode. If not, then the restarted transaction continues executing in restart mode. If there are no more logged output values to compare it to, then the system resumes processing the restarted transaction's output operations in "normal mode," by writing to the display or communication system.

The implementation of this approach can get quite complicated. There are many ways a transaction can perform input and output. Each type of input and output must be logged during the original execution. And for each type of operation the system must be able to reproduce the logged behavior and to detect when the restarted transaction has exhibited different behavior.

The execution of a business process can use this message logging technique to attain a similar level of fault tolerance as it would have using any of the techniques described earlier in this section, namely, a special-purpose runtime, queuing, or pseudo-conversations. However, unlike those earlier approaches, in this case the business process must execute as one transaction and not be decomposed into multiple transactions. Therefore, this technique by itself does not avoid the problems of resource contention and availability, which are two other reasons why it may be undesirable to execute a business process as one transaction. Thus, it's suitable only when they are not critical problems.

5.6 OTHER MODELS OF BUSINESS PROCESSES

The term "business process" has a strong connotation of applying the technology to business procedures in support of large enterprises. However, long-running processes also occur in science and engineering, which also have developed some degree of automation support. Since their capabilities are very similar to those we described for business processes, we summarize them only briefly.

Scientific Workflow

Software systems that support scientific experimentation need to deal with long-running processes. Scientists call these workflows rather than business processes, but the concept is the same. A typical scenario is to use a pipeline of tools that takes raw data from a physical scientific experiment and transforms it into a meaningful interpretation of the result of the experiment. For example, in bioinformatics, an experiment might involve putting the liquid result of a wet-lab experiment into a scientific instrument, such as a mass spectrometer or micro-array. The output of the instrument is a file. That file is then pipelined through a sequence of data analysis tools, ultimately producing results that can be interpreted by a scientist. The analysis may be run thousands of times on different samples.

There are several ways in which automation of workflows can help scientists, such as the following:

- A scientist can write a workflow definition that drives the execution of the multistep experiment. The workflow management system maps the computational steps onto a multiprocessor computing facility and monitors and manages their execution.

- A scientist can review the history of workflow executions. This history, which scientists usually call **provenance**, can give the exact steps that were executed to produce a particular output. The ability to run queries to find the provenance of certain experiments helps enable the reproducibility of experiments. This is especially valuable when the process has manual steps and different executions of the workflow have different manual steps.

- A workflow system can capture the sequence of steps of a process so that it can be replayed many times. Initial experiments may involve many manual steps. But as the process is perfected, the same steps are executed in each replay. It is therefore helpful if the workflow system can transform an execution history into a script that can be re-executed many times.

As of this writing, scientists have their own workflow management systems, which are different from those used for business processes. However, there is a growing awareness of the strong similarities of these two technologies. It therefore seems likely that more technology sharing between these two communities will develop.

Configuration Management Systems

Configuration management systems help engineers manage shared designs. A similar kind of system, called a product data management system, is used for discrete manufacturing. In these systems, design information typically is stored in files, which are grouped into configurations, each of which corresponds to some component being designed. The system offers check-out–check-in functionality. A user checks out the files he or she needs to work on. After the work is completed, the user checks them back in. The work that was done between the check-out and check-in can be thought of as a step in the design process. A design tool may be invoked to evaluate the result of that step. If the result passes the test, it has to be recorded in the project management system where the change request originated. If not, it has to be returned to the engineer to redo the design step.

For the most part, the steps of such a configuration management process are manual. However, they often follow a well-defined engineering process that could be codified as a business process definition. Thus, they can benefit from some degree of software automation to track the state of each process and to review its history long after it executed. Currently, this type of functionality usually is built as a special function in a configuration management product, rather than using general-purpose business process management tools.

Configuration management also is used to manage complex computer systems. This is more of an operational activity than a design activity. However, the business process functionality is largely the same. The steps required to perform certain system management functions are specified as a business process, such as steps to add a new user to the system or to add a new server to the network. Thus, some degree of automation to track process state is valuable here too.

One interesting aspect of configuration management compared to normal TP systems is that the steps of a configuration management process require application-specific logic to make them serializable, due to concurrent checkout steps. For example, suppose Alice checks out file F and then Bob checks out F too. Alice modifies F, thereby creating F', and checks in F'. Then Bob modifies his copy of F, thereby creating F'', and checks in F''. At check-in time, the configuration management system knows that Bob's initial state of F was overwritten by Alice. It therefore knows that it would be incorrect to overwrite Alice's version F' by Bob's version F''. Instead, a configuration management system would ask that Bob's changes to F be merged into F'. The system might help by finding the differences between F and F'', and then helping Bob add those changes to F'. Or it might find the differences between F and F' and the differences between F and F'', merge those changes, and then apply the merged changes to F. In both solutions, the intent is to make it appear that Bob actually made his modifications to F', not to F; that is, to make it appear that Alice's and Bob's modifications ran serially. We will see that this is an instance of a general problem that arises in TP when independent transactions modify different copies of the same data, in this case different copies of F. We discuss a variety of general-purpose solutions to the problem in Section 9.5, *Multimaster Replication*. Those solutions don't solve the problem for configuration management *per se*, but they have the same property of identifying independent and hence conflicting changes and requiring that they be merged together in an application-specific way.

5.7 PRODUCTS AND STANDARDS

This section offers two concrete examples to illustrate the concepts of business process management: the Web Services Business Process Execution Language (WS-BPEL) standard and the Service Broker component of Microsoft SQL Server.

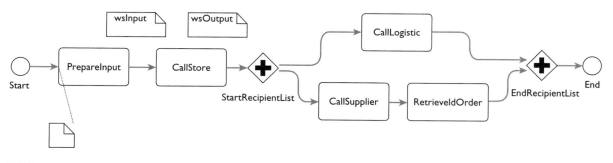

FIGURE 5.7

Sample BPMN Diagram for Order Processing Flow. The rounded rectangles denote steps, the rectangles with folded right corners denote data, and the diamonds with plus signs denote fork and join.

Web Services Business Process Execution Language

WS-BPEL is a standard from the Organization for the Advancement of Structured Information Standards (OASIS), which is responsible for some of the Web Services standards. It specifies an XML syntax and execution semantics for business processes. A business process runtime system is WS-BPEL compliant if it can execute business processes that are expressed in WS-BPEL.

The WS-BPEL standard does not specify a graphical notation or a programming language syntax for expressing processes. Thus, a business process specification tool is WS-BPEL compliant as long as it compiles business process definitions into WS-BPEL—it can offer any notation or language syntax it wants to people who design business processes. There are dozens of such notations and languages. One popular notation is the Business Process Modeling Notation (BPMN), which is a graphical notation standardized by the Object Management Group and supported by many tool vendors. An example is shown in Figure 5.7.[1] BPMN has been mapped successfully to WS-BPEL.

In WS-BPEL, the steps of a business process are called **activities**. WS-BPEL assumes that all activities are performed by Web Services. A process defined in WS-BPEL describes the interfaces between a business process and the Web Services with which it interacts. A WS-BPEL business process can itself be exposed as a Web Service. In addition, a business process describes the control flow of the activities, state management, and exception handling.

A variable in WS-BPEL contains a WSDL message type or an XML Schema (XSD) simple type or element type. For example, a process can use a variable to store a document or message that it receives from one service and that it intends to send later to another service. Or it can use a variable to record state information about a process, as discussed in Section 5.3. A rich expression language is available to assign a value to a variable. In particular, components of a variable can be identified using XPath, which is an expression language for referencing a portion of an XML document.

Each process is itself a service. Each interaction of a process is described by a **partner link**, which connects the process to a partner service. Each partner link has a **partner link type**, which specifies the name of the role of each participant in the link type and the port type over which each participant communicates. Port types are abstract connection points to a service, which are later made concrete through a port definition that includes network information. A partner link specifies the partner link type of which it is an instance and the role that the process and its partner play. In RPC terminology, the partner link type and partner link define a service contract over which service invocations can take place.

---

[1]Example screenshot from the Eclipse SOA Tools Platform Project BPMN Modeler: http://www.eclipse.org/bpmn/images/screenshots/

A process communicates with another service by invoking it via a partner link, either as a one-way or request-reply operation (i.e., an RPC). Since a process is a service, it can also receive such a call from a partner and, if the call is a request-reply operation, the process can subsequently send a reply to the partner.

A process can communicate with a particular instance of a service. To do this, it identifies a set of variables that are input parameters to service calls as a **correlation set**. Messages to a service that have the same values of a correlation set will go to the same instance of that service. That is, the value of the correlation set identifies the instance of the partner service.

A process has the usual control flow structures available, such as a sequential execution of activities, a parallel execution of activities (called a **flow**), if-then-else, a case statement to select among activities (called a **switch**), a wait activity to wait for a duration or for a deadline, and looping constructs (while, repeat-until, for-each). It also offers an event block (called a **pick**) that identifies a set of event-activity pairs, where the first event to fire causes the associated activity to execute.

Each activity defines a scope. Larger scopes consisting of multiple activities can be explicitly defined. Each scope can have an associated fault handler and compensation handler. For example, a compensation handler can be defined using the WS-BusinessActivity protocol of WS-Transactions. There is considerable flexibility in defining the behavior of these handlers to override the default. For example, suppose an employee makes a purchase, which is then billed to his or her department. To cancel this sequence and compensate for it, it may be necessary to cancel the purchase first, to determine if there are cancellation fees that need to be deducted from the credit to the department. This is the opposite order of the default, which is to run compensations for transactions in the reverse order that they executed.

Scopes can also be used to control serializability. If two concurrent scopes are specified as **isolated**, then their execution must be serializable relative to their shared variables and partner links. That is, the effect of read and write operations on shared variables and partner links must be the same as those effects in a serial execution of the two scopes.

A process may be partially specified as an **abstract process**, which leaves out certain details that are needed to execute the process. An abstract process may be useful as a description to business partners who should not see all details of the process or as a stable description that is unaffected by subsequent changes to implementation details.

At the time of this writing, the latest release of the WS-BPEL standard is version 2.0. There are many runtime engines that support some version of the standard.

SQL Server Service Broker

Microsoft SQL Server 2005 includes a queue-based system for managing business processes, called Service Broker. It offers functionality to allow multiple services to cooperate in the execution of a step of a business process and to enable the step to retain persistent state of the business process to be used by later steps. It also reliably and transactionally delivers events and messages to a business process so that the business process can reliably recover from failures without missing or repeating steps.

An application in Service Broker consists of a set of steps, which are implemented by services. Each service is implemented by a program bound to a queue. The program can be a stored procedure or a program external to SQL Server. To invoke a service, a program first creates a session with the service, called a **conversation**, by calling Begin Dialog Conversation. It then sends a message over the conversation, which causes a message to be placed in the service's queue. In the simplest case, the service starts a transaction, receives (i.e., dequeues) the message, does the requested work, and sends a reply message over the same conversation and commits. This causes the reply to be enqueued on the caller's queue. This is essentially the model of queued messaging that we explored in Chapter 4.

Messages within a conversation are processed in the exact order they were placed on the queue. This ordering is maintained even in highly scalable multithreaded and multiprocess services.

Service Broker expands this simple queuing model in a number of ways to support multistep business processes. First, it has an abstraction called **conversation group**. Roughly speaking, a conversation group corresponds to a business process. It has a unique ID, which is meant to be used to identify persistent state that the application associates with the business process. To invoke the first step of a business process, a program creates a conversation without specifying a conversation group, which tells Service Broker to create a new one. If this first step is part of a multistep business process, then the service that executes this step should insert a row into a database table whose key is the conversation group ID. This row is used by this step and subsequent steps to maintain the state of the business process. For each subsequent step, the program invoking the steps should create a conversation (to the service that will perform the step) in the context of the business process's conversation group, so the service can access the business process's state. For example, if the first step S_1 invokes two other steps, S_2 and S_3, then S_1 should create a conversation to the services for S_2 and S_3 in the context of S_1's conversation group, thereby causing the services for S_2 and S_3 to execute in S_1's business process.

It is possible that there are several messages in a queue that pertain to the same conversation group. In the previous example, this could happen if S_2 and S_3 do their work and reply before S_1's service is able to receive either reply. If S_1's service is multithreaded, then when it does get around to receiving S_2's and S_3's replies, it could end up with two separate threads processing those replies. To relieve the application developer from the synchronization that would be required between these two threads, Service Broker has a built-in locking protocol.

Service Broker locks the conversation group for the duration of any transaction that processes a message in the conversation group to ensure that this is the only service invocation (i.e., thread) that can process messages for this conversation group. The service invocation should receive and process the messages for this conversation group one by one. Following this protocol in the example would cause S_1's service to process the replies from S_2 and S_3 in the same transaction with no risk of another service invocation interfering with it.

A service can become idle when there are no messages in its queue. To enable this functionality, Service Broker allows a service to be started in the following ways: (1) when a message arrives in its queue; (2) when an event is received; (3) at a scheduled time (e.g., every night at 11 PM); or (4) when SQL Server starts up. In the first three cases, the service becomes idle after it has processed all the items on its queue. In case (4), the service remains active indefinitely and hence consumes resources even when idle.

To ensure that a service is sent only messages it knows how to process, Service Broker offers some message type management. An application can define message types, each of which includes the name of the message type and a validation criterion. The validation criterion can be none (no criterion), empty (requires the message body to be empty), XML (requires the body to be well-formed XML), or validate with schema collection (requires the body to conform to a given XSD schema). The validation criterion specifies what validation work will be done by the recipient service at runtime for each message of this type that it receives.

When starting a conversation, one can specify a contract that says which message types can be exchanged between the initiator (which is starting the conversation) and the target (the other party to the conversation). To do this, the developer first specifies the contract. For each message type in the contract, it says whether the initiator, target, or both can receive messages of that type. A contract does not constrain the order in which these messages can be sent or whether they can be duplicated; that is up to the services that participate in the conversation.

Service Broker offers a message retention option. This tells Service Broker to maintain a permanent record of the exact sequence of messages that were processed by a conversation; for example, to undo the steps of a business process.

5.8 SUMMARY

Many types of requests need to be executed as a multistep business process, not just as one transaction. Examples include processing an order, arranging a trip, or processing an insurance claim. Business process management is the activity of creating, managing, adapting, and monitoring business processes.

Like any application program, a business process needs to be specified in a formal language. This can be an imperative language with the usual control flow constructs, a finite state machine, or a graphical notation suitable for a visual programming tool.

Usually a business process is supported by a special-purpose runtime system. Since a business process may run for a long time, days or even months, it must be possible for users to interrogate the process's state. Hence, the business process runtime needs to log all the interesting events that occur in a process that affect the process's state. The runtime system needs to offer functions for saving the state of a business process, if the process is idle or in anticipation of a failure, and for restoring the state when the process becomes active again or recovers from a failure.

Breaking up a request into a multitransaction business process loses the benefits of isolation and atomicity. Therefore, a business process needs to pay special attention to maintaining state in a way that avoids interpreting the result of a partially executed process (and thereby break isolation) and that can interpret that state when invoking compensating transactions to cope with the failure of a partially executed process (to ensure atomicity).

There are several ways to maintain process state. There are special-purpose runtime systems that explicitly store state information while the process executes. Some systems use persistent queues to maintain process state. For business processes that engage in back-and-forth communication with a client, the client and business process server can use a pseudo-conversation, which maintains the state of the communication along with some state information in the message. A related technique to cope with interactive transactions is to log its I/O, so if it fails in mid-stream, its I/O can be replayed at recovery time.

Locking

6.1 INTRODUCTION

An important property of transactions is that they are isolated. Technically, this means that the execution of transactions has the same effect as running the transactions serially, one after another, in sequence, with no overlap in executing any two of them. Such an execution is called **serializable**, meaning that it has the same effect as a serial execution. A serializable execution gives each user the easy-to-understand illusion that while the system is processing his or her transaction, it is doing no other work.

The most popular mechanism used to attain serializability is locking. The concept is simple:

- Each transaction reserves access to the data it uses. This reservation is called a **lock**.
- There are **read locks** and **write locks**.[1]
- Before reading a piece of data, a transaction sets a read lock. Before writing the data, it sets a write lock.
- Read locks conflict with write locks, and write locks conflict with both read and write locks.
- A transaction can obtain a lock only if no other transaction has a conflicting lock on the same data item. Thus, it can obtain a read lock on a data item x only if no transaction has a write lock on x. It can obtain a write lock on x only if no transaction has a read lock or write lock on x.

We say that two operations **conflict** if they operate on the same data and at least one of them is a write. The intuition is that the execution order of conflicting operations makes a difference, because it changes either the value read by a transaction (since a read operation reads a different value depending on whether it executes before or after a write operation) or the final value of a data item (since changing the order of two write operations on the same data changes the final value of the data). Since their execution order matters, it's important to control that order.

The intuition behind locking is that it avoids interference between transactions by using conflicting locks to synchronize the execution order of conflicting operations. If a transaction is holding a read lock, then another transaction cannot set a write lock, which avoids the concurrent execution of a conflicting write operation. This works similarly for write locks.

Although the concept of locking is simple, its effects on performance and correctness can be complex, counterintuitive, and hard to predict. Building robust TP applications requires a solid understanding of locking.

---

[1]Many systems call them "shared (or S)" and "exclusive (or X)" locks, instead of "read" and "write" locks. However, as a reminder that there is perfect symmetry between operations and lock types, we use the operation names "read" and "write" instead.

Locking affects performance. When a transaction sets a lock, it delays other transactions that need to set a conflicting lock. Everything else being equal, the more transactions that are running concurrently, the more likely that such delays will happen. The frequency and length of such delays can also be affected by transaction design, database layout, and transaction and database distribution. To understand how to minimize this performance impact, one must understand locking mechanisms and how they are used, and how these mechanisms and usage scenarios affect performance.

Locking also affects correctness. Although locking usually strikes people as intuitively correct, not all uses of locking lead to correct results. For example, reserving access to data before actually doing the access would seem to eliminate the possibility that transactions could interfere with each other. However, if serializability is the goal, then simply locking data before accessing it is not quite enough: The timing of unlock operations also matters.

Correctness and the Two-Phase Rule

To see how unlock operations affect correctness, consider two transactions, T_1 and T_2, which access two shared data items, x and y. T_1 reads x and later writes y, and T_2 reads y and later writes x.[2] For example, x and y could be records that describe financial and personnel aspects of a department. T_1 reads budget information in x and updates the number of open requisitions in y. T_2 reads the current head count and updates the committed salary budget.

To describe executions of these transactions succinctly, we'll use $r_1[x]$ to denote T_1's read of x, $w_1[y]$ to denote T_1's write of y, and similarly for T_2. We'll denote lock operations in a similar way—$rl_1[x]$ to denote that T_1 sets a read lock on x, and $ru_1[x]$ to denote that T_1 unlocks x. Given this notation, consider the following execution E of T_1 and T_2:

$$E = \underbrace{rl_1[x]\ r_1[x]\ ru_1[x]}_{T_1\ \text{reads}\ x}\ \underbrace{rl_2[y]\ r_2[y]\ wl_2[x]\ w_2[x]\ ru_2[y]\ wu_2[x]}_{T_2\ \text{reads}\ y\ \text{and writes}\ x}\ \underbrace{wl_1[y]\ w_1[y]\ wu_1[y]}_{T_1\ \text{writes}\ x}$$

In execution E, each transaction locks each data item before accessing it. (You should check this for each operation.) Yet the execution isn't serializable. We can show this by stripping off the lock and unlock operations, producing the following execution (see Figure 6.1):

$$E' = r_1[x]\ r_2[y]\ w_2[x]\ w_1[y]$$

Since execution E has the same read and write operations as execution E' and the operations are in the same order, E and E' have the same effect on the database (the only difference between them is the lock operations). To show that E' isn't serializable, let's compare it to the two possible serial executions of T_1 and T_2, namely $T_1\ T_2$ and $T_2\ T_1$, and show that neither of them could produce the same result as E':

- In the serial execution $T_1\ T_2 = r_1[x]\ w_1[y]\ r_2[y]\ w_2[x]$, T_2 reads the value of y written by T_1. This isn't what actually happened in E' so this doesn't produce the same effect as E'.
- In the serial execution $T_2\ T_1 = r_2[y]\ w_2[x]\ r_1[x]\ w_1[y]$, T_1 reads the value of x written by T_2. This isn't what actually happened in E' so this too doesn't produce the same effect as E'.

Since T_1T_2 and T_2T_1 are the only possible serial executions of T_1 and T_2, and E' doesn't have the same effect as either of them, E' isn't serializable. Since E has the same effect as E', E isn't serializable either.

---

[2]The example is a bit contrived, in that each transaction updates a data item it didn't previously read. The example is designed to illustrate a variety of concurrency control concepts throughout the chapter.

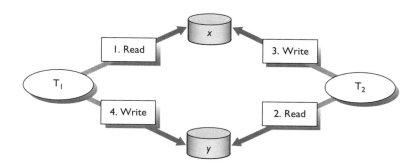

FIGURE 6.1

A Nonserializable Execution, E', That Uses Locking. The numbers 1–4 indicate the order in which operations execute.

Each transaction in E got a lock before accessing the corresponding data item. So what went wrong? The problem is the timing of T_1's unlock operation on x. It executed too soon. By releasing its lock on x before getting its lock on y, T_1 created a window of opportunity for T_2 to ruin the execution. T_2 wrote x after T_1 read it (making it appear that T_2 followed T_1) and it read y before T_1 wrote it (making it appear that T_2 preceded T_1). Since T_2 can't both precede and follow T_1 in a serial execution, the result was not serializable.

The locking rule that guarantees serializable executions in all cases is called **two-phase locking**. It says that a transaction must obtain all its locks before releasing any of them. Or equivalently, a transaction cannot release a lock and subsequently get a lock, as T_1 did in E. When a transaction obeys this rule, it has two phases (hence the name): a growing phase during which it acquires locks, and a shrinking phase during which it releases them. The operation that separates the two phases is the transaction's first unlock operation, which is the first operation of the second phase.

> *Two-Phase Locking Theorem: If all transactions in an execution are two-phase locked, then the execution is serializable.*

Despite the simple intuition behind locking, there are no simple proofs of the Two-Phase Locking Theorem. The original proof by Eswaran et al. appeared in 1976 and was several pages long. The simplest proof we know of is by J. D. Ullman and is presented in the appendix at the end of this chapter.

Transactions Interact Only Via Reads and Writes

Whether or not you take the time to understand the proof, it is important to understand one assumption on which the proof is based, namely, *transactions interact only via read and write operations*. This assumption ensures that the only way that transactions can affect each other's execution is through operations that are synchronized by locking.

One way to break this assumption is to allow transactions to exchange messages through the communication system, as ordinary messages over a communication channel or in main memory, not via transactional queues. For example, consider the following execution: $send_3[msg]$ $receive_4[msg]$ $w_4[x]$ $r_3[x]$ where msg is a message sent by T_3 to T_4. This execution is not serializable: T_4 received msg that was sent by T_3, making it appear that T_4 executed after T_3; but T_3 read the value of x written by T_4, making it appear that T_3 executed after T_4. Obviously, in a serial execution T_3 cannot run both before and after T_4, so the execution is not equivalent to a serial execution and hence is not serializable. Yet two-phase locking would allow this execution to occur, which can be seen by adding locking operations to the execution: $send_3[msg]$ $receive_4[msg]$ $wl_4[x]$ $w_4[x]$ $wu_4[x]$ $rl_3[x]$ $r_3[x]$ $ru_3[x]$.

Since $w_4[x]$ is the last operation of T_4, it is safe for T_4 to unlock x, thereby allowing T_3 to read x. So, we have an execution that is two-phase locked but is not serializable, which seems to contradict the Two-Phase Locking Theorem.

The problem is not that the theorem is wrong, but rather that the execution broke an assumption on which the theorem is based, namely, that transactions interact only via reads and writes. T_3 and T_4 interacted via message passing, and those message passing operations were not locked. Either T_3 and T_4 should not have exchanged messages, or those messages should have been exchanged via a write operation (to send *msg*) and a read operation (to receive *msg*), which would have been synchronized by locks.

Another way of stating the assumption is that "all operations by which transactions can interact must be protected by locks." In other words, it is all right for transactions to issue send[*msg*] and receive[*msg*], provided that locks are set for these operations in a two-phase manner. Later in the chapter, we will see examples of other operations besides read and write that are protected by locks. However, until then, for simplicity, we will assume that reads and writes are the only operations by which transactions can interact and therefore are the only ones that need to be locked.

Preserving Transaction Handshakes

A more subtle way for transactions to communicate is via a human operator. For example, suppose a user reads the output displayed by a transaction T_5 and uses it as input to transaction T_6. The effect here is the same as if T_5 sent a message to T_6. We discussed this example briefly in Figure 1.4. In terms of our example here, Figure 1.4 was concerned that T_5 might abort after the user copied its output into T_6. We therefore recommended that a user wait until a transaction (e.g., T_5) has committed before using that transaction's output as input to another transaction (e.g., T_6). This is called a **transaction handshake**. This solves the problem of a transaction reading input that later is undone by an abort. However, is it safe, in view of the assumption that transactions communicate only via reads and writes? After all, even if the user waits for T_5 to commit before using T_5's output as input to T_6, a message is still effectively flowing from T_5 to T_6.

The following theorem tells us that it is indeed safe.

> ***Transaction Handshake Theorem***[3]: *For every two-phase locked execution, there is an equivalent serial execution that preserves all transaction handshakes.*

In other words, it's all right for a user to wait for T_5 to finish before starting T_6 so that he or she can use T_5's output as input to T_6. It is true that the user is breaking the assumption that transactions only interact via reads and writes. However, this cannot break serializability, because the direction of information transfer, from T_5 to T_6, is consistent with the effective serial order in which the transactions executed.

The Transaction Handshake Theorem seems obvious. To see that it is not, consider the following execution: $r_1[x]\ w_2[x]\ r_3[y]\ w_1[y]$. In this execution, the user may have seen output that was displayed by transaction T_2 and used it as part of the input he or she provided to transaction T_3. The user was careful to use a transaction handshake, to make sure that T_2 committed before providing input to T_3. This execution is serializable, in the order $T_3\ T_1\ T_2$. In fact, $T_3\ T_1\ T_2$ is the only serial ordering of transactions that is equivalent to the given execution. However, this serial ordering does not preserve transaction handshakes. In the original execution, transaction T_2 (consisting of the single operation $w_2[x]$) finished before T_3 (consisting of the single operation $r_3[y]$) started. This is a transaction handshake. But in the only equivalent serial ordering, T_3 *precedes* T_2. This is a problem if the user transferred some of the output of T_2 into T_3.

---

[3]The proof is from Bernstein et al. (1979).

The Transaction Handshake Theorem says that this kind of thing cannot happen when you use two-phase locking. Therefore, the execution $r_1[x]\ w_2[x]\ r_3[y]\ w_1[y]$ must not be obtainable via two-phase locking. To check that this is so, let's try to add lock operations to the execution. We start by locking x for $r_1[x]$: $rl_1[x]\ r_1[x]$ $w_2[x]\ r_3[y]\ w_1[y]$. Now we need to lock x for $w_2[x]$, but we can't do this unless we first release $rl_1[x]$. Since T_1 is two-phase locked, it must get its write lock on y before it releases its read lock on x. Thus, we have $rl_1[x]$ $r_1[x]\ wl_1[y]\ ru_1[x]\ wl_2[x]\ w_2[x]\ wu_2[y]\ r_3[y]\ w_1[y]$. Next, $r_3[y]$ must get a read lock on y, but it can't because T_1 still has its write lock on y and it can't give it up until after $w_1[y]$ executes. So there is no way $r_3[y]$ can run at this point in the execution, which shows that the execution could not have happened if all transactions were two-phase locked.

Automating Locking

An important feature of locking is that it can be hidden from the application programmer. Here's how.

When a transaction issues a read or write operation, the data manager that processes the operation first sets a read or write lock on the data to be read or written. This is done without any special hints from the transaction program, besides the read or write operation itself.

To ensure the two-phase rule, the data manager holds all locks until the transaction issues the Commit or Abort operation, at which point the data manager can release the transaction's locks since it knows the transaction is done. This is later than the rule requires, but it's the first time the data manager can be sure the transaction won't issue any more reads or writes, which would require it to set another lock. That is, if the data manager releases one of the transaction's locks before the transaction terminates, and the transaction subsequently issues a read or write, the system would have to set a lock and thereby break the two-phase rule.

Thus, a transaction program only needs to bracket its transactions. The data manager does the rest. Although a data manager can hide locking from the application programmer, it often gives some control over when locks are set and released. This offers the programmer a measure of performance tuning, often at the expense of correctness. We'll discuss this in more detail later in the chapter.

Notice that we used the term **data manager** here, instead of the more generic term "resource manager" that we use elsewhere in this book. Since there is such a strong connotation that locking is used by database systems, we find it more intuitive to use the terms data manager and data item in this chapter, rather than resource manager and resource. But this is just a matter of taste. We use the terms data manager and resource manager as synonyms, to mean a database system, file system, queue manager, and so on—any system that manages access to transactional resources.

Not all concurrency control algorithms use locks. One popular example is optimistic concurrency control, which is discussed in Sections 6.5 and 6.8. Three other techniques are timestamp ordering, serialization graph testing, and commit ordering. **Timestamp ordering** assigns each transaction a timestamp and ensures that conflicting operations execute in timestamp order. **Serialization graph testing** tracks conflicts and ensures the resulting serialization graph is acyclic. **Commit ordering** ensures that conflicting operations are consistent with the relative order in which their transactions commit, which can enable interoperability of systems using different concurrency control mechanisms. These techniques are rarely used in practice, so we don't discuss them here. See the bibliographic notes for references.

6.2 IMPLEMENTATION

Although an application programmer never has to deal directly with locks, it helps to know how locking is implemented, for two reasons. First, locking can have a dramatic effect on the performance of a TP system.

Most systems offer tuning mechanisms to optimize performance. To use these mechanisms, it's valuable to understand their effect on the system's internal behavior. Second, some of those optimizations can affect correctness. Understanding locking implementation helps to understand when such optimizations are acceptable and what alternatives are possible.

An implementation of locking in a data manager has three aspects: implementing a lock manager, setting and releasing locks, and handling deadlocks, which we discuss in turn next.

Lock Managers

A lock manager is a component that services the operations:

- Lock(transaction-id, data-item, lock-mode): Set a lock with mode *lock-mode* on behalf of transaction *transaction-id* on *data-item*.
- Unlock(transaction-id, data-item): Release transaction *transaction-id's* lock on *data-item*.
- Unlock(transaction-id): Release all transaction *transaction-id's* locks.

Most implementations store locks in a **lock table**. This is a low-level data structure in main memory, much like a control table in an operating system (i.e., not like a SQL table). Lock and unlock operations cause locks to be inserted into and deleted from the lock table, respectively.

Each entry in the lock table describes the locks on a data item. It contains a list of all the locks held on that data item and all pending lock requests that cannot be granted yet.

To execute a Lock operation, the lock manager sets the lock if no conflicting lock is held by another transaction. Consider the lock table state shown in Figure 6.2. In this state the lock manager would grant a request by T_2 for a read lock on z, and would therefore add [trid$_2$, read] to the list of locks being held on z, where trid$_2$ is T_2's transaction ID. If it received a request by T_2 for a write lock on v, it would add an entry in the lock table for data item v and then add [trid$_2$, write] to the list of locks being held on v.

If the lock manager receives a lock request for which a conflicting lock is being held, the lock manager adds a request for that lock, which it will grant after conflicting locks are released. In this case, the transaction that requires the lock is blocked until its lock request is granted. For example, a request by T_2 for a write lock on z would cause [trid$_2$, write] to be added to z's list of lock requests and T_2 to be blocked.

The strategy for granting blocked requests requires some care to avoid indefinite postponement. For example, in Figure 6.2 suppose T_5 requests a read lock on x. In principle, this request could be granted because the only locks on x are read locks. However, following this strategy, a steady stream of requests for read locks on x could indefinitely postpone T_3's request for a write lock, since there might never be a time when there are no read locks on x. Therefore, a safer approach is to add T_5's request for a read lock to the end of the list of lock requests, after T_3's request.

Data item identifiers usually are required to be a fixed length, say 32 bytes. The lock manager does not know what each of these identifiers represents. It could be a table, page, row, or other object. It is up to the

Data Item	List of Locks Being Held	List of Lock Requests
x	[trid$_1$, read], [trid$_2$, read]	[trid$_3$, write]
y	[trid$_2$, write]	[trid$_4$, read] [trid$_1$, read]
z	[trid$_1$, read]	

FIGURE 6.2

A Lock Table. Each entry in a list of locks held or requested is of the form [transaction-id, lock-mode].

caller of the lock manager to compress the name of the object to be locked into a data item identifier of the length supported by the lock manager.

Any data item in a database can be locked, but only a small fraction of them are locked at any one time, because only a small fraction of them are accessed at any one time by a transaction that's actively executing. Therefore, instead of allocating a row in the lock table for every possible data item identifier value, the lock table is implemented as a hash table, whose size is somewhat larger than the maximal number of locks that are held by active transactions. The hash key is the data item identifier.

Lock operations on each data item must be atomic relative to each other. That is, each lock operation must complete before the next one starts. Otherwise, two conflicting lock requests might incorrectly be granted at the same time. For example, if two requests to set a write lock on v execute concurrently, they might both detect that v is unlocked before either of them set the lock. Therefore, both of them might set the lock. To avoid this bad behavior, the lock manager executes each lock or unlock operation on a data item completely before starting the next one on that data item. That is, it executes lock and unlock operations on each data item atomically with respect to each other. Note that lock operations on different data items can safely execute concurrently.

The lock manager could become a bottleneck if it takes too long for a lock to be set or released. Since lock and unlock operations are very frequent, they could consume a lot of processor time. And since lock operations on a data item are atomic, lock requests on popular data items might be delayed because another lock operation is in progress. For these reasons, lock and unlock operations must be very fast, ideally on the order of a few hundred machine language instructions.

Although most systems implement locking using a lock table, this is not the only possible design. An alternative implementation is to store each object's lock with the object itself. For example, a page lock could be stored in the page.

Rather than exposing lock operations to programs that invoke read and write, locks could be set by the data access operations themselves. For example, in an object-oriented system, consider a class C whose instances (i.e., objects) are data items. C could inherit from a generic lock manager class. Each method to access an object of C could be given the responsibility to set the appropriate lock on itself. For example, a get method could set a read lock and a put method could set a write lock. The lock manager class could automatically release all locks when the transaction commits, thereby relieving the object itself from invoking unlock operations. Whether the object's locks are stored in the object's representation or in a lock table is an independent implementation decision.

Setting and Releasing Locks

To understand how higher levels of the data manager choose which data items to lock, we need to know a little bit about data manager architecture. A typical example is a database system that supports the SQL language. Such a system usually is implemented in the following layers (see Figure 6.3):

- Page-oriented files: This is the lowest layer of the system, which communicates directly with the persistent storage device, such as a disk. It offers operations to read and write pages in a file. It also implements a buffer pool that caches recently used pages.

- Access methods: This layer implements record-oriented files by formatting each page as a set of records, each of which can be accessed by a logical address. It also implements indexes, to allow records to be accessed based on field value. Typical operations are GetRecord(logical address), which returns the record with that address; OpenScan(field value), which returns a cursor that points to the first record with that field value; and GetNextRecord(cursor), which returns the record identified by the cursor and advances the cursor to the next record with the field value associated with the cursor.

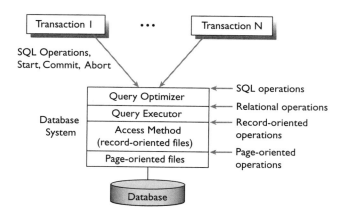

FIGURE 6.3

SQL Database Architecture. A SQL operation issued by a transaction is translated through a series of layers, each of which has the option to set locks.

- Query executor: This layer implements the basic relational database operators, such as project, select, join, update, insert, and delete. It takes as input an expression consisting of one or more of these operations and, in the case of retrieval expressions, returns a set of records. Typically, each table is implemented as a file at the access method layer and each row is implemented as a record. So we treat the following as synonyms in the rest of this chapter: tables and files, columns and fields, and rows and records.

- Query optimizer: This layer takes a SQL statement as input, parses it, and translates it into an optimized expression of relational database operators that is passed to the query executor.

Locks can be set by any or all layers of a data manager that conforms to this SQL database architecture. For example, the page-oriented file layer could set locks on pages, the record-oriented layer could set locks on individual records, and the query executor or query optimizer layer could set locks on tables or columns of tables. The choice is a tradeoff between the amount of concurrency needed, the overhead of locking operations, and the software complexity arising from the combination of locks that are used. We will explore this choice in some detail throughout the chapter. But first, let's take a high level view of the main tradeoff: concurrency versus locking overhead.

Granularity

The size of data items that the data manager locks is called the **locking granularity**. The data manager could lock at a coarse granularity such as files, at a fine granularity such as records or fields, or at an intermediate granularity such as pages. Each approach has its benefits and liabilities.

If it locks at a coarse granularity, the data manager doesn't have to set many locks, because each lock covers so much data. Thus, the overhead of setting and releasing locks is low. However, by locking large chunks of data, the data manager usually is locking more data than a transaction needs to access. For example, with file granularity locking, even if a transaction T accesses only a few records of a file, the data manager will lock the whole file, thereby preventing other transactions from locking any other records of the file, most of which are not accessed by transaction T. This reduces the number of transactions that can run concurrently, which both reduces the throughput and increases the response time of transactions.

If it locks at a fine granularity, the data manager locks only the specific data actually accessed by a transaction. These locks don't artificially interfere with other transactions, as coarse grain locks do. However, the data manager must now lock every piece of data accessed by a transaction, which can generate a lot of locking overhead. For example, if a transaction issues an SQL query that accesses tens of thousands of records, a data manager that does record granularity locking would set tens of thousands of locks, which can be quite costly. In addition to the record locks, locks on associated indexes also are needed, which compounds the problem.

There is a fundamental tradeoff between amount of concurrency and locking overhead, depending on the granularity of locking. Coarse-grained locking has low overhead but low concurrency. Fine-grained locking has high concurrency but high overhead.

One compromise is to lock at the file and page granularity. This gives a moderate degree of concurrency with a moderate amount of locking overhead. It works well in systems that don't need to run at high transaction rates and hence are unaffected by the reduced concurrency. It also works well in systems where transactions frequently access many records per page (such as engineering design applications), so that page locks are not artificially locking more data than transactions actually access. Another benefit is that it simplifies the recovery algorithms for Commit and Abort, as we'll see in Chapter 7. However, for high performance TP, record locking is needed, because there are too many cases where concurrent transactions need to lock different records on the same page.

Multigranularity Locking

Most data managers need to lock data at different granularities, such as file and page granularity; or database, file, and record granularity. For transactions that access a large amount of data, the data manager locks coarse grain units, such as files or tables. For transactions that access a small amount of data, it locks fine grain units, such as pages or records.

The trick to this approach is in detecting conflicts between transactions that set conflicting locks at different granularity, such as one transaction that locks a file and another transaction that locks pages in the file. This requires special treatment, because the lock manager has no idea that locks at different granularities might conflict. For example, it treats a lock on a file and a lock on a page in that file as two completely independent locks and therefore would grant write locks on them by two different transactions. The lock manager doesn't recognize that these locks "logically" conflict.

The technique used for coping with different locking granularities is called **multigranularity locking**. In this approach, transactions set ordinary locks at a fine granularity and **intention locks** at coarse granularity. For example, before read-locking a page, a transaction sets an intention-read lock on the file that contains the page. Each coarse grain intention lock warns other transactions that lock at coarse granularity about potential conflicts with fine grain locks. For example, an intention-read lock on the file warns other transactions not to write-lock the file, because some transaction has a read lock on a page in the file. Details of this approach are described in Section 6.10.

There is some guesswork involved in choosing the right locking granularity for a transaction. For example, a data manager may start locking individual records accessed by a transaction, but after the transaction has accessed hundreds of records, the data manager may conclude that a coarser granularity would work better. This is called lock **escalation** and is commonly supported by database systems. An alternative to lock escalation is program analysis, where the query language compiler estimates how much data will be accessed by a transaction. If it estimates that a lot of data will be accessed, then it generates a hint to lock at coarse granularity. Otherwise, it generates a hint to lock at fine granularity.

Some data managers give the transactions the option of overriding the mechanism that automatically determines lock granularity. For example, in Microsoft SQL Server, a transaction can use the keyword PAGLOCK to insist that the system use a page lock when it would otherwise use a table lock. Similarly, it can use TABLOCK or TABLOCKX to insist that the system use a read or write lock, respectively, on a table. Similarly, in IBM DB2 UDB, you can use the LOCK TABLE statement to set a read or write lock on the entire table. Such overrides are useful when tuning an application whose performance is lacking due to inappropriate automatic selection of lock granularity by the system.

6.3 DEADLOCKS

When two or more transactions are competing for the same lock in conflicting modes, some of them will become blocked and have to wait for others to free their locks. Sometimes, a set of transactions are all waiting for each other; each of them is blocked and in turn is blocking other transactions. In this case, if none of the transactions can proceed unless the system intervenes, we say the transactions are **deadlocked**.

For example, reconsider transactions T_1 and T_2 that we discussed earlier in execution $E' = r_1[x]\ r_2[y]\ w_2[x]\ w_1[y]$ (see Figure 6.4). Suppose T_1 gets a read lock on x (Figure 6.4a) and then T_2 gets a read lock on y (Figure 6.4b). Now, when T_2 requests a write lock on x, it's blocked, waiting for T_1 to release its read lock (Figure 6.4c). When T_1 requests a write lock on y, it too is blocked, waiting for T_2 to release *its* read lock (Figure 6.4d). Since each transaction is waiting for the other one, neither transaction can make progress, so the transactions are deadlocked.

Deadlock is how two-phase locking detects nonserializable executions. At the time deadlock occurs, there is no possible execution order of the remaining operations that will lead to a serializable execution. In the previous example, after T_1 and T_2 have obtained their read locks, we have the partial execution $r_1[x]\ r_2[y]$. There are only two ways to complete the execution, $r_1[x]\ r_2[y]\ w_1[y]\ w_2[x]$ or $r_1[x]\ r_2[y]\ w_2[x]\ w_1[y]$, both of which are nonserializable.

Once a deadlock occurs, the only way for the deadlocked transactions to make progress is for at least one of them to give up its lock that is blocking another transaction. Once a transaction releases a lock, the two-phase locking rule says that it can't obtain any more locks. But since each transaction in a deadlock *must* obtain at least one lock (otherwise it wouldn't be blocked), by giving up a lock it is bound to break the two-phase locking rule. So there's no point in having a transaction release just one lock. The data manager might as well abort the transaction entirely. That is, the only way to break a deadlock is to abort one of the transactions involved in the deadlock.

Deadlock Prevention

In some areas of software, such as operating systems, it is appropriate to prevent deadlocks by never granting a lock request that can lead to a deadlock. For transaction processing, this is too restrictive, because it would

$r_1[x]$

Data Item	Locks Held	Locks Requested
x	T_1,read	
y		

a.

$r_1[x]\ r_2[y]$

Data Item	Locks Held	Locks Requested
x	T_1,read	
y	T_2,read	

b.

$r_1[x]\ r_2[y]\ wl_2[x]\text{-}\{\text{blocked}\}$

Data Item	Locks Held	Locks Requested
x	T_1,read	T_2,write
y	T_2,read	

c.

$r_1[x]\ r_2[y]\ wl_2[x]\text{-}\{\text{blocked}\}\ wl_1[y]\text{-}\{\text{blocked}\}$

Data Item	Locks Held	Locks Requested
x	T_1,read	T_2,write
y	T_2,read	T_1,write

d.

FIGURE 6.4

Execution Leading to a Deadlock. Each step of the execution is illustrated by the operations executed so far, with the corresponding state of the lock table below it.

overly limit concurrency. The reason is that transaction behavior is unpredictable. For example, in the execution in Figure 6.4b, once the system grants T_1's request for a read lock on x and T_2's request for a read lock on y, deadlock is unavoidable; it doesn't matter in which order T_1 and T_2 request their second lock. The only way to avoid deadlock is to delay granting T_2's request to read lock y. This is *very* restrictive. It amounts to requiring that T_1 and T_2 run serially; T_1 must get all of its locks before T_2 gets any of its locks. In this case, a serial execution of T_1 and T_2 is the only serializable execution. But usually, transactions can be interleaved a fair bit and still produce a serializable execution.

The only way to prevent deadlocks and still allow some concurrency is to exploit prior knowledge of transaction access patterns. All operating system techniques to prevent deadlock have this property. In general-purpose TP, it is inappropriate to exploit prior knowledge. It either overly restricts the way transactions are programmed (e.g., by requiring that data be accessed in a predefined order) or overly restricts concurrency (e.g., by requiring a transaction to get all of its locks before it runs). For this reason, all commercial TP products that use locking allow deadlocks to occur. That is, they allow transactions to get locks incrementally by granting each lock request as long as it doesn't conflict with an existing lock, and they detect deadlocks when they occur.

Deadlock Detection

There are two techniques that are commonly used to detect deadlocks: timeout-based detection and graph-based detection. **Timeout-based detection** guesses that a deadlock has occurred whenever a transaction has been blocked for too long. It uses a timeout period that is much larger than most transactions' execution time (e.g., 15 seconds) and aborts any transaction that is blocked longer than this amount of time. The main advantages of this approach are that it is simple and hence easy to implement, and it works in a distributed environment with no added complexity or overhead. However, it does have two disadvantages. First, it may abort transactions that aren't really deadlocked. This mistake adds delay to the transaction that is unnecessarily aborted, since it now has to restart from scratch. This sounds undesirable, but as we'll see later when we discuss locking performance, this may not be a disadvantage. Second, it may allow a deadlock to persist for too long. For example, a deadlock that occurs after one second of transaction execution will be undetected until the timeout period expires.

The alternative approach, called **graph-based detection**, explicitly tracks waiting situations and periodically checks them for deadlock. This is done by building a **waits-for** graph, whose nodes model transactions and whose edges model waiting situations. That is, if transaction T_1 is unable to get a lock because a conflicting lock is held by transaction T_2, then there is an edge $T_1{\rightarrow}T_2$, meaning T_1 *is waiting for* T_2. In general, the data manager creates an edge $T_i{\rightarrow}T_k$ whenever transaction T_i is blocked for a lock owned by transaction T_k. It deletes the edge when T_i becomes unblocked. There is a deadlock whenever the deadlock graph has a cycle, that is, a sequence of edges that loops back on itself, such as $T_1{\rightarrow}T_2{\rightarrow}T_1$ (see Figure 6.5), or $T_1{\rightarrow}T_7{\rightarrow}T_4{\rightarrow}T_2{\rightarrow}T_1$.

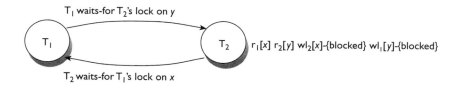

FIGURE 6.5

A Waits-For Graph. The graph on the left represents the waiting situations in the execution on the right (see also Figure 6.4). Since there is a cycle involving T_1 and T_2, they are deadlocked.

Any newly added edge in the waits-for graph could cause a cycle. So it would seem that the data manager should check for cycles (deadlocks) whenever it adds an edge. While this is certainly correct, it is also possible to check for deadlocks less frequently, such as every few seconds. A deadlock won't disappear spontaneously, so there is no harm in checking only periodically; the deadlock will still be there whenever the deadlock detector gets around to look for it. By only checking periodically, the system reduces deadlock detection cost. Like timeout-based detection, it allows some deadlocks to go undetected longer than necessary. But unlike timeout, all detected deadlocks are real deadlocks.

Victim Selection

After a deadlock has been detected using graph-based detection, one of the transactions in the cycle must be aborted. This is called the **victim**. Like all transactions in the deadlock cycle, the victim is blocked. It finds out that it is the victim by receiving an error return code from the operation that was blocked, which says "you have been aborted." It's now up to the application that issued the operation to decide what to do next. Usually, it just restarts the transaction from the beginning, possibly after a short artificial delay to give the other transactions in the cycle time to finish, so they don't all deadlock again.

There are many victim selection criteria that the deadlock detector can use. It could choose the one in the deadlock cycle that:

1. Closed the deadlock cycle: This may be the easiest to identify and is fair in the sense that it is the transaction that actually caused the deadlock.
2. Has the fewest number of locks: This is a measure of how much work the transaction did. Choose the transaction that did the least amount of work.
3. Generated the least amount of log records: Since a transaction generates a log record for each update it performs (to be discussed at length in Chapter 7), this transaction is probably the cheapest to abort.
4. Has the fewest number of write locks: This is another way of selecting the transaction that is probably cheapest to abort.

Instead of the deadlock detector choosing a victim, the application itself can choose one. For example, Oracle Database backs out the statement that caused the deadlock to be detected and returns an error, thereby leaving it up to the application to choose whether to abort this transaction or another one.[4]

Some systems allow the transaction to influence victim selection. For example, in Microsoft SQL Server, a transaction can say "SET DEADLOCK_PRIORITY LOW" or "SET DEADLOCK_PRIORITY NORMAL." If one or more transactions in a deadlock cycle have priority LOW, one of them will be selected as victim. Among those whose priority makes them eligible to be the victim, the system selects the one that is cheapest to abort.

One consideration in victim selection is to avoid **cyclic restart**, where transactions are continually restarted due to deadlocks and thereby prevented from completing. One way this could happen is if the oldest transaction is always selected as victim. For example, suppose T_1 starts running, then T_2 starts, then T_1 and T_2 deadlock. Since T_1 is older, it's the victim. It aborts and restarts. Shortly thereafter, T_1 and T_2 deadlock again, but this time T_2 is older (since T_1 restarted after T_2), so T_2 is the victim. T_2 aborts and restarts and subsequently deadlocks again with T_1. And so on.

One way to avoid cyclic restart is to select the youngest transaction as victim. This ensures that the oldest transaction in the system is never restarted due to deadlock. A transaction might still be repeatedly restarted due to bad luck—if it's always the youngest transaction in the cycle—but this is very unlikely.

---

[4]In *Oracle Database Concepts*,11g Release 1 (11.1), Part Number B28318-05, Chapter 13, "Data Concurrency and Consistency."

The problem can be avoided entirely if the transaction is given the same start time each time it is restarted, so that it will eventually be the oldest in the system. But this requires that the data manager accept the start-time as an input parameter to the Start operation, which few data managers support.

In the end, the application or transactional middleware usually provides the solution by tracking the number of times a transaction is restarted. An application error is reported if a transaction is restarted too many times, whether for deadlock or other reasons, at which point it is an application debugging or tuning problem to determine why the transaction is deadlocking so often.

Distributed Deadlock Detection

In practice many systems use multiple databases. They are introduced for many reasons, for example, to scale up the system, to separate data belonging to different applications, to simplify debugging and maintenance, or to add an application that requires a different data manager product. A system that uses multiple databases is likely to need distributed transactions.

In a distributed system, there are multiple data managers on different nodes of the network. A transaction may access data at more than one data manager. Data managers set locks in the usual way, as if the transaction were not distributed. That is, when a transaction accesses a data item at a data manager, the data manager sets the appropriate lock before performing the access.

As in the nondistributed case, sometimes a lock request becomes blocked. These blocking situations can exist at multiple data managers, which can lead to a deadlock that spans data managers yet is not detectable by any one data manager by itself. For example, let's reconsider our favorite transactions T_1 and T_2, and suppose x and y are stored at different data managers, DM_x and DM_y (see Figure 6.6). T_1 reads x at DM_x, setting a read lock, and T_2 reads y at DM_y, setting a read lock. Now, as before, T_1 tries to set a write lock on y at DM_y but is blocked waiting for T_2, and T_2 tries to set a write lock x at DM_x but is blocked waiting for T_1. This is the same deadlock we observed in Figure 6.4 and Figure 6.5; T_1 is waiting for T_2 at DM_y and T_2 is waiting for T_1 at DM_x. However, neither DM_x nor DM_y alone can see the deadlock. They each just see one waiting situation.

Dozens of algorithms to detect distributed deadlocks have been published by database researchers over the years, but only a few are used in practice. One simple technique is to designate one data manager D as the distributed deadlock detector and have every other data manager periodically send its waits-for graph to D. D has a complete view of waits-for situations across all nodes and can therefore detect distributed deadlocks. This can work well for a set of data managers from a single vendor that are executing on machines that have a high speed interconnect. However, in a more heterogeneous system, this requires more cooperation between data managers than one can reasonably expect. And if communication speeds are slow, frequent exchange of deadlock graphs may be impractical.

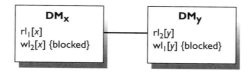

FIGURE 6.6

A Distributed Deadlock. DM_x and DM_y are independent data managers, perhaps at different nodes of the network. At DM_x, T_2 is waiting for T_1, which is waiting for T_2 at DM_y. The transactions are deadlocked, but neither DM_x nor DM_y alone can recognize this fact.

The most popular approach for detecting distributed deadlocks is even simpler, namely, timeout-based detection. The implementation is trivial, it works in heterogeneous systems, and it is unaffected by slow communications (except to select an appropriate timeout period). Moreover, it performs surprisingly well. We will see why in the next section.

6.4 PERFORMANCE

Locking performance is almost exclusively affected by delays due to blocking, not due to deadlocks. Deadlocks are rare. Typically, fewer than 1% of transactions are involved in a deadlock.

One practical reason why deadlocks are rare is that they can have very bad consequences, so database administrators (DBAs) work hard to avoid them. In a poorly constructed system, a deadlock can cause a user's job to sit there for minutes. If too many deadlocks occur, an entire database can be rendered unusable. So DBAs quickly find out about common deadlocks and minimize their frequency of occurrence.

Lock Conversions

One situation that can lead to many deadlocks is lock conversions. **A lock conversion** is a request to upgrade a read lock to a write lock. This occurs when a transaction reads a data item, say x, and later decides to write it, a rather common situation. If two transactions do this concurrently, they will deadlock; each holds a read lock on x and requests a conversion to a write lock, which can't be granted. Notice that it is not safe for a transaction to release its read lock before upgrading it to a write lock, since that would break two-phase locking.

This problem can be prevented if each transaction gets a write lock to begin with and then downgrades it to a read lock if the transaction decides not to write the item. This can be done, provided that the transaction is programmed in a relatively high-level language, such as SQL. To see how, consider a SQL Update statement, which updates the subset of rows in a table that satisfies the predicate in the statement's WHERE clause. A naïve implementation would scan all the rows of the table. For each row, it sets a read lock, checks whether the row satisfies the WHERE clause, and if so, converts the read lock to a write lock and updates the row. To avoid the possible lock conversion deadlock in the last step, it could instead work as follows: For each row, it sets a write lock, checks whether the row satisfies the WHERE clause; if so, it updates the row and if not, it converts the write lock to a read lock.

Downgrading the write lock to a read lock looks like it might be breaking two-phase locking, since reducing the strength of the lock is much like releasing the lock. Ordinarily, two-phase locking would disallow this, but here, since the transaction only reads the row, it's safe: The transaction first sets a write lock, in case it needs that lock later to avoid a deadlock. Once it realizes it will not write the row, it knows that it only needed a read lock, so it downgrades to a read lock.

The approach can be approximated even if the transaction is programmed in a lower level language, where updates are performed by first reading a data item and then later issuing a write operation. However, in this case, the transaction needs to give an explicit hint in the read operation that a write lock is required. Downgrading the lock to a read lock would require another hint; or it may not be done, at the expense of reduced concurrency.

Although getting write locks early can reduce concurrency, the overall performance effect is beneficial since it prevents a likely deadlock. Therefore, many commercial SQL data managers use this approach.

One can improve concurrency somewhat by adding an **update lock mode**. An update lock conflicts with update locks and write locks, but not with read locks. In this approach, when a transaction accesses a data item that it may later update, it sets an update lock instead of a write lock. If it decides to update the data item, it converts the update lock to a write lock. This lock conversion can't lead to a lock conversion deadlock, because at most one transaction can have an update lock on the data item. (Two transactions must try to convert the lock at the same time to create a lock conversion deadlock.) On the other hand, the benefit of this approach is that an update lock does not block other transactions that read without expecting to update later on. The weakness is that the request to convert the update lock to a write lock may be delayed by other read locks. If a large number of data items are read and only a few of them are updated, the tradeoff is worthwhile. This approach is used in Microsoft SQL Server. SQL Server also allows update locks to be obtained in a SELECT (i.e., read) statement, but in this case, it will not downgrade the update locks to read locks, since it doesn't know when it is safe to do so.

Lock Thrashing

By reducing the frequency of lock conversion deadlocks, we have dispensed with deadlock as a major performance consideration, so we are left with blocking situations. Blocking affects performance in a rather dramatic way. Until lock usage reaches a saturation point, it introduces only modest delays—significant, but not a serious problem. At some point, when too many transactions request locks, a large number of transactions suddenly become blocked, and few transactions can make progress. Thus, transaction throughput stops growing. Surprisingly, if enough transactions are initiated, throughput actually decreases. This is called **lock thrashing** (see Figure 6.7). The main issue in locking performance is to maximize throughput without reaching the point where thrashing occurs.

One way to understand lock thrashing is to consider the effect of slowly increasing the **transaction load**, which is measured by the number of active transactions. When the system is idle, the first transaction to run cannot block due to locks, because it's the only one requesting locks. As the number of active transactions grows, each successive transaction has a higher probability of becoming blocked due to transactions already running. When the number of active transactions is high enough, the next transaction to be started has virtually no chance of running to completion without blocking for some lock. Worse, it probably will get some locks before encountering one that blocks it, and these locks contribute to the likelihood that other active transactions will become blocked. So, not only does it not contribute to increased throughput, but by getting some locks that block other transactions, it actually reduces throughput. This leads to thrashing, where increasing the workload decreases the throughput.

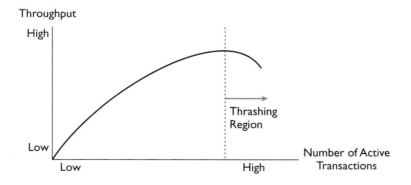

FIGURE 6.7

Lock Thrashing. When the number of active transactions gets too high, many transactions suddenly become blocked, and few transactions can make progress.

There are many techniques open to designers of data managers, databases, and applications to minimize blocking. However, even when all the best techniques are applied, if the transaction load is pushed high enough, lock thrashing can occur, provided other system bottlenecks (such as disk or communications bandwidth) don't appear first.

Tuning to Reduce Lock Contention

Suppose a transaction holds a write-lock L for t seconds. Then the maximum transaction rate for transactions that set L is $1/t$ (i.e., one transaction per t seconds). To increase the transaction rate, we need to make t smaller. Thus, most techniques for minimizing blocking attempt to reduce the time a transaction holds its locks.

One approach is to set lock L later in the transaction's execution, by accessing L's data later. Since a transaction releases its locks when it completes, the later in its execution that it sets a lock, the less time it holds the lock. This may require rearranging application logic, such as storing an update in a local variable and only applying it to the database just before committing the transaction.

A second approach is to reduce the transaction's execution time. If a transaction executes faster, it completes sooner, and therefore holds its locks for a shorter period. There are several ways to reduce transaction execution time:

- Reduce the number of instructions it executes, called its **path length**.
- Buffer data effectively, so a transaction rarely has to read from disk. If data must be read from disk, do the disk I/O before setting the lock, to reduce the lock holding time.
- Optimize the use of other resources, such as communications, to reduce transaction execution time.

A third approach is to split the transaction into two or more shorter transactions. This reduces lock holding time, but it also loses the all-or-nothing property of the transaction, thereby requiring one of the techniques for multitransaction business processes discussed in Chapter 5. This can complicate the application design, but it's the price to be paid for reduced lock contention. For example, instead of one all-or-nothing transaction, there are now two transactions; there needs to be recovery code for the case where the first one succeeds and the second one doesn't, something that wasn't required when there was just one transaction.

Recall that lock granularity affects locking performance. One can reduce conflicts by moving to finer granularity locks. Usually, one relies on the data manager to do this, but there are cases where a database or application designer can affect granularity. For example, suppose a data manager uses record granularity locking. Consider a file that has some frequently updated fields, called **hot** fields, and other infrequently updated ones, called **cold** fields. In this case, it may be worth splitting the file "vertically" into two files, where each record is split in half, with its hot fields in one file and its cold fields in the other. For example, the file may contain information about customer accounts, and we split it with customer number, name, and balance (the hot field) in one file, and customer number, address, and phone number (the cold fields) in the other (see Figure 6.8). Note that customer number, the key, must appear in both files to link the two halves of each record.[5] Before splitting the file, transactions that used the cold fields but not the hot one were delayed by locks held by transactions accessing the hot field. After splitting the file, such conflicts do not arise.

In this example, even though the name field is not frequently updated, it is included with the hot field balance because in this hypothetical application name and balance are usually accessed together by the same transaction. If name were included with the cold fields address and phone number, then a transaction that updates a balance would have to set a read lock on the cold half of the record, which would increase locking overhead and data access cost.

---

[5]In a relational database system, you could make the original table available as a view of the partitioned tables. This avoids rewriting existing programs and offers more convenient access to a transaction that requires both hot and cold fields.

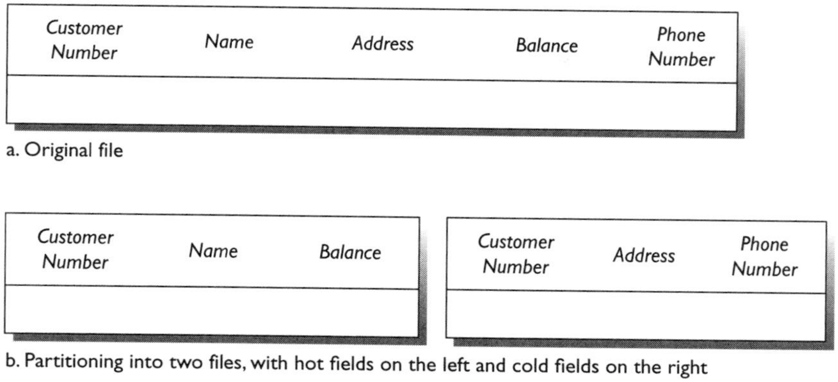

a. Original file

b. Partitioning into two files, with hot fields on the left and cold fields on the right

FIGURE 6.8

Splitting Hot and Cold Fields to Avoid Contention. By moving the cold fields, Address and Phone Number, into a separate file, accesses to those fields aren't delayed by locks on the hot fields, Name and Balance, which are now in a separate file.

When a running system is on the verge of thrashing due to too much blocking, the main way to control the problem is to reduce the transaction load. This is relatively straightforward to do: reduce the maximum number of threads allowed by each data manager. One good measure for determining that the system is close to thrashing is the fraction of active transactions that are blocked. Various studies have shown that a value of about 30% is the point at which thrashing starts to occur. This fraction is available in most systems, which expose the number of active and blocked transactions.

Recall that detecting deadlocks by timeout can make mistakes by aborting transactions that are not really deadlocked. However, if a transaction is blocked for a long time, this suggests that the transaction load is too high, so aborting blocked transactions may be good to do. Of course, to get the full benefit of this load reduction, the aborted transaction should not be immediately restarted, which would keep the transaction load at too high a level. But even if it is restarted immediately, aborting it may have a positive effect by unblocking some transactions that are waiting for the aborted transaction's locks.

Some impractical locking policies are useful to understand, because they provide insight on how locking performance is affected by certain factors. One such policy is **conservative locking**: after a transaction executes the Start operation, it waits until it can set all the locks it needs, at which point it sets all the locks at once. Since blocked transactions hold no locks, this increases the transaction load that can be handled, which is good. However, the approach is impractical for two reasons: First, a transaction must know exactly which locks it needs before it starts. Since it ordinarily does not know this, it would be compelled to set all the locks that it *might* need, typically a much larger set than the exact set it *does* need, which thereby increases lock contention. Second, a transaction may have to try to acquire all its locks many times before it gets all of them, so each attempt to get all its locks must be practically free, which it is not.

Another interesting impractical locking approach is the **pure restart policy**. In this approach, transactions never wait. Rather, if a transaction requests a lock that conflicts with one that is already set, it aborts and waits until the conflicting lock is released before it restarts. If aborts are cheap and there is no contention for other resources (besides locks), a pure restart policy can sustain a higher transaction load than a standard blocking policy (where transactions wait for conflicting locks to be released). Of course, aborts do have a cost and often other resources are in limited supply, which is why the blocking policy is normally used in practice. However, as we'll see in Section 6.8, there is a practical case where a pure restart policy is preferable.

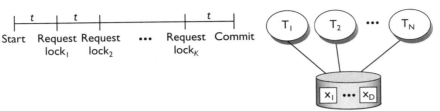

Transaction Model
- K lock requests per transaction
- t seconds average time between lock requests

System Model
- N transactions accessing the database
- D data items in the database

FIGURE 6.9

Mathematical Model of Transactions and System. Using this model, formulas can be derived for probability of conflict and deadlock, and for throughput.

Several other practical approaches to improving locking performance are described in later sections of this chapter: Section 6.5, on hot spot techniques; Section 6.6, on techniques for mixed loads of queries and updates, such as weaker degrees of isolation and multiversion data; and Section 6.8, on optimistic concurrency control.

A Mathematical Model of Locking Performance

Some fairly deep mathematics has been applied to locking performance. Although it isn't necessary to understand the math to know how to reduce lock contention, the math does produce formulas that help explain the observed phenomena. Some of the key formulas can be explained using a fairly simple model, which we describe here. The model can be used to estimate the probability of conflicts and deadlock when designing transactions. Using it in a five-minute calculation can save you a lot of trouble.

In the model each transaction issues requests for K write locks with an average time t between lock requests. The overall database has D data items that can be locked, and there are N transactions running at any given time (see Figure 6.9).

Since each transaction requests K write locks, at any given time each running transaction has $K/2$ write locks on average. Therefore, on average there are $NK/2$ locks held by the system at any given time. When a transaction requests a new lock, if it makes a random selection among the D lockable data items, then the probability it conflicts with an existing lock is $(NK/2)/D$, or $NK/2D$. Since each transaction makes K lock requests, the probability it encounters a conflict sometime during its execution is K times the probability of a conflict, which is $K \times NK/2D$, or $NK^2/2D$.

The probability that two transactions deadlock is the probability that a transaction T_1 is blocked (i.e., $NK^2/2D$) times the probability that another transaction T_2 is blocked waiting for T_1. Since there are N transactions in the system and T_2 is equally likely to conflict with any of them, the probability that T_2 is blocked waiting for T_1 is the probability that T_2 is blocked (i.e., $NK^2/2D$) divided by $N - 1$. To simplify the formula, we'll assume N is large enough that we can use N instead of $N - 1$. So the probability of a deadlock involving two transactions is:

$$(NK^2/2D) \times (NK^2/2D)/N = (N^2 K^4/4D^2)/N = NK^4/4D^2$$

The probability of deadlock cycles that involve three or more transactions is so much smaller than for two transactions that it can be ignored without losing much accuracy. Therefore, dropping the constants, we can summarize the preceding analysis as follows:

- The probability of a conflict is proportional to K^2N/D
- The probability of a deadlock is proportional to K^4N/D^2

Since a typical application might have a K of 20 (for an average transaction) and a D of one million, you can see from the previous two formulas why deadlock is so rare relative to conflict—a deadlock is K^2/D as likely as a conflict, or only 0.0004 as likely.

Now let's look at transaction throughput. If transactions were never blocked, then the throughput would be $N/(t \times (K + 1))$, where $t \times (K + 1)$ is the transaction's execution time. For example, if N is 50 and each transaction executes for 0.5 seconds, then the throughput would be 100 transactions per second. However, at any given time some fraction of transactions are blocked and therefore are not contributing to system throughput. We can estimate that fraction by the probability that a transaction encounters a conflict ($K^2N/2D$) times the fraction of its total execution time (including blocked time) that it spends waiting if it encounters a conflict. Let's use A to denote the latter. Thus, we have the following:

The throughput is proportional to $(N/tt) \times (1 - AK^2N/2D)$, where

- $tt = t \times (K + 1)$ is the transaction's execution time assuming it is never blocked
- A = fraction of total transaction execution time (including blocked time) that a transaction spends waiting given that it encounters a conflict, typically 1/3 to 1/2

Looking at throughput, we see that using finer grain locks increases D, which decreases K^2N/D, thereby increasing throughput (assuming that transactions are really accessing fine-grained data, so that K is unaffected by decreasing lock granularity). Shortening transaction execution time decreases tt, which increases N/tt, and hence increases throughput.

6.5 HOT SPOTS

Even when a system locks fine-grained data items, some of those data items are so frequently updated that they become locking bottlenecks. Such data items are called **hot spots** (i.e., they are so frequently accessed that the data metaphorically "gets hot"). Some common kinds of hot spots are:

- Summary information, such as the amount of money in a bank branch, since every debit and credit transaction needs to update that value
- The end-of-file marker in a file being used primarily for data entry, since each insert operation moves (i.e., updates) the end-of-file marker and therefore needs to lock it
- The next serial number to be sequentially assigned, such as order number or transaction number, since many transaction types need to assign such serial numbers

In these cases, the hot spot is already a fine-grained data item, so moving to a finer granularity to relieve the bottleneck is not an option. Other techniques are needed.

There are four main techniques to relieve hot spot bottlenecks:

1. Keep the hot data in main memory. Since accesses to main memory are fast, the transaction accessing the hot data will hopefully execute quickly and therefore not hold onto its lock for too long.

2. Delay operations on the hot spot until just before the transaction commits. That way, the transaction holds its lock on the hot data for the minimum amount of time.
3. Replace read operations by verification operations that can be delayed until just before the transaction commits.
4. Group operations into private batches and apply the batch to the hot spot data only periodically.

Often, these techniques are used in combination.

The first technique is relatively automatic. Since the data is hot, the data manager's cache management algorithm will probably keep the data in main memory without any special attention. Still, some systems make a special point of nailing down hot data in main memory, so it can't be paged out even if it hasn't been accessed in awhile.

Delaying Operations Until Commit

The second technique can be implemented by carefully programming a transaction so that its updates come at the end. One can automate this approach. Instead of executing operations on data items when they occur, the data manager simply writes a description of each operation in a log.[6] After the transaction is finished and ready to start committing, the data manager actually executes the operations in the transaction's log. The data manager gets locks for the operations only during this actual execution. Since this execution is at the very end of the transaction, the lock holding time will be quite short.

For example, consider a data entry application that is adding records to the end of a file. Each transaction must lock the end-of-file marker from the time it starts its insertion until after it commits. Since every transaction is adding a record, the end-of-file marker is likely to be a lock bottleneck. One can avoid this problem by delaying record insertions until the transaction is ready to commit, thereby reducing the lock holding time on the end-of-file marker. This technique is used in IBM's IMS Fast Path system for data that is declared to be a Data Entry database.

One problem with this technique is read operations. A transaction program usually cannot delay read operations until the end, because the values it reads affect its execution—it affects the values it writes and it affects its control flow via if-statements and the like. For any read operation that must be executed when it is issued (and not delayed until the end of the transaction's execution), the data manager must set a read lock. This is a problem if the read lock is set on a hot spot.

Optimistic Methods

One way to circumvent this problem of read operations is to build reads into higher level operations that don't return data item values to the calling program. For example, consider an operation Decrement(x), which subtracts one from data item x. To decrement x, the operation needs to read the current value of x, but it need not return that value to the caller. It therefore can be deferred until the transaction is ready to commit. However, suppose instead that Decrement(x) subtracts one from x only if x is positive, and it returns True or False to indicate whether or not it actually subtracted one from x. Since Decrement returns a value to its caller, it cannot be deferred. Unfortunately, like the second version of Decrement, many hot spot operations need to return a value and therefore cannot be deferred.

To circumvent the problem of deferring operations that return a value, we need to be a little more devious. Instead of simply deferring the operation until commit, the data manager executes the operation twice: first,

---

[6]This log is local to the transaction. It is unrelated to the shared recovery log to be discussed at length in Chapter 7.

```
void OptimisticTransaction;
  { Start;
     .
     .
     .
     b = Decrement(x) ◄─── System logs "Decrement(x)" and the value returned
     .
     .
     .
     Commit; ◄──────────── System replays the log. If "Decrement(x)" returns a different
                           value than was previously logged, then abort else commit
  }
```

FIGURE 6.10

Using a Decrement Operation with Optimistic Locking. No locks are set when Decrement(*x*) first executes. During the replay of Decrement(*x*), the system sets locks, but aborts if the result Decrement(*x*) changed since the original execution.

when it is initially issued by the application and second, as a deferred operation at commit time (see Figure 6.10). During the operation's first execution, the data manager logs the value returned by the operation along with the operation itself, discards any updates that the operation performs, and releases its lock at the end of the operation. At commit time, the data manager reacquires the necessary lock, executes the logged operation again, but this time it allows the updates to be installed and holds the lock until the transaction is done. In addition, it checks that the operation returns the same value v at commit time as it did initially, by comparing the logged value to v; if they're not the same, it aborts the transaction.

Let's apply this technique to the previous example. If Decrement(*x*) returns True during the first execution of the operation, then its update is thrown out and True is logged, but no lock is held on x. (In terms of the previous paragraph $v = $ True.) When Decrement(*x*) is re-executed at commit time, it sets and holds a lock, its update (if it makes one) is allowed to be installed, and the value returned by Decrement at commit time is compared to the logged value True. If they are different, the transaction is aborted. The reason they could be different is that other transactions decremented x between this transaction's two Decrement operations. The first Decrement executed when x is greater than zero, but by the time the second Decrement executes x equals zero.

To see why this works, consider what happens if the data manager actually sets a lock on the data during the first execution. Then of course the operation would return the same value during the initial and deferred executions, since the data that the operation is reading couldn't change during that period. Instead of setting a lock, the data manager simply checks at commit time that the operation returns the same value, which effectively checks that the execution behaves as if the lock were held.

The reason why this helps is that it allows concurrent conflicting operations on the hot spot data since the data isn't locked during its initial execution. That is, for a given transaction, the value of the data read by the operation can change between its two executions of Decrement, as long as that change doesn't affect the value returned by the operation. For example, suppose a transaction T_1 issues Decrement(*x*) and that when Decrement(*x*) executes the first time, $x = 2$, so it returns True. Suppose that before T_1 commits, another transaction T_2 decrements x and commits. Therefore, when T_1 issues its commit operation, $x = 1$. But that's all right. At commit time, T_1's re-execution of Decrement(*x*) decrements x to zero and returns True, which is the same value that it returned during its first execution. Notice that T_1 and T_2 executed concurrently, even though they both updated x. If they had used ordinary locking, one of them would have been delayed until the other one committed and released its lock.

To illustrate a case where an abort occurs, suppose that initially $x = 1$ instead of $x = 2$. So T_1 executes Decrement(*x*) and returns True. Then T_2 decrements x and commits (before T_1 commits). Then when T_1 re-executes

Decrement(x) at commit time, $x = 0$, so it returns False, which is different than what it returned during its first execution, so T_1 aborts and needs to be restarted. When T_1 is re-executed, it finds $x = 0$ during its first execution of Decrement(x) and takes appropriate action. For example, if x represents the number of available reservations, it would report that there are no more reservations available.

This technique can be effective even for operations that don't do any updates. For example, consider an operation Verify(f), where f is a predicate formula that references data items and evaluates to True or False. Like Decrement(x), this operation can be deferred until the end of the transaction by logging not only the operation, but also the value it returns (i.e., True or False). When the operation is replayed at commit time, it locks any data items it accesses, and if it evaluates to a different value than it did during normal execution, its transaction aborts.

This Verify operation can be used with a deferred Decrement that does not return a value. For example, consider an inventory application that keeps track of the number of items in stock. It can accept orders for an item until there are none in stock. So, suppose that for each inventory item i, it stores the quantity in stock, Quantity(i). A transaction that processes an order for item i should decrement Quantity(i) provided that it doesn't make Quantity(i) negative. It can do this by executing:

> EnoughAvailable = Verify(Quantity(i) $\geq$ 1)
> If EnoughAvailable then Decrement(Quantity(i)) else Print("Insufficient stock.")

The semantics here is surprisingly subtle. For example, this example works only if Decrement is deferred. This method, using a restricted form of the Verify operation, is used in IMS Fast Path in its Main Storage Databases feature.

This idea of executing an operation without setting locks, and checking that the operation is still valid at commit time, is called **optimistic concurrency control**. It is called optimistic because you have to be optimistic that the check at commit time is usually OK. If it fails, the penalty is rather high—you have to abort the whole transaction. In the previous inventory application, for example, the technique would work well only if most items are usually in stock, which is the expected case in most businesses. By contrast, two-phase locking is pessimistic, in that a transaction sets locks in anticipation of conflicts that may never arise. Other scenarios where optimistic concurrency control is useful are presented in Section 6.8.

Batching

Another technique that is used to relieve hot spots is batching. Instead of having each transaction update the hot data when it needs it, it batches its effect across a set of transactions. For example, in a data entry application, instead of appending records to the shared file in each transaction, each transaction appends the record to a local batch (one batch for each thread of executing transactions). Since each thread has a private batch, there is no lock contention for the batch. Periodically, the batch is appended to the shared file. As another example, consider the problem of assigning serial numbers. Instead of reading the latest serial number within each transaction, a batch of serial numbers is periodically set aside for each thread. The thread assigns serial numbers from its private batch until it runs out, at which time it gets another batch.

Batching is effective at relieving hot spots, but it has one disadvantage—failure handling requires extra work. For example, after a failure, the private batches of appended records must be gathered up and appended to the file. Similarly, if it's important that all serial numbers actually be used, then after a failure, unused serial numbers have to be collected and reassigned to threads. Sometimes, the application can allow the failure handling to be ignored, for example, if lost serial numbers are not important.

Partitioning

The load on a hot data item can be reduced by partitioning it. For example, if x represents the number of available reservations and is hot, it can be partitioned into x_1, x_2, and x_3, where the values of x_1, x_2, and x_3 are approximately equal and $x_1 + x_2 + x_3 = x$. Each transaction that decrements x randomly selects one of the partitions to use. Thus, instead of applying 100% of the transaction load to x, one third of the load is applied to each partition. The number of partitions is selected to be large enough so that the load on each partition doesn't create a hot spot bottleneck.

The main problem with partitioning is balancing the load among the partitions. In the previous example, we balanced the load by randomizing each transaction's selection of a partition. However, it's still possible that more transactions are applied to one partition than another. Therefore, it's possible that one partition will run out of available reservations while other partitions still have some reservations left. To ensure that a transaction is denied a reservation only if all partitions have been exhausted, the application would have to try all three partitions. So, once two of the partitions are empty, all transactions are applied to the nonexhausted partition, making it a hot spot. It therefore may be better to deny a reservation immediately, if the partition it selected is empty.

Partitioning x also has the effect of making the value of x more expensive to obtain. To read x, a transaction has to read x_1, x_2, and x_3 and calculate their sum. This isn't very burdensome, unless this value is required frequently. In that case, the read locks on x_1, x_2, and x_3 obtained by each transaction that reads x may cause a locking bottleneck with respect to the transactions that update each partition. It may be satisfactory to read the values of x_1, x_2, and x_3 in separate transactions, which would relieve the bottleneck at the expense of getting an accurate value of x. If not, then one of the techniques described in the next section is needed.

6.6 QUERY-UPDATE PROBLEMS

Another major source of concurrency bottlenecks is queries; that is, read-only requests for decision support and reporting. Queries typically run much longer than update transactions and they access a lot of data. So, if they run using two-phase locking, they often set many locks and hold those locks for a long time. This creates long, often intolerably long, delays of update transactions. There are three popular approaches to circumventing this problem: data warehousing, weaker consistency guarantees, and multiversion databases.

Data Warehousing

A simple way to avoid lock conflicts between queries and updates is to run them against different databases. To do this, one creates a **data warehouse**, which is a snapshot of data that is extracted from TP databases. Queries run against the data warehouse and updates run against the TP databases. Periodically, the contents of the data warehouse is refreshed, either by reloading it from scratch or by extracting only those values from the TP database that have changed since the last time the data warehouse was refreshed.

There are several reasons why it makes sense to use a data warehouse, in addition to relieving lock contention between queries and updates. First, when doing data analysis, it's often important that the data not be changing in between queries. For example, suppose you are trying to understand trends in customer behavior. If the database contents changes after every query you run, then you're never quite sure whether the differences you're seeing are due to changes in the query or changes in the underlying data.

Second, it's often important to run queries against data that is extracted from multiple databases. For example, you may be interested in cross-correlating information in the purchase order, inventory, and sales applications.

Often, such applications are developed independently over a long period of time, which leads to discrepancies between the data in their databases. For example, they may use different ways to encode the same information. Also, since the applications run independently, there may be operational errors that cause their databases to differ. For example, when a shipment arrives, the shipping clerk sometimes types the wrong corresponding purchase order number. For these reasons, it is common practice to transform and "scrub" TP data before putting it in the data warehouse, so that queries see a "clean" database. If queries were run against the TP data, they would see data that is untransformed and partially inconsistent, making the results less useful.

Third, it's important that a TP system has excellent, predictable response time, even under heavy load. For example, if an Internet retail store becomes a bit sluggish, the customer is likely to try a web search to find another store. However, when data analysis queries are running, excellent response time is hard to guarantee, because such queries can put a virtually unbounded load on the data manager. This scenario is avoided by running queries on a data warehouse system, where queries can slow down other queries, but not on-line transactions.

For these reasons, data warehousing is a very popular architecture. Still, there are times when queries need to run against the same database as update transactions, for example, to get an up-to-the-second view of the database. In these situations, solutions to the query-update problem are needed.

Degrees of Isolation

To avoid the query-update problem, many applications just give up on serializability for queries by using weaker locking rules. These rules, sometimes called **degrees of isolation** or **isolation levels**, are codified in the SQL standard and are therefore offered by most SQL database products.

One such rule is called **read committed** (sometimes called **Degree 2**) **isolation**. If a query executes with read committed isolation, then the data manager holds a read lock on a data item only while the query is actually reading the data. As soon as the data is read, it releases the lock.

The benefit of read committed isolation is performance. Some simulation studies of mixed workloads have shown throughput improves by a factor of three over two-phase locking. For some workloads, the performance improvement is even larger.

Read committed isolation is weaker than two-phase locking, which requires the transaction to hold read locks until it has obtained all its locks. Read committed isolation does ensure that the query only reads data that was produced by transactions that committed. That is, if an active update transaction is currently modifying a data item, the query will not be able to lock it until that **updater** (i.e., update transaction) has committed or aborted. However, it does not ensure serializability. For example, if the query reads data items x and y, and an updater is updating those data items, one possible scenario is the following:

- The query reads x and then releases its lock on x.
- Then the updater updates x and y, commits, and releases its locks.
- Then the query reads y.

The query looks like it executed before the updater on x but after the updater on y, a result that would be impossible in a serial execution.

Under read committed isolation, a transaction that reads the same data item twice might read different values for each of the read operations. This can happen because another transaction can update the data in between the two reads. For this reason, we say that read committed isolation allows **nonrepeatable reads**. It's a bit of a misnomer, since the transaction is allowed to repeat a read; it's just that it may get different values each time it executes the read.

A slightly stronger version of read committed isolation, called **cursor stability**, is offered by some SQL database systems. In SQL, the result of a query is a set of rows that is returned to a program as a **cursor**. A program can scan the result of the query by iterating over the cursor, one row at a time. Using read committed isolation, a program would obtain a read lock on the row before reading it and release the lock immediately thereafter. Using cursor stability, the program holds the read lock a little longer, until it asks to move to the next row using the SQL fetch operation. At that point, the database system first releases the lock on the current row and then acquires the lock on the next row. Thus, the row that the cursor currently identifies is stable (i.e., read locked) while the program is looking at it—hence the term, cursor stability.

Using cursor stability, a program can update the current row of the cursor without risking a race condition. Since it is holding a read lock on the row when it issues the update, the data manager can convert the read lock to a write lock. By contrast, if the program used read committed isolation, it would release its read lock on the row immediately after executing its read operation and before issuing its write operation. Thus, two programs could do this concurrently. They each read the record, then they each release their read lock, and then they each update the record, which causes one program to overwrite the other. Cursor stability avoids this outcome.

Given the performance benefits of read committed isolation, many SQL database products make it the default isolation level, so that an application must add special keywords to obtain serializable (i.e., two-phase locked) behavior. Even though the answers could be incorrect, customers don't seem to mind very much. There is no satisfactory technical explanation for this, though there is an intuitive explanation that might be true, at least for queries: Queries often produce summary results about a database. If the database is being updated frequently, then it doesn't matter that there are small discrepancies based on serializability errors, because the query result is somewhat outdated anyway, almost immediately after being presented to the user. Moreover, since this is only a summary for decision support purposes, it doesn't matter that the data isn't exactly right.

One can run queries in an even weaker locking mode, where it holds no locks at all. This is called **read uncommitted** (or **dirty read** or **Degree 1**) **isolation**. In this case, a query can perform **dirty reads**, where it reads uncommitted data—that is, data that may be wiped out when a transaction aborts. This will delay queries even less than read committed, at the cost of further inconsistencies in the values that are read.

Notice that even if queries use either read committed or read uncommitted isolation, update transactions can still use two-phase locking and can therefore be serializable with respect to each other. In this case, the database state is still consistent in the sense that it is the result of a serializable execution of transactions. It's just that queries might read inconsistent versions of that state.

Most SQL database systems offer the option of running update transactions using read committed or even read uncommitted isolation, by executing a statement to set the isolation level. Running a transaction at one of these lower isolation levels violates two-phase locking and can produce a non-serializable execution. The performance may be better, but the result may be incorrect. For example, if two transactions each read and write x (e.g., to increment x), then read committed isolation would allow both of them to read x before either of them write x. This is a non-serializable execution and is almost certainly unsatisfactory to users since it causes one of the updates to be lost.

When using degrees-of-isolation terminology, serializability often is characterized as Degree 3. This is sometimes called **repeatable reads**, because unlike cursor stability, reading a data item multiple times returns the same value since read locks are held throughout a transaction. The strongest level of isolation is called **serializable**, and it means just that: the execution of transactions must be equivalent to a serial execution. A summary of the levels is in Figure 6.11. The degree-of-isolation terminology is used inconsistently in the literature. We've glossed over many of the finer points here. A more thorough discussion of the various terms and their subtle differences appears in Berenson et al. (1995).

Most database systems allow a database administrator to set the degree of isolation per database. Database systems and transactional middleware also usually allow an application developer to override the database's degree of isolation for particular transaction programs. Some database systems allow a transaction to issue an

Degree of Isolation	ANSI SQL Term	Behavior
1	Read uncommitted	Don't set read locks
2	Read committed	Only read committed data
3	Serializable	Serializability

FIGURE 6.11

Degrees of Isolation. Degrees 1 and 2 provide less than serializable behavior, but better performance.

operation that changes its degree of isolation after it has partially executed. Some systems allow the application to discover the degree of isolation, such as .NET's System.Transactions.

Many database systems offer degrees of isolation that are less than serializable but that don't fit neatly into one of the terms of the ANSI SQL standard. For example, Microsoft SQL Server offers a locking option called READPAST. If a transaction is using read committed isolation and specifies the READPAST option in a SQL statement, then the statement will ignore write-locked rows, rather than waiting for those locks to be released. The intuition is that since the application is using read committed isolation, it isn't expecting exact results anyway. So, in some cases, it is worth avoiding the delay of waiting for write locks to be released by simply skipping over write-locked rows.

We will see other examples of weaker degrees of isolation later in the chapter.

Multiversion Data

One good technique for ensuring that queries read consistent data without slowing down the execution of updaters is **multiversion data**. With multiversion data, updates do not overwrite existing copies of data items. Instead, when an updater modifies an existing data item, it creates a new copy of that data item, called a new **version**. So, each data item consists of a sequence of versions, one version corresponding to each update that was applied to it. For example, in Figure 6.12 a data item is a row of the table, so each version is a separate row. There are three versions of employee 3, one of employee 43, and two of employee 19.

To distinguish between different versions of the same data item, each version is tagged by the unique identifier of the transaction that wrote it. Each version of a data item points to the previous version of that data item (the "previous transaction" field in Figure 6.12), so each data item has a chain of versions beginning with the most recent and going back in time. In addition, the data manager maintains a list of transaction IDs of transactions that have committed, called the **commit list**.

Update transactions use two-phase locking and ignore old versions. They therefore behave as if the database has only one version of each data item. That is, when an updater reads a data item x, it sets a read lock on x and reads the latest version of x. When it writes x for the first time, it sets a write lock on x and adds a new version of x. If it writes x again, it simply overwrites the new version that it previously created. Commit and abort work in the usual way. Since update transactions use two-phase locking, they are serializable.

The interesting capability of multiversion data is **snapshot mode**, which allows a query to avoid setting locks and thereby avoid locking delays. When a query executes in snapshot mode, the data manager starts by reading the current state of the commit list and associating it with the query for the query's whole execution. Whenever the query asks to read a data item, say x, the data manager selects the latest version of x that is

Transaction Identifier	Previous Transaction	Employee Number	Name	Department	Salary
174	null	3	Tom	Hat	$20,000
21156	174	3	Tom	Toy	$20,000
21159	21156	3	Tom	Toy	$24,000
21687	null	43	Dick	Finance	$40,000
10899	null	19	Harry	Appliance	$27,000
21687	10899	19	Harry	Computer	$42,000

FIGURE 6.12

An Example Multiversion Database. Each transaction creates a new version of each row that it updates.

tagged by a transaction ID on the query's commit list. This is the last version of x that was committed before the query started executing. There is no need to lock this data because it can't change. An updater will only create new versions and never modify an existing version.

When a query executes in snapshot mode, it is effectively reading the state of the database that existed at the time it started running. Thus, it reads a consistent database state. Any updates that execute after the query started running are issued by transactions that are not on the query's commit list. These updates will be ignored by the data manager when it executes reads on behalf of the query. So although the query reads a consistent database state, that state becomes increasingly out-of-date while it is running.

A popular variation of this technique is **snapshot isolation**, where an update transaction does not use two-phase locking. Instead, it executes reads using snapshot mode and executes writes without setting locks. When an update transaction T commits, the data manager checks that T's updates are still valid. To do this, it checks whether any data that T updated was also updated by another transaction T' that committed while T was running. If so, then T aborts, otherwise it commits. For example, suppose T updated x and while T was running T' also updated x. This is a problem because neither T nor T' read the other transaction's update to x. When T tries to commit, the data manager checks T's updates. If it sees that T' also updated x and already committed, then the data manager aborts T. This is sometimes called "first committer wins," because if two concurrent transactions try to write the same data, then the first one that finishes commits while the second one aborts.

Snapshot isolation provides stronger synchronization than read committed isolation. For example, it prevents a race condition where two transactions try to increment x and both read x before either of them writes x. However, it is not serializable. For example, suppose transaction T_1 copies the value of x into y, so it reads x and then writes y. Transaction T_2 does the opposite. To copy the value of y into x, it reads y and then writes x. If T_1 and T_2 execute concurrently using snapshot isolation, they will swap the values of x and y, which is not equivalent to a serial execution of T_1 and T_2. Snapshot isolation is offered in Oracle Database, Microsoft SQL Server, and PostgreSQL.

In principle, multiversion data can be used to offer read committed isolation. When a transaction reads a data item, if the latest version of that data item currently is locked by an update transaction, then the transaction reads the previous version. The latter was surely written by a committed transaction, so this ensures read committed isolation.

There is obviously some cost in maintaining old versions of data items. However, some of that cost is unavoidable, because recently overwritten old versions are needed to undo updates when a transaction aborts. In a sense, multiversion data is making use of those old versions that are needed anyway for aborting transactions. Implementation details of transaction abort appear in the section on Database Recovery in Chapter 7.

Multiversion Implementation Details

There are two technicalities in making this type of mechanism run efficiently. A user of the mechanism need not be aware of these issues, but for completeness, we describe them here.

First, it is too inefficient to represent the entire commit list as a list of transaction IDs. We can keep the commit list short by assigning transaction IDs sequentially (e.g., using a counter to generate them) and periodically discarding a prefix of the commit list. To do this, we exploit the following observations:

1. If all active transactions have a transaction ID greater than some value, say T-Oldest, and
2. No new transaction will be assigned a transaction ID smaller than T-Oldest, and
3. For every transaction that had a transaction ID ≤ T-Oldest and aborted, its updates are wiped out from the database,
4. Then queries don't need to know about transaction IDs smaller than T-Oldest.

Therefore, the commit list needs to contain only transaction IDs greater than T-Oldest. To see why, suppose the data manager processes a read operation for a query on data item x. As usual, the data manager looks for the latest version of x that is tagged by a transaction ID on the query's commit list. If it finds such a version, it returns it, which is the standard behavior of snapshot mode. If not, then it returns the latest version v of x with transaction ID ≤ T-Oldest. This is the correct version to return because none of the versions later than T-Oldest are on the query's commit list, by (1) and (2) there will not be any other versions of x with transaction ID between that of v and T-Oldest, and by (3) version v must be committed. To keep the list short, the data manager should frequently truncate the small transaction IDs from the commit list based on the previous rule.

One can avoid using a commit list altogether by assigning sequence numbers to transactions, where the sequence numbers are consistent with the effective order in which the transactions executed. This can be done by getting a new sequence number when a transaction starts to commit, thereby ensuring that the sequence number is larger than the sequence number of every committed transaction that it conflicts with. Each version is tagged by the sequence number of the transaction that produced it. When a query starts executing in snapshot mode, instead of reading the commit list, it reads the value of the last transaction sequence number that was assigned, which becomes the sequence number for the query. When it reads a data item, it reads the version of that data item with the largest sequence number tag that is less than or equal to the query's sequence number. This type of technique is used in Oracle Database and in Microsoft SQL Server when snapshot isolation is enabled.

A second problem is that the database can become cluttered with old versions that are useless, because no query will ever read them. A version of data item x is useless if (1) it is not the latest version of x, and (2) all active queries have a commit list that contains the transaction ID of a later version of x, either explicitly or because its T-Oldest value exceeds the transaction ID of some later version of x.

In this case, no active query will read a useless version of x; they'll only read later ones. No new query will look at this version of x either, because it will use an even more up-to-date commit list, which won't include smaller transaction IDs than currently running queries. So this version of x can be discarded.

Since useless versions are harmless, they can be discarded lazily. In some implementations, old versions of a data item are collocated. In this case, when a data item is read, all its versions are brought into main memory. Therefore, when the data manager services the read operation, it can ask a background thread to scan the list of versions to determine if any of them are useless and, if so, delete them.

6.7 AVOIDING PHANTOMS

In the standard locking model that we have been using in this chapter, insert and delete operations are modeled as write operations. We don't treat them specially. However, inside the system, the data manager must be particularly careful with these operations to avoid nonserializable results.

To see the potential problem, consider the database in Figure 6.13. The Accounts table has a row for each account, including the account number, branch location, and balance in that account. The Assets table has the total balance for all accounts at each branch location. Now, suppose we execute the following sequence of operations by transactions T_1 and T_2:

1. T_1: Read Accounts 1, 2, 3.
2. T_1: Identify the Accounts rows where Location = B (i.e., 2 and 3) and calculate the sum of their balances (=150).
3. T_2: Insert a new Accounts row [4, B, 100].
4. T_2: Read the total balance for location B in Assets (returns 150).
5. T_2: Write Assets [B, 250].
6. T_2: Commit.
7. T_1: Read Assets for location B (returns 250).
8. T_1: Commit.

Transaction T_1 is auditing the accounts in location B. It first reads all the accounts in the Accounts table (step 1), adds up the balances in location B (step 2), and then looks up the Assets for location B (step 7) to make sure they match. They don't, because T_1 didn't see the Accounts row inserted by T_2, even though it did see the updated value in the Assets table for location B, which included the result of T_2's insertion.

Accounts

Account Number	Location	Balance
1	A	50
2	B	50
3	B	100

Assets

Location	Total
A	50
B	150

FIGURE 6.13

Accounts Database to Illustrate Phantoms.

This execution is not serializable. If T_1 and T_2 had executed serially, T_1 either would have seen T_2's updates to both the Accounts table and the Assets table, or it would have seen neither of them. However, in this execution, it saw T_2's update to Assets but not its update to Accounts.

The problem is the Accounts row [4, B, 100] that T_2 inserts. T_1 didn't see this row when it read the Accounts table, but did see T_2's effect on Assets that added 100 to B's total balance. The Accounts row [4, B, 100] is called a **phantom**, because it's invisible during part of T_1's execution but not all of it.

The strange thing about this execution is that it appears to be allowed by two-phase locking. In the following, we add the lock operations required by two-phase locking:

1. T_1: Lock rows 1, 2, and 3 in Accounts. Read Accounts 1, 2, 3.
2. T_1: Identify the Accounts rows where Location = B (i.e., 2 and 3) and calculate the sum of their balances (=150).
3. T_2: Insert a new Accounts row [4, B, 100] and lock it.
4. T_2: Lock location B's row in Assets. Read the total balance for location B (returns 150).
5. T_2: Write Assets [B, 250].
6. T_2: Commit and unlock location B's row in Assets and row [4, B, 100] in Accounts.
7. T_1: Lock location B's row in Assets. Read Assets for location B (returns 250).
8. T_1: Commit and unlock location B's row in Assets and rows 1, 2, and 3 in Accounts.

Is it really true that two-phase locking doesn't guarantee serializability when there are insertion operations? Fortunately not. There is some hidden behavior here that would cause an extra lock to be set and that isn't shown in the execution. It all hinges on how T_1 knew there were exactly three rows in the Accounts table. There must have been a data structure of some kind to tell it: an end-of-file marker, a count of the number of rows in the file, a list of pointers to the rows in the file, or something. Since it read that data structure to determine that it should read exactly rows 1, 2, and 3, it had to set a read lock on that data structure. Moreover, since T_2 added a row to the Accounts table, it had to lock that data structure too, in write mode, so it could update it. It would be prevented from doing so by T_1's read lock on that data structure, and thus the previous execution could not occur.

So, the phantom problem is not a problem, provided that the data manager sets locks on all shared data it touches, including system structures that it uses internally on behalf of a transaction's operation.

Performance Implications

This example brings up yet another common scenario that leads to performance problems, one that's closely related to the query-update problems we saw in the previous section. The example has one transaction, T_1, that scans a file (essentially a query), and another transaction, T_2, that inserts a row and therefore is blocked by the scan operation. Since T_1 needs to compare the values it reads in the Accounts table to the values it reads in the Assets table, it must run in a serializable way. Read committed locking isn't good enough. This means that T_1 must lock the entire table in read mode, which delays any update transaction that wants to write an existing row or insert a new one. This reduction in concurrency is bound to cause some transaction delays.

Database systems that support SQL reduce this problem somewhat by locking ranges of key values. In the example, since T_1 only wants to read rows in location B, the system would set a key-range lock on rows with "Location = B." Transaction T_2 would have to get a key-range lock on "Location = B" to insert its new row, so it would be blocked as before. But other update transactions that operate on rows in other locations would be permitted to run, because they would get key-range locks on other key ranges. That is, a key-range lock on "Location = B" does not conflict with one on "Location = A."

Key-range locking works well in SQL because the WHERE clause in SQL has clauses like "Accounts.Location = B," which gives the system a strong hint about which lock to set. In an indexed file system, such as COBOL ISAM implementations, it is much harder to do, since the operations issued by the program don't give such strong hints to the file system to figure out which key-range locks to set. For this reason, key-range locking is widely supported in SQL database systems, but not in many other kinds.

Although key-range locking is effective and relatively inexpensive, it is not free. Therefore, some systems offer a degree of isolation that guarantees serializability except for phantoms. Thus, it is in between read committed and serializable. This is called **repeatable read** in Microsoft SQL Server and in the ANSI SQL 92 standard, and **read stability** in IBM DB2 UDB.

6.8 OPTIMISTIC CONCURRENCY CONTROL

In addition to the hot spot technique described in Section 6.5, optimistic concurrency control is useful in situations where data is cached outside the data manager. For example, a client or middle-tier server may cache data that it retrieves from a data manager that resides on a remote server. In such cases, the cached data may be updated in the data manager at the remote server (e.g., by other clients) without the cache being told about it. Therefore, any transaction that reads the cached data is at risk to use out-of-date data that can lead to a nonserializable execution. As in the hot spot method, the solution is to check at commit time whether the cached data has changed in the data manager in a way that invalidates the transaction's earlier reads. If so, the transaction must abort.

One scenario where this comes up is interactive transactions, where a user is involved in looking at data before deciding whether or how to update it. Since the user may look at the data for several minutes before deciding, it is impractical to lock the data between the time it's read and the time it's updated. Therefore, the application that interacts with the user executes one transaction to read the data and later runs a second transaction to perform the user's updates. In between the two transactions, the user decides which updates to perform. Since the data isn't locked between the reads and writes, an optimistic approach can be used. Namely, the update transaction includes the values of the data items that were read earlier and on which the update depends. The update transaction checks that the values that were read still have the same values in the data manager. If so, then the transaction can perform its updates.

The effect is as if the transaction had set read locks on the data during the first read-only transaction and held them until the update transaction ran. Of course, since it didn't hold the read locks that long, the update transaction may find that some of the data items that were read have changed, and therefore the transaction must abort. In that case, the application needs to get involved by rereading the data that it read during the first transaction, displaying those new values to the user and asking the user if her previous updates are still what she wants.

For example, suppose a building contractor is accessing an on-line supplier from a web browser over the Internet. The contractor wants 20 windows of a certain size, for delivery within two weeks. He issues a request for catalog information on the appropriate type of windows. He shows the windows to his customer and, after some discussion, they select a particular window. That purchase request should include not only the part number of the window to be purchased but also the delivery date. The update transaction that runs on the supplier's server rereads the promised delivery date and compares it to the one in the request; this is to validate the earlier optimistic read of the delivery date. If the delivery date can no longer be met, the application returns an error, else it completes the purchase as requested.

Notice that it's up to the application to figure out the data items that were read earlier and on which the update depends. In the previous example, the application needs to know that the update only depends on the delivery date, not on all the other catalog information that is displayed to the contractor.

Still, under certain assumptions, it's possible for the application to figure out what data items to validate without any hints from the application. For example, in Microsoft SQL Server, a cursor (which contains the result of a SQL query) can be declared as `Optimistic With Values`. In this case, the database rows that are returned in the cursor are not read-locked. Instead, if an application updates a row in the cursor, both the old and new value of the row are sent to the database system. The system processes the update by setting a lock on the row and then checking whether the current value of the row equals the old value that was included with the update. If so, then the new value of the row is installed. If not, then the update is rejected and an exception is returned. A similar option called `Optimistic With Versions` is available, where each row is tagged by a timestamp, which is updated every time the row is modified. So, instead of sending the old value of the row with the update, only the old timestamp needs to be sent. If the timestamp has changed, then the update is rejected.

Note that this SQL Server mechanism implicitly assumes that the update to the row depends only on the previous value of the same row. If the update depended on the previous value of some other rows, then another concurrency control technique would need to be used on those other rows. For example, those rows could be read using the serializable isolation level or the application could reread those rows using serializable isolation level at the time it does the update and check that their values didn't change.

6.9 B-TREE LOCKING

All database systems use some form of index to speed up content-based retrieval of records. An index is a mapping from key values to physical location. For example, in a relational database system an index maps column values to rows; in Figure 6.13 an index on Location values in the Accounts table would map the column value "A" to the first row and "B" to the second and third rows. When a user submits a query to retrieve rows that have a given field value, such as Location = "B," the database system can use the index to access exactly the desired rows, instead of having to scan all rows of the table to find the desired ones.

First, we explain how indexes work. Then we discuss techniques to avoid the special locking bottlenecks that can arise when accessing indexes.

B+ Trees

The most popular data structure used for implementing an index in a database system is the B-tree. A **B-tree** consists of a set of pages organized as a tree. The **leaf pages** (i.e., those that don't point to other pages in the tree) contain the data being indexed, such as rows of a table. The remaining pages, called **internal nodes**, are directories of key values that are used to guide a search.

If the internal nodes contain the data that is associated with the keys, then the tree is called a B-tree. On the other hand, if the internal nodes contain *only* key values and not the associated data, then it is called a **B+ tree**. For the most part, our discussion applies to both B-trees and B+ trees. However, we will use B+ trees in all of our examples since they are more commonly used in practice.

Each page contains a sorted sequence of key values, which subdivides the range of possible key values into subranges. So, a sequence of n key values $[k_1, k_2, ..., k_n]$ creates $n + 1$ subranges: one subrange for key values less than k_1, one for key values from k_1 to k_2, ..., one for key values from k_{n-1} to k_n, and one for key values greater than or equal to k_n. Associated with each subrange is a pointer to the root of a subtree that contains all the keys in that subrange.

For example, the B+ tree in Figure 6.14 has key values that are non-negative integers. The root page, P_0, contains the sorted sequence of key values 125, 490. (In the terminology of the previous paragraph, $n = 2$.) The pointer before 125 points to the root page of a subtree that contains all the keys in the range [0, 125) (i.e., zero up to but not including 125). Similarly, the pointer between 125 and 490 points to a subtree containing the range [125, 490), and the pointer after 490 points to a subtree containing the range [490, ∞). (Only the subtree

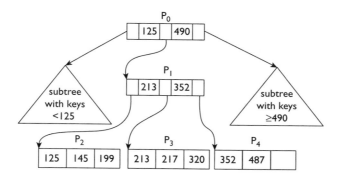

FIGURE 6.14

A B+ Tree. Page P_0 is the root and P_2, P_3, and P_4 are leaves. Each of the two triangular subtrees is an abbreviation for a combination of pages like $P_1 - P_4$.

for the range [125, 490) is shown explicitly.) Thus, the root page partitions the set of all key values into three ranges: [0, 125), [125, 490), and [490, ∞).

Below the root, each page subdivides its key range, which is defined by its parent. Looking again at the figure, we see that page P_1 subdivides the range [125, 490), which is defined by its parent, P_0. The subranges consist of [125, 213), [213, 352), and [352, 490). Notice that P_1's first subrange is [125, 213), not [0, 213), because P_1 subdivides the range [125, 490), not [0, 490). Similarly, the last subrange is [352, 490), not [352, ∞). The leaves of the tree contain the actual key values, such as 125, 145, and 199 in the leaf P_2. These key values may include the data records themselves (such as rows in the Accounts table) or pointers to those records.

To search for a given key value k, you start by examining the root page and finding the key range that contains k. You then follow the pointer associated with that key range to another page. Then repeat the process, moving down the tree. For example, to search for key value 145, you search the root and discover that range [125, 490) contains 145. So you follow the pointer to P_1. In P_1, you find that key range [125, 213) contains 145, so you follow the pointer to P_2. Searching page P_2, you find key 145. To search for key 146, you would follow the same sequence of pages. However, in that case, when reaching P_2, you would find that the page doesn't contain 146. Since this is a leaf page, there is nowhere else to look, so you would conclude that 146 is not contained in the index. Notice that in all cases, the number of pages that are read equals the number of levels of the tree, that is, one more than the number of pointers that need to be followed to get from the root to a leaf.

The B+ tree effectively sorts the keys, as you can see in the leaves P_2, P_3, and P_4 in the figure. You can therefore get all the keys in a given range by searching for the key at the low end of the range and then scanning the leaves in order until you reach the high end of the range. For example, to find all keys in the range 160 to 360, you search for key 160, which takes you to page P_2. Then you scan pages P_2, P_3, and P_4. When you reach key value 487 on P_4, which is the first key value greater than 360, you know you have found all keys in the desired range.

The B+ tree in Figure 6.14 is artificially small, so it can fit on a printed page. In practice, each B+ tree page is the size of a disk page and therefore can hold hundreds of keys. For example, if a page is 8 K bytes, a key is 8 bytes, and a pointer is 2 bytes, then a page can hold up to 819 keys; therefore, a three-level B+ tree can have up to $820^2 = 672{,}400$ leaves. If each leaf holds up to 80 records, that's over 5.3 million records in all. If the tree has four levels, then it can hold up to about 4.4 billion records. As you can see from these numbers, it's very rare for a B+ tree to have more than four levels.

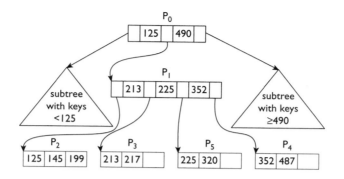

FIGURE 6.15

A B+ Tree After a Split. This shows the B+ tree of Figure 6.14 after inserting key 225, assuming P_1 can hold 3 keys and P_3 can hold 3 records.

B+ trees are intended to live on disk with a portion of them buffered in main memory. The root is always cached in main memory and usually the level below the root is cached too. Levels 3 and 4 are more problematic. How much of them are cached depends on how much memory is available and how frequently the pages are accessed; that is, whether it's worth caching them. However, even if levels 3 and 4 are not cached at all, to search for a key, only two disk pages need to be accessed. It's pretty amazing, if you think about it—you can search for a key in a file of 4 billion records and are guaranteed to find it in two disk accesses.

This great performance of a B+ tree depends on the tree being wide and flat. If the tree were thin and deep—that is, if it had many levels—then the performance would be worse. You would have to read many more pages to search from the root to a leaf. The main trick that makes the B+ tree structure so attractive is that its update algorithms are able to keep the tree wide and flat.

B+ Tree Insertions

To insert a key value into a B+ tree, you simply search for that key value. The search procedure identifies the page where that key value should be stored, so that's where you store it. For example, to insert key value 353 in Figure 6.14, the search would take you to page P_4, so you add the new record to that page.

Inserting 353 was straightforward because there was extra space on that page. What if the desired page is already full? For example, suppose each leaf can hold at most three records and you want to insert key value 225. The search procedure takes you to page P_3, which is full. In this case, you split the page in half. That is, you allocate another page, say P_5, from free space and distribute the keys of P_3 plus 225 evenly between P_3 and P_5, as shown in Figure 6.15. By adding page P_5, you have effectively split the range [213, 352) into two ranges: [213, 225) and [225, 352). This splitting of range [213, 353) must be recorded in P_3's parent, P_1, which is shown in Figure 6.15.

The split shown in Figure 6.15 assumes that there is space in P_1 to store the extra range. If there isn't enough space, then since it's full, P_1 would need to be split, just like P_3 was. The result is shown in Figure 6.16. In this case, P_1 is split into P_1 and P_6. This causes another key range to be propagated up to the root, P_0. But since the root is full, it too must be split into P_0 and P_7. Thus, a new root, P_8, needs to be added, which divides the total key range between P_0 and P_7.

Notice that the tree stays wide and flat as it grows. The technical term is "balanced." It's balanced in the sense that all leaves are the same distance from the root.

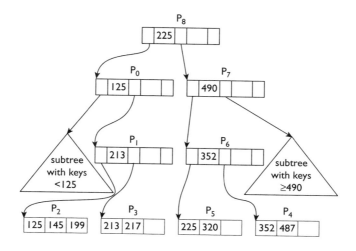

FIGURE 6.16

A B+ Tree After a Recursive Split. This shows the B+ tree of Figure 6.15, after inserting key 225, assuming internal nodes can hold at most two keys. Thus, P_1 must split into P_1 and P_6, which in turn causes P_0 to split into P_0 and P_7, which causes a new root P_8 to be created.

There are many variations of B-trees in the technical literature. The bibliographic notes provide entry points for the interested reader.

Tree Locking

Suppose a transaction is executing a search for key value k_1 in a B+ tree. The search starts by reading the root page and scanning it to find the key range that contains k_1. Since it is reading all of the root, it needs to set a read lock on the entire root page. Similarly, it needs to lock the other pages that it searches, as it travels down the tree toward the leaf that contains k_1. These read locks prevent any updates to the locked pages. If several active transactions are using the B+ tree, then large portions of the tree are read locked, which potentially blocks many update transactions.

This locking bottleneck can be avoided by exploiting the fact that all transactions traverse the B+ tree from root to leaf. Consider a simple tree consisting of a page P (the parent), child C of P, and a child G of C (G is the grandchild of P). Instead of holding read locks on all pages it touches, it is actually safe for a transaction T_i to release its read lock on P after it has set a read lock C, where C covers the key range of interest. This seems more than a little strange, since we have made such a big point in this chapter of being two-phase locked. If T_i continues searching down the tree to lock G, then T_i has broken two-phase locking—it unlocked P and later obtained a lock on G. However, in this special case of traversing a tree, breaking two-phase locking in this way is safe.

The important point is that T_i acquired its lock on C *before* releasing its lock on P. It descends through the tree much like climbing down a ladder, placing one foot firmly on the next lower rung before lifting the other foot from the higher rung. This is called **lock coupling**, or **crabbing** (by analogy to the way a crab walks). The effect is that no transaction that is obtaining conflicting locks can pass T_i on the way down, because T_i is always holding a lock on some page on the path to its final destination.

A bad case would be that some transaction T_k got a write lock on page P after T_i released its read lock on P, but got a write lock on G before T_i got its read lock on G. That would violate serializability because it would appear that T_k came after T_i with respect to P and before T_i with respect to G. But this can't happen. If T_k gets a conflicting lock on P after T_i releases its lock on P, then lock coupling ensures that T_k will follow T_i on the entire path that T_i takes down the tree.

The correctness argument earlier assumes that each transaction gets the same kind of lock on all pages. If it switches between two types of locks, then the argument breaks down. For example, if T_k sets a write lock on P, a read lock on C, and a write lock on G, then a non-serializable execution could arise as follows:

1. T_i read locks P, T_i read locks C, T_i unlocks P. (At this point, T_i has a read lock on C.)
2. T_k write locks P. (So T_k follows T_i at P.)
3. T_k read locks C. (T_i and T_k both have read locks on C.)
4. T_k unlocks P, T_k write locks G, T_k unlocks C, T_k unlocks G. (T_k arrived first at G, then finishes up.)
5. T_i read locks G. (T_i follows T_k at G.)

Since T_k follows T_i at P (step 2) and T_i follows T_k at G (step 5), the result isn't serializable. In this case, where a transaction switches between lock types, lock coupling isn't enough. A commonly used solution is to disallow transactions from getting a weaker lock when traversing down the tree.

After T_i locks the leaf page L that it's looking for, it can release its lock on L's parent. At this point, it is holding a lock on only one page, L. In terms of locking performance, this is much better than before, where T_i would have held a lock on every page on the path from the root to L. Since T_i is only locking L, update transactions can run concurrently as long as they aren't trying to update a key on L.

Insertions cause a problem for lock coupling, due to page splits. Suppose a transaction executes an insert of key value k_2 into the B+ tree. The insert begins by searching down the tree for the leaf that should contain k_2, setting read locks on pages, just like a B+ tree search. When it finds the leaf L, it sets a write lock on it, so that it can insert k_2. If L is full, then it must be split, which requires that a new key be added to L's parent. However, at this point, the transaction doesn't own a lock on L's parent. Reacquiring the lock would break the lock coupling protocol and thereby allow a non-serializable execution to occur.

One solution is to require that the insert procedure obtain write locks as it traverses down the tree. Assume it holds a lock on page P and has just acquired a lock on P's child C. At this point, it checks whether C is full. If not, then it releases its lock on P. If so, then it retains the lock on P because it may have to split C, in which case it will need to update P. This solution is rather expensive, because the insert needs to set write locks from the beginning of its search, including the root, an obvious bottleneck. An alternative solution is to search down the tree using read locks only, keeping track of which pages are full. If the desired leaf turns out to be full, then release its lock and start traversing down from the root again. This time, the insert procedure holds write locks on all the pages that need to be updated, which include the leaf L and its parent P, plus P's parent if P is full, plus P's grandparent if P's parent is full, and so on.

The B-Link Optimization

Lock coupling is a significant performance boost over two-phase locking for B+ trees. However, we can do even better by adding to the B+ tree structure a sideways link from each page to the next page at the same level in key-sequence order. For example, the sideways links in Figure 6.17 are shown as horizontal dashed lines. Notice that links are not only between siblings; that is, between pages that have a common parent. Links may also connect cousins, such as the pointer from P_7 to P_2. Thus, only the last page on each level has no sideways link; in the figure, that's P_4 on level 3, P_1 on level 2, and P_0 on level 1.

These sideways links, called **B-links**, enable the search and insert procedures to hold only one page lock at a time, which improves concurrency over lock coupling. The optimization exploits our knowledge about the kinds of updates to a B+ tree that can alter its structure, namely page splits.

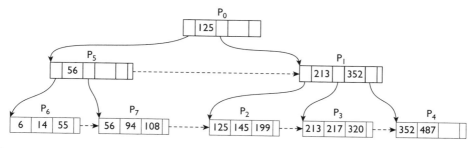

FIGURE 6.17

A B+ Tree with Sideways Pointers. Each page points to the next page at the same level in key sequence order.

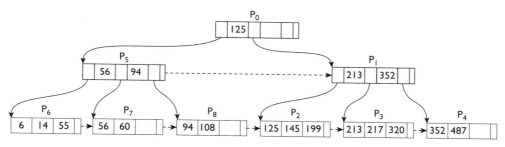

FIGURE 6.18

The B+ Tree of Figure 6.17 After Inserting 60. Page P_7 is split into P_7 and a new page P_8, links are updated, and the boundary key 94 is inserted in page P_5.

When searching down a B+ tree, the search procedure only holds a lock on one page at a time. So, for example, suppose T_1 executes a search for key 94. The search procedure begins by locking P_0, selecting the range [0, 125) as the one that contains 94, getting the associated pointer to P_5, and releasing its lock on P_0. At this point, it holds no locks. It repeats the process on P_5 by locking P_5, selecting the range [56, 125), getting the associated pointer to P_7, and releasing its lock on P_5. Finally, it locks P_7, finds the record with key 94, and releases its lock.

This search procedure looks rather dangerous, because at certain points in its execution, it is holding a pointer to a page that isn't locked. For example, after unlocking P_5, it's holding a pointer to P_7, which is not locked. What if another transaction somehow makes that pointer to P_7 invalid before the search procedure follows the pointer?

Here is where our knowledge of B+ tree behavior comes in. Assume that B+ tree pages are never deleted, which is a common practice since databases rarely shrink significantly. In that case, the only way that P_7 can change in a way that affects the search is if another transaction splits P_7. For example, suppose that when T_1's search holds a pointer to P_7 but no locks, another transaction T_2 inserts key 60 on P_7 causing P_7 to split, yielding the tree in Figure 6.18. Let's look at the split of P_7 in more detail: T_2 write locks P_7, allocates a new page P_8, copies P_7's link (to P_2) into P_8 (so P_8 points to P_2), moves records 94 and 108 from P_7 to P_8, inserts record 60 in P_7, updates P_7's link to point to P_8, and unlocks P_7. At this point, P_5 is inconsistent with P_7 and P_8, so T_2 must update P_5 to add key 94 and a pointer to P_8. However, this update of P_5 has no effect on T_1, which already read P_5 and is holding a pointer to P_7. So, now that T_2 has unlocked P_7, T_1 can push ahead and lock P_7 and read it. Of course, record 94, which T_1 is looking for, isn't in P_7 anymore. Fortunately, T_1 can figure this out. It sees that the largest key in P_7 is 60. So it's possible that record 94 got moved during a split and can be found on the next higher page. This is where the link is used. Instead of giving up after failing to find 94 in P_7, T_1 follows the link to the next higher page, looks there for key 94, and finds it.

Suppose that T_1 was looking for key 95 instead of 94. When it follows the link to P_8, and fails to find 95 on P_8, it looks for the largest key on P_8, which in this case is 108. Since 108 is larger than 95, T_1 knows that there's no point in following P_8's link to P_2, since all keys in P_2 are larger than 108.

6.10 MULTIGRANULARITY LOCKING

At the end of Section 6.2, we briefly explained how a data manager can set locks at different granularities, such as database, file, and record granularity. In this section, we expand on the details. Knowledge of these details can be helpful in understanding the performance characteristics of locking in data managers that use it.

As we explained earlier, the main problem in locking at different granularities is determining when locks at different granularities conflict. For example, if transaction T_1 owns a write lock on file F, we would like T_2 to be prevented from setting a read lock on record R in F. However, as far as the lock manager is concerned, locks on F and R are completely independent, so the lock manager would allow them both to be set.

The trick in multigranularity locking is to require that before setting a fine grain lock on a data item x, a transaction must first set a weak lock, called an **intention lock**, on every coarse grain data item that contains x. Intention locks conflict with read and write locks. In the previous example, since F contains R, T_2 would need to set an **intention read** lock on F before it tried to set a read lock on R. The intention read lock on F conflicts with T_1's write lock on F, so the lock manager recognizes the conflict and T_2 is delayed, as desired.

To know which intention locks to set for a given data item x, a data manager must know which data items contain x. This knowledge is captured in a containment hierarchy, called a **lock type graph**. For example, a simple lock type graph for a SQL database system is shown in Figure 6.19a. This graph says that each row is contained in a table, and each table is contained in a database. So, to set a lock on a row R, the data manager needs to set an intention lock on the table and database that contain R.

Locks must be set in root-to-leaf order, as defined by the lock type graph. For example, consider the **lock instance graph** in Figure 6.19b, which represents a database that conforms to the lock type graph in Figure 6.19a. To set a lock on record R_3, a transaction T_1 first would have to set an intention lock on database DB_A, then set an intention lock on table Tbl_{S2}. If T_1 disobeyed the root-to-leaf order and set a lock on R_3 before setting those intention locks, it might find that another transaction T_2 already owns a lock on Tbl_{S2} that prevents T_1 from setting the intention lock. Thus, T_1 would have a lock on R_3 and T_2 would have a lock on the table Tbl_{S2} that contains R_3, which is exactly the situation we're trying to avoid. Locking from root to leaf prevents this bad outcome.

Note that the hierarchy is only conceptual. It need not be physically stored. That is, the data manager doesn't need a data structure that represents the lock type graph. Rather, the data manager can rely on hard-coded knowledge of the graph to decide which locks to set.

Each lock type has a corresponding intention lock type. That is, there are **intention-to-write** (**iw**) and **intention-to-read** (**ir**) lock types, which correspond to the write and read lock types, respectively. Before setting a read lock on a data item x, a transaction must first set an ir lock on x's ancestors; similarly, for setting a write lock.

The lock conflict rules for intention locks are shown in Figure 6.20. To understand their meaning, consider a data item x (e.g., a table) and data items y and z that are contained by x (e.g., two rows in table x):

- r is compatible with ir, because it's alright if T_1 owns a read lock on x while T_2 owns an ir lock on x and a read lock on, say, y.

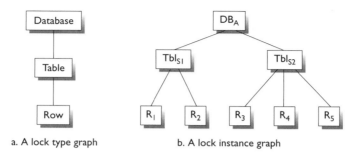

a. A lock type graph   b. A lock instance graph

FIGURE 6.19

Graph That Drives Multigranularity Locking. The lock type graph describes the hierarchy of granularity of object types that can be locked. The lock instance graph shows instances of those types.

		Lock Type Requested				
		r	w	ir	iw	riw
Lock Type Held	r	y	n	y	n	n
	w	n	n	n	n	n
	ir	y	n	y	y	y
	iw	n	n	y	y	n
	riw	n	n	y	n	n

FIGURE 6.20

Lock Type Compatibility Matrix. Each entry says whether the lock type requested can be granted given that another transaction holds the lock type held.

- r is incompatible with iw, because if T_1 owns a read lock on x, then T_2 should not be allowed to own a write lock on y. T_2's attempt to get an iw lock on x (before locking y) will conflict with T_1's read lock.

- w is incompatible with ir or iw, because if T_1 owns a write lock on x, then T_2 should not be allowed to own a read or write lock on y.

- ir and iw locks are compatible with each other, because they indicate only that finer grain locks are being held, possibly on different data items. Suppose T_1 and T_2 own an ir and iw lock on x, respectively. This means T_1 plans to own a read lock on some y contained in x and T_2 plans to own a write lock on some z contained in x. This is a problem only if $y = z$. But in that case T_1 and T_2 will conflict when they both try to lock y. It would be premature to disallow T_1 and T_2 from owning their intention locks on x since in most cases they will lock different fine grained items within x.

The lock type **read-with-intention-to-write** (**riw**) is designed for transactions that are scanning a large number of data items but updating only some of them, such as executing a SQL Update statement. Such a transaction would have to own both an r and iw lock on the same data item, such as a SQL table. It simplifies the lock manager if each transaction is allowed to hold at most one lock on each data item. Therefore, the two lock types, r and iw, are combined into one, riw. Notice that the riw lock type is compatible with another lock type lt if and only if both r and iw are compatible with lt. In Figure 6.20 only lock type ir has this property.

So far, we have treated lock instance graphs that are trees. Trees have the nice property that each data item (except the root) has exactly one parent. Often, we need to handle lock instance graphs that are directed acyclic graphs (DAGs), where a data item may be contained by two or more parents. This requires modifying the rules for setting intention locks, because setting an intention lock on a parent of a data item x does not prevent other transactions from setting a conflicting coarse grain lock on a different parent of x.

Let's look at the most common place where this arises, namely key-range locking, which we used in Section 6.7 to avoid phantoms. In key-range locking, key-range is another type of object that can be locked, as shown in the lock type graph in Figure 6.21a. If a table uses multiple keys, then each row is in multiple key ranges. For example, in Figure 6.22 suppose the Customer and Location columns are used as keys in the Accounts table. Then each row is contained in two different key ranges, one for each key. For example, Account 1 is in the Customer key range for "Eric" and the Location key range for "A." Suppose that transaction T_1 sets an iw lock on DB_A, Accounts, and the key range Customer = "Eric" and then sets a write lock on Account 1. This does not prevent another transaction T_2 from setting an ir lock on DB_A and Accounts and setting a read lock on the key range Location = "A." Since the key range Location = "A" covers the row for Account 1, this means that T_2 implicitly has a read lock on Account 1, which conflicts with T_1's explicit write lock on Account 1. This is an example of the problem described in the previous paragraph: a transaction holds an intention lock on one parent of x (i.e., on key range Customer = "Eric," which is a parent Account 1), but another transaction holds a conflicting lock on a different parent of x (i.e., key range Location = "A").

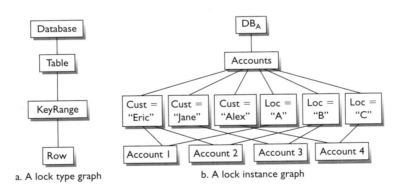

a. A lock type graph　　　b. A lock instance graph

FIGURE 6.21

A DAG That Drives Multigranularity Locking. This extends the graphs of Figure 6.19, to allow each row to have more than one parent, which in this case are key ranges.

Account Number	Customer	Location	Balance
1	Eric	A	50
2	Eric	B	50
3	Jane	B	100
4	Alex	C	75

FIGURE 6.22

Example Database. This database corresponds to the lock instance graph of Figure 6.21b.

To avoid this problem, we modify the multigranularity locking protocol for write locks. We require that to set a write lock or iw lock on an object x, a transaction must have an iw lock on *every* parent of x. In the example, this means that T_1 needs an iw lock on the two key ranges that are parents of Account 1, namely, Customer = "Eric" and Location = "A." The iw lock on Location = "A" would conflict with T_2's read lock on Location = "A." So only one of them can lock the range, thereby avoiding the situation where T_1 and T_2 own conflicting locks on Account 1.

Typically, key range locks are implemented by setting locks on physical index entries. This assumes that each lockable key corresponds to an indexed column. For example, to set a lock on Customer = "Eric," there would need to be an index on the Customer column of the Accounts table. The procedure to set the lock searches for "Eric" in the index and sets the appropriate lock on the index record for Customer = "Eric." A procedure to find the account record for "Eric" needs to look up "Eric" in the index anyway.

6.11 LOCKING NESTED TRANSACTIONS

In this section we discuss locking behavior that is needed to support the nested transaction model described in Section 2.2. Recall that nested transactions behave as follows:

1. If a program is already executing inside a transaction T and issues a Start command, then Start creates a subtransaction S of T. If the program is executing inside a subtransaction S, then Start creates a subtransaction of S. Thus, there is a "nesting hierarchy" among transactions, which can be of any depth.
2. If a program is not already executing inside a transaction and issues a Start command, then Start creates a new, independent top-level transaction, which is not a subtransaction of another transaction.
3. If a subtransaction S aborts, then all of S's operations are undone, including all its subtransactions. However, this does not cause S's parent P to abort. It simply notifies P that S aborted.
4. If a subtransaction S commits, S no longer can issue operations. S's parent is notified of S's commit.
5. While a subtransaction S is executing, data items that it has updated are isolated and hence not visible to other transactions and subtransactions (just like the flat transaction model).

Rule (5) is a requirement on the isolation behavior of nested transactions. If two-phase locking is the mechanism used to obtain isolation, then it needs to be modified slightly in order to satisfy rule (5).

i. Top-level transactions set locks in the same way as they do in a non-nested transaction model.
ii. When a subtransaction S commits or aborts, its locks are inherited by S's parent, which is either a top-level transaction or another subtransaction one level higher in the nesting hierarchy.
iii. A request to lock a data item x on behalf of a subtransaction S is granted if the only conflicting locks on x, if any, are held by ancestors of S in the nesting hierarchy.

The effect of (ii) and (iii) is that subtransactions of the same parent are two-phase locked with respect to each other and hence are serializable with respect to each other. Therefore, even though subtransactions may execute concurrently with much interleaving of their operations, in the end one can think of subtransactions of the same parent as isolated operations.

In Chapter 2, we presented nested transactions as a user-oriented execution model, one that is visible to the application programmer. Nested transactions are also a useful implementation tool when building a data manager. We encountered an example of this in Section 6.9, *B-Tree Locking*, which addressed the problem of implementing operations on a B+ tree index, such as Get Data Item x with Location = "B." The parent transaction that invokes the operation views it as isolated with respect to other operations it invokes. However, the internal execution of the operation has multiple steps that traverse a B+ tree—reading its pages and interpreting their content. The locking protocol that ensures this internal execution is isolated with respect to other B+ tree operations is not two-phase locking. Rather, it's a lock coupling protocol that uses knowledge of the B+ tree structure to enable more concurrency than two-phase locking would allow. However, the goal is the same as nested two-phase locking, namely, ensuring isolation of operations within the same parent.

Another common case where nested transactions arise in a data manager is implementing record-oriented operations on a page-oriented file store. Each page consists of multiple records. An implementation of read and write operations on records involves reading and writing pages and interpreting their contents. We will see an example of nested locking protocols to support this scenario in the next chapter on database recovery.[7]

6.12 SUMMARY

Locking is the most popular mechanism to achieve transaction isolation, that is, to ensure that every execution of a set of transactions is serializable. Each transaction sets read and write locks on data items that it reads and writes, respectively. And it follows the two-phase rule, meaning that it obtains all its locks before releasing any of them. Locks are generally set and released automatically by data managers and therefore are hidden from the application programmer.

A write lock conflicts with a read or write lock on the same data item. Two transactions cannot concurrently hold conflicting locks on the same data item. If a transaction requests a lock that conflicts with one owned by another transaction, it is delayed. This leads to two problems: deadlock and thrashing.

A deadlock occurs when a set of transactions are waiting for each other to release locks. Deadlocks usually are handled automatically by a detection mechanism. The system can use timeouts to identify a transaction that has been waiting too long and is suspected of being in a deadlock. Or it explicitly maintains a waits-for graph and periodically checks for cycles. The system breaks a deadlock by aborting one of the transactions involved in the deadlock.

The main application design problem created by locking is performance delays created by lock conflicts. If too many transactions request conflicting locks, transaction throughput decreases. This is called lock thrashing. To solve it in a running system, the number of active transactions must be decreased by aborting them. Alternatively, one can modify the application, database, or system design to reduce the number of conflicts. The latter is a design activity that involves adjusting the locking granularity or using special locking techniques that reduce the level of conflict, such as the following:

- Use finer grained locks, thereby increasing concurrency, at the expense of more locking overhead, since more locks must be set.
- Reduce the time that locks are held by shortening transaction execution time or delaying lock requests until later in the transaction.
- Use a hot spot technique, such as delaying operations until commit time, using operations that don't conflict, and keeping hot data in main memory to shorten transaction execution time.
- Use a weaker degree of isolation, such as read committed isolation, allowing inconsistent reads by releasing each read lock immediately after reading.
- Use multiversion data, so that queries can access old versions of data and thereby avoid setting locks that conflict with update transactions.

---

[7]See the discussion of latches at the end of Section 7.4. Latches ensure that write-record operations are isolated from each other. Record locks ensure transactions are isolated from each other (i.e., are serializable).

- Use lock coupling or the B-link method to reduce lock contention in B+ tree indexes.
- Use multigranularity locking so that each transaction sets locks at the appropriate granularity for the operation it is performing.

Insert and delete operations require special techniques, such as key-range locking, to avoid phantom updates and thereby ensure serializable executions. Nested transactions require special techniques too, for lock inheritance, to ensure subtransactions of the same parent are isolated from each other.

6.13 APPENDIX: BASIC SERIALIZABILITY THEORY

Serializability theory is one of the standard techniques for arguing the correctness of concurrency control algorithms, such as two-phase locking. In this section, we present the basics—enough to prove that two-phase locking produces serializable executions.

Equivalence of Histories

When we design a concurrency control algorithm, we need to show that every execution of transactions that is permitted by the algorithm has the same effect as a serial execution. So to start, we need a formal model of an execution of transactions. As in Section 6.1, we model an execution as a **history**, which is a sequence of the read, write, and commit operations issued by different transactions. To simplify matters, we do not consider aborted transactions in this analysis, although they can be included with some modest additional complexity to the theory. For clarity, we do include commit operations, denoted by c_i for transaction T_i.

We formalize the concept of "has the same effect as" by the concept of equivalence between two histories. Informally, we say that two histories are equivalent if each transaction reads the same input in both histories and the final value of each data item is the same in both histories. Formally, we say that two histories are **equivalent** if they have the same operations and conflicting operations are in the same order in both histories. This captures the informal notion of "has the same effect as" because changing the relative order of conflicting operations is the only way to affect the result of two histories that have the same operations. For example, the following histories are equivalent:

$$H_1 = r_1[x] \, r_2[x] \, w_1[x] \, c_1 \, w_2[y] \, c_2$$
$$H_2 = r_2[x] \, r_1[x] \, w_1[x] \, c_1 \, w_2[y] \, c_2$$
$$H_3 = r_2[x] \, r_1[x] \, w_2[y] \, c_2 \, w_1[x] \, c_1$$
$$H_4 = r_2[x] \, w_2[y] \, c_2 \, r_1[x] \, w_1[x] \, c_1$$

But none of them are equivalent to

$$H_5 = r_1[x] \, w_1[x] \, c_1 \, r_2[x] \, w_2[y] \, c_2$$

The reason is that $r_2[x]$ and $w_1[x]$ conflict and $r_2[x]$ precedes $w_1[x]$ in $H_1 - H_4$, but $r_2[x]$ follows $w_1[x]$ in H_5.

We model a serial execution as a **serial history**, which is a history where the operations of different transactions are not interleaved. For example, H_4 and H_5 are serial histories, but $H_1 - H_3$ are not.

The Serializability Theorem

One standard way to prove serializability is using a directed graph that describes a history, called a **serialization graph**. It has one node for each transaction. For each pair of conflicting operations by different transactions, it

$$r_1[x] \ r_2[x] \ w_1[x] \ r_3[x] \ w_2[y] \ c_2 \ w_1[y] \ c_1 \ w_3[x] \ c_3$$

$$T_2 \longrightarrow T_1 \longrightarrow T_3$$

FIGURE 6.23

An Execution and Its Serialization Graph. The execution on the left is modeled by the serialization graph on the right.

has an edge from the earlier transaction to the later one. For example, in the history in Figure 6.23, $r_2[x]$ conflicts with and precedes $w_1[x]$, so there is an edge from T_2 to T_1 in the serialization graph. Two conflicts can lead to the same edge. For example, $r_2[x]$ conflicts with and precedes $w_1[x]$, and $w_2[y]$ conflicts with and precedes $w_1[y]$, both of which produce the same edge from T_2 to T_1.

A **cycle** in a directed graph is a sequence of edges from a node back to itself. An **acyclic directed graph** is a directed graph with no cycles. The fundamental theorem of serializability theory is that a history is serializable if its serialization graph is acyclic. For example, the history in Figure 6.23 has an acyclic serialization graph, so it's serializable. In fact, it is equivalent to the following serial history:

$$r_2[x] \ w_2[y] \ c_2 \ r_1[x] \ w_1[x] \ w_1[y] \ c_1 \ r_3[x] \ w_3[x] \ c_3$$

To prove the fundamental theorem, we need to show that if a given history's serialization graph is acyclic, then it is equivalent to a serial history. Let's start by constructing a serial history over the same transactions as the given history where the transactions are in an order that is consistent with the serialization graph. It is surely possible to construct such a serial history because the graph is acyclic. Now observe that each pair of conflicting operations in the given history is in the same order as in the serial history, because the pair corresponds to an edge in the graph. Since all conflicting operations are in the same order, the given history is equivalent to the serial history. Therefore, the given history is serializable, which proves the theorem.

The Two-Phase Locking Theorem

Given this fundamental theorem, we can prove that two-phase locking produces serializable executions by showing that any execution it produces has an acyclic serialization graph. So, consider the serialization graph of a two-phase locked execution, and examine one edge in this graph, say $T_i \rightarrow T_j$. This means there were two conflicting operations, o_i from T_i and o_j from T_j. T_i and T_j each set locks for o_i and o_j, and since the operations conflict, the locks must conflict. (For example, o_i might have been a read and o_j a write on the same data item.) Before o_j executed, its lock was set, and o_i's lock must have been released before then (since it conflicts). So, in summary, given that $T_i \rightarrow T_j$, T_i released a lock before T_j set a lock.

Now, suppose there is a sequence of edges $T_i \rightarrow T_j$ and $T_j \rightarrow T_k$. From the previous paragraph, we know that T_i released a lock before T_j set a lock, and T_j released a lock before T_k set a lock. (They may be different locks.) Moreover, since T_j is two-phase locked, it set all its locks before it released any of them. Therefore, T_i released a lock before T_k set a lock. Avoiding the rigor of an induction argument, it is easy to see that we can repeat this argument for sequences of edges of any length. Therefore, for any sequence of edges $T_i \rightarrow \ldots \rightarrow T_m$, T_i released a lock before T_m set a lock.

To prove that the two-phase locked execution is serializable, we need to show that its serialization graph is acyclic. So, by way of contradiction, suppose there *is* a cycle in the serialization graph $T_i \rightarrow \ldots \rightarrow T_i$. From the previous paragraph, we can conclude that T_i released a lock before T_i set a lock. But this implies T_i was *not* two-phase locked, contradicting our assumption that all transactions were two-phase locked. Therefore the cycle cannot exist and, by the fundamental theorem of serializability, the execution is serializable.

System Recovery

7.1 CAUSES OF SYSTEM FAILURE

A critical requirement for most TP systems is that they be up all the time; in other words, highly available. Such systems often are called "24 by 7" (or 24 × 7), since they are intended to run 24 hours per day, 7 days per week. Defining this concept more carefully, we say that a system is **available** if it is running correctly and yielding the expected results. The **availability** of a system is defined as the fraction of time that the system is available. Thus, a highly available system is one that, most of the time, is running correctly and yielding expected results.

Availability is reduced by two factors. One is the rate at which the system fails. By **fails**, we mean the system gives the wrong answer or no answer. Other things being equal, if it fails frequently, it is less available. The second factor is recovery time. Other things being equal, the longer it takes to fix the system after it fails, the less it is available. These concepts are captured in two technical terms: mean time between failures and mean time to recovery. The **mean time between failures**, or **MTBF**, is the average time the system runs before it fails. MTBF is a measure of system **reliability**. The **mean time to repair**, or **MTTR**, is how long it takes to fix the system after it does fail. Using these two measures, we can define availability precisely as MTBF/(MTBF + MTTR), which is the fraction of time the system is running. Thus, availability improves when reliability (MTBF) increases and when repair time (MTTR) decreases.

In many practical settings, the system is designed to meet a **service level agreement (SLA)**, which is typically a combination of availability, response time, and throughput. That is, it is not enough that the system is available. It must also have satisfactory performance. Of course, poor performance may arise from many sources, such as the database system, network, or operating system. Performance problems are sometimes TP-specific, such as the cases of locking performance discussed in Chapter 6. More often, they are specific to other component technologies. These problems are important, but since they are not specific to the TP aspects of the system, we will not consider them here. Instead, we focus entirely on failures and how to recover from them.

Failures come from a variety of sources. We can categorize them as follows:

- The environment: Effects on the physical environment that surrounds the computer system, such as power, communication, air conditioning, fire, and flood.
- System management: What people do to manage the system, including vendors doing preventative maintenance and system operators taking care of the system.
- Hardware: All hardware devices including processors, memory, I/O controllers, storage devices, etc.
- Software: The operating system, communication systems, database systems, transactional middleware, other system software, and application software.

Let's look at each category of failures and see how we can reduce their frequency.

Hardening the Environment

One part of the environment is communications systems that are not under the control of the people building the computer system, such as long distance communication provided by a telecommunications company. As a customer of communication services, sometimes one can improve communications reliability by paying more to buy more reliable lines. Otherwise, about all one can do is lease more communication lines than are needed to meet functional and performance goals. For example, if one communication line is needed, lease two independent lines instead, so if one fails, the other one will probably still be operating.

A second aspect of the environment is power. Given its failure rate, it's often appropriate to have battery backup for the computer system. In the event of power failure, battery backup can at least keep main memory alive, so the system can restart immediately after power is restored without rebooting the operating system, thereby reducing MTTR. Batteries may be able to run the system for a short period, either to provide useful service (thereby increasing MTBF) or to hibernate the system by saving main memory to a persistent storage device (which can improve availability if recovering from hibernation is faster than rebooting). To keep running during longer outages, an uninterruptible power supply (UPS) is needed. A full UPS generally includes a gas or diesel powered generator, which can run the system much longer than batteries. Batteries are still used to keep the system running for a few minutes until the generator can take over.

A third environmental issue is air conditioning. An air conditioning failure can bring down the computer system, so when a computer system requires an air conditioned environment, a redundant air conditioning system is often advisable.

Systems can fail due to natural disasters, such as fire, flood, and earthquake, or due to other extraordinary external events, such as war and vandalism. There are things one can do to defend against some of these events: build buildings that are less susceptible to fire, that are able to withstand strong earthquakes, and that are secured against unauthorized entry. How far one goes depends on the cost of the defense, the benefit to availability, and the cost of downtime to the enterprise. When the system is truly "mission critical," as in certain military, financial, and transportation applications, an enterprise will go to extraordinary lengths to reduce the probability of such failures. One airline system is housed in an underground bunker.

After hardening the environment, the next step is to replicate the system, ideally in a geographically distant location whose environmental disasters are unlikely to be correlated to those at other replicas. For example, many years ago one California bank built an extra computer facility east of the San Andreas Fault, so they could still operate if their Los Angeles or San Francisco facility were destroyed by an earthquake. More recently, geographical replication has become common practice for large-scale Internet sites. Since a system replica is useful only if it has the data necessary to take over processing for a failed system, data replication is an important enabling technology. Data replication is the subject of Chapter 9.

System Management

System management is another cause of failures. People are part of the system. Everybody has an off day or an occasional lapse of attention. It's only a matter of time before even the best system operator does something that causes the system to fail.

There are several ways to mitigate the problem. One is simply to design the system so that it doesn't require maintenance, such as using automated procedures for functions that normally would require operator intervention. Even preventative maintenance, which is done to increase availability by avoiding failures later on, may be a source of downtime. Such procedures should be designed to be done while the system is operating.

Simplifying maintenance procedures also helps, if maintenance can't be eliminated entirely. So does building redundancy into maintenance procedures, so an operator has to make at least two mistakes to cause the system to malfunction. Training is another factor. This is especially important for maintenance procedures that are needed infrequently. It's like having a fire drill, where people train for rare events, so when the events do happen, people know what actions to take.

Software installation is often a source of planned failures. The installation of many software products requires rebooting the operating system. Developing installation procedures that don't require rebooting is a way to improve system reliability.

Many operation errors involve reconfiguring the system. Sometimes adding new machines to a rack or changing the tuning parameters on a database system causes the system to malfunction. Even if it only degrades performance, rather than causing the system to crash, the effect may be the same from the end user's perspective. One can avoid unpleasant surprises by using configuration management tools that simulate a new configuration and demonstrate that it will behave as predicted, or to have test procedures on a test system that can prove that a changed configuration will perform as predicted. Moreover, it is valuable to have reconfiguration procedures that can be quickly undone, so that when a mistake is made, one can revert to the previous working configuration quickly.

If a system is not required to be 24 × 7, then scheduled downtime can be used to handle many of these problems, such as preventative maintenance, installing software that requires a reboot, or reconfiguring a system. However, from a vendor's viewpoint, offering products that require such scheduled downtime limits their market only to customers that don't need 24 × 7.

Hardware

The third cause of failures is hardware problems. To discuss hardware failures precisely, we need a few technical terms. A **fault** is an event inside the system that is believed to have caused a failure. A fault can be either transient or permanent. A **transient** fault is one that does not reoccur if you retry the operation. A **permanent** fault is not transient; it is repeatable.

The vast majority of hardware faults are transient. If the hardware fails, simply retry the operation; there's a very good chance it will succeed. For this reason, operating systems have many built-in recovery procedures to handle transient hardware faults. For example, if the operating system issues an I/O operation to a disk or a communications device and gets an error signal back, it normally retries that operation many times before it actually reports an error back to the caller.

Of course, some hardware faults are permanent. The most serious ones cause the operating system to fail, making the whole system unavailable. In this case, rebooting the operating system may get the system back into a working state. The reboot procedure will detect malfunctioning hardware and try to reconfigure around it. If the reboot fails or the system fails shortly after reboot, then the next step is usually to reimage the disk with a fresh copy of the software, in case it became corrupted. If that doesn't fix the problem, then repairing the hardware is usually the only option.

Software

This brings us to software failures. The most serious type of software failure is an operating system crash, since it stops the entire computer system. Since many software problems are transient, a reboot often repairs the problem. This involves rebooting the operating system, running software that repairs disk state that might have become inconsistent due to the failure, recovering communications sessions with other systems in a distributed system, and restarting all the application programs. These steps all increase the MTTR and therefore reduce availability. So they should be made as fast as possible. The requirement for faster recovery inspired operating systems vendors in the 1990s to incorporate fast file system recovery procedures, which was a major component of operating system boot time. Some operating systems are carefully engineered for fast boot. For example, highly available communication systems have operating systems that reboot in under a minute, worst case. Taking this goal to the extreme, if the repair time were zero, then failures wouldn't matter, since the system would recover instantaneously, and the user would never know the difference. Clearly reducing the repair time can have a big impact on availability.

Some software failures only degrade a system's capabilities, not cause it to fail. For example, consider an application that offers functions that require access to a remote service. When the remote service is unavailable, those functions stop working. However, through careful application design, other application functions can still be operational. That is, the system degrades gracefully when parts of it stop working. A real example we know of is an application that used a TP database and a data warehouse, where the latter was nice to have but not mission-critical. The application was not designed to degrade gracefully, so when the data warehouse failed, the entire application became unavailable, which caused a large and unnecessary loss of revenue.

When an application process or database system does fail, the failure must be detected and the application or database system process must be recovered. This is where TP-specific techniques become relevant.

7.2 A MODEL FOR SYSTEM RECOVERY

In this section, we will discuss how to cope with the failure and recovery of processes that are running application code. We will look at the failure and recovery of resource managers, notably database systems, starting in Section 7.3.

Detecting Process Failures

Operating system processes are a firewall between the operating system and the application. An application failure may cause the application's process to fail. However, the operating system can continue, so only the process needs to be restarted. This reduces MTTR compared to a system where the application failure causes an operating system reboot. Therefore, most TP systems are built from multiple processes.

We would like each process to be as reliable as possible. But of course, no matter how reliable it is, there are times when it will fail. When it does fail, some agent outside of the process has to observe that fact and ask to recreate the process. Usually that's done by the operating system, database system, or transactional middleware.

The transactional middleware or database system usually has one or more monitoring processes that track when application or database processes fail. There are several ways that are commonly used to detect failures:

- Each process could periodically send an "I'm alive" message to the monitoring process (see Figure 7.1); the absence of such a message warns the monitoring process of a possible failure.
- The monitoring process could poll the other processes with "Are you alive?" messages.
- Each process could own an operating system lock that the monitoring process is waiting to acquire; if the process fails, the operating system releases the process's lock, which causes the monitoring process to be granted the lock and hence to be alerted of the failure.

Whichever approach is taken, it is important to optimize the time it takes for a monitoring process to detect the failure, since that time contributes to the MTTR and therefore to unavailability.

In all these cases, the symptom provides a good reason to suspect that the process failed, but it is not an ironclad guarantee that the process actually did fail. In the first two cases, the process might just be slow to

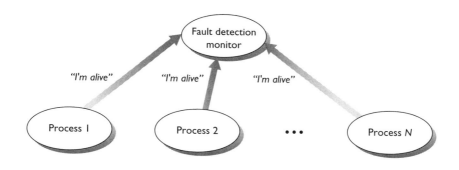

FIGURE 7.1

A Fault Detection Monitor. The monitor detects process failures, in this case by listening for "I'm alive" messages. When it doesn't hear one within its timeout period, it assumes the process has failed.

respond. In the third case, it might have released the lock yet still be operational. The suspicion of a failure is more likely to be true if the detector is executing under the same operating system instance as the process being monitored; that is, on the same machine or virtual machine, though even here it is not a guarantee. This is the scenario we focus on in this chapter, and we will assume that failure detection is accurate.

In a distributed system where the monitor is running on a different machine than the process being monitored, there is a greater chance that the failure symptom is due to a communication failure rather than a process failure. We will explore this issue in Chapters 8 and 9.

A process could fail by returning incorrect values. That is, it could fail to satisfy its specification. For example, the data it returns could have been corrupted by faulty memory, a faulty communication line, or an application bug. We do not consider such errors here. We assume the first two are prevented by suitable error-detecting codes. We do not consider application bugs because we cannot eliminate them by using generic system mechanisms. They are addressed by software engineering technology and methodology, which are outside the scope of this book.

When a process failure is detected, some agent needs to recreate the failed process. The operating system generally is designed only to recreate processes that are needed to keep the system running at all, such as the file system (if it runs as a process) and system monitor processes. The operating system generally does not automatically recreate application processes, except those managed by the operating system's process control system. Therefore, transactional middleware and database systems must step in to detect the failure of application and database system processes, and when they do fail, to recreate them.

Client Recovery

In this discussion of recovery, we assume a basic client–server model: a client process communicates with a server process and the server process uses underlying resources, such as a disk or communications line (see Figure 7.2). A common configuration is to have the client running on a desktop machine and the server on a larger shared machine. Whatever the configuration, the possible technical approaches for system recovery remain the same. We are therefore deliberately vague about the type of machine on which the client and server run.

There are several points of failure in this system: the client, the client-server connection, the server, the server-resource connection, and the resources. If the client fails and later recovers, it needs to reconnect to the server and can start calling it again. Or, if the client loses communication with the server, either because the communication line or server failed, the failure will eventually be repaired and the client will later re-establish

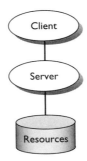

FIGURE 7.2

Basic Client-Server Model. A client process communicates with a server process and the server process uses underlying resources, such as a disk or communication line.

that communication and resume calling the server. In either case, at recovery time, the main issue for the client is to re-establish its state relative to the server.

The state of the client relative to the server consists of the set of its outstanding calls to the server. Therefore, to recover its state, it needs to determine the following:

- What calls were outstanding at the time it failed or lost connectivity with the server?
- What happened to those calls while it was down or not communicating with the server?
- What does it have to do to finish those calls properly before proceeding with new calls?

These are exactly the issues we discussed in Chapter 4, "Queued Transaction Processing." If there is a persistent queue between the client and server, then the client can find out the state of all outstanding calls (called "requests" in Chapter 4) by examining the queue. If not, then it has to use an application-specific technique, such as looking at the database state on the server to determine if the client's previous calls completed, or reissuing in-doubt calls with the same serial number and relying on the server to discard duplicate calls. These techniques too were discussed in Chapter 4.

The remaining issues all focus on server availability, which is the subject of the rest of this section.

Server Recovery

After a server has been recreated, it runs its recovery procedure to reconstruct its state before starting to process new calls. If this is the first time the server has ever run, then the recovery procedure is trivial—the server just initializes its state. If not, then it has some work to do.

To explore how a server reconstructs its state, let's begin from first principles. Suppose the server is a sequential processor of calls and there are no transactions in the picture. The server just receives a call from a client, does what is requested, and returns a result. At the time it failed, the server might have been in the middle of processing such a call.

As we discussed in the previous section on Client Recovery, it is up to the client to determine the state of its outstanding calls. It's always possible that a server (or communications) failure causes a call to get lost, so the client must be able to cope with that fact. Since the client has to be able to deal with lost calls, it would seem that a recovering server could just ignore whatever call it was working on at the time it failed and start afresh. It's up to the client to figure out what to do.

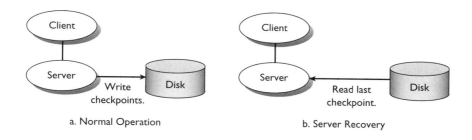

a. Normal Operation   b. Server Recovery

FIGURE 7.3

Server Checkpointing. During normal operation, the server periodically writes a checkpoint. After a failure, it uses its last checkpointed state to recover.

Unfortunately, this doesn't always work, because the server may have performed a non-idempotent operation while it was processing its last call before the failure. For example, it may have printed a check, transferred money, credited a bank account, dispensed cash, or shipped a product. If the client concludes that the server did not execute the call, it will reissue it, thereby causing the server to redo the work. Therefore, if the server performed a non-idempotent operation on behalf of the call it was processing at the time of failure, it must not re-execute the call. Rather, it must complete the call and return a result.

The details of recovering a partially-executed call are complex and are not commonly used in systems that support transactions. However, to appreciate how much easier things are when transactions are available, let us briefly examine what the server would have to do if it could not rely on transactions.

Checkpoint-Based Recovery

Suppose the server partially executed a client's call and then failed. Suppose all the operations that the server executed for that partially-executed call were idempotent. In that case, at recovery time the server can simply reprocess the call from the beginning. Re-executing operations that it executed before the failure does no harm, because all those operations are idempotent.

Suppose the server did perform non-idempotent operations for the last call. Then it must recover itself to a state that came after the last non-idempotent operation it executed before the failure. So, for example, if the server printed a check before the failure, then it must be recovered to a state after the time that it printed the check. If the server continued processing from a state before it printed the check then it would repeat that operation (i.e., print the check again), which is exactly what should not happen. Recreating this state requires some careful bookkeeping before the failure, so the recovering server can look up what was going on at the time of failure, to figure out what it should do.

One general way to prepare for this type of recovery is to have a server save its memory state on nonvolatile storage (e.g., a disk) before it executes a non-idempotent operation. That way, when it recovers, it can recreate that state (see Figure 7.3). Saving memory state is an example of checkpointing. In general, **checkpointing** is any activity that is done during normal processing to reduce the amount of work to redo after a recovery. Saving memory state is a kind of checkpointing, because it ensures that when the server recovers, it won't have to redo any work that it did before saving its state.

Saving the state of the server's memory is not cheap, especially if it has to be done every time a non-idempotent operation is performed. As we'll see in a moment, transactions help reduce this cost.

To recover from a failure, the server restores the last checkpoint state it successfully saved (see Figure 7.4). It must then check if the non-idempotent operation that followed its last checkpoint actually ran. For example,

```
Server Program
    . . .
    Checkpoint;
    // Recovery procedure branches to next line
    If RestartFlag
    { RestartFlag = 0;
      If(check wasn't printed before the failure) print check;
    }
    else print check
    . . .
```

```
Server Recovery Procedure:
    RestartFlag = 1;
    Find last checkpoint on disk;
    Restore checkpoint's memory state;
    Go to next server statement after Checkpoint
```

FIGURE 7.4

Checkpoint-Based Recovery Procedure. The server program checkpoints before its non-idempotent "print check" operation. The server recovery procedure recovers the last checkpoint state and branches to the line after the statement that created the checkpoint. The server program then executes the non-idempotent operation "print check" only if it wasn't done before the failure.

if the server checkpoints its state right before printing a check, then at recovery time reconstituting the server state requires determining whether or not the check was printed. This is the same question we asked in the earlier section on Client Recovery and in Section 4.4, *Handling Non-Undoable Operations*. That is, in this situation, the server is in the role of a client in Section 4.4 that may have called a non-idempotent operation before it failed. Therefore, when the server recovers, it must determine whether that non-idempotent operation ran, and if so it can skip over it.

To summarize: If a server performs non-idempotent operations, then it reconstitutes its state at recovery time to one that comes after the last non-idempotent operation that it performed before the failure. The idea is to start running the process from that state, so that non-idempotent operations it does from that point on don't cause a problem.

Transaction-Based Server Recovery

Transactions simplify server recovery by focusing clients' and servers' attention on the transactions executed by each server, rather than on individual calls within a transaction. That is, the server does all its work within transactions. The client tells the server to start a transaction, the client makes some calls to the server within that transaction, and then the client tells the server to commit the transaction.

If a server that supports transactions fails and subsequently recovers, its state includes the effects of all transactions that committed before the failure and no effects of transactions that aborted before the failure or were active at the time of the failure. Comparing this behavior to a nontransactional server, it is as if the transactional server performs a checkpoint every time it commits a transaction, and its recovery procedure discards all effects of aborted or incomplete transactions. Thus, when a transactional server recovers, it ignores which *calls* were executing when it failed and focuses instead on which *transactions* were executing when it failed. So instead of recovering to a state as of the last partially-executed call (as in checkpoint-based recovery), it recovers to a state containing all the results of all committed transactions and no others.

For this to work, the server must be able to undo all of a transaction's operations when it aborts. This effectively makes the operations redoable when the transaction is re-executed. That is, if an operation was undone, then there's no harm in redoing it later, even if it is non-idempotent. This avoids a problem that was faced in checkpoint-based recovery—the problem of returning to a state after the last non-idempotent operation. This isn't necessary because every non-idempotent operation was either part of a committed transaction (and hence won't be redone) or was undone (and hence can be redone).

FIGURE 7.5

Stateless Servers. An application process stores all its state in resource managers, and is therefore stateless.

If all operations in a transaction must be redoable, then the transaction must not include the non-idempotent operations we encountered in the earlier section, *Server Recovery*, such as printing a check or transferring money. To cope with such a non-idempotent operation, the transaction should enqueue a message that contains the operation. It's safe for the transaction to contain the enqueue operation, because it is undoable. The program that processes the message and performs the non-idempotent operation should use the reply handling techniques in Section 4.4 to get exactly-once execution of the actual operation (printing the check or sending a money-transfer message).

Transactions not only simplify server recovery, they also speed it up. A memory checkpoint is expensive, but transaction commitment is relatively cheap. The trick is that the transactional server is carefully maintaining all its state on disk, incrementally, by writing small amounts to a log file, thereby avoiding a bulk copy of its memory state. It is designed to suffer failures at arbitrary points in time, and to reconstruct its memory state from disk using the log, with relatively modest effort. The algorithms to reconstruct its state in this way are what gives transactions their all-or-nothing and durability properties. Either all of a transaction executes or none of it does. And all of its results are durably saved in stable storage, even if the system fails momentarily after the transaction commits. These algorithms are the main subject of the rest of this chapter.

Stateless Servers

When transactions are used, servers usually are split into two types: application processes and resource managers (see Figure 7.5). An application process receives a client request, starts a transaction, performs application logic, and sends messages to transactional resource managers. It does not directly access transactional resources, such as a database. Resource managers handle the state being shared by transactions—databases, recoverable queues, and so on.

A resource manager behaves just like a transactional server described in the previous section, *Transaction-Based Server Recovery*. That is, it executes all calls within a transaction. And its recovery procedure returns its state to one that includes the effects of all committed transactions and no others.

An application process can use a simpler recovery procedure than resource managers, because it is stateless. That is, it doesn't have any state that might be needed after recovery. It receives a request to run a transaction (from its client), starts a transaction, executes operations that manipulate local memory or call a database system or another application process, commits the transaction, and sends a reply back to the client. At this point, it has no state worth remembering. It simply processes the next request that it receives as if it had been initialized from scratch.

A stateless server doesn't have to do very much to recover from a failure. It just reinitializes its state and starts running transactions again, completely oblivious to whatever it was doing before the failure. Since it maintains all its state in transactional resource managers, it is really up to the resource managers to reconstitute their states after a failure. The resource managers recover to a state that includes all the committed transactions and none of the aborted ones, up to the time of the failure. Now the application process can start processing requests again.

The application processes controlled by transactional middleware usually are designed to be stateless servers so they do not need any recovery code. The only ambiguity is about the state of the last request that a client issued to the application process before the failure (e.g., that a front-end program issued to a request controller). That is, the client is not stateless, since it needs to know the state of that last request. This is where queued request processing comes in—to figure out the state of that last request and thereby determine whether it has to be rerun. For the application process that was actually executing the request, there's no ambiguity at all. It restarts in a clean state, as if it were initialized for the first time.

7.3 INTRODUCTION TO DATABASE RECOVERY

Now that we understand how to recover application processes, it's time to turn our attention to recovering resource managers. As in Chapter 6, "Locking," we will use the term data manager instead of the more generic term resource manager. The most popular type of data manager is a database system. However, the principles apply to any kind of transactional resource manager, such as queue managers and transactional file systems.

To recover from a failure, a data manager needs to quickly return its database to a state that includes the results of all transactions that committed before the failure and no results of transactions that aborted before the failure or were active at the time of failure. Most data managers do an excellent job of this type of recovery. The application programmer doesn't get involved at all.

The mechanisms used to recover from these failures can have a significant effect on performance. However, if a data manager uses a recovery approach that leads to mediocre transaction performance, there is not too much that the application programmer can do about it. This is rather different than locking, where application programming and database design can have a big effect. In view of the lack of control that an application programmer has on the situation, there is no strong requirement that he or she have a deep understanding of how a data manager does recovery.

Still, there are a few ways, though not many, that database and system administrators can work together to improve performance, fault tolerance, and the performance of recovery. For example, they can improve the fault tolerance of a system by altering the configuration of logs, disk devices, and the like. To reason about performance and fault tolerance implications of application and system design, it helps a great deal to understand the main concepts behind database recovery algorithms. We describe these concepts in the rest of this chapter and their implications for application programming.

Types of Failure

Many failures are due to incorrectly programmed transactions and to data entry errors that lead to incorrect parameters to transactions. Unfortunately, these failures undermine the assumption that a transaction's execution preserves the consistency of the database (the "C" in ACID). They can be dealt with by applying software engineering techniques to the programming and testing of transactions, by validating input before feeding it to a transaction, and by semantic integrity mechanisms built into the data manager. However they're dealt with, they are intrinsically outside the range of problems that transaction recovery mechanisms can automatically handle. Since we're interested in problems that transaction recovery mechanisms *can* handle, we will assume that transactions do indeed preserve database consistency.

There are three types of failures that are most important to a TP system: transaction failures, system failures, and media failures. A **transaction failure** occurs when a transaction aborts. A **system failure** occurs when the contents of volatile storage, namely main memory, is corrupted. For example, this can happen to semiconductor memory when the power fails. It also happens when the operating system fails. Although an operating system failure may not corrupt all of main memory, it is usually too difficult to determine which parts were actually corrupted by the failure. So one generally assumes the worst and reinitializes all of main memory. Given the possibility of system failures, the database itself must be kept on a stable storage medium, such as disk. (Of course, other considerations, such as size, may also force us to store the database on stable mass storage media.) By definition, **stable** (or **nonvolatile**) **storage** withstands system failures. A **media failure** occurs when any part of the stable storage is destroyed. For instance, this happens if some sectors of a disk become damaged.

In this chapter we assume that each transaction accesses and updates data at exactly one data manager. This allows us to focus our attention on recovery strategies for a single data manager. In the next chapter we'll consider additional problems that arise when a transaction can update data at more than one data manager.

Recovery Strategies

The main strategy for recovering from failures is quite simple:

- Transaction failure: If a transaction aborts, the data manager restores the previous values of all data items that the transaction wrote.
- System failure: To recover from the failure, the data manager aborts any transactions that were active (i.e., uncommitted) at the time of the failure, and it ensures that each transaction that did commit before the failure actually installed its updates in the database.
- Media failure: The recovery strategy is nearly the same as for system failures, since the goal is to return the database to a state where it contains the results of all committed transactions and no aborted transactions.

We will concentrate on recovery from transaction and system failures for most of the chapter. Recovery from media failures is quite similar to recovery from system failures, so we'll postpone discussing it until the end of the chapter, after we have a complete picture of system recovery mechanisms.

It's easy to see why system and media recovery are so similar. Each recovery mechanism considers a certain part of storage to be unreliable: main memory, in the case of system failures; a portion of stable storage, in the case of media failures. To safeguard against the loss of data in unreliable storage, the recovery mechanism maintains another copy of the data, possibly in a different representation. This redundant copy is kept in another part of storage that it deems reliable: stable storage, in the case of system failures, or another piece of stable storage, such as a second disk or tape, in the case of media failures. Of course, the different physical characteristics of storage in the two cases may require the use of different strategies. But the principles are the same.

The most popular technique for recovering from system and media failures is logging. The log is that second, redundant copy of the data that is used to cope with failures. To understand how a log is used, why it works, and how it affects performance, we need to start with a simplified model of data manager internals, so we have a framework in which to discuss the issues.

7.4 THE SYSTEM MODEL

Locking Assumptions

From the viewpoint of transactions, the recovery system is part of the storage subsystem that processes read, write, commit, and abort operations. The recovery system makes few assumptions about the transactions that use its services. The main one is that the transaction is responsible for setting locks before issuing read and write operations to the storage system, and that it holds onto its write locks until after the transaction commits or aborts.

Since a transaction holds a write lock on any data it updates until after it commits or aborts, no other transaction can read or write that data until then. This avoids three messy recovery situations.

The first messy situation is guaranteeing recoverability. Suppose a transaction is allowed to release write locks before it commits or aborts. Consider a transaction T_2 that reads a data item that was last updated by an active transaction T_1, and T_2 commits while T_1 is still active. If T_1 subsequently aborts, the execution looks like this:

$$E = w_1[x]\, r_2[x]\, \text{commit}_2\, \text{abort}_1$$

The data manager is now stuck. It should abort T_2, because T_2 has read data that is now invalid; but it can't, because T_2 already committed. That is, the data manager is in a state from which it can't recover. It's therefore essential that a transaction not commit if it read any data that was last updated by a transaction that is still active. That is, a transaction T's commit operation must follow the commit of every transaction from which T read. An execution that obeys this rule is called **recoverable**. Holding write locks until after a transaction commits or aborts solves this problem with a sledgehammer; a transaction can't read data that was last updated by a transaction that is still active, because the latter holds a write lock on that data.

The second messy situation is cascading abort. Consider the same situation as in the previous paragraph, where T_2 read data that was last updated by an active transaction T_1. But this time, suppose T_1 aborts while T_2 is still active. That is, the execution looks like this:

$$E' = w_1[x]\, r_2[x]\, \text{abort}_1$$

Then, as before, T_2 would have to abort too, since its input would be invalid. This is called **cascading abort**, since the abort of one transaction (T_1) cascades to the abort of another transaction (T_2). We're certainly better off in this situation than in the previous paragraph, since at least it's legal to abort T_2 (because T_2 is still active). But the system still needs to keep track of which transactions depend on which other transactions—nontrivial bookkeeping. We can avoid this bookkeeping by requiring that a transaction only reads data that was last updated by a transaction that has committed. An execution that obeys this rule is said to **avoid cascading aborts**. A data manager can avoid cascading aborts by ensuring that every transaction holds its write locks until after it commits or aborts.

The third messy situation is being unable to abort a transaction simply by restoring the previous values of data it wrote. This arises if a transaction can overwrite another transaction's uncommitted writes. For example, if T_1 does not hold its write locks until after it commits or aborts, then another transaction can overwrite data written by T_1. The effect is rather nasty, as illustrated by the following execution:

$$E'' = w_1[x]\, w_2[x]\, \text{abort}_1\, \text{abort}_2$$

In execution E'', when transaction T_1 aborts, the system cannot simply restore the value x had before $w_1[x]$, since that would wipe out the result of T_2's write operation, $w_2[x]$. At this point, the system doesn't know whether T_2 will commit or abort. If T_2 later commits, its update to x would be lost. So, the right thing for the data manager to do when T_1 aborts is nothing. Now, when T_2 aborts, the system cannot restore the value x had before $w_2[x]$, since that would reinstall the value written by T_1, which just aborted. So, the right thing for the system to do when T_2 aborts is to restore the value x had before $w_1[x]$. This is a pretty complicated analysis for the recovery mechanism to do, and this is just for two updates by two transactions. If multiple transactions were involved, the analysis would be very tricky indeed. All systems we know of avoid it by allowing a transaction to write a data item only if the previous transaction that updated the data item already committed. Such executions are called **strict**. This is usually implemented by requiring that write locks are held until after the transaction commits or aborts. This ensures that the data manager can abort a transaction simply by restoring the previous values of data that the transaction wrote.

In summary, a lot of recovery problems become much simpler if the recovery system can assume that a transaction holds its write locks until after it commits or aborts. All systems we know of rely on this assumption.

Page Granularity Operations

Locking granularity is another aspect of locking that affects the complexity of recovery mechanisms. Recovery algorithms are a lot simpler when page granularity locking is used. Here's why.

The only truly reliable operation that a data manager has available is writing one page to a disk. Disk hardware is careful to make this an atomic (i.e., all-or-nothing) operation with respect to system failures. That is, if the system fails, then recovers, and then a program reads a page P from disk, the content of P reflects the last complete write to P before the system failed.

Although the hardware is designed to make disk writes atomic, errors are still possible. For example, if a disk malfunctions, it might partially execute a write operation on page P. In that case, the next operation to read P may detect the error, for example, as an erroneous checksum on the page. This is a media failure.

Depending on the hardware, some media failures may not be detectable. For example, consider a disk malfunction where it executes a write operation completely, but stores the data in the wrong location. That is, an operation was issued to write page P, but the disk wrote it to a different location, Q. In this case, when an application reads page P, the value it reads may appear to be correct. However, due to the previous erroneous write, the value of P does not reflect the last write operation to P, but an earlier one. Moreover, the next read of page Q will return a value that appears to be correct (since it reflects a complete write operation), but it too is incorrect because it contains the last value written to page P, not page Q. The latter error can be detected if the checksum on Q is a function of both the address of Q and its content.

We assume that all this complexity is hidden by the hardware and software I/O system that implements read and write operations. That is, each write operation either overwrites the intended page or does nothing. And each read operation returns a complete disk page or an error indicating that the page is corrupted. Recovery algorithms for system failure make heavy use of this property of disks, that page operations are atomic. So if transactions read and write complete pages, the atomicity of page writes offers a clean model we can use to reason about the state of the database after a failure.

Suppose a page can hold multiple records, transactions write records not pages, and the data manager uses record-level locks. In that case, multiple transactions can lock and update different records within a single page. If they do, then at recovery time a page may contain records that were recently updated by different transactions, only some of which have committed. Depending on the state of the page, some of the committed updates may need to be reapplied, while others need to be undone. The bookkeeping to sort this out is quite challenging. This complexity is a problem worth solving, but for pedagogical reasons, it's one we'll postpone for awhile. Instead, to keep things simple, we will use page granularity for everything:

- The database consists of a set of pages.
- Each update by a transaction applies to only one page.

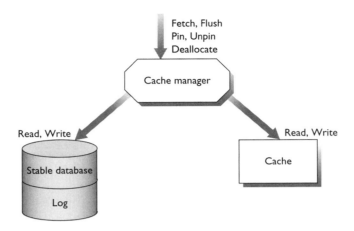

FIGURE 7.6

The Storage Model. The cache manager controls the movement of pages between stable storage (the stable database and log) and volatile storage (the cache).

- Each update by a transaction writes a whole page (not just part of the page).
- Locks are set on pages.

Page granularity simplifies the discussion, but it is too inefficient for high performance systems. After we describe recovery using this assumption, we'll show what happens when we allow finer grained updates and locks on records.

Storage Model

We model storage as two areas: stable storage (usually disk) and volatile storage (usually main memory) (see Figure 7.6). Stable storage contains the **stable database**, which has one copy of each database page. It also contains the log, which we'll discuss in a moment.

Volatile storage contains the database **cache**. The cache contains copies of some of the database pages, usually ones that were recently accessed or updated by transactions. Using a cache is a big performance win, because it helps transactions avoid the high cost of disk accesses for popular pages.

For recovery purposes, it really doesn't matter which pages are in cache, only that there are some. Pages in cache may contain updates that have not yet been written to stable storage. Such pages are called **dirty**. Correctly handling dirty pages is an important responsibility of the recovery system during normal operation.

The **cache manager** keeps track of what is in cache. It is part of the page-oriented file system layer of a data manager, as shown in Figure 6.4. It divides the cache into **slots**, each of which can hold one database page. It uses a table to keep track of what is in each slot. Each row of the table contains a **cache descriptor**, which identifies the database page that is in the cache slot, the main memory address of the cache slot, a bit to indicate whether the page is dirty, and a pin count (explained below; see Figure 7.7). The cache manager supports five basic operations:

- Fetch(P): P is the address of a database page. This reads P into a cache slot (if it isn't already there) and returns the address of the cache slot.

Page	Dirty Bit	Cache Address	Pin Count
P_4	1	104	1
P_{16}	0	376	1
P_5	1	400	0

FIGURE 7.7

Cache Descriptor Table. Each page in a cache slot is described by a row in this table.

- Pin(P): This makes page P's cache slot unavailable for flushing (it is "pinned down"). Usually, a caller pins P immediately after fetching it.
- Unpin(P): Releases the caller's previous pin. The cache manager maintains a **pin count** for each page, which is incremented by each Pin operation and decremented by each Unpin. If the pin count is zero, the page is available for flushing or deallocation.
- Flush(P): If database page P is in a cache slot and is dirty, then this operation writes it to the disk. It does not return until after the disk acknowledges that the write operation is done. That is, a flush is a synchronous write.
- Deallocate(P): Deallocates P so its cache slot can be reused by another page. Does not flush the page, even if the cache slot is dirty. It is up to the cache manager's clients to flush a page (if appropriate) before deallocating it.

Everything else that happens to pages is up to the transactions. If a transaction has fetched and pinned a page, it can do what it wants to the content of that page, as far as the cache manager is concerned. Of course, we know the transaction will have an appropriate lock to read or write the page, but this is at a higher layer than the cache manager, which doesn't know anything about these locks.

The cache manager is heavily used by data manager components that read and write the database. This is usually the record management layer of the data manager (i.e., the Access Method layer in Figure 6.3), which reads and writes records and provides indexed access to data. To read or write data on a page P, this component issues Fetch(P) followed by Pin(P). When it's done reading or updating the page, it calls Unpin(P). It does not call Flush(P).

It is up to two other data manager components to call Flush(P). One is the cache manager's page replacement algorithm. Its job is to make the best use of cache by keeping only those pages that transactions are likely to need in the near future. If a page P hasn't been referenced in awhile, it deallocates P from its page slot. If P is dirty, then it calls Flush(P) before Deallocate(P), so that recent updates to P aren't lost.

The other component that uses Flush(P) is the recovery manager, which is described in the next section.

The Log

The **log** is a sequential file, usually kept on disk, that contains a sequence of records that describes updates that were applied to the database. The record that describes an update includes

- The address of the page that was updated
- The identifier of the transaction that performed the update

- The value of the page that was written, called its **after-image**
- The value of the page before it was written, called its **before-image**

As described here, each log record is over two pages long, which is much too inefficient. Like our other page granularity assumptions, we'll weaken it later on.

This log record is written by the same component that writes to the cache. That is, whenever it updates a cache page, and before it unpins that page, it writes a log record that describes the update. That way, the log is always consistent with the contents of the cache.

The log also contains records that report when a transaction commits or aborts. Such records just contain the identifier of the transaction and an indication whether the transaction committed or aborted.

It is crucial that the log accurately reflects the order in which conflicting operations really executed. That is, if one update precedes and conflicts with another update in the log, then the updates must really have executed in that order. The reason is that after a failure, the recovery system will replay some of the work that happened before the failure. It will assume that the order of operations in the log is the order it should replay work. Note that it is not necessary that the log accurately reflect the ordering of *all* updates, only the conflicting ones, which are the only ones whose relative order makes a difference. Some systems exploit this distinction by logging nonconflicting updates in parallel in "sublogs" and merging those sublogs later, when conflicting updates occur.

Page-level locking ensures this ordering is enforced. If finer granularity locking is used, then two transactions can update a page concurrently, so the database system must ensure that it updates the page and writes the log record on behalf of one transaction before it performs these two actions on behalf of the other. This is done by setting a short-term exclusive lock on the page, called a **latch**, which can simply be a bit in the cache descriptor. The latch brackets the activities of updating the page and logging the update (see Figure 7.8). The latch ensures that if another transaction was concurrently attempting the same sequence, then its update and log operations would either precede or follow those of T.

Setting and releasing latches is done more frequently than setting and releasing locks. It therefore must be very fast—just a few instructions. Thus, in most systems, no deadlock detection is done based on latches. So lots of care is needed to ensure that such deadlocks cannot occur.

Whereas most systems store before-images and after-images in the same log, some use separate logs. This is done because before-images are not needed after a transaction commits and usually are not needed for media recovery. They can therefore be deleted relatively quickly, unlike after-images, which are needed for very long periods. However, this can also lead to extra log writes, since there are now two logs to deal with.

```
Fetch (P)              /* read P into cache */
Pin (P)                /* ensure P isn't flushed */
write lock P           /* for two-phase locking */
latch P                /* get exclusive access to P */
update P               /* update it in the cache */
log the update to P    /* append it to the log */
unlatch P              /* release exclusive access */
Unpin (P)              /* allow P to be flushed */
```

FIGURE 7.8

Using Latches. Obtaining a latch on P ensures that the ordering of log records is consistent with the order of updates to each page.

7.5 DATABASE RECOVERY MANAGER

The recovery manager is the component that is responsible for processing commit and abort operations. It is also responsible for the restart operation, which initiates recovery from a system failure, to bring the database back into a consistent state where it can process transactions again. In summary, the operations should have the following effects (see Figure 7.9):

- Commit(T_i): Permanently installs T_i's updated pages into the stable database. Its effect must be atomic, that is, all-or-nothing, even in the event of a system failure. Also, its effect is irrevocable; once the transaction is committed, it cannot subsequently be aborted.

- Abort(T_i): Restores all the data that T_i updated to the values it had before T_i executed. Like Commit, its effect is irrevocable: once the transaction is aborted, it cannot subsequently be committed.

- Restart: Aborts all transactions that were active at the time of the system failure. Also, any updates by committed transactions that were not installed in the stable database before the failure are installed now. (They may have been written only to the log and may not have made it to the stable database before the failure.) The result should be that the database contains all committed updates and no aborted ones.

To implement these operations, the recovery manager must follow certain rules. The essence of these rules is in controlling when dirty data is flushed to disk.

Implementing Abort

Consider the operation Abort(T_i). Suppose T_i wrote page P and no other transaction wrote P since P was last read from stable storage. If P was not transferred to stable storage after the time that T_i first wrote P, then the recovery manager can simply deallocate P. Otherwise, it has to write P's before-image to the stable database;

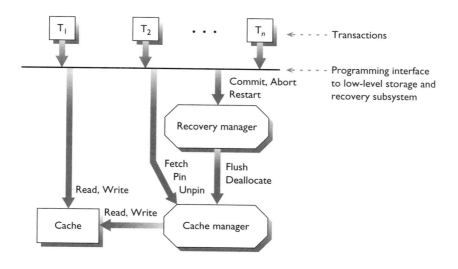

FIGURE 7.9

Recovery Manager Model. The recovery manager calls the cache manager to help it implement the commit, abort, and restart operations.

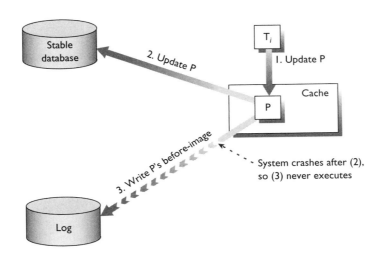

FIGURE 7.10

Why We Need the Write-Ahead Log Protocol. If T_i is active when the system fails, then it can't be aborted after recovery, because P's before-image was lost.

that is, it must restore P's value to what it was before T_i executed. Ordinarily, this is straightforward, since T_i logged its update to P and the log record contains P's before-image. However, what if the abort is being executed to help recover from a system failure? That is, T_i was executing at the time of the system failure and the restart procedure is executing Abort(T_i) to clean things up. It is conceivable that T_i's update to P was transferred to the stable database before the failure, but its update to the log was not transferred to stable storage before the failure (see Figure 7.10). In this case, T_i's update to P cannot be undone, because the before-image has been lost. This unacceptable situation must be prevented by enforcing the following rule:

> **The Write-Ahead Log Protocol:** *Do not flush an uncommitted update to the stable database until the log record containing its before-image has been flushed to the log.*

There is a simple way to avoid the bookkeeping required to enforce this rule, namely, never flush an uncommitted update to the stable database. Just flush it to the log. This is sometimes called a **no-steal** approach, because a cache slot occupied by an updated page is never "stolen" so it can be used to store another page that is read in. After the transaction has committed, then flush the page containing the update to the stable database. That way, you never have to worry whether the before-image is in the log, because it will never be necessary to undo an uncommitted update in the stable database. That is, undo will never be required. For this reason, it is sometimes called a **no-undo** strategy.

Some systems avoid the bookkeeping by maintaining multiple versions of each page, as discussed in Section 6.6, on query-update problems. Instead of overwriting a page, they create a new version of the page. Periodically, old versions that are no longer needed are purged. By keeping old versions in the database itself, before-images need not be logged, so the write-ahead log protocol is automatically satisfied.

Implementing Commit

Now let's consider the operation Commit(T_i), and suppose T_i wrote page P. Since a transaction's results must be durable and Commit is atomic, all of T_i's updates must be in stable storage before the Commit—in the log

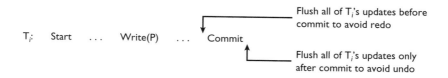

FIGURE 7.11

Avoiding Undo or Redo. Depending on when a transaction's updates are flushed, undo or redo can be avoided.

or in the stable database. In particular, the after-image of T_i's update to P (that is, the value that T_i wrote to P) must be there. This means that the recovery manager must enforce another rule:

> **The Force-at-Commit Rule:** *Do not commit a transaction until the after-images of all its updated pages are in stable storage (in the log or the stable database).*

A simple way to implement the force-at-commit rule is to flush a transaction's updates to the stable database before it commits. This is sometimes called a **force** approach, because all of a transaction's updates are forced to the stable database before commit. This avoids any bookkeeping required to know which updates are not in the stable database and therefore have to be flushed in the log before commit. It also avoids any redo of committed updates, because they are always in the database before they are committed. For this reason, it is sometimes called a **no-redo** strategy. However, it is inefficient for hot pages; that is, those that are frequently updated. As we will see, the best logging algorithms avoid this inefficiency, although it requires some complex bookkeeping.

Notice that the no-steal approach for enforcing the write-ahead log protocol and the force approach for enforcing force-at-commit rule are contradictory (see Figure 7.11). Whichever approach is taken, it would seem that some undo or redo will be required. Although logging algorithms do indeed perform some undo and/or redo, there are techniques that avoid both, which are described in the next section.

The third operation of the recovery manager is restart. Restart requires a fair bit of bookkeeping. It needs to know which transactions were active at the time of the failure, so it can abort them, and which updates of committed transactions were not written to the stable database, so it can redo them. Moreover, restart must be fault-tolerant in the sense that if the system fails when restart is running, it must be possible to re-execute restart. That is, restart must be idempotent. This means that restart must be careful that, at all times, the system is in a state from which restart can correctly execute (which is exactly the same requirement that normal executions have). This requires carefully ordering updates to stable storage.

Given all these rules, we are ready to look at algorithms that implement a recovery manager. A good recovery manager algorithm should add little overhead to the normal processing of transactions. The principal ways it can contribute overhead is by flushing pages too often (creating excess disk traffic) and by logging too much data. A second goal is to recover quickly from a failure, so the system is only down for a short period. The shorter the downtime, the higher the availability. If the system could recover instantly from a failure, then it could fail very often and no one would care (as long as it can commit some transactions!).

7.6 SHADOW-PAGING ALGORITHM

Shadow paging is a simple way to implement a recovery manager. It is one of the easiest recovery algorithms to implement because it does not require a log manager, which is a relatively complex component. It is not widely used in commercial products because it does not scale up to high transaction rates as well as logging. However, since it's simple, we'll describe it first.

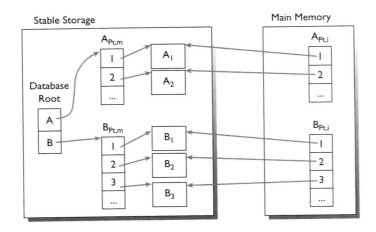

FIGURE 7.12

Tree-structured Database for Shadow Paging. There are two files, A and B. $A_{Pt,m}$ is the master copy of file A's page table that points to the pages of file A, such as A_1 and A_2.

The main idea is to store all of a transaction's updates in a shadow copy of the database. There is also a master copy of the database, whose state represents the execution of all committed transactions and no aborted ones. When the transaction commits, the shadow copy is swapped with the master copy of the database, thereby installing the updates.

To enable this strategy, the master database is structured as a tree of pages. Let's assume that the database consists of a set of files, where each file is a sequence of pages. In this case, the root page of the master database contains pointers to the root page of each file. The root page of a file is a page table that contains a sequence of pointers to the pages of the file. To keep things simple, let's assume that files are small enough that pointers to all of the pages of a file can fit in the file's root page. For example, in Figure 7.12 the database has two files, named A and B. File A has a page table identified by $A_{Pt,m}$, where "m" means "master." The figure shows pointers to the first two pages of the file, A_1 and A_2.

To keep this description simple, let's assume that transactions execute serially. Thus, at most one transaction is active at any given time.

In main memory each transaction has a cached copy of the page table of each file it reads or writes. For example, the cached page tables for transaction T_i are shown in Figure 7.12. Initially, the contents of these cached page tables is the same as their content in stable storage. As the transaction executes, pages are fetched into main memory. The transaction updates some of those pages. When one of those dirty pages is flushed, it is written to an unused location of stable storage. That is, the previous copy of the page is not overwritten. Then, the copy of the page table in main memory is updated to point to the updated page in stable storage, and the updated page table entry is marked as "updated." For example, Figure 7.13 shows the result of flushing a new version of page A_2, where $A_{2,old}$ is the original copy of the page before transaction T_i performed its update and $A_{2,new}$ is the version of the page that includes the update.

To commit a transaction, do the following:

1. For each page P that the transaction updated, if P is dirty in cache, then flush it as described earlier.
2. Initialize a list called UpdatedFiles to include the name of every file updated by the transaction.

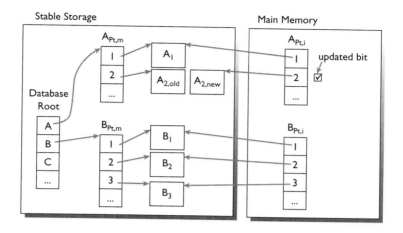

FIGURE 7.13

The Result of Flushing a Dirty Page. An updated version of page A_2 has been flushed to stable storage into an unused location. The main memory page table is updated to point to it and is marked as updated.

3. For each file F in UpdatedFiles, do the following:

   - Set a write lock on F's root page. Let L be its location in stable storage.
   - Read F's root page into cache. Call this the shadow copy of F's page table.
   - For each page of F that is marked as updated in F's cached page table, copy that page's entry from F's cached page table into its shadow page table.
   - Write the shadow copy of F's page table to an unused location L' of stable storage.
   - Replace L by L' in the entry for F in UpdatedFiles.

For example, if a transaction updated page A_2 of file A, and B_1 of file B, then at the end of this procedure, the state of main memory and stable storage would be as shown in Figure 7.14.

When this is done, we repeat essentially the same process for the root page of the database, as follows:

1. Set a write lock on the root page of the database.
2. Read the root page of the database into cache. Call this the shadow copy of the database's page table.
3. For each file F in UpdatedFiles, copy the associated pointer (to F's shadow page table in stable storage) into F's entry in the database's shadow page table.
4. Overwrite the database's root page in stable storage with the shadow copy of the database's root page. This write operation of a single page causes all the transaction's updated pages to become part of the master database.
5. Release all the locks that the transaction obtained on data pages, file page tables, and the database's root page. Discard the UpdatedFiles list and the transaction's cached copies of page tables.

As a result of step 4 (shown in Figure 7.15) the shadow page tables of Figure 7.14 are now master page tables. The former master page tables are now garbage and hence are labeled "g" in the figure ($A_{Pt,g}$ and $B_{Pt,g}$). The old versions of pages updated by the transaction are also garbage, that is, pages $A_{2,old}$ and $B_{1,old}$.

To abort a transaction, simply discard all its updated pages in stable storage and cache. Since the database root page and the page tables it points to are unchanged, none of the pages updated by the aborted transaction are part of the master database. Therefore, there is nothing to undo.

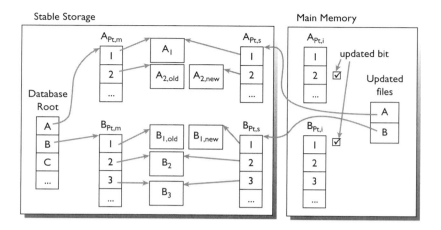

FIGURE 7.14

System State after Partial Commit. Transaction T_i updated pages A_2 and B_1. In the first part of the commit procedure, shadow page tables $A_{Pt,s}$ and $B_{Pt,s}$ are constructed and flushed, and UpdatedFiles points to them.

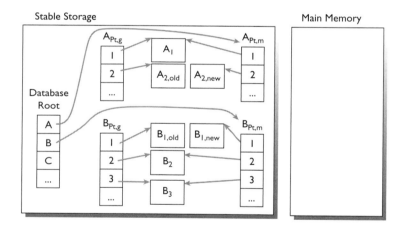

FIGURE 7.15

System State after Commit. The shadow page tables of Figure 7.14 are now master page tables. The former master page tables are now garbage. The UpdatedFiles list and transaction's cached page tables have been deallocated.

One loose end in this story is how to manage available space in stable storage. One approach is to use a list of available space, call it Avail, and treat it as another file. For example, Avail could be a bit map, a binary array where each bit Avail[j] indicates whether page j of stable storage is available.

Suppose Avail fits in one page, and a pointer to Avail is stored in the database's root page. When a transaction flushes a page P for the first time, it needs to allocate a page in stable storage to hold the shadow copy of P. To do this, it reads a copy of Avail into cache (if it is not already there), identifies a page k that is available, clears the bit in Avail, marks Avail[k] as updated, and stores the shadow copy of P in location k. When the transaction commits, the updated entries in the cached copy of Avail are copied into the shadow copy of its page table, which is written to stable storage.

Another loose end is how to allow two or more transactions to execute concurrently. In this case, each transaction has a private copy of the page table of each file it updates. This allows each transaction to keep track of the pages it updated. In addition, to ensure that each transaction reads the last committed value of each page it accesses, a global copy of the master page table is also maintained in cache. When a transaction reads a page for the first time, it uses the pointer in the global cached master page table, not the one in its transaction-local cached page table. To see why, suppose there are two active transactions, T_1 and T_2, and the following sequence of operations executes:

1. T_1 updates page A_1 of file A.
2. T_2 updates page A_2 of file A.
3. T_2 commits.
4. T_1 reads page A_2 of file A.

In step (4), T_1 should read the value of A_2 produced by T_2. However, after T_2 commits, T_1's page table still has a pointer to the original value of A_2, not the one written by T_2. Therefore, when T_1 reads A_2, it needs to use the pointer to A_2 in the master page table.

We began this section by commenting that shadow paging is not used often in commercial products because it does not scale up to high transaction rates. The reason is step one of the commit procedure, which requires that all pages updated by the transaction be written to the stable database. This is a lot of random I/O, which is relatively expensive.

Due to the force-at-commit rule, we cannot avoid writing all the transaction's updates to stable storage before the transaction commits. However, we can do it more efficiently than in shadow paging by appending those updates to a log, which is a sequential file. Sequential writes to disk can be done about 100 times faster than random writes to disk, because they avoid disk head movement and rotational latency. Therefore, a system can reach a much higher transaction rate by writing sequentially to a log than writing randomly to the stable database. Eventually, all updated pages need to be written back to the stable database. However, this can be done lazily, so the rate of random writes has a smaller effect on transaction throughput. The details of making this work are the subject of the next two sections.

7.7 LOG-BASED DATABASE RECOVERY ALGORITHMS

Logging is the most popular technique for implementing a recovery manager. As we described earlier, the log contains a record for each write, commit, and abort operation.

Implementing Commit

To process a commit operation, the recovery manager adds a commit record to the end of the log and flushes the log. The log manager is designed so that it doesn't acknowledge the flush operation until all the log pages in memory, up to and including the one being flushed, have been written to disk and the disk has acknowledged that the disk writes completed successfully. At this point, the transaction has been committed and the recovery manager can acknowledge this fact to its caller.

Since all the transaction's update records precede the commit record in the log, by writing the commit record and then flushing the log, the recovery manager ensures that all the transaction's updates are in stable storage. That is, it ensures that the force-at-commit rule has been satisfied. It doesn't matter whether any of the updated pages have been flushed to the stable database. The updates are in the log, and the log is in stable storage, which is enough to satisfy the rule.

Flushing the log to commit a transaction is a potential bottleneck. If the disk that holds the log can do K sequential disk-writes per second, then K is the maximum number of transactions per second for the whole system. This is too small a number for high performance systems. This is especially annoying because the log page normally isn't full when the flush is invoked, so the full bandwidth of the disk isn't being used. This observation creates an opportunity to improve performance.

A popular way to relieve this bottleneck is an optimization called **group commit**. After adding a commit record to the log, the recovery manager introduces a small artificial delay before flushing the log page, something on the order of $1/K$; that is, a few milliseconds. During that period, if there are other transactions running, they can add records to the end of the log—update records, commit records, and abort records. If the system is busy, then the chances are that the log page will fill up during this period, and when the recovery manager reaches the end of the delay period, it will end up flushing a full page. Thus, each flush operation on the log can commit many transactions, and the recovery manager is getting the full value of the disk bandwidth. If the system is not busy, then it doesn't matter that a partially filled log page is flushed to disk, since not all the disk bandwidth is needed to support the transaction load.

The group commit optimization is an example of a general-purpose technique called **boxcarring**. When there is a high fixed overhead per write operation, it pays to pack a lot of data in each operation. Another place this arises is communication systems that have a high fixed cost to send a message independent of the message's size. The term boxcar is a metaphor for the boxcar in a train, which has a high fixed cost to transport independent of how full it is.

Implementing Abort

To process an abort operation, the recovery manager has to undo the updates of any database pages that were updated by the transaction. It does this by tracing through the transaction's log records, starting from the last one, and installing the before-image of each page that was updated by the transaction.

Sequentially searching the log for the transaction's update records is rather inefficient. To avoid this sequential scan, the recovery manager maintains a linked list of all the transaction's update records in the log. The list header is a **transaction descriptor**, which is a data structure that describes each transaction that it knows about (see Figure 7.16). The descriptor includes a pointer to the last log record that was written by each transaction. Each update record in the log contains a pointer to the previous update record written by the same transaction. So, starting from the transaction descriptor, all the transaction's update records can be scanned.

Maintaining the list is easy. When a transaction writes an update record to the log, it includes a backpointer to the previous log record for that transaction. Then it updates the transaction descriptor to point to the new update record, which is now the last one for the transaction.

There is still the matter of the write-ahead log protocol to consider. The system needs to ensure that it doesn't flush a dirty page from the cache to the stable database unless all the update records that describe updates to that page by uncommitted transactions have already been flushed to the log. To do this, it needs a little help from the cache manager.

We need to add a field to the cache descriptor of each cache slot. This field points to the log page that we need to worry about to enforce the write-ahead log protocol. That is, it contains the address of the log page that contains the update record describing the last update to this cache slot's page (see Figure 7.17). Let's call this the **dependent log page address** (there's no standard term for this). Every time a database page P is updated, the dependent log page address of P's cache slot is also updated to point to the page containing the update's

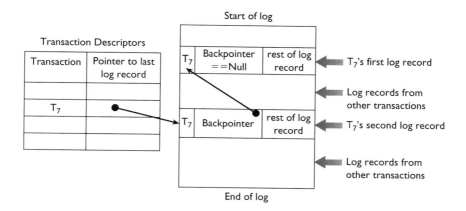

FIGURE 7.16

Data Structure Supporting Abort Processing. Starting from the transaction descriptor, all the transaction's update records can be scanned.

Page	Dirty Bit	Cache Address	Pin Count	Dependent Log Page Address
P_4	I	104	I	1218
P_{16}	0	376	I	null
P_5	I	400	0	1332

FIGURE 7.17

Dependent Log Page Address. Before flushing a page, the cache manager must check that the dependent log page is not in cache and dirty.

log record. Before the cache manager flushes a cache slot, it must check that the dependent log page is not in cache and dirty. If it is, then the dependent log page must be flushed first, to ensure the write-ahead log protocol is satisfied.

Although the cache manager has to check the dependent log page address every time it flushes a page from cache, this rarely generates an extra cache flush of the log page. The reason is this: The log is a sequential file. As soon as a log page fills up, the log manager tells the cache manager to flush it. By the time the cache manager decides to flush a database page, the chances are that the database page has been sitting around in cache for awhile since it was last updated. For example, the cache replacement algorithm notices that the page hasn't been accessed recently and therefore decides to replace it. Since the page hasn't been accessed recently, the chances are that the dependent log page has already been flushed.

As we will see in a moment, even hot pages must eventually be flushed. Since a hot page is updated frequently, it may have update records in the tail of the log. So flushing a hot page may be delayed until its dependent log page has been flushed.

Implementing Restart

To implement restart, the recovery manager scans the log to figure out which transactions need to be aborted and which committed updates need to be redone. As many algorithms of different complexities are in use, we'll start with a simple one and optimize it as we go.

All restart algorithms depend on the recovery manager to perform checkpoint operations periodically, which synchronize the state of the log with the state of the stable database. The simplest checkpoint algorithm does the following:

1. It stops accepting any new update, commit, and abort operations. It waits until all active update, commit, and abort operations have finished.
2. It makes a list of all active transactions along with each transaction's pointer to its last log record.
3. It flushes all the dirty pages in cache.
4. It writes a **checkpoint record** to the log, which includes the list of active transactions and log pointers.
5. It resumes accepting new update, commit, and abort operations again.

At this point, the stable database state is exactly consistent with the state of the log. We'll explain a more efficient checkpointing algorithm in a moment, but for now, let's assume we're using this one.

The restart algorithm scans the log forward and fully processes each log record before proceeding to the next. Its goal is first to redo all updates that executed after the last checkpoint and then to undo the ones that did not commit. It starts at the last checkpoint record. There is no point in looking at log records before the last checkpoint record, because their effects have been fully recorded in the stable database (see Figure 7.18). The restart algorithm maintains lists of committed and aborted transactions, which are initially empty; and a list of active transactions, which is initialized from the last checkpoint record. When the restart algorithm encounters a new log record, it does the following:

- If the log record is an update record, then it writes the after-image of the update to the cache, and it adds the transaction's identifier to the active list if it isn't already there. Notice that even if the update is already in the stable database, there is no harm in writing the after-image, because the after-image contains an entire page image. (Remember our simplifying assumption that each update writes a whole page.) So at worst, it's just redoing work needlessly.

- If the log record is a commit record, it adds the transaction to its commit list and removes it from the active list.

- If the log record is an abort record, it undoes all of the transaction's updates in the same way as it normally processes an abort. Also, it adds the transaction to its abort list and removes it from the active list.

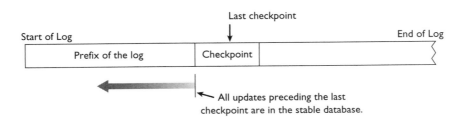

FIGURE 7.18

Basic Checkpointing. All dirty pages are flushed before a checkpoint record is written.

When it reaches the end of the log, it has redone all the updates of committed and active transactions, and wiped out the effects of any aborted transactions. At this point, the active list contains any transactions that started running before the failure but did not commit or abort before the failure. (Notice that since the active list was initialized from the last checkpoint record, this includes transactions that were active at the last checkpoint but did not subsequently commit or abort.) These transactions cannot continue running, since they lost their memory state during the system failure, so the restart algorithm aborts them too. Now the system is ready to process new transactions, since the combined state of the cache and stable database includes all committed updates and no aborted ones.

As long as the restart algorithm is running, users are unable to run transactions. Therefore, it's important to optimize it to minimize its running time and therefore maximize the system's availability. These optimizations are the subject of the next section.

7.8 OPTIMIZING RESTART IN LOG-BASED ALGORITHMS

Fuzzy Checkpointing

Checkpoints are an important way of speeding up the restart algorithm. The more frequently the system runs a checkpoint, the less log that the restart algorithm will have to process, and therefore, the less time it will take to run restart. However, checkpointing isn't free. The checkpointing algorithm described earlier does quite a lot of work and causes the system to stop processing new requests for awhile, until it has finished flushing all the dirty pages in cache. We need a cheaper way to checkpoint, so we can afford to checkpoint often and thereby speed up the restart algorithm.

The solution is called **fuzzy checkpointing**. To do a checkpoint, the recovery manager does the following:

1. It stops accepting any new update, commit, and abort operations.
2. It scans the cache to make a list of all the dirty pages in the cache.
3. It makes a list of all active transactions along with each transaction's pointer to its last log record.
4. It writes a checkpoint record to the log, which includes the list of active transactions and log pointers, and it allows normal operation to resume.
5. It resumes accepting new update, commit, and abort operations.
6. In parallel with running new update, commit and abort operations, it issues flush operations to write to the stable database all the dirty pages on the list it gathered in step (2). These are low priority operations that the cache manager should do only when it has spare capacity. It may take awhile.

The recovery manager is allowed to do another checkpoint operation only after step (6) completes; that is, only after those dirty old pages have been flushed. Thus, by the time the next checkpoint record is written, all the updates that preceded the previous checkpoint record must be in the stable database.

Let's revisit the restart algorithm with this fuzzy checkpointing algorithm in mind. Notice that it's the second-to-last (i.e., penultimate) checkpoint record that has the property we're looking for (see Figure 7.19). All the updates in the log that precede the penultimate checkpoint record must be in the stable database. The checkpointing algorithm would not have written the last checkpoint record until it knew this was true. So, the restart algorithm should start with the penultimate checkpoint record. By contrast, in the simple checkpointing algorithm of the previous section, all updates before the last checkpoint record were in the stable database, so it started with the last checkpoint record, not the penultimate one.

Notice that fuzzy checkpointing is a relatively fast activity. It needs to stop processing momentarily, to examine the cache and write a checkpoint record. It then writes out dirty pages in parallel with normal operation.

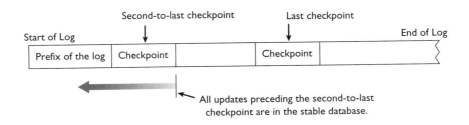

FIGURE 7.19

Fuzzy Checkpointing. After a checkpoint record is written, all dirty cache pages are flushed. The flushes must be completed before the next checkpoint record is written.

If possible, these writes should run at low priority so they don't block reads by active transactions. Assuming there is enough disk bandwidth to process these reads and writes (which is needed in any case), these random writes have very little impact on the performance of active transactions. Thus, checkpointing can be run frequently, to minimize the amount of work that restart has to do.

The fuzzy checkpointing algorithm is so important to transaction performance and restart speed, it is worth optimizing it heavily. Commercial implementations use many optimizations of the algorithm described here.

Operation Logging

It is very inefficient to write the entire before-image and after-image of a page every time a transaction does an update, since most updates modify only a small portion of a page. Worse yet, it does not work correctly if the database system does record-granularity locking. For example, suppose the system logs before-images and after-images of pages, records x and y are on the same page P, and we have the following execution:

$$E = w_1[x] \, w_2[y] \, \text{abort}_1 \, \text{commit}_2$$

When transaction T_1 aborts, we cannot install its before-image of P, since this would wipe out T_2's update to y. This is essentially the same problem we ran into at the beginning of Section 7.4, on Locking Assumptions, where we argued for holding write locks until after the transaction commits.

A solution is to have each update record include only the before-image and after-image of the record that it actually updates on a page. This kills two birds with one stone. It greatly reduces the amount of logging, and it allows us to support record-level locking. It does have one unfortunate side-effect, though. The restart algorithm has to read the page from disk before applying the update. This wasn't needed with page-level logging, because the log contained a complete copy of the page. Since logging is a much more frequent operation than restart, this is a net win, but it does create another activity that needs to be optimized by the restart algorithm.

We can reduce the amount of logging even further by recording only a *description* of the change that was made rather than the entire record. The description must have enough information that we can undo or redo the change, but no more than that. That is, it doesn't necessarily have to include the entire before-image and after-image of the record. For example, if the update modifies only one field of a record, the update record needs to contain only the identity of the record (e.g., its key), the identity of the field (e.g., its byte range within the record), and the before-image and after-image of the modified field, plus the name of the operation being performed (e.g., "update-field"), so the restart algorithm will know how to interpret the log record later. As another example, the update record might describe the insertion of a record, in which case it needs to log only the after-image of the record, since there is no before-image.

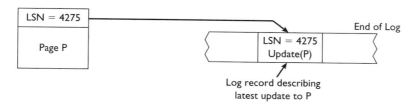

FIGURE 7.20

Storing Log Sequence Numbers (LSNs) in Pages. When updating a page, include the LSN of the log record describing the update.

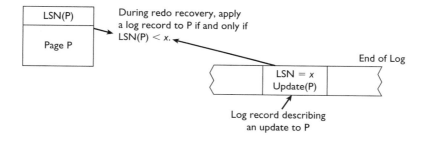

FIGURE 7.21

Interpreting LSNs during Recovery. Redo an update if and only if the page's LSN indicates that the update isn't already there.

By reducing the amount of logging this way, we have complicated the restart algorithm. It can no longer simply start at the penultimate checkpoint record and redo update records, because the redo operations might not be applicable to the stable database page in its current state. For example, it would be wrong to insert a record on a page if that record is already there, because that would put two copies of the record on the page. The reason that the insert is not applicable is because it already executed and it is not idempotent.

The restart algorithm has to know whether an update record is applicable to a page before redoing the update. To do this, each page is given a header that includes the log address of the last log record that was applied to the page (see Figure 7.20). This is called the **log sequence number** (**LSN**). After an update is performed on the page and the log record is written to the log, the LSN is written to the page header before releasing the latch on the page. This allows the restart algorithm to tell whether a page includes an update before redoing it: If LSN(database-page) ≥ LSN(log-record), then the log-record's update is already on the page and should not be redone (see Figure 7.21).

This LSN idea is useful, but it complicates undo operations. When the restart algorithm undoes an update to abort a transaction, T_1, there is no LSN that accurately describes the state of the page relative to the log. To visualize the problem, consider the example in Figure 7.22. Transactions T_1 and T_2 update different records R_1 and R_2, respectively, on the same page, P. T_2 writes to P (at LSN 222) after T_1 and then T_2 commits (at LSN 223). When T_1 aborts (at LSN 224), what LSN should it write in P? It cannot use the LSN of the last update to P that preceded its update (219), since that would say that T_2's update did not execute, which is wrong. It cannot use the LSN of T_2's update either (222), since that says T_1's update was done but not undone.

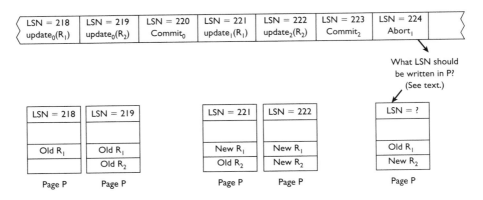

FIGURE 7.22

Installing an LSN during Undo. The state of page P is shown after logging each update. When aborting T_1, there is no LSN to store in P that accurately describes P's state.

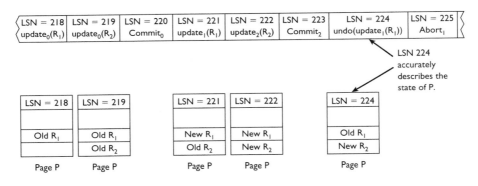

FIGURE 7.23

Using an Undo Log Record. If the undo operation is logged, its LSN can be installed on page P to record the fact that the update was undone.

   A good solution to this problem is to log undo operations. That is, when T_1 aborts, each time it undoes an update operation, say on page P, it writes a log record that describes that undo and it uses the LSN of that log record in P's page header. This is called an **undo record** or **compensation log record**. Now the LSN of the undo record accurately describes the state of the page relative to the log. See Figure 7.23.

   Logging undo's has an interesting side effect: Committed and aborted transactions look exactly the same in the log. They both have a sequence of update operations followed by an operation that says the transaction is done (committed or aborted). The restart algorithm processes both kinds of transactions in the same way, namely, it redoes their updates. For aborted transactions, some of those redo operations are applied to undo records, but the restart algorithm doesn't care. It redoes them just like ordinary update records. The only transactions that the restart algorithm actually has to abort by scanning the log backward are those that were active at the time of the failure.

   Suppose a transaction T is in the midst of aborting when the system fails. That is, T may have written undo records for some but not all of its update records. When the system recovers, the restart algorithm sees that

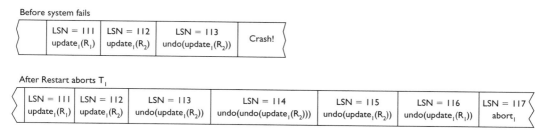

FIGURE 7.24

Undoing Undo Records. During Restart, T_1's undo record at LSN 113 needs to be undone, as does the update at LSN 112, again.

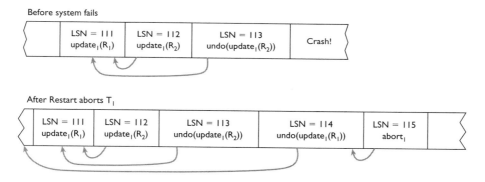

FIGURE 7.25

Splicing Out Undo Records. Each undo record points to the next update record that needs to be undone.

T was active at the time of the failure. Therefore, it undoes all of T's updates, not just the update records for T but also the undo records. For example, in Figure 7.24 transaction T_1 was aborting at the time the system failed. Before the failure, it performed the undo for LSN 112 and recorded that fact in the undo record with LSN 113. However, it didn't complete the abort before the system crashed. After recovery, the restart algorithm sees that T_1 was active when the system crashed, so it performs undo operations for LSN 113, 112, and 111, in that order, thereby writing undo records with LSNs 114, 115, and 116, respectively.

This activity of undoing undo records is redundant. It can be avoided by splicing undo records out of the chain of transaction backpointers, as shown in Figure 7.25. To do this, each undo record points to the next update record to be undone. For example, in the figure the undo record with LSN 113 points to the update record at LSN 111. To finish aborting T_1 during restart, the restart algorithm starts with the last log record for T_1, which is at LSN 113, and follows its backpointer to the next update to be undone, in this case the update at LSN 111.

Another useful optimization is to avoid unnecessary page fetches by recording flush operations in the log. That is, after the cache manager flushes a page and before it allows any further updates to the page, it adds a **flush record** to the log, which includes the address of the page that was flushed. This record tells the restart algorithm that all updates to that page that precede the flush record are already on disk and therefore do not need to be redone. In effect, it is a per-page checkpoint record.

A good way to use flush records during recovery is to pre-analyze the log before the redo phase. To enable this process, in each checkpoint record, each page in the list of dirty pages is augmented with the oldest LSN that must be redone to that page. This requires some additional bookkeeping by the cache manager, which needs to associate that oldest LSN with each cache slot, assign it when a clean page is first updated, and clear it when the page is flushed. This list of dirty pages with their oldest LSNs to redo is called a **dirty page table**.

The pre-analysis phase of the restart algorithm does a preliminary log scan starting at the penultimate checkpoint and moving forward toward the end of the log. The goal is to create a dirty-page table that, to the extent possible, describes the state of the cache at the time of failure. To initialize the undo phase of restart, it also builds a list of active transactions that includes the last LSN of each transaction. During this scan, there are four types of log records of interest: update, flush, commit, and abort.

- $Update_i(P)$: If page P is not in the dirty-page table, then add it and set its oldest LSN to be the LSN of this update record. If transaction T_i is not already on the transaction list, then add it. Set T_i's last LSN to be the LSN of this update record.
- Flush(P): Delete P from the dirty-page table.
- $Commit_i$ or $Abort_i$: Delete T_i from the transaction list.

At the end of this pre-analysis phase, for each page in the dirty-page table there is at least one update record in the log after the last flush record for the page. Therefore, the page needs to be updated during the redo phase. Saying this in reverse: The preanalysis phase avoids redoing any update records for page P if the last update record for P precedes the last flush record for P. Normally, one would expect many update records to satisfy this property, so this preanalysis phase avoids useless page fetches during redo and hence speeds up restart.

The dirty-page table also gives guidance on when a page needs to be fetched. Every page in the dirty-page table needs to be read during restart, since there is at least one update record in the log that follows the last flush record for the page. Since the dirty page table includes the LSN of the oldest update to each page, the restart algorithm can prefetch pages in increasing order of oldest LSN, so the pages will arrive in cache in the order they will be needed by redo scan, which further improves its performance.

The restart algorithm described in this section is called ARIES, and was developed by C. Mohan and his colleagues at IBM. The most important insight is the value of replaying history from the penultimate checkpoint, so that at the end of the redo scan the log and database are mutually consistent. This makes it easy to see that the restart algorithm is correct and enables complex reasoning leading to optimizations like splicing out undo records and using a dirty page table to reduce page fetches during restart. ARIES includes other optimizations not described here, such as taking checkpoints during restart, handling nested transactions and nested top-level actions, and updating index structures. (See the Bibliographic Notes for references.)

Many other tricky problems arise in implementing recovery algorithms, such as redundantly storing pointers to the checkpoint record (so the restart algorithm can find it even if there is a media failure), finding the end of the log (it's too expensive to update a disk-resident pointer to end-of-log every time the log is updated), and handling multipage update records (what if only one of the pages is written before a failure?). These details are of interest mainly to people building recovery algorithms, and are therefore beyond the scope of this book. (See the Bibliographic Notes for further readings.)

User Techniques

Although most optimizations of system recovery are only available to database system implementers, there are a few things that a user can do to speed up restart and thereby improve availability, such as the following:

- If the checkpointing frequency can be adjusted by the system administrator, then increasing it will reduce the amount of work needed at restart. Running a benchmark with different checkpointing frequencies will help determine the expense of using frequent checkpoints to improve recovery time. Depending on the overhead of the checkpointing algorithm used, this might require buying extra hardware, to ensure satisfactory transaction performance while checkpointing is being done.

- Partition the database across more disks. The restart algorithm is often I/O-bound. Although it reads the log sequentially (which is fast), it accesses the database randomly. Spreading the database over more disks increases the effective disk bandwidth and can reduce restart time.

- Increase the system resources available to the restart program. After the operating system recovers from a failure, it runs recovery scripts that include calling the database restart algorithm. It may not allocate main memory resources optimally, if left to its own defaults. The restart algorithm benefits from a huge cache, to reduce its I/O. If memory allocation can be controlled, tuning it can help reduce restart time.

In general, one should benchmark the performance of restart to determine its sensitivity to a variety of conditions and thereby be able to tune it to balance restart running time against checkpointing overhead.

7.9 MEDIA RECOVERY

A media failure is the loss of a portion of stable storage. This usually is detected when an attempt is made to read a portion of the stable database, and the disk responds with an error condition. Failure rates of stable storage devices are sensitive to many factors, and they change over time with changing technologies. That said, a typical failure rate for magnetic disks is 2% to 8% per year, meaning that a system with 100 disks experiences two to eight irreparable disk failures per year. This is a sufficiently frequent occurrence that engineered solutions are needed to shield the system from the effect of a media failure and to enable recovery when a media failure does occur. The latter is similar to recovering from a system failure: Load a usable state of the stable database from some backup device, such as tape or another disk, and then use the log to bring that state up to date.

Mirrored Disks

Media failures are a fairly serious problem, since as we will see, it can take a significant amount of time to recover from one. To avoid it, most TP systems use **mirrored** (or **shadowed**) **disks**. This means they use two physical disks for each logical disk that they need, so each disk has an up-to-date backup that can substitute for it if it fails. The mirroring is usually done in hardware, though operating systems also offer the feature in software. In either case, each write operation is sent to both physical disks, so the disks are always identical. Thus, a read can be serviced from either disk. If one disk fails, the other disk is still there to continue running until a new disk can be brought in to replace the failed one. This greatly reduces the chances of a media failure.

After one disk of a mirrored pair fails, a new disk must be initialized while the good disk is still functioning. Like mirroring itself, this is usually done in the hardware controller. The algorithm that accomplishes it usually works as follows: The algorithm scans the good disk and copies tracks, one by one, to the new disk. It has a temporary variable that identifies the track currently being copied. While it is copying that track, no updates are allowed to the track. Updates to tracks that already have been copied are written to both disks, since these tracks are already identical on both disks. Updates to tracks that have not yet been copied are written only to the good disk, since writing them to the new disk would be useless. This copying algorithm can run in the background while the good disk is handling the normal processing load.

Like restart, it is important that this mirror recovery procedure be as fast as possible. While it is going on, the good disk is a single point of failure. If it dies, then a media failure has occurred, at which point the only hope is to load an old copy of the database and use a redo log to bring it up to date.

Even a fast mirror recovery procedure is intrusive. Mirror recovery does sequential I/O, whereas normal operation performs random I/O. So normal operation slows down mirror recovery and vice versa. Thus, the system needs enough spare disk bandwidth to do mirror recovery while giving satisfactory performance to users.

The failure of a log disk is especially problematic, since it affects all update transactions. There are many creative ways to minimize the effect of mirror recovery on writes to the log. For example, advanced disk-management software lets you set a low priority for repairing that mirror, but then mirror recovery is running much longer, during which time a second log disk failure would be a disaster. Another approach is to populate only a small fraction of the mirrored log disk, say 10%. This cuts the rebuild time and increases the random I/O rate during that rebuild. Or one can build a triple mirror; if a disk fails, wait until a slack time to rebuild the third drive of the mirror. Experienced database administrators build a synthetic load with peak log-write throughput and kill their log mirror to see if the system will continue to support the required service level agreement.

The choice of disk configuration will be greatly affected by the increasing availability of affordable solid state disks (SSDs). These disks perform sequential and random I/O at about the same speed. Therefore, random I/O is less disruptive to mirror recovery than with magnetic disks. However, the cost per gigabyte of SSDs is considerably higher than for magnetic disks, and this gap is expected to continue going forward. It may therefore be desirable to use configurations that contain both SSDs and magnetic disks. It is too early to predict how the cost and performance tradeoffs will play out. However, it seems likely that it will continue to be challenging to design a storage configuration that meets a system's service level agreement at the lowest cost.

A related technology is **RAID**—redundant arrays of inexpensive disks. In RAID, an array of identical disks is built to function like one high-bandwidth disk (see Figure 7.26). A **stripe** is the set of disk blocks consisting of the ith block from each disk, where i is an integer between one and the number of blocks on a disk. If the disk block size is s and there are d disks in the RAID, then a stripe is, in effect, a logical block of size $d \times s$. A RAID is high-bandwidth because the disks are read and written in parallel. That is, it reads or writes a stripe in about the same amount of time that one disk can read or write a single block.

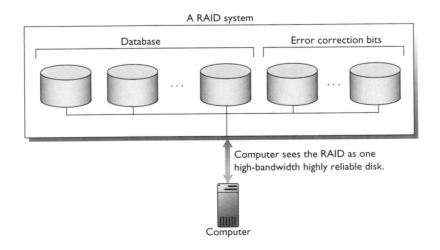

FIGURE 7.26

A Redundant Array of Inexpensive Disks (RAID). An array of disks built to function as one high-bandwidth disk. Using extra disks for error correction bits increases reliability.

Some RAID systems use extra disks in the array to store error correction bits, so they can tolerate the failure of one of the disks in the array without losing data. For example, an array of five disks could store data on four disks and parity bits on the fifth disk. Thus, the RAID can tolerate the loss of one disk without losing data. A write to any of disks 1 through 4 implies a write to disk 5. To avoid having disk 5 be a bottleneck, parity blocks can be distributed across the disks. For example, stripes 1, 6, and 11 store their parity block on disk 1; stripes 2, 7, and 12 store their parity block on disk 2; and so on.

The different RAID configurations are identified by numbers. Striped disks without parity are called RAID 0. Mirroring is called RAID 1 and can use more than two disk replicas. RAID 2 through 6 use parity in different configurations. RAID 10 is a RAID 0 configuration where each disk is actually a mirrored pair (i.e., RAID 1). This is called nested RAID, since it nests RAID 1 disks into a RAID 0 configuration.

Even if it is judged to be uneconomical to use mirrored disks or a RAID for the stable database, one should at least use them for the log. Losing a portion of the log could be a disaster. **Disaster** is a technical term for an unrecoverable failure. There are two ways that a media failure of the log can be unrecoverable:

- After writing an uncommitted update to the stable database, the log may be the only place that has the before-image of that update, which is needed if the transaction aborts. If the tail of the log gets corrupted, it may be impossible to abort the transaction, ever.

- After committing a transaction, some of its after-images may be only in the log and not yet in the stable database. If the tail of the log gets corrupted and the system fails (losing the cache), then the committed after-image is lost forever.

In both cases, manual intervention and guesswork may be needed to recover from the failure. Therefore, it's a good idea to put the log on a separate device and mirror it.

Even with mirrored disks, it is possible that both disks fail before the first failed disk is replaced. When configuring a system, there are some things one can do to reduce this possibility. First, one can try to minimize the amount of shared hardware between two mirrored disks. For example, if the disks share a single controller, and that controller starts scribbling garbage, both disks will be destroyed. Second, one can keep the disks in separate rooms or buildings, so that physical damage, such as a fire, does not destroy both disks. How far to go down these design paths depends on the cost of downtime if data becomes unavailable for awhile due to a media failure.

The general principle here is that protection against media failure requires redundancy. We need two copies of the log to ensure restart can run correctly if one log disk fails. We use mirrored disks or a RAID system that has built-in error correction to avoid requiring media recovery when a database disk fails. If the stable database is not mirrored and a disk fails, or if both mirrors fail, then yet another copy of the stable database—an archive copy—is needed in order to run media recovery.

Archiving

Media recovery requires the system to have an archive (i.e., backup) copy of the stable database that it can use as a starting point. It also needs a copy of the log that includes all committed updates that executed after the archive copy was created. The media recovery algorithm can therefore load the latest archive copy and redo the corresponding log.

To create an archive copy, one can simply copy the entire stable database. If this is done when the system is not processing transactions, it will produce a snapshot of the database that is consistent with the log. If archiving is done on-line, that is, if the system is processing transactions while the archive copy is being made, then different parts of the archive copy will include updates from different transactions. That is, pages copied later will have updates from more transactions than those copied earlier. It seems like this would be hard to sort out when it is time to recover from a media failure. However, essentially the same old restart algorithm that we described for system failures will work here too.

This approach requires that the system keep an archive copy of the log. Therefore, even after a checkpoint has made early parts of the log unnecessary for recovery from system failures, those early parts must still be saved for media recovery. Usually, they are copied to a **media recovery log** on a separate long-term storage device.

To avoid disk head contention between on-line transactions writing to the end of the log and the media recovery log archiver reading from the beginning of the log, it is worthwhile to have two pairs of mirrored log disks. One pair contains the tail of the log for active transactions. The other contains the early part of the log for archiving to the media recovery log. By the time the active transaction log is out of space, the media recovery log archiver should have finished reading the other pair of log disks. So the latter can immediately be reused for the active transaction log and the archiver can turn its attention to the other pair of log disks.

Suppose the recovery manager uses the optimization in *Operation Logging*, in Section 7.8, where it stores on each page the log address of the last update applied to it (i.e., the LSN). This information will be in the archive copy too. So the media recovery manager knows the exact state of the page to recover, in the same way as the restart algorithm.

As for system failures, recovery time for media failures affects availability, so checkpointing frequently is desirable for reducing recovery time. Making an archive copy of the entire stable database is slow. One can speed up archiving by only copying pages that have changed since the last time the archiving algorithm ran. A simple way to do this is to keep an **update-bit** in each page header that indicates whether the page has been updated since it was last archived. This bit is set every time the page is updated. The archive algorithm clears the bit each time it copies the page to the archive. The archive algorithm still needs to read the entire stable database, to look at all the update bits, but it only needs to copy a fraction of those pages to the archive. We can speed things up even further by keeping the update bits in a separate location, so the archiving algorithm needs to read only pages that were recently updated, not all pages.

To recover from the media failure of a disk, one needs to load the most recent archive copy of the disk and process the log that includes all updates that were done since the archive copy was made. This means the archive algorithm should write a checkpoint record to the log, indicating when it started running, and another checkpoint record when it is done. When it is done, all database updates that preceded the first checkpoint record are definitely in the archive (and some later updates too, but we can't tell which ones by looking at the log). So the latter checkpoint record indicates that only updates occurring after the former checkpoint record need to be considered during media recovery.

A useful optimization to reduce the amount of log needed for media recovery is to avoid keeping undo information in the media recovery log, such as before-images. If the archiving procedure archives pages only when their entire contents is committed, then undo information will not be needed at archive recovery time. Therefore, the archiving procedure should write-lock each page before it copies it to the archive, thereby ensuring there are no active transactions writing to the page at the time it does the copy operation. A postprocessing step on the log can strip out all undo information before setting it aside for future use during media recovery.

It is common that a media failure only corrupts a small portion of a disk, such as a few tracks. Depending on how the media recovery algorithm is organized, it may or may not be necessary to recover the entire disk in this case. A distinguishing feature of database systems is whether they can recover from such failures efficiently. For example, instead of reconstructing the entire disk, a database system could offer the ability to recover just the damaged portions of the disk and write them to an empty area of the same disk. Moreover, it could have utilities to postprocess logs, to partition them based on regions of the disk, so that the media recovery algorithm only needs to process a log containing records that are relevant to the damaged portion of the disk.

Not all media failures are permanent failures, where the damaged page is physically destroyed. Some failures are transient, where the content of the page is wrong but it can be repaired simply by rewriting it. For example, a disk may not have written a page atomically (i.e., written out only part of its contents), because the disk arm strayed a bit during the write. Some disks can detect this error immediately and retry the write. However, if the corrupt page is discovered much later when the page is read, then it needs to be recovered. In this case, it is worthwhile to reconstruct the page in place, rather than replacing the disk or relocating the damaged page.

7.10 SUMMARY

TP systems often are expected to be available 24 hours per day, 7 days per week, to support around-the-clock business operations. Two factors affect availability: the mean time between failures (MTBF) and the mean time to repair (MTTR). Improving availability requires increasing MTBF, decreasing MTTR, or both.

Computer failures occur because of:

- Environmental factors (power, air conditioning, communication lines, natural disasters, etc.)
- System management (operations staff errors, software upgrades, preventive maintenance, etc.)
- Hardware (failure of any component, such as memory, disk, network controller, etc.)
- Software (crash of operating system, database system, transactional middleware, or application program)

If the operating system fails, then just reboot it. For other types of software failure, the transactional middleware or database system must detect the failure of a process and recreate it. The recreated process must then run a recovery procedure to reconstruct its state.

When a client recovers it needs to reconnect to its servers. It then should determine which calls were outstanding when it failed, and what it needs to do to complete those calls. This is exactly the problem addressed in Chapter 4, "Queued Transaction Processing."

When a server recovers, it needs to reconstruct a state that is consistent with the last calls that it processed before the failure. This requires taking checkpoints periodically during normal operation, so it can reload the checkpointed state at recovery time. Executing from that recovered state, the server must avoid redoing any non-redoable actions (such as printing a check).

Transactions simplify recovery by allowing a server to focus on restoring its state to contain only the results of committed transactions, rather than recovering to a state that is consistent with the last operations it ran. Transactional servers often are split into two types, resource managers that maintain state and stateless application servers. The latter store all their state in the resource managers and therefore can recover simply by reinitializing.

A database system must be able to recover from several kinds of failure. It recovers from a transaction failure (where a transaction aborts) by undoing all the transaction's updates. It recovers from a system failure (where main memory is lost) or a media failure (where some stable storage is lost) by restoring the database to contain exactly the set of committed updates.

All of today's recovery mechanisms require every transaction to hold its write locks until it commits, to avoid cascading aborts and to ensure that undo can be implemented simply by restoring an update's before-image. For satisfactory performance, locks usually are held at record granularity, though recovery can be simplified considerably if page-granularity locking is used.

The recovery manager uses a cache manager to fetch pages from disk and later flush them. In addition to processing commit and abort operations, it implements a recovery algorithm to recover from system failures. The most popular recovery algorithms use a log, which contains a history of all updates, commits, and aborts.

The recovery manager must carefully control when updates are flushed to ensure the database is always recoverable. In particular, it must enforce two rules:

- The Write-Ahead Log Protocol: Do not flush an uncommitted update to the stable database until the log record containing its before-image has been flushed to the log.
- The Force-at-Commit Rule: Do not commit a transaction until the after-images of all of its updated pages are in stable storage (in the log or the stable database).

The recovery manager tells the cache manager about dependencies between dirty database pages and log pages so the cache manager can enforce the write-ahead log protocol. To implement commit, the recovery manager appends a commit record to the log and flushes it. Since all updates are logged, this implements the force-at-commit rule. To implement abort, the recovery manager follows a linked list of the transaction's log records, undoing each update along the way.

To minimize the amount of log to process at recovery time, the recovery manager periodically does a checkpoint, which synchronizes the state of the log with the stable database. To recover from a system failure, it scans the log from the last or penultimate checkpoint record (depending on the checkpointing algorithm) and redoes updates as required. It can tell whether a log record should be redone by comparing the log record's address (LSN) with the LSN stored in the corresponding database page, since each database page's LSN is updated whenever the page itself is updated. Using LSNs in this way allows the recovery manager to log operation descriptions, rather than before- and after-images, since it redoes an operation only if the page is in the same state as when the operation originally ran.

Recovery time should be short, to maximize availability. Therefore, there are numerous optimizations to reduce checkpoint overhead so it can be done more frequently, and thereby reduce recovery time. For the same reason, there are also many optimizations to speed up the recovery algorithm itself.

To cope with media failures, some redundant storage is required. Mirrored disks or RAID systems commonly are used for the database and for the log. Still, to cope with media failures of the stable database, it's important to periodically make an archive copy of the database plus an archive copy of the log that includes all committed updates that executed after creating the archive database copy. The recovery algorithm for media failures loads the archive copy and redoes committed updates in the log, just like the recovery algorithm for system failures. As for system failures, checkpointing should be frequent and the recovery algorithm should be optimized to run fast, to maximize availability.

Two-Phase Commit

8.1 INTRODUCTION

The previous chapter showed how to use logging to ensure that a transaction is atomic with respect to failures, provided that the transaction updates data only in one resource manager. If two or more resource managers process updates for a transaction, then another technique is needed to ensure that the transaction commits at all resource managers or at none of them. This is called the **two-phase commit** protocol. Chapter 1 briefly introduced the protocol. This chapter develops it in more detail.

The main goal of the protocol is to ensure that a transaction either commits at all the resource managers that it accessed or aborts at all of them. The undesirable outcome that the protocol avoids is that the transaction commits at one resource manager and aborts at another.

Two-phase commit arises whenever the resource managers that processed a transaction's updates can commit the transaction independently. This surely arises if the resource managers execute on different machines. It also arises when the resource managers execute on the same machine but use separate logs. However, when the resource managers use a shared log, they can commit a transaction simultaneously by appending a single commit record to the log. In that case, the resource managers do not independently commit the transaction, so two-phase commit is not required.

At first, it may seem that committing at multiple resource managers is no more difficult than committing at one resource manager: Just send a message telling each resource manager to commit or abort. In the absence of failures, this would work. But failures can make it much harder to commit or abort everywhere. For example, what should be done while committing transaction T in each of the following situations?

- A resource manager that processed some of T's updates fails after T has committed at another resource manager.
- A resource manager that failed while T was committing has now recovered and wants to find out whether T committed or recovered. How does it know who to ask? What should it do if none of the other resource managers that processed T's operations are up and running?
- What if a resource manager R is not responding to messages? Should other resource managers assume R is down, and therefore its active transactions will abort; or that communications is down and R is still operational?

A complete solution must deal with these and all other failure situations that can arise.

In this chapter, we return to using the terms "resource manager" and "resource," instead of the terms "data manager" and "data item" that we used in Chapters 6 and 7. When discussing two-phase commit, it is common practice to talk about resource managers, rather than data managers or database systems. The reason is that when a transaction commits, all the transactional resources it accesses need to get involved in the commitment activity, not just databases. Non-database transactional resources include recoverable scratchpad areas, queues, and other messaging systems.

As in resource manager recovery, application programmers usually do not get involved in two-phase commit. Most database systems and transactional middleware support it and make it transparent to the application. However, if an application needs to directly manage a transactional resource as well as use other resource managers, then the application needs to participate in the two-phase commit protocol. The application programmer needs to know what to do in this case. Some error scenarios require operator intervention. The application needs to expose these situations to the operator in a comprehensible way so the operator can determine the best course of action.

System architects who configure a TP system have a more pressing need to consider the effects of two-phase commit. When configuring a system consisting of different resource managers, such as different database systems supplied by different vendors, one needs to ensure that the two-phase commit implementations of the resource managers interoperate properly. This requires some understanding of how two-phase commit protocols are implemented. Moreover, such multidatabase configurations lead to additional communication overhead for two-phase commit, which can dramatically affect transaction performance. In some cases, that overhead makes it advisable to avoid a multidatabase configuration. For all these reasons, a solid understanding of two-phase commit is needed to build robust TP applications.

8.2 THE TWO-PHASE COMMIT PROTOCOL

Assumptions

The protocol makes the following assumptions about each transaction T:

1. Transaction T accesses resources from time to time. If it experiences a serious error at any time, such as a deadlock or illegal operation, it issues an abort operation. If it terminates normally without any errors, it issues a commit. In response to the commit, the system runs the two-phase commit protocol.

2. Each resource manager can commit or abort its part of T; that is, permanently install or undo T's operations that involve this resource manager. This essentially says that each resource manager has a transactional recovery system, as described in the previous chapter.

3. One and only one program issues the commit operation on T. That is, one program decides when to start committing T by running the two-phase commit protocol, and no other program will later start running the protocol on T independently. In some cases, a second attempt to run two-phase commit while the first attempt is still running will cause the protocol to break; that is, cause it to commit at one resource manager and abort at another. The protocol can be programmed to cope with concurrent attempts to run two-phase commit, but we will not investigate this type of error here. We will just assume it does not happen.

4. Transaction T has terminated executing at all resource managers before issuing the commit operation. If the transaction does all of its communication using RPC, then this is easy to arrange. T can ensure it has finished processing at all resource managers by waiting for all of its RPCs to return, provided that each resource manager finishes all the work it was asked to do before returning from the call. This assumption avoids our having to deal with the complexity of transaction termination here.

In general, termination can be hard to arrange if T uses communications paradigms other than RPC. For example, if the transaction uses peer-to-peer messaging, where each communicating party can send messages to and receive messages from other parties in an application-defined order, then the transaction may need an application-specific protocol to ensure it has terminated. A general-purpose peer-to-peer protocol that ensures termination is IBM's LU6.2, which was described in Section 3.4 of the first edition of this book.

5. Every system and resource manager fails by stopping. That is, the protocol does not make mistakes when a system or a resource manager malfunctions. It either does exactly what the protocol says it should do, or it stops running. It is possible for a failure to cause the protocol to do something that is inconsistent with its specification, such as sending bogus messages. These are called Byzantine failures. There are ways to cope with limited numbers of **Byzantine failures**, but they are quite expensive in terms of the number of messages exchanged and are not used in current TP systems, so they are not discussed here.

In the remainder of this section, we will use the term **coordinator** as the name of the component that runs the two-phase commit protocol on behalf of one transaction. That is, the coordinator is the component that receives the commit or abort request from the application program and drives the execution of the protocol.

In our description of the protocol, the resource managers that did work on behalf of the transaction (by reading and updating resources) are called **participants**. The goal is to ensure that the coordinator and all participants commit the transaction or the coordinator and all participants abort the transaction.

"Coordinator" and "participant" are abstract concepts that don't map exactly to real components of a TP system. In Section 8.5, we will look at how the system is organized into components, including the transaction manager component that actually runs two-phase commit. We will explore how the transaction manager organizes its work, communicates with resource and transaction managers, and interacts with the communication system itself.

Being Prepared

A participant P is said to be **prepared** if all of transaction T's after-images at P are in stable storage. It is essential that T does not commit at *any* participant until *all* participants are prepared. The reason is the force-at-commit rule, which says not to commit a transaction until the after-images of all of its updates are in stable storage. Suppose the rule is violated by having one participant, P_1, commit T before another participant, P_2, is prepared. If P_2 subsequently fails, before it is prepared and after P_1 commits, then T will not be atomic. T already has committed at P_1, and it cannot commit at P_2 because P_2 may have lost some of T's updates when it failed. On the other hand, if P_2 is prepared *before* P_1 commits, then it is still possible for T to be atomic after P_2 fails. When P_2 recovers, it still has T's updates in stable storage (because it was prepared before it failed). After it recovers and finds out that T committed, it too can finish committing T.

Ensuring that all participants are prepared before any of them commits is the essence of two-phase commit. Phase one is when all participants become prepared. Phase two is when they commit. No participant enters phase two until all participants have completed phase one; that is, until all participants are prepared.

The Protocol

The protocol proceeds as follows (see Figure 8.1):

Begin Phase 1:

1. To commit the transaction, the coordinator starts by sending a REQUEST-TO-PREPARE message to each participant.

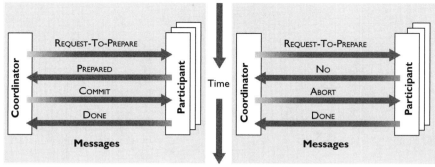

a. The transaction commits   b. The transaction aborts

Horizontal arrows indicate messages between the coordinator and participant.
Time is moving down the page, so the first message in both cases is REQUEST-TO-PREPARE.

FIGURE 8.1

The Two-Phase Commit Protocol. The messages that are shown are exchanged between the coordinator and each participant.

2. The coordinator waits for all participants to "vote" on the request.
3. In response to receiving a REQUEST-TO-PREPARE message, each participant votes by sending a message back to the coordinator, as follows:

   - It votes PREPARED if it is prepared to commit.
   - It may vote NO for any reason, usually because it cannot prepare the transaction due to a local failure.
   - It may delay voting indefinitely, for example, because its system is overburdened with other work or because it failed.

Begin Phase 2:

1. If the coordinator receives PREPARED messages from *all* participants, it decides to commit. The transaction is now officially committed. Otherwise, it either received a NO message or gave up waiting for some participant, so it decides to abort.
2. The coordinator sends its decision to all participants (i.e., COMMIT or ABORT).
3. Participants acknowledge receipt of the commit or abort by replying DONE.
4. After receiving DONE from all participants, the coordinator can **forget** the transaction, meaning that it can deallocate any memory it was using to keep track of information about the transaction.

Performance

The performance of two-phase commit is measured by counting the number of messages required to commit the transaction. There are four rounds of messages to or from all participants, as can easily be seen in Figure 8.1: REQUEST-TO-PREPARE, PREPARED; or NO, COMMIT or ABORT, and DONE.

The transaction actually is committed before all these messages are sent. After the second round, when the coordinator decides to commit, the transaction actually is committed and the coordinator can tell the user that this is true. Of course, there is still another round of messages, the COMMIT messages, before the participants find out that the transaction is committed, at which point they can release their locks. The final round of messages, the

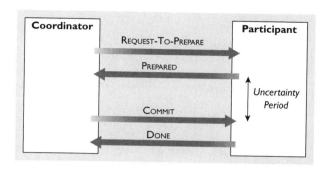

FIGURE 8.2

The Uncertainty Period in Two-Phase Commit. From the time a participant replies PREPARED until it receives the decision from the coordinator, it is uncertain.

DONE messages, is not performance sensitive, since this just tells the coordinator that it can clean up whatever control structures it has used for the transaction. In fact, a participant can avoid an extra message by holding onto the DONE message until it has another message for the coordinator on which it can piggyback the DONE message, such as a PREPARED message for a later transaction.

Blocking

Before a participant votes, it can abort unilaterally, any time it wants. Once it sends PREPARED, and until it receives a message containing the coordinator's decision, it is unable to commit or abort. If it did, it might make a decision opposite to the coordinator's, producing an inconsistent result. During this period, it is said to be **uncertain**[1] (see Figure 8.2).

The coordinator is never uncertain, because it gets to decide. Until it decides, it can abort whenever it wants. And after it decides, it is obviously not uncertain. So, only participants are uncertain.

Uncertainty is a bad property of two-phase commit. If the coordinator fails while a participant is uncertain, the participant is **blocked**; it can neither commit nor abort. The coordinator could be down for a long time. This is a bad situation for the participant, since it is holding locks on data that the transaction accessed. Since the whole point of two-phase commit is to cope with failures (otherwise, one-phase commit would work fine), it is bad news that when a failure does happen, a participant could become blocked.

This leads one to wonder whether two-phase commit is a good protocol after all. Are there other protocols one could adopt that avoid blocking? Unfortunately, the answer is no, as stated in the following theorem.

Theorem 1: For every possible commit protocol (not just two-phase commit), a communications failure can cause a participant to become blocked.

There is a related problem, essentially the recovery-time version of blocking. If a participant fails while it is uncertain, and subsequently recovers, it is possible that when it recovers the coordinator is down. In this case, it is still uncertain and therefore cannot completely recover, since it doesn't know whether to commit or abort the transaction. That is, the participant cannot **independently recover**. Like blocking, this too is unavoidable.

---

[1]This is called "in doubt" in Gray and Reuter (1992).

Theorem 2: No commit protocol can guarantee independent recovery of failed participants.

We may be unhappy about the blocking problem in two-phase commit, but there is no avoiding it. Any other protocol that atomically commits a transaction that accesses multiple resource managers must have the same problem.

Nevertheless, there have been many attempts at circumventing these theorems. One technique for handling blocking situations is to make a **heuristic decision**, which is simply to guess the outcome. The guess may be wrong, but at least the transaction can terminate and release locks. Another is to attempt to find out the decision from other participants, called the cooperative termination protocol, which is described in Section 8.4. Yet another technique is three-phase commit, which avoids blocking if the system has no communications failures. This protocol is much more complex than two-phase commit and still leads to blocking if a communication failure occurs (for details, see Bernstein, Hadzilacos, and Goodman, 1987; Section 7.5). Currently, three-phase commit is not widely used in practice.

8.3 FAILURE HANDLING

The purpose of two-phase commit is to cope with the various failures that can arise. To complete the description of the protocol we need to explain what happens in every possible failure situation.

We assume that all failures of messages and processes are detected by timeout. That is, a caller sets a timer when it sends a message to another process and assumes that a failure has occurred if the timer expires before it receives the reply it was expecting. The length of the timer is called the **timeout period**. The timeout period should be long enough to cover cases where the callee or the communications network is a little slow due to a backlog of work. But it should not be too long, since that will mean that failures are not detected promptly, which would be annoying to users. Notice that if a process detects a timeout, it cannot tell whether the process failed or the communications failed. All it knows is that something has gone wrong.

It is very realistic to assume that all failures are detected by timeout. In most distributed systems, messages are exchanged asynchronously (that is, whenever processes have something to say, rather than synchronously at fixed time intervals). So the only information that a process has about other processes is what it learns from messages it receives from them. If a failure occurs, the only hint it gets about the failure is that a message it was expecting has not arrived.

Sometimes the underlying communication system provides failure detection. A process can ask the communication system to establish a session. Later, if one of the processes or systems stops responding to messages, the communication system tells the other process that the session has failed. In this case, the failure was still detected by timeout, but by the underlying communication system rather than by the process itself.

The coordinator or a participant can fail in two ways. Either it stops running (assumption 5 in Section 8.2) or it times out waiting for a message it was expecting. The latter may happen either because the sender fails or because the communication system isn't functioning properly. The symptom is the same in both cases—the receiver does not get the message.

To analyze the failure cases, let's walk through the protocol from both the coordinator's and participant's viewpoint and explain what happens in each case where a message was expected but does not arrive. Then we will talk about what the coordinator and participant do if they fail and subsequently recover.

Coordinator's view:

1. Send REQUEST-TO-PREPARE messages to all the participants.
   Error handling: None, since it is not expecting any messages in this step.

2. Receive PREPARED messages from all participants, or receive a NO message from at least one participant.
   Error handling: It is waiting for PREPARED or NO messages. If it does not receive all of them within its timeout period, it can simply abort the transaction, just as if one of the participants had voted NO.

3. Depending on the messages received, decide to commit or abort.
   Error handling: None, since it is not expecting any messages in this step.

4. Send COMMIT or ABORT messages to all participants (depending on the decision).
   Error handling: None, since it is not expecting any messages in this step.

5. Receive DONE messages from all participants.
   Error handling: It is waiting for DONE messages. Nothing important depends on when these messages arrive, so it waits indefinitely for them. If its timeout period expires, it can send reminder messages to the participants to resolicit the DONE messages.

6. Forget the transaction.
   Error handling: None, since it is not expecting any messages in this step.

Participant's view:

1. Receive a REQUEST-TO-PREPARE message from the coordinator.
   Error handling: After finishing its work for the transaction, if it does not receive a REQUEST-TO-PREPARE within its timeout period, it can unilaterally abort the transaction. If it later receives a REQUEST-TO-PREPARE from the coordinator, it votes NO (or ignores the message, since a nonvote has the same effect as NO).

2. Prepare the transaction.
   Error handling: None, since it is not expecting any messages in this step.

3. If (2) succeeds, then send a PREPARED message to the coordinator, otherwise send NO to the coordinator.
   Error handling: None, since it is not expecting any messages in this step.

4. Receive a decision message, COMMIT or ABORT.
   Error handling: If it does not receive a decision message within its timeout period, it is blocked. It is in its uncertainty period, so there is nothing it can do without risking a mistake.

5. Send a DONE message.
   Error handling: None, since it is not expecting any messages in this step.

If the coordinator or participant fails and subsequently recovers, then at recovery time it can only use information in stable storage to guide its recovery. This is the same assumption we used for recovering from system failures in the previous chapter. So to ensure that recovery is possible, we need to ensure that the coordinator and participant log information that they may need during the recovery activity.

We say that writing a log record is **eager** (sometimes called forced or synchronous) if it must complete before the corresponding message is sent. Otherwise, it is **lazy** (or asynchronous). Eager log writes have a bigger performance impact than lazy ones, because they must be completed before the protocol can continue and they therefore add to the transaction's response time.

The coordinator needs to write three log records (see Figure 8.3).

- Before it sends a REQUEST-TO-PREPARE, it should log a **start-two-phase-commit record**, which includes a list of the participants. This writing is eager; that is, the coordinator must wait until this record is in the stable log before sending a REQUEST-TO-PREPARE to any participant. Otherwise, if it failed after sending the REQUEST-TO-PREPARE and before the log record was stable, it would not know which participants to notify about the decision.

- Before sending a commit decision, it should log a **commit record**. Indeed, writing the commit record to the log is what actually commits the transaction. This too is eager. Otherwise, if the coordinator failed

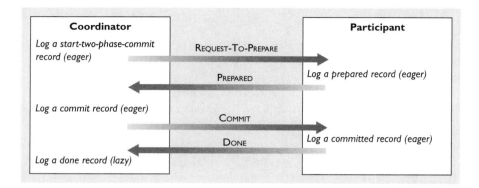

FIGURE 8.3

Log Operations in Two-Phase Commit (the commit case). Each of the eager log writes must be completed before sending the next message, so the process can correctly handle failures that occur after the message is sent (see text).

after sending the COMMIT message and before flushing the commit record to the log, and it subsequently recovered, it would abort the transaction during its recovery procedure, which produces an inconsistent outcome if the participant that received the COMMIT message committed.

- After it receives the DONE messages it writes a **done record**, which records the fact that the transaction is finished. This is lazy.

The participant writes two log records (see Figure 8.3).

- When it gets a REQUEST-TO-PREPARE from the coordinator, it writes a **prepared record** to the log. This is eager; that is, it waits until the prepared record is in the stable log before sending PREPARED to the coordinator. Otherwise, if it failed after sending PREPARED and before flushing the prepared record to the log, and it subsequently recovered, it would abort the transaction during its recovery procedure (since there is no prepared or commit record in the log). But since it sent PREPARED, it gave permission to the coordinator to commit the transaction, which would produce an inconsistent outcome.

- It writes a **commit record** or **abort record**, after it receives the decision message. This too is eager, since once it sends DONE, it gives permission to the coordinator to forget the transaction. If it fails after sending DONE and before the decision message is stable, then at recovery time it might not be able to find out what the decision was. Moreover it holds locks for the transaction until after it commits or aborts, so the sooner it logs the decision, the sooner it can release locks.

We will see ways of turning some of the eager log writes into lazy ones in the next section, on optimizations.

Now that we know what information they log, we can look at how the coordinator and participant recover from failures. First, consider the coordinator. When it recovers it can be in one of four states (see numbered boxes on left side of Figure 8.4):

1. It has no start-two-phase-commit log record for the transaction. It did not start two-phase commit before the failure. So no participant could have received a REQUEST-TO-PREPARE message and therefore all of them either aborted unilaterally while the coordinator was down, or will abort on their own later (if the coordinator was down only briefly).

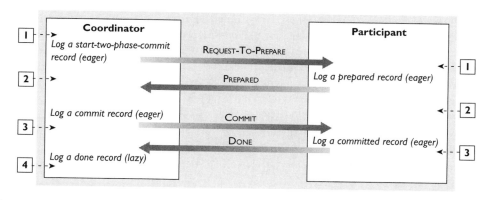

FIGURE 8.4

Possible States from Which a Coordinator or Participant Must Recover. See text for a description of recovery actions for the state labeled by each numbered box.

2. It has a start-two-phase-commit record only, so it did not reach a decision before the failure. It aborts the transaction. It is possible that participants are waiting for this decision, so it sends an abort decision message to all of them. Some of them may ignore the message, because they never got a REQUEST-TO-PREPARE message and therefore unilaterally aborted, but there is no harm in sending the abort decision message.

3. It has a commit or abort record in the log, but no done record. Again, it is possible that participants are waiting for this decision, so it sends a decision message to all of them.

4. It has a done record in the log. All participants acknowledged receiving the decision, so there is nothing to do.

Now, consider a participant. When it recovers it can be in one of three states (see numbered boxes on right side of Figure 8.4):

1. It did not log a prepared record. The transaction could not have committed, so the participant unilaterally aborts the transaction.

2. It logged a prepared record, but did not log a committed or aborted record. This is the bad case, where the participant is blocked. It should run a termination protocol, which will be explained in a moment.

3. It logged the decision, commit, or abort. It can either send another DONE message, or it can wait until the coordinator sends it a reminder message, reminding it of the decision, at which time it sends a DONE message.

A **termination protocol** is what a participant does to try to resolve a blocked transaction when the participant recovers from a failure. The simplest termination protocol is to wait until it re-establishes communication with the coordinator and to resend its vote. If the coordinator sees a redundant vote message, this must mean that the participant hasn't yet received the decision, so it resends the decision.

If communication cannot be re-established in an acceptably short time, then a human operator may need to intervene and guess whether the transaction committed or aborted (perhaps making a telephone call to the operator of the other system to find out the decision). The protocol should log this **heuristic decision**, so that when communication between the two systems is re-established, the systems can detect whether a consistent or inconsistent decision was made. In the latter case, the system can notify an operator that corrective action is needed.

Repairing an inconsistent decision can be difficult. The transaction that incorrectly committed or aborted left some incorrect data in the database. That incorrect data may have been read by later transactions which themselves wrote some data. In this way, the inconsistency may have spread beyond the data that was directly updated by the transaction that terminated inconsistently. Taking corrective action therefore could require some careful analysis of the database and transaction log.

This covers all the failure scenarios—timing out waiting for a message and recovering from a failure. So we now have a complete and correct two-phase commit protocol.

8.4 OPTIMIZATIONS AND VARIATIONS

There are many variations of two-phase commit to handle special transaction communications patterns. We discuss three of them here: reinfection, where a transaction revisits a resource manager after the two-phase commit protocol has started; transfer of coordination, to allow one resource manager to execute one-phase-commit; and phase zero, where a transaction delays sending updates to some resource managers until after it has finished executing.

There are also many optimizations of two-phase commit to save messages and reduce the number of eager log writes. The most obvious is to avoid two-phase commit altogether when there is only one resource manager in a transaction, and run one-phase commit instead. This is a fairly important optimization since many transactions access only one resource manager. If a transaction issues Start and Commit but never accesses a resource manager, then it can run no-phase commit. That is, the coordinator can commit immediately without sending a message to any outside agent. Several other optimizations are described later: presumed abort, to reduce the amount of logging for transactions that abort; reducing a round of messages for read-only resources; and the cooperative termination protocol, to increase the chance that a blocked resource manager can become unblocked.

Reinfection

If the coordinator starts two-phase commit before all the participants have fully completed (thereby violating assumption 4 in Section 8.2), then it's possible that a participant will prepare and later be asked to do work for the same transaction. This is called **reinfection**.

Reinfection can arise if participants want to postpone certain work until after the transaction has completed its regular work, for example, with database triggers that should execute at the end of the transaction. Since the coordinator waits until the transaction completes its normal work before sending REQUEST-TO-PREPARE messages, participant P might use the arrival of a REQUEST-TO-PREPARE message to tell it to execute an end-of-transaction trigger. But the trigger could update data at another participant Q that has already prepared, thereby reinfecting Q. So Q has to prepare again.

This complicates matters. The coordinator already may have received Q's PREPARED message. If the coordinator receives P's acknowledgment of its REQUEST-TO-PREPARE before Q prepares again, it could commit before Q is prepared. To avoid this bad outcome, if Q is reinfected by a call from P, it should not reply to P until it has processed P's request *and* has prepared again by ensuring all updates it made due to the reinfection are in stable storage (see Figure 8.5). That way, when P sends PREPARED to the coordinator, it knows that Q is also prepared (again) and it's safe for the coordinator to commit.

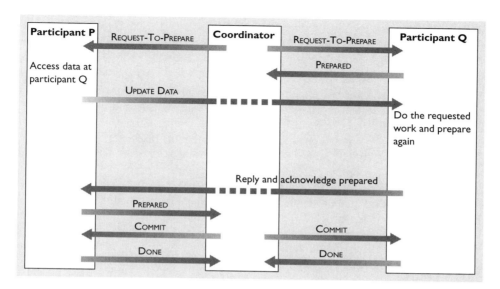

FIGURE 8.5

Reinfection. Participant P reinfects Participant Q after Q prepared. P waits for Q to prepare again and reply to P before P sends PREPARED to the coordinator, thereby ensuring Q is prepared before the coordinator commits.

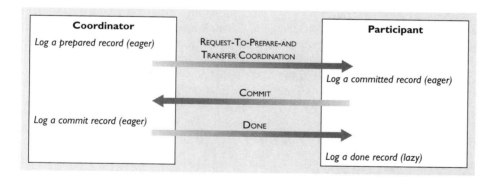

FIGURE 8.6

Transfer of Coordination Optimization. The coordinator prepares and then tells the participant to prepare and commit, and thereby become the coordinator. This saves a message over standard two-phase commit.

Transfer of Coordination

If there is only one participant, then two-phase commit can be done with only three rounds of communication instead of four. The trick is for the coordinator to transfer its "coordinator role" to the participant, which then becomes the coordinator. The optimized protocol works as follows (see Figure 8.6):

- The coordinator prepares and then sends a message to the participant that asks it to prepare *and* to become the coordinator.

- The participant (which is now the coordinator) prepares, commits, and sends a COMMIT message to the former coordinator.
- The coordinator commits and sends DONE to the participant.

Notice that the participant does not need a prepare phase in this case. However, since the participant is now performing the coordinator's role, it must remember the decision until it receives the DONE message from the former coordinator. This covers the case where the COMMIT message is lost, and the former coordinator must later ask the participant what the decision was.

Using this observation, we can run two-phase commit in a system that uses a resource manager that does not support a separate prepare phase and can only commit or abort, as long as there is only one such resource manager in any transaction. To do this, the coordinator goes through the usual first phase of two-phase commit. After all the other participants have acknowledged that they're prepared, the coordinator prepares and transfers coordination to the resource manager that does not support two-phase commit. When the resource manager acknowledges that it committed, the coordinator can finish the job by sending COMMIT messages to the remaining participants.

This can work with only one resource manager that doesn't support the prepare phase. If there were two, then the coordinator would have to tell them both to commit without asking them to prepare. If one committed and the other didn't, the result would be inconsistent, the very situation that two-phase commit is designed to avoid.

Phase Zero

Many systems use a mid-tier or client cache that holds copies of a transaction's updates until the transaction has terminated and is ready to commit. In this case, the cache manager needs to flush the transaction's updates to the appropriate resource manager before the two-phase commit protocol starts to ensure that the resource manager stores a stable copy of the transaction's updates during phase one.

Suppose a participant P is caching transaction updates that P needs to send to a resource manager R before T commits. To ensure that R has all of T's updates, P must send T's updates to R after T invokes Commit (to ensure it has *all* the updates that will perform at R) and before R prepares (to ensure the updates are made stable during phase one). Thus, we need an extra phase, before phase one.

A solution is to allow some participants to enlist for **phase zero** of a transaction. For example, a mid-tier cache manager would enlist for phase zero of transaction T when the cache manager receives the first write on behalf of T. When the transaction manager receives a transaction's request to commit, the transaction manager sends a message to all of the transaction's participants that enlisted for phase zero. A participant who receives such a message can flush its cache or perform any other actions that need to be completed before phase one of two-phase commit begins. The transaction manager waits for all phase zero participants to reply to its phase zero request message before it starts executing phase one of two-phase commit. If it doesn't receive one of those replies within its timeout period, then it aborts the transaction.

Presumed Abort

Ordinarily, the coordinator does an eager write of the start-two-phase-commit log record (see Figure 8.3). By a slight modification of the protocol, the coordinator can avoid logging this record at all—at recovery time, if there is no record of a transaction in the coordinator's log, then the coordinator assumes the transaction must have aborted. This assumption has several implications:

- If a participant asks the coordinator about a transaction, and the coordinator has no information, then the coordinator presumes the transaction aborted. This is more than a presumption; according to this revised protocol, the transaction *must* have aborted.

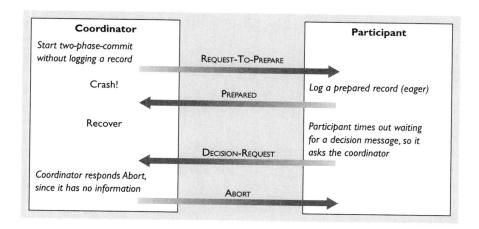

FIGURE 8.7

Presumed Abort Optimization (the Abort Case). The coordinator need not log a start-two-phase-commit record. If it fails before it commits, it has no information about the transaction. In this case, it responds abort to requests for the decision.

- If the transaction aborts, a participant can do a *lazy* log write of an abort decision and need not send DONE to the coordinator.
- If the transaction aborts, the coordinator need not log a done record.

To see why this works, suppose a participant is blocked at recovery time and sends a message to the coordinator. If the transaction aborted, there are two cases to consider: (1) the coordinator has an abort record in the log (it aborted the transaction but failed before sending the ABORT messages), in which case it replies with an abort decision; (2) it has no record at all—it didn't abort the transaction (fully) before the failure—in which case it again replies with an abort decision (the "presumed abort" for the no-information case; see Figure 8.7). If the transaction committed (see Figure 8.8), the coordinator must have a commit record in the log, since it is still obligated to remember commit decisions until all participants have replied DONE (i.e., the two-phase commit protocol is unchanged for the commit case, except that the coordinator doesn't log a start-two-phase-commit record).

Presumed abort is a popular optimization, used by most implementations of two-phase commit.

Read-Only Transactions

If a participant reads but does not write data on behalf of the transaction, then it does not care what the decision is. Whether the transaction commits or aborts, the participant does the same thing, namely, it releases the transaction's read locks. In fact, it need not wait to find out whether the transaction commits or aborts. It can release read locks as soon as it receives a REQUEST-TO-PREPARE, since that signals that the transaction has terminated, at which point it is safe to release read locks, as far as two-phase locking is concerned. Therefore, in response to a REQUEST-TO-PREPARE, it replies PREPARED-READ-ONLY, which tells the coordinator not to bother sending a decision message (see Figure 8.9).

Although this optimization looks very appealing and intuitive, it often cannot be used in practice, because some participants may have more work to do after they receive a REQUEST-TO-PREPARE (again violating assumption 4 in Section 8.2). For example, they may need to execute SQL triggers or integrity constraints, which can involve acquiring more locks. We saw this kind of situation in the section on reinfection. If a read-only participant releases

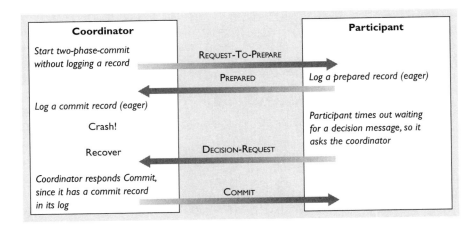

FIGURE 8.8

Presumed Abort Optimization (the Commit Case). The coordinator does not log a start-two-phase-commit record. Since it fails after it commits, it responds commit to the request for the decision, exactly as if the optimization were not used.

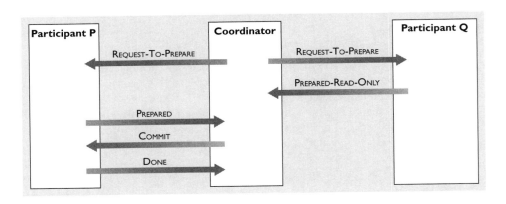

FIGURE 8.9

Read-Only Optimization. Since Participant Q is read-only, it can release locks and finish the transaction when it receives a `REQUEST-TO-PREPARE`, and the coordinator does not have to send it a `COMMIT`.

a lock after receiving a `REQUEST-TO-PREPARE`, and another participant acquires a lock later on while evaluating a trigger, the transaction has broken the two-phase locking protocol and the result may not be serializable.

   If the application knows that a transaction is read-only, then it can get the same effect as the read-only optimization without any help from the transaction manager or resource managers. After the transaction has done its work, it issues an abort instead of a commit. The benefit of aborting is that the coordinator only does one round of messages to abort. And in this case, because the transaction is read-only, an abort has the same effect as a commit; namely, it tells each resource manager to release the transaction's locks. However, notice that this optimization is applicable only if the entire transaction is read-only. This is more restrictive than the read-only optimization, which is applicable as long as the transaction is read-only at one resource manager. Also

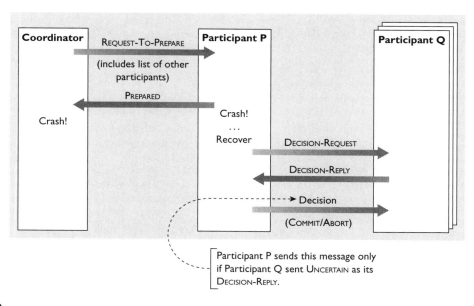

FIGURE 8.10

Cooperative Termination Protocol. When Participant P recovers, the coordinator is down. So Participant P asks other participants what the decision was (via DECISION-REQUEST). Other participants, such as Participant Q, reply with a DECISION-REPLY containing COMMIT, ABORT, or UNCERTAIN. If Participant P learns the decision from some participant, then it sends a decision message to each participant that replied UNCERTAIN in the previous round.

notice that this optimization is the responsibility of the application program, not the transaction manager and resource managers. It can be used only if the application program knows that the transaction did not perform any updates. If application does an RPC to a server whose internal behavior is unknown, then it has to assume the worst and commit, not abort.

Cooperative Termination Protocol

Recall that the bad case when a participant recovers from a failure is that the participant logged a prepared record, but did not log a committed or aborted record. This means the participant is blocked and must run a termination protocol. The participant can find out the decision from the coordinator, if it is alive. If not, it can avoid waiting for the coordinator to recover by using the **cooperative termination protocol**, which asks for help from other participants.

The cooperative termination protocol requires that each participant knows the addresses of the other participants, so that it can contact them if it is blocked during recovery. It therefore needs to get this information from the coordinator in the REQUEST-TO-PREPARE message. At recovery time, it then proceeds as follows (see Figure 8.10):

1. The participant P sends a DECISION-REQUEST message to the other participants.
2. When a participant Q receives a DECISION-REQUEST, it responds as follows:

   ■ If it knows what the decision was (i.e., it got a COMMIT or ABORT from the coordinator), then it replies with the decision (COMMIT or ABORT).

- If it did not prepare the transaction, it replies ABORT. The transaction could not have committed, since this participant did not send a PREPARE to the coordinator. Since another participant is blocked, there is no point in waiting for the decision from the coordinator, since the coordinator is apparently down or not communicating with some participants.
- If it prepared, but does not know what the decision was, then it replies UNCERTAIN. This is the bad case that doesn't help participant P.

3. If any participant replies with a decision, then P acts on the decision and sends the decision to every participant that replied UNCERTAIN, since they want to know the decision too.

If participants are allowed to run the cooperative termination protocol, then it may not be a good idea for them to forget the decision shortly after they receive it from the coordinator, because some other participant may later ask for it when it runs the cooperative termination protocol. Since a participant could fail and be down for a long time, there is no bound on how long participants should remember the decision. There are two ways to handle this problem. First, each participant can simply hold on to each decision for some fixed amount of time, such as one minute, before discarding it. If asked later than that about the decision, it has to reply UNCERTAIN. Second, we could add a fifth round of messages from the coordinator to the participants, after the coordinator receives DONE from all the participants. This final message from the coordinator tells the participants that they can forget the decision, since all other participants know the decision and will not need to run the cooperative termination protocol after a failure. Like DONE messages, these final messages are not urgent and can be piggybacked on other messages from the coordinator to the participants.

8.5 PROCESS STRUCTURING

Independent Transaction Managers

Now that we have studied two-phase commit from a single transaction's viewpoint, it is time to see how a system can manage two-phase commit on behalf of many transactions and resource managers. The usual approach is to have one module, the **transaction manager**, be responsible for running the two-phase commit protocol, performing both the coordinator and participant functions for a group of transactions. The transaction manager usually is packaged with another product, such as the operating system (as in Microsoft Windows and HP's OpenVMS) or transactional middleware (as in IBM's Websphere or Oracle's WebLogic).

One possibility is to have the transaction manager be part of the database system. This works fine for transactions that access multiple copies of one particular database system. But it generally does not work with other database systems, because each database system uses its own two-phase commit protocol, with its own message formats and optimizations. A different approach is needed for transactions to interoperate across different database systems.

The standard solution to this problem is to have the transaction manager be an independent component. It runs two-phase commit for all transactions that execute on its machine. To do this, it communicates with resource managers on its own machine and with transaction managers on other machines.

Although one transaction manager per machine is the standard configuration, it is not the only one. A transaction manager may support multiple machines, or a machine may have multiple transaction managers. In a clustered environment where two or more machines share disks and other resources, there may be one transaction manager for the cluster rather than one per machine. In this case, if the transaction manager's machine fails, then the cluster manager needs to recreate the transaction manager on another machine in the cluster that

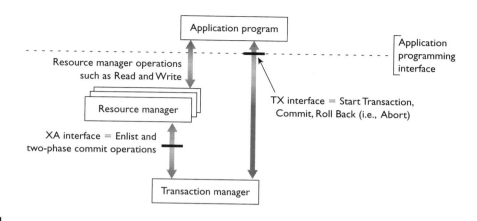

FIGURE 8.11

X/Open Transaction Model. The transaction manager runs two-phase commit for all transactions at its machine and communicates with local resource managers.

has access to the transaction manager's log. Conversely, a machine that runs heterogeneous software may have multiple transaction managers. For example, it may run transactional middleware that has its own transaction manager while executing on a machine whose operating system and database system have transaction managers. This is usually inefficient, due to the logging and communication that each transaction manager requires. But it is unavoidable if the application depends on those heterogeneous components.

This system model of having an independent transaction manager has been standardized by X/Open (now part of The Open Group), which also has defined the interface between transaction managers and resource managers, so that transaction and resource managers from different vendors can be hooked up (see Figure 8.11). Notice that this model defines the transaction bracketing interface (TX) but not the interfaces to resource managers (which are covered by other standards, notably SQL). The application programming interface may also include other operations, which are not shown in the model. Although the X/Open model is widely supported, many transaction managers offer proprietary interfaces too. Section 10.6 describes other transaction management standards, such as the Object Transaction Service and the Java Transaction API.

Enlisting in a Transaction

In this architecture, each transaction manager can be the coordinator of a transaction; its participants are local resource managers accessed by the transaction and, when a transaction is propagated to a remote machine, remote transaction managers on those remote machines. Or, a transaction manager can be a participant, being coordinated by transaction managers on other machines. As we'll see, a transaction manager can be both, even for the same transaction. Since each transaction accesses different resource managers at different machines of the network, the transaction manager must dynamically figure out the coordinator-participant relationships for each transaction. To dynamically manage transactions in this way, each resource manager and transaction manager must **join** or **enlist in** a transaction when it is first accessed on behalf of the transaction.

When the application calls a local resource manager, R, for the first time on behalf of a transaction T, R calls its local transaction manager with Enlist(T), which "enlists R in T." This tells the transaction manager that R needs to be notified about commit and abort operations later (see Figure 8.12). When the transaction manager later receives a commit or abort operation for T, it runs two-phase commit with the local resource managers that enlisted in T.

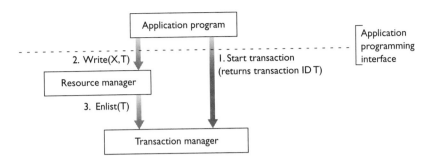

FIGURE 8.12

A Resource Manager Enlists for a Transaction. When an application program executing a transaction first accesses a resource manager, the resource manager enlists with its local transaction manager. This tells the transaction manager to notify the resource manager about this transaction's commit or abort operation later.

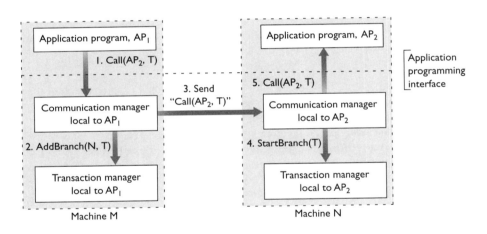

FIGURE 8.13

A Remote Call That Starts a Branch Transaction. Application AP_1 calls application AP_2 at a remote machine N, thereby creating a branch transaction at N. The communication manager tells the transaction managers at machines M and N about the new branch by the AddBranch and StartBranch calls, respectively.

Similarly, when the application calls an application or resource manager at a remote machine M for the first time, the application's local transaction manager and machine M's transaction manager must be notified that the transaction has moved, thereby starting a new **branch** of the transaction at M. This is done by the component that performs remote transactional communications, usually called the **communication manager**. Like the transaction manager, it may be part of the transactional middleware, operating system, or resource manager (for remote resource manager calls).

For example in Figure 8.13, application AP_1 running transaction T at machine M calls application AP_2 at machine N. In addition to sending the message and calling the remote application, the communication manager creates a branch of T at N. This is needed so that M's transaction manager knows to send two-phase commit messages to N's transaction manager. It also tells N's transaction manager to expect Enlist operations on this

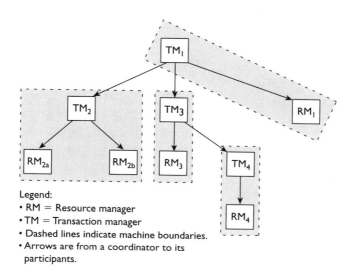

Legend:
- RM = Resource manager
- TM = Transaction manager
- Dashed lines indicate machine boundaries.
- Arrows are from a coordinator to its participants.

FIGURE 8.14

Tree-of-Processes Model. By migrating from machine to machine and accessing resource managers, a transaction creates a tree of coordinators and participants that will run two-phase commit. A particular execution that leads to this tree is described in the text.

transaction from N's resource managers and to expect two-phase commit operations from M's transaction manager. In some systems, M's transaction manager establishes communications with N's transaction manager (if it hasn't already done so) and sends an enlistment message. This tells N's transaction manager where to send the two-phase commit messages later.

It requires a high degree of trust for a transaction manager on one machine to agree to communicate with a transaction manager on another machine. Each transaction manager needs to know that the other transaction manager will make timely and correct progress toward completing the transaction. In particular, if a transaction manager acting as coordinator stops communicating with the other transaction acting as participant, then the participant could become blocked. Each transaction manager needs to believe this is a very unlikely event before agreeing to communicate. This trust relationship is hard to establish between different enterprises, since their systems are autonomous and independently managed. For this reason, two-phase commit rarely is executed between systems in different enterprises. It may even be problematic between systems with a single large enterprise. It is more commonly used between machines that support different parts of the same application, which are controlled by the same system manager.

The Tree-of-Processes Model

A transaction can migrate from machine to machine many times during its execution. This leads to a tree-structured set of transaction managers and resource managers involved in the transaction, called the **tree-of-processes** model of transaction execution. For example, a transaction could migrate as follows (see Figure 8.14):

- It started at machine 1 and accessed resource manager RM_1.
- From machine 1, it made a remote call to machine 2, where it accessed resource managers RM_{2a} and RM_{2b}.
- From machine 1, it made a remote call to machine 3, where it accessed resource manager RM_3.
- From machine 3, it made a remote call to machine 4, where it accessed resource manager RM_4.

In the tree of processes model, the root transaction manager is the coordinator, and its children are participants. So in Figure 8.14, TM_1 is the overall coordinator, and TM_2, TM_3, and RM_1 are its participants. TM_2 is, in turn, the coordinator of RM_{2a} and RM_{2b}, and TM_3 is the coordinator of RM_3 and TM_4. So TM_2 and TM_3 play the roles of both participant (with respect to TM_1) and coordinator (with respect to their children). Similarly, TM_4 is a participant (with respect to TM_3) and coordinator (with respect to RM_4).

In Figure 8.14, suppose the transaction executing on machine 4 calls an application on machine 1. This attempt to execute StartBranch on machine 1 returns a warning that the transaction already is executing on machine 1. This just means that TM_1 does not become a participant with respect to TM_4. This is not an error, so the call to the application at machine 1 succeeds. That application's operations on machine 1's resource managers, such as RM_1, are part of the transaction and are committed or aborted whenever TM_1 tells its local resource managers to commit or abort.

When a transaction manager is both a participant and a coordinator, it must prepare its subtree before it replies prepared to a REQUEST-TO-PREPARE message. For example, in Figure 8.14:

- After TM_3 receives REQUEST-TO-PREPARE from TM_1, it should send a REQUEST-TO-PREPARE to RM_3 and TM_4.
- TM_4 then sends a REQUEST-TO-PREPARE to RM_4.
- After RM_4 replies PREPARED, TM_4 can reply PREPARED to TM_3.
- After TM_4 and RM_3 reply PREPARED, TM_3 can reply PREPARED to TM_1.

A tree-of-processes adds delay to two-phase commit because of the daisy-chain of communication, such as from TM_1, to TM_3, to TM_4 in the example. This delay can be reduced by flattening the tree, so that all transaction managers communicate with the root coordinator. For example, if TM_1 knew about TM_4, it could communicate with TM_4 directly and in parallel with its communication wit h TM_2 and TM_3. This short-circuiting of communications is called **flattening** the tree. It can be done by passing knowledge of new branches back up the tree during normal execution. For example, when the transaction migrates from TM_3 to TM_4, TM_3 could tell TM_1 about the migration, so TM_1 can later communicate with TM_4 directly (see Figure 8.15). Although this flattening is usually desirable, it is not always possible, because some pairs of machines may not be able to communicate directly.

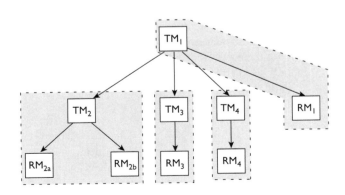

FIGURE 8.15

Flattening the Tree-of-Processes. If TM_3 tells TM_1 about TM_4, then TM_1 can communicate with TM_4 directly. This flattens the tree of Figure 8.14, thereby reducing communication delay from TM_1 to TM_4.

8.6 USER CHECKLIST

There are several aspects of a two-phase commit implementation that are of direct interest to users of TP products. The most obvious is whether two-phase commit is appropriate at all. The communication required for two-phase commit increases transaction execution time and hence lock holding time. This can increase the lock conflict rate and hence reduce throughput. In addition, if the communication connections between resource managers are not extremely reliable, then the probability of blocked transactions may be unacceptably high. In these cases, there are two possible solutions: ensure that each transaction can do its work with just one resource manager, or split the transaction into a multistep business process where each step is a transaction that accesses only one resource manager. Both approaches require extra application development effort. The benefits are better performance or availability.

If transactions do indeed need to perform updates at multiple resource managers, one needs to check whether each resource manager product supports two-phase commit at all. Today, most popular database systems and transactional middleware support it. However, not all combinations of database systems and transactional middleware work correctly together; that is, they don't all **interoperate**. Even if a database system supports the X/Open interfaces, there is still the question of whether it has been tested with a given transactional middleware product and whether it exploits any proprietary optimizations that a given transaction manager offers. Such optimizations can have a big effect on transaction performance.

Although there is increasing support for standard two-phase commit protocols, there is enough variation that this doesn't always guarantee compatibility. Moreover, some transaction manager vendors use their own two-phase commit protocol. In a system that uses transaction managers from different vendors, a transaction might need to access applications or resource managers that use these different transaction managers. To get all-or-nothing behavior, the transaction managers need to interoperate. That is, one of the transaction managers must be willing to communicate using the other transaction manager's two-phase commit protocol.

For the most part, two-phase commit is transparent to system operators. However, when a transaction is blocked due to a failure, an operator may need to get involved. Although this event occurs rarely, when there is a failure, there is a good chance that *some* transaction will be blocked. Therefore, support for heuristic decisions is valuable, along with notification of inconsistent decisions when they are made.

Two-phase commit should be transparent to application programmers. If it isn't, then the vendor's implementation is incomplete. However, if a nonstandard or home-grown database system is used in an application, then it is unlikely to be supported by the TP system's built-in two-phase commit implementation. In this case, it is important that the resource manager interface to the transaction manager be exposed. This interface allows the user to integrate the nonstandard resource manager with the transaction manager, so the resource manager's operations can be included in distributed transactions.

8.7 SUMMARY

The two-phase commit protocol ensures that a transaction either commits at all the resource managers that it accessed or aborts at all of them. It avoids the undesirable outcome that the transaction commits at one resource manager and aborts at another. The protocol is driven by a coordinator, which communicates with participants, which together include all the resource managers accessed by the transaction.

Since failures are unavoidable, the protocol must ensure that if a failure occurs, the transaction can reach a consistent outcome after the failed component recovers. It therefore requires that, during phase one, every resource manager prepares the transaction by recording all the transaction's updates on stable storage. After all resource managers have acknowledged to the coordinator that they "prepared" in phase one, the coordinator starts phase two by committing the transaction and then notifying the participants of this commit decision. If any participant fails to acknowledge phase one, or votes "no," then the coordinator aborts the transaction and notifies the participants of this decision.

The complexity of two-phase commit comes from all the failure scenarios that can arise. The most annoying failure happens after a participant has acknowledged prepared and before it receives the decision, such as a failure of the coordinator or of participant-coordinator communications. This leaves the participant blocked. It can't commit or abort, since the coordinator may have decided the opposite and the participant can't find out the decision. This problem is inherent in any commit protocol when communication failures are possible and not a special weakness of two-phase commit in particular.

The coordinator and participant must log certain changes in their state, so if either of them fails and subsequently recovers, it can tell what it was doing at the time of failure and take appropriate action. In particular, the coordinator must write a log record before beginning the protocol and before sending its decision, and each participant must log a prepared record before acknowledging prepared. Each participant should log the decision when it finds out what it was. Finally, the coordinator should write a log record when it gets all acknowledgments of its decision, so it knows it can forget the transaction. One then must go through a careful analysis to determine what the coordinator and each participant should do in every possible failure situation that can arise.

There are variations of two-phase commit to handle special transaction communications patterns. Three popular ones are reinfection, to handle a transaction that revisits a resource manager after the two-phase commit protocol has started; transfer of coordination, to enable one participant to use one-phase commit; and phase zero, when a mid-tier cache needs to flush its updates before phase one. There are also many optimizations of two-phase commit to reduce the number of log writes and messages. The most popular one is presumed abort, which avoids requiring that the coordinator write a log record before beginning of the protocol and before aborting a transaction.

Two-phase commit is implemented by the transaction manager component, which communicates with local resource managers and remote transaction managers. It plays the role of coordinator or participant, depending on whether the transaction started at its machine or elsewhere. It needs to be notified when a transaction has first accessed a resource manager or moved to another machine, so it will know with whom to communicate when it comes time to run two-phase commit. X/Open has standardized the transaction manager's interfaces with resource managers, called XA. This standard is widely supported, but most systems also have more efficient nonstandard interfaces too. Most transaction managers support a unique proprietary protocol.

Replication

9.1 INTRODUCTION

Replication is the technique of using multiple copies of a server or a resource for better availability and performance. Each copy is called a **replica**.

The main goal of replication is to improve availability, since a service is available even if some of its replicas are not. This helps mission critical services, such as many financial systems or reservation systems, where even a short outage can be very disruptive and expensive. It helps when communications is not always available, such as a laptop computer that contains a database replica and is connected to the network only intermittently. It is also useful for making a cluster of unreliable servers into a highly-available system, by replicating data on multiple servers.

Replication can also be used to improve performance by creating copies of databases, such as data warehouses, which are snapshots of TP databases that are used for decision support. Queries on the replicas can be processed without interfering with updates to the primary database server. If applied to the primary server, such queries would degrade performance, as discussed in Section 6.6, *Query-Update Problems* in two-phase locking.

In each of these cases, replication can also improve response time. The overall capacity of a set of replicated servers can be greater than the capacity of a single server. Moreover, replicas can be distributed over a wide area network, ensuring that some replica is near each user, thereby reducing communications delay.

9.2 REPLICATED SERVERS

The Primary-Backup Model

To maximize a server's availability, we should try to maximize its mean time between failures (MTBF) and minimize its mean time to repair (MTTR). After doing the best we can at this, we can still expect periods of unavailability. To improve availability further requires that we introduce some redundant processing capability by configuring each server as two server processes: a primary server that is doing the real work, and a backup server that is standing by, ready to take over immediately after the primary fails (see Figure 9.1). The goal is to reduce MTTR: If the primary server fails, then we do not need to wait for a new server to be created. As soon as the failure is detected, the backup server can immediately become the primary and start recovering to the state the former primary had after executing its last non-redoable operation, such as sending a message to

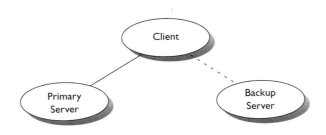

FIGURE 9.1

Primary-Backup Model. The primary server does the real work. The backup server is standing by, ready to take over after the primary fails.

an ATM to dispense money. If it recovered to an earlier state, it would end up redoing the operation, which would be incorrect. Since we are interested primarily in transactional servers, this means recovering to a state that includes the effects of all transactions that committed at the former primary and no other transactions. For higher availability, more backup servers can be used to guard against the possibility that the primary and backup fail.

This technique is applicable to resource managers and to servers that run ordinary applications, such as request controllers and transaction servers. When a server of either type fails, it needs to be recreated. Having a backup server avoids having to create the backup server at recovery time.

If there are many clients and some are connected by slow communication lines, then it can take a long time to recreate sessions with the backup server. To avoid doing this at recovery time, each client connected to the primary server should also have a backup communication session with the backup server. This further decreases (i.e., improves) MTTR.

In general, the degree of readiness of the backup server is a critical factor in determining MTTR. If a backup server is kept up to date so that it is always ready to take over when the primary fails with practically no delay, then it is called a **hot backup**. If it has done some preparation to reduce MTTR but still has a significant amount of work to do before it is ready to take over from the primary, then it is called a **warm backup**. If it has done no preparation, then it is called a **cold backup**.

As in the case of a server that has no backup, when the primary server fails, some external agent, such as a monitoring process, has to detect the failure and then cause the backup server to become the primary. The delay in detecting failures contributes to MTTR, so fast failure detection is important for high availability.

Once the backup server has taken over for the failed primary, it may be worthwhile to create a backup for the new primary. An alternative is to wait until the former primary recovers, at which time it can become the backup. Then, if desired, the former backup (which is the new primary) could be told to fail, so that the original primary becomes primary again and the backup is restarted as the backup again. This restores the system to its original configuration, which was tuned to work well. The cost is a brief period of downtime while the secondary and primary switch roles.

When telling a backup to become the primary, some care is needed to avoid ending up with two servers believing they're the primary. For example, if the monitor process gets no response from the primary, it may conclude that the primary is dead. But the primary may actually be operating. It may just be slow because its system is overloaded (e.g., a network storm is swamping its operating system), and it therefore hasn't sent an "I'm alive" message in a long time, which the monitor interprets as a failure of the primary. If the monitor then tells the backup to become the primary, then two processes will be operating as primary. If both primaries perform operations against the same resource, they may conflict with each other and corrupt that resource. For example, if the

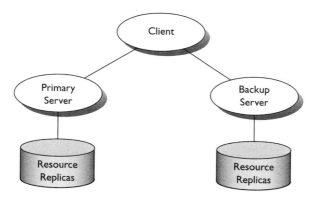

FIGURE 9.2

Replicating a Server and Its Resource. Both the server and the resource are replicated, which enables recovery from a resource failure.

resource is a disk they might overwrite each other, or if the resource is a communications line they may send conflicting messages.

One way to avoid ending up with two primaries is to require the primary to obtain a lock that only one process can hold. This lock could be implemented in hardware as part of the resource. For example, some networking techniques, such as reflective memory, and most disk systems, such as SCSI and Fiber Channel (as it runs over SCSI), allow a lock on a resource over their shared bus. Or it could be implemented in software using a global lock manager, which is supported by some operating systems that are designed for multiserver clusters and as independent components in some distributed systems. Another solution is to use a third "watchdog" process, which is described in Section 9.4, *Primary Recovery with One Secondary*.

Replicating the Resource

A server usually depends on a resource, typically a database. When replicating a server, an important consideration is whether to replicate the server's resource too. The most widely-used approach to replication is to replicate the resource (i.e., the database) in addition to the server that manages it (see Figure 9.2). This has two benefits. First, it enables the system to recover from a failure of a resource replica as well as a failure of a server process. And second, by increasing the number of copies of the resource, it offers performance benefits when access to the resource is the bottleneck. For example, the backup can do real work, such as process queries, and not just maintain the backup replica so it can take over when there is a failure.

The main technical challenge in implementing this approach to replication is to synchronize updates with queries and each other when these operations execute on different replicas. This approach of replicating resources, and its associated technical challenges, is the main subject of this chapter, covered in Sections 9.3 through 9.6.

Replicating the Server with a Shared Resource

Another approach is to replicate the server without replicating the resource, so that all copies of the server share the same copy of the resource (see Figure 9.3). This is useful in a configuration where processors share

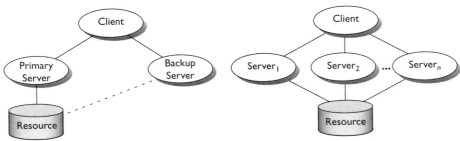

FIGURE 9.3

Replicated Server with Shared Resource. In (a), the primary and backup server share the resource, but only one of them uses the resource at any given time. In (b), many servers share the resource and can concurrently process requests that require access to the resource.

storage, such as a storage area network. In a primary-backup configuration, if the primary fails and the resource is still available, the backup server on another processor can continue to provide service (see Figure 9.3a).

This primary-backup approach improves availability, but not performance. If the server is the bottleneck and not the resource, then performance can be improved by allowing multiple servers to access the resource concurrently, as shown in Figure 9.3b. This approach, often called **data sharing**, introduces the problem of conflicts between transactions that execute in different servers and read and write the same data item in the resource. One solution is to partition the resource and assign each partition to one server. That way, each server can treat the partition as a private resource and therefore use standard locking and recovery algorithms. If a server fails, its partition is assigned to another server, like in the primary-backup approach. Another solution is to allow more than one server to access the same data item. This solution requires synchronization between servers and is discussed in Section 9.7.

9.3 SYNCHRONIZING UPDATES TO REPLICATED DATA

One-Copy Serializability

On possible goal of replication is to have replicas behave functionally like nonreplicated servers. This goal can be stated precisely by the concept of one-copy serializability, which extends the concept of serializability to a system where multiple replicas are present. An execution is **one-copy serializable** if it has the same effect as a serial execution on a one-copy database. We would like a system to ensure that its executions are one-copy serializable. In such a system, the user is unaware that data is replicated.

In a system that produces serializable executions, what can go wrong that would cause it to violate one-copy serializability? The answer is simple, though perhaps not obvious: a transaction might read a copy of a data item, say x, that was not written by the last transaction that wrote other copies of x. For example, consider a system that has two copies of x, stored at locations A and B, denoted x_A and x_B. Suppose we express execution histories using the notation of Section 6.1, where r, w, and c represent read, write, and commit operations, respectively, and subscripts are transaction identifiers. Consider the following execution history:

$$H = r_1[x_A] \, w_1[x_A] \, w_1[x_B] \, c_1 \, r_2[x_B] \, w_2[x_B] \, c_2 \, r_3[x_A] \, w_3[x_A] \, w_3[x_B] \, c_3$$

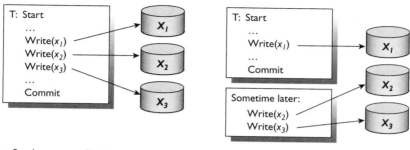

a. Synchronous replication   b. Asynchronous replication

FIGURE 9.4

Synchronous vs. Asynchronous Replication. In synchronous replication, each transaction updates all copies at the same time. In asynchronous replication, a transaction updates only one replica immediately. Its updates are propagated to the other replicas later.

This is a serial execution. Each transaction reads just one copy of x; since the copies are supposed to be identical, any copy will do. The only difficulty with it is that transaction T_2 did not write into copy x_A. This might have happened because copy x_A was unavailable when T_2 executed. Rather than delaying the execution of T_2 until after x_A recovered, the system allowed T_2 to finish and commit. Since we see $r_3[x_A]$ executed after c_2, apparently x_A recovered before T_3 started. However, $r_3[x_A]$ read a stale value of x_A, the one written by T_1, not T_2.

When x_A recovered, it should have been refreshed with the newly updated value of x that is stored in x_B. However, we do not see a write operation into x_A after T_2 committed and before $r_3[x_A]$ executed. We therefore conclude that when $r_3[x_A]$ executed, x_A still had the value that T_1 wrote.

Clearly, the behavior of H is not what we would expect in a one-copy database. In a one-copy database, T_3 would read the value of x written by T_2, not T_1. There is no other serial execution of T_1, T_2, and T_3 that has the same effect as H. Therefore, H does not have the same effect as any serial execution on a one-copy database. Thus, it is not one-copy serializable.

One obvious implication of one-copy serializability is that each transaction that writes into a data item x should write into all copies of x. However, when replication is used for improved availability, this isn't always possible. The whole point is to be able to continue to operate even when some copies are unavailable. Therefore, the not-so-obvious implication of one-copy serializability is that each transaction that reads a data item x must read a copy of x that was written by the most recent transaction before it that wrote into any copy of x. This sometimes requires careful synchronization.

Still, during normal operation, each transaction's updates should be applied to all replicas. There are two ways to arrange this: replicate update operations or replicate requests. In the first case, each request causes one transaction to execute. That transaction generates update operations, each of which is applied to all replicas. In the second case, the request message is sent to all replicas and causes a separate transaction to execute at each replica. We discuss each case, in turn.

Replicating Updates

There are two approaches to sending a transaction's updates to replicas: synchronous and asynchronous. In the **synchronous** approach, when a transaction updates a data item, say x, the update is sent to all replicas of x. These updates of the replicas execute within the context of the transaction. This is called synchronous because all replicas are, in effect, updated at the same time (see Figure 9.4a). Although sometimes this is feasible, often it is not, because it produces a heavy distributed transaction load. In particular, it implies that all transactions that update replicated data have to use two-phase commit, which entails significant communications cost.

Fortunately, looser synchronization can be used, which allows replicas to be updated independently. This is called **asynchronous** replication, where a transaction directly updates one replica and the update is propagated to other replicas later (see Figure 9.4b).

Asynchronous updates from different transactions can conflict. If they are applied to replicas in arbitrary orders, then the replicas will not be identical. For example, suppose transactions T_1 and T_2 update x, which has copies x_A and x_B. If T_1 updates x_A before T_2, but T_1 updates x_B after T_2, then x_A and x_B end up with different values. The usual way to avoid this problem is to ensure that the updates are applied in the same order to all replicas. By executing updates in the same order, all replicas go through the same sequence of states. Thus, each query (i.e., read-only transaction) at any replica sees a state that could have been seen at any other replica. And if new updates were shut off and all in-flight updates were applied to all replicas, the replicas *would* be identical. Therefore, users working with one replica see the same behavior that they would see with any other replica. In this sense, all replicas behave exactly the same way.

Applying updates in the same order to all replicas requires some synchronization. This synchronization can degrade performance, because some operations are delayed until other operations have time to complete. Much of the complexity in replication comes from clever synchronization techniques that minimize this performance degradation.

Whether synchronous or asynchronous replication is used, applying updates to all replicas is sometimes impossible, because some replicas are down. The system could stop accepting updates when this happens, but this is rarely acceptable since it decreases availability. If some replicas do continue processing updates while other replicas are down, then when the down replicas recover, some additional work is needed to recover the failed replicas to a satisfactory state. Some of the complexity in replication comes from ways of coping with unavailable servers and handling their recovery.

Replicas can be down either because a system has failed or because communication has failed (see Figure 9.5). The latter is more dangerous, because it may lead to two or more independently functioning partitions of the network, each of which allows updates to the replicas it knows about. If a resource has replicas in both

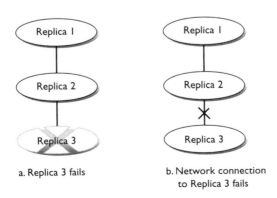

a. Replica 3 fails

b. Network connection to Replica 3 fails

FIGURE 9.5

Node and Communications Failures. Replica 1, Replica 2, and Replica 3 are connected by a network. In (a), Replica 3 fails. In (b), the connection to Replica 3 fails. Replica 1 and Replica 2 cannot distinguish these two situations, yet the system's behavior is quite different.

partitions, those replicas can be independently updated. When the partitions are reunited, they may discover they have processed incompatible updates. For example, they might both have sold the last item from inventory. Such executions are not one-copy serializable, since it could not be the result of a serial execution on a one-copy database. There are two solutions to this problem. One is to ensure that if a partition occurs, only one partition is allowed to process updates. The other is to allow multiple partitions to process updates and to reconcile the inconsistencies after the partitions are reunited—something that often requires human intervention.

Circumventing these performance and availability problems usually involves compromises. To configure a system with replicated servers, one must understand the behavior of the algorithms used for update propagation and synchronization. These algorithms are the main subject of this chapter.

Replicating Requests

An alternative to sending updates to all replicas is to send the **requests** to run the original transactions to all replicas (see Figure 9.6). To ensure that all the replicas end up as exact copies of each other, the transactions should execute in the same order at all replicas. Depending on the approach selected, this is either slow or tricky. A slow approach is to run the requests serially at one replica and then force the requests to run in the same order as the other replicas. This ensures they run in the same order at all replicas, but it allows no concurrency at each replica and therefore would be an inefficient use of each replica's resources.

The trickier approach is to allow concurrency within each replica and use some fancy synchronization across replicas to ensure that timing differences at the different replicas don't lead to different execution orders at different replicas. For example, in HP's Reliable Transaction Router (RTR), a replicated request can be executed at two or more replicas concurrently as a single distributed transaction. Since it runs as a transaction, it is serialized with respect to other replicated requests (which also run as transactions). It therefore can execute concurrently with other requests. Transaction synchronization (e.g., locking) ensures that the requests are processed in the same order at all replicas. As usual, transaction termination is synchronized using two-phase commit. However, unlike ordinary two-phase commit, if one of the replicas fails while a transaction is being committed,

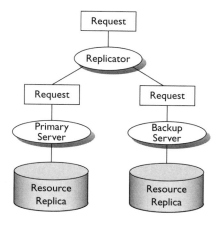

FIGURE 9.6

Replicating Requests. Each transaction runs independently against each replica. In both cases, conflicting updates must be applied in the same order against all replicas.

the other continues running and commits the transaction. This is useful in certain applications, such as securities trading (e.g., stock markets), where the legal definition of fairness dictates that transactions must execute in the order they were submitted, so it is undesirable to abort a transaction due to the failure of a replica.

Replicating updates is a more popular approach than replicating requests, by far. Therefore, we will focus on that approach for the rest of this chapter.

9.4 SINGLE-MASTER PRIMARY-COPY REPLICATION

Normal Operation

The most straightforward, and often pragmatic, approach to replication is to designate one replica as the primary copy and to allow update transactions to read and write only that replica. This is the primary-backup technique illustrated in Figure 9.1. Updates on the primary are distributed to other replicas, called **secondaries**, in the order in which they executed at the primary and are applied to secondaries in that order (see Figure 9.7). Thus, all replicas process the same stream of updates in the same order. In between any two update transactions, a replica can process a local query.

One way to propagate updates is by synchronous replication. For example, in a relational database system, one could define an SQL trigger on the primary table that remotely updates secondary copies of the table within the context of the user's update transaction. This implies that updates are propagated right away, which may delay the completion of the transaction. It also means that administrators cannot control when updates are applied to replicas. For example, in some decision support systems, it is desirable to apply updates at fixed times, so the database remains unchanged when certain analysis work is in progress.

Currently, the more popular approach is asynchronous replication, where updates to the primary generate a stream of updates to the secondaries, which is processed after transactions on the primary commit. For database systems, the stream of updates is often a log. The log reflects the exact order of the updates that were performed at the primary, so the updates can be applied directly to each secondary as they arrive.

One application of primary-copy replication is **database mirroring**, where there are only two replicas, one primary and one secondary. This is a hot backup technique for high availability. Among the first general-purpose

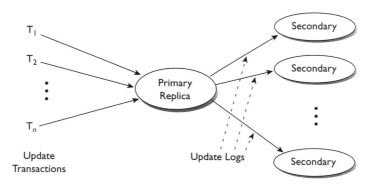

FIGURE 9.7

Propagating Updates from Primary to Secondaries. Transactions update data only at the primary replica. The primary propagates updates to the secondary replicas. The secondaries can process local queries.

systems to do this were IBM's IMS/XRF and Tandem's (now HP's) Non-Stop SQL database systems. Now most database systems offer a database mirroring feature.

With database mirroring, the primary sends its database log to the secondary. The secondary continually runs log-based recovery, so that its database state is very close to that of the primary. If the primary fails, the secondary just needs to finish processing the tail of the log it received before the primary failed, after which it can take over as primary. If synchronous replication is used, then no transactions are lost in this failover. With asynchronous replication, the secondary may not have received the last few updates from the primary. This problem can be mitigated if the primary and secondary are colocated and the secondary can be given access to the primary copy's disk log. In that case, after the secondary is given control, it can read the disk log to pick up the last few log records that it did not receive before the primary failed.

Another application of primary-copy replication is to produce queryable copies of parts of a database. This is a functionally-rich feature that is offered by most relational database products. In this case, there is no real-time requirement to move the log records immediately to the secondary copy, so there is time to postprocess updates from the primary copy in various ways.

Some relational database systems capture updates to each primary table in a log table that is colocated with the primary table (see Figure 9.8b). One approach is to have the system define an SQL trigger on each primary table that translates each update into an insert on the log table. Periodically, the primary creates a new log table to capture updates and sends the previous log table to each secondary where it is applied to the replica. This approach to capturing updates can slow down normal processing of transactions, due to the extra work introduced by the trigger.

Another approach is to postprocess the database log to create the stream of updates to the replicas. If this is done on-line while the log is still in main memory, then it avoids slowing down normal processing of transactions as compared to the trigger approach. In fact, the log can be sent to a different server, where the postprocessing is done.

Since the log can be quite large, one reason to postprocess the log is to reduce its size if possible. One technique is to filter out aborted transactions, since they do not need to be applied to replicas (see Figure 9.8a).

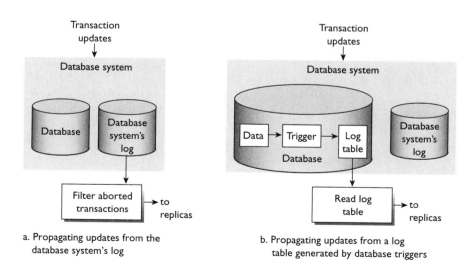

FIGURE 9.8

Generating Update Streams for Replicas. An update stream for replicas can be produced from (a) the database system's log or (b) a log table produced by triggers.

This reduces the amount of data transmission and the cost of processing updates at the replica. However, it requires that the primary not send a log record until it knows that the transaction that wrote the record has committed. This introduces additional processing time at the primary and delay in updating the secondary, which are the main costs of reducing the data transmission. Another technique is to send only the finest granularity data that has changed, e.g., fields of records, rather than coarser-grain units of data, such as entire records.

Another reason to postprocess the log is to group together the updates of each transaction. This is beneficial because it enables transactions to be applied to secondaries serially. After each transaction is applied, the secondary database is in a consistent state. Therefore a query can read a consistent database state without using read locks. If updates were not grouped by transaction, then in order for queries to read a consistent state, updates would have to set write locks and queries would have to set read locks.

Some systems allow different parts of the database to be replicated to different locations. For example, the primary might contain a table describing customers and other tables describing orders. These tables are colocated at the primary, since many transactions require access to all of these tables. However, the customer table may be replicated at different servers than the order tables. To enable this, the log postprocessing splits each transaction's updates into two transactions, one for the customer table and one for the order tables, and adds them to separate streams, one for the customer replicas and one for the order replicas. If there is also a replica that contains all the customer and orders information, then the log postprocessor would generate a third stream for that replica, with all the updates of each transaction packaged in a single transaction in the stream.

Given this complex filtering and transaction splitting, often a "buffer database" is used to store updates that flow from the primary to secondaries. Updates that are destined for different replicas are stored in different areas of the buffer database. This allows them to be applied to replicas according to different schedules.

Some systems allow application-specific logic to be used to apply changes to replicas. For example, the application could add a timestamp that tells exactly when the update was applied to the replica.

Although primary-copy replication normally does not allow transactions to update a secondary before updating the primary, there are situations where it can be made to work. For example, consider an update transaction that reads and writes a replica using two-phase locking. Suppose it keeps a copy of all the values that it read, which includes all the data items that the transaction wrote. When it is ready to commit, it sends the values of data items that it read along with values that it wrote to the primary. Executing within the context of the same transaction, the primary reads the same data items that the transaction read at the secondary, setting locks as in normal two-phase locking. If the values of the data items that it reads at the primary are the same as those that the transaction read at the secondary, then the transaction applies its updates to the primary too, and commits. If not, then it aborts. This is essentially an application of the optimistic concurrency control technique described in Section 6.8.

Most database systems offer considerable flexibility in configuring replication. Subsets of tables can be independently replicated, possibly at different locations. For example, a central office's Accounts table can be split by branch, and the accounts for each branch are replicated at the system at that branch. As the number of replicated tables grows, it can be rather daunting to keep track of which pieces of which tables are replicated at which systems. To simplify management tasks, systems offer tools for displaying, querying, and editing the configuration of replicas.

The replication services of most database systems work by constructing a log stream or log table of updates and sending it to secondary servers. This approach was introduced in Tandem's (now HP's) Non-Stop SQL and in Digital's VAX Data Distributor in the 1980s. Similar approaches currently are offered by IBM, Informix (now IBM), Microsoft (SQL Server), MySQL, Oracle, and Sybase. Within this general approach, products vary in the specific features they offer: the granularity of data that can be replicated (a database, a table, a portion of a table); the flexibility of selecting primaries and secondaries (a server can be a primary server for some data and a secondary for others); how dynamically the configuration of primaries and secondaries can be changed; the options for filtering updates and splitting transactions; and facilities to simplify managing a large set of replicas.

Failures and Recoveries

This primary-copy approach works well as long as the primary and secondaries are alive. How do we handle failures? Let us work through the cases.

Secondary Recovery

If a secondary replica fails, the rest of the system continues to run as before. When the secondary recovers, it needs to catch up processing the stream of updates from the primary. This is not much different than the processing it would have done if it had not failed; it's just processing the updates later. The main new problem is that it must determine which updates it processed before it failed, so it doesn't incorrectly reapply non-idempotent updates. This is the same problem as log-based database recovery that we studied in Chapter 7.

If a secondary is down for too long, it may be more efficient to get a whole new copy of the database rather than processing an update stream. In this case, while the database is being copied from the primary to the recovering secondary, more updates are generated at the primary. So after the database has been copied, to finish up, the secondary needs to process that last stream of updates coming from the primary. This is similar to media recovery, as described in Chapter 7.

Primary Recovery with One Secondary

If the primary fails, recovery can be more challenging. One could simply disallow updates until the primary recovers. This is a satisfactory approach when the main goal of replication is better performance for queries. In fact, it may be hard to avoid this approach if complex filtering and partitioning of updates is supported. Since different secondaries receive a different subset of the changes that were applied to the primary, secondaries are often not complete copies of the primary. Therefore, it would be difficult to determine which secondaries should take over as primary for which parts of the primary's data.

If a goal of replication is improved availability for updates, then it is usually not satisfactory to wait for the primary to recover, since the primary could be down for awhile. So if it is important to keep the system running, some secondary must take over as primary. This leads to two technical problems. First, all replicas must agree on the selection of the new primary, since the system cannot tolerate having two primaries—this would lead to total confusion and incorrect results. Second, the last few updates from the failed primary may not have reached all replicas. If a replica starts processing updates from the new primary before it has received all updates from the failed primary, it will end up in a different state than other replicas that did receive all the failed primary's updates.

We first explore these problems in a simple case of two replicas, one primary and one secondary. Suppose the secondary detects that the primary has failed. This failure detection must be based on timeouts. For example, the secondary is no longer receiving log records from the primary. And when the secondary sends "are you there?" messages to the primary, the secondary receives no reply from the primary. However, these timeouts may be due to a communications failure between the primary and secondary, similar to the one shown in Figure 9.7, and the primary may still be operating.

To distinguish between a primary failure and a primary-secondary communications failure, an external agent is needed to decide which replica should be primary. A typical approach is to add a "watchdog" process, preferably on a different machine than the primary and secondary. The watchdog sends periodic "are you there?" messages to both the primary and secondary. There are four cases to consider (see Figure 9.9):

1. If the watchdog can communicate with the primary and not with the secondary, then it tells the primary of this fact. If the primary can communicate with the secondary, then no action is needed. If not, then the primary creates another secondary, if possible.

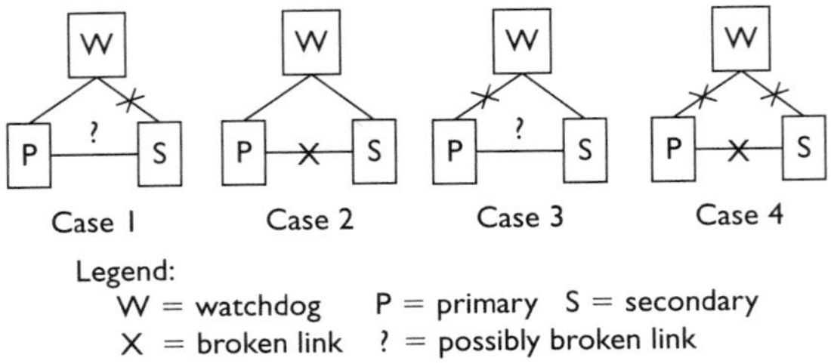

FIGURE 9.9

Failure Cases with a Watchdog. A watchdog process can help sort out failure cases between a primary and secondary.

2. If the watchdog can communicate with both the primary and secondary, but they cannot communicate with each other, then they notify the watchdog of this fact. The watchdog then tells the secondary to fail, since it can no longer function as a replica. It also tells the primary to create another secondary, if possible.

3. If the watchdog can communicate only with the secondary, then it tells the secondary that it believes the primary is down. If the secondary can communicate with the primary, then no action is needed. If not, then it can take over as primary. In this case, if the primary is still operational but is simply unable to communicate with the watchdog, then the primary must self-destruct. Otherwise, the old primary and the new primary (which was formerly the secondary) are both operating as primary. It may therefore be advisable that the watchdog send a message to tell the primary to self-destruct, in case the primary is able to receive messages from the watchdog but its replies are not getting through. In summary, if the secondary loses communications with the primary, then whichever replica can still communicate with the watchdog is now the primary.

4. If neither replica can communicate with the watchdog or with each other, then neither replica can operate as the primary. This is called a **total failure**.

Suppose that the primary did indeed fail and the secondary has been designated to be the new primary. Now we face the second problem: the new primary may not have received all the committed updates performed by the former primary before the former primary failed. One solution to this problem is to have the primary delay committing a transaction's updates until it knows that the secondary received those updates. The primary could wait until the secondary has stored those updates in stable storage, or it could wait only until the secondary has received the updates in main memory. If the system that stores the secondary has battery backup, then the latter might be reliable enough. In either case, we're back to synchronous replication, where the updates to the replica are included as part of the transaction. This extra round of commit-time messages between the primary and secondary is essentially a simple two-phase commit protocol. The performance degradation from these messages can be significant. The choice between performance (asynchronous replication) and reliability (synchronous replication) depends on the application and system configuration. Therefore, database products that offer database mirroring usually offer both options, so the user can choose on a case-by-case basis.

Primary Recovery with Multiple Secondaries

Now let's look at the more general case where there are multiple secondaries and a secondary detects the failure of a primary. There are two ways this could happen. The primary might indeed be down. Or, much worse, there could be a communication failure that partitions the network into independent sets of functioning replicas.

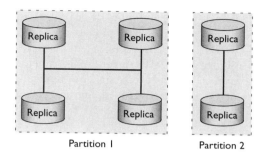

FIGURE 9.10

Majority Consensus. Partition 1 has a majority of the replicas and therefore is allowed to process updates. Partition 2 may not process updates.

In the latter case the primary could still be operational, so the set of replicas that doesn't include the primary must not promote one of the secondaries to be a primary. The same problem can arise even in the first case where the primary is down. In this case, we do want to promote one of the secondaries to become primary. But if there are two independent sets of replicas that are operating, each set might independently promote a secondary to be the primary, a situation that we want to avoid.

To solve this problem, we need a decision criterion by which at most one set of replicas has an operational primary. We need an algorithm by which replicas can reach this decision. And after the replicas have chosen a new primary, we need an algorithm by which they can recover to the latest state before accepting new transactions. The next three sections treat each of these problems in turn.

Majority and Quorum Consensus

One simple way to ensure that only one primary exists is to statically declare one replica to be the primary. If the network partitions, the partition that has the primary is the one that can process updates. This is a feasible approach, but it is useless if the goal is high availability. If the primary is down, each partition has to assume the worst, which is that the primary really is running but not communicating with this partition. Thus, neither partition promotes a secondary to become primary.

A more flexible algorithm for determining which partition can have the primary is called **majority consensus**: a set of replicas is allowed to have a primary if and only if the set includes a majority of the replicas (see Figure 9.10). Since a majority is more than half, only one set of replicas can have a majority. Moreover, each partition can independently figure out if it has a majority. These are the two critical properties of majorities that make the technique work.

Majority consensus is a generalization of the watchdog technique we described for database mirroring. The watchdog adds a third process to the mix. Two communicating processes comprise a majority. Thus, whichever partition has at least two communicating processes is allowed to have the primary: either the existing primary and secondary if the watchdog is down; or the watchdog plus whichever replica(s) it can communicate with. By convention, if the watchdog can communicate with the primary and secondary but the latter cannot communicate with each other, then the secondary is told to fail.

Majority consensus does have one annoying problem: it does not work well when there is an even number of copies. In particular, it is useless when there are just two replicas, since the only majority of two is two; that is, it can operate only when both replicas are available. When there are four replicas, a majority needs at least three, so if the network splits into two groups of two copies, neither group can have a primary.

A fancier approach is the **quorum consensus** algorithm. It gives a **weight** to each replica and looks for a set of replicas with a majority of the weight, called a **quorum** (see Figure 9.11). For example, with two replicas, we could give a weight of two to the more reliable replica and a weight of one to the other. That way, the replica with a weight of two can be primary even if the other replica is unavailable. Giving a weight of two to the most reliable replica helps whenever there is an even number of replicas. If the network partitions into two groups with the same number of copies, the group with the replica of weight two still has a quorum.

Reaching Consensus

During normal operation, the set of operational replicas must agree on which replicas are up and which are down or unreachable. If a replica loses communication with one or more other replicas, then the operational replicas need to reassess whether they still have a majority. (For the purpose of this discussion, we'll assume majority consensus, not quorum consensus.) In fact, the nonoperational replicas that are up also need to do this when they reestablish communications with a replica, since this replica may be the one they need to reach a majority. After some group of replicas is established as having a majority, that group can choose a primary and ensure that all replicas in the group have the most up-to-date state.

To discuss the details, we need some terminology: The **replica set** is the set of all replicas, including those that are up and down; the **current configuration** is the set of operational replicas that are able to communicate with each other and comprise a majority.

An algorithm that enables a set of processes to reach a common decision is called a **consensus algorithm**. In this case, that common decision is agreement on the current configuration by a set of operational replicas. Given our problem context, we'll call the participants replicas instead of processes. But the algorithm we describe works for general consensus, not just for deciding on the current configuration.

One problem with such consensus algorithms is that multiple replicas may be trying to drive a common decision at the same time. It's important that different replicas don't drive the replicas toward different decisions.

Another problem is that the system may be unstable, with replicas and communications links failing and recovering while replicas are trying to reach consensus. There's not much hope in reaching consensus during such unstable periods. However, once the system stabilizes, we do want the algorithm to reach consensus quickly.

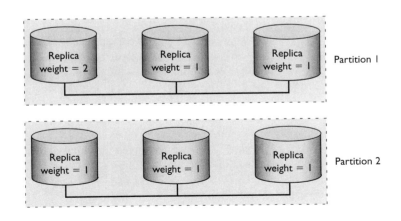

FIGURE 9.11

Quorum Consensus. Partition 1 has a total weight of 4, which is more than half of the total weight of 7. It therefore constitutes a quorum and is allowed to process updates.

There are several variations of algorithms to reach consensus, but they all have a common theme, namely, that there's a unique identifier associated with the consensus, that these identifiers are totally ordered, and that the highest unique identifier wins. We will call that identifier an **epoch number**. It identifies a period of time, called an **epoch**, during which a set of replicas have agreed on the current configuration, called an **epoch set**. An epoch number can be constructed by concatenating a counter value with the unique replica identifier of the replica that generated the epoch number. Each replica keeps track of the current epoch number e in stable storage.

During stable periods, the epoch set with largest epoch number is the current configuration. During unstable periods, the actual current configuration may differ from the current epoch set. The goal of the consensus algorithm is to reach agreement on a new epoch set with associated epoch number that accurately describes the current configuration.

Suppose a replica R is part of the current configuration, which has epoch number e_1. If R detects that the current configuration is no longer valid (because R has detected a failure or recovery), R becomes the leader of a new execution of the consensus algorithm, which proceeds as follows:

1. R generates a new epoch number e_2 that is bigger than e_1. For example, it increments the counter value part of e_1 by one and concatenates it with R's replica identifier.

2. R sends an **invitation** message containing the value e_2 to all replicas in the replica set.

3. When a replica R' receives the invitation, it replies to R with an **accept** message if R' has not accepted another invitation with an epoch number bigger than e_2. R' includes its current epoch number in the accept message. Moreover, if R' was the leader of another instance of the consensus algorithm (which is using a smaller epoch number), it stops that execution. Otherwise, if R' has accepted an invitation with an epoch number bigger than e_2, it sends a **reject** message to R. As a courtesy, it may return the largest epoch number of any invitation it has previously accepted.

4. R waits for its timeout period to expire, to ensure it receives as many replies as possible.

   a. If R receives accept messages from at least one less than a majority of replicas in the replica set, then it has established a majority (including itself) and therefore has reached consensus. It therefore sends a **new epoch** message to all the accepting replicas and stops. The new epoch message contains the new epoch number and epoch set. When a replica receives a new epoch message, it updates its epoch number and the associated list of replicas in the epoch set and writes it to stable storage.

   b. Otherwise, R has failed to reach a majority and stops.

Let's consider the execution of this algorithm under several scenarios. First, assume that only one leader R is running this algorithm. Then it will either receive enough accept messages to establish a majority and hence a new epoch set, or it will fail to reach a majority.

Suppose a leader R_1 fails to establish an epoch set. One reason this could happen is that R_1 may be unable to communicate with enough replicas to establish a majority. In this case, R_1 periodically could attempt to re-execute the algorithm, in case a replica or communication link has silently recovered and thereby made it possible for R_1 to form a majority.

A second reason that R_1 may fail to establish an epoch set is that another replica R_2 is concurrently trying to create a new epoch set using a higher epoch number. In this case, it is important that R_1 not rerun the algorithm right away with a larger epoch number, since this might kill R_2's chance of getting a majority of acceptances. That is, it might turn into an "arms race," where each replica reruns the algorithm with successively higher epoch numbers and thereby causes the other replica's consensus algorithm to fail.

The arms race problem notwithstanding, if R_1 fails to establish an epoch set and, after waiting awhile, receives no other invitations to join an epoch set with higher epoch number, then it may choose to start another round of the consensus algorithm. In the previous round, if it received a reject message with a higher epoch number e_3, then it can increase its chances of reaching consensus by using an epoch number even higher than e_3. This ensures that any replica that is still waiting for the result of the execution with epoch number e_3 will abandon waiting and choose the new, higher epoch number instead.

Establishing the Latest State

After the current configuration has been established as the epoch set, the primary needs to be selected and all the replicas in the current configuration have to be brought up to date. The first step is to determine if the new epoch set includes the primary from the previous epoch. To do this, first observe that since every epoch set has a majority, it overlaps every earlier epoch set. Therefore, there is at least one replica in the new epoch set from the previous epoch set and it has the largest epoch number less than the new epoch number. If one of the replicas with the largest previous epoch number was the primary of that epoch set, then we can simplify recovery by reusing it as the primary of the new epoch set.

Unfortunately, this may not be right, because the last epoch may not have stabilized before it lost its majority and had to reconfigure. If that happened, then the primary of the previous epoch set may not have the latest state. That is, the previous epoch set may have elected the primary but not yet refreshed the new primary's state to be the latest state known to all replicas in the epoch set. To avoid this outcome, the new epoch set needs to identify the last *stable* epoch set. This can be done by having each epoch use a state bit that it sets after it has stabilized and ensured that every replica in the replica set has the latest state. Only then can the epoch set accept new work.

Therefore, the new epoch set should determine if it includes the primary of the last stable epoch set. If so, then it knows that this primary has the most up-to-date state. So to resume normal processing, the primary needs to ensure the secondaries are up to date by determining the state of each secondary and sending it whatever updates it is missing. It then sets the epoch's state bit to stable and broadcasts that to all secondaries.

If the epoch set does not include the primary from the previous epoch, then a new primary must be selected. The choice of primary may be based on the amount of spare capacity on its machine (since a primary consumes more resources than a secondary) and on whether it was a member of the most recent epoch set and thus has the latest or a very recent state (so that it can recover quickly and start accepting new requests).

The latest state of the secondaries that are still alive can be determined by comparing the sequence numbers of the last message received by each secondary from the previous primary. The one with highest sequence number has the latest state and can forward the tail of its update sequence to other secondaries that need it. After a replica receives that state, it acknowledges that fact to the primary. After the new primary receives acknowledgments from all replicas in the epoch set, it can set the epoch's state to stable and start processing new transactions. The new primary should then start off with a message sequence number greater than that of the largest received by any secondary in the previous epoch.

Does the new epoch set actually have the latest state? To answer this question, let C be the set of replicas that were in both the previous epoch and the new one. Since each epoch set has a majority of the replicas, C must include at least one replica. The replicas in C are the only ones that might know the latest state. However, as in the case of database mirroring, it's possible that none of them actually do know the latest state, due to the delay in propagating updates from the primary to the replicas. For example, suppose the epoch set for epoch 1 had replicas P, S_1, and S_2, with P as the primary. Suppose the last transaction was committed by P and S_1, but not S_2. Then they all died, and epoch set 2 was formed, consisting of replicas S_2, S_3, and S_4. Epoch sets 1 and 2 overlap by one replica, S_2, but S_2 doesn't have the latest state.

We encountered this problem when considering secondary recovery for database mirroring. The solution we offered was to propagate updates synchronously. In that case, two-phase commit is needed. This ensures that every replica in C has all the committed updates. However, the last few updates might be in their uncertainty periods and hence blocked. Thus, while synchronous replication reduces the number of transactions that might be lost when a secondary takes over as primary, it doesn't close the gap entirely.

Consistency, Availability, and Partition-Tolerance

In distributed systems, there is an inherent tradeoff between data consistency, system availability, and tolerance to network partitions. A system can offer any two of these three properties, but not all three of them. This is known as the **CAP conjecture**.

The primary-copy approach with synchronous replication ensures data consistency and partition-tolerance, and therefore gives up on availability in some cases. It attains data consistency by writing updates to replicas as part of the transaction that performed the write and using two-phase commit for transaction atomicity. It attains partition-tolerance by using quorum consensus to ensure that there are not two partitions that are both able to run transactions. This leads to a loss of availability in the case where the network partitions, because some operational replicas are not part of the quorum. Therefore, even though they are up and running, they are not available.

Suppose the network partitions and the partition that has a quorum of replicas does not include the former primary. Although the system can ensure the updates are permitted only on the quorum of copies, it cannot guarantee consistency because the last few transactions that executed at the former primary may not have arrived at any of the replicas in the quorum before the network partition occurred. Thus, a decision to allow updates to the quorum of replicas is trading off consistency for availability. A decision to disallow updates to the quorum of replicas is making the opposite tradeoff, namely, trading off availability in order to ensure consistency.

Another aspect of this tradeoff is eventual consistency versus instantaneous consistency. Asynchronous replication ensures eventual consistency but gives up on instantaneous consistency, since there may be a long delay before updates are propagated to some replicas. The weaker level of consistency improves performance by avoiding two-phase commit. It may also improve availability, by allowing a user to be redirected from one replica to another in a slightly different state.

For example, suppose an on-line shopper has started populating her shopping basket and the shopping basket is replicated using primary-copy replication. Suppose the primary fails and is not present in the quorum. To maximize availability, the system could service read requests using another replica while the replicas are being brought up to date. Thus, during this period, the shopper might be given an older state of his or her shopping cart. This may occur even if the last update to the cart is known to the quorum, because the shopper's reads are being serviced by a slightly out-of-date replica. This may be confusing, especially since the shopping cart will return to the latest state after the replicas are brought up to date. However, if the probability of this occurrence is sufficiently low, this loss of consistency may be regarded as a better tradeoff than having the shopping cart be unavailable while the replicas are being brought up to date.

A different set of tradeoffs between consistency, availability, and partition-tolerance is offered by multimaster replication. We will consider these tradeoffs at the end of the next section.

9.5 MULTIMASTER REPLICATION

Partitioned Operation Can Be Useful

Rather than being the result of a communication failure, a partition is sometimes a planned event that happens frequently. For example, a laptop computer might be connected to the network only periodically. It could contain a replica of a database, whose primary resides on a reliable server. When the laptop computer is disconnected, it might still be important that it process updates. For example, consider a laptop that contains a sales database and is used by a sales person. Its database might have a customer table (rarely updated), an orders table (insert-mostly), and a sales-call table (append-only). Even when the laptop is disconnected from the network, the sales person must be able to create an order and change basic customer information, such as address and phone number. In this case, it is not satisfactory to require that only the partition with a quorum of replicas be operative. Indeed, if there are many sales people, there probably is no partition with a quorum of replicas, yet all sales people need to be allowed to update their replicas.

Update Propagation with Multiple Masters

Despite the partition, we could try using the same primary-copy scheme as in the previous section, but allow update transactions to execute at any replica. Each replica logs its updates, as if it were a primary copy. When a replica R reconnects to the network, it sends its logged updates to the real primary that resides on a reliable server, which can process the updates and forward them to other replicas. R can also ask the primary for updates that occurred while it was disconnected.

One problem with this scheme is conflicting updates that originate at different replicas. For example, in Figure 9.12, each transaction executes at a replica. Its updates are applied first to the replica where it executes: transaction T_1 updates x at replica R_1 and T_2 updates x at replica R_2. Each replica sends its update to the primary, which forwards it to the other replica. In the end, these conflicting updates are applied in different orders by different replicas, so the resulting replicas are not identical.

One way to avoid this problem is to design the applications so that most updates do not conflict. Such updates can be applied in different orders by different replicas and still produce the same final state at all replicas. For example, in the sales database, a sales person appends a row to the sales-call table every time the sales person interacts with a customer. This row is unique for each such interaction, so two rows generated by different sales people cannot conflict; they may refer to the same customer, but they describe different interactions. The orders table is also insert-mostly. Each insertion of a new order produces a new row in the order table. With careful

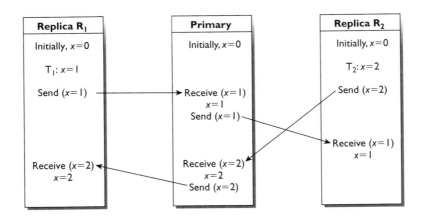

FIGURE 9.12

Conflicting Updates Originating at Different Replicas. The updates to x are applied in different orders by replicas R_1 and R_2, so the resulting replicas are not identical.

design, these insertions do not conflict. For example, to ensure insertions do not conflict, the insertion of a new order must not require reading previous orders; for example, to check that the new order is not a duplicate.

If conflicts can occur, then there are several problems to be solved: (1) detecting the conflicts, (2) resolving the conflicts in the same way at all replicas, and (3) ensuring that replicas eventually converge to be identical. One approach to these problems is to tag each update with a unique timestamp. Unique timestamps can be constructed by concatenating the replica's local clock time with its unique replica identifier, so timestamps generated at different replicas cannot be identical. Each data item at a replica also is tagged with a timestamp. Updates are applied using **Thomas' Write Rule** as follows [Thomas 79] (see Figure 9.13): If an update to data item x arrives at a replica, and the update's timestamp is larger than x's timestamp at the replica, then the update is applied and x's timestamp is replaced by the update's timestamp. Otherwise, the update is discarded.

Thomas' Write Rule addresses these three problems. It detects a conflict when an update to a data item arrives at a replica with an update timestamp lower than the replica's timestamp on that data item. It resolves the conflict by retaining the value that has the larger timestamp. And eventually, each data item x has the same value at all replicas, because at every replica, the update to x with the largest timestamp is the last one that actually was applied.

The deletion of a data item needs to be handled like any other update, to ensure it is not reinserted by an update with a smaller timestamp that arrives after the deletion was processed. That is, a deleted data item must still be known to the replica and have a timestamp that was written by the delete operation, but its value is "deleted." This value is usually called a **tombstone**.

Thomas' Write Rule does not require that clocks be exactly synchronized. However, if the clock at one replica is fast, then its updates will have larger timestamps than updates concurrently generated by other replicas. In conflict situations, the update with the larger timestamp wins, so the replica with a fast clock has an unfair advantage. For this reason, it is beneficial to keep the clocks nearly synchronized when using Thomas' Write Rule.

Nonblind Updates

Thomas' Write Rule works fine for **blind updates**, which are updates that replace the value of a data item with a new value that does not depend on any data that the transaction previously read. We just saw two examples: recording a sales call and inserting a new order. Another example is storing a customer's phone number. In this

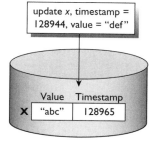

a. The update has smaller timestamp
than the database's timestamp of x,
so it should not be applied

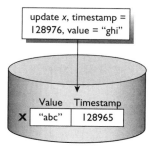

b. The update has larger timestamp
than the database's timestamp of x,
so it should be applied

FIGURE 9.13

Thomas' Write Rule. An update to a data item x is applied only if its timestamp is larger than the one in the database.

case, two updates by different transactions that store a new phone number for the same customer conflict, and if they write different phone numbers then the execution order certainly matters. However, since the updates were submitted concurrently, either execution order is satisfactory as long as all replicas reflect the same execution order. Thomas' Write Rule solves this problem by ensuring that the final value at all replicas is the one written by the update with the higher timestamp.

If the updates are not blind, then Thomas' Write Rule isn't a completely satisfactory solution, because it doesn't diagnose that one update depends on another one. For example, consider Figure 9.14, which is similar to Figure 9.12 except that the transactions increment x instead of performing blind updates to x, and they use Thomas' Write Rule. Each value of x is represented by a [value, timestamp] pair. Initially, $x = 0$ at the primary and replicas and the associated timestamp (ts) is 5. Since transaction timestamps are guaranteed to be unique, T_1 and T_2 update x with different timestamps, namely 6 and 7, respectively. The updates are concurrent in the sense that neither T_1 nor T_2 reads the value of x written by the other. Since T_2 has the larger timestamp, its value is the one that sticks at all three copies. However, the increment operation by T_1 is lost, which is probably not what is desired. The execution is not one-copy serializable, since a serial execution of the two transactions (in either order) on a one-copy database would produce a final value of $x = 3$. The problem is that the nature of the conflict between T_1 and T_2 was not diagnosed. The system simply retained the update with larger timestamp as if both updates were blind, which they were not.

With multimaster replication, situations like Figure 9.14 are unavoidable. That is, in general it's possible for two conflicting transactions to update different copies of the same data item independently at different replicas, such that neither transaction reads the other transaction's updated value.

The way multimaster replication is used can greatly affect the probability of such conflicts. For example, when multimaster replication is used to support disconnected operation, such as laptops that are intermittently connected to the network, replicas can run for long periods without exchanging updates. The longer a replica executes transactions without exchanging its updates with other replicas, the greater the chance that reconciliation will be needed. That is, if updates are exchanged frequently, then the chances are better that an update will be propagated to all replicas before a transaction with a conflicting update executes, thereby avoiding the need for reconciliation.

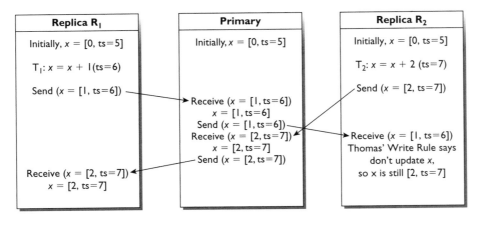

FIGURE 9.14

Conflicting Nonblind Updates. Thomas' Write Rule ensures that $x = 2$ at all replicas, but T_1's update is lost (ts is an abbreviation for timestamp).

When such a conflict occurs, Thomas' Write Rule makes a rather arbitrary choice by applying the one with larger timestamp and discarding the other one. In a variation of the rule, instead of discarding the one with smaller timestamp, the system can save it. The saved update can then be examined later by a person who determines whether it needs to be reconsidered or merged into the primary somehow.

Detecting Replication Conflicts Using Version Vectors

Instead of requiring manual reconsideration of the saved update in all cases, we want to distinguish between real conflicts where reconciliation is required and fake conflicts where a value really should be overwritten by a later update. We can do this using a technique called version vectors.

To explain the use of version vectors, we need the concept of version that was introduced in Section 6.6. Recall that a **version** of a data item x is the value of x written by a particular transaction. That is, each transaction that updates x produces a new version of x. We introduced this notion in the context of multiversion databases, where the database retains all or most of the versions produced by different transactions. Here, we will typically retain only one version of a data item. However, we nevertheless need to refer to different versions of a data item because after a data item is updated, different replicas will store different versions during the period that the update is being propagated between replicas.

To distinguish between real and fake conflicts, we need precise definitions of them. Given two versions x_i and x_k of x, we say that x_i **precedes** x_k (written $x_i \rightarrow x_k$) if there is a sequence of transactions, each of which updates x, such that

- The first transaction in the sequence reads and overwrites x_i.
- Starting with the second transaction in the sequence, each transaction reads and overwrites the version of x produced by the previous transaction in the sequence.
- The last transaction in the sequence produces version x_k.

If x_i does not precede x_k and x_k does not precede x_i then we say that x_i and x_k have a **replication conflict** (i.e., a "real" conflict). If the database started with one version of x, then the presence of a replication conflict implies there is some version of x that was overwritten independently by two transactions that did not see each other's output. This is the essence of the kind of conflict exhibited by transactions T_1 and T_2 in Figure 9.14. If two versions of x are related by the precedes relation, then it's a fake conflict, since the later version clearly should replace the earlier one.

The version vector technique enables us to detect replication conflicts between versions. It requires that each replica maintain an update count. When a transaction updates a data item x for the first time, it associates its local replica ID and current update count with this new version of x, and the update count for the replica is incremented by one. The pair [replica id, update count] uniquely identifies the version and is called a **version ID**. For example, if the current update count for replica R is 8 and the replica runs a transaction T that first updates data item x and then updates y, then T associates version ID [R, 8] with x and [R, 9] with y. If T updates x or y a second time, the version IDs of x and y associated with T needn't be changed. Since each replica has a unique replica ID, each version ID is unique too. By convention, we use the version ID of a data item to uniquely identify the final value (not any intermediate values) written by a transaction into that data item.

To track which versions each replica R has received, R maintains an array of version IDs, called a **version vector**, with one entry in the array for each replica. Each entry in the version vector tells which updates R has received and processed from every other replica. Entry [R_i, c] in the version vector says that R has received all updates generated by R_i with version IDs [R_i, 1], [R_i, 2], ..., [R_i, c]. R's version vector includes an entry for its own latest version ID.

In addition to maintaining a version vector for each replica, we also maintain a version ID and version vector for each data item at the replica. This per-data-item information is used to detect replication conflicts. The version ID and version vector for a data item x is updated when a transaction executing at replica R updates x. After a transaction T executing at R updates a data item x for the first time, it replaces x's version ID by R's version ID, it replaces R's position in x's version vector by R's current version ID, and R increments its version ID. This records the fact that T generated a new version of x at replica R. For example, if T executes at replica R_1, R_1's current update count is 14, and T updates x, then T replaces x's version ID with $[R_1, 14]$, T replaces the version ID formerly in x's version vector, say $[R_1, c]$, by $[R_1, 14]$, and R increments its update count. It must be that $c < 14$, because $[R_1, 14]$ is the largest version ID that R_1 has generated so far.

When replica S (the sender) sends its updated version v of x to another replica R (the receiver), it includes the version ID and version vector along with the value. The version vector tells R which updates were applied to x before v was generated. This gives R enough information to determine whether R's own version of x has a replication conflict with v, and hence whether it should replace its own version by v.

To see how conflict detection works, suppose that the updated version of x that S sends to R has version ID $[S, 10]$ and version vector $[[S,10], [R, 4]]$. Suppose that when R receives the updated version, its value of x has version ID $[R, 5]$ and version vector $[[S, 9], [R, 5]]$. In this case, we have a replication conflict. How can R tell? The version vector $[[S,10], [R, 4]]$ sent by S tells R that S did not receive R's updated version $[R, 5]$ before S executed the update that wrote version $[S, 10]$. On the other hand, R's version vector $[[S, 9], [R, 5]]$ for x tells R that R did not receive S's updated version $[S, 10]$ before it executed update $[R, 5]$. Since neither S nor R saw the other replica's updated version of x before it executed its latest update, R deduces that there is a replication conflict.

We will explain some general approaches to detecting replication conflicts shortly. But first, we describe two other mechanisms that are needed in a complete system, namely, conflict resolution and update propagation.

Conflict Resolution

In the previous example, a simple way for R to deal with the conflict is for it to retain both values of x—the one it already has and the one it just received from S, with the associated version IDs and version vectors. A later conflict resolution process can determine how to reconcile these two values. This is necessarily an application-specific process because it depends on knowing (or assuming) something about the semantics of the transactions that conflicted. For example, if the conflict resolver knows that transactions originating at R increment x by one as opposed to doing a blind write of x, then it can add one to the value of x produced by the other transaction to generate a new final value.

The replication system can help a little bit by allowing an application to register one or more merge procedures for each data item, which can then be invoked automatically when multiple values are stored for that item. Alternatively, the two versions of x can be retained and given to the next transaction that reads x, which then has to determine the correct value of x. In any case, the solution is a matter of application programming.

If the resolution executes as a transaction, then its result propagates to other replicas as a normal updated version. If it propagates fast enough, this avoids the need to execute the resolution procedure at other replicas.

Maintaining the Version Vector

Now let us see how to propagate recently written versions and maintain the per-replica version vector. Suppose that when a replica S sends updated versions to a replica R, S sends all updated versions of all data items that it hasn't previously sent to R. In that case, at the end of the update transfer from S to R, if R has received an updated version with version ID $[S, 10]$ from S, then R knows it has received all updated versions from S with version ID $[S, c]$ for $c \leq 10$.

S needs to send to R not only the updated versions from transactions that S executed since the last time it synchronized with R, but also updated versions that S received from other replicas, such as R'. R may not have received those updated versions and indeed may never have the opportunity to synchronize with R'. For example, S may be a server that is always on the network, and R and R' are portable machines on different continents that are rarely if ever connected to the network at the same time.

This logic about S's version IDs sent by S to R applies to R' too. That is, if S sends an updated version to R with version ID [R', 5], then at the end of the transfer from S to R, R must also have received all of R''s updated versions with version IDs less than 5. This observation holds even if S received R''s updated versions indirectly via other replicas, because every replica along the path from R' to S sent all the updated versions it received earlier from other replicas. That is, R' sent all of its updated versions with version IDs less than or equal to [R', 5] to replica R'', which sent them to R''', and so on, until they reached S, which in turn sent them to R. We can summarize this argument as the following invariant.

> **Version ID invariant**: *If replica R received an updated version with version ID [R_i, c] and there are no transfers to R in progress, then R received all updated versions generated by R_i with version ID [R_i, c'] for all c' ≤ c.*

The version ID invariant implies that R can use a single version ID to summarize which updates it has received from each replica. For example, R can use version ID [R', 5] to summarize the fact that R has received all updated versions generated by replica R' with version IDs [R', 1] through [R', 5]. By doing this for all replicas, R is maintaining a version vector.

Therefore, after R has processed all the updates it received from S, R should merge S's version vector with its own, thereby reflecting the fact that R's state now includes all updates that are known to S. This involves using the maximum count for each entry in the two version vectors. For example, if the R_i entry in the version vectors for S and R are [R_i, c] and [R_i, c'], respectively, then R should replace c' by the maximum of c and c'.

S need not send updated versions that it knows were overwritten. For example, if S executed two or more transactions that updated data item x, S needs to send to R only its last updated version of x. There is no point in sending the earlier updated versions to R because they will be overwritten by later updated versions to x sent by S to R.

Given this observation, we have to modify our earlier explanation of the meaning of version vectors. We said that an entry [R_i, c] in the version vector for replica R means that R has received all updates generated by R_i with version IDs [R_i, 1], [R_i, 2], ..., [R_i, c]. However, this isn't true if overwritten versions are not propagated. Hence, we have to weaken the statement to say that entry [R_i, c] in R's version vector is the largest version ID of any update that was generated by R_i and received by R. Moreover, R's state is the same as if it had received all the versions in the sequence [R_i, 1], ..., [R_i, c].

When two replicas decide to exchange updates, each one needs to figure out which updates to send to the other replica. Version ID's are helpful for this purpose. When replica R wants to receive recent updates from replica S, R sends its current version vector to S. Now S runs a query against its local database that retrieves every version whose version ID is greater than the corresponding version ID in R's version vector and sends these updates to R. For example, if R's version vector has an entry [R_1, 10], then S should send all data items whose version ID is [R_1, b] where b > 10.

Version Vector Update Rules

As a prelude to presenting update rules based on version vectors, we need a few more definitions. To simplify things a bit, let us assume that there are n replicas named R_1 through R_n. This enables us to represent a version vector by a sequence of n integers, where entry i in the vector is the count for replica R_i. For example, a version vector $[[R_1, 7], [R_2, 3], [R_3, 10], [R_4, 7]]$ would be represented by $[7, 3, 10, 7]$.

We say that a version vector V **dominates** another version vector V' if the elements of V and V' cover the same set of replica ID's and for every index position i, $V[i] \geq V'[i]$. For example, if there are three replicas, then version vector $[3, 4, 4]$ dominates $[2, 4, 3]$ and $[3, 4, 3]$. If $V \neq V'$ and neither dominates the other, then we say V and V' are **incomparable**. For example, version vector $[3, 4, 4]$ is incomparable to $[2, 4, 5]$ and $[2, 4]$.

Now that we have the complete picture, let's look at the rules for applying updates, which we call the **version vector-based update rules**. First, let us recall the rule for running a transaction:

VV1. Suppose a transaction T executes at replica R, which has update counter value c, and T updates data item x. Then T replaces x's version ID by $[R, c]$, it sets the R position in x's version vector to c, and it increments R's update counter by 1.

Suppose a version of x moves from replica S to replica R. More precisely, suppose R receives an updated version x_s of some data item x from replica S, where

- The updated version x_s has version ID $[R_i, c]$ and version vector $V_S = [s_1, \ldots, s_n]$, and
- R's stored version x_r of x has version ID $[R_k, d]$ and version vector $V_R = [r_1, \ldots, r_n]$.

Note that R_i and R_k may be different from both R and S. R processes the update from S as follows:

VV2. If V_R dominates V_S, then R discards the updated version x_s sent by S. In effect, this says that x_r should overwrite x_s, but since x_r arrived at R before x_s, R simply discards x_s.

VV3. If V_S dominates V_R, then R replaces its version x_r by x_s, along with version ID $[R_i, c]$ and version vector $[s_1, \ldots, s_n]$.

VV4. If V_R and V_S are incomparable, then there's a conflict and conflict resolution is needed. If R resolves the conflict, then the version that R generates by its conflict resolution procedure has a version vector that's the merge of the version vectors of the conflicting versions (i.e., taking the maximum count for each entry in the two version vectors), except for the position corresponding to R, which has the version ID of the new version generated by R.

As explained in the previous section, after R has processed all the updates it received from S, R should merge S's version vector with its own.

The goal of the rules is to ensure that if a version x_2 overwrites another version x_1, then $x_1 \rightarrow x_2$. Clearly, if a transaction executes according to VV1 or VV4 and overwrites x_1 by x_2, then $x_1 \rightarrow x_2$. The more interesting cases are VV2 and VV3.

In VV2 and VV3, the decisions are governed by version vector dominance. Consider VV2. If V_R dominates V_S, then every vector position of V_R is greater than or equal to the corresponding position of V_S. The only way to create a version vector is to execute a transaction using VV1 or VV4. Each transaction modifies a version vector by increasing one of the elements in the vector. Therefore, the only way that V_R can come into existence is that starting with V_S, there must be a sequence of transactions that generates successive version vectors where each one updates the version of x generated by the previous one and where the last transaction in the sequence generates V_R. By definition of replication conflict, there are no replication conflicts in this sequence. Therefore, if V_R dominates V_S, then $x_s \rightarrow x_r$, so x_r should be retained and x_s should be discarded. This is exactly what rule VV2 does. A symmetric argument holds for VV3.

The remaining possibility is VV4, namely that V_R does not dominate V_S and V_S does not dominate V_R. In that case V_R and V_S are incomparable. Thus, there must be elements r_a, r_b in V_R and s_a, s_b in V_S such that $r_a > s_a$ and $s_b > r_b$. Since $r_a > s_a$, the transaction that produced version $[R_a, r_a]$ was in the sequence of transactions that produced V_R but not in the sequence that produced V_S, so x_r does not precede x_s. Similarly, since $s_b > r_b$, the transaction that produced version $[R_b, r_b]$ was in the sequence of transactions that produced V_S but was not in the sequence that produced V_R, so x_s does not precede x_r. Thus the versions tagged by V_R and V_S exhibit a replication conflict.

Simplified Version Vector Update Rules

Instead of comparing version vectors, it is actually enough to compare version IDs of data items to version vectors of replicas, rather than comparing version vectors for dominance. That is, the rules VV2 and VV3 are modified to the following:

VI2. If $r_i \geq c$, then R discards S's updated version.

VI3. If $s_k \geq d$, then R replaces its version of x by the one sent by S, along with version ID $[R_i, c]$ and version vector $[s_1, \ldots, s_n]$.

As in the previous section, the goal of these rules is to ensure that if a version x_2 overwrites another version x_1 then $x_1 \rightarrow x_2$. Since VV1 and VV4 are unchanged, they ensure this goal as before.

The simplest correctness argument we know of that covers rules VI2 and VI3 involves some fairly subtle reasoning. We provide a proof here. However, you can skip the rest of this section without loss of continuity in understanding the rest of the chapter.

We say that a version ID $v = [R_i, c]$ **is in** a version vector V if the R_i position of V is greater than or equal to c. Notice that the test in VI2 of $r_i \geq c$ is testing whether version ID $[R_i, c]$ is in version vector $[r_1, \ldots, r_n]$. Similarly, the test in VI3 of $s_k \geq d$ is testing whether version ID $[R_k, d]$ is in version vector $[s_1, \ldots, s_n]$.

Suppose we are given two versions x_1 and x_2 of x that have version IDs v_1 and v_2 and version vectors V_1 and V_2, respectively. We want to show that if VI2 or VI3 overwrites x_1 with x_2, then $x_1 \rightarrow x_2$. By the observation of the previous paragraph, this is equivalent to showing that if v_1 is in V_2, then $x_1 \rightarrow x_2$.

First, we restate the definition of $\rightarrow$ recursively as follows: Given versions x_1 and x_2 of x, $x_1 \rightarrow x_2$ if and only if either there exists a transaction T that overwrote version x_1 with x_2 or there exists a transaction T and a version x_3 such that $x_1 \rightarrow x_3$ and T overwrote x_3 with x_2.

We say that a version x_i is **made by** the replica that executed the transaction that created x_i. We say that x_i is **made from** the version x_j that was held by the replica when it executed the transaction that created x_i. When a replica R receives a version x_i from replica S and R replaces its version of x by x_i, we say that x_i **moved** from S to R.

Now we define a total ordering over the versions. For any version held by a replica R, define its **age** to be the number of make and move steps that it took to arrive at this state. For conflict-resolving makes (according to VV4), let its age be one greater than the maximum age over all conflicting versions it is resolving. Our proof is by induction on version age, but we will have to strengthen the statement to be proved to make the induction step work:

For every version x_2 with version ID v_2, version vector V_2, and age c held by replica R, and for every version $x_1 \neq x_2$ with version ID v_1:

1. If v_1 is in V_2 then $x_1 \rightarrow x_2$.
2. If x_1 was made by replica R, x_1 has age c_1, and $c_1 < c$, then $x_1 \rightarrow x_2$. In other words, every version made by a given replica precedes every version that is later held by that replica.

Basis step: If age $= 1$, x_2 must have been created from x_1 by a make step, that is, VV1 or VV4. Clearly, these steps ensure $x_1 \rightarrow x_2$, so both (1) and (2) hold.

Induction step: Suppose x_2 is held by replica R_k and has age c_k and $v_2 = [R_n, c_n]$. Version x_2 was made from some version x_3, possibly resolving a set of conflicting versions, Con. As in the basis step, $x_3 \rightarrow x_2$ and for all versions x_c in Con, $x_c \rightarrow x_2$. Observe that V_2 is the merge of the version vector of x_3 and those of Con, plus with c_n in n^{th} position.

To prove (1), there are two cases:

a. x_1 was not made by R_n. The transaction that made v_2 only updated position n of its version vector. Therefore, if v_1 is in V_2, it must be that v_1 is in the version vector of x_3 or of one of the versions x_c of Con. Since all of these versions are younger than x_2, by part (1) of the induction hypothesis, $x_1 \rightarrow x_3$ or $x_1 \rightarrow x_c$. Since $x_3 \rightarrow x_2$ and for all versions x_c in Con, $x_c \rightarrow x_2$, by transitivity $x_1 \rightarrow x_2$.

b. x_1 itself was made by R_n with an age smaller than c_n. Thus, by induction hypothesis part (2), $x_1 \rightarrow x_3$, and by transitivity $x_1 \rightarrow x_2$.

To prove (2), observe that there are two cases:

c. x_2 was made by R_k (in other words, $R_k = R_n$). In that case, x_3 was held by R_n before it made x_2, and so by induction hypothesis part (2), $x_1 \rightarrow x_3$, and we are done by transitivity.

d. x_2 moved to R_k, overwriting what R_k was holding, say x_4 with version ID v_4. In this case, according to VV_1 and VI_2, v_4 is in V_2. Before x_2 moved, it was younger than it currently is, so we apply part (1) of the induction hypothesis to conclude that $x_4 \rightarrow x_2$. But by induction hypothesis part (2), $x_1 \rightarrow x_4$, and so we are done by transitivity.

Example Revisited

Using these rules, let's revisit the example of Figure 9.14 using version vectors instead of timestamps. The result is shown in Figure 9.15. We rename the primary to be replica R_3, so we can use the more compact version vector

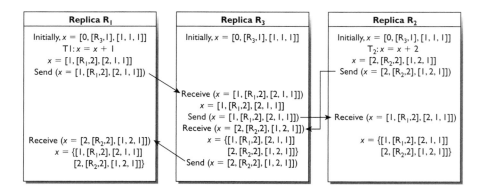

FIGURE 9.15

Using Version Vectors to Reconcile Updates. Initially, x has value 0, produced by version $[R_3, 1]$ in the state characterized by version vector $[1, 1, 1]$. Since T_1 and T_2 produce incomparable version IDs and version vectors, their updated versions conflict and are retained at all replicas.

notation. The version of x is now a triple, comprised of a value, a version ID, and a version vector. Initially, x is 0 at the three replicas. It was last written by a transaction running at replica R_3 that generated version ID $[R_3, 1]$ after which its state is summarized by the version vector $[1, 1, 1]$. The sequence of actions is exactly as before. The interesting cases are when each site receives the second updated version. In each case, the recipient recognizes that the second updated version's version ID and version vector are incomparable to the ones it has stored, so it detects a replication conflict and ends in a state containing both conflicting updates. For example, consider replica R_2 when it receives R_1's updated version $[1, [R_1, 2], [2, 1, 1]]$ from R_3. R_2's local version of x is $[2, [R_2, 2], [1, 2, 1]]$. These versions of x satisfy VV4, which means there is a replication conflict: R_2's local version $[R_2, 2]$ was written without having seen version $[R_1, 2]$, and the version $[R_1, 2]$ sent by R_1 was written without having seen version $[R_2, 2]$.

In this example, it seems like the use of version vectors has only helped a little bit in handling concurrent updates of different replicas of the same data item. It correctly diagnosed the replication conflict but did not fully resolve it. However, there are other cases where the use of version vectors fully resolves the situation.

For example, consider Figure 9.16, which is a variation of the scenario in Figure 9.15 where R_1 sends its update by T_1 directly to R_2 in addition to sending it to R_3. If R_1's updated version arrives at R_2 before R_2 executes T_2, then T_2 will overwrite R_1's updated version of x. R_3 will recognize this fact when it receives R_2's updated version of x from R_2 and will replace R_1's version of x by R_2's updated version. On the other hand, if R_1's updated version arrives at R_2 *after* R_2 executes T_2, then T_2 will not overwrite R_1's updated version of x. R_2 will still send the updated version to R_3, but in this case R_3 will recognize it as a conflict. Notice that timestamps alone cannot make this distinction. For example, if T_2 is assigned a larger timestamp than T_1, then it will always overwrite T_1's updated version at all replicas, whether or not T_2 saw T_1's updated version of x at the time it executed.

Although version vectors do identify replication conflicts, they do not ensure one-copy serializability because they detect conflicts only on a single data item, not across two or more data items. For example, suppose the database has data items x and y that are stored at replicas R_1 and R_2. Initially, x has the version $[3, [R_1, 1], [1, 2]]$ and y has the version $[5, [R_2, 2], [1, 2]]$ at both replicas. Suppose transaction T_1 at R_1 adds x and y and stores the result, 8, into x with version ID $[R_1, 2]$. Suppose transaction T_2 does the same thing, but stores the result, 8, into y with version ID $[R_2, 3]$. Each of them propagates their updated version to the other replica. According to the version ID-based update rules, each replica will apply the updated version that it receives from the other replica. So the final state at both replicas will have $x = [8, [R_1, 2], [2, 2]]$ and $y = [8, [R_2, 2], [1, 3]]$. However, if the transactions ran on a one-copy database, either the resulting value of x would be 11 or the resulting value of y would be 13. So the result is not one-copy serializable.

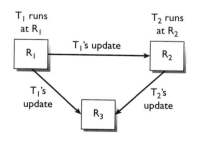

FIGURE 9.16

Diagnosing a Replication Conflict. Using version vectors, when R_3 receives T_2's update, it can tell whether that update ran before or after R_2 received T_1's update.

Consistency, Availability, and Partition-Tolerance Revisited

At the end of Section 9.4 we introduced the tradeoff between data consistency, system availability, and partition-tolerance. We saw that the primary-copy approach with synchronous replication offers data consistency and partition-tolerance at the cost of system availability when a partition occurs. With asynchronous replication, it improves availability in some cases at the cost of data consistency.

The multimaster approach with asynchronous replication offers further improvement of availability and partition-tolerance but with decreased data consistency. If a replica R is up and running, then R can be read or written. R need not be part of a quorum of replicas. In fact, even if R is partitioned from the rest of the network, it is available. However, there is a cost in data consistency. First, since there is delay in propagating updates to replicas, the system is only eventually consistent, not instantaneously consistent. And second, since transactions can update other replicas concurrently with transactions that update R, there may be replication conflicts. Such conflicts represent a loss of data consistency.

As we saw, these conflicts can be detected in certain cases, at which point an application-specific conflict resolution procedure can try to return the data to a consistent state. Still, a conflict resolution procedure may not be able to make the data perfectly consistent, in the sense that it makes the execution one-copy serializable. For example, if replicas are used for flight reservations, and two replicas ran transactions that sold the last seat on a flight, then the best that the conflict resolution procedure can do is run a compensation for one of the ticket holders. This is not a result that would occur in a one-copy system.

Microsoft Sync Framework

As an example of a multimaster replication system that uses version vectors, we consider Microsoft Sync Framework, which was introduced in 2007. Like the approach described in this section, it generates a version ID for each update and maintains a version vector for each replica. Like most multimaster implementations, it uses a number of variations of the basic techniques outlined in this section. We highlight two of them here. First, in most cases it does not attach a version vector to each data item. Instead, it detects replication conflicts using the replica's version vector (not the data item's version vector) and modified version ID-based update rules. Second, it allows a transfer of updates from one replica to another to be interrupted and resumed at another time. This requires additional modifications to the maintenance and use of version vectors.

Like before, suppose that replica R receives from replica S an updated version of some data item x with version ID $[R_i, c]$ and that R's version of x has version ID $[R_k, d]$. At the time R receives the updated version, its current version vector is $[r_1, \ldots, r_n]$ and replica S's current version vector is $[s_1, \ldots, s_n]$. Then R decides how to process the update using the following **modified version ID-based update rules**:

MVI1. If $r_i \geq c$, then discard S's update.
MVI2. If $s_k \geq d$, then replace the value of x at R by the one sent by S, along with version ID $[R_i, c]$.
MVI3. Otherwise, there is a conflict and conflict resolution is needed.

In the case of MVI3, both values of x are retained. The value sent by S is stored with its version ID and with S's version vector $[s_1, \ldots, s_n]$. Thus, some data items have per-data-item version vectors. But these are presumably a small fraction of the data items at the replica. In an application where they are a large fraction of the data items, there is a large number of unresolved replication conflicts, which casts doubt on the value of using multimaster replication in this application.

If a later updated version arrives at R for x, then when deciding whether to overwrite the stored version, R uses the version vector associated with x rather than R's version vector. Similarly, if R forwards this updated version of x to another replica R′, R forwards it with the version vector associated with x and R′ uses that version vector when applying the modified version ID-based update rules, not R's version vector.

The surprising fact about the modified version ID-based update rules is that they have the same effect as the original version ID-based rules.

The second feature of the Microsoft Sync Framework that we discuss is that it allows the transfer of updated versions from replica S to R to be interrupted. Ordinarily, that would cause a problem for R, since it may have received an updated version of some data item x but not some updates on which the version depended. It avoids this problem through a technique similar to conflict detection.

To be more precise, if R receives an updated version with version ID $[R_i, c]$ for data item x and the modified version vector-based update rule says to apply the updated version (either overwriting x or adding a conflicting version of x), then R's state for x is more up to date for x than for other data items. If the transfer is interrupted, R needs to know that S's version vector characterizes the state of updates from S that R has applied. These are called exceptions. Eventually, possibly after several lengthy interruptions, S completes its transfer of updates to R. Now R knows that it is not missing any information earlier than S's version vector. Therefore, any exceptions that it accumulated due to updates it received from R and that are not replication conflicts can be dropped. At that point, S's version vector can be merged with R's version vector, as in the normal case.

Suppose there is a total order over data items; for example, by name or storage address. Then to minimize the number of the exceptions at R, S can send the updated versions to R in data item order. If the transfer is interrupted after R has received items in (say) the range 1 to m, it can summarize its exceptions by the range exception $[1, m]$ and S's version vector. Clearly, this is a much denser representation than enumerating exceptions for each updated data item that was transferred.

Given these techniques, a replica has several sources of knowledge about past updates: a per-replica version vector and per-data-item version vectors for replication conflicts and for exceptions. When a replica R requests recent changes from another replica S, R sends all this knowledge of its current state to S, so that S can avoid sending updates that R already knows about.

There are several other special techniques used in this system; for example, to garbage collect tombstones, to enable replicas to join and leave a system, and to allow different conflict handlers at different replicas. See the bibliographic notes for articles that describe these and other features.

9.6 OTHER REPLICATION TECHNIQUES

Replication algorithms have been an active area of database research for over three decades. Many algorithms have been published beyond those described here, which are the ones that are primarily used in today's database systems. Some interesting other approaches include:

- Nontransactional replication, based on timestamped updates. That is, each original update executes as an atomic action outside the context of any transaction. These algorithms often are used for distributed system services, such as a directory service, where multimaster replication is needed but not transactions.

- Quorum consensus applied to every transaction. Each transaction reads a quorum of copies of each data item it accesses, and uses the most up-to-date value among those copies as input. This approach avoids elections and other reconfiguration algorithms, at the cost of more work for each transaction. It is also one of the first correct replication algorithms published.

- Read-one-write-all-available, where instead of using a primary copy, each transaction writes to all available copies of every data item it updates. One well-known algorithm, called Virtual Partitions, uses this approach along with quorum consensus, to ensure a data item is updatable only if the set of connected sites have a quorum of copies of that item.

See the Bibliographic Notes for further reading.

9.7 DATA SHARING SYSTEMS

A **data sharing system** is one where two data manager processes can both access the same database. This is a case where the server is replicated but not the resource. Data sharing arises in systems where two or more machines have access to the same stable storage devices. In this case, the data managers executing on independent machines have to synchronize their access to shared pages. This usage scenario was made popular in the 1980s in clustered systems, such as VMScluster. Currently, it arises when multiple machines can access the same storage using a storage area network, such as in Oracle Real Application Clusters and IBM DB2 Data Sharing.

Another rather different scenario where data sharing arises is mid-tier caching, where two or more mid-tier machines cache data that is stored on the same backend data manager. Often, the mid-tier machines cache only static data, in which case there are no special concurrency control or recovery problems. However, if the mid-tier machines can update data, then concurrency control problems occur that are similar to those of shared stable storage.

In a data sharing system, it is no longer satisfactory to have the lock manager be local to the data manager, because a lock that is set by one data manager would not be visible to another server that accesses the same database. This changes the locking architecture quite a bit and has some effect on the recovery algorithm.

Locking

In a data sharing system, when a data manager process obtains a lock on a data item it must be sure that no other data manager has a conflicting lock. This usually entails the use of a global lock manager that lives outside of the data manager processes that access it. Thus, invocations of lock and unlock operations are usually more expensive than with an in-process lock manager, due to the expense of a context switch and a message if the lock manager is remote. This expense affects the design of concurrency control algorithms for data sharing. Some systems try to reduce the expense with special hardware or operating system support. Others try to reduce the frequency of calls to the global lock manager.

One way to reduce the number of calls to the global lock manager is to combine it with a local (i.e., in-process) lock manager. When a transaction T accesses a data item x, its data manager S sets a lock at the global lock manager and, if it succeeds, then T sets a lock in the local lock manager. When T commits or aborts, it releases its lock on x at the local lock manager. However, S retains its lock on x at the global lock manager. This allows later transactions running in S to lock x using only the local lock manager.

If a transaction T′ running in another data manager accesses x, its data manager S′ must lock x at the global lock manager. However, it will be unable to do so if S holds a conflicting lock on x. There needs to be a protocol that ensures S will release its lock on x. One way to do this is via a **call-back** from the global lock manager to S. That is, if the global lock manager receives a request by S′ to lock x at a time when S holds a conflicting lock, the global lock manager sends a call-back message to S asking it to release the lock. If there is no active transaction in S that is using x (i.e., that has a local lock on x), then S releases the lock on x at the global lock manager. If there is such a transaction, then S waits until that transaction has completed before releasing its lock on x. If S has other transactions waiting in its local lock manager for the lock on x, then it's a policy question as to whether S releases the lock right away at the global lock manager or waits until there are no active transactions in S that are waiting for the lock.

Caching

In a data sharing system two data manager processes can have a cached copy of the same data item. So they not only need to synchronize access using locks, but they also need to ensure they see each other's cached

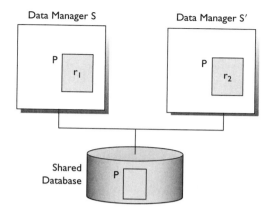

FIGURE 9.17

A Data Sharing System. Page P is stored on disk. Processes S and S' cache P in their private main memory.

updates. For example, in Figure 9.17 data managers S and S' both have a cached copy of page P whose persistent copy resides in a shared database. S sets a lock on P at the global lock manager, executes a transaction T_1 that updates record r_1 on page P, and then releases its lock on P. Now S' sets a lock on P at the global lock manager so that it can run a transaction T_2 that updates a different record r_2 on page P. To ensure that T_1's update to r_1 does not get lost, it's essential that T_2 reads the copy of P that was updated by T_1. This will work fine if S writes P to the shared database on behalf of T_1 before T_1 releases its lock on P.

Since a transaction needs to be durable, it would seem to be obvious that S must write P to the database before T_1 commits. However, as we saw in Section 7.8, often this is not done. Instead, T_1's update to r_1 might be written only to a log, without writing P itself to the database. In this case, S does not need to write P on behalf of each transaction, because later transactions that execute in S will access the cached copy of P and therefore are not in danger of losing earlier transactions' updates. However, before S releases its lock on P at the global lock manager, it needs to ensure that, if another data manager process locks P at the global lock manager, it will access the latest copy of P in the shared database. For example, before releasing its lock on P, S can write P to the shared database. An alternative is for S to set a flag in the global lock for P that indicates it has the latest version of P in cache. When another data manager sets a lock on P, it sees that it should get the latest copy of P from S, not from stable storage.

Continuing the example, let's suppose S writes P to the stable database and releases its global lock on P. Data manager S' gets the global lock on P, reads P from the shared database, runs one or more transactions that update P, and eventually writes P back to the shared database and releases its global lock on P. Now, suppose S has another transaction that wants to access page P. So S sets a global lock on P. However, notice that S might still have a copy of P in its cache. If so, it will use its cached copy rather than reading it from the shared database. Obviously, this would be a mistake since S would ignore the updated value of P that was produced by transactions running in process S'. Therefore, even though S has a cached copy of P, it should invalidate this copy and reread P from the shared database.

What if no other process updated page P between the time S released its global lock on P and the time it set the lock again? In that case, it's safe for S to use its cached copy of P. A simple bookkeeping technique can enable S to recognize this case. Each page header includes a version number. (An LSN could be used for this purpose; see Chapter 7.) The first time that a data manager updates a page P, it increments the version number.

When it releases the global lock on P, it tells the lock manager the version number of the page. Although the lock has been released, the global lock manager retains the lock in its lock table with the associated version number. When a data manager sets a global lock on the page, the lock manager returns the page's version number to the data manager. If the data manager has a cached copy of the page, it can compare this version number to that of its cached copy. If they're the same, then it doesn't need to reread the page from the shared database.

Using this version number technique, locks will remain in the lock manager even if no transaction is holding them. How does a lock disappear from the global lock manager, to avoid having the lock manager become cluttered with locks that are no longer being used? This could be done implicitly by a timer. If a lock is not owned by any data manager and has been unused for a period of time, then the lock can be deallocated. The time period should be long enough that any page that was unused in a data manager's cache for that long is likely to have been deallocated. If the lock manager deallocates a lock too soon, then a data manager may request that lock while it still has the corresponding page in cache. In that case, since the lock manager is unable to tell the data manager the version number of the latest version of the page, the data manager needs to invalidate the cached copy of the page and reread it from stable storage.

Another approach to lock deallocation is to explicitly maintain a reference count of the number of data managers that have a cached copy of the page corresponding to each lock. When a data manager invalidates a cached page, it tells the lock manager to decrement the reference count. There is no urgency to have the lock manager do this decrement, so the data manager could save such calls in a batch and send them to the lock manager periodically.

Synchronizing shared pages between the caches of different data managers is one of the major costs in a data sharing system. One way to reduce this cost is to reduce the chance that a page needs to be accessed by two or more data managers. To take an extreme case, the database could be partitioned so that each data manager has exclusive access to one partition and each transaction only accesses data in one partition. Thus, each transaction uses the data manager that manages the partition needed by the transaction. Two data managers never need the same page, so cache synchronization doesn't arise.

Of course, if all databases and transaction loads could be partitioned in this way, then the mechanism for dynamic cache synchronization would have little value, since each data manager can be assigned a partition statically. However, even if a perfect partitioning isn't possible, an approximate partitioning may be within reach and serve the purpose. That is, each data manager is assigned a partition of the database, but it is allowed to access the rest of the database for the occasional transaction that needs data outside the partition. Similarly, transaction types are partitioned so that each transaction gets most, usually all, of its data from one data manager's partition. Thus, cache synchronization is required only occasionally, since it is relatively unlikely that transactions running in different partitions happen to access the same data page.

For example, consider the debit-credit transaction workload of TPC-B, discussed in Section 1.5. The database could be partitioned by bank branch, so that each branch balance is accessed by at most one data manager. By the nature of the application, tellers are partitioned by bank branch and each account has a home branch. So account records could be organized so that each page has account records with the same home branch. Each request takes an account ID, branch ID, and teller ID as input parameters. The branch ID parameter is used to send the request to that branch's data manager. So the branch balance and teller balance for that branch are guaranteed to be in that data manager's cache. Usually this branch ID for the request is the home branch of the account ID, since people do most of their banking at their home branch. In this case, the account information is very unlikely to be in the cache of any other data manager. Occasionally, the account ID is not for the home branch. In this case, the data manager for the branch is accessing a page of accounts all of which are for another branch. There is a nonnegligible probability that this page is in the cache of the data manager of those accounts' home branch. But it's still a relatively low probability. Therefore, although cache synchronization for such cases does happen, it is relatively rare.

Logging

When logging is used for database recovery, there is one log for each database. The log describes the sequence of updates that was applied to the database. The recovery algorithm uses this sequence to reconstruct the correct database state after a failure, as discussed in Chapter 7.

In a data sharing system, multiple data managers are updating the database and therefore are writing records to the end of the same log. One way to implement this log is to have data managers send "append-log-record" operations to a shared log server process. The append-log-record operation appends the given record to the log and returns the LSN (i.e., log address) of the log record being appended. The append operation has a parameter indicating whether the append must be forced to stable storage before returning to the caller. Since the log is often a bottleneck that limits transaction throughput, it's important that the log server be able to process append operations at a high rate. Therefore, it may be worthwhile for each data manager to send a sequence of append operations in each call to the log server, to amortize the cost of calling the log server across multiple operations.

Another way to implement the log is to allow data mangers to write log pages directly into a shared log file (rather than log records to a shared log server). This is possible because a data sharing system has shared persistent storage, some of which can be used for a shared log file that is directly accessible to all data managers. To ensure that the data managers don't overwrite each others' data at the end of the log, a log space server can be used to allocate log space to each data manager. The log space server supports the "allocate" operation, which returns a range of physical log pages and a range of LSNs that are reserved for the caller. This range of pages may be written only by the data manager to which they were allocated. So the data manager can write into those log pages directly. It can use a local buffer to collect updates to the log and periodically write that buffer to the log pages that are allocated for it. To simplify the following discussion, we assume that the log space server allocates one log page in response to each call to the allocate operation.

In the log server approach, a data manager needs to receive the LSN from the log server to complete each update. By contrast, in this direct writing approach, the data manager has a private pool of LSNs it can use, so it can process updates locally. This helps reduce the amount of communications required for interacting with the log and therefore speeds up the processing of writes.

In both approaches, some care is needed to enforce the write-ahead log protocol. In the log server approach, each data manager needs to be told periodically the LSN of the last log record that was written to disk. This can be one of the return values of every append operation. In the direct writing approach, a data manager uses the same technique as in a system that does not use data sharing. That is, before it flushes a data page, it ensures that the log page containing the last update record to that data page has already been flushed.

To commit a transaction, a commit record is written and the tail of the log is forced to stable storage, possibly after a short delay for group commit. In the direct writing approach, each log page is written by only one data manager. Hence, there may be more partially filled log pages than with the log server approach, where log records from different data managers can be written to the same log page.

The first step of a recovery procedure is to find the end of the log. This is a bit more complicated for the direct writing approach than for the log server approach. Using the direct writing approach, the order in which data managers write their log pages may be different than the order in which those pages were allocated. Therefore, there may be holes in the sequence at the end of the stable log. For example, if pages *n-1* and *n* were the last two log pages that were allocated (to different data managers), it is possible that page *n* was written before the failure but page *n-1* was not. This does not add any cost to the algorithm for finding the end of the log, but it does add some algorithmic complexity.

The final issue relates to transactions that execute in different data managers and update the same data item. Some synchronization is needed to ensure that log records for conflicting updates are written to the log in the same order that the updates themselves executed. With the log server approach, this is automatic, since a data manager does not release a page for use by other data managers until after it has sent its last update record for that page to the log manager.

By contrast, in the direct writing approach it is possible that the update records can appear out of order. For example, suppose a data manager D writes into page P and appends an update record to its log page, say page n. It flushes that log page and then flushes P and releases its lock on P, thereby making P available to other data managers. The next data manager D′ that updates P might be using a log page that precedes n and hence has smaller LSNs than the LSN written by D. If D′ wrote a smaller LSN on P than the one written by D, that would suggest that the update from D′ had been applied to P but the one from D had not, which is incorrect. Thus, the recovery algorithm could no longer use LSNs to determine which updates had or had not been applied to a page before the last failure.

A simple solution is that when D′ updates P, if it sees that P's LSN is larger than the largest LSN currently allocated to D′, then it flushes the remainder of its allocated log and gets new log pages from the log space server. This incurs an extra log flush and increases the likelihood of partially-filled log pages. However, if the database is partially partitioned as described at the end of the previous subsection on *Caching*, then this type of synchronization will be relatively rare.

9.8 SUMMARY

The main goal of replication is to improve availability, since a service is available even if some of its replicas are not. Replication can also improve response time, since the capacity of a set of replicated servers can be greater than the capacity of a single server.

The most widely-used approach to replication is to replicate the resource (i.e., the database) in addition to the server that manages it. This requires synchronizing updates with queries and each other when these operations execute on different replicas, so that the effects are indistinguishable from a nonreplicated system. The synchronization mechanism must allow for replicas or communications between replicas to be down for long periods. Communication failures are especially troublesome, since noncommunicating replicas may process conflicting updates that they are unable to synchronize until after they reconnect.

One popular approach to replication is to designate one replica as the primary copy and to allow update transactions to originate only at that replica. Updates on the primary are distributed and applied to other replicas, called secondaries, in the order in which they executed at the primary. Since all replicas process the same updates in the same order, the replicas converge toward the same state as the primary.

The stream of updates sent from the primary can be quite large, so it is worth minimizing its size by only including data items that are modified and by filtering out aborted transactions. The stream can be generated by processing the resource manager's log or by using triggers to generate the update stream directly from updates on the primary copy.

An alternative to propagating updates is to send the requests to run the original transactions to all secondaries and ensure that the transactions execute in the same order at all secondaries and the primary, either by physically running them in that order, which is slow, or synchronizing their execution between primary and secondaries, which can be tricky.

In any case, when a secondary fails and subsequently recovers, it must catch up processing the updates produced by the primary while it was down. If the primary fails, the remaining secondaries must elect a new primary and ensure it has the most up-to-date view of the updates that executed before the primary failed.

When a primary or secondary fails, the remaining replicas must check that they have a majority or quorum of copies, to ensure that they are the only group of communicating replicas. For if there were two partitions of replicas that could communicate within the partition but not between partitions, then the two partitions could process conflicting updates that would be hard to reconcile after the groups were reunited.

Sometimes partitioning is a planned and frequent event, as with laptop computers that contain replicas but are only periodically connected to the network. This requires that every partition be allowed to process updates, allowing for multiple masters, not just one primary. Some variation of Thomas' write rule often is used for these situations: each data item is tagged by the timestamp of the latest update to it. An update is applied only if its timestamp is larger than the data item's tag in the database. That way, updates can arrive in different orders, sometimes with long delays, yet the replicas will all eventually have the same value, namely the one produced by using the update with the largest timestamp.

The problem with this approach is that an update can be lost if it's overwritten by another update with larger timestamp that didn't see the output of the earlier update. One way to avoid this problem is to use version vectors in place of timestamps. Each version vector tells which updates were received by the replica before producing the current version of the data item. This enables more accurate conflict detection at the cost of more information attached to each data item. An optimization used in Microsoft Sync Framework avoids this per-data-item version vector in most cases, but still requires version vectors for data items involved in a conflict or received out of order.

The CAP conjecture says that a system can offer at most two of the following three properties: data consistency, system availability, and tolerance to network partitions. The primary-copy approach with synchronous replication ensures data consistency and partition-tolerance. It gives up on the availability of replicas that are outside the quorum. Asynchronous replication gives up on instantaneous consistency, ensuring eventual consistency instead, which improves availability further in some cases. Multimaster replication offers availability and partition-tolerance at the cost of data consistency.

The primary copy and multimaster algorithms described here are the ones used most widely in practice. However, since replication has been much studied by database researchers, there are many other published algorithms beyond the ones in this chapter.

Another form of replication is data sharing, where data manager replicas share access to a common resource, such as a database. Since two data managers can access the same page of the database, some synchronization is needed between the data managers. This is usually done with a global lock manager that is accessible to all data managers. A data manager sets a global lock before operating on a page. If it updates a page, then it flushes the page to stable storage before releasing the lock. This ensures the next data manager that reads the page will see the latest version. Synchronization is also needed to enable all the data managers to write to the shared log. This can be done with a global log server. Data managers call the log server to append records to the log. Alternatively, a log space server can be used to allocate log pages to each data manager, which can then write to those log pages without further synchronization.

Transactional Middleware Products and Standards

10.1 INTRODUCTION

In this chapter, we'll survey some popular transactional middleware products and standards, including:

- Current products from Microsoft and Java vendors
- Popular persistence abstractions mechanisms that simplify database access
- Legacy TP monitors, including information on how each product can be reused in a modern system, such as a Service Oriented Architecture (SOA)-based application
- Widely-adopted TP standards

Trends in Transactional Middleware

Over the past 20 years, we have seen a continual repackaging of transactional middleware functionality, both the aggregation of components into transactional middleware packages and the decomposition of packages into independently configurable components. For example, transaction management is a basic capability in most database management systems. It is also offered in enterprise service buses and other products designed for use with an SOA-based application. Some features and functions of front-end programs, request controllers, and transaction servers have migrated from integrated TP monitors and application servers to separate products. Others are migrating into operating systems, such as distributed transaction management. The innovations of large web sites such as Amazon.com, Google, and eBay have also been influential, such as the use of custom transactional middleware components for replicated state management and simple scalable data management.

The goal of this chapter is to give you a feeling for the state of the art of transactional middleware products and some confidence that the technical issues discussed in this book do give you the necessary background to understand transactional middleware. A secondary goal is to help you think about which technology is most appropriate for your specific requirements.

It is not a goal of this chapter to provide sufficiently detailed feature comparisons to help you select the exact products that best suit your needs. Product features change with each succeeding product release, so we recommend that you evaluate the latest information from a product's vendor when making such a decision. It is also not a goal to explain each product in enough detail to enable you to use it. In particular, example programs are meant only to illustrate each product's approach, not to be used as a template for developing applications.

For the most part, when describing each product or technology, we use this book's terminology rather than that of the product or technology. If you know a given product well, it may seem strange to see it described using unfamiliar terms. However, for a reader learning about the product for the first time, we hope this approach makes it easier to gain a basic understanding of how the product is structured and what features it offers.

Transactional Middleware Programming Models

Today's transactional middleware products provide a configurable deployment container for application objects. The goal of the container is to reduce complexity by packaging together system capabilities such as transaction control, threading, and persistence, and enabling a developer to customize them using configuration properties. Deployment of a transactional object into a container requires a configuration step to set its properties. This is the approach described in Section 2.2, *Transaction Bracketing in Object-Oriented Programming*. Both the .NET Framework and Java-based products recommend using container-managed transactions for most applications.

Container-managed transactions are called the **implicit** programming model because an application developer creates TP programs that incorporate the business logic without describing transactional behavior. This simplifies programming by not requiring the developer to think about which parts of the code need to run as transactions. It also helps address the transaction composition problem by enabling programs to be composed in different combinations without being rewritten.

In this model, transactional behavior is defined in another step, perhaps by another person, using configuration properties. Configuration properties can be defined in a separate file associated with the program, as attributes embedded within a program and its interface, or as a combination of the two. Sometimes the separate configuration file is generated from the embedded attributes. Some technologies allow attributes in a configuration file to override embedded attributes. Others do not.

The implicit model is increasingly popular, but there are cases where developers want the flexibility to express transactional behavior in the business logic. To meet this need, both the Java-based and .NET-based transactional middleware systems also offer **explicit** programming control of transactions. In this model, developers use transaction management APIs to explicitly start and end transactions within their objects.

The explicit programming model adds flexibility, but usually at the cost of more difficulty in creating and maintaining complex systems. However, whether developers use explicit or implicit transaction control, the behavior of the underlying transactional system remains the same because the execution of the transaction control operations relies on the same transactional infrastructure.

Java EE and the .NET Framework

Currently, the two primary transactional middleware environments are Java Enterprise Edition-based application servers and Microsoft's .NET Framework. Both environments provide comprehensive capabilities for creating and deploying TP applications.

In keeping with the ongoing trend to repackage transactional middleware functionality, some TP environments use only parts of the Java Enterprise Edition (EE) and .NET Frameworks. Sometimes these parts are combined with legacy TP monitors, for example, to modernize an existing application or to enable new applications to interoperate with older ones.

Comparing the Java EE and .NET Framework environments, one obvious difference is platform coverage. For example, Microsoft's .NET Framework offers a comprehensive and full-featured programming model for developing and deploying TP applications, but it is available only on Windows operating systems. A second significant difference between products is their set of programming interfaces and communication paradigms. For example, .NET Framework APIs differ from Java EE APIs. Although the APIs share many common features, they each offer some unique ones. A third difference is standards conformance. Products typically conform to various TP standards, but not necessarily to the same ones.

We describe the details of the .NET Framework and Java EE in Sections 10.3 and 10.4, respectively. But first, we discuss technologies for developing front-end programs using web browsers, since they are largely common to both environments.

10.2 WEB BROWSER FRONT-END PROGRAMS

As described in Chapter 3, a web browser is a common front-end program for TP applications. Most TP applications support them directly or can be adapted to support them, so we'll cover them as a general topic applicable to any transactional middleware.

A web browser requires a web server to handle HTTP requests and replies. In the multitier architecture the web server may directly interact with the database or with one or more intermediate tiers created using transactional middleware components, as illustrated in Figure 10.1. In some cases the database system can function as a web server. Intermediate tiers typically introduce mechanisms for scalability and availability, such as partitioning, replication, caching, and request routing. HTTP load balancers can be used to scale up browser access to the web server itself. Typical web servers include Microsoft's Internet Information Server (IIS) and the Apache HTTP Server.

One popular type of web browser programming environment is AJAX (Asynchronous JavaScript and XML). AJAX enables browser-based forms and menus to be highly efficient and interactive. Compared to browsers using plain HTML or XML, AJAX introduces three major benefits for TP applications: using AJAX the browser needs to exchange only the changed information with the web server, instead of the entire page, thereby reducing communication expense and improving response time; AJAX allows asynchronous interaction with the web server, which does not block the user's interaction with forms and menus; and AJAX allows the browser to offload the web server by absorbing more of the application processing load.

A simple AJAX program typically involves the exchange of an XML document with a web server and mapping the data into and out of the fields in the menus and forms that users interact with. A more complex AJAX program might handle a REST-style interaction or a Web Service invocation. Java Script Object Notation (JSON) is another popular supported data format for AJAX.

Figure 10.2 illustrates a simplified browser-based form for a money transfer operation. The form obtains account numbers from the user along with the amount to be transferred. This data is sent to the server where

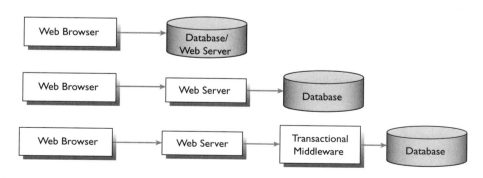

FIGURE 10.1

Web Browsers and Multitier TP Architecture. Web browsers work with TP applications in a variety of ways, including direct database access and multitier architectures using transactional middleware.

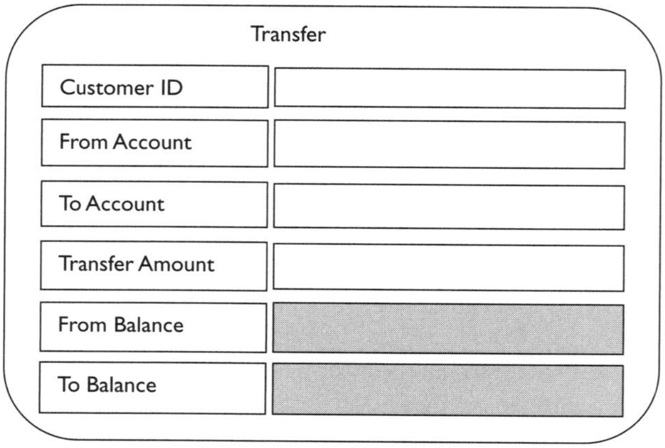

FIGURE 10.2

Simple Web Browser Form. The left boxes are labels. The user types the customer ID, transfer accounts, and transfer amount as input and receives the updated account balances in the shaded boxes as output.

the accounts are updated and the resulting balances for the two accounts are returned to the browser. While this exchange is taking place the user does not leave the form.

Figure 10.3 shows an AJAX program snippet that works for both Microsoft's Internet Explorer and other browsers. Internet Explorer implements AJAX using an ActiveX control (XMLHTTP), which is a mechanism specific to Windows, whereas other browsers typically use the standard XMLHttpRequest class. AJAX support also is included in the .NET Framework Active Server Pages (ASP) .NET library, including integration between AJAX and server-side ASP.NET.

In either case, the XMLHttpRequest class interacts with the web server asynchronously. It provides methods for exchanging data in various formats with the web server, including SOAP, XML, and JSON. Since AJAX is also a popular technology for developing Web Service clients, an AJAX library is available for generating and handling Web Services, called ws.js. Apache CXF provides an option for generating client-side JavaScript from a server-side Web Service definition. In ASP.NET, an AJAX script can be used to call either an ASP.NET Web Service (.asmx) or a Windows Communication Foundation (WCF)-based Web Service (.svc).

Typically, an HTTP GET operation is performed first to display an HTML form. The modified fields are sent to the server as XML elements in an HTTP POST operation, returned in the response message, and displayed on the form. In the example a POST operation sends the URL of the server along with the data from the form (in this case to and from account numbers and the transfer amount). The true parameter in the open method indicates that the HTTP operation is to be performed asynchronously. The onreadystatechange method is used to detect a state change in the data and trigger the data exchange with the server.

Like any other front-end program, the AJAX script creates a request to run a transaction. The subsequent control flow depends on whether the application uses one resource manager, many resource managers, or multiple tiers. Some applications simply connect the web tier to the database tier, so no independent transaction manager is needed. Others introduce tiers in between, some of which may need to control transactions. Still others may introduce a business process layer, which also controls transactions. Each of these back-end designs requires transactional middleware functionality to glue it together. This can be implemented using the .NET Framework and/or Java-EE-based transactional middleware products, which are the subjects of the next two sections.

```
<script type="text/javascript">
var fep = null;

if(navigator.appName == "Microsoft Internet Explorer") {
  fep = new ActiveXObject("Microsoft.XMLHTTP");
} else {
  fep = new XMLHttpRequest();
}

function transfer(Customer) {
 fep.open("POST", "document"+CustomerID, FromAccountNo, ToAccountNo,
        TransferAmt, true);
 fep.onreadystatechange=function() {
   if(fep.readyState == 4) {
      document.getElementById('account1Balance').innerHTML = fep.responseText1
      document.getElementById('account2Balance').innerHTML = fep.responseText2;
}
 }
fep.send(document);
}
</script>

<h1>Transfer</h1>

<form>
  <input type="text" />
  <div id="Customer">
  </div>
  <input type="int" />
  <div id="FromAccountNo">
  </div>
  <input type="int" />
  <div id="ToAccountNo">
  </div>
  <input type="int" />
  <div id="TransferAmt">
  </div>
  <input type="int" />
  <div id="FromAccountBalance">
  </div>
  <input type="int" />
  <div id="ToAccountBalance">
  </div>

</form>
```

FIGURE 10.3

Sample AJAX Program for Browser-Based Funds Transfer Operation. The AJAX program is divided between its related JavaScript and HTML elements. After it detects the user input, it obtains the changed information from the form, sends it asynchronously to the web server, and then displays the results.

10.3 .NET FRAMEWORK

Microsoft's .NET Framework provides a complete environment for developing and deploying multitier TP applications, including:

- Windows Presentation Foundation (WPF), ASP.NET, and Silverlight for developing PC-based or browser-based front-end programs.

- Windows Communication Foundation (WCF) and the Internet Information Server (IIS) for developing and deploying request controllers and transaction servers.
- Host Integration Server (HIS) and BizTalk Server adapters for integration with legacy environments. In some instances of the multitier architecture, the transaction server and/or resource manager can be hosted within a legacy environment. Interoperability tools such as these can include them into the .NET Framework environment.
- Windows Workflow Foundation (WF) and WS-BPEL support in BizTalk Server for creating and executing business processes, including those that combine multiple services.

Except for HIS and BizTalk Server, these components are bundled into Windows operating systems, starting with the Vista release. Most components are also available as downloads for prior versions of Windows.

Figure 10.4 shows that a front-end program can be written to run in a web browser and connect to a web server acting as a request controller. Or it can connect directly to the database acting as a web server (not shown) or transaction server.

A native PC program created using WPF can also connect to a web server. Or it can communicate directly with either a request controller or a transaction server. Similarly, a Web Services client can communicate directly with an application process or the database (not shown in the figure).

A request controller can be developed to run in a web server or as an application process using WCF. A transaction server can be implemented to run as an application process using WCF or as a stored procedure in a database system.

An application developed using the .NET Framework transactional middleware components can therefore implement a two-tier, three-tier, or multitier architecture to meet scalability, availability, and other TP application requirements.

Any server-side component or combination of components can use the transaction management capabilities of the platform through either the implicit or explicit programming models, either with or without using WCF.

A variety of deployment functions also are supported to meet TP application requirements for scalability, availability, and reliability. These include Windows operating system services, IIS application spaces, and Windows Server clusters.

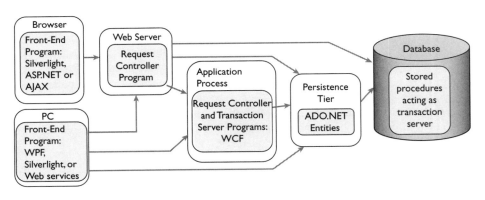

FIGURE 10.4

.NET Framework Multitier Transactional Middleware Architecture. The components of the .NET Framework multitier architecture provide multiple options for developing and deploying front-end programs, request controllers, and transaction servers.

A WCF program can use Web Services standards to interoperate with a legacy TP monitor or Java-based product, such as a Java-EE-compliant application server.

Developing Front-End Programs

In the .NET Framework the technologies used for front-end programs include:

- Windows Presentation Foundation for PC- or browser-based GUIs
- ASP.NET and Silverlight for web browser-based GUIs

The Windows Presentation Foundation (WPF) provides a comprehensive environment for developing front-end programs that implement menus and forms with high levels of interactivity, control, and graphical capability. WPF is intended to consolidate and replace prior generations of Windows-based graphical user interface (GUI) frameworks. WPF also can be used to create a GUI that runs in a web browser.

ASP.NET provides a complete development and deployment environment for web-based applications. A second option, Silverlight, provides a subset of WPF and .NET for cross-platform use; that is, for multiple operating systems and web browsers.

Windows Presentation Foundation

WPF uses **XAML (Extensible Application Markup Language**, pronounced "zammel"), which is an XML syntax for initializing structured values. In WPF, these structured values define components of a GUI. WPF commands are expressed using XAML, or alternatively using a CLR-based programming language such as C# or Visual Basic (VB).

Front-end programs developed using XAML commands can be deployed in a browser or in a native PC environment, which Microsoft calls a standalone application. A standalone application can be hosted in its own window or in a special window provided by WPF that offers basic navigation features. WPF can directly access data in a database or other resource. The .NET Framework provides several options for this, including ADO.NET, LINQ (Language-Integrated Query), and various mechanisms to execute a stored procedure in SQL Server (see Section 10.5 for further information). WPF also can be used in combination with WCF to connect to request controllers and transaction servers in a multitier architecture.

A complete front-end program requires a combination of a XAML markup file to define the display characteristics, a CLR-based program for the execution logic, and a configuration file to bind the display characteristics to the program. The configuration file generates an executable file for deployment in the target hosting environment (Visual Studio, standalone, or web browser).

Figure 10.5 illustrates a simple front-end program snippet defined using WPF. XAML commands exist within the XAML namespace. The XAML commands are contained within a top-level structure called a **page**,

```
<Page
  xmlns="http://schemas.microsoft.com/winfx/2006/xaml/presentation"
  xmlns:x="http://schemas.microsoft.com/winfx/2006/xaml"
  x:Class="Transfer.HomePage"
  WindowTitle="Transfer Funds"
  Title="Transfer - Home"
  WindowWidth="550" WindowHeight="380">
</Page>
```

FIGURE 10.5

Simple XAML Commands for WPF. These sample XAML commands define a form title and the form's position on the screen.

which is similar to an operating system window or a web page. The top-level page is called a **home page**, which in the example is the Transfer page. A single front-end program can have multiple pages corresponding to multiple display panels for additional menus and forms.

The display panel defined by the home page in the example is given the title "Transfer Funds." The Transfer class is set as the namespace for all subpages and programs associated with this display. The display width and height are specified in pixels. Additional controls typically are added to define fields and buttons and to map data into and out of the page. For example, input fields could be added in C# to capture the user's bank account numbers and transfer amount for an update operation.

The C# snippet in Figure 10.6 illustrates a program associated with the Transfer home page. Additional C# logic typically is added to handle GUI events, such as what steps to perform on a button click or pressing Enter. In WPF terminology this is called a **code behind** file to handle events defined in the XAML file. The code behind file is merged with the code generated by processing the XAML definitions. For example, the XAML steps would obtain from the user the account number and amount to transfer between bank accounts and the C# code would execute the actual transfer operation. A build step combines any XAML files and associated C# files into an executable that can be run from a command line or within Visual Studio for testing and debugging.

The .NET Framework environment supports the use of multiple approaches for front-end program construction. In particular, a front-end program developed independently of .NET can use standard HTTP, the REST/HTTP protocol, or another Web Service invocation mechanism compatible with WCF to invoke a .NET Framework request controller or transaction server.

ASP.NET and Silverlight

ASP.NET supports the development and deployment of web-based applications, including components to create a GUI for a web browser and a hosting environment in the IIS web server for processing requests. ASP.NET applications can be developed using any CLR-based language and can use any of the classes in the .NET Framework, including capabilities for security, transactions, and system administration. ASP.NET also supports Web Services development and deployment.

```
using System;
using System.Windows;
using System.Windows.Controls;
using System.Windows.Navigation;
namespace Transfer
{
    public partial class HomePage : Page
    {
        public HomePage()
        {
            InitializeComponent();
            void Button(object sender, FormInput e)
        }
    }
}
```

FIGURE 10.6

Sample C# Class Associated with a WPF Page. The C# code is merged with code generated from the corresponding XAML file, for example to implement a button object that submits form input data.

Silverlight is used similarly to WPF to develop front-end programs that can be used natively on Windows or with any web browser. Silverlight programs can be included within static HTML files and server-generated pages (e.g., using PHP, Python, or Ruby scripts). Like WPF, Silverlight programs include XAML files and code in the form of class files that are associated with the XAML files.

Silverlight supports a JavaScript/AJAX programming model and a cross-platform, cross-browser version of the .NET Framework. This allows developers of front-end programs to write Silverlight applications using any .NET language (including VB, C#, JavaScript, IronPython, and IronRuby) and deploy it on a range of operating systems and web browsers. Silverlight supports REST, Web Services, XML over HTTP, RDF Site Summary (RSS), and standard HTTP communication protocols for interaction with web servers and WCF services.

Developing Request Controllers and Transaction Servers

WCF provides a set of capabilities that can be used to connect a front-end program to a request controller or transaction server developed using the .NET Framework. WCF implements a service-oriented interaction model that can be configured for CLR objects created using Visual Basic .NET and C#. Many of the WCF libraries are also available to programs created using C++, J#, and JScript. WCF supports both implicit and explicit transaction programming models and works with all Microsoft SQL Server versions and ADO.NET compliant resource managers. WCF also includes .NET libraries that work with COM and COM+ components.

For communications WCF supports a variety of configurable messaging models and data formats, including native remote procedure call (RPC), Web Services, and asynchronous queuing (using Microsoft Message Queuing). WCF also supports custom-developed protocols and formats.

A WCF service requires an explicit **contract**, which is an interface to a .NET Framework object. The interface must be associated with an executable class file that contains the program logic. It must also be associated with a binding that specifies the data format, communication protocol, and additional characteristics of the communication session (such as reliability, security, or transaction propagation) for the operations in the interface.

A WCF interface describes a service that can be invoked remotely and defines any additional distributed computing characteristics for each method. For example, the interface shown in Figure 10.7 is called

```
[ServiceContract]
Interface ITransfer
{
    [OperationContract]
    void AccountBalance (decimal AccountNumber, decimal);

    [OperationContract]
    void WithdrawAccount (decimal AccountNumber, decimal Amount);

    [OperationContract]
    void DepositAccount (decimal AccountNumber, decimal Amount);

    [OperationContract]
    void Transfer(decimal FromAccountNumber, decimal ToAccountNumber,
                decimal Amount);
}
```

FIGURE 10.7

WCF Interface Definition. An interface that exposes a service remotely is a core feature of WCF. Multiple bindings can be configured for an interface, including Web Services and native.

ITransfer and includes four methods: AccountBalance, WithdrawAccount, DepositAccount, and Transfer. The interface is marked as a service using [ServiceContract], and each method in the service is marked as being remotely accessible using [OperationContract]. Not all methods have to be made available remotely, but when they are they must be tagged with the [OperationContract] attribute.

Transactions

Three main attributes affect the transaction behavior of a method:

- TransactionFlowOption is specified on the interface to the method and tells whether the method will accept a transaction context propagated from its caller.
- TransactionScopeRequired property of the OperationBehavior attribute is specified on an implementation of the method and tells whether the method must execute within a transaction.
- TransactionFlow is specified on the binding that the caller uses to invoke the method and tells whether the caller's transaction context can flow across the binding.

The [TransactionFlow] attribute on an interface has three possible values: Mandatory, Allowed, and NotAllowed. The Mandatory attribute shown in Figure 10.8 indicates that the WithdrawAccount operation must receive a transaction context when invoked by another method. Allowed means that the service accepts a transaction context if one is received with the message, but it does not require the message to contain one. NotAllowed is the default and means that the service ignores a propagated transaction context.

An annotated class implements a WCF interface definition. The class defines the execution logic for each of the methods listed in the service, such as methods that access a database, do computation, or invoke other services. The TransactionScopeRequired attribute on each method is set to true or false, indicating whether or not the operation must be executed within a transaction. For example, in Figure 10.9 the WithdrawAccount

```
[OperationContract]
        [TransactionFlow(TransactionFlowOption.Mandatory)]
        void WithdrawAccount(int AccountNumber,int Amount);
```

FIGURE 10.8

Using the TransactionFlow Attribute to Require Propagation. Adding attributes to the WCF interface controls transaction propagation.

```
class TransferService : Transfer
{
    [OperationBehavior(TransactionScopeRequired = true)]
    public void WithdrawAccount (int accountNumber, decimal amount)
}
{
    [OperationBehavior(TransactionScopeRequired = true)]
    public void DepositAccount (int accountNumber, decimal amount)
    ...
}
```

FIGURE 10.9

Defining the Object Class for the Interface. Each operation in a WCF interface has a method in a corresponding object class for its implementation.

and `DepositAccount` methods have a `TransactionScopeRequired` attribute of `true`, so they must always execute in the context of a transaction.

Suppose the binding between the caller and the service indicates that the caller's transaction context can flow across the binding (details are in the next section). The combination of values for `TransactionFlowOption` and `TransactionScopeRequired` lead to a variety of possible behaviors. For example:

- If the caller is executing a transaction, the `TransactionFlowOption` on the method is `Mandatory` or `Allowed`, and `TransactionScopeRequired` is `true`, then the method executes in the caller's transaction.
- If the caller is executing a transaction, the `TransactionFlowOption` is `NotAllowed`, and `TransactionScopeRequired` is `true`, then the method executes in a new transaction.
- If the caller is *not* executing a transaction and `TransactionScopeRequired` is `true`, then the method executes in a new transaction, no matter what value is specified for `TransactionFlowOption`.

Transaction termination depends on the successful completion of each method executed within the transaction. That is, a transactional object is considered a participant in the transaction and must provide a completion vote for the transaction to commit. If the `TransactionAutoComplete` attribute is `true` (which is the default), then the transaction is completed automatically if it exits without throwing an unhandled exception. Such an exception means the transactional object will vote to abort.

A one-way flow (i.e., a one-way asynchronous message exchange) is not allowed to propagate a transaction context, although a correlated request/reply message exchange using an asynchronous communication protocol is allowed to propagate a context.

So far nothing has indicated which wire format is used. The type of transaction context is specified in the WCF binding.

Bindings

Internally, WCF is based on the **chain of responsibility** architecture, in which a series of **handlers** (sometimes called **interceptors**) are inserted into the call chain between client and server, including a handler that propagates transaction context for a remote service. The chain of responsibility pattern can be implemented as an extension to the RPC mechanism. When the proxies and stubs are generated from the interface, the code for the handlers is inserted into the call chain to implement any additional characteristics associated with the interface defined using configuration metadata. Handlers are inserted into the call chain in a predetermined order, according to the type of functionality they provide. For example, a message serialization handler must execute before a handler that dispatches the serialized message onto the communications protocol.

The call chain handlers in WCF are called **channels** and are visible to developers in collections called **bindings**. A binding is basically a collection of related channels designed to fulfill a specific task, such as transmit a Web Services request using HTTP. A binding contains an ordered collection of **binding elements**, such as the `TransactionFlowBindingElement` in a transaction propagation channel. The various communication and transaction propagation capabilities offered by WCF therefore are expressed in the collection of available channels. Custom bindings can also be defined. A local optimization of a WCF binding is used when services are deployed into the same address space.

An extended HTTP binding, `WSHttpBinding`, shown in Figure 10.10, is used for messages that need binding elements for SOAP headers defined in extended Web Services specifications such as WS-Security for message-based security, WS-ReliableMessaging for reliable message exchange, and WS-AtomicTransaction for transaction context propagation. A simpler HTTP binding, `BasicHttpBinding`, which is aimed at WS-I Basic Profile conformance, is used to transmit a basic SOAP-formatted message over HTTP. In the simpler binding, HTTP security is used for basic encryption, authentication, and authorization, and transactions are not supported.

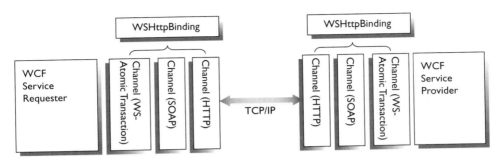

FIGURE 10.10

WCF Bindings Consist of a Collection of Channels. The WSHttpBinding combines channels for Web Service transaction context propagation, message formatting, and transport.

```
<endpoint
    address  = "http://localhost:8002/TransferService.svc"
             bindingConfiguration = "TransactionalHTTP"
             binding  = "wsHttpBinding"
             contract = "ITransfer"/>
```

FIGURE 10.11

Endpoint Definition for a WCF Service. The endpoint definition maps an interface to one or more bindings, such as WSHttpBinding for transactional Web Services.

The example in Figure 10.11 illustrates a configuration for the Transfer service. The executable service logic, interface contract, and communications binding are combined in an **endpoint** definition. The endpoint identifies the executable file for the service as TransferService.svc and gives its network address as a URL. The service uses the WSHttpBinding for the interface contract ITransfer, and a TransactionalHTTP binding configuration, which will propagate the transaction context using WS-AtomicTransaction.

WCF also offers a binding, called NetTcpBinding, for directly sending a binary message over TCP/IP. The message format is optimized for internal communications and available for use only among WCF services. The NetTcpBinding supports transaction propagation and a configurable selection of formats for the transaction context. The format choices include OLE Transactions, WS-AtomicTransaction 2004, or WS-AtomicTransaction 1.1.

A WCF service can be configured to support multiple bindings and thus multiple communication protocols and data formats. For example, a developer may want to publish a service over NetTcpBinding for optimized WCF-WCF communications and over WSHttpBinding to allow access from external Web Services clients. This simply requires specifying multiple bindings for the service in its associated endpoint configuration file. To propagate transaction context, however, it's always necessary to choose a transactional binding; that is, one that can include a TransactionFlowBindingElement.

The code in Figure 10.12 illustrates a WCF service endpoint that uses two bindings, TransactionalTCP and TransactionalHTTP. This makes TransferService available over each protocol on a different port number (8001 and 8002, respectively). In the binding definitions for NetTCPBinding and WsHttpBinding, the transactionFlow attribute is set to true (the default is false). In this case both bindings are transaction-aware and the flow attribute requires transaction context to propagate. In other words, the TransferService is configured to accept a transactional service invocation over both TCP and HTTP. The TCP channel will receive OLE-Transactions context and the HTTP channel will receive WS-Transaction's WS-AT context.

```
<?xml version = "1.0" encoding = "utf-8" ?>
<configuration>
   <system.serviceModel>
      <services>
         <service name = "TransferService">
            <endpoint
               address = "net.tcp://localhost:8001/TransferService/"
               bindingConfiguration = "TransactionalTCP"
               binding  = "netTcpBinding"
               contract = "ITransfer"
            />
            <endpoint
               address  = "http://localhost:8002/TransferService/"
               bindingConfiguration = "TransactionalHTTP"
               binding  = "wsHttpBinding"
               contract = "ITransfer"
            />
         </service>

      <bindings>
         <NetTcpBinding>
            <binding name = "TransactionalTCP"
               transactionFlow = "true"
            />
         </NetTcpBinding>
         <WsHttpBinding>
            <binding name = "TransactionalHTTP"
               transactionFlow = "true"
            />
         </WsHttpBinding>
      </bindings>
   </system.serviceModel>
</configuration>
```

FIGURE 10.12

Configuration File Example for WCF Services. Transactional bindings for both binary and HTTP-based protocols can be configured for the same service, using different port numbers.

Discussion

The implicit programming model was first implemented in .NET as a single attribute associated with an interface that applied to all methods of the interface. The attribute defined both how the method would handle a transaction context when invoked, and whether or not the method would create a new transaction if it did not receive a context on the invocation. That is, a single setting controlled whether or not a method would accept a transaction context propagation and whether or not the called method would create a new transaction if it didn't receive one. This is still the model use in Java EE.

This changed in WCF. First, attributes are associated with individual methods, not the entire interface. Second, WCF uses separate attributes to demarcate a transaction and to control the propagation of transaction context. This allows a potential separation of roles between a developer and system integrator. A developer wants to require that his method executes in a transaction because it accesses transactional resources. But he wants to allow the method to be called by another method that is already operating inside a transaction. He does not necessarily want to define an exception handler, because the exception handler's behavior may be different depending on whether the transaction is demarcated by his method or a method that invokes his method.

Consider a system integrator who is reusing an existing transactional method M in a larger application. He or she may need to control whether M executes in the context of the caller's transaction. For example, if M logs a security violation, it needs to run as a transaction, which the developer of M can specify. The system integrator needs to control whether or not the security violation will be logged even if the caller's transaction aborts. He or she can do this by deciding whether or not the caller's transaction context is propagated to M. If so, then M will run in the caller's transaction. If not, then M will run as a top-level transaction and commit independently of the caller. The system integrator can configure two different callers so that one propagates transaction context and the other doesn't.

In the earlier model, the decisions of transaction demarcation and context propagation were linked. That is, a single attribute controlled whether M executes as a transaction and whether it executes in the context of the caller's transaction. In WCF, these decisions are made separately.

REST/HTTP Support

REST/HTTP support in NET is provided using enhancements to WCF, including templates for constructing and using URLs with HTTP verbs, and attributes for defining REST-based operations in a WCF interface. WCF provides a nontransactional binding for REST/HTTP style services called `WebHttpBinding`.

WCF Deployment Options

WCF supports several hosting options, including IIS running on Windows Server clusters for scalability and availability. For production, one option is to use a Windows hosted "service" (not to be confused with a WCF service). WCF programs can also be hosted using IIS worker processes. Or they can be included in ASP.NET applications.

Initially, the IIS hosting environment was available only for HTTP-based communications. As of the Windows Vista release, the application hosting environment portion of IIS is packaged separately, so it can now accept incoming requests over any communication protocol that WCF supports.

In a Windows Server cluster environment, it's possible to configure the transaction manager to manage transactions centrally or per machine. When configured per machine, if one machine fails, then a transaction manager on another machine can assume responsibility for coordinating transactions for the failed machine's transaction manager. A clustered transactional application must use a cluster-aware transaction manager to ensure correct results and meet availability requirements. In general, performance is improved by colocating the transaction manager in a cluster with the resource manager(s) being coordinated.

Transaction Management Using `System.Transactions`

The runtime infrastructure for creating transactional services and objects in the .NET Framework is delivered in the `System.Transactions` API. The API supports both implicit and explicit transaction programming models, either for .NET programs running on their own or for those defined within WCF. The .NET transaction management infrastructure uses a context called an **ambient transaction**, which is created for any Windows operating system thread that runs transactional code. If an ambient transaction already exists when an object needs a transaction context, then the existing ambient transaction is used. If not, then a new one is created.

Two transaction managers are used in .NET. The general-purpose transaction manager for transactions that use multiple resource managers (RMs) is the Microsoft Distributed Transaction Coordinator (DTC). There is also the Lightweight Transaction Manager (LTM), which can handle any number of volatile resources and at most one persistent resource. LTM is cheaper than DTC because it doesn't require a log.

```
using (TransactionScope tx = new TransactionScope())
{
  //...
  AccountCredit = 100.00M;
  AccountID = 77392;
  AccountDeposit(AccountID, AccountCredit);
  //...

  tx.Complete();
}
```

FIGURE 10.13

Explicit Transaction Management Using `TransactionScope( )`. The `TransactionScope( )` class code snippet shown picks up an existing ambient transaction or initiates a new transaction and votes to successfully complete the transaction if no exception is thrown.

To minimize transaction overhead, `System.Transactions` optimizes transaction coordination by attempting to use the LTM when possible. A transaction starts out being managed by LTM. If the transaction only accesses volatile resources, then LTM coordinates the transaction. If the transaction accesses a persistent resource, such as SQL Server or the transactional NT File System (TxF), then an optimization strategy called **Promotable Single Phase Enlistment (PSPE)** comes into play. It transparently promotes the lightweight in-memory transaction to a persistent single-phase transaction. To coordinate the transaction, LTM commits the volatile resources and then transfers commit coordination responsibility to the durable RM. If the transaction accesses a second durable RM, propagates the transaction to another process, or takes other actions that are beyond LTM's ability to manage, then LTM delegates the transaction coordination to DTC.

SQL Server version 2005 and higher are compatible with PSPE and can therefore handle the delegation or promotion of control when a transaction is started by `System.Transactions`. DTC supports any XA-compliant RM, such as Oracle Database and IBM's DB2, and can include them within a DTC managed transaction.

The Explicit Programming Model

The explicit model in `System.Transactions` incorporates transaction management APIs directly into application code. Developers use the methods in the `Transaction` class to manage transactional behavior. Similar to the implicit programming model, the explicit programming model can be used in any .NET programming language, within or outside of WCF.

A typical approach to manage transactions explicitly is to set a transaction scope on a `using` or `try` block. All operations on data within the block execute within the scope of the transaction. This includes any methods called from within the block, unless explicitly excluded.

An example is shown in Figure 10.13. The `TransactionScope( )` object is instantiated within a `using` block, and the `AccountDeposit` operation within the block is contained within the transaction. Instantiating a `TransactionScope( )` object starts a new transaction or joins an ambient transaction, if one exists. The default `TransactionScopeOption` is `Required`. In the explicit model, the transaction is completed using the `complete` method instead of using the `Autocomplete` attribute. However, the result is the same—the transaction is committed if all participants vote complete and the execution of all methods is successful (i.e., no unhandled exceptions are thrown).

The `System.Transactions` explicit model API also can be used to bracket multiple SQL connections. In Figure 10.14 a new transaction scope is created explicitly. The first `using` block creates an initial SQL

```
using (TransactionScope scope =

  new TransactionScope(TransactionScopeOption.Required))
  {
    using (SqlConnection connection =
      new SqlConnection(connectionString))
    {
      SqlCommand command = connection.CreateCommand();
      command.CommandText = "Insert....";

      connection.Open();
      command.ExecuteNonQuery();
      connection.Close();

      using (SqlConnection connection2 =
        new SqlConnection (connectionString)
      {
        SqlCommand command2 = connection2.CreateCommand();
        command2.CommandText = "Update....";

        connection.Open();

        command2.ExecuteNonQuery();
      }
    }
    scope.Complete();
  }
```

FIGURE 10.14

Bracketing Multiple SQL Connections. In this example, nested using blocks are defined to connect to two SQL databases and coordinate a transaction across both.

connection that executes an insert command. A second using block creates a second SQL connection that executes an update command. After both SQL commands complete successfully, the scope.complete() operation indicates the work of this method is done, and the method is prepared for the transaction to be committed. For simplicity, exception handling logic that typically is added to the using blocks has been omitted.

The TransactionScopeOption choices are:

- Required: Join the existing ambient transaction, or create a new one if one does not exist.
- RequiresNew: Create a new transaction whether or not an ambient transaction was present.
- Suppress: Execute outside the scope of a transaction, that is, suppress the ambient transaction.

A transaction context is associated with a scope object created when a transaction is initiated. The decision to create a new transaction depends on the TransactionScopeOption attribute defined for the object.

The explicit programming model offered by System.Transactions allows a developer to control transaction bracketing without decomposing transactions into separate methods. It also offers more control over the details of transaction management, such as getting and manipulating the transaction context and logging transaction IDs. For example, a program can obtain a reference to the ambient transaction context as follows:

```
Transaction ambientTransaction = Transaction.Current;
```

This enables a program to pass its ambient transaction to another party. The ambient transaction can be changed by setting Transaction.Current, which enables a program to control its transaction context explicitly.

Integration with Legacy TP Monitors

The .NET Framework includes the Microsoft Host Integration Server to access CICS and IMS transactions and DB2 databases. BizTalk Server Adapters for Host Systems can be used to integrate with other existing systems and legacy TP monitors. The Line of Business adapter toolkit in WCF and BizTalk Server can be used to develop a custom adapter where no packaged adapter exists.

Transactional integration with existing systems and legacy TP monitors is offered specifically for CICS and IMS using a two-phase commit bridge between DTC and mainframe transaction managers using the LU6.2 protocol in the Host Integration Server product. Transactional integration also is offered generically via Web Services transactions in WCF and XA support in DTC, both of which can also be used with BizTalk Server. Existing systems also can be wrapped using Web Services and accessed via WCF, either standalone or together with BizTalk Server.

Host Integration Server offers a direct connection to DB2 databases from the .NET Framework. Programs that access mainframe transactions from the .NET Framework can be developed using Visual Studio, including the ability to import metadata from legacy environments in the form of COBOL Copy Books and RPG data definitions. A data access tool provides a mapping to the DB2 data sources. It's also possible to manage database connections to mainframe databases from the .NET Framework environment and integrate them with connections to SQL Server data sources.

Host Integration Server also supports an option for using IBM 3270 terminal communications protocol over TCP/IP.

10.4 JAVA ENTERPRISE EDITION

Java Enterprise Edition (Java EE) refers to an umbrella specification that groups 79 API specifications (as of Java EE 5) designed for enterprise computing applications such as transaction processing. Java EE API features work together to provide a complete environment for developing and deploying TP applications, including:

- The Swing Library, Servlets, Java Server Pages, and Java Server Faces for developing front-end programs, including interactive menu and forms capabilities for web browsers and native PC and UNIX programs
- Enterprise Java Beans (EJBs), a distributed computing component model for developing request controllers and transaction servers that support a variety of front-end programs
- The Java Persistence API (JPA), a lightweight object-relational mapping integrated with EJBs to interact with persistent entities stored in a relational database
- The Java Connector Architecture (JCA) API, a programming environment for integration with legacy systems that includes a standard client and adapter toolkit
- The Java Transaction API (JTA), an infrastructure and programming environment for transaction management, used in both the implicit and explicit programming models for Java EE
- A WS-BPEL engine for business process management, which is also provided by most Java EE vendors

Java EE is defined through the Java Community Process, a consortium of Java vendors chaired by Sun Microsystems. Java EE originally was released in December 1999, and has gone through several iterations since then. Its original name was Java 2 Enterprise Edition, or J2EE, which was changed to Java EE as of its fourth release, called Java EE 5. A major difference between the enterprise edition and the standard edition of Java is the addition of EJBs. The current version, EJB3, represents a significant change from earlier versions of EJB (1.1 through 2.1), with a lighter weight container, JPA in place of entity beans, and the use of Java 5 annotations for transaction demarcation and other EJB functions.

Java EE APIs are delivered in Java-EE-compliant application server products from IBM, Oracle, Red Hat, and others. Java-EE-compliant vendors must pass a set of conformance tests to receive a certification from the Java Community Process, which indicates that the vendor has successfully implemented each of the required APIs. Examples of certified products include IBM's WebSphere Application Server, Oracle's WebLogic Application Server, and Red Hat's JBoss Application Server. These products are available on UNIX, Windows, and zOS operating systems. Java-EE-compliant application servers typically include vendor-specific mechanisms for server clustering and failover, sometimes including state caching and replication. However, these features are not included in the Java EE APIs and are therefore beyond the scope of this book.

In contrast to the Microsoft transactional middleware, which runs only on Windows operating systems, Java-based transactional middleware runs on virtually any operating system. But operating system portability has its costs. In particular, .NET Framework components are generally better integrated with the operating system than Java-based components. As might be expected, the specific details of how to create and deploy transactional programs with Java EE and the .NET Framework are different, even though the technologies and underlying concepts are very similar.

Figure 10.15 illustrates the relationships among the transactional middleware components of the Java EE architecture. It includes two types of front-end programs, those designed to run in a web browser and those designed to run on a desktop PC or UNIX system. The Java EE architecture is very similar to the .NET Framework in this respect, but a significant difference is the presence of EJBs, which are programs and associated containers that were specifically designed for use in TP applications.

Typically, a browser-based front-end program communicates with the web tier, which in turn calls the EJB tier. The EJB tier then invokes one or more JPA entities at the persistence tier. An EJB may also use JCA to invoke a back-end system, such as a legacy TP monitor, or may directly access a database using SQL commands through Java Database Connectivity (JDBC).

The standard protocol for remote communication between the web tier and the EJB tier is the Java Remote Method Invocation over the CORBA Internet Inter-Orb Protocol (RMI/IIOP). Other communication protocols can also be used. SOAP over HTTP is supported from a Web Services client to the EJB tier. Java EE vendors typically offer proprietary communications protocols and data formats specifically tuned for their individual products. It is also fairly common practice for the web tier to communicate locally with the EJB tier.

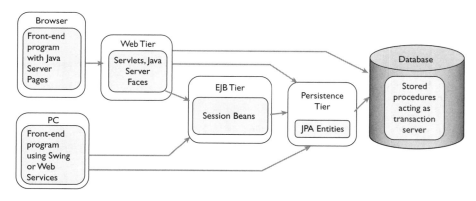

FIGURE 10.15

Java EE Multitier Transactional Middleware Architecture. The components of the Java EE environment provide several options for developing and deploying front-end programs, request controllers, and transaction servers.

An application developed using Java-EE-compliant transactional middleware components can therefore implement a two-tier, three-tier, or multitier architecture to meet scalability, availability, and other TP application requirements. For example:

- When a web browser is used for the front-end program, a web server can function as the request controller by including an EJB that routes the request to a transaction server program.
- When a PC- or UNIX-based front-end program is used, the EJB tier can be used to fulfill the request controller function on its own, without a web server.
- When multiple tiers are needed, EJBs can be used to fulfill both the request controller and transaction server functions (including the persistence tier).
- Stored procedures can also fulfill the transaction server function for web server hosted or plain EJB-based request controllers.

As in the .NET environment, both implicit and explicit transaction programming models are supported, and the implicit model is recommended for most applications.

Developing Front-End Programs

In Java EE the technologies used for front-end programs include:

- The Swing Library for PC- and UNIX-based GUIs
- Servlets, Java Server Pages (JSP), and Java Server Faces (JSF) for web browser-based GUIs

Swing is the name of a collection of libraries and functions used to develop highly interactive PC- and UNIX-based front-end programs. The Swing Library is comparable to the .NET Framework's WPF and Silverlight. Library functions define a screen's area and layout, menus, scroll bars, tabs, buttons, sliders, tables, frames, toolbars, and so on. The example in Figure 10.16 uses the Swing libraries to display a table of information. As shown in the figure, Swing classes can be used to construct a variety of GUI features. In this case the JTable class is used to create a table of a customer's accounts. Although the main program thread exits at the end of the example, Swing supplies a second thread that continues processing in the background to handle GUI components.

A Java **servlet** extends the capability of a standard web server to support dynamic content generation. The Java Servlet API is an alternative to web server callout mechanisms such as Common Gateway Interface (CGI) scripts and web server APIs such as Apache API or ISAPI (IIS). Servlets handle HTTP sessions and route requests to Java objects, EJBs, or databases. Servlets also handle REST and Web Services communications. The server can use any technique to maintain session state, typically using cookies or URL rewriting. All Java-EE-based application server products include a servlet engine. Apache Tomcat is an example of a popular standalone servlet engine.

Java Server Pages (JSP) layer on servlets and replace static HTML and XML pages with dynamic content generated using JSP tags embedded in HTML or XML pages. The tags access and generate content that is then formatted into HTML or XML. When the page request is executed, a JSP is converted to a servlet for handling the content to be displayed in the browser.

The example in Figure 10.17 illustrates the use of JSP tags to generate information within an HTML bulleted list. When executed, the JSP tags dynamically generate the content for the bank name, the account balance, and the current date of the web server access. **Java Server Faces (JSF)** components are server-side controllers of browser-based menu and form components such as buttons, tables, and graphics. JSF and JSP technologies can work together, for example when JSFs are used to create JSPs, and JSPs generate content for JSF-defined menu and form elements. JSPs and JSFs can work in combination to drive server-side and client-side user interaction scenarios. For example, the JSF custom library can be used by the JSP to generate content and GUI elements for the browser.

```
import java.awt.*;
    import javax.swing.*;

    public class SimpleTable extends JFrame {
        public SimpleTable() {
            super("Transfer");
            setSize(300, 200);
            setDefaultCloseOperation(EXIT_ON_CLOSE);
            JTable jt = new JTable(
              new String[][] {
              {"John Smith", "Savings", "100.0"} },
              new String[] { "Customer", "Account", "Balance"}
            );
            JScrollPane scp = new JScrollPane(jt);
            getContentPane().add(scp, BorderLayout.CENTER);
        }

        public static void main(String args[]) {
            SimpleTable st = new SimpleTable();
            st.setVisible(true);
        }
    }
```

FIGURE 10.16

Code for a Java Swing-Based Table. The Swing client displays a list of accounts and balances for a customer.

```
<UL>
  <LI> Web Bank name: ${account.bankName}
  <LI> Current Balance: ${account.balance}
  <LI><B> JSP 1.2 expression: </B><BR>
   Current date: <%= new java.util.Date()%>
</UL>
```

FIGURE 10.17

JSP Tags Generate Content for an HTML List. JSP 2.0 tags inside an HTML list include an expression that finds the web bank's name, an account balance, and a directive that gets and displays the current date.

The example in Figure 10.18 illustrates a simple form defined using JSF tag libraries. The JSF component classes maintain the component's state and the rendering tags define how to render the content for the user. For example, the commandButton tag is rendered as a button. The example also illustrates a validation function to check a username when the button is clicked. When a JSP is created using JSF, a tree of components is mapped into memory from which a response to a browser request is generated.

REST Support

REST support in Java EE environments is provided by the Java API for Restful Web Services (JAX-RS). JAX-RS defines a set of annotations and interfaces that can be used in Java objects to expose them as RESTful web resources. JAX-RS objects can be deployed to either a standalone servlet engine or a servlet engine within a Java EE application server. JAX-RS enables front-end programs to call the objects using HTTP as the network protocol, using HTTP content types to define the data formats.

```
<%@ taglib uri="http://java.sun.com/jsf/html" prefix="h" %>
  <%@ taglib uri="http://java.sun.com/jsf/core" prefix="f" %>
  <body bgcolor="white">
  <f:view>
  <h:form id="Sign In Form">
  <h2>Username:</h2>
      <h:inputText id="username" value="#{UserNameBean.userName}"
          validator="#{UserNameBean.validate}"/>
      <h:commandButton id="submit" action="success" value="Submit"/>
  </h:form>
  </f:view>
```

FIGURE 10.18

JSF Components Prompt for a Username and Create a Submit Button. This JSF component prompts the user for his or her name and checks it with the server-side username validation program.

Developing Request Controllers and Transaction Servers

An **Enterprise Java Bean (EJB)** refers both to a type of Java program designed for TP applications and to a container within which such a program is deployed. An EJB abstracts transactional middleware functionality, such as threading, transaction control, and security. EJBs originally were designed for compatibility with legacy TP monitors, although the most popular implementations of EJBs have been written from scratch. EJBs have evolved significantly from their initial definition. Compared to EJB2, EJB3 beans feature a lighter weight container, dependency injection, and Java 5 attributes for expressing configuration properties.

In Java EE, a request controller can be developed for the web tier or the EJB tier. When developed for the web tier, the request controller typically is implemented using a servlet engine running inside a web server, which routes the request to an EJB. The EJB can execute in the web server or in a separate process.

EJB types include:

- Session beans: Designed for hosting an interactive session with the front-end program. A session bean can be stateless or stateful and can manage transactions.
- Message-driven beans: Designed for interacting with asynchronous messaging systems that conform to the Java Messaging Service (JMS) API.

EJB2 defined a third EJB type, an entity bean. Entity beans are preserved in EJB3 for compatibility with EJB2 applications. In EJB3, entity beans are replaced by JPA entities (covered next and in Section 10.6).

An EJB can manage transactions and participate in transactional compositions. A message-driven bean can also manage transactions, but cannot be composed into a transaction started by another bean.

A session bean is allocated to a single instance of a front-end program and is terminated when the front-end program terminates. A stateful session bean maintains the state of its instance variables for the duration of its interaction with the front-end program; a stateless session bean does not.

Stateful session bean state is volatile and not transactional. For a web browser front-end program, session state management also can be provided by the HttpSession object. For PC- or UNIX-based Swing clients stateful session beans are the only mechanism available to preserve in-memory conversational state across multiple interactions between the front-end program and the request controller.

As with any stateless design, the advantage of a stateless session bean is that the application server can maintain a reusable pool of stateless session beans, allocate them to any request on demand, and deallocate them once a bean finishes executing the request. With a stateful bean the application server has to direct a subsequent call by a given front-end program to the same bean instance so that it has access to the state of its conversation with the front end.

A stateless session bean can have a Web Service interface, allowing a Web Service client to invoke an EJB method. Web Services support is included in the Java EE specifications through the inclusion of the Java API for XML-Based Web Services (JAX-WS) specification. Therefore, all Java-EE-complaint application server products offer toolkits that generate a Web Service interface from an EJB interface.

A session bean can query and update a relational database by using one or more JPA entities. The data members of a JPA entity are transactionally persistent, and a session bean can access that state by issuing operations on the JPA `EntityManager`. Like a web server, however, a session bean also has the option to access a database directly to execute embedded SQL or to invoke a stored procedure using JDBC. Direct database access is commonly used in practice.

A **bean implementation class** is an ordinary Java class file that contains the method implementations for the EJB. An implementation class exposes a **business interface** for remote and local access to business logic methods. Restrictions on the Java class and methods used for an EJB ensure that everything works correctly when deployed within a container, such that they must be public, cannot be final, and cannot be abstract.

A bean implementation class becomes an EJB by importing one or more EJB libraries and either including one or more EJB annotations or declaring it an EJB in an associated descriptor file (see Figure 10.24). EJB annotations control the abstractions of the container and generate deployment metadata. As of EJB3 the embedded annotations can be used to generate the descriptor file. As with entity beans, a manually coded descriptor file (i.e., created without using annotations) is supported for backward compatibility with EJB2. In EJB3, the embedded annotations typically are used to generate the deployment metadata, including any vendor-specific variations.

The EJB type annotations are:

- `@javax.ejb.Stateless`
- `@javax.ejb.Stateful`
- `@javax.ejb.MessageDriven`

The first two define a session bean as being either stateless or stateful. The third defines a message-driven bean (i.e., one that interacts with JMS message queues). The `Stateless` annotation is more commonly used than `Stateful`. In EJB3, the `@javax.ejb.entity` annotation is used only to include an EJB 2.1 entity bean into an EJB3-compliant application server.

Other annotations specify transaction control, security, and how to handle messages and resources. Each of the annotations other than the EJB type has a default value if not specified. For example, if a transaction control annotation is not specified, the default is to require a transaction for each method in a class.

The example in Figure 10.19 illustrates a stateless session bean for a group of methods that can perform several operations for a fictitious bank account management application. A session bean typically is invoked by the servlet engine, although it can also be invoked using a Web Service, another EJB, or a Swing client. Since no `@TransactionAttribute` annotation is included, the bean uses default of container-managed transactions with a transaction required for the execution of each method. Thus, if a method is called from another method, the calling method's transaction will be used. Otherwise a new transaction will be created.

An EJB **reference** is needed to invoke a bean, with the exception of a Web Service invocation of a stateless session bean method. The EJB reference can be injected or retrieved using a directory lookup. A typical directory service for a Java EE-based application server is the Java Naming and Directory Interface (JNDI). Figure 10.20 shows an example of a client with an EJB reference injected using the `@EJB` annotation to provide the reference that can be used to invoke the `Transfer` EJB. The `@Resource` annotation also can be used to inject a variety of other external information, such an environment variable, an EJB context, a JMS destination, a connection factory, or a data source.

The default for accessing an interface is local access; that is, from an EJB client running in the same address space. A remotely accessible interface needs to be explicitly identified using the `@javax.ejb.Remote` annotation. The `@javax.ejb.Local` annotation explicitly restricts an interface to local access.

```
import javax.ejb.Stateless;

@Stateless
public class AccountOperationBean implements AccountOperation {

    public double balance(int accountNumber) {
        Account acct = this.getAccount(accountNumber);
        return acct.getBalance();
    }

    public void deposit(int accountNumber, double amount) {
        Account acct = this.getAccount(accountNumber);
        acct.setBalance(acct.getBalance() + amount);
    }

    public void withdraw(int accountNumber, double amount) {
        Account acct = this.getAccount(accountNumber);
        if (acct.getBalance() < amount) {
            throw new InsufficientFundsException();
        }
        acct.setBalance(acct.getBalance() - amount);
    }

    private Account getAccount(int accountNumber) {
        // Code to retrieve the Account balance
    }
}
```

FIGURE 10.19

Stateless Session Bean. This stateless EJB implements the operations of the AccountOperation interface to check a customer's account balance and to withdraw or deposit funds.

```
import javax.naming.Context;
import javax.naming.InitialContext;

public class TransferClient
{
public static void main(String [] args)
  {
    @EJB Transfer myTransfer;
    myTransfer.transfer(123, 456, 100.00);
  }
}
```

FIGURE 10.20

Sample EJB Reference for Transfer Class. An EJB reference can be injected to allow a front-end program or request controller to invoke an EJB.

The @TransactionManagement annotation defines whether the implicit or explicit programming model is used for a bean. Valid values for this attribute are:

- TransactionManagementType.CONTAINER
- TransactionManagementType.BEAN

When the value is CONTAINER the implicit programming model is used, which is called **container managed** in EJB terminology. When it's BEAN, the explicit programming model is used, called **bean managed**.

The @javax.ejb.ApplicationException annotation marks an application exception that can be thrown by a method in a bean managed transaction. The exception is reported directly to the EJB client when it occurs. The rollback attribute of the annotation can be used to define whether the exception automatically causes a rollback.

The @TransactionAttribute is used to control the operations of the implicit programming model, such as whether or not the container is required to start a new transaction before executing each method in the class. The next section lists the valid values for this attribute.

A **JPA entity** can be defined within an EJB to map its data to a relational database, using an object-relational mapping. The @javax.persistence.Entity annotation defines a Java class as a JPA entity. A JPA entity can be used from within a session bean or a plain Java class.

In previous versions of EJB this functionality was called bean-managed or container-managed persistence. JPA is lighter weight, easier to use, and more efficient than the previous EJB approach. A JPA entity maps the data items and attributes of a Java class to one or more rows in one or more database tables. Optional attributes can be used to specify fine-grained control over which data items are persisted.

The example in Figure 10.21 shows a stateless session bean that uses a JPA EntityManager to create a new account record. Bean methods access and update the persistent resource. Operations to create or update an entity should execute in the context of a transaction, which is why the @TransactionAttribute annotation is set to REQUIRED. It creates a new Account record based on parameters passed to the createAccount method, and then calls the em.persist method to add a row to the database table. When used in an EJB, a JPA entity participates in the global transaction managed by the Java Transaction API (JTA; described later in this section). When used outside of an EJB, a JPA entity can use a JDBC managed transaction or a global transaction managed by JTA.

Transaction Management in Java

Java developers creating TP applications may choose to use a persistence abstraction from a plain Java object or from within an EJB. If using a plain Java object, a session can be established with a single resource manager

```
import javax.ejb.Stateless;
import javax.ejb.TransactionManagement;
import javax.persistence.PersistenceContext;
import javax.persistence.EntityManager;
...

@Stateless
@TransactionAttribute(REQUIRED)
public class AccountCreationBean implements AccountCreation {
    @PersistenceContext(unitName="AccountSystem")
    private EntityManager em;
    public void createAccount(String customerName, int accountNumber,
                              double initialDeposit) {
        Account acct = new Account(accountNumber);
        acct.setCustomerName(customerName);
        acct.setBalance(initialDeposit);
        em.persist(acct);
    }
}
```

FIGURE 10.21

Using a JPA Entity to Create an Account Record. A JPA entity manager retrieves and updates persistent items in a database.

to directly control its transactions. If using a persistence abstraction within an EJB, JTA is used to control the transaction.

An EJB does not have an equivalent mechanism to the .NET Framework `set.complete()` method because an EJB is not treated as a transaction participant. Nor does the EJB specification include a concept directly comparable to an ambient transaction; that is, one that exists independently of the lifecycle of an object for which a transaction is started. However, Java EE does offer the `setRollbackOnly` command for a subobject to tell the top-level object to abort.

The Implicit Programming Model

In the implicit programming model the EJB container automatically starts and terminates a transaction when a transactional EJB method is invoked. Successful completion commits the transaction and an exception can be set to cause an automatic abort.

By default, the EJB container automatically invokes a business method within a transaction context and automatically decides whether to commit or abort the transaction, depending on whether the method completes successfully or not. A transaction annotation can be specified on the entire bean class, or on individual methods to override the default behavior. An annotation at the method level overrides an annotation at the class level, if both are specified.

Valid values for the `@TransactionAttribute` annotation are:

- `REQUIRES_NEW`
- `REQUIRED`
- `SUPPORTS`
- `NOT_SUPPORTED`
- `MANDATORY`
- `NEVER`

The transaction attribute values instruct the container to perform the following operations:

- `REQUIRES_NEW`. Every invocation of the method starts executing in a new transaction, whether or not the caller was already executing in a transaction.
- `REQUIRED`. If the caller is already running within a transaction, then the called method executes within that transaction. If not, then the called method starts executing in a new transaction.
- `SUPPORTS`. If the caller is already running within a transaction, then the called method executes within that transaction. If not, then the called method does not execute within a transaction.
- `NOT_SUPPORTED`. The called method does not execute within a transaction, even if the caller is running within a transaction.
- `MANDATORY`. If the caller is already running within a transaction, then the called method executes within that transaction. If not, an exception is raised.
- `NEVER`. If the caller is already running within a transaction, an exception is raised.

If the transaction attribute of a message-driven bean is `REQUIRED`, then the bean executes as a top-level transaction. The transaction includes its operations on the message queue and on any other transactional resources. Operations in a message-driven bean cannot join the transactional operations of any other bean. When the transaction attribute is `NOT_SUPPORTED`, the message-driven bean's operations do not execute in the context of a transaction. A container-managed transaction is required to coordinate operations on message queues with operations on other persistent resources.

An EJB always uses JTA unless the `NOT_SUPPORTED` attribute is specified. JTA implementations use a one-phase commit optimization whenever there's a single resource manager. This optimization is sufficient for most applications. However, unlike the PSPE optimization in .NET's System.Transactions, it still involves the application server's transaction manager. There are workarounds, but they involve the EJB doing explicit transaction control with the RM.

Figure 10.22 illustrates a session bean that uses the REQUIRED attribute to invoke two methods within the same transaction. The REQUIRED attribute means that if the caller is executing in a transaction, then any called methods also execute within the caller's transaction. If the caller is not executing a transaction, the method executes in a new top-level transaction.

An exception class can be defined so that when the execution of a transaction throws an exception, the application can catch it in the exception handler and throw an application-specific exception. In the example in Figure 10.23 the @ApplicationException annotation sets the rollback attribute to true, meaning that when the exception handler catches an exception of the defined type, a TransferException is raised, and a rollback is signaled for the transaction.

```
public class TransferBean implements Transfer {
    @EJB AccountOperation op;
    ...
    @TransactionAttribute(REQUIRED)
    public void transfer(int acct1, int acct2, double amount) {
        op.withdraw(acct1, amount);
        op.deposit(acct2, amount);
    }
}
```

FIGURE 10.22

Transactional Session Bean Invoking Two Methods. Both the Withdraw and Deposit methods are invoked within the same transaction.

```
>>> Exception class:
import javax.ejb.ApplicationException;
@ApplicationException(rollback = true)
public class TransferException extends RuntimeException {}

>>> Session bean class:
import javax.ejb.*;
@Stateless
@TransactionManagement(TransactionManagementType.CONTAINER)
public class TransferBean implements Transfer {

    @TransactionAttribute(TransactionAttributeType.REQUIRES_NEW)
    public void transfer(int acct1, int acct2, double amount) {
      try {
          <<do transfer>>
      } catch (Exception e1) {
          <<log>>
          throw new TransferException(e1);
      }
    }
}
```

FIGURE 10.23

Using a Try Block to Catch an Exception. The try block allows an exception to be caught and transferred for the transaction.

Transaction control attributes can be specified either as embedded annotations and attributes in EJB3 or in a deployment descriptor file, which is illustrated in Figure 10.24. A descriptor file can be either hand-coded or generated from annotations and attributes. For each EJB listed in the example file, the implicit programming model is specified (`transaction-type` is `container`) and a transaction control attribute is associated with either all methods of a class (using an asterisk) or with a particular method of the class (for example, `transfer`).

The Explicit Programming Model

In the Java EE environment, explicit transaction programming directly uses the Java Transaction API (JTA) in a bean-managed transaction. JTA has three major functional areas:

- Simple transaction demarcation: `javax.transaction.UserTransaction`
- Transaction manger control: `javax.transaction.TransactionManager`
- A Java mapping of the XA API for resource integration: `javax.transaction.xa.XAResource`

```
<ejb-jar>
  ...
  <session>
    <ejb-name>AccountOperationBean</ejb-name>
    ...
    <transaction-type>Container</transaction-type>
  </session>
  <session>
    <ejb-name>TransferBean</ejb-name>
    ...
    <transaction-type>Container</transaction-type>
  </session>

  <assembly-descriptor>
     ...
    <container-transaction>
      <method>
        <ejb-name>AccountOperationBean</ejb-name>
        <method-name>*</method-name>
      </method>
      <trans-attribute>Required</trans-attribute>
    </container-transaction>

    <container-transaction>
      <method>
        <ejb-name>TransferBean</ejb-name>
        <method-name>transfer</method-name>
      </method>
      <trans-attribute>RequiresNew</trans-attribute>
    </container-transaction>

  </assembly-descriptor>
</ejb-jar>
```

FIGURE 10.24

Using an EJB Deployment Descriptor to Specify Transaction Control Attributes. The EJB descriptor file associates EJB method names with attributes that define whether the program in the bean uses the explicit or implicit programming model, and whether or not a transaction context is required to invoke the method.

```
@Stateless
@TransactionManagement(TransactionManagementType.BEAN)
public class TransferBean implements Transfer {

@Resource private UserTransaction utx;

public void transfer(int acct1, int acct2, double amount) {
    try {
        utx.begin();
        <<do transfer>>
        utx.commit();
    } catch (Exception e1) {
        try { utx.rollback(); } catch (Exception e2) {}
        <<log>>
        throw new TransferException(e1);
    }
}
}
```

FIGURE 10.25

Explicit Transaction Control in a Stateless Session Bean. A stateless session bean can explicitly manage a transaction that includes updates to multiple resource managers.

The UserTransaction part of the API is used for bean managed transactions; that is, for explicit transaction programming in an EJB. The TransactionManager part of the API typically is used by application server vendors to access and control the functions of an independent transaction manager, such as a Java Transaction Service (JTS) compliant transaction manager. Some application server products explicitly prohibit its use. The XAResource portion of the API is a Java mapping of the standard XA interface that the application server uses to include XA-compliant resource managers into JTA-managed transactions.

The underlying implementation of JTA isn't explicitly defined and may vary from vendor to vendor. JTS specifies one implementation, using the Object Management Group's Object Transaction Service (OTS, described in Section 10.8) and General Inter-ORB Protocol (IIOP). Vendors typically use a combination of JTS and XA-compliant libraries. Transaction interoperability between transactional Java EE application servers is optional, but if supported it must use JTS/OTS.

JTA can be used in a Java EE environment. It can also be used outside a Java EE environment when an independent implementation of JTA is available, such as Atomikos or the JBoss Transaction Manager.

Figure 10.25 illustrates the use of explicit transaction management within a stateless session bean. The UserTransaction part of the JTA API is used in a stateless EJB to start (utx.begin()) and terminate (utx.commit()) a transaction. A transaction has to be started and completed in the same method, although the transaction context (as in the implicit model) can be propagated to other methods. As shown in the example, an exception handler can be defined to issue the utx.rollback()command and throw an exception to the client if there's a problem.

Integration with Legacy TP Monitors

The Java Connector Architecture (JCA) defines a standard way for Java-EE-compliant transactional middleware to connect to legacy TP monitors and other existing systems such as packaged applications. JCA provides a set of APIs and system programming interfaces for developing and deploying connections and adapters to existing systems. JCA can propagate a transaction context from an EJB to a legacy TP monitor, depending on the compatibility of the application server's and legacy TP monitor's transaction protocols.

JCA defines a set of system-level contracts between a Java EE application server and an existing system. They include contracts for communications, security, and transaction management. JCA defines a common client interface that allows an EJB to call an adapter written for an existing technology's external client or a custom-developed adapter. It can propagate application server features using one or more connection contracts, such as one that propagates transaction context. JCA calls such a contract a **resource adapter**. A resource adapter plugs into the application server as a protocol and functional bridge between an application server and an existing system.

Transaction management is integrated with JTA and is based on wrapping each existing transactional environment as an XA resource so it can be coordinated using the application server's transaction manager. JCA offers the application server the option to delegate transaction management to the local resource when a single resource manager is involved in the transaction, saving the overhead of two-phase commit coordination when it isn't needed. Transaction propagation works with both the implicit and explicit programming models.

Existing systems such as legacy TP monitors typically support external clients, for example ECI for CICS and TP Web Connector for ACMS. Vendors also have the option of providing their own JCA-compliant adapter. JCA adapters are capable of bidirectional communication, including transactions, between existing systems and application servers.

Spring Transactions

The Spring Framework is a popular open source programming model for developing enterprise applications, such as TP applications, using plain old Java objects (POJOs) and EJBs. Spring objects, called Spring Beans, can be deployed into Java-EE-compliant application servers, standalone servlet engines that don't support EJBs, or OSGi Frameworks such as Eclipse Equinox and Apache Felix.

The Spring Framework offers a widely-adopted lightweight alternative to EJBs, including transactional middleware functions. Spring works with popular EJB containers and standalone JTA-compliant transaction managers such as the JBoss Transaction Manager, the Atomikos transaction manager, or the Java Open Transaction Manager (JOTM) from the OW2 Consortium. The Spring Framework extends transaction processing applications outside of the Java-EE-compliant application server environment and offers a lightweight alternative for single resource transactions.

Spring supports two models for transaction management:

- Local: Delegates transaction management to the persistence abstraction mechanism (e.g., JDBC or JPA)
- JTA: Uses the JTA API from within the Spring Platform Transaction Manager API explicitly to initiate and terminate transactions

Spring supports both implicit and explicit programming models for either the local or JTA transaction management models. The implicit and explicit models are called **declarative** and **programmatic demarcation**, respectively. Declarative demarcation uses embedded annotations whereas programmatic demarcation uses the JTA API. Spring Beans using transactions can be deployed within an EJB container or independently of an EJB container as long as the requisite transaction management infrastructure is available (i.e., a transactional persistence abstraction mechanism and/or a standalone JTA implementation).

Spring transaction management uses the Spring Platform Transaction Manager API to abstract the transaction management and programming models. The local and JTA transaction management models are **strategies**. A transaction management strategy is defined or altered using a configuration file associated with a Spring

```
public interface PlatformTransactionManager {
    TransactionStatus getTransaction(TransactionDefinition definition)
        throws TransactionException;
    void commit(TransactionStatus status) throws TransactionException;
    void rollback(TransactionStatus status) throws TransactionException;
}
```

FIGURE 10.26

The Spring Framework Abstract Interface for Transaction Management. The interface is used internally by the Spring Framework to set the transaction strategy, which is defined in an associated configuration file. It can also be used explicitly by developers to control the transaction strategy programmatically.

```
DefaultTransactionDefinition def = new DefaultTransactionDefinition();
    def.setName("Transfer");
    def.setPropagationBehavior(TransactionDefinition.PROPAGATION_REQUIRED);

TransactionStatus status = txManager.getTransaction(def);
    try {
        //execute your business logic here
    }
    catch (MyException ex) {
        txManager.rollback(status);
        throw ex;
    }
    txManager.commit(status);
```

FIGURE 10.27

Using the Spring Framework for Explicit Transaction Management. A new transaction is defined for the Transfer method along with its propagation behavior. The transaction is initiated and completed within the try block, which also can throw the rollback exception.

Bean. The Spring Framework focuses primarily on local transaction management as the most common use of two-phase commit; that is, coordinating transactional resources that reside on the same machine.

The Spring Framework supports local propagation of transaction context across method invocations using either strategy. Remote propagation of transaction context uses a JTA-aware communication protocol (e.g., RMI and RMI/IIOP) and requires explicit JTA programming.

The Spring Framework allows TP application developers to define which exceptions will cause a rollback, a capability that is also available in EJB3.

As shown in Figure 10.26, the Spring Framework uses the PlatformTransactionManager interface to implement the transaction strategy declared for a Spring Bean. The strategy can choose a transaction manager that provides a JTA API, or it can use the transaction management capabilities of a JDBC connection. However, it is also possible for a Java programmer to use this interface directly from a Spring Bean to programmatically set the strategy.

In Figure 10.27 the PROPAGATION_REQUIRED attribute is set to ensure that the method is invoked within a transaction context. Note that remote context propagation requires the use of the explicit programming model. The example also illustrates the way in which the Spring Framework allows a rollback to be associated with an application defined exception, such as MyException.

```
@Transactional(propagation=Propagation.REQUIRES_NEW)
    public void withdrawFunds(Account Amount) {
        ...
    }
```

FIGURE 10.28

Spring Transactions Implicit Model. Spring uses the @Transactional annotation to declaratively specify transaction control for a method (method code not shown).

```
<tx:annotation-driven/>
<bean id="transactionManager"
 class="org.springframework.jdbc.datasource.DataSourceTransactionManager">
    <property name="dataSource" ref="myTargetDataSourceBean"/>
</bean>
 <tx:annotation-driven/>

<bean id="transactionManager"
 class="org.springframework.transaction.jta.JtaTransactionManager"/>
```

FIGURE 10.29

Switching Transaction Strategies. Spring transactions use configuration to switch transaction management strategies.

The implicit model implements declarative demarcation using Spring's @Transactional annotation. This works similarly to EJB's annotation system. Spring supports the EJB @TransactionAttribute values and extends them for defining a custom isolation level or a read-only transaction, or to control cache flushing.

In the example in Figure 10.28, the @Transactional annotation indicates using the Propagation. REQUIRES_NEW property that a new transaction must be started before executing the withdrawFunds method, even when a transaction context is propagated on the method invocation. Spring supports EJB propagation options and adds a NESTED option to support nested transactions. This can be used by persistence abstraction mechanisms that support savepoints, such as a JDBC3 driver or Apache OpenJPA.

Switching the transaction management strategy from local to JTA is accomplished using a configuration change. For example, the first part of Figure 10.29 configures the local Spring transaction management strategy to use a JDBC driver and the second part configures a JTA strategy. A configuration change to a JTA strategy may be necessary when a Spring Bean accesses multiple resource managers within the same transaction, or needs to propagate transaction context remotely.

10.5 SERVICE-ORIENTED ARCHITECTURE

The SOA style of design provides many benefits, including functional reuse across multiple applications, improved flexibility in developing new applications, and interoperability across disparate software systems, such as .NET, Java EE, and legacy TP monitors. SOA-based applications can include services created from Java EE or .NET Framework objects, legacy TP monitor procedures, asynchronous message queues, or databases. SOA products create and manage services for these and other environments. They also combine services into business process flows. Interoperability across disparate software systems enhances the benefits of SOA for reuse and flexibility, but presents additional challenges for transaction management.

Applications based on the Service-Oriented Architecture (SOA) style of design began to appear in the late 1990s and early 2000s using products such as Progress Software's CORBA-compliant Orbix and IBM's WebSphere MQ. Some applications based on the SOA design use both, such as the well-documented Credit Suisse Information Bus.

More recently, Web Services have become a popular technology for SOA. As mentioned in the .NET Framework and Java EE sections, both of those technology suites support Web Services. They also support REST/HTTP, another popular technology for SOA. We will discuss both technologies for SOA.

Products and services specifically designed for use with SOA are offered by HP, IBM, Microsoft, Oracle, Progress Software, Red Hat, Software AG, TIBCO Software, and others. Most SOA products support a two-phase commit protocol for services that execute as a transaction. Some products also include a compensation-based protocol for services that execute as a business process. SOA-based applications often include both kinds of services, sometimes in the same application. Sometimes these two types of services are called fine-grained and coarse-grained, or tightly-coupled and loosely-coupled, respectively.

The exact characteristics and details of the SOA products vary, but they tend to fall into these general categories:

- Service enablement: Create Web Service interfaces and REST/HTTP access to existing and new programs, objects, databases, and message queues.
- Business process management: Compose and execute flows of sequences of services.
- Governance: Store and retrieve service metadata, including development lifecycle support.
- Management: Monitor runtime service execution and enforce policy contracts such as security and availability.

In a typical SOA-based application, a request type can invoke a transaction that uses cooperating services within a single application environment, or a business process that invokes multiple services in sequence. In the first case, any transaction protocol can be used, such as a native two-phase commit or the WS-AT protocol from WS-Transactions. For a business process, however, a compensation-based protocol is more likely to be required, such as the WS-BusinessActivity protocol from WS-Transactions.

Several factors apply to the choice of Web Services or REST/HTTP based technologies for an SOA-based application. In general, requirements for RPC communications and for wrapping existing systems favor the use of Web Services, and requirements for hosting applications on the Web favors the use of REST/HTTP. Other factors include whether the application is a purely web-based application, or whether the application is a mixture of web components and transactional middleware components. Web Services are readily available for transactional middleware environments, including legacy TP monitors. However, given the success of the Web, developers would do well to prepare for a web-based architecture whenever possible.

Web Services-Based SOA

Web Services use SOAP as the message format, with parameters expressed in XML and interfaces expressed in Web Services Definition Language (WSDL). Some implementations allow a SOAP message to contain a single XML document instead of RPC-style arguments. Optional headers are added to SOAP messages to express requirements for system functions such as security, reliability, and transaction propagation.

One popular application of Web Services is interoperability between native RPC protocols, such as Java EE's RMI and the Microsoft RPC. This is done by programs that understand both formats, translating native RPC messages into and out of the SOAP format.

In Figure 10.30, the SOAP message is created using a C# object linked with a proxy generated from a WCF interface that uses a Web Services binding. The SOAP processor in the WCF environment obtains the

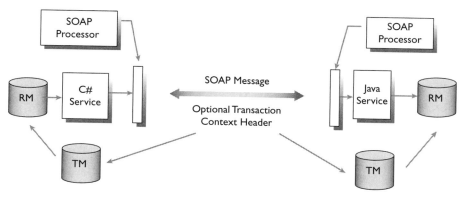

FIGURE 10.30

Web Services Interoperability. Two different execution environments can interoperate using SOAP, potentially including a transaction context.

WSDL interface from the remote service, perhaps using a registry, and marshals the C# data types into XSD data types using the message definition in the remote service's WSDL file. The caller uses the Web Services address, or obtains the address of the remote service from the WSDL file as well as the transport to be used, typically HTTP. The WSDL file may also include a WS-Policy assertion that requires a transaction context to invoke the remote service. In that case the WCF SOAP processor includes in the SOAP message header a transaction context conforming to the policy assertion.

When the remote Java service receives the request message, its SOAP processor unmarshals the XSD data types into Java data types (perhaps using the Java Architecture for XML Binding (JAXB)). The SOAP processor checks whether any SOAP headers need to be interpreted, such as a transactional context, and then uses the service name in the interface to dispatch the request to a local Java object for processing. When a transaction context header is received, the SOAP processor calls a transaction manager to enroll the local transaction in a transaction initiated by the service requester and propagated on the request. Results are returned in the response message, following this path in reverse. If an exception occurs, it is passed back to the calling service using a SOAP Fault message. The WS-Transactions standard defines how the transaction context is propagated and how the commitment protocol is executed.

The style of Web Services illustrated in this example focuses on their use within the .NET Framework and Java EE-based application server environment. However, SOA vendors also provide products that do not depend upon either of these transactional middleware systems. Instead, they use a **mediator** to process a SOAP message and submit requests to programs, queues, and databases. A mediator is software that sits between the service requester and the service provider. It is also typically responsible for processing any optional SOAP headers for security, reliability, or transactions.

Another popular application of Web Services is to encapsulate a series of fine-grained services inside a business process, exposed using a coarse-grained service. A coarse-grained service may not need the RPC-oriented mechanisms described in the previous example. Instead, an XML payload may be consumed directly. However, the message can still carry optional SOAP headers such as a WS-Security or WS-Transactions context.

The transaction context for the fine-grained services shown in Figure 10.31 executes within a business process and uses a compensation-based protocol such as WS-Transactions' WS-BA to undo the results of transactions executed within the steps of the business process. A compensation-based protocol can also be used for

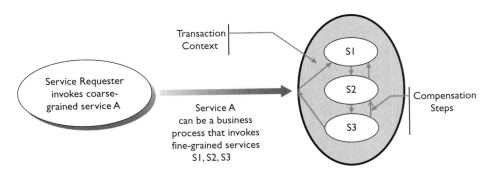

FIGURE 10.31

Encapsulating Fine-Grained Services in a Business Process. In an SOA environment, the service requester may invoke a coarse-grained service that encapsulates and invokes a series of fine-grained services within a compensation-based transaction context.

recovery from failures in interactions among coarse-grained services, especially those using asynchronous communication protocols.

REST/HTTP-Based SOA

In the REST/HTTP approach to SOA, interfaces such as WSDL are not used. Nor are message headers such as those defined for SOAP. Instead, HTTP headers are used and resource representations are exchanged and processed. Resource representations typically use XML or JavaScript Object Notation (JSON) formats. Information contained within the resources tells the client what it's allowed to do. The server accepts HTTP verb requests (GET, PUT, DELETE) or interprets information it receives from the client on a POST request. Therefore, typical RPC artifacts aren't necessary, such as an interface compiler, proxies and stubs, and marshaled parameters in the form of method arguments.

Instead, REST/HTTP assigns a URI to a resource and exchanges representations of the resource using HTTP verbs. For example, the resource could be a database and the exchanged representation could be an XML representation of rows retrieved from or to be stored in a database table.

Unlike Web Services, transaction propagation for REST/HTTP isn't defined. However, transactions can be supported by representing each transaction as a unique resource with which HTTP verbs interact. To start a transaction T, the server creates a resource R_T that represents the transaction. All of T's operations on (other) transactional resources R' (such as rows of database tables) are sent to R_T, so that it can keep track of before- and after-images of R'. T finishes by sending a commit or abort operation to R_T, which does the corresponding action and then deletes R_T.

The reason for representing the transaction as a resource is that REST/HTTP doesn't support shared session state. Since there is no session on which to propagate the transaction context, the resource is used to hold that context. Indeed, it holds the entire transaction state. The client maintains its application state and drives the state changes of the server resource that represents the transaction.

REST/HTTP is often a good choice for communication between companies, in which the cost of processing a self-describing XML message isn't justified due to the relatively small volume of such messages. The REST/HTTP approach is also simpler than the RPC style of interaction more commonly used with Web Services, and thus is easier to use. A multistep REST/HTTP-based exchange between two companies can use a compensation-based transaction protocol.

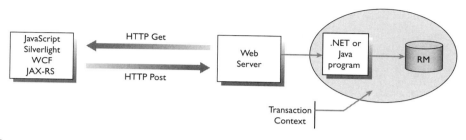

FIGURE 10.32

REST/HTTP Architecture for SOA. A program capable of using HTTP verbs constructs a document to exchange as a representation of a server-side resource. The service requester receives a hypermedia document representing a resource, which can direct the requester with URIs and forms to POST information back to the resource to effect changes.

Figure 10.32 illustrates clients that understand REST/HTTP, such as Silverlight, WCF, Java EE (through the JAX-RS API), and Java Script. These interact with the web server via HTTP verbs. The web server typically dispatches the document received via REST/HTTP to a program on the server side, such as a .NET Framework or Java EE object to interact with the resource, such as a database.

REST/HTTP architectures typically use reliable messaging to capture and process messages after they are received. Large web businesses also typically deploy redundant hardware and software systems to ensure reliable request capture and processing. For example, a REST/HTTP request message may be durably stored before sending it to the transaction server and processing it against the database. Reliable schemes also include the ability to detect and filter duplicate messages, or to design messages as idempotent.

An SOA project initially should define a blueprint or style of design before identifying a particular technology or how to apply it. The examples in this section illustrate some possible implementations, highlighting the relationship between transaction management and SOA designs using popular technologies. However, many more approaches are possible.

10.6 PERSISTENCE ABSTRACTION MECHANISMS

Much of the application code in a TP system makes direct use of database functionality. Some of this functionality is closely related to transactional middleware, namely, database sessions and stored procedures. Therefore, even though database APIs are beyond the scope of this book, this chapter on transactional middleware products and standards would be incomplete without some discussion of these closely-related topics.

Early database systems for enterprise computing executed in the same address space as the application and therefore could be invoked directly as a runtime library. With the advent of client-server architectures in the 1980s, these database systems were redesigned to execute in a separate process, that is, as a database server. This enables the database system to run on a separate machine from the applications that use the database. In this architecture, the application and database system need to communicate using messages. This communication requires that a fair bit of context is shared between the application and database system, such as the identity of the database that the application is using (since a database server may have access to multiple databases), the security credentials of the application for access control, and the transaction ID of the transaction that the application is currently executing. It would be expensive and cumbersome to pass this context information back and forth between the application and database system with every message. To avoid this, a session is needed to maintain the shared context between the application and database server.

A database session API has two main kinds of operations: operations to create, destroy, and update the session; and operations to send and receive database commands and data over the session. In addition, there are provider interfaces that enable vendors to plug in drivers that enable the session API to be used with different database server products.

When it became clear that the session API would be a part of every database application, various efforts were undertaken to standardize it, notably the SQL Access Group (originally an independent consortium whose activities were transferred to the Open Group). To make it easy for PCs to access database servers, Microsoft developed the Open Database Connectivity (ODBC) specification in conjunction with the SQL Access Group, publishing the first version in September 1992. The corresponding Java Database Connectivity (JDBC) standard for Java objects, modeled on ODBC, was first published in 1997.

Since then, there has been a steady stream of new APIs introduced, some of which include an ODBC or JDBC session. Many of the new APIs make it easier to access data from an object-oriented programming language and add support for a wider range of data types. Some also support access to other types of resources in addition to SQL databases. Examples include the Java Persistence API (JPA), OASIS Service Data Objects (SDO), Microsoft's OLE DB (Object Linking and Embedding, Database), and Microsoft's ActiveX Data Objects (ADO). There are also APIs that support more flexible mappings between the application's view of the database schema and the schema supported by the underlying database system, such as Red Hat's Hibernate, Oracle's TopLink, and Microsoft's ADO.NET Entity Framework and Language Integrated Query (LINQ).

These APIs can be used independently of, or in conjunction with, transactional middleware. In either case, their use has to be considered as part of a multitier TP architecture. The following sections briefly describe ODBC and JDBC and the use of stored procedures as transaction servers.

ODBC and JDBC

The architecture used for ODBC and JDBC defines a client-side driver for use by the application program. The client-side driver exposes a standard interface on top of the store-specific functions and protocols. These functions and protocols receive and execute application commands against the database on behalf of the client. The client and server usually run in different address spaces. The use of ODBC and JDBC drivers allows client-side SQL statements to be created dynamically and passed to the server for execution. ODBC can be used by a variety of programming languages. JDBC is intended for use by Java applications.

ODBC and JDBC provide a common architecture for accessing database products, ensuring some level of application portability and application interoperation with different database systems. ODBC clients and drivers ship with every version of the Windows operating system and most versions of Linux. ODBC and JDBC drivers are supported by most database products, including Microsoft SQL Server, IBM's DB2, Oracle Database, MySQL, and PostgreSQL. Bridges are also available to layer JDBC on ODBC and vice versa.

ODBC access starts by defining a data source, as follows:

```
DSN = mydsn;attribute1 = value;attribute2 = value;attributeN = value;
```

The data source definition includes a data source name (DSN) and attributes of the connection, such as security requirements, server address, and isolation level. JDBC uses a very similar format.

Given a data source definition, an application starts by opening a data source connection and then creates SQL statements to send to the connection. For example, a Java object using JDBC instantiates a driver manager object to connect to the database and execute SQL statements against it. Once ODBC or JDBC establishes a connection object to the database the application executes methods on the connection object.

For example, the code fragment in Figure 10.33 starts by instantiating a connection using the `DriverManager` object, thereby logging into the database. Then it instantiates a `Statement` object in the context of the connection and uses it to execute a SQL statement. The result of the query is assigned to a

```
Connection con = DriverManager.getConnection
        ("jdbc:myDriver:Wombat", "Login","Password");

Statement stmt = con.createStatement();
ResultSet rs = stmt.executeQuery("SELECT a, b, c FROM Table1");
while (rs.next()) {
        int x = rs.getInt("a");
        String s = rs.getString("b");
        float f = rs.getFloat("c");
        }
```

FIGURE 10.33

JDBC Connection and SQL Statement Execution. JDBC (and ODBC, not shown) establishes a connection by providing a login username and password and then sends SQL statements to the connection.

```
con.setAutoCommit(false);
PreparedStatement DepositAccount = con.prepareStatement(
    "UPDATE ACCOUNT SET Balance = Balance + ?");
DepositAccount.setInt(1, 100);
DepositAccount.executeUpdate();

PreparedStatement WithdrawAccount = con.prepareStatement(
    "UPDATE ACCOUNT SET Balance = Balance - ?");
WithdrawAccount.setInt(1, 100);
WithdrawAccount.executeUpdate();
con.commit();
```

FIGURE 10.34

Disabling Auto Commit for a JDBC Connection. When AutoCommit is disabled, it's possible to group multiple operations into the same transaction, such as these statements that execute withdrawal and deposit operations.

ResultSet object, which in general can contain many rows. The program executes a simple while loop to retrieve results from those rows.

ODBC and JDBC features include transaction control. An ODBC or JDBC connection is created in AutoCommit mode by default, meaning that each SQL statement automatically is committed after it is completed. Turning off AutoCommit allows two or more SQL statements to be grouped into the same transaction and committed using the commit() method on the connection object. Similarly, the rollback() method aborts all SQL statements that executed after the last commit() or rollback() on the connection object. JDBC and ODBC both support savepoints for partial rollback.

In Figure 10.34, AutoCommit mode is disabled for the connection, allowing the two statements, DepositAccount and WithdrawAccount, to commit their updates together when the commit() method is called. The question marks in the SQL statements act as a placeholder for the substituted amount, which in the example is simply hardcoded for convenience.

A popular function for an ODBC/JDBC driver is to execute a stored procedure, as in the following example.

```
CallableStatement proc = conn.prepareCall("{ ? = call TransferFunds(?, ?) }");
```

Executing the proc command in the client causes the driver program to request the execution of the TransferFunds stored procedure. The application program assigns values to the second and third question-mark parameters before executing the statement and gets the value of the first question mark parameter after the statement executes.

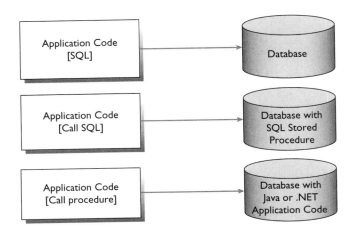

FIGURE 10.35

Options for Using a SQL in Application Code or as a Stored Procedure. Stored procedures offer an application the choice of executing SQL statements inside the database instead of in the application code, using a proprietary SQL stored procedure language, Java, or a .NET language.

Object-relational mapping solutions generate mappings from classes and their members to tables and columns of a relational database. For example, the Java Persistence API (JPA), which is part of Java EE, maps Java objects to rows in a relational database system. The ADO.NET Entity Framework provides similar functionality for the .NET Framework. Other APIs support data item mappings to other types of resource managers and allow multiple resource managers to be combined in a single program access.

Stored Procedures

Most relational database systems support stored procedures, which can be used to implement a transaction server. Stored procedures can be called directly from application code from any tier in a multitier TP architecture.

Database system products typically offer a stored procedure language derived from SQL. Often it's a proprietary one because the SQL/PSM standard is not widely implemented. The Oracle Database calls its stored procedure language PL/SQL, SQL Server calls it Transact-SQL, and IBM's DB2 calls it the SQL procedure language. Database systems typically also support stored procedures written using standard programming languages such as Java or a CLR-based language from the .NET Framework, such as C#.

As with proprietary language stored procedures, the rules vary by product as to how much of the Java and .NET languages are supported, and how to deploy Java or .NET classes into the database. For example, in Oracle Java methods must be public and static. The LoadJava command is used to prepare a Java class for loading. Rules for deploying Java in DB2 include "fencing" the Java code (i.e., restricting its capabilities), configuring it, and determining the argument types to be supported. For example, no user-defined signal handlers are permitted in DB2.

The inclusion of Java and CLR-based language procedures in the database provides the ability to run all or part of the transaction server code within the database process. This gives developers the flexibility to write transaction server code before deciding how much of it to run as stored procedures and how much to deploy in another address space, whether on the same machine or on a remote machine (see Figure 10.35). Parts of the

```
CREATE PROCEDURE Transfer (@fromAccount int, @toAccount int, @amount int)
BEGIN TRAN
   UPDATE Account SET Balance = Balance - @amount WHERE AccountID = @fromAccount
   UPDATE Account SET Balance = Balance + @amount WHERE AccountID = @toAccount
COMMIT TRAN
END
```

FIGURE 10.36

Transact-SQL Stored Procedure for Transfer Operation. Execution of the stored procedure, whether directly from within object code or using an ODBC or JDBC connection, results in the transfer of the given amount from one of the customer's accounts to the other.

application that frequently invoke SQL statements should execute in a stored procedure, to minimize context switching overhead. Parts of the application that are processor-intensive and make infrequent calls to SQL should execute outside the stored procedure, so they can run on a different machine and not limit the scalability of the database server, which is often a bottleneck.

SQL Server Stored Procedure Examples

We show some examples of stored procedures using Microsoft SQL Server. Stored procedures in other database products work similarly. The example in Figure 10.36 illustrates the native SQL Server stored procedure language, Transact-SQL. This could be accessed from a web server or application process using an ODBC connection by executing the @Transfer command. In SQL Server, the stored procedure can also be invoked using a Web Service. The procedure allocates variables using the @-sign prefix and executes SQL statements such as SELECT and SET. A stored procedure is created using the database CREATE command and can accept input arguments and return output arguments.

Figure 10.37 illustrates the use of SQL commands in a stored procedure written in C#. The stored procedure needs to include the partial class StoredProcedures and manages the connection to SQL server as it would in a WCF service. In either case, transaction control can group multiple operations on data. Transaction bracketing operations are the same for proprietary SQL and CLR-based or Java-based stored procedures. However, nested transactions and savepoints are supported only by proprietary SQL stored procedures.

Using the .NET Framework's ambient transaction feature, it's possible to delegate transaction control from the middleware to the stored procedure, and to include multiple resource managers in the same transaction, whether control is defined in the middleware or the stored procedure.

Java Persistence API

The Java Persistence API (JPA) defines a standard for object-relational mapping between Java objects and relational databases. JPA can be used independently from an EJB in a plain Java object and also can be used within a stateless or stateful session bean. JPA was developed as part of the EJB3 specification as a replacement for EJB2 entity beans, which were used in EJB2's container-managed persistence and bean-managed persistence object-relational mappings. EJB2 entity beans continue to be supported in EJB3 for backward compatibility.

The JPA specification is intended to unify multiple object-relational mechanisms for Java, such as JDO, Hibernate, and entity beans. In doing so JPA abandoned the heavyweight EJB2 persistence model that integrated container-managed transactions, security, and concurrency within a single entity bean. JPA is based on the lightweight persistent model made popular by products such as Red Hat's Hibernate and Oracle's TopLink.

```
using System;
using System.Data;
using System.Data.Sql;
using System.Data.SqlTypes;
using Microsoft.SqlServer.Server;

public partial class StoredProcedures
{
    [Microsoft.SqlServer.Server.SqlProcedure]
    public static void Transfer()
    {
        SqlConnection conn = new SqlConnection();
        conn.ConnectionString = "Context Connection=true";

        SqlCommand cmd = new SqlCommand();
        cmd.Connection = conn;
        cmd.CommandText = @"SELECT ToAccount, [Number]
                            FROM Account ;"

        conn.Open();

        SqlDataReader rdr = cmd.ExecuteReader();
        SqlContext.Pipe.Send(rdr);

        rdr.Close();
        conn.Close();
    }
};
```

FIGURE 10.37

Stored Procedure Written in C#. This stored procedure retrieves all matching account numbers.

JPA uses Java 5 annotations and XML descriptors to map the data items and attributes of a Java class to relational database tables. JPA also includes a runtime EntityManager API for processing queries and updates against the objects mapped to the database, using an object-level query language called Java Persistence Query Language (JPQL).

Each JPA entity maps to a particular row in one or more tables and is uniquely identified by one or more fields or properties that comprise an identifier. The identifier of each entity is unique within the scope of an inheritance hierarchy for that entity. It can be used both by clients for querying and by the implementation for maintaining instance identity throughout the transactional or persistence context.

An implementation of JPA is called a **JPA provider**. Examples of JPA providers include Oracle's Kodo, Red Hat's Hibernate, the Eclipse Foundation's EclipseLink, and Apache OpenJPA. The JPA specification also defines a service provider interface that describes how an EJB container hosts a JPA entity, using such mechanisms as EntityManager injection, propagation of persistence contexts, and Java classloading. Through these mechanisms, any EJB3-compliant application server can plug in any JPA provider and run it within the host container. The Spring Framework's container is also capable of hosting a JPA provider.

JPA can be used outside of an EJB in a plain Java environment. In plain Java, the EntityManager API is used directly to initiate and terminate transactions, which are always local to the EntityManager that created them (see Figure 10.38). JPA transactions in a plain Java environment are simple JDBC-level single-RM transactions.

```
EntityManager em = emf.getEntityManager();
EntityTransaction tx = em.getTransaction();
try
{
    tx.begin();
      {user code to persist objects}
    tx.commit();
}
done
{
    if (tx.isActive())
    {
        tx.rollback();
    }
}
em.close();
```

FIGURE 10.38

JPA Uses Locally Managed Transactions in Plain Java. An `EntityManager` API transaction is associated with a local JDBC transaction when used outside of an EJB.

```
@Stateless
@TransactionManagement(TransactionManagementType.BEAN)
public class TransferBean implements Transfer {
    @PersistenceContext EntityManager em;
    @Resource UserTransaction tx;

    public boolean transfer(int sourceAcct, int destAcct, int amount) {
        Account src = em.find(Account.class, sourceAcct);
        Account dest = em.find(Account.class, destAcct);
        if (src == null || dest == null) return false;
        try {
            tx.begin();
            src.setBalance(src.getBalance() - amt);
            dest.setBalance(dest.getBalance() + amt);
            tx.commit();
        } catch  (Exception ex) {
            try { tx.rollback(); } catch (Exception e) {}
            return false;
        }
        return true;
    }
}
```

FIGURE 10.39

JPA Transactions Enlist with a JTA Managed Transaction When Used within an EJB. The example illustrates a bean-managed transaction using JPA with JTA to update two account records.

When running in an EJB the `EntityManager` transaction joins the global transaction managed by JTA (see Figure 10.39). Updates to JPA entities can then be coordinated with updates to any other transactional resources enlisted in the same transaction for the EJB.

A JPA entity can be used in any stateful or stateless session bean with either the implicit or explicit programming models.

ADO.NET and the ADO.NET Entity Framework

ADO.NET provides a consistent abstraction for .NET programs to access data resources, such as SQL Server databases, XML files, and other resources accessible through OLE DB or ODBC. It offers generic classes for accessing the data, such as `DataTableCollection` to access the tables in a database and `DataTable` to access the schema and rows of a table. A client program can directly retrieve data, update data, or run a stored procedure. A client can also retrieve data into a `DataSet` object, which is an in-memory relational database. Data that is modified in the `DataSet` object can optionally be transferred back to the data source.

ADO.NET connects to a resource manager through an adaptor called a **data provider**. There are built-in data providers for SQL Server, Oracle, OLE DB, and ODBC. Various database vendors also offer ADO.NET data providers.

In addition to ADO.NET, there is a newer data-access API called the ADO.NET Entity Framework, which offers access to data expressed in a new data model called the **entity data model (EDM)**. EDM is based on the extended entity-relationship model commonly used for database design. It has constructs for inheritance, associations (i.e., relationships), and complex types. The Entity Framework simplifies programmatic access to relational data by mapping a conceptual schema expressed in EDM into an underlying relational database, which is connected to the Entity Framework using an ADO.NET data provider.

The Entity Framework differs from an object-relational mapping because an EDM schema represents an abstract definition of data separate from either the programming object or the relational database. Relationships among entities are explicitly defined within the model, eliminating the need to join relational tables using foreign keys. Multiple different EDM schemas can be mapped to the same physical database.

The Entity Framework offers four ways to access data. First, data can be accessed as entities using Entity SQL, which is an extension of SQL that can manipulate data that conforms to an EDM schema. This enables access using standard database interfaces, such as query builders and report writers. Second, the Entity Framework can generate an object-oriented interface that corresponds to the EDM schema. This provides strongly-typed read and write access through object-oriented programming languages, such as C# and VB. Third, queries against this object-oriented representation can be expressed in the language-integrated query (LINQ) mechanism of the .NET Framework. LINQ enables compile-time checking of queries against the schema. Finally, data can be represented as web resources that are addressed by URIs and accessed using HTTP commands.

For example, consider an EDM schema `BankDB` that has two entity sets, `Customers` and `Accounts`, and a relationship between them called `CustomerAccounts`. The entity type `Accounts` has a role `Customer` that relates each account to the customer that owns it. Figure 10.40 illustrates an Entity SQL statement that finds the balance for a given customer account. In this case, `acct.Customer.CustomerName` navigates the relationship between the `Customers` and `Accounts` sets to retrieve the `CustomerName` from the appropriate entity.

```
SELECT acct.Customer.CustomerName, acct.Balance
FROM BankDB.Accounts AS acct
WHERE acct.AccountNumber = @acctNum
```

FIGURE 10.40

Entity SQL Example. The Entity Framework's Entity SQL is similar to SQL but abstracts data access mechanics to use a mapping layer called an entity provider.

ADO.NET Data Services offers REST-style access to EDM data, returning data in the format of ATOM/XML or JSON. ADO.NET Data Services are implemented using a specialized version of a WCF service to which instructions are sent via URL parameters. For example, the following URI accesses `Customers` of `BankDB`:

`http://www.BankDB.com/transfer.svc/Customers`

If customer number is the key of Customers, then a query to return CustomerName of customer number 345 could be expressed like this:

```
http://www.BankDB.com/transfer.svc/Customers(345)/CustomerName
```

An EDM schema is defined in a separate schema file, expressed as an XML document. A mapping from a conceptual EDM schema into a relational database schema is expressed in a similar format. These files can be generated by a graphical schema and mapping editor or created manually. The mapping is compiled into an internal form that the runtime layer uses to translate operations on the conceptual schema into operations on the relational database.

If an application accesses an EDM database as a set of objects, then the Entity Framework generates a class for the EDM database derived from the class ObjectContext. This class includes a connection to the database, metadata that describes the EDM schema, and the state of objects in the client cache. It tracks each object handed out through a query, notes any objects that change, and generates the required statements for implicitly updating the objects when they are returned to the entity provider. The Entity Framework uses a form of optimistic concurrency control in which the user optionally specifies a subset of properties to be used to track changes (for example, a timestamp or version property), along with the identity properties of any entities to be updated. During update operations, if the values on the server no longer match the values obtained by the original query, the update fails and the framework throws an exception. The application then decides whether to refresh the client objects with the values on the server or commit the changes made on the client. An application can explicitly issue an update using the SaveChanges() command. Figure 10.41 shows an example of a transaction that updates two accounts, very similar to the JPA example in Figure 10.39.

```
public class TransferClass implements Transfer {
  public bool transfer(int sourceAcct, int destAcct, int amount) {
    // Connection string for BankDB is specified in a configuration file
    BankDB db = new BankDB();
    var src = from a in db.Accounts
              where a.AccountNumber = sourceAcct
              select a;
    var dest = from a in db.Accounts
               where a.AccountNumber = destAcct
               select a;
    try {
      src.FirstOrDefault().Balance = src.FirstOrDefault().Balance - amt);
      dest.FirstOrDefault().Balance = dest.FirstOrDefault().Balance + amt);
      db.SaveChanges();
    } catch  (OptimisticConcurrencyException) {
      try {
        db.Refresh(src, RefreshMode.StoreWins);
        db.Refresh(dest, RefreshMode.StoreWins); }
      catch (Exception) {}
      return false;
    } catch  (NullReferenceException) {
      return false;
    }
    return true;
  }
}
```

FIGURE 10.41

A Transaction in the ADO.NET Entity Framework. This example illustrates a transaction that updates two accounts. The queries assigned to src and dest are expressed in LINQ.

10.7 LEGACY TP MONITORS

Transactional middleware products began with the development and deployment of dedicated hardware and software systems, designed specifically for use in processing transactions. The first such system, called SABRE, was developed by IBM and American Airlines in the late 1950s and early 1960s as an automated way of reserving seats on airplanes. Later it was adapted for use by other airlines. The operating system layer became an IBM product called ACP (Airline Control Program) with PARS (Programmed Airline Reservation System) as one of the applications. An offshoot named PARS-Financial was used in the finance industry. The product introduced many useful innovations, such as system performance modeling prior to system construction, replicated writes, fast restart (at most 5 seconds), intelligent terminal controller, client failover, and workload migration. However, in one respect, it was quite bare-bones by today's standards: ACID transaction semantics was implemented by the application. Many years later, acknowledging its use outside the airline industry, IBM renamed it TPF (Transaction Processing Facility). TPF is still used for airline reservations some 40 years later, and by several financial institutions, for example to process credit card payments.

In the late 1960s, IBM released two TP monitor products with much more functionality, IMS (Information Management System) and CICS (Customer Information Control System). CICS was developed before IMS, by IBM's field engineering group, initially for one specific customer, but was not released as a product until after IMS. All of these TP monitors were designed for the mainframe environment and typically were used on machines dedicated to a single application.

During the minicomputer area, roughly from 1980 to 2000, a new generation of distributed TP monitors emerged. Operating systems for these machines were designed to work well with many more processes than mainframe systems. So these TP monitors make heavier use of processes, which enable them to scale up an application by moving processes onto more machines. This is in contrast to earlier mainframe TP monitors, where scaling up usually involves buying a larger mainframe machine.

Legacy TP monitors typically include a lot of product-specific components. They are part of the TP monitor because they're essential for the construction and deployment of TP applications but were not part of the underlying platform at the time the TP monitor product was developed. Examples include specialized resource managers such as database management systems, indexed files, and queues; specialized presentation technology for vendor-specific terminals; program development tools; and system management environments. Today, many of these components are available as general-purpose technology, such as general-purpose system management tools, display devices, and database systems.

Many applications still exist that are based on legacy TP monitors, because the applications work well and the cost of rewriting the application exceeds the expected savings in moving to commodity technologies. This section describes some of these products—ones that you may still encounter, for example in the context of a legacy modernization, interoperability, or SOA project.

One challenge with modernization, interoperability, and SOA projects is finding a good point of entry for an external call into the legacy application. Many older applications are not very modular, due to poor initial design, tight integration of components to meet stringent performance requirements, or many changes made to the application over the years. Sometimes this means that the applications themselves have to be modified to complete the project, and it can be difficult finding programmers who are qualified to work in the legacy computing environment.

The legacy TP monitors described in this section all are popular enough that interfaces to modern TP environments have been built for them, such as Web Services wrappers, Java EE connectors, CORBA interfaces, and message queue adapters. In some cases capabilities such as these have been added directly into the legacy TP monitors themselves. And as we have already seen, both the .NET Framework and Java EE transactional middleware environments include capabilities specifically designed for integration with these (and other) legacy environments.

CICS Transaction Server

CICS is IBM's most popular legacy TP monitor. It pioneered many of the technologies and approaches found in modern transactional middleware products, including two-phase commit and transactional RPC.

Developed in 1968 to improve the efficiency of mainframe operating system environments, CICS is now a family of products running on the VSE and z/OS operating systems. A version of the CICS product called TX Series runs on the UNIX and Windows operating systems. Although there is some variation of features between the different implementations, the products all support essentially the same "command level" API.

Commands are embedded using the prefix EXEC CICS in any of the supported languages: COBOL, PL/I, Assembler, C/C++, and Java. The commands are translated by a precompiler into CICS function calls to carry out the requested operations. For example, the following are commands to send a form to a terminal, receive a form from a terminal, and link to another CICS program:

```
EXEC CICS SEND...
EXEC CICS RECEIVE...
EXEC CICS LINK...
```

IBM and various third-party vendors offer toolkits for enabling Web Service access of CICS applications, allowing them to participate in SOA-based applications. These convert existing COBOL data types to XML and generate SOAP messages and WSDL interfaces from the COBOL metadata (often called the Copy Book or **COMMAREA**). CICS supports HTTP as a transport, which allows SOAP and plain XML messages to be exchanged with CICS transactions.

Other approaches to legacy integration employ an intermediate node, such as a UNIX or Windows system running the TX Series version of CICS. The intermediate node runs Web Services or other formats and protocols, which are converted into legacy formats and protocols. Deploying the integration solution on an intermediate machine can avoid having to modify the mainframe CICS application or install additional integration software on the mainframe.

Most CICS remote communication today uses TCP/IP and HTTP. LU6.2 gateways are still in use but IIOP, RMI, and WebSphere MQ protocols are more typical. IBM also has ported WebSphere Application Server to the mainframe, which can invoke EJB Session Beans hosted in CICS.

System Architecture

CICS offers a process-like abstraction called a **region**. A region is an address space that can execute multiple threads. CICS implements its own middleware-level threading abstraction (see Section 2.3). A region can own resources, such as terminals, programs, communications, and databases. The failure of an application is scoped to a region; that is, when a failure occurs, it affects only the region. The unit of distribution likewise is a region.

Each CICS resource type is described by a table, whose entries list resources of that type (see Figure 10.42). In early mainframe versions of CICS, it was common practice to have all resources of a TP application be owned by a single region. Early communications mechanisms were limited and had high overhead, so this was the most efficient structure. It amounts to running all tiers of a TP application in a single process. Today, communications capabilities are much improved, so the recommended practice is to partition an application into three regions that correspond roughly to the multitier transactional middleware model: a terminal region (the front-end program), an application region (request controller), and a data region (transaction server).

A CICS region can communicate with another region and with an external application using a dynamic program link (DPL), an RPC-style mechanism specific to CICS. Inter-region communication points offer good opportunities for integration with applications based on other technologies, including through an external client.

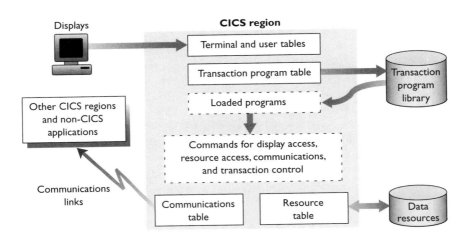

FIGURE 10.42

A CICS Region. A region provides multithreading and controls application resources, including devices, transaction programs, data resources, and communications links.

In a terminal region, the terminal table identifies the terminals attached to the region. When a user logs in, the user is authenticated via a password; later accesses to data resources are controlled via an access control list external to CICS. The region can support geographical entitlement by optionally checking that the user is authorized to operate from the given terminal within a given time period and to fulfill a given role (such as the master terminal operator).

"Transaction" is the CICS term for a request. Each request entered by a user includes a four-character transaction code. Using the region's transaction table, the request can be sent to a region that can process it. In CICS, this is called **transaction routing**. In our model, it corresponds to using a request controller to route a request from a front-end program to a transaction server.

Requests that arrive at a region are classified based on request type, user, and terminal ID. Once the request is scheduled, the program table checks whether or not this request type can be processed locally, and whether the user and terminal are authorized to run this request. It then loads the application program if it's not already loaded. (Multiple users can share the same copy of a transaction program.) Then CICS creates a **task**, which is the execution of a transaction program for a given user and request, assigns it an execution thread, and automatically starts a transaction using the chained transaction model. Each execution thread is reclaimed for use by another program when the reply message is sent.

Front-End Program

Before the widespread adoption of PCs, most CICS systems were accessed by IBM 3270 block-mode terminals, which send and receive a screen of data at a time. This is still a popular mode of access, sometimes with 3270 emulation software running on the PC or other displays that conform to the 3270's data stream communications protocol. Thus, one way for an external system to communicate with a CICS application is to emulate a 3270 terminal and communicate using the 3270 protocol. A function called the external programming interface (EPI) provides this support. EPI is also used to connect a variety of external clients.

CICS has a built-in forms manager, called Basic Mapping Services (BMS), which maps between a device-oriented view of the data and program-oriented data structures. BMS can be used to interact with 3270 terminals and

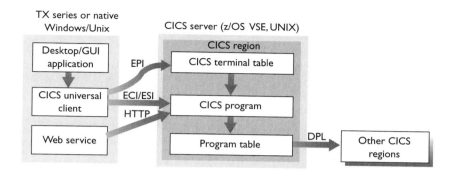

FIGURE 10.43

Communications from CICS Clients and External Interfaces. CICS provides multiple communications options for distributed processing and interoperability with external platforms, including the integration of browsers, PCs, and UNIX Servers.

other types of devices. Typical Web Service enablement and other interoperability tools support COMMAREA direct calls (DPL style), 3270 emulation, and BMS emulation.

TP Communications

CICS offers applications a variety of ways to call remote programs. We have already encountered EPI. Some others are:

- Distributed Program Link (DPL), which is a programming model similar to a remote procedure call. DPL is synchronous, that is, the application waits for the results (see Figure 10.43).

- Multiregion Operation (MRO) and Inter-Systems Communication (ISC), which are available on CICS VSE and zOS, are transport mechanisms that enable communications between regions running on the same mainframe (i.e., transaction routing and DPL can be implemented using MRO or ISC).

- Distributed Transaction Processing (DTP), which is the interface to a peer-to-peer communications transport. It uses the LU6.2 protocol, which is a session-based protocol that associates a transaction with each session using the chained transaction model. It propagates transaction context across send-message operations and includes a two-phase commit protocol. LU6.2 is part of IBM's proprietary network architecture called SNA (System Network Architecture).

The COMMAREA is the standard place in main memory to put information to pass via inter-region communications facilities such as DPL. Web Services toolkits for CICS also use the COMMAREA to obtain message definitions. COMMAREA data types typically are converted to XML data types for use in Web Services.

The CICS Universal Client product from IBM includes programming libraries for Visual Basic, C/C++, and COBOL, and supports both TCP/IP and SNA-based communication protocols.

Database Access

CICS initially was implemented on mainframe operating systems that did not support efficient multithreading. Thus, multithreading was implemented by CICS. Recall from Section 2.3 that such an implementation must not allow application programs to issue blocking operations, since they would delay all the threads in the process. Therefore, applications issued all of their database operations to CICS, which could thereby switch threads if a database operation would ordinarily cause the process to be blocked.

Early versions of CICS did most of their database processing through COBOL indexed files, accessing the VSAM (Virtual Sequential Access Method) file store. CICS and VSAM include services for buffer management, block management, indexed access, and optional logging for rollback. CICS was among the first TP systems to offer remote data access, using a facility called **function shipping**, which allows an application to access a remote VSAM file.

Later, support was added for IMS databases via the DL/I interface and, more recently, for relational databases including IBM's DB2 family via the SQL interface. Implementations of all continue to be found in production.

IMS

IMS (Information Management System) is another popular TP monitor product from IBM. IMS was designed with Rockwell and Caterpillar for the Apollo space program. IMS's challenge was to inventory the very large bill-of-materials for the Saturn V moon rocket and Apollo space vehicle. Thus, its design originally centered around its powerful hierarchical database.

IMS was released in 1968 for IBM mainframes. It was among the first products to offer online database and transaction processing at a time when nearly all data processing was done in batch. IMS runs in both online and batch modes, allowing the incremental conversion of an application from batch to online. Like many TP applications, most IMS applications still contain a large portion of batch programming.

IMS consists of both a TP monitor called IMS Transaction Manager (TM) and a hierarchical-style database system called IMS Database Manager (DB). The TP monitor and database systems are independent and can be configured separately, which allows considerable flexibility. For example, the IMS DB can be used with the CICS TP monitor, or IMS TM can be used with DB2, IBM's relational database product. Multiple IMS systems can be configured for distributed processing environments and as standby systems for high availability. In addition, IMS supports multiple optimizations for fast performance.

IMS TM is among the first queued messaging systems dedicated to TP. Like CICS, IMS TM can be accessed from devices, PCs, and UNIX systems outside the mainframe environment. It has specific external access points for XML, Web Services, Java EE, and BPEL. A variety of third-party products provide support for Web Service enablement and interoperability with IMS, such as Orbix, WebSphere MQ, and WebSphere Application Server. IMS DB includes support for XML data mapping, JDBC drivers, and XML Query.

Basic System Architecture

Applications run in a **system**, which contains the application program itself and the facilities required to support the application. In contrast to CICS, which manages its own address space, an IMS application runs in an operating system process and accesses TP monitor services such as threading, dispatching, and program loading through a call interface to a system library (instead of using an embedded command style language). An example appears in Figure 10.44. Multiple applications can run in separate processes to take advantage of zSeries symmetric multiprocessing.

The basic IMS TM model is queued. An end user inputs some data on a device (see Figure 10.45). IMS extracts the data, adds a transaction ID, formats the input into a request message, and enqueues it on the input queue. IMS then loads the program associated with the transaction, if it is not already running. Then IMS dequeues the input message (starting the transaction), translates the transaction ID into the transaction program name, and routes the message to the application, which executes the transaction program using the input data. Dequeuing a message starts a transaction. When the transaction program completes, the application enqueues

```
PROCEDURE DIVISION.

ENTRY-LINKAGE.
     ENTRY 'DLITCBL' USING I-O-PCB DB-PCB.

MAIN PROGRAM.
     PERFORM GET-MSG-ROUTINE THRU GET-MESSAGE-ROUTINE-EXIT
                   UNITL I-O-STATUS-CODE EQUAL NO-MORE-MESSAGES.
     GO BACK
```

FIGURE 10.44

IMS COBOL Example. The PROCEDURE DIVISION starts with a loop that executes until no more messages are found on the queue. The first time a request is issued for this program, IMS loads it and keeps it loaded until all requests for the program are completed.

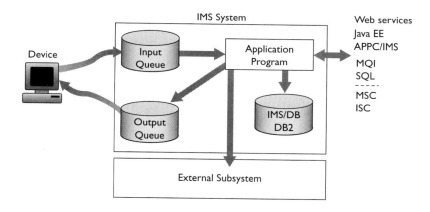

FIGURE 10.45

Basic IMS System Architecture. Request and reply messages move between a device and an application via queues. Various gateways connect IMS to external communications systems and resource managers.

a reply message to the output queue associated with the input device or program. There are options to enqueue the reply message to a different device, another application, or a specific user, instead of or in addition to the input device.

IMS TM also offers an optimization called Fast Path, which essentially allows the application to bypass the queuing system (i.e., request controller) and send simple request messages directly from the device to the transaction program, using a predefined mapping that is kept resident in main memory. Requests identify the fast path transaction programs, which are preloaded and ready to process the requests. The fast path can also use a special main memory database, with advanced concurrency control features, as described in Section 6.5 on Hot Spot locking.

An interface called the Open Transaction Manager Access (OTMA), allows multiple communications managers to connect to IMS. Using OTMA, IMS receives transaction requests from any source on the network and routes responses back.

Security options include device security (which controls the entry of IMS commands), password security, and access control on transactions, commands, control regions, and application programs.

Front-End Program

IMS TM includes a built-in forms manager, called Message Format Service (MFS), and an optional Screen Definition Facility (SDF) that defines and formats IBM 3270 terminal screens and collects the input data and transaction ID for the request message.

TP Communications

IMS TM is based on a queued TP model, rather than a direct TP model such as RPC. This has enhanced recovery compared to most TP monitors, at the cost of extra transactions and I/O, as described in Chapter 4.

Applications access the input and output queues using calls to retrieve input messages, to return output messages to the sending device, and to send output messages to other application programs and devices. MFS assists in translating messages between device format (originally the terminal format) and the application program format.

Extensions to IMS allow it to accept a remote call from a PC or workstation, access an IMS database via SQL, use APPC for LU6.2 conversational communications with CICS, access the message queue interface (MQI) to interoperate with WebSphere MQ, and accept calls from a CORBA wrapper, EJB, or Web Service. IMS also supports TCP/IP sockets for LU6.2-style conversations. And IMS supports IBM's Intersystem Communication (ISC), which allows communication among multiple IMS systems or between an IMS system and a CICS region; and Multiple Systems Coupling (MSC), which allows communication among multiple IMS systems.

Database Access

The native database system that comes with IMS is based on a hierarchical model, which preceded the development of relational database systems. The higher performance of the hierarchical model is one of the reasons IMS-based applications are still in production. Today's IMS applications can also use DB2, in addition to or in place of the IMS DB database. The database access runs using the application's thread. A data propagation utility is available that moves data updates from IMS DB to DB2, or vice versa, automatically. Java library support allows IMS DB to invoke stored procedures hosted in DB2. Other tools allow data to be moved between IMS and non-IBM relational databases.

Tuxedo

Tuxedo is a legacy TP monitor from Oracle. Tuxedo runs on a variety of UNIX and Windows platforms. Oracle owns the rights for Tuxedo, as do a few resellers who customize the product for their own platforms (e.g., UNISYS and Bull). AT&T's Bell Laboratories created Tuxedo in 1984, primarily to service telecommunication applications, which remains its largest market. The Tuxedo design is based on IMS, and originally was intended to replace IMS at the US telephone companies (who are large IMS users).

Tuxedo supports several options for interoperability with external systems, including Java EE, Web Services, and CORBA.

Tuxedo was the basis for many of the X/Open DTP standards, including the DTP model itself, XA, TX, and XATMI. Tuxedo also implements OTS via its CORBA API.

System Architecture

Tuxedo provides two main APIs. One is called the **Application Transaction Monitor Interface (ATMI)**, which is a collection of runtime services that are called directly by a C, C++, or COBOL application. The other is the CORBA C++ API. Tuxedo runtime services provide support for communications, distributed transactions, and system management. In contrast to the full-featured CICS API, ATMI relies heavily on UNIX system libraries and external database system services for filling some TP application requirements.

The ATMI function `tpcall()` invokes a Tuxedo service. A typical `tpcall` is shown in the following example:

```
tpcall( "TRANS", (char *)reqfb, 0, (char **)&reqfb, (long *)&reqlen, );
```

Tuxedo services can be developed using C, C++, or COBOL. Native Tuxedo API clients can be developed using C, C++, COBOL, and Java. Tuxedo services can be written using Java when they are hosted on the Oracle WebLogic Server using its domain gateway feature. And CORBA-compliant Tuxedo API clients and servers can be developed using C++.

Tuxedo's services are implemented using a shared memory area called the **bulletin board**, which contains configuration information (similar to CICS tables) that supports many TP monitor functions (see Figure 10.46). For example, it contains transaction service names, a mapping of transaction service names to transaction server addresses, parameter-based routing information, and configuration options for transaction services and servers.

In a distributed environment, one system at a time is designated as having the master bulletin board. The bulletin board at each node is loaded into shared memory from a configuration file when Tuxedo boots. Changes to the master bulletin board are written to the configuration file, which is propagated at boot time if it has changed since the last boot. The master copy of the bulletin board is propagated at the boot of a new machine. Other nodes reload the file to see the updated state. Servers and services can be added, modified, or removed dynamically.

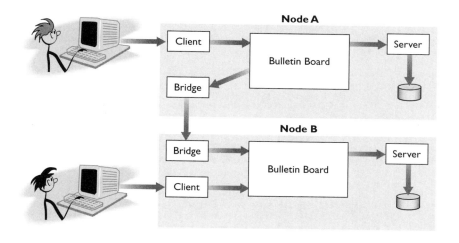

FIGURE 10.46

Tuxedo Client/Server Architecture. Requests are routed to the correct server process using the bulletin board, whether on a local or remote node.

A Tuxedo system consists of client and server processes. Clients typically provide presentation services to users. That is, they interact with devices that issue requests and do not access transactional resource managers. Unlike CICS and IMS, a Tuxedo client is allowed to issue a Start operation, which may optionally be forwarded to the server (request controller or transaction server) to actually start the transaction.

Tuxedo systems are configured in a **domain**, which defines the scope of computers in the network that participate in a given application. The domain concept essentially represents an administrative boundary around participating client and server processes in a network and represents the scope of shared access to bulletin board metadata. A domain also can be federated with other domains to increase the scalability of large Tuxedo installations.

Although the bulletin board typically is used for the request controller, a Tuxedo server can perform the functions of request controller, transaction server, or both. This flexibility allows an application to be structured into a multitier architecture, but doesn't require it.

In Tuxedo, a **service** is the name of a server interface. When a client calls a service, the bulletin board forwards the call to a server that supports the service, similar to how IMS routes a queued message to a transaction program. The server might be on a different node than the client, in which case the bulletin board routes the request via a bridge to the other node. When a service becomes available, the server advertises the service by posting the service name to the bulletin board. Each server process has a main memory queue that is used for incoming messages (see Figure 10.47). A call to a service causes a message to be put into its queue. As in IMS, the server dequeues messages sent by the client and does the requested work, optionally in priority order. When it's done, the server sends a reply message to a message queue associated with the client, which includes a status that tells whether the call completed successfully or resulted in an error. The client dequeues the message and processes the reply.

The Tuxedo API offers programmers explicit transaction control primitives—for example, `tpbegin`, `tpcommit`, and `tpabort`.

Flags can be set in the client program and in the configuration file to place the execution of transaction programs in automatic, or implicit, transaction mode. In implicit transaction mode, a transaction is started automatically when the transaction program receives control from the front-end program (or client program, in Tuxedo terminology), and is automatically committed if the execution of the server program is successful.

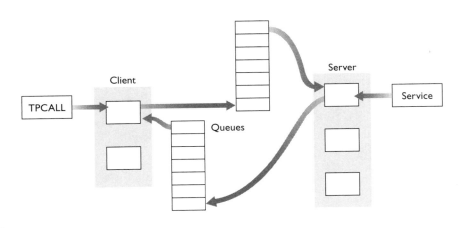

FIGURE 10.47

Tuxedo Request Message Flow. Requests are routed between client and server processes using input and output queues.

If the client program starts a transaction, automatic transaction mode detects the existing transaction and includes the called transaction program in the same transaction. An execution error (that is, a return of bad status) results in an automatic transaction abort. This is similar to the way CICS handles transactions for DPL-invoked programs.

An explicit programming model option is asynchronous commit processing, where an application can continue without waiting for the second phase to complete in a two-phase commit operation.

Error handling is at the application level. The program examines a global variable to get an error message, and checks this error status after every call, as in IMS programming.

Front-End Program

Some legacy applications still use Tuxedo's Data Entry System forms package, originally designed for use on character cell terminals. The input on such a form contains the desired transaction type's service name and a typed buffer that contains the input data. It also includes flags that select various options, such as automatically starting a transaction for the server being called and automatically retrying after an operating system interrupt signal.

Native communication messages are constructed using Tuxedo's Field Manipulation Language (FML). This creates typed buffers, which are similar to the CICS COMMAREA.

Tuxedo offers several options for external client access, including the /WS package for UNIX and PC clients, web browser and Web Services clients, CORBA clients, and a Java client for use with Oracle's WebLogic application server. Tuxedo also supports interoperability with JMS-based message queues.

TP Communications

Processes using the ATMI protocol can communicate using a choice of peer-to-peer message passing, remote procedure calls, or an event posting mechanism. An RPC can be synchronous (i.e., the application waits for the results) or asynchronous (i.e., the application asks sometime later for the results). Using peer-to-peer message passing, the programmer can establish a conversational session between the front-end program and the transaction server and exchange messages in an application-defined order, rather than in the strict request-reply style of RPC. A subscription service puts events on the bulletin board, and an event posting mechanism allows a server to raise an event, which sends an unsolicited message to one or more clients (in the case of multiple clients this represents a type of broadcast facility).

Servers developed using the CORBA API can communicate using the RMI/IIOP protocol. Tuxedo servers can interact bidirectionally with an HTTP Web Service through Tuxedo's SALT (Services Architecture Leveraging Tuxedo) gateway. Tuxedo also includes a variety of mainframe connectivity options, including TCP/IP, SNA, and OSI TP-based protocols with specific support for invoking CICS and IMS transactions.

When a server calls another server, the caller can specify whether the callee runs in the same transaction or outside of the transaction context.

Database Access

TUXEDO has a built-in transaction manager that supports two-phase commit. It can use any XA-compliant resource manager, such as Oracle, Sybase, DB2, or SQL Server.

ACMS

ACMS (Application Control and Management System) is a legacy TP monitor from HP. ACMS was developed by Digital Equipment Corporation in the early 1980s as part of an effort to gain market share in commercial applications. (Digital's initial strength was in scientific computing.) ACMS runs on the HP OpenVMS operating system.

ACMS was originally released in 1984 as part of the integrated VAX Information Architecture product set along with Rdb (relational database system), DBMS (CODASYL database system), TDMS (original forms system), DECforms (a newer forms system), CDD (Common Data Dictionary), and Datatrieve (query and report writer for record-oriented files and databases). ACMS pioneered many transactional RPC and abstraction concepts, and remains a popular TP monitor for the HP OpenVMS environment.

System Architecture

ACMS uses a three-process TP monitor model in which each of the three tiers is mapped to a different operating system process, very similar to our multitier architecture: front-end program, request controller, and transaction server (see Figure 10.48). The processes communicate via a proprietary RPC.

ACMS applications accept a request for the execution of a transaction from a terminal or other display device connected to the process running the front-end program, called the **Command Process**. It is multithreaded to handle multiple devices concurrently. The front-end program sends a request message to the request controller process, called the **Task Server**. (A **task** is a program in a request controller that controls a request.) The request controller is also multithreaded to handle multiple requests concurrently. The request controller calls a procedure running in the transaction server, which ACMS calls the **Procedure Server**. Since the transaction server is single-threaded, it is typically deployed as a server class consisting of multiple server processes. ACMS monitors the workload on transaction servers to determine whether enough server process instances are active to handle the application workload. If there are too few, it automatically starts another server instance. If a server is idle for too long, ACMS automatically deletes it to conserve system resources.

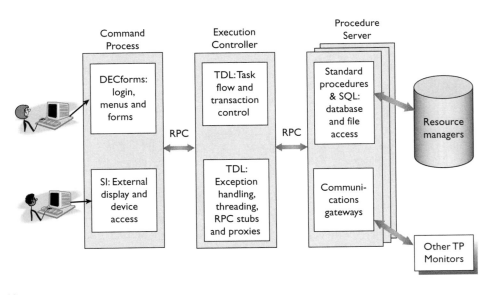

FIGURE 10.48

ACMS Three-Process Model. Remote procedure calls communicate among predefined processes tuned for specific types of application work. The Task Definition Language defines the workflow and controls transactions.

In contrast to CICS, IMS, and Tuxedo, ACMS has a specialized compiled language, the Task Definition Language (TDL), for specifying request control. It supports features that were required by the ACMS model but not present in traditional imperative languages in the early 1980s when ACMS was designed, such as RPC, multithreading, transaction control, and structured exception handling. TDL is designed to work in conjunction with TDMS and DECforms for menu and forms handling and with any OpenVMS language for transaction server development. It was standardized by X/Open as the Structured Transaction Definition Language (STDL). ACMS was also the basis of the X/Open Transactional RPC specification (TxRPC). Figure 10.49 contains an example of TDL calls to transaction server procedures.

When an exception occurs, control is passed to the ACTION portion of the task. Certain exceptions automatically abort the transaction before branching to the exception handler, as in CICS or automatic transaction mode of Tuxedo. A single resource transaction can be started in the procedure server.

ACMS offers an open, call-level interface to its RPC, called the Systems Interface (SI) API, for connecting specialized devices such as ATMs, gas pumps, and telecom switches. The SI also has been used to create clients external to ACMS, such as .NET clients, web browsers, and Java EE clients.

TP Communications

All process-to-process communication is via a proprietary RPC protocol, including calling a procedure in another process on the same machine. It is possible to change a local call (i.e., in the same process) to a remote call via a configuration change.

```
REPLACE TASK TRANSFER

WORKSPACES ARE  CUSTOMER_WKSP,
                ACCOUNTS_WKSP;

TASK ARGUMENTS ARE CUSTOMER_WKSP WITH ACCESS READ,
                   ACCOUNTS_WKSP WITH ACCESS MODIFY;
BLOCK
    ...
        BLOCK WORK WITH TRANSACTION IS

            PROCESSING WORK IS
            CALL WITHDRAW_PROC USING CUSTOMER_WKSP, ACCOUNT_WKSP;
            CALL DEPOSIT_PROC USING CUSTOMER_WKSP, ACCOUNT_WKSP;

            EXCHANGE WORK IS  ...

            ACTION IS  ...

        END BLOCK WORK;

    END BLOCK;

    END DEFINITION;
```

FIGURE 10.49

ACMS TDL Example for the Transfer Task. The ACMS task definition declares the data to be passed to a procedure using record definitions and can call multiple procedures within the same transaction block.

TDL includes an interface definition language called the **task group**. The TDL compiler uses the task group information to generate proxy and stub programs to be linked with the RPC caller and callee. The callee typically would be a procedure server developed using any of the OpenVMS supported languages, such as COBOL, C, FORTRAN, Basic, Pascal, and Ada. This allows callers to use standard procedure call syntax, rather than explicitly constructing a specially-formatted buffer and then passing it in the call (as in CICS and Tuxedo). Information about the request, such as the security context and display identifier, is automatically placed in hidden arguments and is forwarded transparently to the server, where it becomes part of the server's context.

ACMS uses OpenVMS cluster technology to support high availability for applications, by automatically redirecting an RPC from a failed node to a surviving node. It uses the OpenVMS transaction manager, DECdtm, for two-phase commit. It also uses the OpenVMS database, Rdb (now owned by Oracle Corp), for automatic failover in an OpenVMS cluster. That is, the database is available from multiple nodes in the cluster, and the application can fail over automatically from a database connection on one machine to a database connection on another machine, using the OpenVMS lock manager. Using these mechanisms, ACMS is able to achieve very high levels of availability.

ACMS has been extended using a product called TP Ware that includes support for .NET Framework clients, Java clients, web browsers, and Web Services clients running on the Windows operating system. A product called the Web Services Integration Toolkit, running on OpenVMS, exposes ACMS tasks as EJBs and Web Services. ACMS server procedures can include HP's APPC/LU6.2 gateway for interoperability with CICS-based applications. TP Ware basically replaces the command process in the three-tier architecture with web browser, .NET, and Java clients, providing libraries and an API to directly invoke a task in the task server, bypassing the Command Process.

Database Access

Transaction server programs directly access any database or resource manager. Certain specialized databases are directly accessible from TDL. ACMS includes a queue manager for durable request queue operations.

If a transaction is bracketed within a TDL program (in a request controller), then ACMS controls the commitment activity using DECdtm. If it is bracketed within the transaction server, then ACMS is uninvolved in the commitment process. This is useful for database systems that are not integrated with DECdtm, or that offer specialized options that can only be set in the transaction bracket statements.

Pathway TS/MP

Pathway with NonStop Transaction Services (TS/MP) is another legacy TP monitor from HP. It was developed originally by Tandem Computers and released in the mid-1980s as a TP development platform for Tandem's Guardian operating system running on their fault-tolerant platform.

Tandem later teased apart its operating system into a kernel portion, the NonStop Kernel (NSK), with two layers on top: one that supports the Guardian API, and one that supports a POSIX (UNIX) API, called Open System Services (OSS). OSS supports a native port of Tuxedo and a nonnative port of a Java EE application server (Oracle's WebLogic). Pathway and Tandem in general, was a pioneer of high availability, fault tolerance, and data replication technologies.

Pathway is based on a client/server process structure and a transaction abstraction. NonStop TS/MP provides server process management (e.g., load balancing and automatic server restart). Transaction management is implemented using infrastructure called the NonStop Transaction Management Facility (TMF). This TP infrastructure supports all application environments, including Pathway, NonStop Tuxedo, NonStop CORBA, NonStop JSP, NonStop SOAP, and NonStop Web Server. TS/MP recently has been completely rearchitected

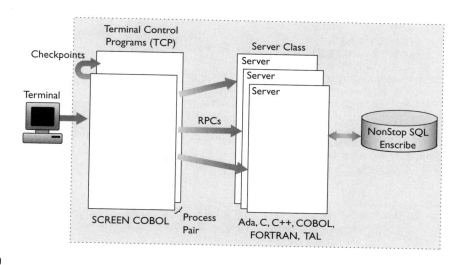

FIGURE 10.50

Pathway Monitor Two-Process Model. The Terminal Control Program interprets SCREEN COBOL programs to interact with the display and format requests, and to call servers via RPC. The servers access the Tandem resource managers. TCPs are implemented using process pairs for fault-tolerance.

using a new component called Application Cluster Services that extends server management and load balancing capabilities to the new generation of HP Integrity NonStop processors.

System Architecture

Pathway uses a two-process model to implement its client/server architecture, which is called requester/server (see Figure 10.50). The client is a multithreaded Terminal Control Program (TCP), which handles multiple simultaneous interactions with end users. It supports both front-end program and request controller functions. The TCP interpretively executes programs written in Tandem's COBOL dialect, SCREEN COBOL, which includes features for terminal handling and communication with single-threaded transaction servers. An example of SCREEN COBOL is in Figure 10.51. Enhancements to the NonStop environment have allowed the development of multithreaded transaction servers. Similarly to ACMS, transaction servers execute compiled object code written in a standard language with embedded SQL and run in server classes. Supported languages include C/C++, COBOL, Java, and TAL (Transaction Application Language, which is proprietary to HP NonStop).

The TCP interprets a SCREEN COBOL application program to display menus, paint and read a screen, validate the input data, and format a request message with the name of the target server class. The application program then starts a transaction and executes a SEND command to issue an RPC to a transaction server in the server class named by the request.

The RPC mechanism establishes a new link to a server in the requested server class, if it doesn't already have one or if all existing links are busy processing other requests. The server accepts the message and does the work of the request, accessing a database if appropriate. When the server program completes, it sends a reply message to the TCP. The TCP's application program can invoke many such RPCs before forwarding the reply to the terminal and committing the transaction. Finally, the reply message is displayed.

The Guardian operating system implements software fault-tolerance through **process pairs**, a mechanism by which a given operating system process has a second, shadow process as a backup to each primary process.

```
PROCEDURE DIVISION.
000-BEGIN SECTION.
ACCEPT INPUT-MSG.
  BEGIN-TRANSACTION.
  MOVE ACCOUNT-ID OF INPUT-MSG TO ACCOUNT-ID OF DBCR-MSG.
  MOVE AMOUNT OF INPUT-MSG TO AMOUNT OF DBCR-MSG.
  SEND MESSAGE DBCR-MSG TO /LOCAL
      REPLY CODE STATUS.
  MOVE BALANCE OF DBCR-MSG TO BALANCE1 OF CONFIRM-MSG.
  SEND MESSAGE DBCR-MSG TO /REMOTE
      REPLY CODE STATUS.
  END-TRANSACTION.
```

FIGURE 10.51

SCREEN COBOL Example. The program accepts input from the display, begins a transaction, and sends messages to two servers, one locally for the debit operation and the other to a remote node for the credit operation.

A configuration option tells Pathway to run each TCP as a process pair. A server monitoring feature called Pathmon, which is also implemented as a process pair, monitors Pathway servers and restarts them in the event of a process or processor failure. The primary and backup processes in a process pair configuration run on different processors so that at least one of them will survive any processor failure.

At the beginning of each transaction, Pathway checkpoints the display context (essentially, the request), which means that it copies this state from the primary process to its backup process. It checkpoints again just before commit (essentially, the reply). If the primary fails during the transaction execution, the transaction aborts and the backup can re-execute the transaction using the checkpointed display context, without asking the user to re-enter the data. If the transaction executes without any failures and commits, then the precommit checkpoint replaces the start-of-transaction checkpoint, and can be sent to the display. The checkpoints play a similar role to queue elements in queued TP. The NonStop process pair and checkpoint/restart capability is unique in the TP industry.

Servers are typically stateless, which allows successive calls to a server class within the same transaction to be handled by different servers. Servers are automatically restarted in the event of process or processor failure.

Transactions are managed by the TMF. Updates to data are logged to an audit file, from which TMF manages various types of recovery. There is one log per node. TMF provides a system logging service for both itself (as a transaction manager), and for the NonStop resource managers (NonStop SQL and Enscribe). All updates by a transaction are written as a single log write, no matter how many resource managers are involved, thereby minimizing the number I/Os per transaction to improve performance and scalability.

NonStop resource managers provide fault tolerance through disk mirroring and hot backup, and provide upward scalability through data partitioning and parallel processing. System server processes typically run as process pairs to ensure high availability.

Front-End Program

Pathway was introduced in the days of low-function terminals. So its front-end program, TCP, supports terminal devices via a multithreaded process, where each thread maintains a context for a terminal and initiates a request on behalf of the user. Later on, the TCP interface was opened up for access from PCs, workstations, and other devices, such as ATMs, gas pumps, and bar code readers.

External client support has been added for web browsers, Web Services, .NET, CORBA, JMS, and Tuxedo using a set of special gateway processes that replace the TCP for modern display devices and interoperability solutions. A Web Services toolkit is available to generate a WSDL interface from a Pathway interface so that a standard Web Services client can access a Pathway server. Similarly, the NonStop JSP product, together with the NonStop Web Server product, supports direct access to Pathway servers from standard HTTP clients.

TP Communications

A NonStop system (or node) is a loosely-coupled cluster of processors, connected by a high-speed bus called ServerNet. Processors do not share memory, but this architecture is supported by the common operating system environment that provides high performance, availability, and scalability.

The NonStop operating system uses a transactional interprocess communications mechanism based on the NonStop messaging system, between processes both on the same node and on remote nodes. The communication mechanism is accessed using the PathSend API.

Database Access

The NonStop environment includes an SQL-compliant resource manager called NonStop SQL and a transactional file system called Enscribe. Both resource managers support parallel processing and distributed processing features of the NonStop platform. When it was released in the mid-1980s, NonStop SQL was the first distributed, parallel relational database system product.

Mirrored disks are supported for local backup, and the Remote Database Facility (RDF) supports a remote hot backup. RDF uses the process pair architecture to forward log records from the primary database to the remote replica, where another process pair applies the log records to the database replica.

Multiple processors can execute separate SQL requests simultaneously or divide a large single request for parallel processing on multiple processors. The resource managers support the standard locking and logging approaches described in Chapters 6 and 7, including record locking, relaxed isolation levels for improved read performance, and logs for undo-redo recovery. Online reconfiguration is supported for such things as moving a partition or splitting an index.

10.8 TP STANDARDS

Historically, standardization has been very challenging for TP technologies, due to the broad variety of implementation architectures, programming models, communications protocols, and integration points among modern and legacy products. The main goals of TP standardization are:

- Portability: Allowing the same transaction program to run on different transactional middleware products
- Interoperability: Allowing multiple transactional middleware products to exchange data or control information while executing within the same transaction
- Integration: Allowing components from multiple transactional middleware products that perform different functions to work in combination

We will focus primarily on standards pertinent to the .NET Framework and Java EE transactional middleware and touch only briefly on other related standardization efforts. The primary standard for transactional interoperability is defined by the Web Services transactions set of specifications. We describe the following standards:

- The Web Services Transactions (WS-Transactions) set of specifications from OASIS
- The XA protocol from the Open Group

- The Object Transaction Service (OTS) from the Object Management Group
- The Java Transaction API (JTA) from the Java Community Process

These last three standards are related. The XA protocol is incorporated into OTS, and both XA and OTS are incorporated into JTA. The XA protocol is perhaps the most successful TP standard. Most transactional resource managers support it for two-phase commit, including relational database systems and asynchronous message queues.

We also briefly mention the emerging Service Component Architecture (SCA), OSGi enterprise edition, and Advanced Message Queuing Protocol (AMQP) specifications since they support transactions.

WS-Transactions

WS-Transactions is a set of transactional interoperability specifications standardized by OASIS. It extends basic Web Services (i.e., SOAP and WSDL) by including a transaction context in a SOAP header and defining a protocol for transactional interoperability across Web Services. Both vendor and open source products implement it, including Microsoft's Windows Communications Framework, IBM's WebSphere Application Server, Red Hat's JBoss Application Server, Progress Software's Artix ESB, Sun's Metro, and Apache's Kandula2.

WS-Transactions includes three specifications:

- WS-Coordination (WS-C) is the core specification, defining a generic state machine coordinator that supports pluggable protocols for various transaction models, such as WS-AT and WS-BA.
- WS-AtomicTransactions (WS-AT) defines a durable and volatile variation of the classic two-phase commit protocol that plug into WS-C.
- WS-BusinessActivity (WS-BA) defines an "open nested" transaction protocol with compensation actions that plugs into WS-C. It can be used with long running transaction flows such as those defined using WS-BPEL.

An implementation of WS-C is a prerequisite for WS-AT and/or WS-BA. However, it is also possible to implement WS-C without implementing either WS-AT or WS-BA, for example by defining a new protocol to plug into WS-C, such as a notification, publish/subscribe, consensus, or three-phase commit protocol.

The WS-C specification defines how a Web Service implementation interacts with a transaction coordinator to obtain and manage the context for a given transaction type. The WS-AT and WS-BA specifications define specific context formats for WS-C to manage. The context is obtained from WS-C and passed from a Web Service requester to a Web Service provider using SOAP headers. A WS-Policy assertion can be attached to the Web Service's WSDL interface to advertise its transactional requirements.

For example, in Figure 10.52 the .NET client obtains a WSDL interface from the Java EE application server that includes a policy requiring WS-AT. It therefore knows it has to start a transaction and obtain a WS-AT context for propagation to the remote service. The context is included in the header of the SOAP message that invokes the remote EJB server. When the service provider receives the SOAP header it recognizes the WS-AT context and registers the transaction with a WS-C coordinator—either a local coordinator that contacts the remote coordinator on its behalf, or directly with the remote coordinator.

Figure 10.53 shows an example of the context structure for WS-AT. It includes URIs that identify the coordination (i.e., context) type, the coordinator, and the address of the coordinator with which to register the context.

The two-phase commit protocol includes volatile and durable variations. The open nested model defined in WS-BA allows a nested transaction to commit without requiring the top-level or root transaction to commit. However, if the top-level transaction aborts, a compensation action must be applied to any subtransaction that previously committed. WS-BA includes two variations: one for participant completion and the other for coordinator completion.

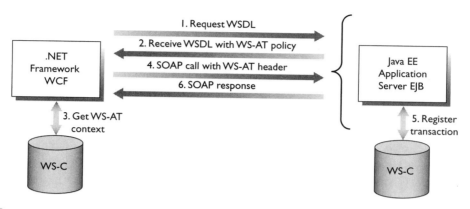

FIGURE 10.52

The .NET Client Obtains a WSDL Interface Requiring WS-AT. The example illustrates a transactional Web Service invocation that coordinates Java EE and NET Framework resources.

```
<SOAP11:Envelope xmlns:S11="http://www.w3.org/2003/05/soap-envelope">
    <SOAP11:Header>
        . . .
        <wscoor:CoordinationContext
            . . .
            <wscoor:Identifier>
                uuid:1234567890
            </wscoor:Identifier>
            . . .
            <wscoor:CoordinationType>
                http://docs.oasis-open.org/ws-tx/wsat/2006/06
            </wscoor:CoordinationType>

            <wscoor:RegistrationService>
                <wsa:Address>
                http://WWW.MyLargeBank.com/CoordinationService/registration
                </wsa:Address>
            </wscoor:RegistrationService>
    </SOAP11:Header>
    . . .
</SOAP11:Envelope>
```

FIGURE 10.53

WS-Transactions Context for WS-Atomic Transactions. The context type for WS-AT is included in the SOAP header along with the URL for the coordinator.

WS-Transactions uses the Web Services Policy (WS-Policy) Framework as the format for the policies it defines for association with a WSDL interface. In WS-Policy the policy items, called **assertions**, are used to advertise the transactional capabilities of a Web Service. For example, an assertion can tell the service requester whether or not a transaction context is required in order to invoke the service. Each WSDL operation can have its own policies.

```
<wsdl:operation name="Transfer">
    <wsp:PolicyReference URI-"#TransactedPolicy" wsdl:required="true" />
    <!-- omitted elements -->
</wsdl:operation>

<wsp:Policy wsu:Id="TransactedPolicy" >
    <wsat:ATAssertion/>
</wsp:Policy>
```

FIGURE 10.54

Policy Assertion Requiring a Transaction for the `Transfer` **Operation.** The Transfer operation has a reference to a `wsp:Policy` element that contains a `wsat:ATAssertion` indicating that a transaction context is required for this operation.

For example, Figure 10.54 defines the transacted policy for the `Transfer` operation. It indicates that a transaction context, such as the WS-AT context, is required in order to request this service. If a SOAP message arrives for the `Transfer` operation without a transaction context an exception will be generated.

The XA Interface

The XA specification originally was developed by X/Open in 1991 as part of a family of specifications defining a complete distributed transaction processing environment. XA is supported by most relational database products, including Oracle, Sybase, IBM's DB2, Microsoft's SQL Server, and Sun's MySQL. XA is also supported by most asynchronous message queuing products, including IBM's WebSphere MQ, TIBCO Software's Enterprise Message Service, Progress Software's SonicMQ, and the Apache Foundation's ActiveMQ.

X/Open was established to define portability and interoperability standards for UNIX. X/Open is now part of The Open Group, Inc., which was formed in 1994 by combining X/Open with the Open Software Foundation. X/Open's original goal was to promote application portability through the development of API standards for UNIX. In fact, The Open Group owns the UNIX brand.

Although the complete family of X/Open specifications failed to gain adoption, the X/Open Distributed Transaction Processing (DTP) model remains a good framework for identifying both the components involved in a distributed transaction and the appropriate areas for standardization (see Figure 10.55). It divides a distributed TP system into three major components—transaction manager, resource manager, and application—and defines the interfaces between them.

Within the X/Open DTP model, the XA specification defines a bidirectional interface between the transaction manager (TM) and the resource manager (RM). Today it's common to think of the .NET Framework or Java EE defining the transaction demarcation API instead of the TX API. SQL is the most widely-used API for RM access, but there are others for access to queues and other nonrelational resources. XA is intended primarily for transactions that span multiple resource managers. For example, a common application of XA is to coordinate a transaction that includes a database and a message queue.

The XA specification defines the protocol to allow the transactional work of an RM to be externally coordinated by a TM in a distributed transaction. XA is a presumed-abort, two-phase commit protocol with optimizations that enable a TM to chose a one-phase commit when there is only a single RM involved in the transaction. When an application starts a transaction the TM creates a new transaction and assigns it a global transaction ID (which XA calls an **XID**). When the application calls the RM (for example, using an SQL statement), the runtime hosting the application passes the ID it obtained from the TM to the RM. The RM's transaction manager recognizes the ID as coming from an independent TM (i.e., it's not a transaction that the RM

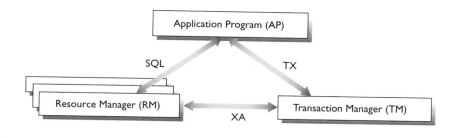

FIGURE 10.55

X/Open DTP Model. In the X/Open DTP model an application program typically uses the TX API to access transaction management services and SQL to access a resource manager. The XA standard allows different vendors' transactional middleware and resource managers to interoperate.

initiated) and enlists its transaction with the TM's transaction using the address of the TM, which is passed as part of the transaction context. At termination, the TM notifies all registered participants of the transaction outcome.

Object Transaction Service

The Object Transaction Service (OTS) was defined in 1994 by the Object Management Group (OMG), an industry consortium. OMG was founded to develop the Common Object Request Broker Architecture (or CORBA) specifications and now is responsible for a variety of standards, including the well-known Unified Modeling Language (UML). OTS is one of the CORBA services that extend the core interfacing and interoperability technology for use in enterprise applications such as transaction processing.

OTS is incorporated into Java EE as the interoperable format for transaction context propagation on remote EJB requests. JTA provides the local Java interfaces in Java EE for TX and XA protocols. Implementations of CORBA and OTS include Progress Software's Orbix, Borland Software's VisiBroker, Oracle's Tuxedo, HP's NonStop Kernel, and Hitachi's TP Broker. OTS often is mapped to Java Transaction Service (JTS) implementations. And the WS-Transactions approach is derived from the OMG's *Additional Structuring Mechanisms for the OTS Specification*, which first included the concept of separating the coordinator from the transaction protocol.

The OTS model (as of V1.4) includes a transactional server and recoverable server, which correspond to the request controller and transaction server in our multitier model (see Figure 10.56).

Objects in the transactional clients and servers communicate with each other using the ORB. They also access the transaction service to initiate and terminate a transaction and to register resources for a transaction. The transactional server does not directly interact with persistent resources, but calls one or more objects in the recoverable server to do so.

In XA terms, the transactional client, transactional server, and recoverable server comprise the application (AP) and the transaction service implements the transaction manager (TM). The RM is the same as in XA and, in fact, interacts with the TM using the XA protocol.

OTS supports both implicit and explicit programming models. The implicit programming model uses an object called **current** to associate a context with the execution thread. The begin command initializes the current context. Once a context is associated with the execution thread, it can be automatically propagated to any other transactional object invoked from that thread, depending on the transactional policy associated with

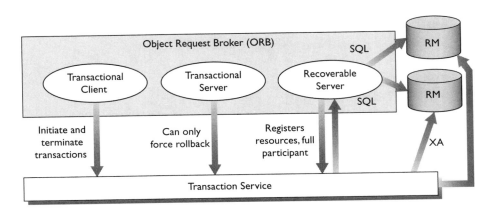

FIGURE 10.56

Object Transaction Service Architecture. The ORB provides the communication among objects participating in an OTS transaction while the transaction service provides transaction coordination.

the target object. The scope of a transaction is determined by the extent of the context sharing among objects, whether explicit or implicit.

The following properties can be associated with an object's interoperable object reference (IOR) to define whether or not it will accept implicit context propagation:

- REQUIRES: A transaction context must be present when the object is invoked.
- FORBIDS: A transaction context must not be present when the object is invoked.
- ADAPTS: The object can be invoked whether or not a transaction context is present.

Properties cannot be set on individual methods in an object. A transactional object can perform both transactional and nontransactional work.

The explicit programming model uses the complete set of methods on the current object to explicitly start a transaction, get a context object, control the transaction through the methods on the object, and propagate the context to other transactional objects.

Transaction semantics in OTS are compatible with XA, and transactions can be exported and imported between the two environments. OTS supports subtransactions but they are not widely implemented in resource managers.

An OTS coordinator can become a resource to another coordinator. This is called **interposition**, in which a coordinator acts as a resource to the root coordinator. Interposition was designed for network efficiency. When multiple remote resources are included in the transaction, it's more efficient for the root coordinator to exchange remote messages with an interposed coordinator than it would be with all the remote resources individually. The interposed coordinator receives messages from the root coordinator and passes them along to the local resources enrolled with it. An interposed coordinator can also reduce the number of sessions a given resource manager has to support, and can help enforce security for a given domain. This is essentially the tree-of-processes model discussed in Section 8.5.

JTA

The Java Transaction API (JTA) defines the Java interfaces for the TX and XA protocols. JTA originally was defined in 1999 and joins OTS and XA within a common Java programming environment. JTA is used in JCA,

JDBC, and JMS, and is included in any Java-EE-compliant application server product. See Section 10.4, *The Explicit Programming Model* for additional examples.

JTA consists of three main parts:

- An interface that allows an application to explicitly initiate, propagate, and terminate a transaction
- A Java language mapping of the XA interface (XAResource)
- An interface between the TM and other application server components such as containers and cache managers to support enlistment of durable and volatile resources (XAResources and Synchronizations).

The `javax.transaction.UserTransaction` interface defines an explicit transaction programming model that can be used by Java clients and EJBs.

The `javax.transaction.TransactionManager` interface defines a programming model for the application server vendor to control transactions that use the implicit programming model. When an EJB container manages the transaction state for a transactional EJB, the container uses the `TransactionManager` interface to create, manage, and propagate a transaction context for a given thread of execution.

The `javax.transaction.xa.XAResource` interface is a Java mapping of the industry standard XA interface. As of JTA 1.1, the `javax.transaction.TransactionSynchronizationRegistry` interface defines a distinct set of operations for components such as persistence managers that typically would not have access to the full `TransactionManager` interface.

Service Component Architecture

The OASIS Service Component Architecture (SCA) defines a set of metadata for identifying services for an SOA, mapping them into a component model for deployment, and assembling them into various applications. SCA also includes a mechanism for attaching policies to the components and identifies a way in which Java programs can include SCA metadata as annotations.

Transactions are incorporated into SCA components using extended policy information incorporating the WS-Policy specification from W3C. For example, when deploying an SCA component or assembly of components into a Java EE runtime environment, the transaction policies attached to the SCA components are translated into Java EE transaction attributes. See the Section 10.4, *The Implicit Programming Model*, for information on Java EE transaction attributes. When SCA components are deployed onto other runtimes, the policies are mapped into WS-Policy elements as defined in the WS-TX set of specifications, described earlier in this section.

OSGi Alliance

The OSGi Alliance creates and maintains the OSGi specifications, which define a core framework for Java modularization and an associated set of framework services for discovery, security, logging, and so on. The OSGi Alliance was created as the Open Server Gateway initiative in 1998 based on Java Specification Request 8. Its original goal was to modularize Java for embedded devices, such as those intended for home automation, allowing the dynamic loading and unloading of selected sets of Java libraries needed to support the device's resource constraints and capability requirements. OSGi technology had mixed early adoption in various embedded applications, including automotive and mobile telephone application.

Following the adoption of the OSGi platform by the Eclipse Foundation in 2004, the OSGi framework became popular as a deployment mechanism for Java-based products such as IBM's WebSphere Application Server, Oracle's WebLogic, Red Hat's JBoss, Spring Source's dm Server, and the Apache Foundation's ServiceMix, among others.

The OSGi framework defines a dynamic component model for Java, and addresses other shortcomings of the standalone Java virtual machine environment, such as improved classloading, versioning, and lifecycle control. Applications can be defined as a set of cooperating components that can be remotely installed, started, stopped, updated, and uninstalled dynamically (i.e., without requiring application reboot). A service registry allows modules to detect the addition of new services or the removal of services, and to adapt dynamically, including the automatic installation of new components as required by the application.

The enterprise release of the OSGi specifications, R 4.2, extends the OSGi framework to meet the requirement of enterprise Java applications, including components for distributed computing, extensions to the component model itself (based on the Spring Framework's component model), and a mapping of various Java EE components such as JTA, JDBC, JPA, JNDI, and Web applications. The Java EE and other enterprise components are accessible from application code using the OSGi service model. That means web applications, transaction, persistence abstractions, and other enterprise components are available as dynamically-loadable services for OSGi-compliant applications.

Advanced Message Queuing Protocol

The Advanced Message Queuing Protocol (AMQP) is an open standard originally defined by JP Morgan Chase and then submitted to an independent consortium, which maintains and improves it. AMQP focused initially on defining a wire format interoperability standard for asynchronous messaging systems, such as JMS-based message queues.

JMS defines a standard API for message queuing, but it does not define a data format. Among the goals of the AMQP Working Group is achieving interoperability across multiple asynchronous message queuing technologies and products. AMQP supports XA transactions for coordinating queue operations with operations on another resource. Current implementations include Red Hat's Enterprise MRG, Apache Qpid, iMatix's OpenAMQ, and Cohesive FT and LShift's RabbitMQ.

Members of the AMQP Working Group consortium include Cisco Systems; Credit Suisse; Deutsche Borse Systems; Envoy Technologies; Goldman Sachs; iMatix Corporation; JP Morgan Chase Bank & Co.; Microsoft Corporation; Novell; Progress Software; Rabbit Technologies (a joint venture of CohesiveFT and LShift); Red Hat, Inc.; Twist Process Innovations; WSO2, Inc.; and 29West, Inc.

10.9 SUMMARY

Transactional middleware products meet the requirements of multitier TP applications. Twenty years ago, transactional middleware was delivered to market as a single product category, the TP (or OLTP) monitor. Many of these products are still in production, but the most popular transactional middleware environments are now delivered in the Java EE and .NET Framework environments.

As the new environments have gained popularity, components of the original monolithic TP monitors now are sold as independent products. Examples include forms products, database management systems, system management consoles, distributed computing communications systems, and application development environments. Modern TP applications often include server components of legacy TP monitors, general purpose products, and components from the .NET Framework, Java EE-compliant application servers, or both. We expect the trend toward componentization to continue. Yet the features and functions of transactional middleware remain unchanged—to help scale up, improve performance, reliability, security, manageability, maintenance, transaction control, recovery, and availability.

TP applications typically consist of two or more tiers that provide the functions of the front-end program, request controller, and transaction server. In their simplest and most direct design, a front-end program might directly access the transaction server in a database. However, since connections between front-end programs and databases can be expensive to maintain, one or more middle tiers often are introduced to improve scalability and performance. Transactions can be controlled by the resource manager or the transactional middleware. Different transactional middleware systems provide different options for composing multiple resources into local and distributed transactions.

Most transactional middleware systems also support the use of web servers as request controllers, and rich Internet applications such as AJAX deliver desktop-like levels of interactivity and features to the web browser. All transactional middleware, including legacy TP monitors, supports access from web browsers either directly or through an intermediary.

Transactional middleware products typically support both an implicit and explicit programming model for transaction control. The implicit model uses configuration properties of abstract runtime containers to automatically begin, propagate, and terminate a transaction. The explicit model relies on APIs incorporated directly into programs. The tradeoffs are generally between ease of use of the implicit model and flexibility of control of the explicit model.

Legacy TP monitors such as CICS, IMS, ACMS, Tuxedo, and Pathway continue to be used in many production environments. They now include support for modern front ends such as .NET, Java, and Web Services, for integration with newer applications and SOA-based designs.

Microsoft's .NET Framework includes multiple technologies for creating front-end programs, such as WPF, Silverlight, and ASP.NET. WCF can be used to develop request controllers and transaction servers. SQL Server can run stored procedures, which functions as a complete transaction server in some environments.

Transaction management in the .NET Framework uses the `System.Transactions` API set. It underlies the implicit programming model in WCF and can also be accessed explicitly from .NET Framework objects. When used with WCF, attributes embedded within .NET objects cause them to execute as transactions. Annotations can also be embedded in programs and interfaces to automatically complete and propagate a transaction.

The Java EE environment includes multiple technologies for creating front-end programs, such as Swing, JSP, JSF, and servlets. EJBs can be used to develop request controllers and transaction servers, and can include JPA beans for object-relational persistence. SQL database systems run stored procedures, which can function as transaction servers.

Transaction management in the Java EE environment uses the Java Transaction API (JTA), which underlies the implicit programming model in EJBs, and can also be accessed directly from Java objects. As in WCF, annotations embedded in EJBs control transaction initiation, termination, and propagation. In the Java world, the Spring Framework is emerging as an alternative for TP application development. It includes a transaction management abstraction API that's configurable for either JDBC- or JTA-managed transactions.

In Java EE the same set of annotations is used for transaction control and propagation, whereas these functions can be controlled separately in the .NET Framework. Another difference between the environments is that the .NET Framework automatically promotes a single resource transaction to a multiresource transaction when it detects an application accessing a second resource manager. `System.Transactions` can automatically reassign coordination responsibility from the resource manager's transaction manager to an independent transaction manager (i.e., DTC). In the Java EE environment, such a change has to be explicitly programmed.

SOA-based designs are gaining adoption for TP applications using various technologies, such as Web Services and REST/HTTP. The transactional models differ for these two approaches. In Web Services, transactional RPC and compensation protocols are formalized in the WS-Transactions specifications, which make mapping transactional capabilities fairly straightforward. With REST/HTTP, a transaction can be modeled as a resource. The server maintains the state of the resource and the front-end program maintains the application state separately. Representations of state changes are exchanged using HTTP verbs.

Persistence abstractions enable easier access to resource managers, especially relational databases. The initial abstraction was designed to improve the use of remote database connections, and was formalized in ODBC and JDBC, which are still widely used. Newer abstractions include object-relational mappings such as JPA and entity data models such as ADO.NET Entity Framework. The abstraction mechanisms typically include transaction management capabilities.

TP standards help promote interoperability of TP environments and portability of applications. The most widely adopted is the XA protocol, which defines the relationship between a resource manager and an independent transaction manager, so resource managers and transaction managers from different vendors can easily integrate. Other widely-adopted standards include the Object Transaction Service from OMG, which is included in Java EE's JTA, JTA itself, and WS-Transactions for Web services transactions. Emerging standards gaining adoption include SCA, OSGi's enterprise edition, and AMQP.

Future Trends

11.1 INTRODUCTION

Although the principles of transaction processing change very slowly, the technology that implements those principles changes all the time. Some of these changes involve repackaging well-known mechanisms to fit into new software architectures. For example, over the years we have seen transactional RPC appear in TP monitors, client-server database systems, object request brokers, application servers, and web services. Other changes are driven by cost reductions in hardware and communications that put additional applications within reach. For example, airline reservation systems evolved from simply keeping track of the number of available seats to adding applications for frequent flyer programs, special meals, seat assignments, complex fares, and notifications via e-mail and text messaging. Banking and stock brokerage systems have undergone a similar evolution. We are now seeing a growing use of mobile devices to access TP applications, such as managing a doctor's appointments.

A third driver of changes are web-based enterprises with large TP sites. When off-the-shelf technology fails to meet their needs, they often roll their own. Forty years ago, early corporate on-line TP application developers rolled their own middleware. Later, transactional middleware products, such as TP monitors, came along with general-purpose implementations of the same functionality. We expect to see this trend continue, with custom solutions for the largest e-commerce sites migrating into transactional middleware and database system products.

This chapter highlights four areas where we expect that technological changes will have a major effect on the design of TP systems and products: cloud computing, scalable distributed computing, flash memory, and stream processing. Since these areas are changing rapidly, anything we say about the technology is likely to become quickly outdated. So we will focus on overall trends, not on technical detail.

11.2 CLOUD COMPUTING

Cloud computing is a computing service offered over the Internet. That is, a customer plugs into the "network cloud" and uses computing capabilities owned and operated by another company called the **service provider**. The service provider may be a large company with many data centers containing hundreds of thousands of machines, such as Microsoft, Google, Yahoo!, Amazon.com, IBM, or Salesforce.com.

Roughly speaking, a computing service can be an application-specific service or a generic service. An application-specific service offers a particular application, such as e-mail, search, enterprise resource planning

(ERP), customer relationship management (CRM), or social networking. An application-specific service usually is offered both as a web site that can be accessed from a browser and as a web service that can be invoked by other applications. The application is usually customizable and extensible.

A generic service offers a general-purpose computing service, such as raw storage, record-oriented data storage, data warehousing, or raw processing power. The latter often is provided in the form of a virtual machine (VM) into which the customer can load any kind of software.

An application-specific service may be combined with generic services. For example, a social networking application may run in one cloud service but store large media files on another service provider's cloud service.

The customer may use the generic service as extra data center capacity, for processing, storage, or both. For example, a company could use cloud computing services to test new functionality or to handle temporary workload spikes. Or the customer may use the service as its primary computing infrastructure. Sometimes, the customer starts using it as extra capacity and, after gaining confidence in the service, evolves into using it as its primary computing facility.

One of the attractions of most cloud computing services is that they gracefully scale up or down to meet the current workload. That is, the customer pays only for the capacity that's needed at any given moment. For example, if a company is suddenly front-page news and hence gets a huge burst of traffic, the cloud computing service can quickly respond by scaling up the company's application to run on triple the number of machines to handle the load.

A set of generic services can be packaged together, much like system software components that are packaged into transactional middleware. For example, a service may offer a combination of computing, storage, and database management. A customer writes his or her application to the service's API in much the same way he or she would write it to a transactional middleware API. The service provider ensures that any application written to their API will scale up. Usually, this requires that the API restricts functionality in certain ways; for example, to minimize or avoid the use of two-phase commit or database queries that span many machines. These restrictions are designed to ensure that data and computation can be partitioned efficiently across many machines, and that the partitioning automatically adjusts to changing the load by dynamically repartitioning across more machines and balancing the load among them.

Another attraction of cloud computing services is that the customer benefits from the economies of scale that are available to the service provider. A large-scale service provider can invest in complex system management software to minimize the staff required to run the service, something that is beyond the reach of most customers today. They can buy communications bandwidth at wholesale rates. They can design custom hardware with lower power requirements. And they can reduce the need for expensive backup electrical power by geo-replicating applications, so if a data center goes off-line another can immediately pick up the load. These cost savings can be shared with the customer, so that both customer and service provider benefit.

Today, to obtain economies of scale, a generic service typically runs a fixed small set of components of each type, often just one. For example, it may support only one message queuing system and two database system products. Thus, by choosing a generic service, customers are choosing the software platform on which their applications will run. Over time, service providers may compete by the range of platforms they offer.

Multitenant Systems

This book is about the technology for building application-specific services for TP applications. However, we have not covered one important aspect of such applications that arise in cloud computing, that of supporting independent enterprises using the same service provider's computing infrastructure. This is called **multitenant** support. Consider a CRM service that supports many enterprise customers. When an enterprise signs up as a customer of the service, the service provider needs to **provision** the system; that is, assign resources that are required to serve the customer. For example, it might need to allocate storage space, adjust the configuration so that requests from this customer are serviced by server machines that have access to the customer's database, and update the network name service with a customer-specific URL that is directed to the service provider's network address.

The service provider faces architectural decisions about how to isolate customers from each other. For example, it could create a separate database for each customer. This ensures that data from different customers isn't accidentally comingled. However, this doesn't scale very well if the service provider supports a large number of small customers, due to the fixed overhead of each separate database. An alternative is to have one database that serves all customers, where the customer ID is a field of every table in the database. In this case, the service provider's application needs to be very careful to give each customer access only to those database records that have that customer's ID.

Virtual machine technology can also be used to isolate customers from each other. A virtual machine can be configured for each customer with all the customer's required resources. Since an application has access only to the resources assigned to its virtual machine, this approach reduces the chance that one customer's data leaks to another customer.

11.3 SCALABLE DISTRIBUTED COMPUTING

With a corporate TP application, the users are known—usually, they are the employees of the company. The load is fairly predictable, especially for back-office applications and customer-facing applications whose load is bounded by physical constraints, such as the number of cash registers or gas pumps where a customer can be served. And downtime for upgrades and maintenance can be scheduled since the application is running inside of the business.

By contrast, the web environment is less predictable and controllable. Large web sites have to be prepared to react immediately to huge spikes in application load, to maintain higher levels of availability, and to upgrade their systems without taking them out of service.

Many of these requirements are not easily met by traditional transactional middleware products, since they were designed to meet the requirements of internal systems. Still, the mechanisms required to meet these requirements are well known. Indeed, many of them were covered in this book. What changes is how the mechanisms are assembled into a complete system that has satisfactory availability, performance, scalability, security, manageability, and so on. By looking at the largest e-commerce web sites, many trends can be identified:

- More use of caching: While browsing, a user expects instant response time. To do this in a cost-effective way, systems exploit skewed access patterns by caching frequently accessed information. This is done at every layer of the multitier architecture—in HTTP proxy servers, web servers, application servers, and database servers. Ordinarily, the system refreshes its cache frequently, especially for items that change rapidly. During workload spikes, the system may use fewer of its resources to refresh its cache, thereby giving good response time to more users but offering more stale results. Cache management has become so important that it has become a separate product category.

- More use of updatable caches: Not all cached data is static. When cached data is updated, the update must flow to all the caches that store it. We described the approaches in Chapter 9: primary copy, where the update is first applied to the master and then propagated to the caches; and multimaster, where an update can be directly applied to any cache and then propagated lazily to the other caches. In either case, the replication model is one of eventual consistency, not instantaneous consistency. In many cases, this weaker model offers acceptable behavior to end users, while yielding better availability and partition tolerance.

- More use of queued transactions: After a user has finished browsing and is ready to take action, such as placing an order, it is usually enough that the system captures the request reliably and quickly. It is usually not necessary to process the request instantly. Thus, if there is a burst of traffic the system can give a good customer experience as long as the queuing system can handle the load. When combined with caching, this sometimes leads to rejected requests, because the user issued the request based on information that turned out to be too stale, such as quantity on hand or highest bid. In effect, rejecting such requests is a form of optimistic concurrency control. This occasional undesirable result usually is regarded as an acceptable compromise in return for better scalability.

- More use of business processes: This is a natural consequence of increased use of queued transactions. Since an instant response isn't required, it is not critical that the entire request run as a single transaction. Therefore, for all the reasons discussed in Chapter 5, it makes sense to break up the request into multiple steps, which often execute on different systems. This is a form of partitioning, which makes the system more scalable. Also, the system can be made more available by continuing to offer some level of service even when some subsystems are down. This leads to more application programming for compensating transactions and more system support to automate their invocation.

- More use of dynamic partitioning: When a server becomes overloaded, its workload needs to be spread over more servers. This entails installing the application on those servers and often partitioning the database across those servers. Some systems have made this an automated process, thereby enabling graceful growth.

- More physical componentization of applications: With the use of service-oriented architecture and object-oriented design, applications are more componentized and reusable in multiple contexts. For easier manageability, it is beneficial to partition these application components on different systems. This isolates their workload for easier performance management and enables them to be independently upgraded without affecting other applications on the web site.

- More exploitation of user requirements: Some technology problems can be addressed by trading off customer requirements. For example, users have learned to accept communication errors as a fact of life, since they can occur for a broader set of reasons and are largely outside their control. Therefore, following a communication error, customers may prefer fast resubmission of requests rather than ensuring reliable capture of all input. Another example of a tradeoff is relaxing immediate consistency of some data to ensure only eventual consistency, but gaining performance and availability in the face of network partitions.

- More use of cloud computing: A TP system needs to be configured for its peak workload. If the workload increases rapidly, a common occurrence when an Internet site becomes popular, a "success disaster" can occur where the system is unable to grow fast enough to handle the increasing load. As a result, customers leave in frustration. Instead of each system paying for spare capacity that it probably will not need, a cloud-based service can be configured with enough headroom to handle load spikes from a few of its many tenants. The cost of the headroom is therefore spread across many more applications, reducing the system cost for all of them.

The current generation of transactional middleware and database systems is not flexible enough to enable the cost-effective construction of the largest web sites, such as those managed by Amazon, Google, eBay, and Microsoft. These companies have therefore invested heavily in building out their own solutions. The older technologies are often in the mix, but play designated roles rather than serving as the primary infrastructure.

We expect the system architecture for assembling such sites to stabilize, at which point we expect to see a new generation of transactional middleware products modeled on that architecture. These may be packaged products, like classical transactional middleware, or cloud-based platforms that are made available to application tenants. Whatever form they take, we expect them to borrow heavily from the solutions adopted by today's largest web sites.

11.4 MEMORY TECHNOLOGY

Magnetic disks were one of the main technologies that enabled the development of the first TP systems in the 1960s. Until very recently, it has remained the only nonvolatile storage medium for on-line random access to large databases. We are now beginning to see nonvolatile solid state devices that are viable alternatives to disk, particularly those based on flash memory. Given the high demand for flash memory for use in digital cameras, music players, and cell phones, manufacturers have been able to ramp up production to very high volumes. As a consequence, the cost and capacity of flash memory has been dropping rapidly.

There are three main performance metrics for nonvolatile storage:

- Capacity: The number of gigabytes it can store
- Bandwidth: The rate at which data can be streamed onto or off of the device
- Latency: The time required for a random read or write

Although the capacity of magnetic disks has improved dramatically, their bandwidth and latency have improved much more slowly. There are physical limits to how fast the disk can spin, which along with bit density determine disk bandwidth. And there are limits to how quickly a head can seek to a new cylinder, which determines disk latency.

Semiconductor devices offer much shorter latency than magnetic disks, roughly two orders of magnitude shorter. However, until recently, they were too expensive per gigabyte to offer a meaningful alternative to magnetic disk. This is now changing due to the availability of higher-density flash memory chips, which reduce the cost per gigabyte. Solid state disk devices are now available that use flash memory, have the capacity of a small magnetic disk drive, and are competitively priced. Given that fast random access to nonvolatile storage is a major determinant of TP performance, it is likely that these solid state storage devices will become a popular alternative to magnetic disks for TP systems.

Other solid state memory technologies are under development, which have characteristics that make them potentially competitive with dynamic RAM (DRAM) and flash memory. Current examples are magnetoresistive RAM (MRAM), memristors, and phase-change memory (PCM or PRAM). It is too soon to tell whether any of these technologies will reach commodity status and hence be candidates to dislodge today's market dominance of DRAM and flash. However, they are sufficiently promising to be worth tracking as a possible source of disruptive change to the storage device market.

11.5 STREAMS AND EVENT PROCESSING

One source of inputs for a TP system are real-time devices that detect events in the physical world. Example applications include processing streams of price changes in financial markets, monitoring events in a computer network, tracking packages using RFID tags, and monitoring automobile movement for traffic control.

Such applications take as input streams of messages—essentially requests in our terminology. In many of these applications it is inappropriate or infeasible to store messages in a persistent database before taking action based on that data. It may be inappropriate because it introduces too much delay before the input event is processed. It may be infeasible because the incoming data rate is too high. This breaks the classical TP paradigm, where the message causes a transaction to execute, the transaction stores the data in a database, and users query that data later.

Instead, the messages need to be processed while they pass through main memory on their way to persistent storage (if they are stored at all). This processing usually involves a query that filters the data for events that determine whether the data is of special interest and, if so, what action to take. The query may need to access a persistent database to compare the new message to past behavior, for example, to identify an unusual price change for electronic trading or an unusual purchase for fraud detection. It may also need to access a range of recent messages, to determine a trend or a break in a trend in a financial market. It may need to deal with erroneous and out-of-order messages, which requires retracting query results, much like a compensating transaction.

This style of application is reminiscent of messaging applications that are supported by message-oriented middleware, as described in Chapter 5. What makes them different are primarily the performance requirements: response time, throughput, and scalability. These requirements create challenges for conventional transactional middleware and database systems, where data must be stored before it can be processed. This has led to the development of specialized database systems for stream processing.

Stream processing functionality is already becoming an important capability of database systems. It is important for TP as well, and this importance is likely to continue growing for some time. Contributing factors include the decreasing cost and increasing function of sensor devices, the growth and declining cost of wireless networks, and the desire to monitor more events of the physical world in real time.

11.6 SUMMARY

Businesses continually adapt to changing technology capabilities and pricing. Although transaction processing principles have remained fairly constant during the past 20 years or so, the technologies that implement the principles have been evolving. Recent changes starting to impact transactional middleware products include cloud computing, highly scalable computing designs, solid state memory, and streaming event processing. These changes are too recent for us to predict with any certainty what impact they'll have on the next generation of transactional middleware, but we can at least identify the trends to watch.

Cloud computing is a computing service offered over the Internet. A service provider may offer a complete application, such as e-mail, search, enterprise resource planning (ERP), customer relationship management (CRM), or social networking. Or they may offer generic infrastructure services such as providing processing and storage capacity on demand. Some cloud computing systems provide a combination of these capabilities. Usually, the service can scale up quickly when the workload increases, and the customer pays only for the capacity that actually is used.

The largest web sites are innovating in the use of custom designs for scalable computing. This customization is needed to cope with the unpredictability of workloads and the need to optimize fast response times for a good customer experience. Such customization is reminiscent of the early years of transaction processing technologies, where companies developed middleware for their internal applications. Among the techniques now being employed are additional caching at every level of the multitier TP architecture to improve performance and ensure good response time, increased use of queued transactions and business processes, and more dynamic application partitioning.

The evolution of nonvolatile solid state memory as an alternative to magnetic disk is another trend influencing TP system design. Flash memory is now being used for solid state disks. Its capacity is continually increasing, while its cost is decreasing. Its latency is much smaller than that of magnetic disk, making it very attractive for TP applications. Solid state memory is also likely to have a significant impact on mid-tier caching solutions for scalability.

Finally, the growing importance of processing data and event streams is another trend likely to affect transactional middleware products. Stream processing technology enables data to be processed in real time, while it is in flight—that is, before it is persisted. This is similar to message processing, but with higher performance and throughput.

Glossary of Acronyms

The following acronyms are used in this book. If an acronym is specific to a company, organization, or product, the company, organization, or product name is appended.

2PC	two-phase commit
3270	block-mode terminal—IBM
4GL	fourth-generation language
ACID	atomicity, consistency, isolation, durability (properties of a transaction)
ACMS	Application Control and Management System—HP
ACP	Airline Control Program—IBM
ADO	ActiveX Data Objects—Microsoft
AJAX	Asynchronous JavaScript And XML
AMD	Advanced Micro Devices
ANSI	American National Standards Institute
AP	application program
API	application programming interface
APPC	Advanced Program to Program Communication—IBM
AQ	Advanced Queuing—Oracle
ARM	Advanced RISC Machine – ARM Holdings
ASP	Active Server Pages—Microsoft
ATM	automated teller machine
ATMI	Application Transaction Manager Interface—Oracle
BMS	Basic Mapping Services—IBM
BPM	business process management
BPMN	Business Process Modeling Notation—OMG
CAP	consistency, availability, and partition-tolerance
CCI	Common Client Interface (part of JCA)—JCP
CDR	Common Data Representation—OMG
CGI	Common Gateway Interface—W3C
CICS	Customer Information and Control System—IBM
CLR	Common Language Runtime—Microsoft
COM	Component Object Model—Microsoft
COM+	Component Object Model plus—Microsoft
CORBA	Common Object Request Broker Architecture—OMG
CRM	customer relationship management
DAG	directed acyclic graph
DB	database manager
DBA	database administrator
DL/I	Data Language/I—IBM
DM	data manager
DNS	Domain Name System—IETF
DPL	Distributed Program Link—IBM
DRAM	dynamic random access memory
DSN	data source name
DTC	Distributed Transaction Coordinator—Microsoft
DTP	distributed transaction processing
ECI	external call interface (part of CICS)—IBM
EDI	Electronic Data Interchange—UN/EDIFACT
EDM	entity data model
EAI	enterprise application integration

EJB	Enterprise Java Beans—Java Enterprise Edition
EPI	external programming interface (part of CICS)—IBM
ERP	enterprise resource planning
ESB	enterprise service bus
FML	Field Manipulation Language—Oracle
GUI	graphical user interface
HIS	Host Integration Server—Microsoft
HTML	Hypertext Markup Language—W3C
HTTP	Hypertext Transfer Protocol—IETF
HTTPS	HTTP/TLS—IETF
ID	identifier
IDE	interactive development environment
IDL	interface definition language
IETF	Internet Engineering Task Force
IIOP	Internet Inter-Orb Protocol—OMG
IIS	Internet Information Server—Microsoft
IMS	Information Management System—IBM
I/O	input/output
ISAPI	Internet Server Application Programming Interface—Microsoft
ISC	Intersystem Communication—IBM
Java EE	Java Enterprise Edition—JCP
Javax	Java extensions—JCP
JAXB	Java Architecture for XML Binding—JCP
JAX-RS	Java API for Restful Web Services—JCP
JAX-WS	Java API for XML Web Services—JCP
JCA	Java Connector Architecture—JCP
JCP	Java Community Process
JDBC	Java Database Connectivity—JCP
JMS	Java Messaging Service—JCP
JNDI	Java Naming and Directory Interface—JCP
JPA	Java Persistence Architecture—JCP
JSON	JavaScript Object Notation—JSON.org
JSF	Java Server Faces—JCP
JSP	Java Server Pages—JCP
JTA	Java Transaction API—JCP
JTS	Java Transaction Service—JCP
LAN	Local Area Network
LINQ	Language-Integrated Query—Microsoft
LOB	Line of Business adapter—Microsoft
LSN	log sequence number
LTM	Lightweight Transaction Manager—Microsoft
LU6.2	Logical Unit 6.2 protocol—IBM
MFS	Message Format Service—IBM
MQ	message queue
MQI	Message Queue Interface—IBM
MRAM	magnetoresistive random access memory
MRO	Multiregion Operation—IBM
MSC	Multiple Systems Coupling—IBM
MSMQ	Microsoft Message Queue—Microsoft
MTBF	mean time between failures
MTTR	mean time to repair
MVI	modified version ID
NSAPI	Netscape Server API—Sun
NSK	NonStop Kernel—HP
OASIS	Organization for the Advancement of Structured Information Standards

ODBC	Open Database Connectivity—SQL Access Group
OLE	Object Linking and Embedding—Microsoft
OLE DB	Object Linking and Embedding, Database—Microsoft
OLTP	on-line transaction processing
OMG	Object Management Group
OpenVMS	Open Virtual Management System—HP
OO	object-oriented
OSI TP	Open Software Interconnect Transaction Processing—ISO
OSS	Open System Services—HP
OTMA	Open Transaction Manager Access—IBM
OTS	Object Transaction Service—OMG
PARS	Programmed Airline Reservation System—IBM
PC	personal computer
PCM	phase change memory
PL/SQL	Procedural Language/Structured Query Language—Oracle
POJO	plain old Java object
POWER	Performance Optimization With Enhanced RISC—IBM
PowerPC	Power Performance Computing—Apple, IBM, and Motorola
PRAM	parameter random access memory
PSPE	Promotable Single Phase Enlistment—Microsoft
RAID	redundant array of inexpensive disks
RAM	random access memory
RCP	Rich Client Platform—Eclipse
RDF	Remote Database Facility—HP
REST	representational state transfer
RFID	radio frequency identification
RM	resource manager
RMI	Remote Method Invocation—JCP
RMI/IIOP	RMI over IIOP—JCP
RPC	remote procedure call
RSS	RDF Site Summary—RSS-DEV Working Group
RTR	Reliable Transaction Router—HP
SABRE	Semi-Automated Business Research Environment—Sabre Holdings
SALT	Services Architecture Leveraging Tuxedo—Oracle
SCA	Service Component Architecture—OASIS
SCSI	Small Computer System Interface—ANSI
SDF	Screen Definition Facility—IBM
SDO	Service Data Objects—OASIS
SI	Systems Interface—HP
SLA	service level agreement
SMP	symmetric multiprocessor
SNA	System Network Architecture—IBM
SOA	service-oriented architecture
SPARC	Scalable Processor Architecture—Sun
SPI	system programming interface
SQL	Structured Query Language—ISO
SQL/PSM	Structured Query Language/Persistent Stored Modules—ANSI
SSL	Secure Socket Layer—IETF
STDL	Structured Transaction Definition Language—The Open Group (formerly X/Open)
TAL	Transaction Application Language—HP
TCP	Terminal Control Program—HP
TCP/IP	Transmission Control Protocol/Internet Protocol—IETF
TDL	Task Definition Language—HP
TLS	Transport Layer Security—IETF
TM	transaction manager

TMF	Transaction Management Facility—HP
TP	transaction processing
TPC	Transaction Processing Performance Council
TPC-A, -B, -C, -E, -H	Transaction Processing Performance Council benchmarks A, B, C, E, and H
TPF	Transaction Processing Facility—IBM
tpm	transactions per minute
tpmC	transactions per minute—TPC-C
tps	transactions per second
tpsE	transactions per second—TPC-E
$/tpsE	cost per transaction per second—TPC-E
TX	Transaction Demarcation API—The Open Group (formerly X/Open)
TxF	Transactional NT File System—Microsoft
TxRPC	Transactional Remote Procedure Call—The Open Group (formerly X/Open)
UDDI	Universal Description, Discovery, and Integration – OASIS
UML	Unified Modeling Language—OMG
UN/EDIFACT	United Nations/ Electronic Data Interchange For Administration, Commerce, and Transport
URI	Uniform Resource Identifier—W3C
URL	Uniform Resource Locator—W3C
VAX	Virtual Address Extension—HP
VB	Visual Basic—Microsoft
VM	virtual machine
VSAM	Virtual Sequential Access Method—IBM
VSE	Virtual Storage Extended
W3C	World Wide Web Consortium
WAN	wide area network
WCF	Windows Communication Foundation—Microsoft
WF	Windows Workflow Foundation—Microsoft
WPF	Windows Presentation Foundation—Microsoft
WSDL	Web Services Description Language—W3C
WS-AT	Web Services Atomic Transaction—OASIS
WS-BA	Web Services Business Activity—OASIS
WS-BPEL	Web Services Business Process Execution Language—OASIS
WS-C	Web Services Coordination—OASIS
WS-I	Web Services Interoperability Organization
WWW	World Wide Web
WYSIWYG	What you see is what you get
XA	Interface between TM and RM—The Open Group (formerly X/Open)
XAML	Extensible Application Markup Language—Microsoft
XATMI	X/Open Application Transaction Manager Interface—The Open Group (formerly X/Open)
XDR	External Data Representation—IETF
XHTML	Extensible Hypertext Markup Language—W3C
XID	X/Open transaction ID—The Open Group (formerly X/Open)
XML	Extensible Markup Language—W3C
XPath	XML Path Language—W3C
XRF	extended recovery facility—IBM
XSD	XML Schema Definition language—W3C
XSL	Extensible Stylesheet Language—W3C
XSLT	XSL Transformations—W3C

Bibliographic Notes

The goal of these bibliographic notes is to provide some historical context and offer places to find additional material on each topic. It is not intended to be a comprehensive bibliography.

The definitive work on TP technology is *Transaction Processing: Concepts and Techniques*, by Jim Gray and Andreas Reuter (1992). Most of the topics in this book are covered there in more detail, usually from the viewpoint of someone developing a database system or transactional middleware. For the reader who wants to dig deeper into TP technology, this is an excellent place to look. However, it is no longer the last word on some topics, since there has been technical progress since it was published. For a more up-to-date view on any particular topic, see the following bibliographic notes.

Most articles on advanced transaction processing technology are published in the database research field. A very complete bibliography search engine called DBLP is available at http://www.sigmod.org/dblp/db/index.html. Most of the relevant conference proceedings can be obtained from the ACM SIGMOD Anthology (http://www.sigmod.org/sigmod/anthology/index.htm) and the ACM Digital Library (http://portal.acm.org/dl.cfm).

More extensive bibliographic notes for Chapters 6 through 9 can be found in Bernstein et al. (1987) and for Chapters 6 through 8 in Weikum and Vossen (2002). These are academic-style textbooks that cover the material in more depth. Other books on transaction processing are Claybrook (1992) and Lewis et al. (2002).

CHAPTER 1 INTRODUCTION

The concepts of transaction and TP monitor appeared in the early 1970s. There is a rich literature on the theory of transactions, starting from the mid 1970s (see Bernstein, Hadzilacos, and Goodman, 1987, for references), and on their implementation (first summarized in Gray, 1978, and later in Gray and Reuter, 1992). SOA and Web Services are described in Newcomer and Lomow (2004). REST is described in Richardson and Ruby (2007). For references on transactional middleware, see the Bibliographic Notes for Chapter 3.

An early influential paper on the transaction concept was Eswaran et al. (1976), which includes some earlier references. The acronym ACID was coined in Härder and Reuter (1983). For references on the two-phase commit protocol, see the Bibliographic Notes for Chapter 7.

The most up-to-date information on TPC benchmarks can be found at the Transaction Processing Performance Council web site, http://www.tpc.org. A description of the evolution of TPC-A/B into TPC-C is in Levine et al. (1993). Articles about many database and TP benchmarks can be found in Gray (1993). Much of Section 1.6 on availability is from Gray (1986).

CHAPTER 2 TRANSACTION PROCESSING ABSTRACTIONS

The material on transaction bracketing is mostly from the authors' experience in designing and using transaction APIs. Descriptions of the use of transaction attributes in object-oriented programming in .NET can be found at the Microsoft web site, http://msdn.microsoft.com. For Java EE, see http://java.sun.com/javaee. The nested transaction model described here is from Moss (1985); see also Lynch et al. (1993) for a mathematical treatment and Liskov (1988) for a language that embodies the model. Details about threads can be found in any modern operating systems textbook, such as Silberschatz et al. (2008). The core material on RPC is from Birrell and Nelson (1984), the classic research paper on this topic.

CHAPTER 3 TRANSACTION PROCESSING APPLICATION ARCHITECTURE

The three-tier TP application architecture model is from Bernstein (1990) and Bernstein et al. (1991). See also Gray and Edwards (1995) and Chapter 5 of Gray and Reuter (1992). The more up-to-date view of multitier TP application architecture is based on the authors' knowledge of current products. The REST architectural pattern was introduced in Chapter 5 of Fielding (2000). Details of the Secure Socket Layer can be found in Rescorla (2001). Kaufman et al. (2002) give a general treatment of network security. Howard and LeBlanc (2003) give a more prescriptive view of how to ensure code is secure. See the Bibliographic Notes for Chapter 10 for specific product references.

CHAPTER 4 QUEUED TRANSACTION PROCESSING

Much of this chapter evolved from Bernstein et al. (1990), which in turn was influenced by many sources, such as Gray (1978) and Pausch (1988). A good place to find more details about the publish-subscribe paradigm is in books about the Java Messaging Service or at http://java.sun.com/products/jms/. Further information on Websphere MQ and Oracle Streams AQ can be found at http://www.ibm.com and http://www.oracle.com, respectively. The Advanced Message Queue Protocol is described at www.amqp.org.

CHAPTER 5 BUSINESS PROCESS MANAGEMENT

Jajodia and Kerschberg (1997) is an anthology of business process models, written by many top researchers working in that field. Leymann and Roller (2000) present a broad overview of business process technology from requirements and design through run-time deployment. The WS-BPEL standard and associated documents are at http://www.oasis-open.org/. Wolter (2006) explains the technology of SQL Server Service Broker and how to use it. Documents about the Business Process Modeling Notation are at http://www.omg.org. WS-BPEL is described at http://www.oasis-open.org/committees/tc_home.php?wg_abbrev=wsbpel. Other relevant material about business processes can be found at the web site of the Workflow Management Coalition (http://www.wfmc.org).

CHAPTER 6 LOCKING

Two-phase locking was introduced in Eswaran et al. (1976). The deadlock discussion is from Chapter 3 of Bernstein et al. (1987). The description of lock managers is from Gray (1978). The view of locking performance is from Tay (1987) and Thomasian (1996, 1998); for further reading, see Shasha and Bonnet (2002). Most of the hot spot methods originated in IMS Fast Path (Gawlick and Kinkade 1985). Degrees of isolation originated in Gray et al. (1976); see Berenson et al. (1995) for an updated presentation. Chan et al. (1982) describes an early implementation of multiversion data. The phantom problem was introduced in Eswaran et al. (1976). The use of index locking to avoid phantoms appears in Lomet (1993). Optimistic concurrency control was introduced in Kung and Robinson (1981).

B-trees were introduced in Bayer and McCreight (1972). There are many papers on B-tree variations and optimizations. An early survey is Comer (1979). The prefix B-tree optimization is in Bayer and Unterauer (1977). The lock coupling protocol is from Bayer and Schkolnick (1977) and Kedem and Silberschatz (1980). The B-link optimization is by Lehman and Yao (1981).

Multigranularity locking was introduced in Gray et al. (1975, 1976). The nested transaction model was introduced in Reed (1978). The locking protocol for nested transactions is from Moss (1985).

Timestamp ordering and serialization graph testing are described in Chapter 4 of Bernstein et al. (1987). Commit ordering is presented in Raz (1992).

CHAPTER 7 SYSTEM RECOVERY

The introduction that summarizes causes of failure was inspired by Gray (1986). The explanation of recovery and checkpointing techniques in Section 7.2 was developed for this book, but was heavily influenced by ideas in early products from Tandem Computers. The model of recovery management in Sections 7.4 and 7.5 is an expanded version of material in Chapter 6 of Bernstein et al. (1987), which was in turn heavily influenced by Gray (1978) and Härder and Reuter (1983). The shadow-paging algorithm in Section 7.6 is from Lorie (1977).

Many logging algorithms have been published, going back at least to Gray (1978). The use of LSNs in pages are discussed in Lindsay (1980). The ARIES algorithm is described in Mohan et al. (1992). Mohan (1999) gives a retrospective of ARIES and its variations with an extensive bibliography. Other details about logging can be found in Gray and Reuter (1992), Lomet (1992), Lomet and Tuttle (2003), and Weikum and Vossen (2002). Kumar and Hsu (1998) is an anthology that includes many of these articles and others.

Disk failure rates are presented in Gray and Van Ingen (2005) and Pinheiro et al. (2007). RAID was introduced in Patterson et al. (1988).

CHAPTER 8 TWO-PHASE COMMIT

The two-phase commit protocol was first published in Lampson and Sturgis (1976) and explained further in Gray (1978) and Lampson (1981). The tree of processes model is from Lindsay et al. (1984) and the presumed abort optimization is from Mohan et al. (1986). This particular description borrows heavily from Chapter 7 of Bernstein et al. (1987).

The X/Open model is published in The Open Group (1992). For descriptions of particular products, see Laing et al. (1991) for Digital's VMS transaction manager, and Microsoft (2000) for Microsoft's Distributed Transaction Coordinator.

CHAPTER 9 REPLICATION

One-copy serializability was introduced in Attar et al. (1984). The primary copy approach was first published in Stonebraker (1979). Majority consensus comes from Thomas (1979), and was extended in Gifford (1979) to quorum consensus. The behavior of timestamps is explained in Lamport (1978).

There are many articles on how to reach consensus, not limited to the problem of deciding which replicas are alive and which is primary. An early such algorithm for data replication is the Virtual Partitions algorithm in El Abbadi et al. (1985) and El Abbadi and Toueg (1989). The algorithm for reaching consensus near the end of Section 9.4 is a variation of the Paxos algorithm in Oki and Liskov (1988) and Lamport (1998). An implementation is described in Chandra et al. (2007).

The CAP conjecture was posed in Brewer (2000). It was proved in Gilbert and Lynch (2002).

The multimaster implementation of Lotus Notes is described in Kawell et al. (1988). Early use of version vectors for replication are Fischer and Michael (1982) and Parker et al. (1983). A later algorithm is described in Ladin et al. (1992) with an extensive bibliography. The algorithms described here are based on Microsoft's WinFS and Sync Framework, described in Novik et al. (2006) and Malkhi et al. (2007). Terry (2008) presents an excellent survey of replication techniques for mobile computing. DeCandia et al. (2007) describes multimaster techniques used by Amazon.com.

The description of data sharing was modeled on Oracle's Rdb/VMS, described in Lomet et al. (1992). Data sharing in IBM DB2 is described in Josten et al. (1997). Concurrency control for data sharing is also discussed in Mohan and Narang (1991) and Rahm (1993).

CHAPTER 10 TRANSACTIONAL MIDDLEWARE PRODUCTS AND STANDARDS

Primary sources were used for most of the information in this chapter. The most significant web references are listed next. MSDN was our source of most of the information about the .NET Framework. An excellent source of general information on Java EE and EJB3 is Burke and Monson-Haefel (2006). Java Swing is described in Loy et al. (2003). Further information about Java TP technologies, standards, and programming techniques are in Little et al. (2004).

SOA design principles and concepts, with case studies and a detailed description of the Credit Suisse SOA-based application, is in Krafzig et al. (2004). Richardson and Ruby (2007) explore how to use REST/HTTP for web services and SOA. Another view of RESTful services is in Vinoski (2008a,b).

Alonso et al. (2004) give an overview of Web Services. Detailed descriptions of Web Services standards and their relationships is in Werrawarana et al. (2005).

The following books were used for the first edition as source material on legacy TP monitors, and much of the information remains relevant: Andrade et al. (1996), for Tuxedo; LeBert (1989), for CICS; UNIX International (1992), for Tuxedo and CICS; and Willis (1994), for OpenVMS.

Other general sources of product and standards information are http://www.infoq.com/, http://www.theserverside.com/, and of course http://www.wikipedia.org/.

Apache

General: http://www.apache.org/
Apache HTTP Server: http://httpd.apache.org/
Apache CXF: http://cxf.apache.org/
Apache OpenJPA: http://openjpa.apache.org/
Apache Tomcat: http://tomcat.apache.org/
Apache ActiveMQ: http://activemq.apache.org/

Eclipse

General: http://www.eclipse.org/
SOA Tools Platform Project BPMN Editor Screenshot examples: http://www.eclipse.org/projects/project_summary.php?projectid = stp.bpmnhttp://www.eclipse.org/bpmn/images/screenshots/

HP

ACMS: http://h71000.www7.hp.com/commercial/acms/index.html
NonStop Software/Pathway: http://h20219.www2.hp.com/NonStopComputing/cache/76380-0-0-230-470.html

IBM

IMS: http://www.ibm.com/software/data/ims/
CICS: http://www.ibm.com/software/htp/cics/
DB2: http://www.ibm.com/software/data/db2/
WebSphere: http://www.ibm.com/software/websphere/

Java Enterprise Edition (Java EE)

General: http://java.sun.com/javaee/
Enterprise Java Beans: http://java.sun.com/products/ejb/
J2EE Connector Architecture: http://java.sun.com/j2ee/connector/
Java Message Service: http://java.sun.com/products/jms/
Java Persistence API: http://java.sun.com/javaee/technologies/persistence.jsp
Java Server Faces: http://java.sun.com/javaee/javaserverfaces/
Java Server Pages: http://java.sun.com/products/jsp/
Java Servlets: http://java.sun.com/products/servlet/index.jsp
Java Swing: http://java.sun.com/javase/6/docs/technotes/guides/swing/
Java Transaction API: http://java.sun.com/javaee/technologies/jta/
JDBC: http://java.sun.com/products/jdbc/overview.html
REST- JAX-RS: http://jcp.org/aboutJava/communityprocess/final/jsr311/index.html
Web services- JAX-WS: http://jcp.org/en/jsr/detail?id=224

Microsoft

NET Framework Overview: http://msdn.microsoft.com/en-us/netframework/default.aspx
ADO.NET: http://msdn.microsoft.com/en-us/data/default.aspx
BizTalk Server: http://www.microsoft.com/biztalk/en/us/default.aspx
Host Integration Server: http://www.microsoft.com/hiserver/default.mspx
Internet Information Services: http://msdn.microsoft.com/en-us/library/aa737439.aspx
Open Database Connectivity (ODBC): http://msdn.microsoft.com/en-us/library/ms710252(VS.85).aspx
Silverlight: http://silverlight.net/
SQL Server: http://www.microsoft.com/sqlserver/2008/en/us/default.aspx
System.Transactions: http://msdn.microsoft.com/en-us/library/system.transactions.aspx
Visual Studio: http://msdn.microsoft.com/en-us/vstudio/default.aspx
Windows Communication Foundation: http://msdn.microsoft.com/en-us/library/ms735119.aspx
Windows Presentation Foundation: http://msdn.microsoft.com/en-us/netframework/aa663326.aspx
Windows Workflow Foundation: http://msdn.microsoft.com/en-us/netframework/aa663328.aspx

Oracle

Database: http://www.oracle.com/database/index.html
Tuxedo: http://www.oracle.com/products/middleware/tuxedo/tuxedo.html
WebLogic Server: http://www.oracle.com/appserver/weblogic/enterprise-edition.html

Red Hat

JBoss: http://www.jboss.com/

Object Management Group (OMG)

General: http://www.omg.org/
Object Transaction Service: http://www.omg.org/technology/documents/formal/transaction_service.htm

The Open Group

General: http://www.opengroup.org/
DTP Model: http://www.opengroup.org/pubs/catalog/c193.htm
XA: http://www.opengroup.org/onlinepubs/009680699/toc.pdf

Organization for the Advancement of Structured Information Standards (OASIS)

General: http://www.oasis-open.org/home/index.php
WS-Transactions: http://www.oasis-open.org/committees/tc_home.php?wg_abbrev=ws-tx

OSGi Alliance

General: http://www.osgi.org/

Service Composition Architecture (SCA)

General: http://www.oasis-opencsa.org/sca

The Web Services Interoperability Organization (WS-I)

General: http://www.ws-i.org/

World Wide Web Consortium (W3C)

General: http://www.w3.org/
Web Services Activity: http://www.w3.org/2002/ws/

Bibliography

Alonso, G., Casati, F., Kuno, H., Machiraju, V., 2004. Web Services. Springer-Verlag, Berlin.

Andrade, J.M., Carges, M.T., Dwyer, T.J., Felts, S.D., 1996. The TUXEDO System, Software for Constructing and Managing Distributed Business Applications. Addison Wesley, Reading, MA.

Attar, R., Bernstein, P.A., Goodman, N., 1984. Site initialization, recovery, and backup in a distributed database system. IEEE Trans. Software Eng. 10 (6), 645–650.

Bayer, R., McCreight, E.M., 1972. Organization and maintenance of large ordered indices. Acta Inform. 1, 173–189.

Bayer, R., Schkolnick, M., 1977. Concurrency of operations on B-trees. Acta Inform. 9 (1), 1–21.

Bayer, R., Unterauer, K., 1977. Prefix B-Trees. ACM Trans. Database Syst. 2 (1), 11–26.

Berenson, H., Bernstein, P.A., Gray, J.N., Melton, J., O'Neil, E., O'Neil, P., 1995. Levels of isolation. In: Proceedings of the 1995 ACM SIGMOD Conference on Management of Data, pp. 1–10.

Bernstein, P.A., 1990. Transaction processing monitors. Commun. ACM 33 (11), 75–86.

Bernstein, P.A., Emberton, W., Trehan, V., 1991. DECdta: digital's distributed transaction processing architecture. Digital Tech. J. 3 (1), 10–17.

Bernstein, P.A., Hadzilacos, V., Goodman, N., 1987. Concurrency Control and Recovery in Database Systems. Addison-Wesley, Reading, MA. Freely downloadable at: http://research.microsoft.com/~philbe.

Bernstein, P.A., Hsu, M., Mann, B., 1990. Implementing recoverable requests using queues. In: Proceedings of the 1990 ACM SIGMOD Conference on Management of Data, pp. 112–122.

Bernstein, P.A., Shipman, D.W., Wong, W.S., 1979. Formal aspects of serializability in database concurrency control. IEEE Trans. Software Eng. SE-5 (3), 203–215.

Birrell, A.D., Nelson, B.J., 1984. Implementing remote procedure calls. ACM Trans. Comput. Syst. 2 (1), 39–59.

Brewer, E.A., 2000. Towards robust distributed systems (abstract). In: Proceedings of the Nineteenth Annual ACM Symposium on Principles of Distributed Computing, p. 7.

Burke, B., Monson-Haefel, R., 2006. Enterprise Java Beans, fifth ed. O'Reilly Media, Sebastopol, CA.

Chan, A., Fox, S., Lin, W.T.K., Nori, A., Ries, D.R., 1982. The implementation of an integrated concurrency control and recovery scheme. In: Proceedings of the 1982 ACM SIGMOD Conference on Management of Data, pp. 184–191.

Chandra, T.D., Griesemer, R., Redstone, J., 2007. Paxos made live: an engineering perspective. In: Proceedings of the 1988 ACM Conference on Principles of Distributed Computing, pp. 398–407.

Claybrook, B.J., 1992. OLTP—Online Transaction Processing Systems. J. Wiley & Sons, New York.

Comer, D., 1979. The ubiquitous B-Tree. ACM Comput. Surv. 11 (2), 121–137.

DeCandia, G., Hastorun, D., Jampani, M., Kakulapati, G., Lakshman, A., Pilchin, A., Sivasubramanian, S., Vosshall, P., Vogels, W., 2007. Dynamo: amazon's highly available key-value store. In: Proceedings of the 21st ACM Symposium on Operating Systems Principles, pp. 205–220.

El Abbadi, A., Skeen, D., Cristian, F., 1985. An efficient, fault-tolerant protocol for replicated data management. In: Proceedings of the 1985 Symposium on Principles of Database Systems, pp. 215–229.

El Abbadi, A., Toueg, S., 1989. Maintaining availability in partitioned replicated databases. ACM Trans. Database Syst. 14 (2), 264–290.

Eswaran, K.P., Gray, J.N., Lorie, R.A., Traiger, I.L., 1976. The notions of consistency and predicate locks in a database system. Commun. ACM 19 (11), 624–633.

Fielding, R.T., 2000. Architectural Styles and the Design of Network-based Software Architectures. University of California, Irvine, http://www.ics.uci.edu/~fielding/pubs/dissertation/top.htm.

Fischer, M.J., Michael, A., 1982. Sacrificing serializability to attain high availability of data in an unreliable network. In: Proceedings of the 1982 Symposium on Principles of Database Systems, pp. 70–75.

Gawlick, D., Kinkade, D., 1985. Varieties of concurrency control in IMS/VS fastpath. IEEE Database Eng. 8 (2), 3–10.

Gifford, D.K., 1979. Weighted voting for replicated data. In: 7th ACM SIGOPS Symposium on Operating System Principles, pp. 150–159.

Gilbert, S., Lynch, N., 2002. Brewer's conjecture and the feasibility of consistent, available, partition-tolerant web services. ACM SIGACT News 33 (2), 51–59.

Gray, J.N., 1978. Notes on database operating systems. In: Operating Systems: An Advanced Course, Springer-Verlag Lecture Notes in Computer Science, vol. 60. Springer-Verlag, New York.

Gray, J.N., 1981. The transaction concept: virtues and limitations (Invited Paper). In: Proceedings of the 7th International Conference on Very Large Data Bases. IEEE Press, pp. 144–154.

Gray, J.N., 1986. Why do computers stop and what can we do about it. In: 5th Symposium on Reliability in Distributed Software and Database Systems. IEEE Computer Society Press, pp. 3–12. Early version available at: http://research.microsoft.com/~gray/papers/TandemTR85.7_WhyDoComputersStop.pdf.

Gray, J.N. (Ed.), 1993. The Benchmark Handbook for Database and Transaction Processing Systems, second ed. Morgan Kaufmann Publishers, San Francisco.Online at: http://research.microsoft.com/users/gray/BenchmarkHandbook/TOC.htm.

Gray, J.N., Edwards, J., 1994. Scale up with TP monitors. Byte Mag. April.

Gray, J.N., Lorie, R.A., Putzolu, G.R., Traiger, I.L., 1976. Granularity of locks and degrees of consistency in a shared database. In: Modeling in Data Base Management Systems. Elsevier, Amsterdam.

Gray, J.N., Lorie, R.A., Traiger, I.L., 1975. Granularity of locks in a shared data base. In: Proceedings of 1975 International Conference on Very Large Data Bases, pp. 428–451.

Gray, J.N., Reuter, A., 1992. Transaction Processing: Concepts and Techniques. Morgan Kaufmann, San Francisco.

Gray, J.N., Van Ingen, C., 2005. Empirical measurements of disk failure rates and error rates. In: Microsoft Research Technical Report MSR-TR-2005-166. http://research.microsoft.com/research/pubs.

Härder, T., Reuter, A., 1983. Principles of transaction-oriented database recovery. ACM Comput. Surv. 15 (4), 287–317.

Howard, M., LeBlanc, D., 2003. Writing Secure Code. Microsoft Press, Redmond, WA.

Jajodia, S., Kerschberg, L. (Eds.), 1997. Advanced Transaction Models and Architecture. Springer-Verlag, Berlin.

Josten, J.W., Mohan, C., Narang, I., Teng, J.Z., 1997. DB2's use of the coupling facility for data sharing. IBM Sys. J. 36 (2), 327–351.

Kaufman, C., Perlman, R., Speciner, M., 2002. Network Security–PRIVATE Communication in a PUBLIC World. Prentice Hall PTR, Upper Saddle River, NJ.

Kawell Jr. L., Beckhardt, S., Halvorsen, T., Ozzie, R., Greif, I., 1988. Replicated document management in a group communication system. In: Proceedings of the 1988 ACM Conference on Computer-Supported Cooperative Work. Online at the ACM Digital Library.

Kedem, Z.M., Silberschatz, A., 1980. Non-two-phase locking protocols with shared and exclusive locks. In: Proceedings of 1980 International Conference on Very Large Data Bases, pp. 309–317.

Krafzig, D., Banke, K., Slama, D., 2004. Enterprise SOA: Service-Oriented Architecture Best Practices (Coad Series). Prentice Hall PTR, Upper Saddle River, NJ.

Kumar, V., Hsu, M., 1998. Recovery Mechanisms in Database Systems. Prentice Hall PTR, Upper Saddle River, NJ.

Kung, H.T., Robinson, J.T., 1982. On optimistic methods for concurrency control. ACM Trans. Database Syst. 6 (2), 213–226.

Ladin, R., Liskov, B., Shrira, L., Ghemawat, S., November 1992. Providing high availability using lazy replication. ACM Trans. Comput. Syst. 10 (4), 360.

Laing, W.A., Johnson, J.E., Landau, R.V., 1991. Transaction management support in the VMS operating system kernel. Digital Tech. J. 3 (1), 33–44.

Lamport, L., 1978. Time, clocks, and the ordering of events in a distributed system. Commun. ACM 21 (7), 558–565.

Lamport, L., 1998. The part-time parliament. ACM Trans. Comput. Syst. 16 (2), 133–169.

Lampson, B.W., 1981. Atomic transactions. In: Goos, G., Hartmanis, J. (Eds.), Distributed Systems—Architecture and Implementation: An Advanced Course. LNCS 105. Springer Verlag, Berlin, pp. 246–265.

Lampson, B.W., Sturgis, H., 1976. Crash recovery in a distributed data storage system. In: Technical Report, Computer Science Laboratory, Xerox Palo Alto Research Center, Palo Alto, CA.

LeBert, J.J., 1989. CICS for microcomputers. McGraw Hill, New York.

Lehman, P.L., Yao, S.B., 1981. Efficient locking for concurrent operations on B-trees. ACM Trans. Database Syst. 6 (4), 550–670.

Levine, C., Gray, J.N., Kiss, S., Kohler, W., 1993. The Evolution of TPC Benchmarks: Why TPC-A and TPC-B are Obsolete. Tandem Technical Report 93.1, Tandem Computers. Online at: http://www.hpl.hp.com/techreports/tandem/TR-93.1.pdf.

Lewis, P.M., Bernstein, A., Kifer, M., 2002. Databases and Transaction Processing, An Application-Oriented Approach. Addison-Wesley, Boston.

Leymann, F., Roller, D., 2000. Production Workflow, Concepts and Techniques. Prentice Hall PTR, Upper Saddle River, NJ.

Lindsay, B.G., Haas, L.M., Mohan, C., Wilms, P.F., Yost, R.A., 1984. Computation and communication in R*: a distributed database manager. ACM Trans. Comput. Syst. 2 (1), 24–38.

Liskov, B., 1988. Distributed programming in Argus. Commun. ACM 31 (3), 300–312.

Little, M., Maron, J., Pavlik, G., 2004. Java Transaction Processing. Prentice Hall PTR, Upper Saddle River, NJ.

Lomet, D.B., 1992. MLR: A recovery method for multi-level systems. In: Proceedings of the 1992 ACM SIGMOD Conference on Management of Data, pp. 185–194.

Lomet, D.B., 1993. Key range locking strategies for improved concurrency. In: Proceedings of the 1993 International Conference on Very Large Data Bases, pp. 655–664.

Lomet, D.B., Anderson, R., Rengarajan, T.K., Spiro, P., 1992. How the Rdb/VMS data sharing system became fast. In: Technical Report CRL 92/4, Digital Equipment Corp., Cambridge Research Lab. http://www.hpl.hp.com/techreports/Compaq-DEC/CRL-92-4.pdf.

Lomet, D.B., Tuttle, M.R., 2003. A theory of redo recovery. In: Proceedings of the 2003 ACM SIGMOD Conference on Management of Data, pp. 397–406.

Lomet, D.B., Weikum, G., 1998. Efficient and transparent application recovery in client-server information systems. In: Proceedings of the 1995 ACM SIGMOD Conference on Management of Data, pp. 460–471.

Lorie, R.A., 1977. Physical integrity in a large segmented database. ACM Trans. Database Syst. 2 (1), 91–104.

Loy, M., Eckstein, R., Wood, D., Elliot, J., Cole, B., 2003. Java Swing, second ed. O'Reilly Media Examples: http://examples.oreilly.com/jswing2/code/.

Lynch, N., Merritt, M., Weihl, W.E., Fekete, A., 1993. Atomic Transactions in Concurrent and Distributed Systems. Morgan Kaufmann Publishers, San Francisco.

Malkhi, D., Novik, L., Purcell, C., 2007. P2P replica synchronization with vector sets. Operating Syst. Rev. 41 (2), 68–74.

Microsoft Corporation, 2000. COM + Developer's Reference Library. Microsoft Press, Redmond, WA.

Mohan, C., 1999. Repeating history beyond ARIES. In: Proceedings of the 1999 International Conference on Very Large Data Bases, pp. 1–17.

Mohan, C., Haderle, D., Lindsay, B., Pirahesh, H., Schwarz, P., 1992. ARIES: a transaction recovery method supporting fine-granularity locking and partial rollback using write-ahead logging. ACM Trans. Database Syst. 17 (1), 94–162.

Mohan, C., Lindsay, B.G., Obermarck, R., 1986. Transaction management in the R* distributed database management system. ACM Trans. Database Syst. 11 (4), 378–396.

Mohan, C., Narang, I., 1991. Recovery and coherency-control protocols for fast intersystem page transfer and fine-granularity locking in a shared disks transaction environment. In: Proceedings of the 1991 International Conference on Very Large Databases, pp. 193–207.

Moss, E., 1985. Nested Transactions: An Approach to Reliable Distributed Computing. MIT Press, Boston.

Newcomer, E., Lomow, G., 2004. Understanding SOA with Web Services. Addison-Wesley, Upper Saddle River, NJ.

Novik, L., Hudis, I., Terry, D.B., Anand, S., Jhaveri, V., Shah, A., Wu, Y., 2006. Peer-to-peer replication in WinFS. In: Microsoft Research Technical Report MSR-TR-2006-78.

Oki, B.M., Liskov, B., 1988. View stamped replication: a general primary copy. In: Proceedings of the 1988 ACM Symposium on Principles of Distributed Computing, pp. 8–17.

Parker Jr., D.S., Popek, G.J., Rudisin, G., Stoughton, A., Walker, B.J., Walton, E., Chow, J.M., Edwards, D., Kiser, S., Kline, C., 1983. Detection of mutual inconsistency in distributed systems. IEEE Trans. Software Eng. 9 (3), 240–247.

Patterson, D.A., Gibson, G., Katz, R.H., 1988. A case for redundant arrays of inexpensive disks (RAID). In: Proceedings of the 1988 ACM SIGMOD Conference on Management of Data, pp. 109–116.

Pausch, R., 1988. Adding input and output to the transaction model. Ph.D. Thesis, Computer Science Dept., Carnegie Mellon University, August (CMU-CS-88-171).

Pinheiro, E., Weber, W.-D., Barroso, L.A., 2007. Failure trends in large disk drive populations. In: Proceedings of the 5th USENIX Conference on File and Storage Technologies (FAST '07), pp. 17–28.

Rahm, E., 1993. Empirical performance evaluation of concurrency and coherency control protocols for database sharing systems. ACM Trans. Database Syst. 18 (2), 333–377.

Raz, Y., 1992. The principle of commitment ordering, or guaranteeing serializability in a heterogeneous environment of multiple autonomous resource managers using atomic commitment. In: Proceedings of the 1992 International Conference on Very Large Data Bases, pp. 292–312.

Reed, D.P., 1978. Naming and synchronization in a decentralized computer system. Ph.D. Dssertation, Department of Electrical Engineering and Computer Science, MIT., Cambridge, MA. Technical Report TR-205, Laboratory for Computer Science, Cambridge, MA.

Rescorla, E., 2001. SSL and TLS—Designing and Building Secure Systems. Addison-Wesley, Upper Saddle River, NJ.

Richardson, L., Ruby, S., 2007. RESTful Web Services. O'Reilly Media, Sebastopol, CA.

Shasha, D., Bonnet, P., 2002. Database Tuning: Principles, Experiments, and Troubleshooting Techniques. Morgan Kaufmann Publishers, San Francisco.

Silberschatz, A., Galvin, P.B., Gagne, G., 2008. Operating System Concepts, seventh ed. Wiley, Hoboken, NJ.

Stonebraker, M., 1979. Concurrency control and consistency of multiple copies of data in distributed INGRES. IEEE Trans. Software Eng. 3 (3), 188–194.

Tay, Y.C., 1987. Locking Performance in Centralized Databases. Academic Press, Orlando, FL.

Terry, D.B., 2008. Replicated data management for mobile computing. In: Synthesis Lectures on Mobile and Pervasive Computing #5, Morgan & Claypool Publishers.

The Open Group, 1992. Distributed TP: The XA Specification. http://www.opengroup.org/bookstore/catalog/c193.htm.

Thomas, R., 1979. A majority consensus approach to concurrency control for multiple copy databases. ACM Trans. Database Syst. 4 (2), 180–209.

Thomasian, A., 1996. Database Concurrency Control: Methods, Performance, and Analysis. Kluwer Academic Publishers, Boston.

Thomasian, A., 1998. Concurrency control: methods, performance, and analysis. ACM Comput. Surv. 30 (1), 70–119.

UNIX International, 1992. Open Enterprise Transaction Processing: Integrating the TUXEDO System with Mainframe CICS.

Vinoski, S., 2008a. RPC and REST—dilemma, disruption, and displacement. IEEE Internet Comput. September/October, 92–95, Toward Integration Column.

Vinoski, S., 2008b. RESTful web services development checklist. IEEE Internet Comput. November/December, 94–96, Toward Integration Column.

Weerawarana, S., Curbera, F., Leymann, F., Storey, T., Ferguson, D., 2005. Web Services Platform Architecture: SOAP, WSDL, WS-Policy, WS-Addressing, WS-BPEL, WS-Reliable Messaging, and More. Prentice-Hall, Upper Saddle River, NJ.

Weikum, G., Vossen, G., 2002. Transactional Information Systems—Theory, Algorithms, and the Practice of Concurrency Control and Recovery. Morgan Kaufmann Publishers, San Francisco.

Willis, J.M., 1994. TP Software Development for OpenVMS. CBM Books, Horsham, PA.

Wolter, R., 2006. The Rational Guide to SQL Server 2005 Service Broker. Rational Press, Rollinsford, NH.

Index

Page numbers followed by "f" indicate figures.